WASHINGTON CAMPING

WASHINGTON CAMPING

The Complete Guide to
More Than 650 Campgrounds

FIRST EDITION

Stephani & Tom Stienstra

AVALON
TRAVEL

FOGHORN OUTDOORS:
WASHINGTON CAMPING
The Complete Guide to
More Than 650 Campgrounds

First Edition

Stephani and Tom Stienstra

Published by
Avalon Travel Publishing
5855 Beaudry Street
Emeryville, CA 94608, USA

Please send all comments, corrections,
additions, amendments, and critiques to:

ⒻOGHORN OUTDOORS®
WASHINGTON CAMPING
AVALON TRAVEL PUBLISHING
5855 BEAUDRY ST.
EMERYVILLE, CA 94608, USA
email: atpfeedback@avalonpub.com
website: www.foghorn.com

Printing History
1st edition-June 2002
5 4 3 2 1

ISBN: 1-56691-469-8
ISSN: 1537-8551

Editor: Kevin McLain
Series Manager: Marisa Solís
Copy Editor: Ginjer Clarke
Graphics Coordinator: Melissa Sherowski
Illustrations: Bob Race
Production Coordinator: Darren Alessi
Cover Design: Jacob Goolkasian
Map Editor: Olivia Solís
Cartographers: CHK America, Mike Morgenfeld,
  Katherine Kalamaras, Suzanne Service
Index: Rachel Kuhn

Front cover photo: © 1988 Joel W. Rogers

Distributed by Publishers Group West

Printed in the United States by Bertelsmann Services

About the Authors

©TOM STIENSTRA

© KURT ROGERS

This book by Stephani and Tom Stienstra would never have been written without a little bit of destiny at play.

The two first met in 1976 on the staff of the San Jose State *Spartan Daily*. Years later, Tom came across a magazine article by chance, where Stephani had been interviewed about a wildlife issue. To his surprise, he was able to track her down in minutes, and in 1998, they were married at Lake Tahoe, California.

During the 20 years in between, Stephani's extensive travels were highlighted by boating, watersports, and climbing the West's highest summits, including Mt. Whitney and Mt. Shasta. In addition to her work as author and research editor, she has taught English and journalism, served in a wildlife advisory capacity, and run successful businesses.

Meanwhile, Tom nearly left home in the late 1980s, having decided to move to Alaska and become a bush pilot and fishing guide. In the course of being certified as a pilot, he found himself looking down from airplanes, shocked by the high number of remote lakes, streams, and campsites sprinkled across vast amounts of landscape. Instead of moving, he chose to dedicate himself to searching out and exploring little-known spots throughout the Pacific Northwest and California.

Tom's adventure stories are distributed across the nation on *The New York Times* News Service. He has been twice honored with the Presidents Award by the Outdoors Writers Association of America as the national Outdoor Writer of the Year for the newspaper division.

To complete this book, Stephani and Tom flew their small plane, drove, hiked, boated, and fished across Washington in search of the best of the outdoors.

They live with their two sons, Jeremy and Kris, and can be reached directly on the Internet at www.TomStienstra.com, where their other books are available.

Contents

SPECIAL TOPICS

Maps

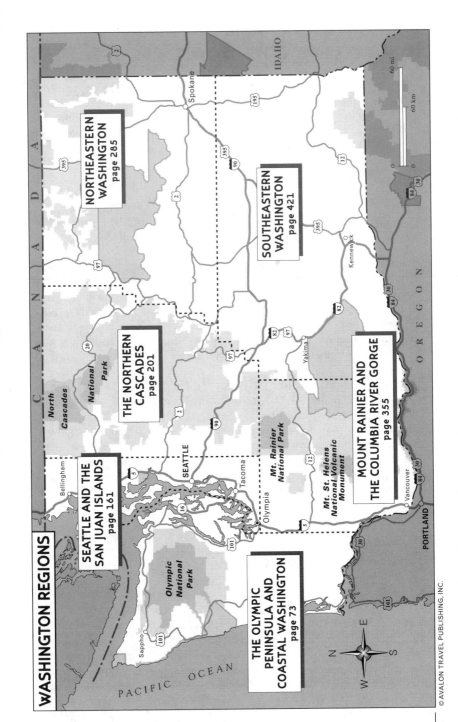

WASHINGTON REGIONS

NORTHEASTERN WASHINGTON
page 285

SOUTHEASTERN WASHINGTON
page 421

THE NORTHERN CASCADES
page 201

MOUNT RAINIER AND THE COLUMBIA RIVER GORGE
page 355

SEATTLE AND THE SAN JUAN ISLANDS
page 161

THE OLYMPIC PENINSULA AND COASTAL WASHINGTON
page 73

CANADA

IDAHO

OREGON

PACIFIC OCEAN

North Cascades National Park

Olympic National Park

Mt. Rainier National Park

Mt. St. Helens National Volcanic Monument

Bellingham
Spokane
Sappho
SEATTLE
Tacoma
Olympia
Kennewick
Yakima
Vancouver
PORTLAND

60 mi
60 km

© AVALON TRAVEL PUBLISHING, INC.

How to Use This Book

Washington Camping is divided into six sections, one for each region of the state: the Olympic Peniosula and Coastal Washington, Seattle and the San Juan Islands, the Norhtern Cascades, Northeastern Washington, and Mt. Rainier and the Columbia River Gorge. Maps at each chapter's beginning show where all the campgrounds in that region are located.

You can search for the ideal campsite in two ways:

1. If you know the name of the specific campground where you would like to stay, or the name of the surrounding geographical area or nearby feature (town, national or state park or forest, mountain, lake, river, etc.), look it up in the index and turn to the corresponding page.
2. If you know the general area you want to visit, you can determine which chapter covers that territory by checking the Washington map. Then turn to the regional map at the beginning of that chapter. Each regional map is broken down into grids, which show by number all the hikes in that chapter. Opposite the map will be a chapter table of contents listing each campground in the chapter by its map number and profile page number. Turn to the corresponding page for complete information on the campground that interests you.

About the Campground Profiles

Each campground in this book begins with a brief overview of its setting. Topics such as facilities, amenities, nearby or on-site recreation options, historical trivia, and ambience may also be addressed. The practical information you need to plan your trip is broken down further into the following categories:

Location— This category provides the general location of the campround by naming its proximity to the nearest major town or landmark. Following this information is a number and letter grid reference to help you locate the campground on the chapter map. The entire entry will be written like this: "Northwest of San Juan Island; see Seattle and the San Juan Islands, map 1, grid a8."

Campsites, facilities— This section provides the number of campsites for both tents and RVs and whether hookups are available. Facilities such as restrooms, picnic areas, recreation areas, laundry, and dump stations will be addressed, as well as the availability of piped water, showers, playgrounds, and stores, among others. The campground's pet policy is also mentioned here.

Reservations, fees— This section notes whether reservations are accepted, and the rates for tent sites and RV sites. If there are additional fees for parking or pets, or discounted weekly or seasonal rates, that will also be noted here. This section also provides the dates that the campground is open. Some campgrounds in Washington are closed during the winter and may not open until the snow melts and roads re-open. If you are planning a late spring or early summer trip, call the campground ahead of time to make sure it's open.

Directions— This section provides mile-by-mile driving directions to the campground from the nearest major town.

Contact— This section provides an address, phone number, and Internet address, if available, for the campground.

About the Icons

The icons in this book are designed to provide at-a-glance information on activities that are available on-site or nearby each campground. Some icons have been selected to also represent facilities available or services provided. They are not meant to represent every activity or service, but rather those that are most significant.

— Hiking trails are available.

— Biking trails or routes are available. This usually refers to mountain biking, although it may represent road cycling as well. Refer to the text for that campground for details.

— Swimming opportunities are available.

— Fishing opportunities are available.

— Boating opportunities are available. Various types of vessels apply under this umbrella activity, including motorboats and personal watercrafts (Jet Skis). Refer to the text for that campground for more detail, including mph restrictions and boat ramp availability.

— Hunting is permitted. Campers need to be aware of the hunting season in a particular state, and that they may be near hunters when camping in some state parks or in the backcountry.

— Winter sports are available. This general category may include activities such as downhill skiing, cross-country skiing, snowshoeing, snow mobiling, snowboarding, and ice skating. Refer to the text for that campground for more detail on which sports are available.

— Hot or cold springs are located nearby. Refer to the listing text for more information.

— Pets are permitted. Campgrounds that allow pets may require an additional fee or that pets be leashed. Campgrounds may also restrict pet size or behavior. Refer to the text for that campground for specific instructions or call in advance.

— A playground is available. A campground with a playground can be desireable for campers traveling with children.

— Wheelchair access is provided, as advertised by campground managers. However, concerned persons are advised to call the contact number of a campground to be certain that their specific needs will be met.

— RV sites are provided.

— Tent sites are provided.

About the Ratings

Each campground in this book has been rated on a scale of 1 to 10 for its scenic beauty. Ratings are based solely on scenic appeal and do not reflect quality issues such as the cleanliness of the camp or the temperament of the management, which can change from day to day.

About the Maps

The maps in this book are designed to show the general location of campgrounds and are not meant to substitute for more detailed road maps. Readers are advised to take additional maps when heading out to any campground, particularly when venturing into the wilderness.

Our Commitment

We are committed to making *Foghorn Outdoors: Washington Camping* the most accurate, thorough, and enjoyable camping guide to the state. Every campground in this book has been thoroughly researched and is accompanied by the most up-to-date information. Be aware that with the passing of time, some of the fees listed may have changed, and a change in season or weather patterns may have had some ill effects on a campground. You may also have a specific need or concern. With all of this in mind, it's usually best to call the location ahead of time.

If you would like to comment on the book, whether to suggest a campground we have overlooked or to let us know about any noteworthy experience—good or bad—that occurred while using *Foghorn Outdoors: Washington Camping* as your guide, we would appreciate hearing from you. Please address your correspondence to:

Foghorn Outdoors: Washington Camping
Avalon Travel Publishing
5855 Beaudry Street
Emeryville, CA 94608
email: atpfeedback@avalonpub.com

Acknowledgements

U.S. Forest Service

Nan Berger, Colville National Forest, Newport Ranger District

Dortha Sattler, Colville National Forest, Republic Ranger District

Leon Beam, Colville National Forest, Sullivan Lake Ranger District

George McNicholl, Colville National Forest, Three Rivers Ranger District

Diana Baxter, Colville National Forest, Three Rivers Ranger District, Colville Office

Jack Thorne, Gifford Pinchot National Forest, Cowlitz Ranger District

Ross Bluestone, Gifford Pinchot National Forest, Mount Adams Ranger District

Tom Linde, Gifford Pinchot National Forest, Mount Adams Ranger District, Wind River Work Center

Theresa Newton, Gifford Pinchot National Forest, Mount St. Helens National Volcanic Monument

Diane Holz and Diane Boyd, Mt. Baker-Snoqualmie National Forest, Darrington Ranger District

Eli Warren, Mt. Baker-Snoqualmie National Forest, Mount Baker Ranger District

Kelly Redfield, Mt. Baker-Snoqualmie National Forest, North Bend Ranger District

Pam Young, Mt. Baker-Snoqualmie National Forest, Skykomish Ranger District

Mary Coughlin, Mt. Baker-Snoqualmie National Forest, White River Ranger District

Margie Peterson, Okanogan and Wenatchee National Forests, Chelan Ranger District

Mike Ames, Okanogan and Wenatchee National Forests, Cle Elum Ranger District

Les Julian, Okanogan and Wenatchee National Forests, Entiat Ranger District

Susan Peterson, Okanogan and Wenatchee National Forests, Lake Wenatchee Ranger District

Robin Wanner, Okanogan and Wenatchee National Forests, Leavenworth Ranger District

Patricia Boley and Kathy Corrigan, Okanogan and Wenatchee National Forests, Methow Valley Visitor Center

Mikel Davis, Okanogan and Wenatchee National Forests, Naches Ranger District

Howard Christensen, Okanogan and Wenatchee National Forests, Tonasket Ranger District

Susan Graham, Olympic National Forest, Hood Canal Ranger District

Molly Erickson, Olympic National Forest, Pacific Ranger District

Steve Ricketts, Olympic National Forest, Quilcene Ranger District

Pete Erben and Daniel Hull, Olympic National Forest, Quinault Ranger District

Monte Fujishin, Umatilla National Forest, Pomeroy Ranger District

U.S. Army Corps of Engineers

Rich Hess, Portland District
Barbara Logston, Walla Walla District

National Parks

Lynne Brougher, Lake Roosevelt National Recreation Area
Steve Harvey and Patty Wold, Mount Rainier National Park
Joyce Brown and Nancy Holman, North Cascades National Park
Kathy Steichen and Maurie Sprague, Olympic National Park

State Parks

Thuy Luu-Beams, Public Information Officer
Judy Sabin, Eastern Region Office
Billy Hoppe, San Juan Marine Area
John Clayton, Bogachiel State Park
Kay Keck, Spencer Spit State Park
Teri Ockwell, Central Ferry State Park
Andy Kallinen, Horsethief Lake State Park
John Scarola, Maryhill State Park
Mike Sternback, Sun Lakes State Park
Tom Poplawski, Steamboat Rock State Park
George Eidson, Daroga State Park
Rick Lewis, Pearrygin State Park
Rob Wilson, Lincoln Rock State Park
Matt Morrison, Wenatchee Confluence State Park
Jack Hartt, Riverside State Park
Robert Meyer, Birch Bay State Park
Barb Buman, Moran State Park
Kevin Kratochvil, Rasar State Park
Steve Shively, Fort Worden State Park
Bob Fisher, Fort Ebey State Park
Greg John, Bay View State Park
Brian Hageman and Josh Lancaster, Deception Pass State Park
Tom Riggs, Illahee State Park
Eric Plunkett, Beacon Rock State Park
John Ernster, Paradise Point State Park
Aaron Tritto, Kopachuck State Park
Janet Shonk, Jarrell Cove State Park
Dave Rush, Rainbow Falls State Park
Pam Ripp, Lewis and Clark State Park
Seth Mason-Todd, Millersylvania State Park
Terry Carlton, Ocean City State Park
JoAnne Gardner, Twin Harbors State Park
Tracy Zuern, Fort Canby State Park

State Department of Natural Resources
Sarah Thirtyacre, Darrell Fields, and Bud Clark, Central Region
Andrew Spenbeck, Northeast Region
Stan Kurowski, Northwest Region
Elena Kuo-Harrison, Olympic Region
Jon Byerly and Walt Pulliam, South Puget Sound Region
Jim Munroe, Southeast Region
Kris Aanzerud and Dee Becker, Southwest Region

Other
Paul Rehse and Gary Rinta, Tacoma Power
Bob Reynolds, Whitman County
Michelle Brooks, City of Entiat
Joe Miller, Snohomish County
Connie Thomas, City of Omak
Peggy Reifsnyder, City of Coulee City
Paul Wilson, Pend Oreille County
Lee Reynolds, City of Chelan
Scott Green, Skagit County
Cathy Mulhall, Chelan County
Rosemary Morrison, City of Oak Harbor
Valora Mendum, City of Anacortes
Bill Karruf, Snohomish County Parks
Laura Eastman, City of Auburn
Galin Downing, Clallam County

Dear Campers,

If this book looks different from anything you have ever seen about Washington, that's because it is. We have made it a personal mission to win your trust and put the best of Washington's great outdoors in the palms of your hands with this book.

In this mission to make *Washington Camping* your book of choice, we started by incorporating the information collected over the course of 25 years of roaming around the West as full-time outdoors writers. We then faxed out 700 pages of galley proofs to more than 100 rangers and recreation specialists at field offices, as well as to the owners of each privately owned and operated park. In the process, each word of every page has been reviewed by three or four specialists, with hundreds of people involved in polishing the final product.

We wrote this book for several reasons. The first reason was simple: We never wanted to get stuck again for the night without a spot. That is why we searched them out. In the end, that is the best public value of the book: You will never get stuck for the night again. With this book, your days of being a prisoner of hope are over.

Another reason was that our publisher found that other guidebooks available were extremely incomplete, loaded with mistakes, and often included directions to destinations that were simply wrong or incoherent. If you have an old edition of *Pacific Northwest Camping,* for instance, throw it on your campfire because thousands of changes have been made since that book was first published. A lot of other books out there deserve a far less honorable fate.

We have written every direction in the book as if a person in the passenger seat is reading to the person who is driving. Compare the directions and maps in this book with anything else out there, and this feature alone can make *Washington Camping* your book of choice.

One note is that in every case, the prices listed for each campground were provided to us for the 2002 season. Over the course of seasons and years, prices increase. Count on it. If price is a bottom-line concern, call the contact number listed before planning your visit.

We also wrote this book because many of the most beautiful places on earth are in Washington. When our families and friends heard we were writing this book, some were outraged. They feared that all of their favorite spots would be revealed to all. After reviewing the manuscript, though, they've decided we're all right, after all. They have discovered, as we have, that Washington is filled with beautiful, little-used campgrounds that are perfect jumping-off points for adventures—and they represent hundreds of outstanding destinations, in addition to their sprinkling of favorites.

Some of the highlights of this book include:

—Over 650 campgrounds, featuring national forests; local, county, state, and national parks; land managed by the Department of Natural Resources; and privately owned and operated parks

—15,000 updates and upgrades from anything previously published

—45 extremely detailed maps
—Directions that are the easiest to use (and that have been fact-checked) of any outdoor book in the state
—Detailed and fact-checked information about each camp's setting, facilities, fees, reservation policies, and nearby recreation
—Helpful and anecdotal information about how to put the fun into every trip, including tips on catching fish, dealing with bears, and finding the best camp tents, bags, food, water purifiers, and more
—Icons that quickly identify activities at each camp
—Individually confirmed and reviewed telephone numbers

As guidebook authors, we get tons of emails and read each one carefully. These comments have often been beneficial. In the process, we have incorporated dozens of suggestions from readers to make this the book they want it to be. Your comments are always welcome and appreciated.

As you might have realized, this is not a hobby for us, as it is for some part-time writers who publish books. This is our full-time job. Because we spend 200 days a year in the field, traveling an average of 40,000 miles per year, we understand how seriously people take their fun, what they need to know to make their trips work, and their underlying fears of getting stuck for the night without a spot.

Our advice is to never go anywhere in Washington without this book on your front seat!

See you out there!

—Stephani and Tom Stienstra
website: www.TomStienstra.com

©TOM STIENSTRA

Introduction

Going on a camping trip can be like trying to put hiking boots on an octopus. You've tried it too, eh? Instead of the relaxing and fun trip full of adventure you hoped for, it turns into a scenario called You Against the World. You might as well try to fight a volcano.

But it doesn't have to be that way, and that's what this book is all about. If you give it a chance, it can put the mystery, excitement, and fun back into your camping vacations—and remove the fear of snarls, confusion, and occasional temper explosions of volcanic proportions that keep people at home, locked away from the action.

Mystery? There are hundreds of hidden, little-used campgrounds listed and mapped in this book that you have never dreamed of.

Excitement? At many of them, you'll find the sizzle with the steak, the hike to a great lookout, the big fish at the end of the line.

Fun? The how-to section of this book can help you take the futility out of your trips and put the fun back in. Add it up, put it in your cash register, and you can turn a camping trip into the satisfying adventure it's meant to be, whether it's just an overnight quicky or a month-long expedition.

It has been documented that 95 percent of American vacationers use only 5 percent of the available recreation areas. With this book, you can leave the herd, wander and be free, and join the inner circle, the Five Percenters who know the great hidden areas used by so few people. Take a hard look at the maps for the areas you wish to visit and the corresponding listings of campgrounds. As you study the camps, you'll start to feel a sense of excitement building, a feeling that you are about to unlock a door and venture into a world that is rarely viewed. When you feel that excitement, act on it. Parlay that energy into a great trip.

The campground maps and listings can serve in two ways: (1) If you're on the road late in the day and you're stuck for a spot for the night, you can likely find one nearby; or (2) if you are planning a trip, you can tailor a vacation to fit exactly into your plans rather than heading off and hoping—maybe praying—it turns out all right.

For the latter option, you may wish to obtain additional maps, particularly if you are venturing into areas governed by the U.S. Forest Service or Department of Natural Resources. Both agencies offer low-cost maps detailing all hiking trails, lakes, streams, and backcountry camps reached via logging roads. How to obtain these and other maps is described in the Resource Guide.

Backcountry camps listed in this book are often in primitive and rugged settings but provide the sense of isolation you may want from a trip. They also provide good jumping-off points for backpacking trips, if that's your calling. These camps are often free, and we have listed hundreds of them.

At the other end of the spectrum are the developed parks for RVs. They offer a home away from home, with everything from full hookups to a grocery store and laundry room. These spots are just as important as the remote camps with no facilities. Instead of isolation, an RV park provides a place to shower and get outfitted for food and clean clothes. For RV cruisers, it's a place to stay in high style while touring the area. RV parks range in price from $15 to $30 per night, depending on location, and an advance deposit may be necessary in summer months.

Somewhere between the two extremes—the remote, unimproved camps and the highly developed RV parks—are hundreds of campgrounds that provide a compromise: beautiful settings and some facilities, with a small overnight fee. Drinking water, vault toilets, and picnic tables tend to come with the territory, along with a fee that usually ranges from $6 to $15, with the higher-priced sites located near population centers. Because they offer a bit of both worlds, these sites are in high demand. Reservations are usually advised, and at state parks, particularly during the summer season, you can expect company. Most state parks have set up quotas so that you don't feel as if you've been squeezed in with a shoehorn. For another option, the same parks are often uncrowded during the off-season or on weekdays.

Before starting your trip, you'll want to get organized, and that's where you must start putting socks on that giant octopus. The trick to organization for any task is breaking it down into its key components, then solving each element independent of the others. Remember the octopus. Grab a moving leg, jam on a boot, and make sure it's on tight before reaching for another leg. Do one thing at a time, in order, and all will get done quickly and efficiently.

In the section that follows, we have isolated the different elements of camping, and you should do the same when planning your trip. There are separate tips for each of the following primary ingredients for a successful trip:

- Food and cooking gear
- Clothing and weather protection
- Hiking and foot care (and how to choose the right boots and socks)
- Sleeping gear
- First aid and insect protection
- Catching fish, avoiding bears, and having fun
- Outdoors with kids
- Weather prediction
- How to beat the time trap

We've also included sections on boat-in and desert camping, ethics in the outdoors, and a camping gear checklist.

Getting organized is an unnatural act for many people, but you can become completely organized for your trip in just one week, spending a little time planning each evening. By splitting up the tasks, you take the pressure out of planning and put the fun back in.

As full-time outdoors writers, the question we are asked more than any other is: "Where are you going this week?" All of the answers are in this book.

Camping Tips

Food and Cooking Gear

It was a warm, crystal clear day, the kind of day when if you had ever wanted to go skydiving, you would go skydiving. That was exactly the case for my old pal Foonsky, who had never before tried the sport. But a funny thing happened after he jumped out of the plane and pulled on the rip cord: His parachute didn't open.

In total freefall, Foonsky watched the earth below getting closer and closer. Not one to panic, he calmly pulled the rip cord on the emergency parachute. Again, nothing happened. No parachute, no nothing.

The ground was getting ever closer, and as he tried to search for a soft place to land, Foonsky detected a small object shooting up toward him, growing larger as it approached. It looked like a camper.

Figuring this was his last chance, Foonsky shouted as they passed in midair, "Hey, do you know anything about parachutes?"

The other fellow just yelled back as he headed off into space, "Do you know anything about lighting camping stoves?"

Well, Foonsky got lucky and his parachute opened. As for the other guy, well, he's probably in orbit like a NASA weather satellite. If you've ever had a mishap while lighting a camping stove, you know exactly what I'm talking about.

When it comes to camping, all gear is not created equal. Nothing is more important than lighting your stove easily and having it reach full heat without feeling as if you're playing with a short fuse to a miniature bomb. If your stove does not work right, your trip can turn into a disaster, regardless of how well you have planned the other elements. In addition, a bad stove will add an underlying sense of foreboding to your day. You will constantly have the inner suspicion that your darn stove is going to foul up again.

Camping Stoves

If you are buying a camping stove, remember this one critical rule: Do not leave the store with a new stove unless you have been shown exactly how to use it.

Know what you are getting. Many stores that specialize in outdoor recreation equipment now provide experienced campers/employees who will demonstrate the use of every stove they sell and, while they're at it, describe their respective strengths and weaknesses.

An innovation by Peak 1 is a two-burner backpacking stove that allows you to boil water and heat a pot of food simultaneously. While that has long been standard for car campers using Coleman's legendary camp stove, it was previously unheard of for wilderness campers in high-elevation areas. Another recent invention is the flameless stove (no kidding) that allows campers to cook in a tent safely.

A stove that has developed a cultlike following is the little Sierra, which burns small twigs and pinecones, then uses a tiny battery-driven fan to develop increased heat and cooking ability. It's an excellent alternative for long-distance backpacking trips because it solves the problem of carrying a fuel bottle, especially on expeditions for which large quantities of fuel would otherwise be needed. Some tinkering with the flame (a very hot one) is required, and they are legal and functional only in the alpine zone where dry wood is available. Also note that in years with high fire danger, the U.S. Forest Service will enact rules prohibiting open flames, and fires are also often prohibited above an elevation of 10,000 feet.

I prefer a small, lightweight stove that uses white gas so I can closely gauge fuel consumption. My pal Foonsky uses one with a butane bottle because it lights so easily. We have contests to see who can boil a pot of water faster, and the difference is usually negligible. Thus, other factors are important when choosing a stove.

Of these, ease of cleaning the burner is the most important. If you camp often, especially with a smaller stove, the burner holes will eventually become clogged. Some stoves have a built-in cleaning needle—a quick twist of the knob and you're in business. Others require disassembly and a protracted session using special cleaning tools. If a stove is difficult to clean, you will tend to put off doing it, and your stove will sputter and pant while you feel humiliated watching the cold pot of water sitting there.

Before making a purchase, have the salesperson show you how to clean the burner head. Except in the case of large, multiburner family camping stoves,

*Stoves are available in many styles and burn a variety of fuels. These are three typical examples. Top: **White gas** stoves are the most popular because they are inexpensive and easy to find; they do require priming and can be explosive. Middle: **Gas canister** stoves burn propane, butane, isobutane, and mixtures of the three. These are the easiest to use but have two disadvantages: 1) Because the fuel is bottled, determining how much fuel is left can be difficult. 2) The fuel is limited to above-freezing conditions. Bottom: **Liquid fuel** stoves burn Coleman fuel, denatured alcohol, kerosene, and even gasoline; these fuels are economical and have a high heat output, but most must be primed.*

which rarely require cleaning, this test can do more to determine the long-term value of a stove than any other factor.

Fuels for Camping Stoves

White gas and butane have long been the most popular camp fuels, but a newly developed fuel could dramatically change that. Liquid petroleum gas (LPG) comes in cartridges for easy attachment to a stove or lantern. At room temperature, LPG is delivered in a combustible gaseous form. When you shake the cartridge, the contents sound liquid; that is because the gas liquefies under pressure, which is why it is so easy to use. Large amounts of fuel are compressed into small canisters.

While convenience has always been the calling card for LPG, recent innovations have allowed it to become a suitable choice for winter and high-altitude mountaineering expeditions, coming close to matching white gas performance specs. For several years now, MSR, Epi (Coleman), Coleman, Primus, Camping Gaz, Markill, and other makers have been mixing propane, butane, and isobutane to improve performance capabilities.

Two important hurdles that stood in the way of LPG's popularity were recently leaped. Coleman, working in cooperation with the U.S. Postal Service, has developed a program in which three-packs of 170-gram Coleman Max fuel cartridges can be shipped by mail to any address or post office in the 50 states and Puerto Rico. Also, each Coleman Max fuel cartridge is now made of aluminum and comes with a special device that allows the consumer to puncture the cartridge safely once the fuel is gone and toss it into any aluminum recycling container.

The following details the benefits and drawbacks of other available fuels:

White gas: White gas is the most popular camp fuel because it can be purchased at most outdoor recreation stores and many supermarkets and is inexpensive and effective. It burns hot, has virtually no smell, and evaporates quickly when spilled. If you are caught in wet, miserable weather and can't get a fire going, you can use white gas as an emergency fire starter; however, if you do so, use it sparingly and never on an open flame.

White gas is a popular fuel both for car campers, who use the large, two-burner stoves equipped with a fuel tank and a pump, and for hikers who carry a lightweight backpacking stove. On the latter, lighting can require priming with a gel called priming paste, which some people dislike. Another problem with white gas is that it can be extremely explosive.

As an example, I once almost burned my beard completely off in a mini-explosion while lighting one of the larger stoves designed for car camping. I was in the middle of cooking dinner when the flame suddenly shut down. Sure enough, the fuel tank was empty, and after refilling it, I pumped the tank about 50 times to regain pressure. When I lit a match, the sucker ignited from three feet away. The resulting explosion was like a stick of dynamite going off, and immediately the smell of burning hair was in the air. In a flash, my once thick, dark beard had been reduced to a mass of little yellow burned curlicues.

My error? After filling the tank, I forgot to shut the fuel cock off while pumping up the pressure in the tank. As a result, the stove burners were slowly producing the gas/air mixture as I pumped the tank, filling the air above the stove. Then strike a match from even a few feet away and—ka-boom!

Butane: The explosive problem can be solved by using stoves that burn bottled butane fuel. Butane requires no pouring, pumping, or priming, and butane stoves are the easiest to light. Just turn a knob and light—that's it. On the minus side, because it comes in bottles, you never know precisely how much fuel you have left. And when a bottle is empty, you have a potential piece of litter. (Never litter. Ever.)

The other problem with butane is that it just plain does not work well in cold weather or when there is little fuel left in the cartridge. Because you cannot predict mountain weather in spring or fall, you can wind up using more fuel than originally projected. That can be frustrating, particularly if your stove starts wheezing when there are still several days left to go in your trip. In addition, with most butane cartridges, if there is any chance of the temperature falling below freezing, you often have to sleep with the cartridge to keep it warm or forget about using it in the morning.

Coleman Max Performance Fuel: This new fuel offers a unique approach to solving the consistent burn challenge facing all pressurized gas cartridges: operating at temperatures at or below 0° Fahrenheit. Using a standard propane/butane blend for high-octane performance, Coleman gets around the drop-off in performance that other cartridges experience by using a version of fuel injection. A hose inside the cartridge pulls liquid fuel into the stove, where it vaporizes—a switch from the standard approach of pulling only a gaseous form of the fuel into a stove. By drawing liquid out of the cartridge, Coleman gets around the tendency of propane to burn off first and allows each cartridge to deliver a consistent mix of propane and butane to the stove's burners throughout the cartridge's life.

Butane/Propane: This blend offers higher octane performance than butane alone, solving the cold temperature doldrums somewhat; however, propane burns off before butane, so there will be a performance drop-off as the fuel level in the cartridge lowers.

Propane: Now available for single-burner stoves using larger, heavier cartridges to accommodate higher pressures, propane offers the best performance of any of the pressurized gas canister fuels.

Primus Tri-Blend: This blend is made up of 20 percent propane, 70 percent butane, and 10 percent isobutane and is designed to burn with more consistent heat and efficiency than standard propane/butane mixes.

Denatured alcohol: Although this fuel burns cleanly and quietly and is virtually explosion proof, it generates much less heat than pressurized or liquid gas fuels.

Kerosene: Never buy a stove that uses kerosene for fuel. Kerosene is smelly and messy, generates low heat, needs priming, and is virtually obsolete as a camp fuel in the United States. As a test, I once tried using a kerosene stove. I could scarcely boil a pot of water. In addition, some kerosene leaked out when the stove was packed, ruining everything it touched. The smell of kerosene never did go away. Kerosene remains popular in Europe only because most campers there haven't yet heard much about white gas. When they do, they will demand it.

Building Fires

One summer expedition took me to the Canadian wilderness in British Columbia for a 75-mile canoe trip on the Bowron Lake Circuit, a chain of 13 lakes, six rivers, and seven portages. It is one of the truly great canoe trips in the world—a loop that ends just a few hundred feet from its starting point. But at the first camp at Kibbee Lake, my stove developed a fuel leak at the base of the burner, and the nuclearlike blast that followed just about turned Canada into a giant crater.

As a result, the final 70 miles of the trip had to be completed without a stove, cooking on open fires each night. The problem was compounded by the weather. It rained 8 of the 10 days. In Canada, raindrops the size of silver dollars fall so hard they actually bounce on the lake surface. We had to stop paddling a few times to empty the rainwater out of the canoe. At the end of the day, we'd make camp and then face the test: either make a fire or go to bed cold and hungry.

With an ax, at least we had a chance for success. As soaked as all the downed wood was, I was able to make my own fire-starting tinder from the chips of split logs; no matter how hard it rains, the inside of a log is always dry.

In miserable weather, matches don't stay lit long enough to get the tinder started. Instead we used either a candle or the little waxlike fire-starter cubes that remain lit for several minutes. From those we could get the tinder going. Then we added small, slender strips of wood that had been axed from the interior of the logs. When the flame reached a foot high, we added the logs, their dry interior facing in. By the time the inside of the logs had caught fire, the outside would be drying from the heat. It wasn't long before a royal blaze was brightening the rainy night.

That's a worst-case scenario, and hopefully you will never face anything like it. Nevertheless, being able to build a good fire and cook on it can be one of the more satisfying elements of a camping trip. At times just looking into the flames can provide a special satisfaction at the end of a good day; however, you should never expect to build a fire for every meal or, in some cases, even to build one at all.

Many state and federal campgrounds have been picked clean of downed wood, or forest fire danger forces rangers to prohibit fires altogether during the fire season. In either case, you must use your camp stove or go hungry.

But when you can build a fire and the resources for doing so are available, it will enhance the quality of your camping experience. Of the campgrounds listed in this book, those where you are permitted to build fires usually have fire rings. In primitive areas where you can make your own fire, you should dig a ring eight inches deep, line the edges with rock, and clear all the needles and twigs in a five-foot radius. The next day, when the fire is dead, you can discard the rocks, fill over the black charcoal with dirt, and scatter pine needles and twigs over it. Nobody will even know you camped there. That's the best way I know to keep a secret spot a real secret.

> During high fire danger, the U.S. Forest Service will enact rules prohibiting open flames. Fires are also often prohibited above an elevation of 10,000 feet.

When you start to build a campfire, the first thing you will notice is that no matter how good your intentions, your fellow campers will not be able to resist moving the wood around. Watch. You'll be getting ready to add a key piece of wood at just the right spot, and your companion will stick his mitts in, confidently believing he has a better idea. He'll shift the fire around and undermine your best-thought-out plans.

So I enforce a rule on camping trips: One person makes the fire while everybody else stands clear or is involved with other camp tasks such as gathering wood, getting water, putting up tents, or planning dinner. Once the fire is going strong, then it's fair game; anyone adds logs at his or her discretion. But in the early, delicate stages of the campfire, it's best to leave the work to one person.

Before a match is ever struck, you should gather a complete pile of firewood. Then start small, with the tiniest twigs you can find, and slowly add larger twigs

---

Keep It Wild Tip 1: Campfires

1. Fire use can scar the backcountry. If a fire ring is not available, use a lightweight stove for cooking.
2. Where fires are permitted, use existing fire rings away from large rocks or overhangs.
3. Don't char rocks by building new rings.
4. Gather sticks from the ground that are no larger than the diameter of your wrist.
5. Don't snap branches of live, dead, or downed trees, which can cause personal injury and scar the natural setting.
6. Put the fire "dead out" and make sure it's cold before departing. Remove all trash from the fire ring and sprinkle dirt over the site.
7. Remember that some forest fires can be started by a campfire that appears to be out. Hot embers burning deep in the pit can cause tree roots to catch fire and burn underground. If you ever see smoke rising from the ground, seemingly from nowhere, dig down and put the fire out.

as you go, criss-crossing them like a miniature tepee. Eventually you will get to the big chunks that will produce high heat. The key is to get one piece of wood burning into another, which then burns into another, setting off what I call the chain of flame. Conversely, single pieces of wood set apart from each other will not burn.

On a dry summer evening at a campsite where plenty of wood is available, about the only way you can blow the deal is to get impatient and try to add the big pieces too quickly. Do that and you'll get smoke, not flames, and it won't be long before every one of your fellow campers is poking at your fire. It will drive you crazy, but they just won't be able to help it.

Cooking Gear

I like traveling light, and I've found that all I need for cooking is a pot, small frying pan, metal pot grabber, fork, knife, cup, and matches. If you want to keep the price of food low and still cook customized dinners each night, a small pressure cooker can be just the ticket. (See "Keeping the Price Down.") I store all my gear in one small bag that fits into my pack. If I'm camping out of my four-wheel-drive rig, the little bag of cooking gear is easy to keep track of. Going simple, not complicated, is the key to keeping a camping trip on the right track.

You can get more elaborate by purchasing complete kits with plates, a coffeepot, large pots, and other cookware, but what really counts is having a single pot that makes you happy. It needs to be just the right size—not too big or small—and stable enough so it won't tip over, even if it is resting at a slight angle on a fire, full of water at a full boil. Mine is just 6 inches wide and 4.5 inches deep. It holds more than a quart of water and has served me well for several hundred camp dinners.

The rest of your cook kit is easy to complete. The frying pan should be small, light-gauge aluminum, and Teflon-coated, with a fold-in handle so it's easy to store. A pot grabber is a great addition. It's a little aluminum gadget that clamps to the edge of pots and allows you to lift them and pour water with total control without burning your fingers. For cleanup, take a plastic scrubber and a small bottle filled with dish cleaner, and you're in business.

A sierra cup, a wide aluminum cup with a wire handle, is an ideal item to carry because you can eat out of it and use it for drinking. This means no plates to scrub after dinner, so cleanup is quick and easy. In addition, if you go for a hike, you can clip it to your belt with its handle.

If you want a more formal setup complete with plates, glasses, silverware, and the like, you can end up spending more time preparing and cleaning up from meals than you do enjoying the country you are exploring. In addition, the more equipment you bring, the more loose ends you will have to deal with, and loose ends can cause plenty of frustration. If you have a choice, go simple.

And remember what Thoreau said: "A man is rich in proportion to what he can do without."

Food and Cooking Tricks

On a trip to the Bob Marshall Wilderness in western Montana, I woke up one morning, yawned, and said, "What've we got for breakfast?"

The silence was ominous. "Well," finally came the response, "we don't have any food left."

"What!?"

"Well, I figured we'd catch trout for meals every other night."

On the return trip, we ended up eating wild berries, buds, and, yes, even roots (not too tasty). When we finally landed the next day at a suburban pizza parlor, we nearly ate the wooden tables.

Running out of food on a camping trip can do more to turn reasonable people into violent grumps than any other event. There's no excuse for it, not when a system for figuring meals can be outlined with precision and little effort. You should not go out and buy a bunch of food, throw it in your rig, and head off for yonder. That leaves too much to chance. If you've ever been in the woods and real hungry, you'll know it's worth taking a little effort to make sure a day or two of starvation will not occur. Here's a three-step solution:

1. Draw up a general meal-by-meal plan and make sure your companions like what's on it.

2. Tell your companions to buy any specialty items (like a special brand of coffee) on their own and not to expect you to take care of everything.

3. Put all the food on your living room floor and literally plan out every day of your trip, meal by meal, putting the food in plastic bags as you go. That way you will know exact food quotas and will not go hungry.

Fish for your dinner? There's one guarantee as far as that goes: If you expect to catch fish for meals, you will most certainly get skunked. If you don't expect to catch fish for meals, you will probably catch so many they'll be coming out of your ears. I've seen it happen a hundred times.

Keeping the Price Down

"There must be some mistake," I said with a laugh. "Who ever paid $750 for camp food?"

But the amount was as clear as the digital numbers on the cash register: $753.27.

"How is this possible?" I asked the clerk.

"Just add it up," she responded, irritated.

Then I started figuring. The freeze-dried backpack dinners cost $6 apiece. A small pack of beef jerky went for $2, the beef sticks for 75 cents, granola bars for 50 cents. Multiply it all by four hungry men, including Foonsky, for 21 days. This food was to sustain us on a major expedition—four guys hiking 250 miles over three weeks from Mount Whitney to Yosemite Valley.

The dinners alone cost close to $500. Add in the usual goodies—jerky, granola bars, soup, dried fruit, oatmeal, Tang, candy, and coffee—and I felt as if an earthquake had struck when I saw the tab.

How to Make Beef Jerky in Your Own Kitchen

Start with a couple pieces of meat: lean top round, sirloin, or tri-tip. Cut it into 3/16-inch strips across the grain, trimming out the membrane, gristle, and fat. Marinate the strips for 24 hours in a glass dish. The fun begins in picking a marinade. Try two-thirds teriyaki sauce, one-third Worcestershire sauce. You can customize the recipe by adding pepper, ground mustard, bay leaf, red wine vinegar, garlic, and, for the brave, Tabasco sauce.

After a day or so, squeeze out each strip of meat with a rolling pin, lay the strips in rows on a cooling rack over a cookie sheet, and dry them in the oven at 125 degrees for 12 hours. Thicker pieces can take as long as 18 to 24 hours.

That's it. The hardest part is cleaning the cookie sheet when you're done. The easiest part is eating your own homemade jerky while sitting at a lookout on a mountain ridge. The do-it-yourself method for jerky may take a day or so, but it is cheaper and can taste better than any store-bought jerky.

A lot of campers have received similar shocks. In preparation for their trips, campers shop with enthusiasm. Then they pay the bill in horror.

Well, there are solutions, lots of them. You can eat gourmet style in the outback without having your wallet cleaned out. But it requires do-it-yourself cooking, more planning, and careful shopping. It also means transcending the push-button I-want-it-now attitude that so many people can't leave behind when they go to the mountains.

The secret is to bring along a small pressure cooker. A reader in San Francisco, Mike Bettinger, passed this tip on to me. Little pressure cookers weigh about two pounds, which may sound like a lot to backpackers and backcountry campers. But when three or four people are on a trip, it actually saves weight.

The key is that it allows campers to bring items that are difficult to cook at high altitudes, such as brown and white rice; red, black, pinto, and lima beans; and lentils. You pick one or more for a basic staple and then add a variety of freeze-dried ingredients to make a complete dish. Available are packets of meat, vegetables, onions, shallots, and garlic. Sun-dried tomatoes, for instance, reconstitute wonderfully in a pressure cooker. Add herbs, spices, and maybe a few rainbow trout, and you will be eating better out of a backpack than most people do at home.

"In the morning, I have used the pressure cooker to turn dried apricots into apricot sauce to put on the pancakes we made with sourdough starter," Bettinger said. "The pressure cooker is also big enough for washing out cups and utensils. The days when backpacking meant eating terrible freeze-dried food are over. It doesn't take a gourmet cook to prepare these meals, only some thought beforehand."

Now when Foonsky, Mr. Furnai, Rambob, and I sit down to eat such a meal, we don't call it "eating." We call it "hodgepacking" or "time to pack your hodge." After a particularly long day on the trail, you can do some serious hodgepacking. If your trip is a shorter one, say for a weekend, you can bring more fresh food to add some sizzle to the hodge. You can design a hot soup/stew mix that is good enough to eat at home.

Start by bringing a pot of water to a full boil, then adding pasta, ramen noodles, or macaroni. While it simmers, cut in a potato, carrot, onion, and garlic clove, and cook for about 10 minutes. When the vegetables have softened, add in a soup mix or two, maybe some cheese, and you are just about in business. But you can still ruin it and turn your hodge into slodge. Make sure you read the directions on the soup mix to determine cooking time. It can vary widely. In addition, make sure you stir the whole thing up; otherwise, you will get these hidden dry clumps of soup mix that taste like garlic sawdust.

How do I know? Well, it was up near Kearsage Pass in the Sierra Nevada, where, feeling half-starved, I dug into our nightly hodge. I will never forget that first bite—I damn near gagged to death. Foonsky laughed at me, until he took his first bite (a nice big one) and turned green.

Another way to trim food costs is to make your own beef jerky, the trademark staple of campers for more than 200 years. A tiny packet of beef jerky costs $2, and for that 250-mile expedition, I spent $150 on jerky alone. Never again. Now we make our own and get big strips of jerky that taste better than anything you can buy. (See the sidebar, "How To Make Beef Jerky in Your Own Kitchen.")

If all this still doesn't sound like your idea of a gourmet but low-cost camping meal, you are forgetting the main course—rainbow trout. Remember: If you don't plan on catching them for dinner, you'll probably snag more than you can finish in one night's hodgepacking. Some campers go to great difficulties to cook their trout, bringing along frying pans, butter, grills, tinfoil, and more, but all you need is some seasoned salt and a campfire.

Rinse the gutted trout, and while it's still wet, sprinkle on a good dose of seasoned salt, both inside and out. Clear any burning logs to the side of the campfire, then lay the trout right on the coals, turning it once so both sides are cooked. Sound ridiculous? Sound like you are throwing the fish away? Sound like the fish will burn up? Sound like you will have to eat the campfire ash? Wrong on all counts. The fish cooks perfectly, the ash doesn't stick, and after cooking trout this way, you may never fry trout again.

But if you can't convince your buddies, who may insist the trout should be fried, then make sure you have butter to fry them in, not oil. Also make sure you cook them all the way through, so the meat strips off the backbone in two nice, clean fillets. The fish should end up looking like one that Sylvester the Cat just drew out of his mouth—only the head, tail, and a perfect skeleton.

You can supplement your eats with sweets, nuts, freeze-dried fruits, and drink mixes. In any case, make sure you keep the dinner menu varied. If you and your buddies look into your dinner cups and groan, "Ugh, not this again," you will soon start dreaming of cheeseburgers and french fries instead of hiking, fishing, and finding beautiful campsites.

If you are car camping and have a big ice chest, you can bring virtually anything to eat and drink. If you are on the trail and don't mind paying the price, the newest freeze-dried dinners provide another option.

Some of the biggest advances in the outdoors industry have come in the freeze-dried dinners now available to campers. Some of them are almost good enough to serve in restaurants. Sweet-and-sour pork over rice, tostadas, Burgundy chicken—it sure beats the goop we used to eat, like the old soupy chili-mac dinners that tasted bad and looked so unlike food that consumption was near impossible, even for my dog, Rebel. Foonsky usually managed to get it down, but just barely.

To provide an idea of how to plan a menu, consider what my companions and I ate while hiking 250 miles on California's John Muir Trail:

- Breakfast: instant soup, oatmeal (never get plain), one beef or jerky stick, coffee or hot chocolate
- Lunch: one beef stick, two jerky sticks, one granola bar, dried fruit, half cup of pistachio nuts, Tang, one small bag of M&Ms
- Dinner: instant soup, one freeze-dried dinner, one milk bar, rainbow trout

What was that last item? Rainbow trout? Right! Unless you plan on it, you can catch them every night.

Clothing and Weather Protection

What started as an innocent pursuit of a perfect campground evolved into one heck of a predicament for Foonsky and me.

We had parked at the end of a logging road and then bushwhacked our way down a canyon to a pristine trout stream. On my first cast—a little flip into the plunge pool of a waterfall—I caught a 16-inch rainbow trout, a real beauty that jumped three times. Magic stuff.

Then just across the stream, we saw it: The Perfect Camping Spot. On a sandbar on the edge of the forest, there lay a flat spot, high and dry above the river. Nearby was plenty of downed wood collected by past winter storms that we could use for firewood. And, of course, this beautiful trout stream was bubbling along just 40 yards from the site.

But nothing is perfect, right? To reach it, we had to wade across the river, although it didn't appear to be too difficult. The cold water tingled a bit, and the river came up surprisingly high, just above the belt. But it would be worth it to camp at The Perfect Spot.

Once across the river, we put on some dry clothes, set up camp, explored the woods, and fished the stream, catching several nice trout for dinner. But late that afternoon, it started raining. What? Rain in the summertime? Nature makes its own rules. By the next morning, it was still raining, pouring like a Yosemite waterfall from a solid gray sky.

That's when we noticed The Perfect Spot wasn't so perfect. The rain had raised the river level too high for us to wade back across. We were marooned, wet, and hungry.

"Now we're in a heck of a predicament," said Foonsky, the water streaming off him.

Getting cold and wet on a camping trip with no way to warm up is not only unnecessary and uncomfortable, but it can also be a fast ticket to hypothermia, the number one killer of campers in the woods. By definition, hypothermia is a condition in which body temperature is lowered to the point that it causes illness. It is particularly dangerous because the afflicted are usually unaware it is setting in. The first sign is a sense of apathy, then a state of confusion, which can eventually lead to collapse (or what appears to be sleep), then death.

You must always have a way to get warm and dry in short order, regardless of any conditions you may face. If you have no way of getting dry, then you must take emergency steps to prevent hypothermia. Those steps are detailed in the first-aid section.

But you should never reach that point. For starters, always have spare sets of clothing tucked away so no matter how cold and wet you might get, you have something dry to put on. On hiking trips, I always carry a second set of clothes, sealed to stay dry, in a plastic garbage bag. I keep a third set waiting back at the truck.

If you are car camping, your vehicle can cause an illusory sense of security. But with an extra set of dry clothes stashed safely away, there is no illusion. The security is real. And remember, no matter how hot the weather is when you start your trip, always be prepared for the worst. Foonsky and I learned the hard way.

So both of us were soaking wet on that sandbar, and with no other choice we tried holing up in the tent for the night. A sleeping bag with Quallofil or another polyester fiberfill can retain warmth even when wet, because the fill is hollow and retains its loft. So as miserable as it was, we made it through the night.

The rain stopped the next day and the river dropped a bit, but it was still rolling big and angry. Using a stick as a wading staff, Foonsky crossed about 80 percent of the stream before he was dumped, but he made a jump for it and managed to scramble to the riverbank. He waved for me to follow. "No problem," I thought.

It took me 20 minutes to reach nearly the same spot where Foonsky had been dumped. The heavy river current was above my belt and pushing hard. Then in the flash of an instant, my wading staff slipped on a rock. I teetered in the river current and was knocked over like a bowling pin. I became completely submerged. I went tumbling down the river, heading right toward the waterfall. While underwater I looked up at the surface, and I can remember how close it seemed yet how out of control I was. Right then this giant hand appeared, and I grabbed it. It was Foonsky. If it weren't for that hand, I would have sailed right over the waterfall.

My momentum drew Foonsky right into the river, and we scrambled in the current, but I suddenly sensed the river bottom under my knees. On all fours, the two of us clambered ashore. We were safe.

"Thanks ol' buddy," I said.

"Man, we're wet," he responded. "Let's get to the rig and get some dry clothes on."

The Art of Layering

The most important element in enjoying the outdoor experience in any condition is to stay dry and warm. There is no substitute. You must stay dry and you must stay warm.

Thus comes the theory behind layering, which suggests that as your body temperature fluctuates or the weather shifts, you simply peel off or add available layers as needed—and have a waterproof shell available in case of rain.

The introduction of a new era of outdoor clothing has made it possible for campers to turn choosing clothes into an art form. Like art, it comes much more expensive than throwing on a pair of blue jeans, a T-shirt, and some flannel, but for many it is worth the price.

In putting together your ideal layering system, there are some general considerations. What you need to do is create a system that effectively combines elements of breathability, wicking, rapid drying, insulation, durability, wind resistance, and water repellence while still being lightweight and offering the necessary freedom of movement, all with just a few garments.

The basic intent of a base layer is to manage moisture. Your base layer will be the first article of clothing you put on and the last to come off. Because your skin will be churning out the perspiration, the goal of this second skin is to manage the moisture and move it away from you without trapping your body's heat. The only time cotton should become a part of your base layer is if you wish to keep cool, not warm, such as in a hot desert climate where evaporative cooling becomes your friend, not your enemy.

That is why the best base layer available is from bicomponent knits; that is, blends of polyester and cotton, which work to provide wicking and insulating properties in one layer. The way it works is that the side facing your skin is water hating, while the side away from your skin is water loving; thus it pulls or "wicks" moisture through. You'll stay dry and happy, even with only one layer on, something not possible with old single-function weaves. The best types include Thermax, Capilene, Driclime, Lifa, and Polartec 100.

Stretch fleece and microdenier pile also provide a good base layer, although they can be used as a second layer as well. Microdenier pile can be worn alone or layered under or over other pieces, and it has excellent wicking capability as well as more windproof potential.

The next layer should be a light cotton shirt or a long-sleeved cotton/wool shirt, or both, depending on the coolness of the day. For pants, many just wear blue jeans when camping, but blue jeans can be hot and tight, and once wet, they tend to stay that way. Putting on wet blue jeans on a cold morning is a torturous way to start the day. (I tell you this from experience because I have suffered that fate a number of times.) A better choice is pants made from a cotton/canvas mix, which are available at outdoors stores. They are light, have a lot of give, and dry quickly. If the weather is warm, roomy shorts can be the best choice.

Finally, you'll top the entire ensemble off with a thin windproof, water-resistant layer. You want this layer to breathe like crazy, yet not be so porous that rain runs through it like floodwaters through a leaking dike. Patagonia's Velocity shell is one of the best. Its outer fabric is durable water-repellent (DWR) treated, and the coating is by Gore. Patagonia calls it Pneumatic. (Gore now calls it Activent, while Marmot, Moonstone, and North Face all offer their own versions). Although condensation will still build up inside, it manages to get rid of enough moisture.

It is critical to know the difference between "water-resistant" and "waterproof." This distinction is covered later in the chapter under the "Rain Gear" section.

But hey, why does anybody need all this fancy stuff just to go camping? Fair question. Like the introduction of Gore-Tex years ago, all this fabric and fiber mumbo-jumbo has its skeptics, including me. You don't have to opt for this aerobic-function fashion statement; it is unnecessary on many camping trips. But the fact is you must be ready for anything when you venture into the outdoors. And the truth is that the new era of outdoor clothing works, and it works better than anything that has come before.

Regardless of what you choose, weather should never be a nuisance or cause discomfort, regardless of what you experience. Instead it should provide a welcome change of pace.

About Hats

One final word of advice: Always pack a warm hat for those times when you need to seal in warmth. You lose a large percentage of heat through your head. I almost always wear a wide-brimmed hat, something like the legendary outlaws wore 150 years ago. There's actually logic behind it: My hat is made out of kangaroo skin (waterproof), is rigged with a lariat (it can be cinched down when it's windy), and has a wide brim that keeps the tops of my ears from being sunburned (years ago they once were burned to a red crisp on a trip where I was wearing a baseball hat). But to be honest, I mostly like how it looks, kind of like my pal Waylon Jennings.

Vests and Parkas

In cold weather, you should take the layer system one step further with a warm vest and a parka jacket. Vests are especially useful because they provide warmth without the bulkiness of a parka. The warmest vests and parkas are either filled with down or Quallofil, or are made with a cotton/wool mix. Each has its respective merits and problems. Down fill provides the most warmth for the amount of weight but becomes useless when wet, closely resembling a wet dishrag. Quallofil keeps much of its heat-retaining quality even when wet but is expensive. Vests made of cotton/wool mixes are the most attractive and are warm, but they can be as heavy as a ship's anchor when wet.

Sometimes the answer is combining the two. One of my best camping companions wears a good-looking cotton/wool vest and a parka filled with Quallofil. The vest never gets wet, so weight is not a factor.

Rain Gear

One of the most miserable nights I ever spent in my life was on a camping trip where I didn't bring my rain gear or a tent. It was early August, the temperature had been in the nineties for weeks, and if anybody had said it was going to rain,

I would have told him to consult a brain doctor. But rain it did. And as I got wetter and wetter, I kept saying to myself, "Hey, it's summer, it's not supposed to rain." Then I remembered one of the 10 commandments of camping: Forget your rain gear and you can guarantee it will rain.

To stay dry, you need some form of water-repellent shell. It can be as simple as a $5 poncho made out of plastic or as elaborate as a Gore-Tex jacket-and-pants set that costs $300. What counts is not how much you spend, but how dry you stay.

The most important thing to realize is that waterproof and water-resistant are completely different things. In addition, there is no such thing as rain gear that is both waterproof and breathable. The more waterproof a jacket is, the less it breathes. Conversely, the more breathable a jacket is, the less waterproof it becomes.

If you wear water-resistant rain gear in a downpour, you'll get soaked. Water-resistant rain gear is appealing because it breathes and will keep you dry in the light stuff, such as mist, fog, even a little splash from a canoe paddle. But in rain? Forget it.

So what is the solution?

I've decided that the best approach is a set of fairly light but 100 percent waterproof rain gear. I recently bought a hooded jacket and pants from Coleman, and my assessment is that it is the most cost-efficient rain gear I've ever had. All I can say is, it works: I stay dry, it doesn't weigh much, and it didn't cost a fortune.

You can also stay dry with any of the waterproof plastics and even heavy-duty rubber-coated outfits made for commercial fishermen. But these are uncomfortable during anything but a heavy rain. Because they are heavy and don't breathe, you'll likely get soaked anyway (that is, from your own sweat), even if it isn't raining hard.

On backpacking trips, I still stash a super lightweight water-repellent slicker for day hikes and a poncho, which I throw over my pack at night to keep it dry. But otherwise I never go anywhere—*anywhere*—without my rain gear.

Some do just fine with a cheap poncho, and note that ponchos can serve other uses in addition to a raincoat. Ponchos can be used as a ground tarp, as a rain cover for supplies or a backpack, or can be roped up to trees in a pinch to provide a quick storm ceiling if you don't have a tent. The problem with ponchos is that in a hard rain, you just don't stay dry. First your legs get wet, then they get soaked. Then your arms follow the same pattern. If you're wearing cotton, you'll find that once part of the garment gets wet, the water will spread until, alas, you are dripping wet, poncho and all. Before long you start to feel like a walking refrigerator.

Waterproof: impervious to water. Though rain won't penetrate waterproof material, if you're at all mobile, you'll soon find yourself wet from perspiration that can't evaporate.

Water-resistant: resistant but not impervious to water. You'll stay dry using water-resistant material only if it isn't pouring.

One high-cost option is buying a Gore-Tex rain jacket and pants. Gore-Tex is actually not a fabric as is commonly believed, but a laminated film that coats a breathable fabric. The result is lightweight, water-repellent, breathable jackets and pants. They are perfect for campers, but they cost a fortune.

Some hiking buddies of mine have complained

that the older Gore-Tex rain gear loses its water-repellent quality over time; however, manufacturers insist that this is the result of water seeping through seams, not leaks in the jacket. At each seam, tiny needles have pierced the fabric, and as tiny as the holes are, water will find a way through. An application of Seam Lock, especially at major seams around the shoulders of a jacket, can usually fix the problem.

If you don't want to spend the big bucks for Gore-Tex rain gear but want more rain protection than a poncho affords, a coated nylon jacket is the compromise that many choose. They are inexpensive, have the highest water-repellency of any rain gear, and are warm, providing a good outer shell for your layers of clothing. But they are not without fault. These jackets don't breathe at all, and if you zip them up tight, you can sweat a river.

My brother Rambob gave me a nylon jacket before I embarked on a mountain climbing expedition. I wore that $20 special all the way to the top with no complaints; it's warm and 100 percent waterproof. The one problem with nylon is that when temperatures drop below freezing, it gets so stiff that it feels as if you are wearing a straitjacket. But at $20, it seems like a treasure, especially compared to a $180 Gore-Tex jacket.

There's one more jacket-construction term to know: durable water-repellent (DWR) finish. All of the top-quality jackets these days are DWR treated. The DWR causes water to bead up on the shell. When the DWR wears off, even a once-waterproof jacket will feel like a wet dishrag.

Also note that ventilation is the key to coolness. The only ventilation on most shells is often the zipper. But waterproof jackets need additional openings. Look for mesh-backed pockets and underarm zippers, as well as cuffs, waists, and hems that can be adjusted to open wide. Storm flaps (the baffle over the zipper) that close with hook-and-loop material or snaps let you leave the zipper open for airflow into the jacket.

Other Gear—and a Few Tips

What are the three most commonly forgotten items on a camping trip? A hat, sunglasses, and lip balm.

A hat is crucial, especially when you are visiting high elevations. Without one you are constantly exposed to everything nature can give you. The sun will dehydrate you, sap your energy, sunburn your head, and in worst cases, cause sunstroke. Start with a comfortable hat. Then finish with sunglasses, lip balm, and sunscreen for additional protection. They will help protect you from extreme heat.

To guard against extreme cold, it's a good idea to keep a pair of thin ski gloves stashed away with your emergency clothes, along with a wool ski cap. The gloves should be thick enough to keep your fingers from stiffening up, but pliable enough to allow full movement so you don't have to take them off to complete simple tasks, like lighting a stove. An alternative to gloves is glovelets, which look like gloves with no fingers. In any case, just because the weather turns cold doesn't mean your hands have to.

If you fall into a river as Foonsky and I did—well, I hope you have a set of dry clothes waiting back at your rig. Oh, and a hand reaching out to you.

Hiking and Foot Care

We had set up a nice little camp in the woods, and my buddy, Foonsky, was strapping on his hiking boots, sitting against a big Douglas fir.

"New boots," he said with a grin. "But they seem pretty stiff."

We decided to hoof it down the trail for a few hours, exploring the mountain wildlands that are said to hide Bigfoot and other strange creatures. After just a short while on the trail, a sense of peace and calm seemed to settle in. The forest provides the chance to be purified with clean air and the smell of trees, freeing you from all troubles.

But it wasn't long before a look of trouble appeared on Foonsky's face. And no, it wasn't from seeing Bigfoot.

"Got a hot spot on a toe," he said.

Immediately we stopped. He pulled off his right boot, then his socks, and inspected the left side of his big toe. Sure enough, a blister had bubbled up, filled with fluid, but hadn't popped. From his medical kit, Foonsky cut a small piece of moleskin to fit over the blister and taped it to hold it in place. In a few minutes we were back on the trail.

A half hour later, there was still no sign of Bigfoot. But Foonsky stopped again and pulled off his other boot. "Another hot spot." On the little toe of his left foot was another small blister, over which he taped a Band-Aid to keep it from further chafing against the inside of his new boot.

In just a few days, ol' Foonsky, a strong, 6-foot-5-inch, 200-plus-pound guy, was walking around like a sore-hoofed horse that had been loaded with a month's worth of supplies and ridden over sharp rocks. It wasn't the distance that had done Foonsky in; it was those blisters. He had them on 8 of his 10 toes and was going through Band-Aids, moleskin, and tape like a walking emergency ward. If he used any more tape, he would've looked like a mummy from an Egyptian tomb.

If you've ever been in a similar predicament, you know the frustration of wanting to have a good time, wanting to hike and explore the area where you have set up a secluded camp, only to be turned gimp-legged by several blisters. No one is immune—all are created equal before the blister god. You can be forced to bow to it unless you get your act together. That means wearing the right style boots for what you have in mind and then protecting your feet with carefully selected socks. If you are still so unfortunate as to get a blister or two, it means knowing how to treat them fast so they don't turn your walk into a sore-footed endurance test.

What causes blisters? In almost all cases, it is the simple rubbing of a foot against the rugged interior of a boot. That can be worsened by several factors:
• A very stiff boot or one in which your foot moves inside as you walk, instead of the boot flexing as if it were another layer of skin.
• Thin, ragged, or dirty socks. This is the fastest route to blisters. Thin socks will

allow your feet to move inside your boots, ragged socks will allow your skin to chafe directly against the boot's interior, and dirty socks will wrinkle and fold, also rubbing against your feet instead of cushioning them.

- Soft feet. By themselves, soft feet will not cause blisters, but in combination with a stiff boot or thin socks, they can cause terrible problems. The best way to toughen up your feet is to go barefoot. In fact, some of the biggest, toughest-looking guys you'll ever see, from Hell's Angels to pro football players, have feet that are as soft as a baby's butt. Why? Because they never go barefoot and don't hike much.

Selecting the Right Boots

One summer I hiked 400 miles, including 250 miles in three weeks, along the crest of California's Sierra Nevada, and another 150 miles over several months in an earlier general training program. In that span I got just one blister, suffered on the fourth day of the 250-miler. I treated it immediately and suffered no more. One key is wearing the right boot, and for me, that means a boot that acts as a thick layer of skin that is flexible and pliable to my foot. I want my feet to fit snugly in them, with no interior movement.

There are three kinds of boots: mountaineering boots, hiking (or backpacking) boots, and canvas walking shoes. Select the right one for you or pay the consequences.

Mountaineering Boots

The stiffest of the lot is the mountaineering boot. These boots are often identified by midrange tops, laces that extend almost as far as the toe area, and ankle areas that are as stiff as a board. The lack of "give" is what endears them to mountaineers. Their stiffness is preferred when rock climbing, walking off-trail on craggy surfaces, or hiking down the edge of streambeds where walking across small rocks can cause you to turn your ankle. Because these boots don't give on rugged, craggy terrain, they reduce ankle injuries and provide better traction.

The drawback to stiff boots is that if you don't have the proper socks and your foot starts slipping around in the boot, you will get a set of blisters that would raise even Foonsky's eyebrows. But if you just want to go for a walk or a good tromp with a backpack, then hiking shoes or backpacking boots will serve you better.

Backpacking Boots

My preference is for a premium backpacking boot, the perfect medium between the stiff mountaineering boot and the soft canvas walking shoe. The deep lug bottom provides traction, the high ankle coverage provides support, yet the soft, waterproof leather body gives each foot a snug fit. Add it up and that means no blisters. On the negative side, they can be quite hot, weigh a ton, and if they get wet, take days to dry.

There are a zillion styles, brands, and price ranges to choose from. If you wander about comparing all their many features, you will get as confused as a kid in a toy store. Instead, go into the store with your mind clear about what you want, find it, and buy it. If you want the best, expect to spend $85 to $110 for canvas walking shoes, from $130 to $180 and sometimes more for hiking or mountaineering boots. I have spent as much as $250 for hiking boots that I have worn for close to 2,000 miles. Yet another time I spent $185, thinking I was getting stellar quality, but they turned out to be miserable blister makers, and even after a year of trying to get my money's worth, they never worked right on the trail and now occupy a dark place deep in my closet.

This is one area where you don't want to scrimp, so try not to yelp about the high cost. Instead, walk out of the store believing you deserve the best, and that's exactly what you just paid for. Another trick I have learned is to bring several pairs of different style hiking boots on adventures, then change them constantly according to the terrain. Use heavy boots for steep trails with loose footing, lightweight models for flat routes with a hard surface. This works wonders to avoid blisters and muscle soreness because you are constantly changing what I call "the point of attack."

If you plan on using the advice of a shoe salesperson, first look at what kind of boots he or she is wearing. If he or she isn't even wearing boots, then any advice the salesperson might tender may not be worth a plugged nickel. Most people I know who own quality boots, including salespeople, will wear them almost daily if their job allows because boots are the best footwear available; however, even these well-meaning folks can offer sketchy advice. Every hiker I've ever met will tell you he wears the world's greatest boot.

Instead, enter the store with a precise use and style in mind. Rather than fish for suggestions, tell the salesperson exactly what you want, try two or three brands of the same style, and always try on both boots in a pair simultaneously so you know exactly how they'll feel. If possible, walk up and down stairs with them. Are they too stiff? Are your feet snug yet comfortable, or do they slip? Do they have that "right" kind of feel when you walk?

If you get the right answers to those questions, then you're on your way to blister-free, pleasure-filled days of walking.

Canvas Walking Shoes

Canvas walking shoes are the lightest of all boots, designed for day walks or short backpacking trips. Some of the newer models are like rugged tennis shoes, designed with a canvas top for lightness and a lug sole for traction. These are perfect for people who like to walk but rarely carry a backpack. Because they are flexible, they are easy to break in, and with fresh socks they rarely cause blister problems. Because they are light, general hiking fatigue is greatly reduced.

On the negative side, because canvas shoes have shallow lug soles, traction can be far from good on slippery surfaces. In addition, they provide less than ideal ankle support, which can be a problem in rocky areas, such as along a stream where you might want to go trout fishing. Turn your ankle and your trip can be ruined.

Keep It Wild Tip 2: Travel Lightly

1. Visit the backcountry in small groups.
2. Below tree line, always stay on designated trails.
3. Don't cut across switchbacks.
4. When traveling cross-country where no trails are available, follow animal trails or spread out with your group so no new routes are created.
5. Read your map and orient yourself with landmarks, a compass, and an altimeter. Avoid marking trails with rock cairns, tree scars, or ribbons.

Socks

The poor gent was scratching his feet as if ants were crawling over them. I looked closer. Huge yellow calluses covered the bottoms of his feet, and at the ball and heel, the calluses were about a quarter inch thick, cracking and sore.

"I don't understand it," he said. "I'm on my feet a lot, so I bought a real good pair of hiking boots. But look what they've done to my feet. My feet itch so much I'm going crazy."

People can spend so much energy selecting the right kind of boot that they virtually overlook wearing the right kind of socks. One goes with the other.

Your socks should be thick enough to cushion your feet and fit snugly. Without good socks, you might try to get the bootlaces too tight—and that's like putting a tourniquet on your feet. You should have plenty of clean socks on hand, or plan on washing what you have on your trip. As socks are worn, they become compressed, dirty, and damp. Any one of those factors can cause problems.

My camping companions believe I go overboard when it comes to socks, that I bring too many and wear too many. But it works, so that's where the complaints stop. So how many do I wear? Well, it varies. On day hikes, I have found a sock called a SmartWool that makes my size thirteens feel as if I'm walking on pillows. But on long expeditions, the 200-milers, I sometimes wear three socks on each foot, believe it or not. It may sound like overkill, but each has its purpose, and like I said, it works.

The interior sock is thin, lightweight, and made of polypropylene or silk synthetic materials designed to transport moisture away from your skin. With a poly interior sock, your foot stays dry when it sweats. Without a poly sock, your foot can get damp and mix with dirt, which can cause a hot spot to start on your foot. Eventually you get blisters, lots of them.

The second sock is for comfort and can be cotton, but a thin wool-based composite is ideal. Some made of the latter can wick moisture away from the skin, much like polypropylene does. If wool itches your feet, a thick cotton sock can be suitable, though cotton collects moisture and compacts more quickly than other socks. If you're on a short hike though, cotton will do just fine.

The exterior sock should be made of high-quality, thick wool—at least 80 percent wool. It will cushion your feet, provide that just-right snug fit in your boot, and give you additional warmth and insulation in cold weather. It is critical to keep the wool sock clean. If you wear a dirty wool sock over and over again, it will compact and lose its cushion and start wrinkling while you hike. Then your feet will catch on fire from the blisters that start popping up. Of course, when wearing multiple socks, especially a wool composite, you will likely need to go up a boot size so they fit comfortably.

A Few More Tips

If you are like most folks—that is, the bottoms of your feet are rarely exposed and quite soft—you can take additional steps in their care. The best tip is keeping a fresh foot pad made of sponge rubber in your boot. Another cure for soft feet is to get out and walk or jog on a regular basis before your camping trip.

If you plan to use a foot pad and wear three socks, you will need to use these items when sizing boots. It is an unforgiving error to wear thin cotton socks when buying boots and later try to squeeze all this stuff, plus your feet, into them. There just won't be enough room.

The key to treating blisters is fast work at the first sign of a hot spot. But before you remove your socks, check to see if the sock has a wrinkle in it, a likely cause of the problem. If so, either change socks or pull them tight, removing the tiny folds, after taking care of the blister. Cut a piece of moleskin to cover the offending toe, securing the moleskin with white medical tape. If moleskin is not available, small Band-Aids can do the job, but these have to be replaced daily, and sometimes with even more frequency. At night, clean your feet and sleep without socks.

Two other items that can help your walking is an Ace bandage and a pair of gaiters. For sprained ankles and twisted knees, an Ace bandage can be like an insurance policy to get you back on the trail and out of trouble. Over the years, I have had serious ankle problems and have relied on a good wrap with a four-inch bandage to get me home. The newer bandages come with the clips permanently attached, so you don't have to worry about losing them.

Gaiters are leggings made of plastic, nylon, or Gore-Tex that fit from just below your knees, over your calves, and attach under your boots. They are of particular help when walking in damp areas or in places where rain is common. As your legs brush against ferns or low-lying plants, gaiters will deflect the moisture. Without them, your pants will be soaking wet in short order.

Should your boots become wet, a good tip is never to try to force dry them. Some well-meaning folks will try to dry them quickly at the edge of a campfire or actually put the boots in an oven. While this may dry the boots, it can also loosen the glue that holds them together, ultimately weakening them until one day they fall apart in a heap.

A better bet is to treat the leather so the boots become water repellent. Silicone-based liquids are the easiest to use and least greasy of the treatments available.

A final tip is to have another pair of lightweight shoes or moccasins that you can wear around camp and in the process give your feet the rest they deserve.

Sleeping Gear

One mountain night in the pines on an eve long ago, my dad, brother, and I had rolled out our sleeping bags and were bedded down for the night. After the pre-trip excitement, a long drive, an evening of trout fishing, and a barbecue, we were like three tired doggies who had played too much. But as I looked up at the stars, I was suddenly wide awake. This kid was still wired. A half hour later? No change—wide awake.

And as little kids can do, I had to wake up ol' dad to tell him about it. "Hey, Dad, I can't sleep."

"This is what you do," he said. "Watch the sky for a shooting star and tell yourself that you cannot go to sleep until you see at least one. As you wait and watch, you will start getting tired, and it will be difficult to keep your eyes open. But tell yourself you must keep watching. Then you'll start to really feel tired. When you finally see a shooting star, you'll go to sleep so fast you won't know what hit you."

Well, I tried it that night and I don't even remember seeing a shooting star, I went to sleep so fast. It's a good trick, and along with having a good sleeping bag, ground insulation, maybe a tent, or a few tricks for bedding down in a pickup truck or motor home, you can get a good night's sleep on every camping trip.

More than 20 years after that camping episode with my dad and brother, we made a trip to the planetarium at the Academy of Sciences in San Francisco to see a show on Halley's comet. The lights dimmed, and the ceiling turned into a night sky, filled with stars and a setting moon. A scientist began explaining phenomena of the heavens.

After a few minutes, I began to feel drowsy. Just then, a shooting star zipped across the planetarium ceiling. I went into a deep sleep so fast it was as if I was in a coma. I didn't wake up until the show was over, the lights were turned back on, and the people were leaving.

Feeling drowsy, I turned to see if ol' Dad had liked the show. Not only had he gone to sleep too, but he apparently had no intention of waking up, no matter what. Just like a camping trip.

Sleeping Bags

Question: What could be worse than trying to sleep in a cold, wet sleeping bag on a rainy night without a tent in the mountains?

Answer: Trying to sleep in a cold, wet sleeping bag on a rainy night without a tent in the mountains when your sleeping bag is filled with down.

Water will turn a down-filled sleeping bag into a mushy heap. Many campers do not like a high-tech approach, but the state-of-the-art polyfiber sleeping bags can keep you warm even when wet. That factor, along with temperature rating and weight, is key when selecting a sleeping bag.

A sleeping bag is a shell filled with heat-retaining insulation. By itself, it is not warm. Your body provides the heat, and the sleeping bag's ability to retain that heat is what makes it warm or cold.

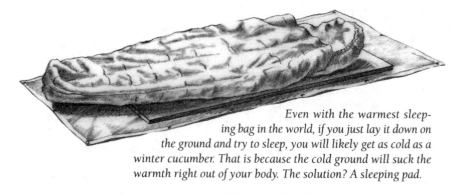

Even with the warmest sleeping bag in the world, if you just lay it down on the ground and try to sleep, you will likely get as cold as a winter cucumber. That is because the cold ground will suck the warmth right out of your body. The solution? A sleeping pad.

The old-style canvas bags are heavy, bulky, cold, and when wet, useless. With other options available, their use is limited. Anybody who sleeps outdoors or backpacks should choose otherwise. Buy and use a sleeping bag filled with down or one of the quality polyfills. Down is light, warm, and aesthetically pleasing to those who don't think camping and technology mix. If you choose a down bag, be sure to keep it double wrapped in plastic garbage bags on your trip to keep it dry. Once wet, you'll spend your nights howling at the moon.

The polyfiber-filled bags are not necessarily better than those filled with down, but they can be. Their one key advantage is that even when wet, some polyfills can retain up to 85 percent of your body heat. This allows you to sleep and get valuable rest even in miserable conditions. My camping experience is that no matter how lucky you may be, there comes a time when you will get caught in an unexpected, violent storm and everything you've got will get wet, including your sleeping bag. That's when a polyfill bag becomes priceless. You either have one and can sleep or you don't have one and suffer. It is that simple. Of the synthetic fills, Quallofil made by DuPont is the industry leader.

But just because a sleeping bag uses a high-tech polyfill doesn't necessarily make it a better bag. There are other factors.

The most important are a bag's temperature rating and weight. The temperature rating of a sleeping bag refers to how cold it can get before you start actually feeling cold. Many campers make the mistake of thinking, "I only camp in the summer, so a bag rated at 30 or 40°F should be fine." Later they find out it isn't so fine, and all it takes is one cold night to convince them of that. When selecting the right temperature rating, visualize the coldest weather you might ever confront, and then get a bag rated for even colder weather.

For instance, if you are a summer camper, you may rarely experience a night in the low 30s or high 20s. A sleeping bag rated at 20°F would be appropriate, keeping you snug, warm, and asleep. For most campers, I advise bags rated at 0 or 10°F.

If you buy a polyfilled sleeping bag, never leave it squished in your stuff sack between camping trips. Instead, keep it on a hanger in a closet or use it as a blanket. One thing that can reduce a polyfilled bag's heat-retaining qualities is if you lose the loft out of the tiny hollow fibers that make up the fill. You can avoid this with proper storage.

The weight of a sleeping bag can also be a key factor, especially for backpackers. When you have to carry your gear on your back, every ounce becomes important. Sleeping bags that weigh just three pounds are available, although they are expensive. But if you hike much, it's worth the price to keep your weight to a minimum. For an overnighter, you can get away with a 4- or 4.5-pound bag without much stress; however, bags weighing five pounds and up should be left back at the car.

I have two sleeping bags: a seven-pounder that feels like a giant sponge and a little three-pounder. The heavy-duty model is for pickup truck camping in cold weather and doubles as a blanket at home. The lightweight bag is for hikes. Between the two, I'm set.

Insulation Pads

Even with the warmest sleeping bag in the world, if you just lay it down on the ground and try to sleep, you will likely get as cold as a winter cucumber. That is because the cold ground will suck the warmth right out of your body. The solution is to have a layer of insulation between you and the ground. For this you can use a thin Insulite pad, a lightweight Therm-a-Rest inflatable pad, or a foam pad or mattress, an air bed, or a cot. Here is a capsule summary of all three categories:

- **Insulite pads:** They are light, inexpensive, roll up quick for transport, and can double as a seat pad at your camp. The negative side is that in one night, they will compress, making you feel that you are sleeping on granite.
- **Therm-a-Rest pads:** These are a real luxury because they do everything an Insulite pad does, but also provide a cushion. The negative side is that they are expensive by comparison, and if they get a hole in them, they become worthless without a patch kit.
- **Air beds, foam mattresses, and cots:** These are excellent for car campers. The new line of air beds available are outstanding, especially the thicker ones, and inflate quickly with an electric motor inflator that plugs into a power plug or cigarette lighter in your vehicle. Foam mattresses are also excellent, in fact, the most comfortable of all, but their size precludes many from considering them. I've found that cots work great, too. I finally wore out an old wooden one just before this book went to press and replaced it immediately with one of the new high-tech, light metal ones. For camping in the back of a pickup truck with a camper shell, the cots with three-inch legs are best.

A Few Tricks

When surveying a camp area, the most important consideration should be to select a good sleeping spot. Everything else is secondary. Ideally, you want a flat spot that is wind sheltered and on ground soft enough to drive stakes into. Yeah, and I want to win the lottery, too.

Sometimes that ground will have a slight slope to it. In that case, always sleep with your head on the uphill side. If you sleep parallel to the slope, every time you roll over, you'll find yourself rolling down the hill. If you sleep with your head on the downhill side, you'll get a headache that feels as if an ax is embedded in your brain.

When you've found a good spot, clear it of all branches, twigs, and rocks. A good tip is to dig a slight indentation in the ground where your hip will fit. Since your body is not flat, but has curves and edges, it will not feel comfortable on flat ground. Some people even get severely bruised on the sides of their hips when sleeping on flat, hard ground. For that reason alone, they learn to hate camping. What a shame, especially when the problem is so easily solved with a Therm-a-Rest pad, foam insulation, an air bed, or a cot.

After the ground is prepared, throw a ground cloth over the spot, which will keep much of the morning dew off you. In some areas, particularly where fog is a problem, morning dew can be heavy and get the outside of your sleeping bag quite wet. In that case, you need overhead protection, such as a tent or some kind of roof, like a poncho or tarp with its ends tied to trees.

Tents and Weather Protection

All it takes is to get caught in the rain once without a tent and you will never go anywhere without one again. A tent provides protection from rain, wind, and mosquito attacks. In exchange, you can lose a starry night's view, although some tents now even provide moon roofs.

A tent can be as complex as a four-season, tubular-jointed dome with a rain fly or as simple as two ponchos snapped together and roped up to a tree. They can be as cheap as a $10 tube tent, which is nothing more than a hollow piece of plastic, or as expensive as a $500 five-person deluxe expedition dome model. They vary greatly in size, price, and put-up time. If you plan on getting a good one, plan on doing plenty of shopping and asking lots of questions. With a little bit of homework, you can get the right answers to these questions:

Will It Keep Me Dry?

On many one-person and two-person tents, the rain fly does not extend far enough to keep water off the bottom side-walls of the tent. In a driving rain, water can also drip from the rain fly and to the bottom sidewalls of the tent. Eventually, the water can leak through to the inside, particularly through the seams where the tent has been sewn together.

You must be able to stake out your rain fly so it completely covers all of the tent. If you are tent shopping and this does not appear possible, then don't buy the tent. To prevent potential leaks, use a seam water-proofer such as Seam Lock, a gluelike substance, to close potential leak areas on tent seams. For large umbrella tents, keep a patch kit handy.

Another way to keep water out of your tent is to store all wet garments outside the tent, under a poncho. Moisture from wet clothes stashed in the tent will condense on the interior tent walls. If you bring enough wet clothes into the tent, by the next morning you can feel as if you're camping in a duck blind.

How Hard Is It To Put Up?

If a tent is difficult to erect in full sunlight, you can just about forget it at night. Some tents can go up in just a few minutes, without requiring help from another camper. This might be the kind of tent you want.

The way to compare put-up time of tents when shopping is to count the number of connecting points from the tent poles to the tent and the number of stakes required. The fewer the better. Think simple. My tent has seven connecting points and, minus the rain fly, requires no stakes. It goes up in a few minutes. If you need a lot of stakes, it is a sure tipoff to a long put-up time. Try it at night or in the rain, and you'll be ready to cash your chips and go for broke.

Another factor is the tent poles themselves. Some small tents have poles that are broken into small sections that are connected by bungee cords. It takes only an instant to convert them to a complete pole.

Some outdoor shops have tents on display on their showroom floor. Before buying the tent, have the salesperson take the tent down and put it back up. If it takes him more than five minutes, or he says he doesn't have time, then keep looking.

*A-frame style **tents** have gone the way of the dinosaur. With the world going high-tech, tents of today vary greatly in complexity, size, price, and put-up time. And they wouldn't be fit for this new millennium without offering options such as moon roofs, rain flies, and tent wings. Be sure to buy the one that's right for your needs.*

Is It Roomy Enough?

Don't judge the size of a tent on floor space alone. Some tents small on floor space can give the illusion of roominess with a high ceiling. You can be quite comfortable in them and snug.

But remember that a one-person or two-person tent is just that. A two-person tent has room for two people plus gear. That's it. Don't buy a tent expecting it to hold more than it is intended to.

How Much Does It Weigh?

If you're a hiker, this becomes the preeminent question. If it's much more than six or seven pounds, forget it. A 12-pound tent is bad enough, but get it wet and it's like carrying a piano on your back. On the other hand, weight is scarcely a factor if you camp only where you can take your car. My dad, for instance, used to have this giant canvas umbrella tent that folded down to a neat little pack that weighed about 500 pounds.

Family Tents

It is always worth spending the time and money to purchase a tent you and your family will be happy with. Although many good family tents are available for $125 to $175, particularly from Coleman, Cabela's, and Remington, here is a synopsis of two of the best tents available anywhere, without regard to cost, generally ranging from $350 to $600:

Sierra Designs Mondo 5CD

800/736-8551

10.14 pounds

82 square feet / 20-square-foot covered entry / Inside peak height: five feet, five inches

If your family likes to head for distant camps, then this is your tent. It's light enough to pack along, yet big enough to accommodate a family of four. Using speed clips, this tent is by far the easiest and quickest to set up of any family tent I've used. A generous rain fly and covered entry area (new adjustment features allow various awning configurations) mean ample protection from the elements, no matter how hard they are pelting down.

Kelty Domolite 6

800/423-2320

16.4 pounds

81.5 square feet / Inside peak height: five feet, seven inches

Using three 18-foot-long fiberglass poles, the Domolite boasts a sleek, low profile that slips the wind nicely. Each pole slides easily through continuous pole sleeves, thanks to rubber-tipped ends, making setup a snap. Kelty has an optional covered entry area, since without it, the tent is barely adequate shelter should you have to weather a deluge in cramped quarters. Floor seams are taped for added waterproofness. A great package.

Bivouac Bags

If you like going solo and choose not to own a tent at all, a bivy bag (short for bivouac bag) can provide the weather protection you require. A bivy bag is a water-repellent shell in which your sleeping bag fits. It is light and tough, and for some is the perfect alternative to a heavy tent. My bivy weighs 31 ounces and cost me $240, made by Outdoor Research, and I just plain love the thing on expeditions. On the downside, however, it can be a bit difficult getting settled just right in it, and some say they feel claustrophobic in the close quarters. My biggest fear was the idea of riding out a storm. You can hear the rain hitting you, and sometimes even feel the pounding of the drops through the bivy bag. For some, it can be unsettling to try and sleep under such circumstances. On the other hand, I've always looked forward to it. In cold weather, it also helps keep you warm.

Pickup Truck Campers

If you own a pickup truck with a camper shell, you can turn it into a self-contained campground with a little work. This can be an ideal way to go: it's fast, portable, and you are guaranteed a dry environment.

But that does not necessarily mean it is a warm environment. In fact, without insulation from the metal truck bed, it can be like trying to sleep on an iceberg because the metal truck bed will get as cold as the air temperature, which is often much colder than the ground temperature. Without insulation, it can be much colder in your camper shell than it would be on the open ground.

When I camp in my rig, I use a large piece of foam for a mattress and insulation. The foam measures 4 inches thick, 48 inches wide, and 76 inches long. It makes a bed as comfortable as anything one might ask for. In fact, during the winter, if I don't go camping for a few weeks because of writing obligations, I sometimes throw the foam on the floor, lie down the old sleeping bag, light a fire, and camp right in my living room. It's in my blood, I tell you. Air beds and cots are also extremely comfortable, and I've used both many times. Whatever you choose, just make sure you have a comfortable sleeping unit. Good sleep makes for great camping trips.

Keep It Wild Tip 3: Camp with Care

1. Choose an existing, legal site. Restrict activities to areas where vegetation is compacted or absent.
2. Camp at least 75 steps (200 feet) from lakes, streams, and trails.
3. Always choose sites that won't be damaged by your stay.
4. Preserve the feeling of solitude by selecting camps that are out of view when possible.
5. Don't dig trenches or build structures or furniture.

RVs

The problems RVers encounter come from two primary sources: lack of privacy and light intrusion. The lack of privacy stems from the natural restrictions of where a land yacht can go. Without careful use of the guide portion of this book, motor home owners can find themselves in parking lot settings, jammed in with plenty of neighbors. Because RVs often have large picture windows, you lose your privacy, causing some late nights; then, come daybreak, light intrusion forces an early wakeup. The result is that you get shorted on sleep.

The answer is to carry inserts to fit over the inside of your windows. This closes off the outside and retains your privacy. If you don't want to wake up with the sun at daybreak, you don't have to. It will still be dark.

First Aid and Insect Protection

The mountain night could not have been more perfect, I thought, as I lay in my sleeping bag. The sky looked like a mass of jewels and the air tasted sweet and smelled of pines. A shooting star fireballed across the sky, and I remember thinking, "It just doesn't get any better."

Just then, as I was drifting into sleep, a mysterious buzz appeared from nowhere and deposited itself inside my left ear. Suddenly awake, I whacked my ear with the palm of my hand, hard enough to cause a minor concussion. The buzz disappeared. I pulled out my flashlight and shined it on my palm, and there, lit in the blackness of night, lay the squished intruder: a mosquito, dead amid a stain of blood.

Satisfied, I turned off the light, closed my eyes, and thought of the fishing trip planned for the next day. Then I heard them. It was a squadron of mosquitoes flying landing patterns around my head. I tried to grab them with an open hand, but they dodged the assault and flew off. Just 30 seconds later another landed in my left ear. I promptly dispatched the invader with a rip of the palm.

Now I was completely awake, so I got out of my sleeping bag to retrieve some mosquito repellent. But en route, several of the buggers swarmed and nailed me in the back and arms. After I applied the repellent and settled snugly again in my sleeping bag, the mosquitoes would buzz a few inches from my ear. After getting a whiff of the poison, they would fly off. It was like sleeping in a sawmill.

The next day, drowsy from little sleep, I set out to fish. I'd walked but 15 minutes when I brushed against a bush and felt this stinging sensation on the inside of my arm, just above the wrist. I looked down: A tick had his clamps in me. I ripped it out before he could embed his head into my skin.

After catching a few fish, I sat down against a tree to eat lunch and just watch the water go by. My dog, Rebel, sat down next to me and stared at the beef jerky I was munching as if it were a T-bone steak. I finished eating, gave him a small piece, patted him on the head, and said, "Good dog." Right then, I noticed an itch on my arm where a mosquito had drilled me. I unconsciously scratched it. Two days later, in that exact spot, some nasty red splotches started popping up. Poison oak. By petting my dog and then scratching my arm, I had transferred the oil residue of the poison oak leaves from Rebel's fur to my arm.

When I returned home, Foonsky asked me about the trip.

"Great," I said. "Mosquitoes, ticks, poison oak. Can hardly wait to go back."

"Sorry I missed out," he answered.

Mosquitoes, No-See-Ums, Gnats, and Horseflies

On a trip to Canada, Foonsky and I were fishing a small lake from the shore when suddenly a black horde of mosquitoes could be seen moving across the lake toward us. It was like when the French army looked across the Rhine and saw the Wehrmacht coming. There was a buzz in the air. We fought them off for a few minutes, then made a fast retreat to the truck and jumped in, content the buggers had been fooled. But somehow still unknown to us, the mosquitoes gained entry to the truck. In 10 minutes, we squished 15 of them as they attempted to plant their oil drills into our skin. Just outside the truck, the black horde waited for us to make a tactical error like rolling down a window. It finally took a miraculous hailstorm to foil the attack.

When it comes to mosquitoes, no-see-ums, gnats, and horseflies, there are times when there is nothing you can do. In most situations, however, you can muster a defense to repel the attack.

The first key with mosquitoes is to wear clothing too heavy for them to drill through. Expose a minimum of skin, wear a hat, and tie a bandanna around your neck, preferably one that has been sprayed with repellent. If you try to get by with just a cotton T-shirt, you will be declared a federal mosquito sanctuary.

So first your skin must be well covered, exposing only your hands and face. Second, you should have your companion spray your clothes with repellent. Third, you should dab liquid repellent directly on your skin.

At night, the easiest way to get a good sleep without mosquitoes buzzing in your ear is to sleep in a bug-proof tent. If the nights are warm and you want to see the stars, new tent models are available that have a skylight covered with mosquito netting. If you don't like tents on summer evenings, mosquito netting rigged with an air space at your head can solve the problem. Otherwise, prepare to get bitten, even with the use of mosquito repellent.

Mosquito repellent: Taking vitamin B1 and eating garlic are reputed to act as natural insect repellents, but I've met a lot of mosquitoes that are not convinced. A better bet is to examine the label of the repellent in question for N,N di-ethyl-m-toluamide, commonly known as DEET. That is a poison, and the percentage of it in the container must be listed and will indicate that brand's effectiveness. Inert ingredients are mainly fluids used to fill the bottles.

If your problems are with no-see-ums or biting horseflies, then you need a slightly different approach. No-see-ums are tiny black insects that look like nothing more than a sliver of dirt on your skin. Then you notice something stinging, and when you rub the area, you scratch up a little no-see-um. The results are similar to mosquito bites, making your skin itch, splotch, and when you get them bad, swell. In addition to using the techniques described to repel mosquitoes, you should go one step further.

The problem is that no-see-ums are tricky little devils. Somehow they can actually get under your socks and around your ankles, where they will bite to their hearts' content all night long while you sleep, itch, sleep, and itch some more. The best solution is to apply a liquid repellent to your ankles, then wear clean socks.

Horseflies are another story. They are rarely a problem, but when they get their dander up, they can cause trouble you'll never forget.

One such episode occurred when Foonsky and I were paddling a canoe along the shoreline of a large lake. This giant horsefly, about the size of a fingertip, started dive-bombing the canoe. After 20 minutes, it landed on Foonsky's thigh. He immediately slammed it with an open hand, then let out a blood-curdling "Yeeeee-ow!" that practically sent ripples across the lake. When Foonsky whacked it, the horsefly had somehow turned around and bit him on the hand, leaving a huge red welt.

In the next 10 minutes, that big fly strafed the canoe on more dive-bomb runs. I finally got my canoe paddle, swung it as if it were a baseball bat, and nailed that horsefly as if I'd hit a home run. It landed about 15 feet from the boat, still alive and buzzing in the water. While I was trying to figure what it would take to kill this bugger, a large rainbow trout surfaced and snatched it out of the water, finally avenging the assault.

If you have horsefly or yellow jacket problems, you'd best just leave the area. One, two, or a few can be dealt with. More than that and your fun camping trip will be about as fun as being roped to a tree and stung by an electric shock rod.

On most trips, you will spend time doing everything possible to keep from getting bitten by mosquitoes or no-see-ums. When that fails, you must know what to do next, and fast, if you are among those ill-fated campers who get big red lumps from a bite inflicted from even a microscopic mosquito.

A fluid called After Bite or a dab of ammonia should be applied immediately to the bite. To start the healing process, apply a first-aid gel (not a liquid), such as the one made by Campho-Phenique.

DEET Versus "Natural" Repellents

What is DEET? You're not likely to find the word DEET on any repellent label. That's because DEET stands for N,N diethyl-m-toluamide. If the label contains this scientific name, the repellent contains DEET. Despite fears of DEET-associated health risks and the increased attention given to natural alternatives, DEET-based repellents are still acknowledged as by far the best option when serious insect protection is required.

What are the health risks associated with using DEET? A few deaths and several medical problems have been attributed in the press to DEET in recent years—events that those in the DEET community vehemently deny as being specifically DEET related, pointing to reams of scientific documentation as evidence. It does seem logical to assume that if DEET can peel paint, melt nylon, destroy plastic, wreck wood finishes, and damage fishing line, then it must be hell on the skin—perhaps worse.

On one trip, I had a small bottle of mosquito repellent in the same pocket as a Swiss army knife. Guess what happened? The mosquito repellent leaked a bit and literally melted the insignia right off the knife. DEET will also melt synthetic clothes. That is why in bad mosquito country, I'll expose a minimum of skin, just hands and face (with full beard), and apply the repellent only to my cheeks and the back of my hands, perhaps wear a bandanna sprinkled with a few drops as well. That does the trick, with a minimum of exposure to the repellent.

Although nothing definitive has been published, there is a growing belief among the scientific community that repeated applications of products containing low percentages of DEET can be potentially dangerous. It is theorized that this practice actually puts consumers at a greater risk for absorbing high levels of DEET into the body than if they had just used one application of a 30 to 50 percent DEET product with an efficacy of four to six hours. Also being studied is the possibility that low levels of DEET, which might not otherwise be of toxicologic concern, may become hazardous if they are formulated with solvents or dilutents (considered inert ingredients) that may enhance the absorption rate.

Are natural alternatives a safer choice? To imply that essential oils are completely safe because they are a natural product is not altogether accurate. Essential oils, while derived from plants that grow naturally, are chemicals too. Some are potentially hazardous if ingested, and most are downright painful if they find their way into the eyes or onto mucus membranes. For example, pennyroyal is perhaps the most toxic of the essential oils used to repel insects and can be deadly if taken internally. Other oils used include citronella (perhaps the most common, it's extracted from an aromatic grass indigenous to Southern Asia), eucalyptus, cedarwood, and peppermint.

Three citronella-based products, Buzz Away (manufactured by Quantum), Avon's Skin-So-Soft, and Natrapel (manufactured by Tender), have received Environmental Protection Agency (EPA) registration and approval for sale as repellents for use in controlling mosquitoes, flies, gnats, and midges.

How effective are natural repellents? While numerous studies are cited by those on the DEET and citronella sides of the fence, the average effective repelling time of a citronella product appears to range from 1.5 to 2 hours. Tests conducted at Cambridge University, England, comparing Natrapel to DEET-based Skintastic (a low-percentage DEET product) found citronella to be just as effective in repelling mosquitoes. The key here is effectiveness and the amount of time until reapplication.

Citronella products work for up to two hours and then require reapplication (the same holds true for other natural formulations). Products using a low-percentage level of DEET also require reapplication every two hours to remain effective. So if you're going outside for only a short period in an environment where insect bites are more an irritant than a hazard, you would do just as well to go natural.

What other chemical alternatives are there? Another line of defense against insects is the chemical permethrin, which is used on clothing, not on skin. Permethrin-based products are designed to repel and kill arthropods or crawling insects, making them a preferred repellent for ticks. The currently available products will remain effective, repelling and killing mosquitoes, ticks, and chiggers, for two weeks and through two launderings.

Ticks

Ticks are nasty little vermin that will wait in ambush, jump on unsuspecting prey, and then crawl to a prime location before filling their bodies with their victim's blood.

I call them Dracula bugs, but by any name they can be a terrible camp pest. Ticks rest on grass and low plants and attach themselves to those who brush against the vegetation (dogs are particularly vulnerable). Typically, they are no more than 18 inches above ground, and if you stay on the trails, you can usually avoid them.

There are two common species of ticks. The common coastal tick is larger, brownish in color, and prefers to crawl around before putting its clamps on you. The latter habit can be creepy, but when you feel it crawling, you can just pick it off and dispatch it. The coastal tick's preferred destination is usually the back of your neck, just where the hairline starts. The other species, the wood tick, is small and black, and when he puts his clamps in, it's immediately painful. When a wood tick gets into a dog for a few days, it can cause a large red welt. In either case, ticks should be removed as soon as possible.

Keep It Wild Tip 4: Sanitation

If no refuse facility is available:
1. Deposit human waste in "cat holes" dug six to eight inches deep. Cover and disguise the cat hole when finished.
2. Deposit human waste at least 75 paces (200 feet) from any water source or camp.
3. Use toilet paper sparingly. When finished, carefully burn it in the cat hole, then bury it.
4. If no appropriate burial locations are available, such as in popular wilderness camps above tree line in granite settings, then all human refuse should be double-bagged and packed out.
5. At boat-in campsites, chemical toilets are required. Chemical toilets can also solve the problem of larger groups camping for long stays at one location where no facilities are available.
6. To wash dishes or your body, carry water away from the source and use small amounts of biodegradable soap. Scatter dishwater after all food particles have been removed.
7. Scour your campsites for even the tiniest piece of trash and any other evidence of your stay. Pack out all the trash you can, even if it's not yours. Finding cigarette butts, for instance, provides special irritation for most campers. Pick them up and discard them properly.
8. Never litter. Never. Or you become the enemy of all others.

If you have hiked in areas infested with ticks, it is advisable to shower as soon as possible, washing your clothes immediately. If you just leave your clothes in a heap, a tick can crawl out and invade your home. They like warmth, and one way or another, they can end up in your bed. Waking up in the middle of the night with a tick crawling across your chest can really give you the creeps.

Once a tick has its clampers on you, you must decide how long it has been there. If it has been a short time, the most painless and effective method for removal is to take a pair of sharp tweezers and grasp the little devil, making certain to isolate the mouth area, then pull him out. Reader Johvin Perry sent in the suggestion to coat the tick with Vaseline, which will cut off its oxygen supply, after which it may voluntarily give up the hunt.

If the tick has been in longer, you may wish to have a doctor extract it. Some people will burn a tick with a cigarette or poison it with lighter fluid, but this is not advisable. No matter how you do it, you must take care to remove all of it, especially its clawlike mouth.

The wound, however small, should then be cleansed and dressed. This is done by applying liquid peroxide, which cleans and sterilizes, and applying a dressing coated with a first-aid gel such as First-Aid Cream, Campho-Phenique, or Neosporin.

Lyme disease, which can be transmitted by the bite of the deer tick, is rare but common enough to warrant some attention. To prevent tick bites, some people tuck their pant legs into their hiking socks and spray tick repellent, called Permamone, on their pants.

The first symptom of Lyme disease is that the bite area develops a bright red, splotchy rash. Other possible early symptoms include headache, nausea, fever, and/or a stiff neck. If this happens, or if you have any doubts, you should see your doctor immediately. If you do get Lyme disease, don't panic. Doctors say it is easily treated in the early stages with simple antibiotics. If you are nervous about getting Lyme disease, carry a small plastic bag with you when you hike. If a tick manages to get its clampers into you, put it in the plastic bag after you pull it out. Give it to your doctor for analysis to see if the tick is a carrier of the disease.

During the course of my hiking and camping career, I have removed ticks from my skin hundreds of times without any problems; however, if you are worried about ticks, you can purchase a tick removal kit from any outdoors store. These kits allow you to remove ticks so that their toxins are guaranteed not to enter your bloodstream.

If you are particularly wary of ticks or perhaps even have nightmares of them, wear long pants that are tucked into the socks, as well as a long-sleeved shirt tucked securely into the pants and held with a belt. Clothing should be light in color, making it easier to see ticks, and tightly woven so ticks have trouble hanging on. On one hike with my mom, Eleanor, I brushed more than 100 ticks off my blue jeans in less than an hour, while she did not pick up a single one on her polyester pants.

Perform tick checks regularly, especially on the back of the neck. The combination of DEET insect repellents applied to the skin and permethrin repellents applied directly to clothing is considered to be the most effective line of defense against ticks.

Poison Oak

After a nice afternoon hike, about a five-miler, I was concerned about possible exposure to poison oak, so I immediately showered and put on clean clothes. Then I settled into a chair with my favorite foamy elixir to watch the end of a baseball game. The game went 18 innings; meanwhile, my dog, tired from the hike, went to sleep on my bare ankles.

A few days later, I had a case of poison oak. My feet looked as though they had been on fire and put out with an ice pick. The lesson? Don't always trust your dog, give him a bath as well, and beware of extra-inning ball games.

You can get poison oak only from direct contact with the oil residue from the leaves. It can be passed in a variety of ways, as direct as skin-to-leaf contact or as indirect as leaf to dog, dog to sofa, sofa to skin. Once you have it, there is little you can do but itch yourself to death. Applying Caladryl lotion or its equivalent can help because it contains antihistamines, which attack and dry the itch.

A tip that may sound crazy but seems to work is advised by my pal Furniss. You should expose the afflicted area to the hottest water you can stand, then suddenly immerse it in cold water. The hot water opens the skin pores and gets the "itch" out, and the cold water then quickly seals the pores.

In any case, you're a lot better off if you don't get poison oak to begin with. Remember that poison oak can disguise itself. In the spring, it is green; then it gradually turns reddish in the summer. By fall, it becomes a bloody, ugly-looking red. In the winter, it loses its leaves altogether and appears to be nothing more than barren, brown sticks of a small plant; however, at any time and in any form, its contact with skin can quickly lead to infection.

Some people are more easily afflicted than others, but if you are one of the lucky few who aren't, don't cheer too loudly. While some people can be exposed to the oil residue of poison oak with little or no effect, the body's resistance can gradually be worn down with repeated exposure. At one time, I could practically play in the stuff and the only symptom would be a few little bumps on the inside of my wrist. Now, more than 15 years later, my resistance has broken down. If I merely rub against poison oak, in a few days the exposed area can look as if it were used for a track meet.

So regardless of whether you consider yourself vulnerable or not, you should take heed to reduce

Avoiding Poison Oak
Remember the old Boy Scout saying: "Leaves of three, let them be."

your exposure. That can be done by staying on trails when you hike and making sure your dog does the same. Remember, the worst stands of poison oak are usually brush-infested areas just off the trail. Protect yourself by dressing so your skin is completely covered, wearing long-sleeved shirts, long pants, and boots. If you suspect you've been exposed, immediately wash your clothes and then wash yourself with aloe vera, rinsing with a cool shower.

And don't forget to give your dog a bath as well.

Sunburn

The most common injury suffered on camping trips is sunburn, yet some people wear it as a badge of honor, believing that it somehow enhances their virility. Well, it doesn't. Neither do suntans. And too much sun can lead to serious burns or sunstroke.

Sunburn is easy enough to avoid. Use a high-level sunscreen on your skin, apply lip balm with sunscreen, and wear sunglasses and a hat. If any area gets burned, apply first-aid cream, which will soothe and provide moisture for your parched, burned skin.

The best advice is not to get even a suntan. Those who do are involved in a practice that can be eventually ruinous to their skin and possibly lead to cancer.

A Word about Giardia and Cryptosporidium

You have just hiked in to your backwoods spot, you're thirsty and a bit tired, but you smile as you consider the prospects. Everything seems perfect—there's not a stranger in sight, and you have nothing to do but relax with your pals.

You toss down your gear, grab your cup, dip it into the stream, and take a long drink of that ice-cold mountain water. It seems crystal pure and sweeter than anything you've ever tasted. It's not until later that you find out it can be just like drinking a cup of poison.

Whether you camp in the wilderness or not, if you hike, you're going to get thirsty. And if your canteen runs dry, you'll start eyeing any water source. Stop! Do not pass Go. Do not drink.

By drinking what appears to be pure mountain water without first treating it, you can ingest a microscopic protozoan called *Giardia lamblia*. The pain of the ensuing abdominal cramps can make you feel that your stomach and intestinal tract are in a knot, ready to explode. With that comes long-term diarrhea that is worse than even a bear could imagine.

Doctors call the disease *giardiasis*, or giardia for short, but it is difficult to diagnose. One friend of mine who contracted giardia was told he might have stomach cancer before the proper diagnosis was made.

Drinking directly from a stream or lake does not mean you will get giardia, but you are taking a giant chance. There is no reason to assume such a risk, potentially ruining your trip and enduring weeks of misery.

A lot of people are taking that risk. I made a personal survey of campers in the Yosemite National Park wilderness and found that roughly only 1 in 20 was equipped with some kind of water-purification system. The result, according to the Public Health Service, is that an average of 4 percent of all backpackers and campers suffer *giardiasis*. According to the Parasitic Diseases Division of the Center for Infectious Diseases, the rates range from 1 percent to 20 percent across the country.

Treating Your Water Means Avoiding Diarrhea: The only sure way to beat giardia and other waterborne diseases is to filter or boil your water before drinking, eating, or brushing your teeth. The best way to prevent the spread of giardia is to bury your waste products at least eight inches deep and 100 feet away from natural waters.

But if you get giardia, you are not going to care about the statistics. "When I got giardia, I just about wanted to die," said Henry McCarthy, a California camper. "For about 10 days, it was the most terrible thing I have ever experienced. And through the whole thing, I kept thinking, 'I shouldn't have drunk that water, but it seemed all right at the time.'"

That is the mistake most campers make. The stream might be running free, gurgling over boulders in the high country, tumbling into deep, oxygenated pools. It looks pure. Then in a few days, the problems suddenly start. Drinking untreated water from mountain streams is a lot like playing Russian roulette. Sooner or later, the gun goes off.

Filters

There's really no excuse for going without a water filter: Handheld filters are getting more compact, lighter, easier to use, and often less expensive. Having to boil water or endure chemicals that leave a bad taste in the mouth has been all but eliminated.

With a filter, you just pump and drink. Filtering strains out microscopic contaminants, rendering the water clear and somewhat pure. How pure? That depends on the size of the filter's pores—what manufacturers call pore-size efficiency. A filter with a pore-size efficiency of one micron or smaller will remove protozoa like *Giardia lamblia,* and cryptosporidium, as well as parasitic eggs and larva, but it takes a pore-size efficiency of less than 0.4 microns to remove bacteria. All but one of the filters recommended here do that.

A good backcountry water filter weighs less than 20 ounces, is easy to grasp, simple to use, and a snap to clean and maintain. At the least, buy one that will remove protozoa and bacteria. (Several cheap, pocket-size filters remove only *Giardia lamblia* and cryptosporidium. That, in my book, is risking your health to save money.) Consider the flow rate, too: One liter per minute is good.

All filters will eventually clog—it's a sign that they've been doing their job. If you force water through a filter that's becoming difficult to pump, you risk injecting a load of microbial nasties into your bottle. Some models can be backwashed, brushed, or, as with ceramic elements, scrubbed to extend their useful lives. If the filter has a pre-filter to screen out the big stuff, use it: It will give your filter a boost in mileage, which can then top out at about 100 gallons per disposable element. Any of the filters reviewed here will serve well on an outing into the wilds, providing you always play by the manufacturer's rules. They cost about $35 to $75, up to more than $200, depending on the volume of water they are constructed to filter.

- **First Need Deluxe:** The 15-ounce First Need Deluxe from General Ecology does something no other handheld filter will do: It removes protozoa, bacteria, and viruses without using chemicals. Such effectiveness is the result of a fancy three-stage matrix system. Unfortunately, if you drop the filter and unknowingly crack the cartridge, all the little nasties can get through. General Ecology's solution is to include a bottle of blue dye that indicates breaks. The issue hasn't scared off too many folks, though: the First Need has been around since 1982. Additional cartridges cost $30. A final note: The filter pumps smoothly and puts out more than a liter per minute. This one is a favorite of mine.

- **PentaPure Oasis:** The PentaPure Oasis Water Purification System from WTC/Ecomaster offers drinkable water with a twist: You squeeze and sip instead of pumping. Weighing 6.5 ounces, the system packages a three-stage filter inside a 21-ounce-capacity sport bottle with an angled and sealing drinking nozzle, ideal for mountain bikers. The filter removes and/or kills protozoa, bacteria, and viruses, so it's also suitable for world travel. It's certainly convenient: just fill the bottle with untreated water, screw on the cap, give it a firm squeeze (don't expect the easy flow of a normal sport bottle; there's more work being done), and sip. The Oasis only runs into trouble if the water source is shallow; you'll need a cup for scooping.

- **Basic Designs Ceramic:** The Basic Designs Ceramic Filter Pump weighs eight ounces and is as stripped-down a filter as you'll find. The pump is simple, easy to use, and reliable. The ceramic filter effectively removes protozoa and bacteria, making it ideal and cost effective

Water filters are a wise investment since all wilderness water should be considered contaminated. Make sure the filter can be easily cleaned or has a replaceable cartridge. The filter pores must be 0.4 microns or less to remove bacteria.

for backpacking, but it won't protect against viruses. Also, the filter element is too bulbous to work directly from a shallow water source; like the PentaPure, you'll have to decontaminate a pot, cup, or bottle to transfer your unfiltered water. It's a great buy, though, for anyone worried only about *Giardia lamblia* and cryptosporidium.

- **SweetWater WalkAbout:** The WalkAbout is perfect for the day hiker or backpacker who obsesses on lightening the load. The filter weighs just 8.5 ounces, is easily cleaned in the field, and removes both protozoa and bacteria: a genuine bargain. There are some trade-offs, however, for its diminutiveness. Water delivery is a tad slow at just under one liter per minute, but redesigned filter cartridges ($12.50) are now good for up to 100 gallons.
- **MSR MiniWorks:** Like the WalkAbout, the bargain-priced MiniWorks has a bigger and more expensive water-filtering brother, but in this case the differences are harder to discern. The new 14.3-ounce MiniWorks looks similar to the $140 WaterWorks II, and like the WaterWorks is fully field-maintainable, while guarding against protozoa, bacteria, and chemicals. But the Mini is the best-executed, easiest-to-use ceramic filter on the market, and it attaches directly to a standard one-quart Nalgene water bottle. Too bad it takes 90 seconds to filter that quart.
- **PUR Explorer:** The Explorer offers protection from all the bad guys—viruses as well as protozoa and bacteria—by incorporating an iodine matrix into the filtration process. An optional carbon cartridge ($20) neutralizes the iodine's noxious taste. The Explorer is also considered a trusty veteran among water filters because of its smooth pumping action and nifty back-washing feature: With a quick twist, the device switches from filtering mode to self-cleaning mode. It may be on the heavy side (20 ounces) and somewhat pricey, but the Explorer works well on iffy water anywhere.
- **Katadyn U.S.A. Mini Filter:** The Mini Filter is a much more compact version of Katadyn's venerable Pocket Filter. This one weighs just eight ounces—ideal for the minimalist backcountry traveler—and it effectively removes protozoa and bacteria. A palm-of-the-hand-size filter, however, makes it challenging to put any kind of power behind the pump's tiny handle, and the filtered water comes through at a paltry half-liter per minute. It also requires more cleaning than most filters, although the good news is that the element is made of long-lasting ceramic. Ironically, one option lets you purchase the Mini Filter with a carbon element instead of the ceramic. The pumping is easier, the flow rate is better, and the price is way down ($99), but I'd only go that route if you'll be pumping from clear mountain streams.
- **MSR WaterWorks II Ceramic:** At 17.4 ounces, the WaterWorks II isn't light, but for the same price as the Katadyn, you get a better flow rate (90 seconds per liter), an easy pumping action, and—like the original Mini Filter—a long-lasting ceramic cartridge. This filter is a good match for the person who encounters a lot of dirty water—its three-stage filter weeds out protozoa, bacteria, and chemicals—and is mechanically inclined. The MSR can be completely disassembled afield for troubleshooting and cleaning. (If you're not so endowed, take the filter apart at home only because the potential for confusion is somewhat high.) By the way, the company has corrected the clogging problem that plagued a previous version of the WaterWorks.

The big drawback with filters is that if you pump water from a mucky lake, the filter can clog in a few days. Therein lies the weakness. Once plugged up, it is useless, and you have to replace it or take your chances. One trick to extend the filter life is to fill your cook pot with water, let the sediment settle, then pump from there. As an insurance policy, always have a spare filter canister on hand.

Boiling Water

Except for water filtration, this is the only treatment you can use with complete confidence. According to the federal Parasitic Diseases Division, it takes a few minutes at a rolling boil to be certain you've killed *Giardia lamblia*. At high elevations, boil for three to five minutes. A side benefit is that you'll also kill other dangerous bacteria that live undetected in natural waters.

But to be honest, boiling water is a thorn for most people on backcountry trips. For one thing, if you boil water on an open fire, what should taste like crystal-pure mountain water tastes instead like a mouthful of warm ashes. If you don't have a campfire, it wastes stove fuel. And if you are thirsty *now*, forget it. The water takes hours to cool.

The only time boiling always makes sense, however, is when you are preparing dinner. The ash taste will disappear in whatever freeze-dried dinner, soup, or hot drink you make.

Water-Purification Pills

Pills are the preference for most backcountry campers, and this can get them in trouble. At just $3 to $8 per bottle, which can figure up to just a few cents per canteen, they do come cheap. In addition, they kill most of the bacteria, regardless of whether you use iodine crystals or potable aqua iodine tablets.

The problem is they just don't always kill *Giardia lamblia*, and that is the one critter worth worrying about on your trip. That limitation makes water-treatment pills unreliable and dangerous.

Another key element is the time factor. Depending on the water's temperature, organic content, and pH level, these pills can take a long time to do the job. A minimum wait of 20 minutes is advised. Most people don't like waiting that long, especially when they're hot and thirsty after a hike and end up thinking, "What the heck, the water looks fine."

Then there is the taste. On one trip, my water filter clogged and we had to use the iodine pills instead. It doesn't take long to get tired of the iodine-tinged taste of the water. Mountain water should be one of the greatest tasting beverages of the world, but the iodine kills that.

No Treatment

This is your last resort and, using extreme care, can be executed with success. One of my best hiking buddies, Michael Furniss, is a nationally renowned hydrologist, and on wilderness trips he has showed me the difference between safe and dangerous water sources.

Long ago, people believed that just finding water running over a rock was a guarantee of its purity. Imagine that. What we've learned is that safe water sources are almost always small springs located in high, craggy mountain areas. The key is making sure no one has been upstream from where you drink.

Furniss mentioned that another potential problem in bypassing water treatment is that even in settings free of *Giardia lamblia*, you can still ingest other bacteria that cause stomach problems.

Hypothermia

No matter how well planned your trip might be, a sudden change in weather can turn it into a puzzle for which there are few answers. Bad weather or an accident can set in motion a dangerous chain of events.

Such a chain of episodes occurred for my brother Rambob and me on a fishing trip one fall day just below the snow line. The weather had suddenly turned very cold, and ice was forming along the shore of the lake. Suddenly, the canoe became terribly imbalanced, and just that quick it flipped. The little life vest seat cushions were useless, and using the canoe as a paddleboard, we tried to kick our way back to shore, where my dad was going crazy at the thought of his two sons drowning before his eyes.

It took 17 minutes in that 38°F water, but we finally made it to shore. When they pulled me out of the water, my legs were dead, not strong enough even to hold up my weight. In fact, I didn't feel so much cold as tired, and I just wanted to lie down and go to sleep. I closed my eyes, and my brother-in-law, Lloyd Angal, slapped me in the face several times, then got me on my feet and pushed and pulled me about.

In the celebration over our making it to shore, only Lloyd had realized that hypothermia was setting in. Hypothermia is the condition in which the temperature of the body is lowered to the point that it causes poor reasoning, apathy, and collapse. It can look like the afflicted person is just tired and needs to sleep, but that sleep can be the first step toward a coma.

Ultimately, my brother and I shared what little dry clothing remained. Then we began hiking around to get muscle movement, creating internal warmth. We ate whatever munchies were available because the body produces heat by digestion. Most important, we got our heads as dry as possible. More body heat is lost through wet hair than any other single factor.

A few hours later, we were in a pizza parlor replaying the incident, talking about how only a life vest can do the job of a life vest. We decided never again to rely on those little flotation seat cushions that disappear when the boat flips.

Almost by instinct we had done everything right to prevent hypothermia: Don't go to sleep, start a physical activity, induce shivering, put dry clothes on, dry your head, and eat something. That's how you fight hypothermia. In a dangerous situation, whether you fall in a lake or a stream or get caught unprepared in a storm, that's how you can stay alive.

After being in that ice-bordered lake for almost 20 minutes and then finally pulling ourselves to the shoreline, we discovered a strange thing. My canoe was flipped right-side up and almost all of its contents were lost: tackle box, flotation cushions, and cooler. But remaining were one paddle and one fishing rod, the trout rod my grandfather had given me for my 12th birthday.

Lloyd gave me a smile. "This means that you are meant to paddle and fish again," he said with a laugh.

Getting Unlost

You could not have been more lost. But there I was, a guy who is supposed to know about these things, transfixed by confusion, snow, and hoofprints from a big deer.

I discovered it is actually quite easy to get lost. If you don't get your bearings, getting found is the difficult part. This occurred on a wilderness trip where I'd hiked in to a remote lake and then set up a base camp for a deer hunt.

"There are some giant bucks up on that rim," confided Mr. Furnai, who lives near the area. "But it takes a mountain man to even get close to them."

That was a challenge I answered. After four-wheeling it to the trailhead, I tromped off with pack and rifle, gut-thumped it up 100 switchbacks over the rim, then followed a creek drainage up to a small but beautiful lake. The area was stark and nearly treeless, with bald granite broken only by large boulders. To keep from getting lost, I marked my route with piles of small rocks to act as directional signs for the return trip.

But at daybreak the next day, I stuck my head out of my tent and found eight inches of snow on the ground. I looked up into a gray sky filled with huge, cascading snowflakes. Visibility was about 50 yards, with fog on the mountain rim. "I better get out of here and get back to my truck," I said to myself. "If my truck gets buried at the trailhead, I'll never get out."

After packing quickly, I started down the mountain. But after 20 minutes, I began to get disoriented. You see, all the little piles of rocks I'd stacked to mark the way were now buried in snow, and I had only a smooth white blanket of snow to guide me. Everything looked the same, and it was snowing even harder now.

Five minutes later, I started chewing on some jerky to keep warm, then suddenly stopped. Where was I? Where was the creek drainage? Isn't this where I was supposed to cross over a creek and start the switchbacks down the mountain?

Right then I looked down and saw the tracks of a huge deer, the kind Mr. Furnai had talked about. What a predicament: I was lost and snowed in and seeing big hoofprints in the snow. Part of me wanted to abandon all safety and go after that deer, but a little voice in the back of my head won out. "Treat this as an emergency," it said.

The first step in any predicament is to secure your present situation; that is, to make sure it does not get any worse. I unloaded my rifle (too easy to slip, fall, and have a misfire), took stock of my food (three days' worth), camp fuel (plenty), and clothes (rain gear keeping me dry). Then I wondered, "Where the hell am I?"

I took out my map, compass, and altimeter, then opened the map and laid it on the snow. It immediately began collecting snowflakes. I set the compass atop the map and oriented it to north. Because of the fog, there was no way to spot landmarks, such as prominent mountaintops, to verify my position. Then I checked the altimeter, which read 4,900 feet. Well, the elevation at my lake was 5,320 feet. That was critical information.

I scanned the elevation lines on the map and was able to trace the approximate area of my position, somewhere downstream from the lake, yet close to a 4,900-foot elevation. "Right here," I said, pointing to a spot on the map with a finger. "I should pick up the switchback trail down the mountain somewhere off to the left, maybe just 40 or 50 yards away."

Slowly and deliberately, I pushed through the light, powdered snow. In five minutes, I suddenly stopped. To the left, across a 10-foot depression in the snow, appeared a flat spot that veered off to the right. "That's it! That's the crossing."

In minutes, I was working down the switchbacks, on my way, no longer lost. I thought of the hoofprints I had seen, and now that I knew my position, I wanted to head back and spend the day hunting. Then I looked up at the sky, saw it filled with falling snowflakes, and envisioned my truck buried deep in snow. Alas, this time logic won out over dreams.

In a few hours, now trudging through more than a foot of snow, I was at my truck at a spot called Doe Flat, and next to it was a giant, all-terrain U.S. Forest Service vehicle and two rangers.

"Need any help?" I asked them.

They just laughed. "We're here to help you," one answered. "It's a good thing you filed a trip plan with our district office in Gasquet. We wouldn't have known you were out here."

"Winter has arrived," said the other. "If we don't get your truck out now, it will be stuck here until next spring. If we hadn't found you, you might have been here until the end of time."

They connected a chain from the rear axle of their giant rig to the front axle of my truck and started towing me out, back to civilization. On the way to pavement, I figured I had learned some of the more important lessons of my life. Always file a trip plan and have plenty of food, fuel, and a camp stove you can rely on. Make sure your clothes, weather gear, sleeping bag, and tent will keep you dry and warm. Always carry a compass, altimeter, and map with elevation lines, and know how to use them, practicing in good weather to get the feel of it.

And if you get lost and see the hoofprints of a giant deer, well, there are times when it is best to pass them by.

Catching Fish, Avoiding Bears, and Having Fun

Feet tired and hot, stomachs hungry, we stopped our hike for lunch beside a beautiful little river pool that was catching the flows from a long but gentle waterfall. My brother Rambob passed me a piece of jerky. I took my boots off, then slowly dunked my feet into the cool, foaming water.

I was gazing at a towering peak across a canyon when suddenly, Wham! There was a quick jolt at the heel of my right foot. I pulled my foot out of the water to find that, incredibly, a trout had bitten it.

My brother looked at me as if I had antlers growing out of my head. "Wow!" he exclaimed. "That trout almost caught himself an outdoors writer!"

It's true that in remote areas trout sometimes bite on almost anything, even feet. On one high-country trip I caught limits of trout using nothing but a bare hook. The only problem is that the fish will often hit the splitshot sinker instead of the hook. Of course, fishing isn't usually that easy, but it gives you an idea of what is possible.

America's wildlands are home to a remarkable abundance of fish and wildlife. Deer browse with little fear of man, bears keep an eye out for your food, and little critters like squirrels and chipmunks are daily companions. Add in the fishing, and you've got yourself a camping trip.

Your camping adventures will evolve into premium outdoor experiences if you can work in a few good fishing trips, avoid bear problems, and occasionally add a little offbeat fun with some camp games.

Trout and Bass

He creeps up on the stream as quiet as an Indian scout, keeping his shadow off the water. With his little spinning rod, he'll zip his lure within an inch or two of its desired mark, probing along rocks, the edges of riffles, pocket water, or wherever he can find a change in river habitat. Rambob is trout fishing, and he's a master at it.

In most cases, he'll catch a trout on his first or second cast. After that, it's time to move up the river, giving no spot much more than five minutes' due. Stick and move, stick and move, stalking the stream like a bobcat zeroing in on an unsuspecting rabbit. He might keep a few trout for dinner, but mostly he releases what he catches. Rambob doesn't necessarily fish for food. It's the feeling that comes with it.

You don't need a million dollars' worth of fancy gear to catch fish. What you need is the right outlook, and that can be learned. That goes regardless of whether you are fishing for trout or bass, the two most popular fisheries in the United States. Your fishing tackle selection should be as simple and clutter free as possible.

At home, I have every piece of fishing tackle you might imagine, more than 30 rods and many tackle boxes, racks, and cabinets filled with all kinds of stuff. I've got one lure that looks like a chipmunk and another that resembles a miniature can of beer with hooks. If I hear of something new, I want to try it and usually do. It's a result of my lifelong fascination with the sport.

Why We Fish: Fishing can give you a sense of exhilaration, like taking a hot shower after being coated with dust. On your walk back to camp, the steps come easy. You suddenly understand what John Muir meant when he talked of developing a oneness with nature, because you have it. That's what fishing can provide.

But if you just want to catch fish, there's an easier way to go. When I go fishing, I take that path. I don't try to bring everything. It would be impossible. Instead, I bring a relatively small amount of gear. At home, I scan my tackle boxes for equipment and lures, make my selections, and bring just the essentials. Rod, reel, and tackle will fit into a side pocket of my backpack or a small carrying bag.

So what kind of rod should be used on an outdoor trip? For most camper/anglers, I suggest the use of a light, multipiece spinning rod that will break down to a small size. The lowest-priced, quality six-piece rod on the market is the Daiwa 6.5-foot pack rod, No. 6752, which is made of a graphite/glass composite that gives it the quality of a much more expensive model. It comes in a hard plastic carrying tube for protection. Other major rod manufacturers, such as Fenwick, offer similar premium rods. It's tough to miss with any of them.

The use of graphite/glass composites in fishing rods has made them lighter and more sensitive, yet stronger. The only downside to graphite as a rod material is that it can be brittle. If you rap your rod against something, it can crack or cause a weak spot. That weak spot can eventually snap under even light pressure, like setting a hook or casting. Of course, a bit of care will prevent that from ever occurring.

If you haven't bought a fishing reel in some time, you will be surprised at the quality and price of micro spinning reels on the market. The reels come tiny and strong, with rear-control drag systems. Sigma, Shimano, Cardinal, Abu, and others all make premium reels. They're worth it. With your purchase, you've bought a reel that will last for years and years.

The one downside to spinning reels is that after long-term use, the bail spring will weaken. The result is that after casting and beginning to reel, the bail will sometimes not flip over and allow the reel to retrieve the line. Then you have to do it by hand. This can be incredibly frustrating, particularly when stream fishing, where instant line pickup is essential. The solution is to have a new bail spring installed every few years. This is a cheap, quick operation for a tackle expert.

You might own a giant tackle box filled with lures, but on your fishing trip you are better off to fit just the essentials into a small container. One of the best ways to do that is to use the Plano Micro-Magnum 3414, a tiny two-sided tackle box for trout anglers that fits into a shirt pocket. In mine, I can fit 20 lures in one side of the box and 20 flies, splitshot, and snap swivels in the other. For bass lures, which are bigger, you need a slightly larger box, but the same principle applies.

There are more fishing lures on the market than you can imagine, but a few special ones can do the job. I make sure these are in my box on every trip. For trout, I carry a small black Panther Martin spinner with yellow spots, a small gold Kastmaster, a yellow Roostertail, a gold Z-Ray with red spots, a Super Duper, and a Mepps Lightning spinner.

You can take it a step further using insider's wisdom. My old pal Ed "the Dunk" showed me his trick of taking a tiny Dardevle spoon, spray painting it flat black, and dabbing five tiny red dots on it. It's a real killer, particularly in tiny streams where the trout are spooky.

The best trout catcher I've ever used on rivers is a small metal lure called a Met-L Fly. On days when nothing else works, it can be like going to a shooting gallery. The problem is that the lure is nearly impossible to find. Rambob and I consider the few we have remaining so valuable that if the lure is snagged on a rock, a cold swim is deemed mandatory for its retrieval. These lures are as hard to find in tackle shops as trout can be to catch without one.

For bass, you can also fit all you need into a small plastic tackle box. I have fished with many bass pros, and all of them actually use just a few lures: a white spinner bait, a small jig called a Gits-It, a surface plug called a Zara Spook, and plastic worms. At times, as when the bass move into shoreline areas during the spring, shad minnow imitations like those made by Rebel or Rapala can be dynamite. My favorite is the one-inch, blue-silver Rapala. Every spring, as the lakes begin to warm and the fish snap out of their winter doldrums, I like to float and paddle around in my small raft. I'll cast that little Rapala along the shoreline and catch and release hundreds of bass, bluegill, and sunfish. The fish are usually sitting close to the shoreline, awaiting my offering.

Fishing Tips

There's an old angler's joke about how you need to think like a fish. But if you're the one getting zilched, you may not think it's so funny.

The irony is that it is your mental approach, what you see and what you miss, that often determines your fishing luck. Some people will spend a lot of money on tackle, lures, and fishing clothes. That done, they just saunter up to a stream or lake, cast out, and wonder why they are not catching fish. The answer is their mental outlook. They are not attuning themselves to their surroundings.

You must live on nature's level, not your own. Try this and you will become aware of things you never believed even existed. Soon you will see things that allow you to catch fish. You can get a head start by reading about fishing, but to get your degree in fishing, you must attend the University of Nature.

On every fishing trip, regardless of what you fish for, try to follow three hard-and-fast rules:

1. Always approach the fishing spot so you will be undetected.
2. Present your lure, fly, or bait in a manner so it appears completely natural, as if no line was attached.
3. Stick and move, hitting one spot, working it the best you can, then move to the next.

Approach

No one can just walk up to a stream or lake, cast out, and start catching fish as if someone had waved a magic wand. Instead, give the fish credit for being smart. After all, they live there.

Your approach must be completely undetected by the fish. Fish can sense your presence through sight and sound, although this is misinterpreted by most people. By sight, this rarely means the fish actually see you; more likely, they will see your shadow on the water or the movement of your arm or rod while casting. By sound, it doesn't mean they hear you talking, but that they will detect the vibrations of your footsteps along the shore, kicking a rock, or the unnatural plunking sound of a heavy cast hitting the water. Any of these elements can spook them off the bite. In order to fish undetected, you must walk softly, keep your shadow off the water, and keep your casting motion low. All of these keys

The rule of the wild is that wildlife will congregate wherever there is a distinct change in habitat. To find **where fish are hiding,** look where a riffle pours into a small pond, where a rapid plunges into a deep hole and flattens, and around submerged trees, rock piles, and boulders in the middle of a long riffle.

become easier at sunrise or sunset, when shadows are on the water. At midday, a high sun causes a high level of light penetration in the water, which can make the fish skittish to any foreign presence.

Like hunting, you must stalk the spots. When my brother Rambob sneaks up on a fishing spot, he is like a burglar sneaking through an unlocked window.

Presentation
Your lure, fly, or bait must appear in the water as if no line were attached, so it looks as natural as possible. My pal Mo Furniss has skin-dived in rivers to watch what the fish see when somebody is fishing.

"You wouldn't believe it," he said. "When the lure hits the water, every trout within 40 feet, like 15, 20 trout, will do a little zigzag. They all see the lure and are aware something is going on. Meanwhile, onshore the guy casting doesn't get a bite and thinks there aren't any fish in the river."

If your offering is aimed at fooling a fish into striking, it must appear as part of its natural habitat, like an insect just hatched or a small fish looking for a spot to hide. That's where you come in.

After you have sneaked up on a fishing spot, you should zip your cast upstream and start your retrieval as soon as it hits the water. If you let the lure sink to the bottom and then start the retrieval, you have no chance. A minnow, for instance, does not sink to the bottom, then start swimming. On rivers, the retrieval should be more of a drift, as if the "minnow" is in trouble and the current is sweeping it downstream.

When fishing on trout streams, always hike and cast upriver and retrieve as the offering drifts downstream in the current. This is effective because trout will sit almost motionless, pointed upstream, finning against the current. This way they can see anything coming their direction, and if a potential food morsel arrives, all they need to do is move over a few inches, open their mouths, and they've got an easy lunch. Thus you must cast upstream.

Conversely, if you cast downstream, your retrieval will bring the lure from behind the fish, where he cannot see it approaching. I've never seen a trout that had eyes in its tail. In addition, when retrieving a downstream lure, the river current will tend to sweep your lure inshore to the rocks.

Finding Spots
A lot of anglers don't catch fish, and a lot of hikers never see any wildlife. The key is where they are looking.

The rule of the wild is that fish and wildlife will congregate wherever there is a distinct change in the habitat. This is where you should begin your search. To find deer, for instance, forget probing a thick forest, but look for where it breaks into a meadow or a clear-cut has splayed a stand of trees. That's where the deer will be.

In a river, it can be where a riffle pours into a small pool, a rapid that plunges into a deep hole and flattens, a big boulder in the middle of a long riffle, a shoreline point, a rock pile, a submerged tree. Look for the changes. Conversely, long, straight stretches of shoreline will not hold fish—the habitat is lousy.

On rivers, the most productive areas are often where short riffles tumble into small oxygenated pools. After sneaking up from the downstream side and staying low, you should zip your cast so the lure plops gently into the white water just above the pool. Start your retrieval instantly; the lure will drift downstream and plunk into the pool. Bang! That's where the trout will hit. Take a few more casts and then head upstream to the next spot.

With a careful approach and lure presentation and by fishing in the right spots, you have the ticket to many exciting days on the water.

Of Bears and Food

The first time you come nose-to-nose with a bear can make your skin quiver. Even the sight of mild-mannered black bears, the most common bear in America, can send shock waves through your body. They weigh 250 to 400 pounds and have large claws and teeth that are made to scare campers. When they bound, the muscles on their shoulders roll like ocean breakers.

Bears in camping areas are accustomed to sharing the mountains with hikers and campers. They have become specialists in the food-raiding business. As a result, you must be able to make a bearproof food hang or be able to scare the fellow off. Many campgrounds provide bear- and raccoon-proof food lockers. You can also stash your food in your vehicle, but that limits the range of your trip.

If you are staying at one of the easy backpack sites listed in this book, there will be no food lockers available. Your car will not be there, either. The solution is to make a bearproof food hang, suspending all of your food wrapped in a plastic garbage bag from a rope in midair, 10 feet from the trunk of a tree and 20 feet off the ground. (Counterbalancing two bags with a rope thrown over a tree limb is effective, but finding an appropriate limb can be difficult.)

This is accomplished by tying a rock to a rope, then throwing it over a high but sturdy tree limb. Next, tie your food bag to the rope and hoist it in the air. When you are satisfied with the position of the food bag, tie off the end of the rope to another tree. In an area frequented by bears, a good food bag is a necessity—nothing else will do.

I've been there. On one trip, my pal Foonsky and my brother Rambob left to fish, and I was stoking up an evening campfire when I felt the eyes of an intruder on my back. I turned around and saw a big bear heading straight for our camp. In the next half hour, I scared the bear off twice, but then he got a whiff of something sweet in my brother's pack.

The bear rolled into camp like a truck, grabbed the pack, ripped it open, and plucked out the Tang and the Swiss Miss. The 350-pounder then sat astride a nearby log and lapped at the goodies like a thirsty dog drinking water.

Once a bear gets his mitts on your gear, he considers it his. I took two steps toward the pack, and that bear jumped off the log and galloped across the camp right at me. Scientists say a man can't outrun a bear, but they've never seen how fast I can go up a granite block with a bear on my tail.

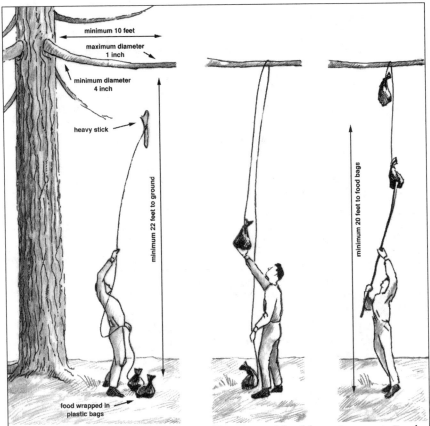

*In an area frequented by bears, a good **bear-proof food hang** is a must. Food should be stored in a plastic bag 10 feet from the trunk of the tree and at least 20 feet from the ground.*

Shortly thereafter, Foonsky returned to find me perched on top of the rock and demanded to know how I could let a bear get our Tang. It took all three of us, charging at once and shouting like madmen, to clear the bear out of camp and send him off over the ridge. We learned never to let food sit unattended.

The Grizzly

When it comes to grizzlies, my friends, you need what we call an attitude adjustment. Or that big ol' bear may just decide to adjust your attitude for you, making your stay at the park a short one.

Grizzlies are nothing like black bears. They are bigger, stronger, have little fear, and take what they want. Some people believe there are many different

Bear Territory

If you are hiking in a wilderness area that may have grizzlies, you should wear bells on your pack. That way the bear will hear you coming and likely get out of your way. Keep talking, singing, or maybe even debating the country's foreign policy, but do not fall into a silent hiking vigil. If a breeze is blowing in your face, you must make even more noise (a good excuse to rant and rave about the government's domestic affairs). Noise is important because your smell will not be carried in the direction you are hiking, and the bear will not smell you coming.

If a bear can hear you and smell you, it will tend to get out of the way and let you pass without your knowing it was even close by. The exceptions are if you are carrying fish or lots of sweets in your pack or if you are wearing heavy, sweet deodorants or makeup. All of these are bear attractants.

species of this critter, like Alaskan brown, silvertip, cinnamon, and Kodiak, but the truth is they are all grizzlies. Any difference in appearance has to do with diet, habitat, and life habits, not speciation. By any name, they all come big.

The first thing you must do is determine if there are grizzlies in the area where you are camping. That can usually be done by asking local rangers. If you are heading into Yellowstone or Glacier National Park, or the Bob Marshall Wilderness of Montana, you don't have to ask. They're out there, and they're the biggest and potentially most dangerous critters you could run into.

One general way to figure the size of a bear is from its footprint. Take the width of the footprint in inches, add one to it, and you'll have an estimated length of the bear in feet. For instance, a nine-inch footprint equals a 10-foot bear. Any bear that big is a grizzly, my friends. In fact, most grizzly footprints average about 9 to 10 inches across, and black bears (though they may be brown in color) tend to have footprints only 4.5 to 6 inches across.

Most encounters with grizzlies occur when hikers fall into a silent march in the wilderness with the wind in their faces, and they walk around a corner and into a big, unsuspecting grizzly. If you do this and see a big hump just behind its neck, don't think twice. It's a grizzly.

Then what should you do? Get up a tree, that's what. Grizzlies are so big that their claws cannot support their immense weight, and thus they cannot climb trees. Although their young can climb, they rarely want to get their mitts on you.

If you do get grabbed, every instinct in your body will tell you to fight back. Don't believe it. Play dead. Go limp. Let the bear throw you around a little, because after awhile you become unexciting play material and the bear will get bored. My grandmother was grabbed by a grizzly in Glacier National Park and, after a few tosses and hugs, was finally left alone to escape.

Some say it's a good idea to tuck your head under his chin, since that way the bear will be unable to bite your head. I'll take a pass on that one. If you are taking action, any action, it's a signal that you are a force to be reckoned with, and he'll

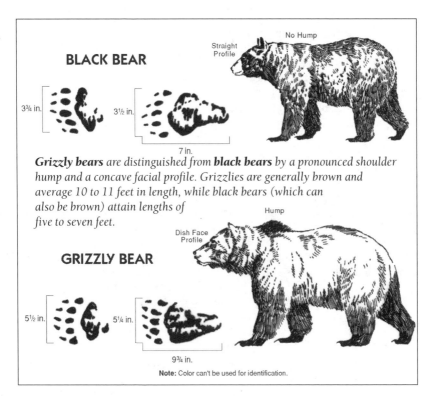

BLACK BEAR

No Hump

Straight Profile

3¾ in.

3½ in.

7 in.

Grizzly bears are distinguished from black bears by a pronounced shoulder hump and a concave facial profile. Grizzlies are generally brown and average 10 to 11 feet in length, while black bears (which can also be brown) attain lengths of five to seven feet.

Hump

Dish Face Profile

GRIZZLY BEAR

5½ in.

5¼ in.

9¾ in.

Note: Color can't be used for identification.

likely respond with more aggression. Bears don't lose many wrestling matches.

What grizzlies really like to do, believe it or not, is to pile a lot of sticks and leaves on you. Just let them, and keep perfectly still. Don't fight them, and don't run. When you have a 100 percent chance (not 98 or 99) to dash up a nearby tree, that's when you let fly. Once safely perched in a tree, you can hurl down insults and let your aggression out.

In a wilderness camp, you should take special precautions. Always hang your food at least 100 yards downwind of camp and get it high—30 feet is reasonable. In addition, circle your camp with rope and hang the bells from your pack on it. Thus, if a bear walks into your camp, he'll run into the rope, the bells will ring, and everybody will have a chance to get up a tree before ol' griz figures out what's going on. Often, the unexpected ringing of bells is enough to send him off in search of a quieter environment.

You see, more often than not, grizzlies tend to clear the way for campers and hikers. So be smart, don't act like bear bait, and always have a plan if you are confronted by one.

My pal Foonsky had such a plan during a wilderness expedition in Montana's northern Rockies. On our second day of hiking, we started seeing scratch marks on the trees 13 to 14 feet off the ground.

"Mr. Griz made those," Foonsky said. "With spring here, the grizzlies are coming out of hibernation and using the trees like a cat uses a scratch board to stretch the muscles."

The next day, I noticed Foonsky had a pair of track shoes tied to the back of his pack. I just laughed. "You're not going to outrun a griz," I said. "In fact, there's hardly any animal out here in the wilderness that man can outrun."

Foonsky just smiled. "I don't have to outrun a griz," he said. "I just have to out-run you!"

Fun and Games

"Now what are we supposed to do?" the young boy asked his dad.

"Yeah, Dad, think of something," said another son.

Well, Dad thought hard. This was one of the first camping trips he'd taken with his sons, and one of the first lessons he learned was that kids don't appreciate the philosophic release of mountain quiet. They want action and lots of it. With a glint in his eye, Dad searched around the camp and picked up 15 twigs, breaking them so each was four inches long. He laid them in three separate rows—three twigs in one row, five twigs in another, and seven in the other.

"OK, this game is called 3-5-7," said Dad. "You each take turns picking up sticks. You are allowed to remove all or as few as one twig from a row, but here's the catch: You can pick only from one row per turn. Whoever picks up the last stick left is the loser."

I remember this episode well because those two little boys were my brother Bobby, as in Rambobby, and me. To this day, we still play 3-5-7 on campouts, with the winner getting to watch the loser clean the dishes. What I have learned since that original episode is that it does not matter what age you are: campers need options for camp fun.

Some evenings, after a long hike or ride, you are likely to feel too wornout to take on a serious romp downstream to fish or a climb up to a ridge for a view. That is especially true if you have been in the outback for a week or more. At that point, a lot of campers spend their time resting and gazing at a map of the area, dreaming of the next day's adventure, or just take a seat against a rock, watching the colors of the sky and mountain panorama change minute by minute. But kids in the push-button video era, and a lot of adults too, want more. After all, they think, "I'm on vacation. I want some fun."

There are several options, like the 3-5-7 twig game, and they should be just as much a part of your trip planning as arranging your gear. For kids, plan on games, the more physically challenging the competition, the better. One of the best games is to throw a chunk of wood into a lake and challenge the kids to hit it by throwing rocks. It wreaks havoc on the fishing, but it can keep kids totally absorbed for some time. Target practice with a wrist-rocket slingshot is also all consuming for kids, firing rocks away at small targets like pine cones set on a log.

You can also set kids off on little missions near camp, such as looking for the footprints of wildlife, searching out good places to have a "snipe hunt," picking up twigs to get the evening fire started, or having them take the water purifier to a stream to pump some drinking water into a canteen. The latter is an easy, fun, yet important task that will allow kids to feel a sense of equality they often don't get at home.

For adults, the appeal should be more to the intellect. A good example is star and planet identification. While you are staring into space, you're bound to spot a few asteroids or shooting stars. A star chart can make it easy to locate and identify many distinctive stars and constellations, such as Pleiades (the Seven Sisters), Orion, and others from the zodiac, depending on the time of year. With a little research, this activity can add a unique perspective to your trip. You could point to Polaris, one of the most easily identified of all stars, and note that navigators in the 1400s used it to find their way. Polaris, of course, is the North Star and is at the end of the handle of the Little Dipper. Pinpointing Polaris is easy. First find the Big Dipper and then locate the outside stars of the ladle of the Big Dipper. They are called the "pointer stars" because they point right at Polaris.

A tree identification book can teach you a few things about your surroundings. It is also a good idea for one member of the party to research the history of the area you have chosen and another to research the geology. With shared knowledge, you end up with a deeper love of wild places.

Another way to add some recreation to your trip is to bring a board game, many of which have been miniaturized for campers. The most popular are chess, checkers, and cribbage. The latter comes with an equally miniature set of playing cards. If you bring those little cards, that opens a vast set of other possibilities. With kids along, for instance, just take three queens out of the deck and you can play Old Maid.

But there are more serious card games, and they come with high stakes. Such occurred on one high-country trip where Foonsky, Rambob, and I sat down for a late afternoon game of poker. In a game of seven-card stud, I caught a straight on the sixth card and felt like a dog licking on a T-bone. Already I had bet several Skittles and peanut M&Ms on this promising hand.

Then I examined the cards Foonsky had face up. He was showing three sevens and acting as happy as a grizzly with a pork chop—or a full house. He matched my bet of two peanut M&Ms, then raised me three SweetTarts, one Starburst, and one sour apple Jolly Rancher. Rambob folded, but I matched Foonsky's bet and hoped for the best as the seventh and final card was dealt.

Just after Foonsky glanced at that last card, I saw him sneak a look at my grape stick and beef jerky stash. "I raise you a grape stick," he said.

Rambob and I both gasped. It was the highest bet ever made, equivalent to a million dollars laid down in Las Vegas. Cannons were going off in my chest. I looked hard at my cards. They looked good, but were they good enough?

Even with a great hand like I had, a grape stick was too much to gamble, my last one with 10 days of trail ahead of us. I shook my head and folded my cards. Foonsky smiled at his victory. But I still had my grape stick.

Old Tricks Don't Always Work

Most people are born honest, but after a few camping trips, they usually get over it. I remember some advice I got from Rambob, normally an honest soul, on one camping trip. A giant mosquito had landed on my arm and he alerted me to some expert advice.

"Flex your arm muscles," he commanded, watching the mosquito fill with my blood. "He'll get stuck in your arm, then he'll explode."

For some reason, I believed him. We both proceeded to watch the mosquito drill countless holes in my arm.

Alas, the unknowing face sabotage from their most trusted companions on camping trips. It can arise at any time, usually in the form of advice from a friendly, honest-looking face, as if to say, "What? How can you doubt me?" After that mosquito episode, I was a little more skeptical of my dear old brother. Then the next day, when another mosquito was nailing me in the back of the neck, out came this gem:

"Hold your breath," he commanded. I instinctively obeyed. "That will freeze the mosquito," he said, "then you can squish him."

But in the time I wasted holding my breath, the little bugger was able to fly off without my having the satisfaction of squishing him. When he got home, he probably told his family, "What a dummy I got to drill today!"

Over the years, I have been duped numerous times with dubious advice:

On a grizzly bear attack: "If he grabs you, tuck your head under the grizzly's chin; then he won't be able to bite you in the head." This made sense to me until the first time I came face-to-face with a nine-foot grizzly 40 yards away. In seconds, I was at the top of a tree, which suddenly seemed to make the most sense.

On coping with animal bites: "If a bear bites you in the arm, don't try to jerk it away. That will just rip up your arm. Instead force your arm deeper into his mouth. He'll lose his grip and will have to open it to get a firmer hold, and right then you can get away." I was told this in the Boy Scouts, and when I was 14, I had a chance to try it out when a friend's dog bit me as I tried to pet it. What happened? When I shoved my arm deeper into his mouth, he bit me three more times.

Keep It Wild Tip 5: Keep the Wilderness Wild

1. Let nature's sound prevail. Avoid loud voices and noises.
2. Leave radios and tape players at home. At drive-in camping sites, never open car doors with music playing.
3. Careful guidance is necessary when choosing any games to bring for children. Most toys, especially any kind of gun toys with which children simulate shooting at each other, shouldn't be allowed on a camping trip.
4. Control pets at all times or leave them with a sitter at home.
5. Treat natural heritage with respect. Leave plants, rocks, and historical artifacts where you find them.

On cooking breakfast: "The bacon will curl up every time in a camp frying pan. So make sure you have a bacon stretcher to keep it flat." As a 12-year-old Tenderfoot, I spent two hours looking for the bacon stretcher until I figured out the camp leader had forgotten it. It was several years until I learned there is no such thing.

On preventing sore muscles: "If you haven't hiked for a long time and you are facing a rough climb, you can keep from getting sore muscles in your legs, back, and shoulders by practicing the 'Dead Man's Walk.' Simply let your entire body go slack, and then take slow, wobbling steps. This will clear your muscles of lactic acid, which causes them to be so sore after a rough hike." Foonsky pulled this one on me. Rambob and I both bought it and tried it while we were hiking up Mount Whitney, which requires a 6,000-foot elevation gain in six miles. In one 45-minute period, about 30 other hikers passed us and looked at us as if we were suffering from some rare form of mental aberration.

Fish won't bite? No problem: "If the fish are not feeding or will not bite, persistent anglers can still catch dinner with little problem. Keep casting across the current, and eventually, as they hover in the stream, the line will feed across their open mouths. Keep reeling and you will hook the fish right in the side of the mouth. This technique is called 'lining.' Never worry if the fish will not bite, because you can always line 'em." Of course, heh, heh, heh, that explains why so many fish get hooked in the side of the mouth.

How to keep bears away: "To keep bears away, urinate around the borders of your campground. If there are a lot of bears in the area, it is advisable to go right on your sleeping bag." Yeah, surrrrrre.

What to do with trash: "Don't worry about packing out trash. Just bury it. It will regenerate into the earth and add valuable minerals." Bears, raccoons, skunks, and other critters will dig up your trash as soon as you depart, leaving one huge mess for the next camper. Always pack out everything.

Often the advice comes without warning. That was the case after a fishing trip with a female companion, when she outcaught me two to one, the third such trip in a row. I explained this to a shopkeeper, and he nodded, then explained why: "The male fish are able to detect the female scent on the lure, and thus become aroused into striking." Of course! That explains everything!

Getting Revenge

I was just a lad when Foonsky pulled the old snipe-hunt trick on me. It took nearly 30 years to get revenge.

You probably know about snipe hunting. That is where the victim is led out at night in the woods by a group, then is left holding a bag.

"Stay perfectly still and quiet," Foonsky explained. "You don't want to scare the snipe. The rest of us will go back to camp and let the woods settle down. Then when the snipe are least expecting it, we'll form a line and charge through the forest with sticks, beating bushes and trees, and we'll flush the snipe out right to you. Be ready with the bag. When we flush the snipe out, bag it. But until we start our charge, make sure you don't move or make a sound or you will spook the snipe and ruin everything."

I sat out there in the woods with my bag for hours, waiting for the charge. I waited, waited, and waited. Nothing happened. No charge, no snipe. It wasn't until well past midnight that I figured something was wrong. When I finally returned to camp, everybody was sleeping.

Well, I tell ya, don't get mad at your pals for the tricks they pull on you. Get revenge. Some 25 years later, on the last day of a camping trip, the time finally came.

"Let's break camp early," Foonsky suggested to Mr. Furnai and me. "Get up before dawn, eat breakfast, pack up, and be on the ridge to watch the sun come up. It will be a fantastic way to end the trip."

"Sounds great to me," I replied. But when Foonsky wasn't looking, I turned his alarm clock ahead three hours. So when the alarm sounded at the appointed 4:30 A.M. wakeup time, Mr. Furnai and I knew it was actually only 1:30 A.M.

Foonsky clambered out of his sleeping bag and whistled with a grin. "Time to break camp."

"You go ahead," I answered. "I'll skip breakfast so I can get a little more sleep. At the first sign of dawn, wake me up, and I'll break camp."

"Me, too," said Mr. Furnai.

Foonsky then proceeded to make some coffee, cook a breakfast, and eat it, sitting on a log in the black darkness of the forest, waiting for the sun to come up. An hour later, with still no sign of dawn, he checked his clock. It now read 5:30 A.M. "Any minute now, we should start seeing some light," he said.

He made another cup of coffee, packed his gear, and sat there in the middle of the night, looking up at the stars, waiting for dawn. "Anytime now," he said. He ended up sitting there all night long.

Revenge is sweet. Before a fishing trip at a lake, I took Foonsky aside and explained that the third member of the party, Jimbobo, was hard of hearing and sensitive about it. "Don't mention it to him," I advised. "Just talk real loud."

Meanwhile, I had already told Jimbobo the same thing. "Foonsky just can't hear very good."

We had fished less than 20 minutes when Foonsky got a nibble.

"GET A BITE?" shouted Jimbobo.

"YEAH!" yelled back Foonsky, smiling. "BUT I DIDN'T HOOK HIM!"

"MAYBE NEXT TIME!" shouted Jimbobo with a friendly grin.

Well, they spent the entire day yelling at each other from the distance of a few feet. They never did figure it out. Heh, heh, heh.

That is, I thought so, until we made a trip salmon fishing. I got a strike that almost knocked my fishing rod out of the boat. When I grabbed the rod, it felt as if Moby Dick were on the other end. "At least a 25-pounder," I said. "Maybe bigger."

The fish dove, ripped off line, and then bulldogged. "It's acting like a 40-pounder," I announced, "Huge, just huge. It's going deep. That's how the big ones fight."

Some 15 minutes later, I finally got the "salmon" to the surface. It turned out to be a coffee can that Foonsky had clipped on the line with a snap swivel. By maneuvering the boat, he made the coffee can fight like a big fish.

This all started with a little old snipe hunt years ago. You never know what your pals will try next. Don't get mad. Get revenge.

Camping Options

Boat-in Seclusion

Most campers would never think of trading in their car, pickup truck, or RV for a boat, but people who go by boat on a camping trip enjoy virtually guaranteed seclusion and top-quality outdoor experiences.

Camping with a boat is a do-it-yourself venture in living under primitive circumstances. Yet at the same time you can bring along any luxury item you wish, from giant coolers, stoves, and lanterns to portable gasoline generators. Weight is almost never an issue.

Many outstanding boat-in campgrounds in beautiful surroundings are available in Washington. The best are on the shores of lakes accessible by canoe or skiff and at offshore islands reached by saltwater cruisers. Several boat-in camps are detailed in this book.

If you want to take the adventure a step further and create your own boat-in camp, perhaps near a special fishing spot, this is a go-for-it deal that provides the best way possible to establish your own secret campsite. But most people who set out freelance style forget three critical items for boat-in camping: a shovel, a sunshade, and an ax. Here is why these items can make a key difference in your trip:

Shovel: Many lakes and virtually all reservoirs have steep, sloping banks. At reservoirs subject to drawdowns, what was lake bottom in the spring can be a campsite in late summer. If you want a flat area for a tent site, the only answer is to dig one out yourself. A shovel gives you that option.

Sunshade: The flattest spots to camp along lakes often have a tendency to support only sparse tree growth. As a result, a natural shield from sun and rain is rarely available. What? Rain in the summer? Oh yeah, don't get me started. A light tarp, set up with poles and staked ropes, solves the problem.

Ax: Unless you bring your own firewood, which is necessary at some sparsely wooded reservoirs, there is no substitute for a good, sharp ax. With an ax, you can almost always find dry firewood, since the interior of an otherwise wet log will be dry. When the weather turns bad is precisely when you will most want a fire. You may need an ax to get one going.

In the search to create your own personal boat-in campsite, you will find that the flattest areas are usually the tips of peninsulas and points, while the protected back ends of coves are often steeply sloped. At reservoirs, the flattest areas are usually near the mouths of the feeder streams and the points are steep. On rivers, there are usually sandbars on the inside of tight bends that make for ideal campsites.

Almost all boat-in campsites developed by government agencies are free of charge, but you are on your own. Only in extremely rare cases is piped water available.

Any way you go—by canoe, skiff, or power cruiser—you end up with a one-in-a-million campsite you can call your own.

Desert Outings

It was a cold, snowy day in Missouri when 10-year-old Rusty Ballinger started dreaming about the vast deserts of the West.

"My dad was reading aloud from a Zane Grey book called *Riders of the Purple Sage*," Ballinger said. "He would get animated when he got to the passages about the desert. It wasn't long before I started to have the same feelings."

That was in 1947. Ballinger, now in his sixties, has spent a good part of his life exploring the West, camping along the way. "The deserts are the best part. There's something about the uniqueness of each little area you see," Ballinger said. "You're constantly surprised. Just the time of day and the way the sun casts a different color. It's like the lady you care about. One time she smiles, the next time she's pensive. The desert is like that. If you love nature, you can love the desert. After awhile, you can't help but love it."

A desert adventure is not just an antidote for a case of cabin fever in the winter. Whether you go by RV, pickup truck, car, or on foot, it provides its own special qualities.

If you go camping in the desert, your approach has to be as unique as the setting. For starters, don't plan on any campfires, but bring a camp stove instead. Unlike in the mountains, do not camp near a water hole because an animal such as a badger, coyote, or desert bighorn might be desperate for water, and if you set up camp in the animal's way, you may be forcing a confrontation.

In some areas, there is a danger of flash floods. An intense rain can fall in one area, collect in a pool, then suddenly burst through a narrow canyon. If you are in its path, you could be injured or drowned. The lesson? Never camp in a gully.

"Some people might wonder, 'What good is this place?'" Ballinger said. "The answer is that it is good for looking at. It is one of the world's unique places."

Camp Ethics and Politics

The perfect place to set up a base camp turned out to be not so perfect. In fact, according to Doug Williams of California, it did not even exist.

Williams and his son, James, had driven deep into Angeles National Forest, prepared to set up camp and then explore the surrounding area on foot. But when they reached their destination, no campground existed.

"I wanted a primitive camp in a national forest where I could teach my son some basics," said the senior Williams. "But when we got there, there wasn't much left of the camp, and it had been closed. It was obvious that the area had been vandalized."

It turned out not to be an isolated incident. A lack of outdoor ethics practiced by a few people using the unsupervised campgrounds available on national forestland has caused the U.S. Forest Service to close a few of them and make extensive repairs to others.

Keep It Wild Tip 6: Respect Other Users

1. Horseback riders have priority over hikers. Step to the downhill side of the trail and talk softly when encountering horseback riders.
2. Hikers and horseback riders have priority over mountain bikers. When mountain bikers encounter other users, even on wide trails, they should pass at an extremely slow speed. On narrow trails, they should dismount and get off to the side so hikers or horseback riders can pass without having their trip disrupted.
3. Mountain bikes aren't permitted on most single-track trails and are expressly prohibited in designated wilderness areas and all sections of the Pacific Crest Trail. Mountain bikers breaking these rules should be confronted and told to dismount and walk their bikes until they reach a legal area.
4. It's illegal for horseback riders to break off branches that may be in the path of wilderness trails.
5. Horseback riders on overnight trips are prohibited from camping in many areas and are usually required to keep stock animals in specific areas where they can not damage the landscape.

"There have been sites closed, especially in Angeles and San Bernardino national forests in Southern California," said David Flohr, regional campground coordinator for the U.S. Forest Service. "It's an urban type of thing, affecting forests near urban areas, and not just Los Angeles. They get a lot of urban users and they bring with them a lot of the same ethics they have in the city. They get drinking and they're not afraid to do things. They vandalize and run. Of course, it is a public facility, so they think nobody is getting hurt."

But somebody is getting hurt, starting with the next person who wants to use the campground. If the ranger district budget doesn't have enough money to pay for repairs, the campground is then closed for the next arrivals. Just ask Doug and James Williams.

In an era of considerable fiscal restraint for the U.S. Forest Service, vandalized campgrounds could face closure instead of repair in the next few years. Williams had just a taste of it, but Flohr, as camping coordinator, gets a steady diet.

"It starts with behavior," Flohr said. "General rowdiness, drinking, partying, and then vandalism. It goes all the way from the felt tip pen things (graffiti) to total destruction, blowing up toilet buildings with dynamite. I have seen toilets destroyed totally with shotguns. They burn up tables, burn barriers. They'll burn up signs for firewood, even the shingles right off the roofs of the bathrooms. They'll shoot anything, garbage cans, signs. It can get a little hairy. A favorite is to remove the stool out of a toilet building. We've had people fall in the open hole."

The National Park Service had a similar problem some years back, especially with rampant littering. Park Director Bill Mott responded by creating an interpretive program that attempts to teach visitors the wise use of natural areas, and to have all park workers set examples by picking up litter and reminding others to do the same.

The U.S. Forest Service has responded with a similar program, making brochures available that detail the wise use of national forests. The four most popular brochures are titled: "Rules for Visitors to the National Forest," "Recreation in the National Forests," "Is the Water Safe?" and "Backcountry Safety Tips." These include details on campfires, drinking water from lakes or streams, hypothermia, safety, and outdoor ethics. They are available for free by writing to Public Affairs, U.S. Forest Service, 630 Sansome Street, San Francisco, CA 94111.

Flohr said even experienced campers sometimes cross over the ethics line unintentionally. The most common example, he said, is when campers toss garbage into the outhouse toilet, rather than packing it out in a plastic garbage bag.

"They throw it in the vault toilet bowls, which just fills them up," Flohr said. "That creates an extremely high cost to pump it. You know why? Because some poor guy has to pick that stuff out piece by piece. It can't be pumped."

Two Dogs: "There are two dogs inside of you," my dad once said, "a good one, and a bad one. The one you feed is the one that will grow. Always try to feed the good dog."

At most backcountry sites, the U.S. Forest Service has implemented a program called "Pack it in, pack it out," even posting signs that remind all visitors to do so. But a lot of people don't do it, and others may even uproot the sign and burn it for firewood.

On a trip to a secluded lake near Carson Pass in the Sierra Nevada, I arrived at a small, little-known camp where the picnic table had been spray painted and garbage had been strewn about. A pristine place, the true temple of God, had been defiled.

Getting Along with Fellow Campers

The most important thing about a camping, fishing, or hunting trip is not where you go, how many fish you catch, or how many shots you fire. It often has little to do with how beautiful the view is, how easy the campfire lights, or how sunny the days are.

Oh yeah? Then what is the most important factor? The answer: The people you are with. It is that simple.

Who would you rather camp with? Your enemy at work or your dream mate in a good mood? You get the idea. A camping trip is a fairly close-knit experience, and you can make lifetime friends or lifelong enemies in the process. That is why your choice of companions is so important. Your own behavior is equally consequential.

Yet most people spend more time putting together their camping gear than considering why they enjoy or hate the company of their chosen companions. Here are 10 rules of behavior for good camping mates:

1. **No whining:** Nothing is more irritating than being around a whiner. It goes right to the heart of adventure, since often the only difference between a hardship and an escapade is simply whether an individual has the spirit for it. The people who do can turn a rugged day in the outdoors into a cherished memory. Those who don't can ruin it with their incessant sniveling.

2. **Activities must be agreed upon:** Always have a meeting of the minds with your companions over the general game plan. Then everybody will possess an

equal stake in the outcome of the trip. This is absolutely critical. Otherwise they will feel like merely an addendum to your trip, not an equal participant, and a whiner will be born (see No. 1).

3. **Nobody's in charge:** It is impossible to be genuine friends if one person is always telling another what to do, especially if the orders involve simple camp tasks. You need to share the space on the same emotional plane, and the only way to do that is to have a semblance of equality, regardless of differences in experience. Just try ordering your mate around at home for a few days. You'll quickly see the results, and they aren't pretty.

4. **Equal chances at the fun stuff:** It's fun to build the fire, get the first cast at the best fishing spot, and hoist the bagged food for a bearproof food hang. It is not fun to clean the dishes, collect firewood, or cook every night. So obviously there must be an equal distribution of the fun stuff and the not-so-fun stuff, and everybody on the trip must get a shot at the good and the bad.

5. **No heroes:** No awards are bestowed for achievement in the outdoors, yet some guys treat mountain peaks, big fish, and big game as if they are prizes in a trophy competition. Actually, nobody cares how wonderful you are, which is always a surprise to trophy chasers. What people care about is the heart of the adventure, the gut-level stuff.

6. **Agree on a wakeup time:** It is a good idea to agree on a general wakeup time before closing your eyes for the night. That goes regardless of whether you want to sleep in late or get up at dawn. Then you can proceed on course regardless of what time you crawl out of your sleeping bag in the morning, without the risk of whining (see No. 1).

7. **Think of the other person:** Be self-aware instead of self-absorbed. A good test is to count the number of times you say, "What do you think?" A lot of potential problems can be solved quickly by actually listening to the answer.

8. **Solo responsibilities:** There are several essential camp duties on all trips, and while they should be shared equally, most should be completed solo. That means that when it is time for you to cook, you don't have to worry about me changing the recipe on you. It means that when it is my turn to make the fire, you keep your mitts out of it.

9. **Don't let money get in the way:** Of course, everybody should share equally in trip expenses, such as the cost of food, and it should be split up before you head out yonder. Don't let somebody pay extra, because that person will likely try to control the trip. Conversely, don't let somebody weasel out of paying a fair share.

10. **Accordance on the food plan:** Always have complete agreement on what you plan to eat each day. Don't figure that just because you like Steamboat's Sludge, everybody else will, too, especially youngsters. Always, always, always check for food allergies such as nuts, onions, or cheese, and make sure each person brings his or her own personal coffee brand. Some people drink only decaffeinated; others might gag on anything but Burma monkey beans.

Obviously, it is difficult to find companions who will agree on all of these elements. This is why many campers say that the best camping buddy they'll ever have is their mate, someone who knows all about them and likes them anyway.

Outdoors with Kids

How do you get a boy or girl excited about the outdoors? How do you compete with the television and remote control? How do you prove to a kid that success comes from persistence, spirit, and logic, which the outdoors teaches, and not from pushing buttons?

The answer is in the **Ten Camping Commandments for Kids.** These are lessons that will get youngsters excited about the outdoors, and will make sure adults help the process along, not kill it. I've put this list together with the help of my own kids, Jeremy and Kris, and their mother, Stephani. Some of the commandments are obvious, some are not, but all are important:

1. Take children to places where there is a guarantee of action. A good example is camping in a park where large numbers of wildlife can be viewed, such as squirrels, chipmunks, deer, and even bears. Other good choices are fishing at a small pond loaded with bluegill or hunting in a spot where a kid can shoot a .22 at pine cones all day. Kids want action, not solitude.

2. Enthusiasm is contagious. If you aren't excited about an adventure, you can't expect a child to be. Show a genuine zest for life in the outdoors, and point out everything as if it is the first time you have ever seen it.

3. Always, always, always be seated when talking to someone small. This allows the adult and child to be on the same level. That is why fishing in a small boat is perfect for adults and kids. Nothing is worse for youngsters than having a big person look down at them and give them orders. What fun is that?

4. Always *show* how to do something, whether it is gathering sticks for a campfire, cleaning a trout, or tying a knot. Never tell—always show. A button usually clicks to "off" when a kid is lectured, but kids can learn behavior patterns and outdoor skills by watching adults, even when the adults are not aware they are being watched.

5. Let kids be kids. Let the adventure happen, rather than trying to force it within some preconceived plan. If they get sidetracked watching pollywogs, chasing butterflies, or sneaking up on chipmunks, let them be. A youngster can have more fun turning over rocks and looking at different kinds of bugs than sitting in one spot, waiting for a fish to bite.

6. Expect short attention spans. Instead of getting frustrated about it, use it to your advantage. How? By bringing along a bag of candy and snacks. Where there is a lull in the camp activity, out comes the bag. Don't let them know what goodies await, so each one becomes a surprise.

7. Make absolutely certain the child's sleeping bag is clean, dry, and warm. Nothing is worse than discomfort when trying to sleep, but a refreshing sleep makes for a positive attitude the next day. In addition, kids can become scared of animals at night. A parent should not wait for any signs of this,

but always play the part of the outdoor guardian, the one who will take care of everything.

8. Kids quickly relate to outdoor ethics. They will enjoy eating everything they kill, building a safe campfire, and picking up all their litter, and they will develop a sense of pride that goes with it. A good idea is to bring extra plastic garbage bags to pick up any trash you come across. Kids long remember when they do something right that somebody else has done wrong.

9. If you want youngsters hooked on the outdoors for life, take a close-up photograph of them holding up fish they have caught, blowing on the campfire, or completing other camp tasks. Young children can forget how much fun they had, but they never forget if they have a picture of it.

10. The least important word you can ever say to a kid is "I." Keep track of how often you are saying "Thank you" and "What do you think?" If you don't say them often, you'll lose out. Finally, the most important words of all are: "I am proud of you."

Predicting the Weather

Foonsky climbed out of his sleeping bag, glanced at the nearby meadow, and scowled hard. "It doesn't look good," he said. "Doesn't look good at all."

I looked at my adventure companion of 20 years, noting his discontent. Then I looked at the meadow and immediately understood why: *"When the grass is dry at morning light, look for rain before the night."*

"How bad you figure?" I asked him.

"We'll know soon enough, I reckon," Foonsky answered. "Short notice, soon to pass. Long notice, long it will last."

When you are out in the wild, spending your days fishing and your nights camping, you learn to rely on yourself to predict the weather. It can make or break you. If a storm hits the unprepared, it can quash the trip and possibly endanger the participants. But if you are ready, a potential hardship can be an adventure.

You can't rely on TV weather forecasters, people who don't even know that when all the cows on a hill are facing north, it will rain that night for sure. God forbid if the cows are all sitting. But what do you expect from TV's talking heads?

Foonsky made a campfire, started boiling some water for coffee and soup, and we started to plan the day. In the process, I noticed the smoke of the campfire: It was sluggish, drifting and hovering.

"You notice the smoke?" I asked, chewing on a piece of homemade jerky.

Keep It Wild Tip 7: Plan Ahead and Prepare

1. Learn about the regulations and issues that apply to the area you're visiting.
2. Avoid heavy-use areas.
3. Obtain all maps and permits.
4. Bring extra garbage bags to pack out any refuse you come across.

"Not good," Foonsky said. "Not good." He knew that sluggish, hovering smoke indicates rain.

"You'd think we'd have been smart enough to know last night that this was coming," Foonsky said. "Did you take a look at the moon or the clouds?"

"I didn't look at either," I answered. "Too busy eating the trout we caught." You see, if the moon is clear and white, the weather will be good the next day. But if there is a ring around the moon, the number of stars you can count inside the ring equals the number of days until the next rain. As for clouds, the high, thin clouds called cirrus indicate a change in the weather.

We were quiet for a while, planning our strategy, but as we did so, some terrible things happened: A chipmunk scampered past with his tail high, a small flock of geese flew by very low, and a little sparrow perched on a tree limb quite close to the trunk.

"We're in for trouble," I told Foonsky.

"I know, I know," he answered. "I saw 'em, too. And come to think of it, no crickets were chirping last night either."

"Damn, that's right!"

These are all signs of an approaching storm. Foonsky pointed at the smoke of the campfire and shook his head as if he had just been condemned. Sure enough, now the smoke was blowing toward the north, a sign of a south wind. *"When the wind is from the south, the rain is in its mouth."*

"We'd best stay hunkered down until it passes," Foonsky said.

I nodded. "Let's gather as much firewood now as we can, get our gear covered up, then plan our meals."

"Then we'll get a poker game going."

As we accomplished these camp tasks, the sky clouded up, then darkened. Within an hour, we had gathered enough firewood to make a large pile, enough wood to keep a fire going no matter how hard it rained. The day's meals had been separated out of the food bag so it wouldn't have to be retrieved during the storm. We buttoned two ponchos together, staked two of the corners with ropes to the ground, and tied the other two with ropes to different tree limbs to create a slanted roof/shelter.

As the first raindrop fell with that magic sound on our poncho roof, Foonsky was just starting to shuffle the cards.

"Cut for deal," he said.

Just as I did so, it started to rain a bit harder. I pulled out another piece of beef jerky and started chewing on it. It was just another day in paradise.

Weather lore can be valuable. Small signs provided by nature and wildlife can be translated to provide a variety of weather information. Here is the list I have compiled over the years:

When the grass is dry at morning light,
Look for rain before the night.

Short notice, soon to pass.
Long notice, long it will last.

When the wind is from the east,
'Tis fit for neither man nor beast.

When the wind is from the south,
The rain is in its mouth.

When the wind is from the west,
Then it is the very best.

Red sky at night, sailors' delight.
Red sky in the morning, sailors take warning.

When all the cows are pointed north,
Within a day rain will come forth.

Onion skins very thin, mild winter coming in.
Onion skins very tough, winter's going to be very rough.

When your boots make the squeak of snow,
Then very cold temperatures will surely show.

If a goose flies high, fair weather ahead.
If a goose flies low, foul weather will come instead.

A thick coat on a woolly caterpillar means a big, early snow is coming.

Chipmunks will run with their tails up before a rain.

Bees always stay near their hives before a rainstorm.

When the birds are perched on large limbs near tree trunks, an intense but short storm will arrive.

On the coast, if groups of seabirds are flying a mile inland, look for major winds.

If crickets are chirping very loud during the evening, the next day will be clear and warm.

If the smoke of a campfire at night rises in a thin spiral, good weather is assured for the next day.

If the smoke of a campfire at night is sluggish, drifting, and hovering, it will rain the next day.

If there is a ring around the moon, count the number of stars inside the ring, and that is how many days until the next rain.

If the moon is clear and white, the weather will be good the next day.

High, thin clouds, or cirrus, indicate a change in the weather.

Oval-shaped lenticular clouds indicate high winds.

Two levels of clouds moving in different directions indicate changing weather soon.

Huge, dark, billowing clouds, called cumulonimbus, suddenly forming on warm afternoons in the mountains mean that a short but intense thunderstorm with lightning can be expected.

When squirrels are busy gathering food for extended periods, it means good weather is ahead in the short term, but a hard winter is ahead in the long term.

And God forbid if all the cows are sitting down. . . .

Beating the Time Trap

If the great outdoors is so great, then why don't people enjoy it more? The answer is because of the time trap, and I will tell you exactly how to beat it.

For many, the biggest problem is finding the time to go, whether it is camping, hiking, fishing, boating, backpacking, biking, or even just for a good drive in the country. The solution? Believe it or not, the answer is to treat your fun just as you treat your work, and I'll tell you how.

Consider how you treat your job: Always on time? Go there every day you are scheduled? Do whatever it takes to get there and get it done? Right? No foolin' that's right. Now imagine if you took the same approach to the outdoors. Suddenly your life would be a heck of a lot better.

The secret is to schedule all of your outdoor activities. For instance, I go fishing every Thursday evening, hiking every Sunday morning, and on an overnight trip every new moon (when stargazing is best). No matter what, I'm going. Just like going to work, I've scheduled it. The same approach works with longer adventures. The only reason I have been able to complete hikes ranging from 200 to 300 miles was that I scheduled the time to do it. The reason I spend 125 to 150 days a year in the field is that I schedule them. In my top year, I had nearly 200 days where at least part of the day was enjoyed taking part in outdoor recreation.

If you get out your calendar and write in the exact dates you are going, then you'll go. If you don't, you won't. Suddenly, with only a minor change in your life plan, you can be living the life you were previously dreaming about.

THE OLYMPIC PENINSULA
AND COASTAL WASHINGTON

The Olympic Peninsula and Coastal Washington

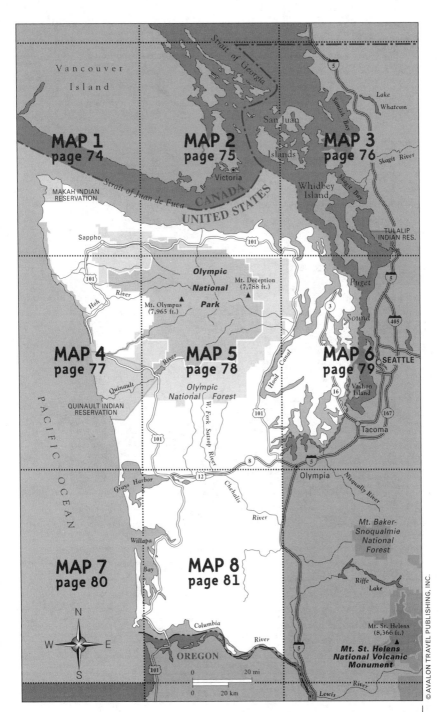

The Olympic Peninsula and Coastal Washington 73

Map 1

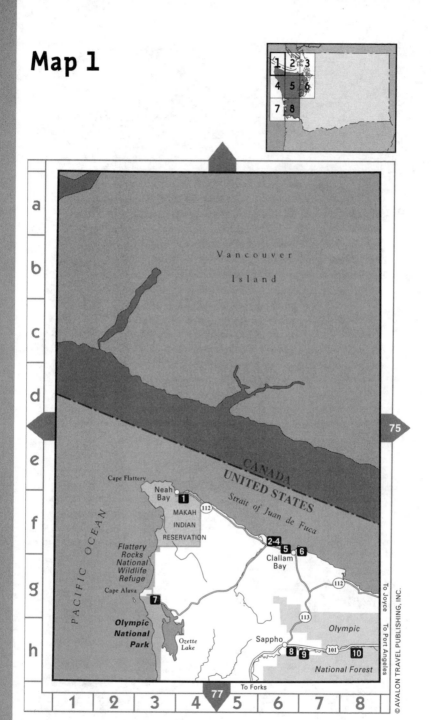

Map 2

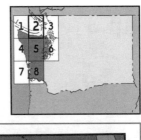

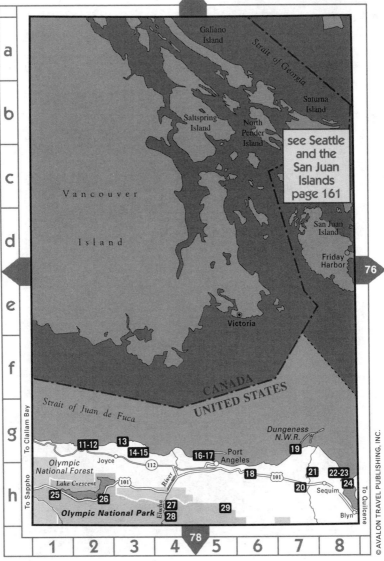

Galiano Island

Strait of Georgia

Saturna Island

Saltspring Island

North Pender Island

Vancouver

Island

see Seattle and the San Juan Islands page 161

San Juan Island

Friday Harbor

76

Victoria

CANADA
UNITED STATES

Strait of Juan de Fuca

Dungeness N.W.R.

To Clallam Bay

11-12   13
14-15
Joyce   112

16-17   Port Angeles

19

Olympic National Forest

To Sappho   Lake Crescent

101

18   101   21   22-23

20   24

Sequim

25   26   River   27   29   Blyn

Olympic National Park   28

Elwha

To Quilcene

78

© AVALON TRAVEL PUBLISHING, INC.

Map 3

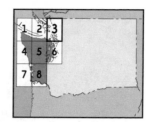

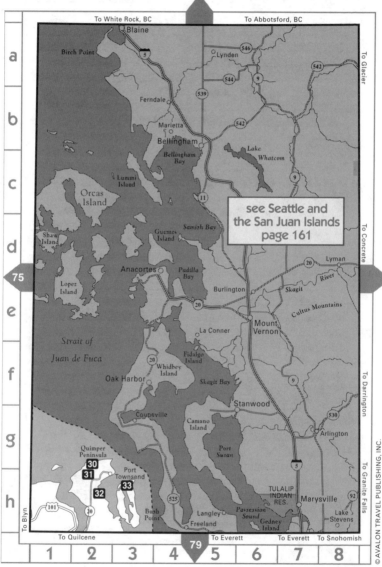

To White Rock, BC   To Abbotsford, BC

To Glacier

Blaine

Birch Point

Lynden

5

546

544

542

9

539

Ferndale

Marietta

542

Bellingham

Lake
Whatcom

Bellingham
Bay

Lummi
Island

9

Orcas
Island

11

**see Seattle and
the San Juan Islands
page 161**

Shaw
Island

Guemes
Island

Samish Bay

Loper
Island

Anacortes

Padilla
Bay

To Concrete

Lyman

20

Skagit

River

Burlington

Cultus Mountains

Strait of
Juan de Fuca

La Conner

Mount
Vernon

20

Fidalgo
Island

Whidbey
Island

Oak Harbor

Skagit Bay

To Darrington

Coupeville

Stanwood

9

530

Camano
Island

Arlington

Quimper
Peninsula

30

31

Port
Suzan

Port
Townsend

32

33

5

To Granite Falls

101

20

TULALIP
INDIAN
RES.

Marysville

92

To Blyn

Bush
Point

525

Langley

Possession
Sound

Lake
Stevens

Freeland

Gedney
Island

To Quilcene   To Everett   To Everett   To Snohomish

© AVALON TRAVEL PUBLISHING, INC.

Map 4

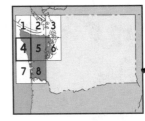

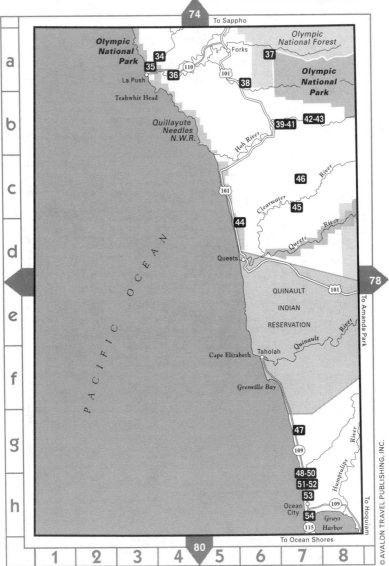

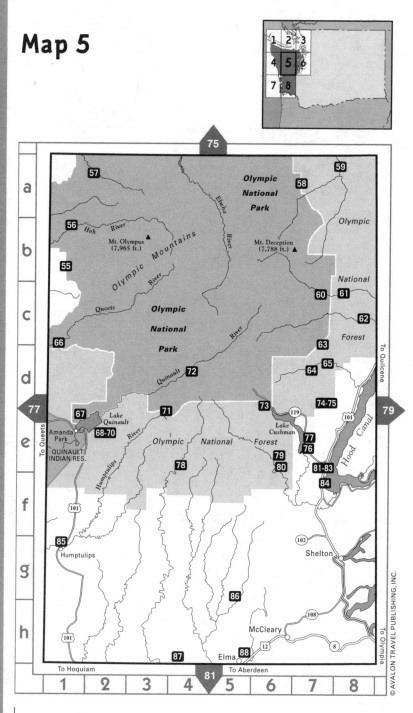

Map 5

Map 6

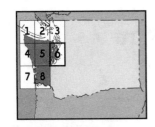

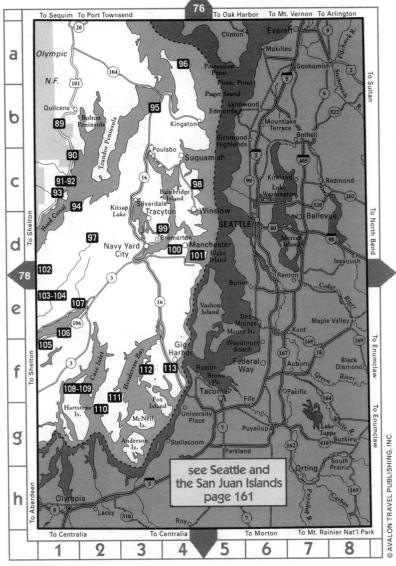

To Sequim To Port Townsend — **76** — To Oak Harbor To Mt. Vernon To Arlington

a

Olympic
N.F.

20
104
101

Quilcene
89
Bolton Peninsula

Clinton
Everett
Mukilteo
Possession Point
Picnic Point
Puget Sound
Lynnwood
Edmonds
Snohomish
5
2
522
9

96

b

95

Kingston

Mountlake Terrace
Bothell
Richmond Highlands

90

Poulsbo
Suquamish

5
99
405

c

91-92
93
94

16
98
Bainbridge Island
Silverdale
Tracyton

Kirkland
Lake Washington
Redmond
520
202

Kitsap Lake
Winslow
SEATLE
Bellevue

d

97

Navy Yard City
99
Bremerton
100
Manchester
101
Blake Island

Mercer Island
40
90
Issaquah

78 — **102**

103-104
107

3

Burien
Renton
Cedar River

e

106
105

106
16

Vashon Island
Des Moines
Maury Is.
Woodmont Beach
Kent
Maple Valley
169
169

f

108-109
111
110

Gig Harbor
112 **113**
Ruston
Brown Pt.
Tacoma
Fife

Federal Way
Auburn
167
18
Black Diamond
Green River

McNeil Is.
University Place
Pacific
164

g

Hartstene Is.
Anderson Is.
Steilacoom

Puyallup
Lake Tapps
Buckley
162
410
South Prairie
165

Parkland
Orting
Carbon R.

h

Olympia
Lacey
8
510

5
Roy
7

To Aberdeen

see Seattle and
the San Juan Islands
page 161

To Centralia — To Centralia — To Morton — To Mt. Rainier Nat'l Park

1 2 3 4 5 6 7 8

© AVALON TRAVEL PUBLISHING, INC.

Map 7

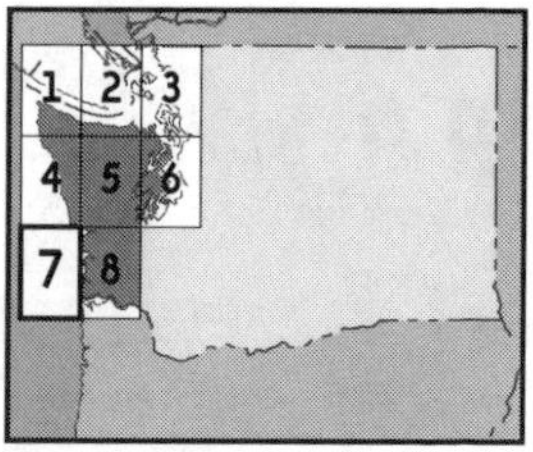

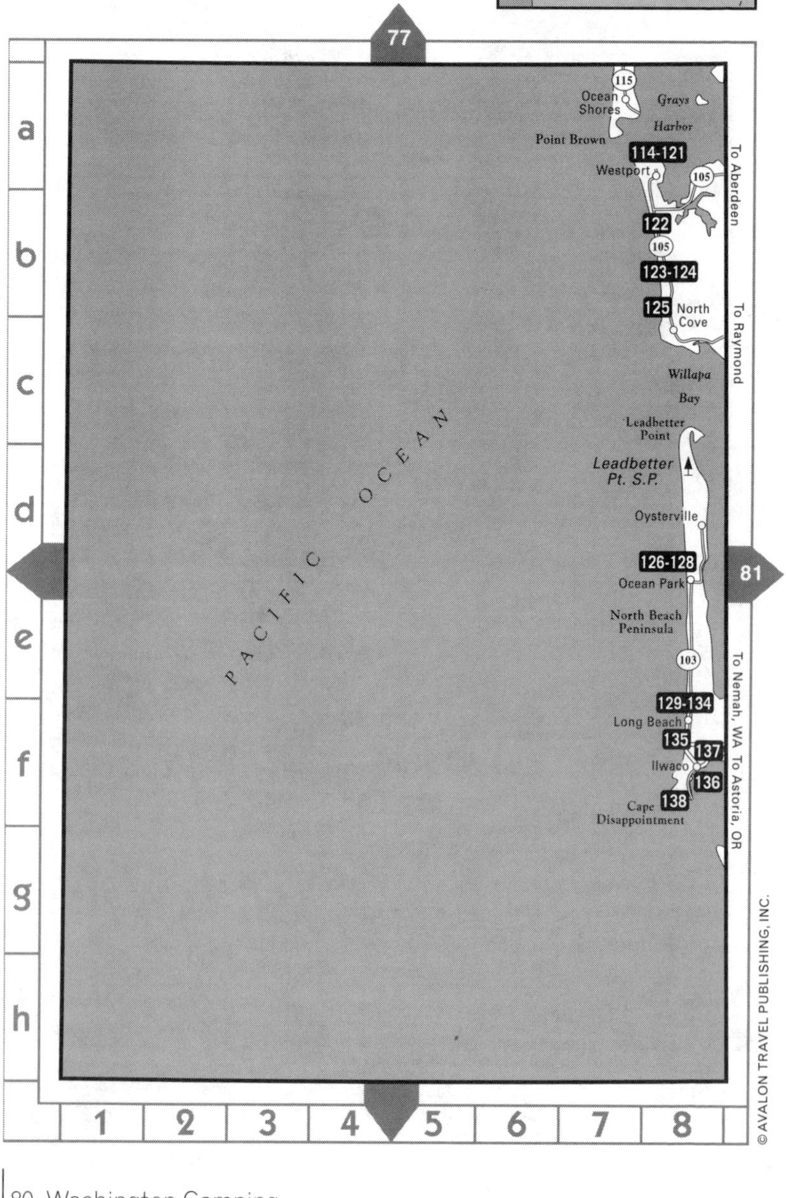

115
Ocean
Shores
Grays
Harbor
Point Brown
114-121
Westport
105

122
105

123-124

125 North
Cove

Willapa
Bay

Leadbetter
Point

*Leadbetter
Pt. S.P.*

Oysterville

126-128
Ocean Park

North Beach
Peninsula

103

129-134
Long Beach
135
137
Ilwaco **136**
138
Cape
Disappointment

PACIFIC OCEAN

To Aberdeen

To Raymond

To Nemah, WA To Astoria, OR

81

a b c d e f g h

1 2 3 4 5 6 7 8

© AVALON TRAVEL PUBLISHING, INC.

Map 8

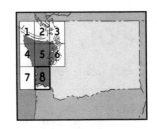

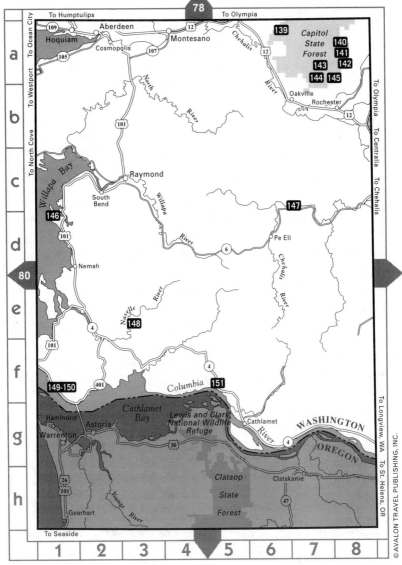

© AVALON TRAVEL PUBLISHING, INC.

The Olympic Peninsula and Coastal Washington

(CONTINUED ON NEXT PAGE)

Vast, diverse, and beautiful, the Olympic Peninsula is like no other landscape in the world. The region is bordered by water on three sides: the Pacific Ocean to the west, the Strait of Juan de Fuca to the north, and the inlets of the Hood Canal to the east. At its center are Olympic National Park and Mt. Olympus, with rainforests on its slopes feeding rivers and lakes that make up the most dynamic river complex in America.

Only heavy rainfall for months on end from fall through spring and coastal fog in the summer have saved this area from a massive influx of population. At the same time, those conditions make it outstanding for getaways and virtually all forms of recreation. A series of stellar campgrounds ring the perimeter foothills of Mt. Olympus, both in Olympic National Park and at state parks and areas managed by the Department of Natural Resources. Your campsite can be your launch pad for adventure—just be sure to bring your rain gear.

In winter, campers can explore the largest array of steelhead rivers anywhere—there is no better place in America to fish for steelhead. Almost every one of these rivers provides campsites, often within walking distance of prime fishing spots.

■ Tyee Motel and RV Park

 5

For RVs and trailers only, this private, developed campground is located near the northwestern tip of the Olympic Peninsula. It's a fairly plain-looking park, with two long strips of spaces, but a few sites have views of the Strait of Juan de Fuca. Fishing for halibut, salmon, and rockfish can be excellent in this area. Recreation options include the world-renowned Makah Museum, which details the history of the Makah Indian tribe, and the half-mile hike to Cape Flattery, the northwestern tip of the continental United States. Cape Flattery offers many hiking trails and opportunities for viewing whales, seals, and walrus. Nearby Makah Bay has a beautiful beach and is a popular spot for surfing.

Location: In Neah Bay; see the Olympic Peninsula and Coastal Washington, map 1, grid f4.

Campsites, facilities: There are 20 pull-through sites for trailers or RVs of any length. Electricity, drinking water, and sewer hookups are provided. Restrooms with toilets and coin-operated showers are available nearby, and sanitary services are available on the property. A store, café, ice, and laundry facilities are located within a few blocks. Boat docks, launching facilities, and boat rentals are located across the street. Leashed pets and motorbikes are permitted.

Reservations, fees: Reservations accepted. Sites are $17 per night, $1 per extra vehicle per night, $7 per pet per night. Major credit cards accepted. Open year-round.

Directions: From Aberdeen, drive north on U.S. 101 and drive 119 miles to Sappho and Highway 113. Turn north on Highway 113 and drive 18 miles to Clallam Bay. Continue on Highway 113 for 20 miles to Neah Bay. Continue to the middle of town to the park on the left.

Contact: Tyee Motel and RV Park, P.O. Box 193, Neah Bay, WA 98357; 360/645-2223.

■ Van Riper's Resort

 7

Part of this campground is on the waterfront and the other part is on a hill overlooking the Strait of Juan de Fuca. Most sites are graveled, many with views of the strait. Other sites are grassy, without views. Hiking, fishing, and boating are among the options here, with salmon fishing being the principal draw. The beaches in the area are a mixture of sand and gravel, and rockhounding for agates and fossils is popular.

Location: On Clallam Bay in Sekiu; see the Olympic Peninsula and Coastal Washington, map 1, grid f6.

Campsites, facilities: There are 150 sites with full or partial hookups for tents or RVs of any length; 60 are drive-through sites. There are also two cabins, mobile homes, a house, and 12 motel rooms. Electricity, drinking water, and picnic tables are provided. Sanitary services, toilets, showers, and ice are available. A store, café, and laundry facilities are located within one mile. Firewood is available for a fee. Boat docks, launching facilities, and rentals are available in spring and summer. Leashed pets and motorbikes are permitted. No pets are allowed in cabins or other buildings. Some facilities are wheelchair-accessible.

Reservations, fees: No reservations for campsites. Sites are $11 to $18 per night. Open from April through September. Major credit cards accepted.

Directions: From Aberdeen, drive north on U.S. 101 for 119 miles to Sappho and Highway 113. Turn north on Highway 113 and drive nine miles to Clallam Bay. Continue north on Highway 113/112 for two miles to Sekiu and Front Street. Turn right and drive one quarter-mile to the resort on the right.

Contact: Van Riper's Resort, P.O. Box 246, Sekiu, WA 98381; 360/963-2334; website: www.vanripersresort.com.

3 Olson's Resort

 5

This full-service camp is large and private. The marina nearby is salmon fishing headquarters. In fact, the resort caters to anglers, offering all-day salmon fishing trips and boat moorage. Chartered trips can be arranged by reservation. A tackle shop, cabins, houses, and a motel are also available. See the description of Van Riper's for details on the Sekiu area.

Location: In Sekiu; see the Olympic Peninsula and Coastal Washington, map 1, grid f6.

Campsites, facilities: There are 100 sites for RVs of any length and tents, 64 sites for RVs with full hookups. Seven cabins, 14 motel rooms, and four houses are also available. Picnic tables, drinking water, sanitary services, flush toilets, showers, a laundry room, a store, and ice are available. Boat docks, launching facilities, boat rentals, bait, tackle, a fishing-cleaning station, gear storage, gas, and diesel fuel are also available on-site. Call for pet policy. A restaurant is located one mile away.

Reservations, fees: No reservations. Sites are $12 to $16 per night, $2 per person per night for more than two people. Cabins and other lodging are $45 to $110 per night. Major credit cards accepted. Open year-round.

Directions: From Aberdeen, drive north on U.S. 101 and drive 119 miles to Sappho and

Highway 113. Turn north on Highway 113 and drive nine miles to a fork with Highway 112. Continue straight on Highway 112 and continue to Sekiu and Front Street. Turn right and drive one block to the resort on the right.

Contact: Olson's Resort, P.O. Box 216, Sekiu, WA 98381; 360/963-2311.

4 Coho RV Park and Marina

 5

The camp is set just across the highway from water. A feature is that there is no concrete at the campsites. They are mainly gravel, and some have grass. This is one of several camps in the immediate area. A full-service marina nearby provides boating access. See the descriptions of Van Riper's Resort Hotel, Olson's Resort, and Surfside Resort for information on the area.

Location: Near Sekiu; see the Olympic Peninsula and Coastal Washington, map 1, grid f6.

Campsites, facilities: There are 100 sites for tents and 108 for tents, trailers, or RVs of any length; 60 are full-hookup sites and the remainder are partial hookups with electricity and water. Cable TV is available at a few sites. Sanitary services, toilets, coin-operated showers, a café, a restaurant, laundry facilities, and ice are available. A store is located within one mile. A full-service marina with docks, launching facilities, and gas is available. Leashed pets are permitted.

Reservations, fees: No reservations. Sites are $12 to $16 per night, $1 per person per night for more than two people. No credit cards are accepted. Open from April through September.

Directions: From Aberdeen, drive north on U.S. 101 for 119 miles to Sappho and Highway 113. Turn north on Highway 113 and drive nine miles to a junction with Highway 112. Continue straight on Highway 112 and continue toward Sekiu. The campground is located between Mileposts 15 and 16, about three-quarters of a mile before the town of Sekiu.

Contact: Coho Resort and Trailer Park, 15572 Highway 112, Sekiu, WA 98381; 360/963-2333.

5 Surfside Resort

   7

This park is smaller, less crowded, and more secluded than many in the area. Campers can enjoy the park's private beach and panoramic views of the Strait of Juan de Fuca and Vancouver Island to the north. Nearby recreation options include marked hiking and bike trails within 30 miles, beachcombing, a full-service marina, and the finest fishing for miles.

Location: In Sekiu; see the Olympic Peninsula and Coastal Washington, map 1, grid f6.

Campsites, facilities: There are 10 tent sites and 10 drive-through sites for trailers or RVs of any length. Fire rings, picnic tables, electricity, and sewer hookups are provided. Drinking water, toilets and showers, sanitary services, and cable TV are available. Bottled gas, a store, a café, coin-operated laundry facilities, and ice are available within one mile. Boat docks, launching facilities, and rentals are located within one mile. Leashed pets and motorbikes are permitted.

Reservations, fees: Reservations recommended. Sites are $10 to $18 per night. No credit cards accepted. Open year-round.

Directions: From Aberdeen, drive north on U.S. 101 for 119 miles to Sappho and Highway 113. Turn north on Highway 113 and drive nine miles to a junction with Highway 112. Continue straight on Highway 112 and drive to Clallam Bay. Continue about one mile west; the campground is located on the left,

halfway between the towns of Clallam Bay and Sekiu.

Contact: Surfside Resort, P.O. Box 39, Sekiu, WA 98381; 360/963-2723.

6 Sam's Trailer and RV Park

  5

This is an alternative to Van Riper's Resort, Olson's Resort, Surfside Resort, and Coho Resort and Trailer Park on Clallam Bay. It's a family-oriented park, with grassy sites and many recreation options nearby. Beaches and shopping are within walking distance. Those wanting to visit Cape Flattery, Hoh Rain Forest, or Port Angeles will find this a good central location.

Location: On Clallam Bay; see the Olympic Peninsula and Coastal Washington, map 1, grid f7.

Campsites, facilities: There are four tent sites and 25 sites with full hookups for trailers or RVs of any length; 10 are drive-through sites. One RV rental is available. Picnic tables are provided. Restrooms, showers, sanitary services, cable TV, and coin-operated laundry facilities are available. Bottled gas, a store, a café, and ice are located within one mile. Boat docks, launching facilities, and rentals are located within one mile. Leashed pets are permitted.

Reservations, fees: Reservations accepted. Sites are $9 to $16 per night. Senior discount available. No credit cards accepted. Open year-round.

Directions: From Aberdeen, drive north on U.S. 101 for 119 miles to Sappho and Highway 113. Turn north on Highway 113 and drive nine miles to Clallam Bay and Highway 112. Continue straight on Highway 112 and drive into Clallam Bay. Just as you come into town, the campground is on the right at 17053 Highway 112.

Contact: Sam's Trailer and RV Park, P.O. Box 45, Clallam Bay, WA 98326; 360/963-2402.

7 Ozette

 6

Many people visit this site set on the shore of Lake Ozette just a few miles from the Pacific Ocean. This camp is a favorite for both hikers and boaters. It is set close to a trailhead road and ranger station, with multiple trailheads nearby. This is a popular campground and one of the first to fill in the park.

Location: On Lake Ozette in Olympic National Park; see the Olympic Peninsula and Coastal Washington, map 1, grid g3.

Campsites, facilities: There are 13 sites for tents or RVs up to 21 feet long. Drinking water, picnic tables, vault toilets, and fire grills are available. Leashed pets are permitted.

Reservations, fees: No reservations. Sites are $10 per night, plus $10 national park entrance fee per vehicle. Senior discount available. Open year-round.

Directions: From Port Angeles, drive west on U.S. 101 to the junction with Highway 112. Bear right on Highway 112 and drive to Hoko-Ozette Road. Turn left and drive 21 miles to the ranger station. The camp parking lot is across from the ranger station on the northwest corner of Lake Ozette.

Contact: Olympic National Park, 600 East Park Avenue, Port Angeles, WA 98362; 360/565-3130, fax 360/565-3147.

8 Bear Creek Motel and RV Park

 7

This quiet little spot is set where Bear Creek empties into the Sol Duc River. It's private and developed, with a choice of sunny or shaded sites in a wooded setting. There are many recreation options in the area, including fishing, hunting, and nature and hiking trails leading to the ocean. Sol Duc Hot Springs is 25 miles north and well worth the trip. A restaurant next to the camp serves family-style meals.

Location: On Bear Creek; see the Olympic Peninsula and Coastal Washington, map 1, grid h6.

Campsites, facilities: There are 12 drive-through sites for trailers or RVs of any length. Electricity, drinking water, sewer hookups, and picnic tables are provided. Restrooms, showers, sanitary services, a café, coin-operated laundry, and firewood are available. A motel is also available on the premises. Boat-launching facilities are located within a half mile. Leashed pets are permitted.

Reservations, fees: No reservations. Sites are $15 per night. Major credit cards accepted. Open year-round.

Directions: From Aberdeen, drive north on U.S. 101 to Forks. Continue past Forks for 15 miles to Milepost 205 (just past Sappho) to the campground on the right at 205860 Highway 101 West.

Contact: Bear Creek Motel and RV Park, P.O. Box 236, Beaver, WA 98305; 360/327-3660; website: www.hungrybearcafemotel.com.

9 Bear Creek

 8

Fishing for salmon and hiking along the Sol Duc River make this a good launch point for recreation. There are also good opportunities for wildlife viewing and photography, including a wheelchair-accessible viewing platform overlooking the Sol Duc River. Note: No drinking water. This campsite is also popular in the fall with hunters.

Location: On the Sol Duc River; see the Olympic Peninsula and Coastal Washington, map 1, grid h7.

Campsites, facilities: There are 10 tent sites. Vault toilets and fire pits are available, but there is no drinking water. Some facilities are wheelchair-accessible. Leashed pets are permitted.

Reservations, fees: No reservations; no fee. Open year-round.

Directions: From Olympia on I-5, take Exit 104 and drive north on U.S. 101 to the Aberdeen/Highway 8 exit. Turn west on Highway 8 and drive 36 miles to Aberdeen. Continue through Aberdeen four miles to U.S. 101 and turn north and drive to Forks. Continue past Forks for 15 miles to Milepost 206 (two miles past Sappho) to the campground on the right.

Contact: Department of Natural Resources, Olympic Region, 411 Tillicum Lane, Forks, WA 98331-9797; 360/374-6131, fax 360/374-5446.

⑩ Klahowya

  8

Klahowya features great views of Lake Crescent and Mt. Olympus. It makes a good choice if you don't want to venture far from U.S. 101 yet want to retain the feel of being in the Olympic National Forest. Set along the Sol Duc River, this 32-acre camp is pretty and wooded, with hiking trails in the area. A favorite is across the river, the Kloshe Nanitch Lookout Trail, tromping up to the actual lookout on Snider Ridge overlooking Sol Duc Valley. The Pioneer Path Interpretive Trail starts in the camp, an easy 0.3-mile loop trail that is wheelchair-accessible. Fishing can be good about a quarter-mile downstream from camp for salmon and steelhead, in season; always check regulations. This camp gets medium use.

Location: On the Sol Duc River in Olympic National ; see the Olympic Peninsula and Coastal Washington, map 1, grid h8.

Campsites, facilities: There are 54 sites for trailers or RVs up to 30 feet long and two walk-in sites requiring a 700-foot walk. Picnic tables are provided. Drinking water, vault and flush toilets, and wheelchair-accessible restrooms are available. An amphitheater with summer interpretive programs is also available. A boat ramp is nearby. Leashed pets are permitted.

Reservations, fees: No reservations. Sites are $12 per night. The campground is open from May to late September with full service. Limited service is available in the off-season. Senior discount available.

Directions: From I-5 at Olympia, turn north on U.S. 101 and drive about 122 miles to Port Angeles. Continue on U.S. 101 for past Port Angeles for about 36 miles (nine miles west of Lake Crescent) to the campground on the right side of the road, close to Milepost 212. (Coming from the other direction on U.S. 101, drive eight miles east of Sappho to the campground.)

Contact: Olympic National Forest, Pacific Ranger District, 437 Tillicum Lane, Forks, WA 98331; 360/374-6522, fax 360/374-1250.

⑪ Lyre River

   7

This prime spot is one of the rare free campgrounds on the Olympic Peninsula. Although quite primitive, it does offer drinking water and an even more precious commodity in these parts—privacy. The camp is set along the Lyre River, about 15 miles from where it enters the ocean. This is a popular camp for anglers, often with good salmon fishing during fish migrations; always check regulations. A wheelchair-accessible fishing pier is available.

Location: On the Lyre River; see the Olympic Peninsula and Coastal Washington, map 2, grid g2.

Campsites, facilities: There are 10 primitive tent sites. Picnic tables, fire grills, tent pads, vault toilets, and drinking water are provided. A roofed group shelter is available. Leashed pets are permitted.

Reservations, fees: No reservations; no fee. Open year-round.

Directions: From Olympia on I-5, take U.S. 101 and drive north 127 miles to a fork with Highway 112 (five miles past the town of Port Angeles). Turn west (right) on Highway 112 and drive about 15 miles to Milepost 46. Look to the right for a paved road between Mileposts 46 and 47; then turn north and drive 0.4 mile to the camp entrance road on the left.

Contact: Department of Natural Resources, Olympic Region, 411 Tillicum Lane, Forks, WA 98331-9797; 360/374-6131, fax 360/374-5446.

Lyre River Park

   9

This beautiful 23-acre camp is situated in a wooded area tucked between the Strait of Juan de Fuca and the Lyre River, with open space surrounding the park. Freshwater and saltwater beaches are available, giving the park a unique flavor. Kids can give their rods a try in the pond stocked with trout (a fee charged), while adult anglers can head for excellent fishing in the Lyre River (steelhead are tops during migrations) and the nearby shoreline (for perch). Tubing down the river is popular here, and bike and hiking trails are available nearby.

Location: Near the Lyre River; see the Olympic Peninsula and Coastal Washington, map 2, grid g2.

Campsites, facilities: There are 97 sites for tents, trailers, or RVs of any length; 55 have full hookups and 30 are drive-through sites. Picnic tables are provided and some sites have fire rings. Restrooms, bottled gas, sanitary services, a store, a coin-operated laundry, and ice are available. Showers and firewood are available for a fee. Leashed pets are permitted.

Reservations, fees: Reservations accepted. Sites are $14 to $25 per night for two campers, $2 per person per night for more than two people. Group reservations welcome with an advance deposit. Major credit cards accepted. Open year-round.

Directions: From Olympia on I-5, take U.S. 101 and drive north 127 miles (five miles past the town of Port Angeles) to a fork with Highway 112. Turn west on Highway 112 and drive 15 miles to West Lyre River Road. Turn right and drive a half mile to the park on the right.

Contact: Lyre River Park, 596 West Lyre River Road, Port Angeles, WA 98363; 360/928-3436.

Whiskey Creek Beach

   7

Located on the beach along the Strait of Juan de Fuca, this campground covers 30 acres, set next to a timberland acreage. It is popular with rock hounds. Surf fishing for perch and other species is popular, and this is an excellent launch point for sea kayaking. The setting is rustic, with 1.25 miles of beach access. Olympic National Park is located five miles away and offers numerous recreation possibilities, including miles of stellar hiking trails. This camp is a good option if the national park camps are full, but note that almost one-half of the campground is permanently rented out.

Location: On the Strait of Juan de Fuca; see the Olympic Peninsula and Coastal Washington, map 2, grid g3.

Campsites, facilities: There are 30 sites for tents and RVs, including six with full hookups and five with partial hookups, plus seven cabins on the beach. Picnic tables and fire rings are provided. Drinking water and pit toilets are available. Launching facilities for small boats are on site. A cave, a store, a gas station, and a coin-operated laundry are available within three miles. Leashed pets are permitted.

Reservations, fees: Reservations accepted. Sites are $15 per night, cabins are $60 to $75 per night, pets $1 per night. No credit cards are accepted. Open from May to late October; cabins available year-round.

Directions: From Olympia on I-5, take U.S. 101 and drive north 127 miles (five miles past the town of Port Angeles) to a fork with Highway 112. Turn west (right) on Highway 112 and drive 13 miles (three miles past Joyce) to Whiskey Creek Beach Road. Turn right and continue 1.5 miles to the campground on the right (well marked).

Contact: Whiskey Creek Beach, P.O. Box 130, Joyce, WA 98343; 360/928-3489, fax 360/928-3218.

ⅤⅣ Crescent Beach RV

 6

Set on a half-mile stretch of sandy beach, this campground makes a perfect weekend spot. Popular activities include swimming, fishing, surfing, sea kayaking, and beachcombing. It borders Salt Creek Recreation Area, with direct access available. Numerous attractions and recreation options are available in Port Angeles.

Location: On the Strait of Juan de Fuca; see the Olympic Peninsula and Coastal Washington, map 2, grid g3.

Campsites, facilities: There are 41 sites for tents, trailers, or RVs with full or partial hookups, with a separate area for tent camping. Picnic tables and fire rings are provided. Restrooms, showers, a coin-operated laundry, a pay phone, a recreation field, and horseshoe pits are available. A dump station is nearby. Leashed pets are permitted.

Reservations, fees: Reservations recommended. Sites are $25 to $30 per night, $5 per person per night for more than two people, $5 per extra vehicle per night unless towed, $5 per night for pets. Weekly and monthly rates available. Open year-round.

Directions: From Olympia on I-5, take U.S. 101 and drive north 127 miles (five miles past the town of Port Angeles) to a fork with Highway 112. Turn west (right) on Highway 112 and drive 10 miles to Camp Hayden Road (between Mileposts 53 and 54). Turn right on Camp Hayden Road and drive four miles to the campground on the left, on the beach.

Contact: Crescent Beach RV, 2860 Crescent Beach Road, Port Angeles, WA 98363; 360/928-3344; website: www.olypen.com/crescent.

ⅤⅤ Salt Creek Recreation Area

 8

This is the former site of Camp Hayden, a World War II–era facility. It's a great spot for gorgeous ocean views, fishing, and hiking near Striped Peak, which overlooks the campground. Only a small beach area is available because of the rugged coastline, but there is an exceptionally good spot for tide pool viewing on the west side of the park. The park covers 192 acres and overlooks the Strait of Juan de Fuca. Recreation options include nearby hiking trails, swimming, fishing, horseshoes, and field sports. It's a good layover spot if you're planning to take the ferry out of Port Angeles to Victoria, British Columbia. Reservations are strongly advised, with the camp filling up quickly most summer weekends.

Location: Near the Strait of Juan de Fuca; see the Olympic Peninsula and Coastal Washington, map 2, grid g3.

Campsites, facilities: There are 92 sites for tents, trailers, or RVs of any length. Picnic tables are provided. A restroom, flush toilets, coin-operated showers, a dump station, and a playground are available. Firewood is available for a fee. Some facilities are wheelchair-accessible. Leashed pets are permitted.

Reservations, fees: No reservations. Sites are $8 to $10 per night, $3 per extra vehicle per night; six campers maximum per site. Open year-round.

Directions: From Olympia on I-5, take U.S. 101 and drive north 127 miles (five miles past the town of Port Angeles) to a fork with Highway 112. Turn west (right) on Highway 112 and drive six miles to Camp Hayden Road. Turn right (north) and drive 3.5 miles to the campground.

Contact: Salt Creek Recreation Area, Clallam County, 3506 Camp Hayden Road, Port Angeles, WA 98363; 360/928-3441; website: www.clallam.net/park.

16 Peabody Creek RV Park

 5

This three-acre RV park is right in the middle of town but offers a wooded, streamside setting. Nearby recreation options include salmon fishing, an 18-hole golf course, marked biking trails, a full-service marina, and tennis courts. The park is within walking distance of shopping and ferry services.

Location: In Port Angeles; see the Olympic Peninsula and Coastal Washington, map 2, grid g5.

Campsites, facilities: There are 36 sites with full hookups for trailers or RVs of any length, but note that 19 are permanent rentals. Sanitary services, restrooms with coin-operated showers, ice, and coin-operated laundry facilities are available. A cable TV hookup is available for $3 per night. A store and a café are located within one block. Boat docks, launching facilities, and boat rentals are located within 1.5 miles. Leashed pets are permitted.

Reservations, fees: Reservations accepted. Sites are $22 per night. No credit cards accepted. Open year-round.

Directions: From I-5 at Olympia, turn north on U.S. 101 and drive about 122 miles to Port Angeles and Lincoln Street. Bear left on Lincoln and drive one-half mile to Second Street and the park entrance on the right.

Contact: Peabody Creek RV Park, 127 South Lincoln, Port Angeles, WA 98362; 360/457-7092 or 800/392-2361; website: www.peabodyrv.tripod.com.

17 Al's RV Park

  8

This adult-oriented campground is a good choice for RV owners. The campground is set in the country at about 1,000 feet, yet is centrally located and not far from the Strait of Juan de Fuca. Nearby recreation options include an 18-hole golf course and a full-service marina. Olympic National Park and the Victoria ferry are a short drive away.

Location: Near Port Angeles; see the Olympic Peninsula and Coastal Washington, map 2, grid g5.

Campsites, facilities: There are 31 sites with full hookups, including some drive-through, for trailers or RVs up to 40 feet long, 20 sites for tents, and one rental trailer for up to four people. No fires are allowed. Picnic tables are provided. Restrooms, drinking water, flush toilets, showers, cable TV, a clubhouse, and laundry facilities are available. Telephone service is available for all sites. A store, a café, bottled gas, and ice are located within one mile. Boat docks and launching facilities are located within two miles. Some facilities are wheelchair-accessible. Leashed pets are permitted.

Reservations, fees: Reservations accepted at 360/457-9844 (preferred) or 800/357-1553. Sites are $14 to $21 per night, $2 per person per night for more than two people. Trailer is $25 per night, Weekly and monthly rates available. Major credit cards accepted. Open year-round.

Directions: From Port Angeles, take U.S. 101 west for two miles to North Brook Avenue. Turn right (north) on North Brook Avenue, then left (almost immediately) on Lees Creek Road, and drive a half mile to the park on the right.

Contact: Al's RV Park, 521 North Lees Creek Road, Port Angeles, WA 98362; 360/457-9844.

18 KOA Port Angeles-Sequim

   5

This is a private, developed camp covering 13 acres in a country setting. It is a pleasant park, a typical KOA complete with pool, recreation hall, and playground. Horseshoe pits and a sports field are also available. Hay rides are available in summer. Miniature golf, an 18-hole golf course, marked hiking trails, and tennis courts are nearby recreation options. Nearby side trips feature Victoria, Butchart Gardens, and whale-watching tours.

Location: Near Port Angeles; see the Olympic Peninsula and Coastal Washington, map 2, grid h6.

Campsites, facilities: There are 90 sites with full and partial hookups, including 45 drive-through, for tents, trailers, or RVs of any length, and 12 cabins. Picnic tables are provided. Restrooms, drinking water, flush toilets, showers, cable TV, bottled gas, firewood, a dump station, a store, a coin-operated laundry, ice, a playground, miniature golf, a recreation room, and a swimming pool are available. A café is located within two miles. Some facilities are wheelchair-accessible. Leashed pets are permitted.

Reservations, fees: Reservations accepted at 800/562-7558. Sites are $21 to $35 per night, $4 per person per night for more than two people, $5 per extra vehicle per night. Cabins are $44 to $60 per night. No charge for ages 5 and under. Major credit cards accepted. Open mid-March through mid-November.

Directions: From I-5 at Olympia, turn north on U.S. 101 and drive 116 miles to O'Brien Road, six miles southeast of Port Angeles. Turn left on O'Brien Road and drive half a block to the campground on the right.

Contact: KOA Port Angeles-Sequim, 80 O'Brien Road, Port Angeles, WA 98362; 360/457-5916, fax 360/417-0759.

19 Dungeness Recreation Area

   5

This park overlooks the Strait of Juan de Fuca and is set near the Dungeness National Wildlife Refuge. It is very popular and fills up on summer weekends. The refuge is a highlight, set on a seven-mile lot spit with a historic lighthouse at its end. Bald eagles are often spotted in the wildlife refuge. Nearby recreation options include marked hiking trails, fishing, and golfing. The toll ferry at Port Angeles can take you to Victoria, British Columbia.

Location: Near the Strait of Juan de Fuca; see the Olympic Peninsula and Coastal Washington, map 2, grid g7.

Campsites, facilities: There are 65 sites, with full hookups, including five drive-through, for tents, trailers, or RVs of any length. Picnic tables and fire grills are provided. Restrooms, drinking water, flush toilets, coin-operated showers, firewood, a dump station, and a playground are available. Leashed pets are permitted.

Reservations, fees: No reservations. Sites are $8 to $10 per night, $3 per extra vehicle per night. Open February to October, with facilities limited to day use in the winter. Entrance gates close at dusk year-round.

Directions: From Sequim, drive north on U.S. 101 for four miles to Kitchen-Dick Road. Turn right on Kitchen-Dick Road and drive four miles to the park on the left.

Contact: Dungeness Recreation Area, Clallam County, 554 Voice of America Road, Sequim, WA 98382; 360/683-5847.

20 Sunshine RV Park

 5

This is a 5.7-acre private camp that is set in a wooded area outside of Sequim. Although primarily an RV park, tents are permitted. It has paved, shaded sites, horseshoe pits, and a recreation room, and is close to an 18-hole golf course and a full-service marina at Sequim Bay.

Location: Near Sequim; see the Olympic Peninsula and Coastal Washington, map 2, grid h7.

Campsites, facilities: There are 44 sites with full hookups for trailers or RVs of any length, and 20 sites for tents. Picnic tables are provided. Restrooms, drinking water, flush toilets, showers, cable TV, a recreation room, and a coin-operated laundry are available. A dump station, a store, and a café are located within one mile. Leashed pets are permitted.

Reservations, fees: Reservations accepted. Sites are $15 to $20 per night, $2 per person per night for more than two people. Senior discount available. Major credit cards accepted. Open year-round.

Directions: From Sequim, drive west on U.S. 101 for four miles to the park (along the highway) on the left.

Contact: Sunshine RV Park, 259790 Highway 101, Sequim, WA 98382; 360/683-4769 or 888/383-4769.

21 Sequim West Inn & RV Park

 5

This two-acre camp is near the Dungeness River and within 10 miles of Dungeness Spit State Park. It's a pleasant spot, with full facilities and an urban setting. An 18-hole golf course and a full-service marina at Sequim Bay are close by.

Location: Near the Dungeness River; see the Olympic Peninsula and Coastal Washington, map 2, grid h7.

Campsites, facilities: There are 27 drive-through sites with full hookups for tents, trailers, or RVs of any length, and 17 cabins and 21 motel rooms. Picnic tables are provided. Restrooms, drinking water, flush toilets, showers, cable TV, a coin-operated laundry, a pay phone, and ice are available. Bottled gas, a store, and a café are located within one mile. Leashed pets are permitted.

Reservations, fees: Reservations accepted. Sites are $15 to $22, $1 per person per night for more than two people (under 18 free). Cabins are $49 to $150 per night. Major credit cards accepted. Open year-round.

Directions: From Sequim and U.S. 101, take the Washington Street exit and drive west on Washington Street for 2.7 miles to the park on the left.

Contact: Sequim West Inn & RV Park, 740 West Washington Avenue, Sequim, WA 98382; 360/683-4144 or 800/528-4527, fax 360/683-6452; website: www.olypen.com/swi.

Rainbow's End RV Park

     6

This park on Sequim Bay is pretty and clean, with a rainbow trout pond and a creek running through the campground. There is a weekly potluck dinner in the summer, with free hamburgers and hot dogs, and a special landscaped area available for reunions, weddings, and other gatherings. Recreation seekers will find an 18-hole golf course, marked bike trails, a full-service marina, and tennis courts nearby.

Location: On Sequim Bay; see the Olympic Peninsula and Coastal Washington, map 2, grid h8.

Campsites, facilities: There are 39 sites with full hookups, including some drive-through sites, for trailers or RVs of any length, and 10 tent sites. Telephone and cable TV hookups are provided at RV sites. Picnic tables and fire grills are provided at tent sites. Restrooms, drinking water, flush toilets, showers, a dump station, bottled gas, a coin-operated laundry, and a clubhouse are available. A store, a café, and ice are located within one mile. Firewood is available for a fee. Leashed pets are permitted.

Reservations, fees: Reservations accepted. Weekly and monthly rates are available. Sites are $10 to $23 per night, $2 per person per night for more than two people. Major credit cards accepted. Open year-round.

Directions: From Sequim, drive west on U.S. 101 for one mile past the River Road exit to the park on the right (along the highway).

Contact: Rainbow's End RV Park, 261831 Highway 101, Sequim, WA 98382; 360/683-3863, fax 360/683-2150.

Sequim Bay Resort

   5

This is Sequim Bay headquarters for salmon anglers. The camp is set in a wooded, hilly area, close to many activity centers, and with an 18-hole golf course nearby.

Location: On Sequim Bay; see the Olympic Peninsula and Coastal Washington, map 2, grid h8.

Campsites, facilities: There are 43 sites with full hookups, including 34 drive-through, for trailers or RVs of any length, and eight cabins. No tent camping. Restrooms, drinking water, flush toilets, showers, cable TV, and a coin-operated laundry are available. Boat docks and launching facilities are located across the street from the resort. Leashed pets are permitted.

Reservations, fees: Reservations recommended. Sites are $21.50 per night, $3 per person per night for more than two people. Cabins are $35 to $65 per night, and rented by night with a two-night minimum from May to September, and by the month the rest of the year. Open year-round.

Directions: From Olympia on I-5, turn north on U.S. 101 and drive about 100 miles (near Sequim) to Whitefeather Way (located between Mileposts 267 and 268, 2.5 miles east of Sequim). Turn north on Whitefeather Way and drive one-half mile to West Sequim Bay Road. Turn left (west) and drive one block to the park on the left.

Contact: Sequim Bay Resort, 2634 West Sequim Bay Road, Sequim, WA 98382; 360/681-3853.

24 Sequim Bay State Park

  8

Sequim translates to "quiet waters," and that is an appropriate description of this area. It is set in the heart of Washington's rain show, a region with far less rainfall than the surrounding areas. Sequim's average rainfall is only 17 inches. The park features 4,909 feet of saltwater shoreline, and two natural overlapping sand bars protect the bay waters from the rough waves and currents of the Strait of Juan de Fuca. The park has only one mile of hiking trails. An underwater park for scuba divers is a highlight of this 90-acre camp on Sequim Bay.

Location: On Sequim Bay Bay; see the Olympic Peninsula and Coastal Washington, map 2, grid h8.

Campsites, facilities: There are 60 developed sites for tents, trailers, or self-contained RVs, 16 sites with full hookups for trailers or RVs up to 30 feet long, and three primitive tent sites. Picnic tables and fire grills are provided. Restrooms, drinking water, flush toilets, showers, a dump station, a picnic area with kitchen shelters, an amphitheater, athletic fields, a basketball court, and a playground are available. Boat docks, launching facilities, and boat mooring are available. Facilities are wheelchair-accessible. Leashed pets are permitted.

Reservations, fees: Reservations at 888/CAMP-OUT (888/226-7688); website: www.parks.wa.gov/reservations ($7 reservation fee). Sites are $6 to $22 per night, $6 per extra vehicle per night; boat mooring is $10 to $16 per night. Major credit cards

accepted. Senior discount available. Open year-round.

Directions: From Olympia on I-5, turn north on U.S. 101 and drive 100 miles (near Sequim) to the park entrance on the right (along the highway). The park is located four miles southeast of the town of Sequim.

Contact: Sequim Bay State Park, 360/683-4235; State Park information, 360/902-8844.

25 Fairholm

   6

This camp is set on the shore of Lake Crescent, a pretty lake situated within the boundary of Olympic National Park. These campsites are set on the western end of the lake, in a cove with a boat ramp. It's located less than one mile off U.S. 101 and gets heavy use during tourist months; some highway noise is audible at some sites. A naturalist program is often available in the summer. The elevation is 580 feet. Water skiing is permitted at Lake Crescent, but personal watercraft are prohibited.

Location: On Lake Crescent in Olympic National Park Bay; see the Olympic Peninsula and Coastal Washington, map 2, grid h1.

Campsites, facilities: There are 88 sites for tents, trailers, or RVs up to 21 feet long. Picnic tables and fire grills are provided. A sanitary disposal station, restrooms, and drinking water are available. Some facilities are wheelchair-accessible. A store and a café are located within one mile. Boat-launching facilities and rentals are nearby on Lake Crescent. Leashed pets are permitted.

Reservations, fees: No reservations. Sites are $10 per night, plus $10 national park entrance fee. Senior discount available. Open year-round, weather permitting.

Directions: From Port Angeles, drive west on U.S. 101 for about 26 miles and continue along Lake Crescent to North Shore Road. Turn right and drive one-half mile to the camp on North Shore Road on the right.

Contact: Olympic National Park, 600 East Park Avenue, Port Angeles, WA 98362; 360/565-3130, fax 360/565-3147.

26 Log Cabin Resort

  8

This pretty camp along the shore of Lake Crescent is a good spot for boaters, with many sites near the water with excellent views. Fishing and swimming are two options at this family-oriented resort. Note the fishing became catch-and-release in 2000. It is home for the strain of Beardslee trout. Water skiing is permitted, but no personal watercraft are allowed. A marked hiking trail traces the lake's 22-mile shoreline. Note that this camp is extremely popular in the summer months and reservations can be necessary 6 to 12 months in advance.

Location: On Lake Crescent in Olympic National Park Bay; see the Olympic Peninsula and Coastal Washington, map 2, grid h2.

Campsites, facilities: There are 38 sites with full hookups for trailers or RVs of any length, and 28 cabins. Picnic tables and fire barrels are provided. Sanitary services, restrooms, a store, a café, laundry facilities, ice, and a recreation field are available. Showers and firewood are also available for a fee. Boat docks, launching facilities, and boat rentals and hydrobikes are available nearby. Some facilities are wheelchair-accessible. Leashed pets are permitted.

Reservations, fees: Reservations accepted. Sites are $30.33 per night, $2.34 per person per night for more than two people, $6.50 per pet per night; cabins $58 to $135 per night. Open from April through October. Major credit cards accepted.

Directions: From I-5 at Olympia, turn north on U.S. 101 and drive about 122 miles to Port Angeles. Continue on U.S. 101 past Port Angeles for about 18 miles to East Beach Road. Turn right and drive three miles (along Lake Crescent) to the camp on the left.

Contact: Log Cabin Resort, 3183 East Beach Road, Port Angeles, WA 98363; 360/928-3325, fax 360/928-2088; website: www.logcabin resort.net.

27 Elwha

 7

The Elwha River is the backdrop for this popular camp, with excellent hiking trails close by in Olympic National Park; check at one of the visitors centers for maps and backcountry information. Also see the description of neighboring Altaire for more information. The elevation is 390 feet.

Location: On the Elwha River in Olympic National Park Bay; see the Olympic Peninsula and Coastal Washington, map 2, grid h4.

Campsites, facilities: There are 41 sites for tents, trailers, or RVs up to 21 feet long. Picnic tables and fire grills are provided. Restrooms and drinking water are available. Some facilities are wheelchair-accessible. Leashed pets are permitted.

Reservations, fees: No reservations. Sites are $10 per night, plus $10 national park entrance fee per vehicle. Senior discount available. Open year-round.

Directions: From Port Angeles, drive west on U.S. 101 for about nine miles (just past Lake Aldwell) to the signed entrance road on the left. Turn left at the entrance road and drive three miles south along the Elwha River to the campground on the left.

Contact: Olympic National Park, 600 East Park Avenue, Port Angeles, WA 98362; 360/565-3130, fax 360/565-3147.

Altaire

 8

This camp is set on the Elwha River about one mile from Lake Mills, a pretty and well-treed camp with easy highway access. Fishing is good in season; check regulations. The elevation is 450 feet. It also can make for a nice layover spot for one night before taking the ferry at Port Angeles to Victoria, British Columbia.

Location: On the Elwha River in Olympic National Park Bay; see the Olympic Peninsula and Coastal Washington, map 2, grid h4.

Campsites, facilities: There are 30 sites for tents, trailers, or RVs up to 21 feet long. Picnic tables and fire grills are provided. Restrooms and drinking water are available. Some facilities are wheelchair-accessible. Leashed pets are permitted.

Reservations, fees: No reservations. Sites are $10 per night, plus $10 national park entrance fee per vehicle. Senior discount available. Open June to September.

Directions: From I-5 at Olympia, turn north on U.S. 101 and drive about 122 miles to Port Angeles. Continue on U.S. 101 past Port Angeles for about nine miles (just past Lake Aldwell). Turn left at the signed entrance road and drive four miles south along the Elwha River.

Contact: Olympic National Park, 600 East Park Avenue, Port Angeles, WA 98362; 360/565-3130, fax 360/565-3147.

Heart O' the Hills

 9

Heart O' the Hills is nestled on the northern edge of Olympic National Park. You can drive into the park on Hurricane Ridge Road and take one of numerous hiking trails. Little Lake Dawn is less than one-half mile to the west, but note that most of the property around this lake is privately owned. This camp is set at 1,807 feet. Naturalist programs are available in summer months.

Location: In Olympic National Park Bay; see the Olympic Peninsula and Coastal Washington, map 2, grid h5.

Campsites, facilities: There are 105 sites for tents, trailers, or RVs up to 21 feet long. Picnic tables and fire grills are provided. Restrooms and drinking water are available. Some facilities are wheelchair-accessible. Leashed pets are permitted.

Reservations, fees: No reservations. Sites are $10 per night, plus $10 national park entrance fee per vehicle. Senior discount available. Open year-round, weather permitting.

Directions: From I-5 at Olympia, turn north on U.S. 101 and drive about 122 miles to Port Angeles to Hurricane Ridge Road. Turn left and drive five miles to the camp on the left. (Access roads can be impassable in severe weather.)

Contact: Olympic National Park, 600 East Park Avenue, Port Angeles, WA 98362; 360/565-3130, fax 360/565-3147.

Fort Worden State Park

 9

This park is set on the northeastern tip of the Olympic Peninsula, at the northern end of Port Townsend, set on a high bluff overlooking Puget Sound. Highlights here include great lookouts and two miles of trails over the Strait of Juan de Fuca as it feeds into Puget Sound. This park covers 433 acres at historic Fort Worden (on which construction was begun in 1897 and decommissioned in 1953) and includes buildings from the turn of the 20th century. It has 11,020 feet of saltwater shoreline. Recreation options include 12 miles of marked hiking and biking trails, including five miles of wheelchair-accessible trails. The Coast Artillery Museum, Rothschild House, and the Marine Science Center are open during the summer season. A ferry at Port Townsend will take you across the strait to Whidbey Island.

Location: Near Puget Sound; Bay; see the Olympic Peninsula and Coastal Washington, map 3, grid g2.

Campsites, facilities: There are 80 sites with full or partial hookups, including some drive-through, for tents, trailers, or RVs up to 60 feet long, and five primitive, hike-in or bike-in tent sites. Picnic tables and fire grills are provided. Restrooms, drinking water, flush toilets, coin-operated showers, a laundry room, a store, and firewood for sale are available. A restaurant, conference facilities, a sheltered amphitheater, athletic fields, and interpretive activities are available nearby. Boat docks, buoys, floats, and launching facilities are nearby. Wheelchair-accessible facilities are available. Several golf courses are located nearby. Leashed pets are permitted.

Reservations, fees: Reservations available at 360/344-4400. Sites are $6 to $22 per night, $6 per extra vehicle per night; moorage is $10 to $16 per night. Senior discount available. Open year-round.

Directions: From Olympia, turn north on U.S. 101 and drive 86 miles to Highway 20 (Port Townsend turnoff). Turn north on Highway 20 and drive 13 miles to Port Townsend. Continue through Port Townsend to Cherry Street. Turn left at Cherry Street and drive 1.75 miles to the park entrance at the end of the road.

Contact: Fort Worden State Park, 200 Battery Way, Port Townsend, WA 98638; 360/344-4400; State Park information, 360/902-8844.

31 Point Hudson Resort & Marina

   5

Point Hudson Resort is located near the beach on the site of an old Coast Guard station in a part of Port Townsend. The park features ocean views and 2,000 feet of beach frontage. Port Townsend is called Washington's Victorian seaport, known for its Victorian architecture. Fishing and boating are popular here, and nearby recreation possibilities include an 18-hole municipal golf course, a full-service marina, Old Fort Townsend State Park, Fort Flagler State Park, and Fort Worden State Park. Note that the past concessionaire's lease with the Port of Port Townsend expired in spring of 2002 and changes are likely.

Location: In Port Townsend; see the Olympic Peninsula and Coastal Washington, map 3, grid h2.

Campsites, facilities: There are 60 sites, most drive-through with full hookups, for trailers or RVs of any length. No tents are allowed. Restrooms, drinking water, flush toilets, showers, three restaurants, and a coin-operated laundry are available. A 100-plus slip marina is on site. Leashed pets are permitted.

Reservations, fees: Reservations encouraged. Sites are $15 to $20 per night. Major credit cards accepted. Open year-round.

Directions: From Port Townsend on State Route 20, take the Water Street exit. Turn left (north) and continue (the road becomes Sims Way and then Water Street) to the end of Water Street at the marina. Turn left for registration.

Contact: Point Hudson Resort, 103 Hudson Street, Port Townsend, WA 98368; 360/385-2828 or 800/826-3854.

32 Old Fort Townsend State Park

    10

This 367-acre park features thickly wooded landscape and nearly 4,000 feet of saltwater shoreline on Port Townsend Bay. There are 6.5 miles of hiking trails. Built in 1856, the historic fort is one of the oldest remaining in the state. The scenic campground has access to a good clamming beach, and visitors can take a short self-guided walking tour. Note that the nearest boat ramps are at Port Townsend, Fort Flagler, and Hadlock. Mooring buoys are located one mile south of Glenn Cove on the west side of Port Townsend Bay.

Location: Near Quilcene; see the Olympic Peninsula and Coastal Washington, map 3, grid h2.

Campsites, facilities: There are 40 sites for tents, trailers, or RVs up to 40 feet long, three primitive tent sites, and one group site. Picnic tables and fire grills are provided. Restrooms, drinking water, flush toilets, coin-operated showers, a playground, boat buoys, firewood, a dump station, and a picnic area with kitchen shelter are available. Leashed pets are permitted.

Reservations, fees: No reservations for family sites. Group site reservations required at 360/385-4730. Sites are $7 to $15 per night, $6 per extra vehicle per night. Senior discount available. Open mid-April through mid-September.

Directions: From Port Townsend and State Route 20, drive south on State Route 20 for two miles to Old Fort Townsend Road. Turn left and drive 0.5 mile to the park entrance road.

Contact: Old Fort Townsend State Park, Route 1, Port Townsend, WA 98368; 360/385-3595; State Park information, 360/902-8844.

33 Fort Flagler State Park

  10

This beautiful park sits on a high bluff overlooking Puget Sound with views of the Olympic and Cascade mountains. The park covers 784 acres and is surrounded on three sides by 19,100 feet of saltwater shoreline. Highlights include five miles of trails for hiking and biking, an interpretive trail, and a military museum featuring gun batterys that is open in the summer. Historic Fort Flagler is a pretty, unique state park, set on Marrowstone Island east of Port Townsend. The RV sites are situated right on the beach. Anglers like this spot for year-round rockfish and salmon fishing, and crabbing and clamming are good in season. The park offers an underwater park and is popular with scuba divers. Tours of Fort Flagler are available. You will learn that construction started in 1897 and virtually was continued on some level until the fort was closed in 1953. There is a youth hostel in the park.

Location: Near Port Townsend; see the Olympic Peninsula and Coastal Washington, map 3, grid h3.

Campsites, facilities: There are 101 tent sites, 15 sites with partial hookups (water and electricity) for trailers or RVs up to 50 feet long, and two primitive tent sites. Picnic tables and fire grills are provided. Restrooms, drinking water, flush toilets, coin-operated showers, interpretive activities, a dump station, a store, a café, boat buoys, floats, and a launch are available. Facilities are wheelchair-accessible. Leashed pets are permitted.

Reservations, fees: Reserve at 888/CAMP-OUT (888/226-7688); website: www.parks.wa.gov/reservations ($7 reservation fee). Sites are $6 to $22 per night. Senior discount available. Major credit cards accepted. Open March through October, weather permitting.

Directions: From Port Townsend at Highway 20, drive east on Highway 20 for three miles to Ness' Corner Road (at the traffic light). Continue straight onto Highway 19 and go eight miles to Oak Bay Road/State Route 116. Turn left and drive two miles through Port Hadlock (turning left to stay on State Route 116). Continue about eight miles to the entrance.

Contact: Fort Flagler State Park, 360/385-1259; State Park information, 360/902-8844.

34 Mora

    8

At an elevation of 50 feet, this is a good out-of-the-way choice near the Pacific Ocean and the Olympic Coast Marine Sanctuary. The Quillayute River feeds into the ocean near the camp, and upstream is the Bogachiel, a prime steelhead river in winter months. A naturalist program is available during the summer. This camp includes eight sites requiring short walks, several of which are stellar sites.

Location: Near the Pacific Ocean in Olympic National Park; see the Olympic Peninsula and Coastal Washington, map 4, grid a4.

Campsites, facilities: There are 94 sites for tents or RVs up to 21 feet long, and 8 walk-in sites. Picnic tables and fire grills are provided. Restrooms, drinking water, and a dump station are available. Some facilities are wheelchair-accessible. A naturalist program is available in summer months. Leashed pets are permitted.

Reservations, fees: No reservations. Sites are $10 per night, plus $10 national park entrance fee per vehicle. Senior discount available. Open year-round.

Directions: From Aberdeen, drive north on U.S. 101 for 108 miles to Forks. Continue past Forks for two miles to La Push Road (High-

way 110). Turn west (left) and drive 12 miles to the campground on the left (well marked along route).

Contact: Olympic National Park, 600 East Park Avenue, Port Angeles, WA 98362; 360/565-3130, fax 360/565-3147.

35 Lonesome Creek RV Resort

     8

This private, developed park is set along the Pacific Ocean and the coastal Dungeness National Wildlife Refuge. It has some of the rare ocean sites available in the area. It offers recreation options such as fishing, beachcombing, boating, whale-watching, and sunbathing.

Location: On the Pacific Ocean; see the Olympic Peninsula and Coastal Washington, map 4, grid a3.

Campsites, facilities: There are 36 sites for trailers or RVs and 10 sites for tents. Picnic tables and fire rings are provided. Restrooms, coin-operated showers, a coin-operated laundry, gasoline and bottled gas, and a store with a deli and ice are available. Boat docks and launching facilities are located within one mile. Leashed pets are permitted.

Reservations, fees: Reservations accepted for RV sites and are recommended for ocean-front sites; phone 360/374-4338. Sites are $18 per night for tent sites and $28 to $32 for RV sites. Major credit cards accepted. Open year-round.

Directions: From Aberdeen, drive north on U.S. 101 for 108 miles to Forks. Continue past Forks for two miles to La Push Road/Highway 110. Turn west (left) and drive 14 miles to the campground on the left.

Contact: Lonesome Creek RV Resort, P.O. Box 130, La Push, WA 98350; 360/374-4338.

36 Three Rivers Resort

 8

This small, private camp is set where three rivers come together—the Quillayute, Sol Duck, and Bogachiel. The campground is situated above this confluence, about six miles upstream from the ocean. It is a pretty spot with wooded, spacious sites. Hiking and fishing are popular here. Salmon and steelhead migrate upstream here, best on the Sol Duc and Bogachiel Rivers; anglers should check regulations. The coastal Dungeness National Wildlife Refuge and Pacific Ocean are a short drive to the west, with whale-watching often good in the spring. Hoh Rain Forest, a worthwhile side trip, is about 45 minutes away.

Location: On the Quillayute River; see the Olympic Peninsula and Coastal Washington, map 4, grid a4.

Campsites, facilities: There are 10 sites for tents, trailers, or RVs of any length, and 14 sites for RVs only with full or partial hookups, plus five rental cabins. Picnic tables are provided. Restrooms, coin-operated showers, a store, a café, a coin-operated laundry, and ice are available. Firewood is available for a fee. Leashed pets are permitted.

Reservations, fees: Reservations accepted. Sites are $8 to $12 per night; cabins are $39 to $59 per night, $5 per pet per night. Major credit cards accepted. Open year-round.

Directions: From Aberdeen, drive north on U.S. 101 for 108 miles to Forks. Continue past Forks for two miles to La Push Road/Highway 110. Turn west (left) and drive eight miles to the campground on the right.

Contact: Three Rivers Resort, 7764 La Push Road, Forks, WA 98331; 360/374-5300; website: www.northolympic.com/threerivers.

37 Klahanie

 8

This camp was closed for several years before reopening in 2002, so it is likely off the radar scope of many travelers. It features sites amid large, old-growth spruce, with lots of ferns. It is quite pretty, set along a riparian zone along the North Fork Klahamie River, with a hiking trail along the river for one quarter-mile.

Location: On the North Fork Klahanie River; see the Olympic Peninsula and Coastal Washington, map 4, grid a6.

Campsites, facilities: There are 15 sites for tents, trailers, or RVs of any length. Picnic tables and fire grills are provided. Drinking water and vault toilets are available. Garbage must be packed out. Some facilities are wheelchair-accessible. Leashed pets are permitted.

Reservations, fees: No reservations; $5 per site per night. Senior discount available. Open May to late September with facilities listed. Open with limited facilities in off-season.

Directions: From Aberdeen, drive north on U.S. 101 to Forks. Continue past Forks for one miles to Forest Road 29. Turn right (east) and drive five miles to the campground on the right.

Contact: Olympic National Forest, Pacific Ranger District, 437 Tillicum Lane, Forks, WA 98331; 360/374-6522, fax 360/374-1250.

38 Bogachiel State Park

 6

This is a good base camp for salmon or steelhead fishing trips. This 123-acre park is set on the Bogachiel River, with marked hiking trails in the area. It can be noisy at times because a logging mill is located directly across the river from the campground. Also note that there is highway noise, and you can see the highway from some campsites. A one-mile hiking trail is nearby. Hunting is popular in the adjacent national forest. This region is heavily forested, with lush vegetation fed by 140 to 160 inches of rain on the average each year.

Location: On the Bogachiel River; see the Olympic Peninsula and Coastal Washington, map 4, grid a6.

Campsites, facilities: There is one primitive tent site, 36 developed tent sites, and six sites with water and electrical hookups for trailers or RVs up to 30 feet long. Picnic tables and fire grills are provided. Restrooms, drinking water, coin-operated showers, a sanitary disposal station, and a picnic area are available. A store, ice, and firewood are located within one mile. A primitive boat ramp is nearby. Leashed pets are permitted.

Reservations, fees: No reservations. Sites with hookups are $15 to $22 per night; tent sites are $7 to $9 per night, $6 per extra vehicle per night. Senior discount available. Open year-round.

Directions: From Olympia on I-5, take Exit 104 and drive north on U.S. 101 to the Aberdeen/Highway 8 exit. Turn west on Highway 8 and drive 36 miles to Aberdeen. Continue through Aberdeen four miles to U.S. 101. Turn north on U.S. 101 and drive 102 miles to the park (six miles south of Forks) on the left (west) side of the road.

Contact: Bogachiel State Park, Northwest Region, 185983 Highway 101, Forks, WA 98331; 360/902-8844 or 360/374-6356.

39 Hoh River Resort

 6

This is a nice camp along U.S. 101 with a choice of grassy or graveled shady sites, most popular as a fishing camp. Although the Hoh River is nearby, you cannot see the river from the campsites. Marked hiking trails are in the area. It's a pleasant little park, with steelhead and salmon fishing available and elk hunting in the fall. Horseshoe pits and a recreation field are provided for campers.

Location: On the Hoh River; see the Olympic Peninsula and Coastal Washington, map 4, grid b7.

Campsites, facilities: There are 23 sites for tents, trailers, or RVs of any length, some with full hookups, some with electrical hookups only. Fire pits and picnic tables are provided. Restrooms, coin-operated showers, a coin-operated laundry, a store, a gas station, and ice are available. Firewood is available for a fee. A boat launch is available nearby. Leashed pets are permitted.

Reservations, fees: Reservations accepted. Sites are $10 to $15 per night, $3 per extra vehicle per night, $5 per person per night for more than two people. No credit cards accepted. Open year-round.

Directions: From Aberdeen, drive north on U.S. 101 for 90 miles to the resort (15 miles south of Forks) on the left.

Contact: Hoh River Resort, 175443 Highway 101 South, Forks, WA 98331; 360/374-5566.

40 Cottonwood

 8

This primitive camp is set along the Hoh River, providing an alternative to Hoh Oxbow, Willoughby Creek, and Minnie Peterson campgrounds. Like Hoh Oxbow, Cottonwood offers the bonus of a boat launch. Its distance from the highway makes it quieter here.

Location: On the Hoh River; see the Olympic Peninsula and Coastal Washington, map 4, grid b7.

Campsites, facilities: There are nine sites for tents or small trailers. Picnic tables, fire grills, and tent pads are provided. No drinking water is available. Vault toilets and a boat launch are available. Some facilities are wheelchair-accessible. Leashed pets are permitted.

Reservations, fees: No reservations; no fee. Open year-round.

Directions: From Olympia on I-5, take Exit 104 and drive north on U.S. 101 to the Aberdeen/Highway 8 exit. Turn west on Highway 8 and drive 36 miles to Aberdeen. Continue through Aberdeen four miles to U.S. 101. Turn north on U.S. 101 and drive 92 miles to Oil City Road between Mileposts 177 and 178. Turn west on Oil City Road and drive 2.3 miles. Turn left on Road H4060 (gravel) and drive one mile to the camp at the end of the road.

Contact: Department of Natural Resources, Olympic Region, 411 Tillicum Lane, Forks, WA 98331-9797; 360/374-6131, fax 360/374-5446.

41 Hoh Oxbow

 7

This is the most popular of the five camps on the Hoh River. It's primitive and close to the highway, and the price is right. The adjacent boat launch makes this the camp of choice for anglers, best in fall and winter for salmon and steelhead; check regulations. It is also a popular hunter's camp in the fall. A downer is that there is some highway noise within range of the campsites. You can't see the traffic, but you can hear it, which can be irritating for those who want perfect quiet.

Location: On the Hoh River; see the Olympic Peninsula and Coastal Washington, map 4, grid b7.

Campsites, facilities: There are seven sites for tents or small trailers up to 16 feet. Picnic tables, fire grills, and tent pads are provided. Vault toilets and a hand boat launch are available, but there is no drinking water.

Some facilities are wheelchair-accessible. Leashed pets are permitted.

Reservations, fees: No reservations; no fee. Open year-round.

Directions: From Aberdeen, drive north on U.S. 101 for 90 miles to the campground (15 miles south of Forks). Exit between Mileposts 176 and 177 and look for the campground on the right, next to the river.

Contact: Department of Natural Resources, Olympic Region, 411 Tillicum Lane, Forks, WA 98331-9797; 360/374-6131, fax 360/374-5446.

42 Willoughby Creek

 9

This little-known camp along Willoughby Creek and the Hoh River is tiny and rustic, with good fishing nearby, for steelhead and salmon during peak migrations in season. The area gets heavy rainfall. Other campground options in the vicinity are Hoh Oxbow, Cottonwood, and Minnie Peterson.

Location: In Hoh Clearwater State Forest; see the Olympic Peninsula and Coastal Washington, map 4, grid b7.

Campsites, facilities: There are three campsites for tents or trailers up to 16 feet long. Picnic tables, fire grills, and tent pads are provided. Vault toilets are available, but there is no drinking water. Leashed pets are permitted.

Reservations, fees: No reservations; no fee. Open year-round.

Directions: From Olympia on I-5, take Exit 104 and drive north on U.S. 101 to the Aberdeen/Highway 8 exit. Turn west on Highway 8 and drive 36 miles to Aberdeen. Continue through Aberdeen four miles to U.S. 101. Turn north on U.S. 101 and drive about 90 miles. Exit between Mileposts 178 and 179. At Hoh Rain Forest Road/Upper Hoh Valley Road, turn east and drive 3.5 miles to the campground on the right.

Contact: Department of Natural Resources, Olympic Region, 411 Tillicum Lane, Forks, WA 98331-9797; 360/374-6131, fax 360/374-5446.

Minnie Peterson

 9

Not many folks know about this primitive camp, set on the Hoh River on the edge of the Hoh Rain Forest. It's quite pretty and forested with Sitka spruce and western hemlock, with nice riverside sites. Bring your rain gear.

Location: On the Hoh River; see the Olympic Peninsula and Coastal Washington, map 4, grid b7.

Campsites, facilities: There are eight campsites for tents or small trailers. Picnic tables, fire grills, and tent pads are provided. Vault toilets are available. No drinking water is available, and discharging firearms is prohibited. Some facilities are wheelchair-accessible. Leashed pets are permitted.

Reservations, fees: No reservations; no fee. Open year-round.

Directions: From Olympia on I-5, take Exit 104 and drive north on U.S. 101 to the Aberdeen/Highway 8 exit. Turn west on Highway 8 and drive 36 miles to Aberdeen. Continue through Aberdeen four miles to U.S. 101. Turn north on U.S. 101 and drive about 90 miles. Exit between Mileposts 178 and 179. At Hoh Rain Forest Road/Upper Hoh Valley Road, turn east and drive 4.5 miles to the campground on the left.

Contact: Department of Natural Resources, Olympic Region, 411 Tillicum Lane, Forks, WA 98331-9797; 360/374-6131, fax 360/374-5446.

Kalaloch

 10

This camp is located on a bluff above the beach, with some wonderful oceanview sites.

That is why this camp is popular and can fill quickly. Like other camps set on the coast of the Olympic Peninsula, heavy rain in winter and spring is common, and it's often foggy in the summer. A naturalist program is offered in the summer months. There are several good hiking trails in the area; check out the visitors center for maps and information.

Location: Near the Pacific Ocean in Olympic National Park; see the Olympic Peninsula and Coastal Washington, map 4, grid d6.

Campsites, facilities: There are 175 sites for tents or RVs up to 21 feet long, and one group site. Picnic tables and fire grills are provided. Restrooms, drinking water, wheelchair-accessible facilities, and a dump station are available. A store and a restaurant are located within one mile. Leashed pets are permitted in the campground.

Reservations, fees: Reservations for group site only, phone 360/962-2271; individual sites are $12 per night, group site is $20 per night plus $2 per person, plus $10 national park entrance fee per vehicle. Senior discount available. Open year-round.

Directions: From Aberdeen, drive north on U.S. 101 for 83 miles to the campground on the left. It is located near the mouth of the Kalaloch River five miles north of the U.S. 101 bridge over the Queets River.

Contact: Olympic National Park, 600 East Park Avenue, Port Angeles, WA 98362; 360/565-3130, fax 360/565-3147.

Coppermine Bottom

 9

Few tourists ever visit this primitive, hidden campground with river dory launching facilities. It's set on the Clearwater River, a tributary of the Queets River, which runs to the ocean. The boat launch is a bonus and makes this a perfect camp for anglers and river runners who want to avoid the usual U.S. 101 crowds. Salmon fishing is popular here during the migratory journey of this anadramous fish. Good news: The access road once washed out in a flood is again open.

Location: On the Clearwater River; see the Olympic Peninsula and Coastal Washington, map 4, grid c7.

Campsites, facilities: There are nine campsites for tents or trailers up to 16 feet long. Picnic tables, fire grills, and tent pads are provided. Vault toilets, a group shelter, and a hand boat launch are available, but there is no drinking water. Leashed pets are permitted.

Reservations, fees: No reservations; no fee. Open year-round.

Directions: From Olympia on I-5, take Exit 104 and drive north on U.S. 101 to the Aberdeen/Highway 8 exit. Turn west on Highway 8 and drive 36 miles to Aberdeen. Continue through Aberdeen four miles to U.S. 101. Turn north on U.S. 101 and drive about 60 miles to Milepost 147. Turn north on Clearwater Mainline Road and drive about 14 miles to C-3000 Road. Turn east on C-3000 Road (a gravel one-lane road) and drive two miles to C-1010 Road. Turn right on C-1010 Road and drive one mile. The camp is on the left.

Contact: Department of Natural Resources, Olympic Region, 411 Tillicum Lane, Forks, WA 98331-9797; 360/374-6131, fax 360/374-5446.

46 Upper Clearwater

 8

Upper Clearwater is one of the three primitive camps set along the Clearwater River. This is a great camp—it's very pretty, unused by most tourists, and has a boat ramp and other amenities. Best of all, it's free. It is set amid a forest of western hemlock, red alder, and big leaf maple.

Location: On the Clearwater River; see the Olympic Peninsula and Coastal Washington, map 4, grid c7.

Campsites, facilities: There are seven sites for tents or trailers up to 16 feet long. Picnic tables, fire grills, tent pads, and vault toilets are provided, but there is no drinking water. There are unimproved boat-launching facilities for small crafts, such as river dories, rafts, canoes, and kayaks. Leashed pets are permitted.

Reservations, fees: No reservations; no fee. Open year-round.

Directions: From Olympia on I-5, take Exit 104 and drive north on U.S. 101 to the Aberdeen/Highway 8 exit. Turn west on Highway 8 and drive 36 miles to Aberdeen. Continue through Aberdeen four miles to U.S. 101. Turn north on U.S. 101 and drive about 60 miles to Milepost 147. Turn north on Hoh Clearwater Mainline Road and drive about 13 miles to C-3000 Road (a gravel one-lane road). Turn right and drive 3.3 miles to the camp entrance on the right.

Contact: Department of Natural Resources, Olympic Region, 411 Tillicum Lane, Forks, WA 98331-9797; 360/374-6131, fax 360/374-5446.

47 Pacific Beach State Park

 10

This is the only state park campground in Washington where you can see the ocean from your campsite. It is set on just nine acres, within the town of Pacific Beach, but with 2,300 feet of beachfront. This spot is great for long beach walks, although it can be windy, especially in the spring and early summer. Because of those winds, this is a great place for kite flying. Clamming (for razor clams) is permitted only in season. Note that rangers advise no swimming or body surfing because of strong riptides. Vehicle traffic is allowed seasonally on the uppermost portions of the beach, but ATVs are not allowed in the park, on the beach, or on sand dunes. This camp is popular and often fills up quickly.

Location: On the Pacific Ocean; see the Olympic Peninsula and Coastal Washington, map 4, grid g7.

Campsites, facilities: There are 30 developed tent sites, 31 sites with partial hookups (electricity) for trailers or RVs up to 50 feet long, and two primitive tent sites. Picnic tables are provided. Restrooms, drinking water, flush toilets, coin-operated showers, a dump station, and a picnic area are available. No fires are permitted. Some facilities are wheelchair-accessible. Leashed pets are permitted.

Reservations, fees: Reserve at 888/CAMP-OUT (888/226-7688); website: www.parks.wa.gov/reservations ($7 reservation fee). Sites are $6 to $22 per night. Senior discount available. Major credit cards accepted. Open year-round.

Directions: From Hoquiam, drive north on State Route 109 for 37 miles to Pacific Beach and the park on the right.

Contact: Pacific Beach State Park, 148 State Route 115, Hoquiam, WA 98550; 360/276-4297; State Park information, 360/902-8844.

48 Driftwood Acres Ocean Campground

 7

Driftwood Acres spreads over some 150 acres. Most find the camp is family friendly, with beach access, spacious RV sites, secluded tent spots, evergreens, and marked hiking trails. It is located along a tidal river basin, out of the wind. Clamming is often good in the area. Additional facilities within five miles include an 18-hole golf course and a riding stable.

Location: In Copalis Beach; see the Olympic Peninsula and Coastal Washington, map 4, grid g7.

Campsites, facilities: There are 45 tent sites and 17 sites with partial hookups (water and electricity) for trailers or RVs of any length. Picnic tables and fire pits are provided. Restrooms, drinking water, flush toilets, coin-operated showers, a free bundle of firewood, a recreation hall, and a dump station are available. A clam-cleaning station is nearby. Bottled gas, a store, a café, and ice are located within one mile. Leashed pets are permitted, but no Rottweilers, pitbulls, Dobermans, or aggressive dogs of any type.

Reservations, fees: Reservations accepted. Sites are $15 to $25 per night, $5 per extra vehicle per night. Open year-round.

Directions: From Hoquiam, drive west on State Route 109 for 21 miles to Copalis Beach. Continue one-half mile north to the camp on the left, between Mileposts 21 and 22.

Contact: Driftwood Acres Ocean Campground, P.O. Box 216, 3209 State Route 109, Copalis Beach, WA 98535; 360/289-3484.

49 Surf and Sand RV Park, Copalis Beach

 5

Although not particularly scenic, this five-acre park is a decent layover for an RV vacation and will do the job if you're tired and ready to get off U.S. 101. It does have beach access, possible with a 15-minute walk, but as of spring 2002, the creek had washed out the nearby road to the ocean, so check for status. The surrounding terrain is flat and grassy.

Location: In Copalis Beach; see the Olympic Peninsula and Coastal Washington, map 4, grid h7.

Campsites, facilities: There are 50 sites with full or partial hookups, including 20 drive-through, for trailers or RVs of any length, and 16 tent sites. Picnic tables and fire grills are provided. Restrooms, drinking water, flush toilets, showers, cable TV hookups, a coin-operated laundry, a café, a recreation room with kitchen facilities, and ice are available. Bottled gas is available within one mile. Leashed pets are permitted.

Reservations, fees: Reservations accepted. Sites are $15 to $29, $4 per extra vehicle per night. Major credit cards accepted. Open year-round.

Directions: From Hoquiam, drive west on State Route 109 for 21 miles to Copalis Beach and Heath Road. Turn left (west) on Heath Road and 0.2 mile to the campground.

Contact: Surf and Sand RV Park, Copalis Beach, P.O. Box 208, No. 8 McCullough, Copalis Beach, WA 98535; 360/289-2707.

🔢 Riverside RV Resort

 8

River access is a bonus at this nice and clean six-acre park. Most sites have a river view. Salmon fishing can be good in the Copalis River, and a boat ramp is available nearby for anglers. Swimming and beachcombing are two other options.

Location: Near Copalis Beach; see the Olympic Peninsula and Coastal Washington, map 4, grid h7.

Campsites, facilities: There are 53 sites with full hookups, including 20 drive-through, for trailers or RVs of any length, and 15 tent sites. Picnic tables and fire grills are provided. Restrooms, drinking water, flush toilets, showers, a dump station, a hot tub, firewood, and a recreation hall are available. A café is located within one mile. A boat dock and launching facilities are nearby. Leashed pets are permitted.

Reservations, fees: Reservations accepted. Sites are $15 to $20 per night, $2 per person per night for more than two people. Senior discount available. Major credit cards accepted. Open year-round.

Directions: From Hoquiam, drive west on State Route 109 for 22 miles to Copalis Beach. The park is off the highway on the left.

Contact: Riverside RV Resort, P.O. Box 307, No. 11 Condra Road, Copalis Beach, WA 98535; 360/289-2111; website: www.riversidervresort.net.

🔢 Tidelands Resort

 7

This flat, wooded campground covers 47 acres and provides beach access and a great ocean view. It's primarily an RV park, and the sites are pleasant and grassy. Ten sites are set on sand dunes, while the remainder are in a wooded area. In the spring, azaleas and wildflowers abound. Horseshoe pits and a sports field offer recreation possibilities. Clamming is available in season. This option is more remote than the other sites in the area. Various festivals are held in the area from spring through fall. Remodeling is scheduled for 2002.

Location: Near Copalis Beach; see the Olympic Peninsula and Coastal Washington, map 4, grid h7.

Campsites, facilities: There are 100 tent sites, 55 with full or partial hookups, including some drive-through, for trailers or RVs of any length, and one three-bedroom trailer and three two-bedroom cabins. Picnic tables and fire rings are provided. Restrooms, drinking water, flush toilets, coin-operated showers, a dump station, firewood, ice, cable TV, and a playground are available. Boat docks and a café are located within one mile. A golf course is located nearby. A casino and horseback riding are within five miles. Leashed pets are permitted.

Reservations, fees: Reservations accepted. Sites are $12 to $16 per night; cabins and trailers are $65 to $85 per night. Senior discount available. Major credit cards accepted. Open year-round.

Directions: From Hoquiam, drive west on State Route 109 for about 20 miles to the campground on the left. It is located between Mileposts 20 and 21, about one mile south of Copalis Beach.

Contact: Tidelands Resort, P.O. Box 36, Copalis Beach, WA 98535; 360/289-8963; website: www.tidelandsresort.com.

52 Rod's Beach Resort

 8

This well-maintained 10-acre park has large, flat, grassy sites among cedar, spruce, and a beach, plus nice sunsets, and can be a prime spot for RVers. Access to the ocean and fishing are highlights.

Location: Near Copalis Beach; see the Olympic Peninsula and Coastal Washington, map 4, grid h7.

Campsites, facilities: There are 80 sites with full hookups, including 25 drive-through, for trailers or RVs of any length, and lodging units with kitchenettes. No tents are allowed. Restrooms, drinking water, flush toilets, showers, cable TV, a dump station, a recreation hall, a store, ice, and a playground are available. Bottled gas and a café are located within one mile. A seasonal swimming pool is available for a fee. Leashed pets are permitted.

Reservations, fees: Reservations accepted. Sites are $12 to $16 per night. Major credit cards accepted. Open April through October.

Directions: From Hoquiam, drive west on State Route 109 for 20 miles to the campground on the left. It's located about one mile south of Copalis Beach at Milepost 20.

Contact: Rod's Beach Resort, P.O. Box 507, 2961 State Route 109, Copalis Beach, WA 98535; 360/289-2222.

53 Ocean Mist Resort

 9

Always call to determine whether space is available before planning a stay here. This is a membership resort RV campground, and members always come first. If space is available, they will rent sites to the public. Surf fishing is popular in the nearby Pacific Ocean, and there are salmon fishing and canoeing opportunities in the Capellis River. It's about a one-block walk to the beach. There's a golf course within five miles.

Location: On Conners Creek; see the Olympic Peninsula and Coastal Washington, map 4, grid h7.

Campsites, facilities: There are 120 sites, most with full hookups, for trailers or RVs, an area for dispersed camping for up to 20 tents, and three trailers. Picnic tables are provided. Restrooms, drinking water, flush toilets, showers, cable TV, a dump station, two community fire pits, a hot tub, and a coin-operated laundry are available. A grocery store is within one mile in Ocean City. Leashed pets are permitted.

Reservations, fees: Reservations required in the summer; phone 360/289-3656 or fax 360/289-2807. Sites are $20 to $30 per night, trailers are $60 per night. Major credit cards accepted. Open year-round.

Directions: From Hoquiam, drive west on State Route 109 for 19 miles to the campground on the left (one mile north of Ocean City)

Contact: Ocean Mist Resort, 2781 State Route 109, Ocean City, WA 98569; 360/289-3656, fax 360/289-2807.

54 Ocean City State Park

 9

This 170-acre oceanfront camp features ocean beach, dunes, and dense thickets of pine surrounding freshwater marshes. It is an excellent example of coastal wetlands and dune succession. The Ocean Shores Interpretive Center is located on the south end of Ocean Shores near the marina (open summer season only). This area is part of the Pacific Flyway, and just offshore is the migratory route for gray whales and other marine mammals. Spring wildflowers are excellent, including lupine, buttercups, and wild strawberry. This is also a good area for surfing and kite flying, with springs typically windy. Beachcombing, clamming, and fishing are possibilities at this park. An 18-hole golf course is nearby.

Location: Near Hoquiam; see the Olympic Peninsula and Coastal Washington, map 4, grid h7.

Campsites, facilities: There are 149 standard sites for tents, trailers, or RVs, 29 sites with full hookups, including some drive-through, for trailers or RVs up to 55 feet long, and three primitive tent sites. Picnic tables and fire rings are provided. Restrooms, drinking water, flush toilets, showers, a dump station, a sheltered picnic area, and firewood are available. Some facilities are wheelchair-accessible. Leashed pets are permitted.

Reservations, fees: Reserve at 888/226-7688 (CAMP-OUT); website: www.parks.wa.gov /reservations ($7 reservation fee). Sites are $6 to $22 per night. Senior discount available. Open year-round.

Directions: From Hoquiam, drive northwest on State Route 109 for 16 miles to State Route 115. Turn left and drive 1.2 miles south to the park on the right (1.5 miles north of Ocean Shores).

Contact: Ocean City State Park, 148 State Route 115, Hoquiam, WA 98550; 360/289-3553; State Park information, 360/902-8844.

55 South Fork Hoh

 10

This rarely used, beautiful camp set along the cascading South Fork of the Hoh River is way out there. It's tiny and primitive but offers a guarantee of peace and quiet, something many U.S. 101 cruisers would cheerfully give a limb for after a few days of fighting crowds. Fishing for steelhead can be excellent; check regulations.

Location: In Hoh Clearwater State Forest; see the Olympic Peninsula and Coastal Washington, map 5, grid b1.

Campsites, facilities: There are three campsites for tents or small trailers. Picnic tables, fire grills, vault toilets, and tent pads are provided. No drinking water is available. Leashed pets are permitted.

Reservations, fees: No reservations; no fee. Open year-round.

Directions: From Olympia on I-5, take Exit 104 and drive north on U.S. 101 to the Aberdeen/Highway 8 exit. Turn west on Highway 8 and drive 36 miles to Aberdeen. Continue through Aberdeen four miles to U.S. 101. Turn north on U.S. 101 and drive about 94 miles. Exit at Milepost 176. At Hoh Mainline Road turn east and drive 6.5 miles. Turn left on Road H1000 and drive 7.5 miles to the campground on the right. Obtaining a Department of Natural Resources (DNR) map is advised.

Contact: Department of Natural Resources, Olympic Region, 411 Tillicum Lane, Forks, WA 98331-9797; 360/374-6131, fax 360/374-5446.

56 Hoh

 10

This camp at a trailhead leading into the interior of Olympic National Park is located in the beautiful heart of a temperate, old-growth rainforest. Hoh Oxbow, Cottonwood, Willoughby Creek, and Minnie Peterson campgrounds are nearby, set downstream on the Hoh River, outside national park boundaries. In the summer, there are naturalist programs, and a visitors center is nearby. This is one of the most popular camps in the park. The elevation is 578 feet.

Location: In Olympic National Park; see the Olympic Peninsula and Coastal Washington, map 5, grid b1.

Campsites, facilities: There are 88 sites for tents or RVs up to 21 feet long. Picnic tables and fire grills are provided. Restrooms and drinking water are available A dump station is available nearby. Some facilities are wheelchair-accessible. Leashed pets are permitted.

Reservations, fees: No reservations. Sites are $10 per night, plus $10 national park entrance fee per vehicle. Senior discount available. Open year-round.

Directions: From Aberdeen, drive north on U.S. 101 for about 90 miles to Milepost 176. Turn east on Hoh River Road and drive 19 miles to the campground on the right (near the end of the road).

Contact: Olympic National Park, 600 East Park Avenue, Port Angeles, WA 98362; 360/565-3130, fax 360/565-3147.

57 Sol Duc

 10

This site is a nice hideaway, with Sol Duc Hot Springs near the campground a highlight.

The problem is that this camp is very popular. The camp fills up quickly on weekends, and a fee is charged to use the hot springs, which have been fully developed since the early 1900s. The camp is set at 1,680 feet along the Sol Duc River. A naturalist program is available in the summer.

Location: On the Sol Duc River in Olympic National Park; see the Olympic Peninsula and Coastal Washington, map 5, grid a2.

Campsites, facilities: There are 82 sites for tents or RVs up to 21 feet long, and one group site. Picnic tables and fire grills are provided. Restrooms and drinking water are available. Some facilities are wheelchair-accessible. A dump station is available nearby, and a store and a café are within one mile. Leashed pets are permitted.

Reservations, fees: Reservations for group site only, phone 360/327-3534 from April 16 through October 31, phone 360/928-3380 from November 1 to April 15. Individual sites are $12 per night, group sites are $20 per night and $1 per person, plus $10 national park entrance fee per vehicle. Senior discount available. Open from May to late October, with limited winter facilities.

Directions: From I-5 at Olympia, turn north on U.S. 101 and drive about 122 miles to Port Angeles. Continue on U.S. 101 for past Port Angeles for 27 miles, just past Lake Crescent. Turn left at the Sol Duc turnoff and drive 12 miles to the camp.

Contact: Olympic National Park, 600 East Park Avenue, Port Angeles, WA 98362; 360/565-3130, fax 360/565-3147.

58 Deer Park

 9

This camp is set in the Olympic Peninsula's high country at 5,400 feet, just below 6,000-foot Blue Mountain. There are numerous trails in the area, including a major trailhead into the backcountry of Olympic National Park and the Buckhorn Wilderness.

Location: Near Blue Mountain in Olympic National Park; see the Olympic Peninsula and Coastal Washington, map 5, grid a7.

Campsites, facilities: There are 14 tent sites. Picnic tables and fire grills are provided. Vault toilets and drinking water are available. Leashed pets are permitted.

Reservations, fees: No reservations. Sites are $8 per night, $10 per vehicle park entrance fee. Senior discount available. Open mid-June to late September, with limited winter facilities.

Directions: From Port Angeles, drive east on U.S. 101 for about five miles to Deer Park Road. Turn south and drive 18 miles to the campground at the end of the road. Note that the last six miles are gravel, steep and narrow, closed to RVs and trailers, and often closed to all vehicles in winter.

Contact: Olympic National Park, 600 East Park Avenue, Port Angeles, WA 98362; 360/565-3132, fax 360/565-3147.

59 Dungeness Forks

 7

This pretty, wooded spot is nestled at the confluence of the Dungeness and Gray Wolf Rivers. It offers seclusion, yet easy access from the highway. The campsites are set in forest. If you want quiet, you'll often find it here. The Upper Dungeness Trailhead, located about seven miles south of camp, provides access to Buckhorn Wilderness and Olympic National Park. The trailhead for the Gray Wolf Trail is four miles from camp, but note that portions of this trail are closed due to slides; check with rangers before embarking on a long trip here. The Gray Wolf River is closed to fishing year-around to protect salmon. The elevation is 1,000 feet.

Location: On the Dungeness and Gray Wolf Rivers in Olympic National Forest; see the Olympic Peninsula and Coastal Washington, map 5, grid a8.

Campsites, facilities: There are 10 tent sites. Picnic tables and fire rings are provided. Drinking water and vault toilets are available. Garbage must be packed out. Leashed pets are permitted.

Reservations, fees: No reservations. Sites are $10 per night, $10 per vehicle park entrance fee. Open May through September.

Directions: From Olympia on I-5 at, turn north on U.S. 101 and drive approximately 100 miles to Palo Alto Road, located 1.5 miles north of Sequim Bay State Park and 3 miles southeast of Sequim. Turn south (left) on Palo Alto Road and drive about seven miles to Forest Road 2880. Turn right (west) and drive one mile (after crossing Dungeness River Bridge) to the campground on the right. Obtaining a U.S. Forest Service map is advised. Trailers and RVs are not recommended because of steep, narrow, and unpaved access road.

Contact: Olympic National Forest, Quilcene Ranger District, P.O. Box 280, Quilcene, WA 98376; 360/765-2200, fax 360/765-2202.

60 Dosewallips

 7

Dosewallips is a more remote option to Elkhorn and Collins. Set on the Dosewallips River at 1,500 feet, the camp provides a major trailhead into the backcountry of Olympic National Park. The trail follows the Dosewallips River over Anderson Pass, proceeds along the Quinault River, and ultimately reaches Quinault Lake. Note that as of spring 2002, this trail was not accessible to Quinault Lake because of a bridge closure; check the status before departing. Other hiking trails are available nearby.

Location: On the Dosewallips River in Olympic National Park; see the Olympic Peninsula and Coastal Washington, map 5, grid c7.

Campsites, facilities: There are 30 tent sites. Picnic tables and fire grills are provided. Restrooms, drinking water, and flush toilets are available. Some facilities are wheelchair-accessible. Leashed pets are permitted.

Reservations, fees: No reservations. Sites are $10 per night, $10 park entrance fee. Senior discount available. Open mid-May to late September.

Directions: From Olympia on I-5, drive north on U.S. 101 for 60 miles to a signed turnoff near Brinnon (located about one mile north of Dosewallips State Park) for Forest Road 2610 (County Road 2500). Turn west and drive 15 miles along the Dosewallips River to the camp at the end of the road. Note that the access road is not paved and is not recommended for RVs or trailers.

Contact: Olympic National Park, 600 East Park Avenue, Port Angeles, WA 98362; 360/565-3132, fax 360/565-3147.

61 Elkhorn

 8

This eight-acre, wooded camp is set on the Dosewallips River at 600 feet, with river access. Some campsites are set along the north bank of the river. The surrounding landscape features old-growth forest, with deer and a variety of birds often spotted. It's not far from Olympic National Park, which makes a good side trip.

Location: On the Dosewallips River in Olympic National Forest; see the Olympic Peninsula and Coastal Washington, map 5, grid c8.

Campsites, facilities: There are 20 sites for tents, trailers, or RVs up to 21 feet long.

Picnic tables and fire pits are provided. Drinking water and vault toilets are available. Leashed pets are permitted.

Reservations, fees: No reservations. Sites are $10 per night. Senior discount available. Open mid-May through September.

Directions: From Olympia on I-5, drive north on U.S. 101 for 60 miles to a signed turnoff near Brinnon (about one mile north of Dosewallips State Park) for Forest Road 2610 (County Road 2500). Turn west and drive 10 miles along the Dosewallips River. Look for the camp on the left. Note that the last four miles of the road has a lot of potholes.

Contact: Olympic National Forest, Quilcene Ranger District, P.O. Box 280, Quilcene, WA 98376; 360/765-2200, fax 360/765-2202.

62 Collins

 7

Most vacationers cruising U.S. 101 don't have a clue about this quiet spot set on a great launch point for adventure, yet it's only five or six miles from the highway. This four-acre camp is set on the Duckabush River at 200 feet elevation. It has small, shaded sites, river access nearby, and plenty of fishing and hiking; check fishing regulations. Just one mile from camp is the Duckabush Trail, which connects to trails in Olympic National Park. The Murhut Falls Trail starts about three miles from the campground, providing access to a 0.8-mile trail to the falls. It's a 1.5-mile drive to nearby Dosewallips State Park and a 30- to 35-minute drive to Olympic National Park.

Location: On the Duckabush River in Olympic National Forest; see the Olympic Peninsula and Coastal Washington, map 5, grid c8.

Campsites, facilities: There are six tent sites and 10 sites for trailers or RVs up to 21 feet long. Picnic tables and fire rings are provided. Drinking water and vault toilets are available. Some facilities are wheelchair-accessible. Leashed pets are permitted.

Reservations, fees: No reservations. Sites are $10 per night. Senior discount available. Open mid-May through September.

Directions: From Olympia on I-5, drive north on U.S. 101 for 59 miles to Forest Road 2510 (near Duckabush). Turn left on Forest Road 2510 and drive five miles west to the camp on the left.

Contact: Olympic National Forest, Hood Canal Ranger District, Hoodsport Office, P.O. Box 68, Hoodsport, WA 98548; 360/877-5254.

63 Lena Lake Hike-In

 8

Lena Lake is one of the most popular lakes on the Olympic Peninsula. Compared to other sites, it is crowded in the summer, yet you can usually get a site. The 55-acre lake is nestled along the Hamma Hamma drainage among rugged peaks, adjacent to the Brothers Wilderness. It takes a three-mile hike-in from the trailhead at Lena Creek to reach this camp. This adventure is suitable for the entire family—an outstanding way to turn youngsters onto backpacking. It's a lovely setting, too, with a pleasantly mild climate in summer. The lake is good for swimming and fishing for rainbow trout. The elevation is 1,800 feet.

Location: Near the Hamma Hamma River in Olympic National Forest; see the Olympic Peninsula and Coastal Washington, map 5, grid c7.

Campsites, facilities: There are 29 primitive sites at this hike-in campground. There is no drinking water. Vault toilets are available. Leashed pets are permitted.

Reservations, fees: No reservations. There is no fee for camping, but you must obtain a

$25 annual Trail Park Pass or pay $3 per day to park at the trailhead. Open year-round, weather permitting.

Directions: From Olympia on I-5, turn north on U.S. 101 and drive about 37 miles to Hoodsport. Continue north on U.S. 101 from 14 miles to Forest Road 25. Turn west on Forest Road 25 and drive eight miles to the Lena Creek Camp and the trailhead. Hike 3.2 miles north to Lena Lake. Campsites are scattered around the lake.

Contact: Olympic National Forest, Hood Canal Ranger District, P.O. Box 68, Hoodsport, WA 98548; 360/877-5254, fax 360/352-2569.

64 Lena Creek

7

This seven-acre camp is set where Lena Creek empties into the Hamma Hamma River. The camp is set amid both conifers and hardwoods. This is a popular trailhead camp. A trail from the camp leads three miles to Lena Lake and seven miles to Upper Lena Lake. A map of Olympic National Forest details the trail and road system. The camp is rustic with some improvements.

Location: On the Hamma Hamma River in Olympic National Forest; see the Olympic Peninsula and Coastal Washington, map 5, grid d7.

Campsites, facilities: There are 14 sites for tents, trailers, or RVs up to 21 feet long. Picnic tables and fire rings are provided. Drinking water and vault toilets are available. Some facilities are wheelchair-accessible. Leashed pets are permitted.

Reservations, fees: No reservations. Sites are $10 per night. Senior discount available. Open mid-May through September.

Directions: From Olympia on I-5, turn north on U.S. 101 and drive about 37 miles to Hoodsport. Continue north on U.S. 101 for

14 miles to Forest Road 25. Turn west on Forest Road 25 and drive eight miles to the camp on the left.

Contact: Olympic National Forest, Hood Canal Ranger District, Hoodsport office, P.O. Box 68, Hoodsport, WA 98548; 360/877-5254, fax 360/352-2569.

65 Hamma Hamma

 7

This camp is set on the Hamma Hamma River at an elevation of 600 feet. It's small and primitive, but it can be preferable to some of the developed camps on the U.S. 101 circuit. The Civilian Conservation Corps is memorialized in a wheelchair-accessible interpretive trail that begins in the campground and leads one quarter-mile along the river. The camps are set among conifers and hardwoods.

Location: On the Hamma Hamma River in Olympic National ; see the Olympic Peninsula and Coastal Washington, map 5, grid d7.

Campsites, facilities: There are three tent sites and 12 sites for trailers or RVs up to 21 feet long. Picnic tables and fire rings are provided. Hand-pumped water and vault toilets are available. Some facilities are wheelchair-accessible. Leashed pets are permitted.

Reservations, fees: No reservations. Sites are $10 per night. Senior discount available. Open May through September.

Directions: From Olympia on I-5, turn north on U.S. 101 and drive 37 miles to Hoodsport. Continue on U.S. 101 for 14 miles north to Forest Road 25. Turn left on Forest Road 25 and drive 6.5 miles to the camp on the left side of the road.

Contact: Olympic National Forest, Hood Canal Ranger District, Hoodsport Office, P.O. Box 68, Hoodsport, WA 98548; 360/877-5254, fax 360/352-2569.

66 Queets

 6

This primitive camp on the shore of the Queets River is a gem if you don't mind bringing your own water or purifying river water. A trailhead is available for hikes into the interior of Olympic National Park. The elevation is 290 feet.

Location: On the Queets River in Olympic National Park; see the Olympic Peninsula and Coastal Washington, map 5, grid c1.

Campsites, facilities: There are 20 primitive tent sites. Picnic tables and fire grills are provided. Toilets are available, but there is no drinking water. Some facilities are wheelchair-accessible. Leashed pets are permitted.

Reservations, fees: No reservations. Sites are $8 per night, plus $10 national park entrance fee per vehicle. Senior discount available. Open year-round.

Directions: From Aberdeen, drive north on U.S. 101 for 38 miles to Lake Quinault, and continue for 19 miles to a signed turnoff for the campground. Turn right (northeast) on an unpaved road and drive 14 miles along the Queets River. The campground is at the end of the unpaved road, which is not recommended for RVs or trailers.

Contact: Olympic National Park, 600 East Park Avenue, Port Angeles, WA 98362; 360/565-3130, fax 360/565-3147.

67 July Creek Walk-In

 7

This walk-in camp is set on the north shore of Quinault Lake near where July Creek empties into the lake. Full supplies are available on the south shore, where there's a marina. This is a good choice for hikers looking to avoid crowds. The walk to the campsites is short.

Location: On Quinault Lake in Olympic National Park; see the Olympic Peninsula and Coastal Washington, map 5, grid e1.

Campsites, facilities: There are 28 walk-in tent sites. Picnic tables and fire grills are provided. Vault toilets and drinking water are available. Leashed pets are permitted.

Reservations, fees: No reservations. Sites are $10 per night, plus $10 national park entrance fee per vehicle. Senior discount available. Open year-round.

Directions: From Aberdeen, drive north on U.S. 101 for 38 miles to Lake Quinault and the town of Amanda Park. Continue two miles north on U.S. 101 to North Shore Road. Turn right (east) and drive two miles along the north shore of Quinault Lake to the camp on the right.

Contact: Olympic National Park, 600 East Park Avenue, Port Angeles, WA 98362; 360/565-3130, fax 360/565-3147.

68 Willaby

 8

This pretty, 14-acre wooded camp is set on the shore of Lake Quinault at 200 feet elevation, adjacent to where Willaby Creek empties into the lake. The lake is part of the Quinault Indian Reservation and is closed to fishing. The campsites vary, with some open with lake views, while others are more private, with no views. The tree cover is Douglas fir, western red cedar, western hemlock, and bigleaf maple. The forest floor is covered with wall-to-wall greenery, with exceptional moss growth. The Quinault Rain Forest Nature Trail and the Quinault National Recreation Trail System are nearby. Quinault Lake covers about six square miles. This camp is concessionaire operated.

Location: On Lake Quinault in Olympic National Forest; see the Olympic Peninsula and Coastal Washington, map 5, grid e2.

Campsites, facilities: There are 22 drive-in sites for tents, trailers, or RVs up to 16 feet long. Picnic tables and fire pits are provided. Drinking water, flush toilets, and electricity in the restrooms are available. Some facilities are wheelchair-accessible. Launching facilities and rentals are available at nearby Quinault Lake. Leashed pets are permitted.

Reservations, fees: No reservations. Sites are $11 to $14 per night. Senior discount available. Open from Memorial Day weekend through September.

Directions: From Olympia on I-5, take Exit 104 and drive north on U.S. 101 to the Aberdeen/Highway 8 exit. Turn west on Highway 8 and drive 36 miles to Aberdeen. Continue through Aberdeen four miles to U.S. 101. Turn north on U.S. 101 and drive about 45 miles to the Lake Quinault turnoff and South Shore Road. Turn northeast on South Shore Road and drive 1.5 miles to the camp set on the southern shore of the lake.

Contact: Olympic National Forest, Pacific Ranger District, Quinault Office, P.O. Box 9, Quinault, WA 98575; 360/288-2525, fax 360/352-2676.

69 Falls Creek

 8

This scenic, wooded three-acre camp is set where Falls Creek empties into Quinault Lake. A canopy of lush bigleaf maple hangs over the campground. The elevation is 200 feet. The campsites feature both drive-in and walk-in sites, with the latter requiring about a 125-yard walk. The Quinault Rain Forest Nature Trail and Quinault National Recreation Trail System are nearby. The camp is located adjacent to the Quinault Ranger Station and historic Lake Quinault Lodge.

Location: On Lake Quinault in Olympic National Forest; see the Olympic Peninsula and Coastal Washington, map 5, grid e2.

Campsites, facilities: There are 11 tent sites and 20 sites for trailers or RVs up to 16 feet long. Picnic tables and fire pits are provided. Drinking water, flush toilets, and electricity in the restrooms are available. A camp host has firewood for sale nearby. Some facilities are wheelchair-accessible. Four picnic sites are available nearby. Launching facilities and boat rentals are available at nearby Quinault Lake. Leashed pets are permitted.

Reservations, fees: No reservations. Sites are $11 to $14 per night. Senior discount available. Open Memorial Day through Labor Day.

Directions: From Aberdeen, drive north on U.S. 101 for 38 miles to Quinault and South Shore Road. Turn right (northeast) and drive 2.5 miles to the camp on the southeast shore of Lake Quinault.

Contact: Olympic National Forest, Pacific Ranger District, Quinault Office, P.O. Box 9, Quinault, WA 98575; 360/288-2525, fax 360/352-2676.

70 Gatton Creek Walk-In

 9

This five-acre wooded camp is set on the shore of Lake Quinault (elevation 200 feet), where Gatton Creek empties into it. Reaching the campsites requires about a 100-yard walk from the parking area. A highlight is great views across the lake to the forested slopes of Olympic National Park. The lake is part of the Quinault Indian Nation, which has jurisdiction here. Rules allow a 24-mph speed limit on the lake, but no towing and no personal watercraft. Salmon fishing is catch-and-release only, and fishing opportunities

can vary from year to year; always check regulations. Quinault Lake covers about six square miles. The Quinault Rain Forest Nature Trail and the Quinault National Recreation Trail System are nearby. About nine miles of loop trails are accessible here. This camp, like the others on the lake, is concessionaire operated.

Location: On Lake Quinault in Olympic National Forest; see the Olympic Peninsula and Coastal Washington, map 5, grid e2.

Campsites, facilities: There are five tent sites and eight overflow RV sites (in a parking area). Picnic tables and fire pits are provided. Vault toilets, firewood, and a picnic area are available. Some facilities are wheelchair-accessible. Leashed pets are permitted.

Reservations, fees: No reservations. Sites are $11 per night. There is no charge for picnicking. Open from May through September.

Directions: From Aberdeen, drive north on U.S. 101 for 38 miles to the Lake Quinault turnoff and South Shore Road. Turn right (northeast) and drive 3.5 miles to the camp on the southeast shore of Lake Quinault.

Contact: Olympic National Forest, Pacific Ranger District, Quinault Office, P.O. Box 9, Quinault, WA 98575; 360/288-2525, fax 360/352-2676.

71 Campbell Tree Grove

8

This 14-acre camp is set amid dense, old-growth forest featuring stands of both conifers and hardwoods, with licorice ferns growing on the trunks and branches of the bigleaf maples. The camp is a favorite for hikers, with trailheads nearby that provide access to the Colonel Bob Wilderness. One of the best is the 3,400-foot climb to the Colonel Bob Summit, a four-mile round-trip accessible from camp, much of it a great buttkicker. The West Fork of the Humptulips River runs near the camp, and the Humptulips Trail provides access. Fishing is an option here as well; check state regulations.

Location: On the Humptulips River in Olympic National Forest; see the Olympic Peninsula and Coastal Washington, map 5, grid e3.

Campsites, facilities: There are eight tent sites and three sites for trailers or RVs up to 16 feet long. Picnic tables are provided. Vault toilets and drinking water (well water) are available. Some facilities are wheelchair-accessible. Leashed pets are permitted.

Reservations, fees: No reservations; no fee. The campground is open June through October.

Directions: From Aberdeen, drive north on U.S. 101 for 22 miles to Humptulips and continue for another five miles to Forest Road 22 (Donkey Creek Road). Turn right and drive eight miles to Forest Road 2204. Turn left (north) and drive 17 miles to the campground.

Contact: Olympic National Forest, Pacific Ranger District, Quinault Office, P.O. Box 9, Quinault, WA 98575; 360/288-2525, fax 360/352-2676.

Graves Creek

 6

This camp located at an elevation of 540 feet is a short distance from a trailhead leading into the backcountry of Olympic National Park. See an Olympic National Park and U.S. Forest Service map for details. The East Fork Quinault River is nearby, and there are lakes in the area. As of spring 2002, this campground was closed due to damage to a bridge on the access road from the flood of 1999. Call for current status before planning a trip here.

Location: Near the Quinault River in Olympic National Park; see the Olympic Peninsula and Coastal Washington, map 5, grid d4.

Campsites, facilities: There are 30 sites for tents or RVs up to 21 feet long. Picnic tables, fire grills, drinking water, and restrooms are available. Some facilities are wheelchair-accessible. Leashed pets are permitted.

Reservations, fees: No reservations. There is a $10 per-night fee, plus $10 national park entrance fee per vehicle. Senior discount available. Camp opening pending repairs to bridge on access road.

Directions: From Aberdeen, drive north on U.S. 101 for 38 miles to the Lake Quinault turnoff and South Shore Road. Turn east on South Shore Road and drive 15 miles (the road becomes unpaved) to the campground at the end of the road. The Graves Creek Ranger Station is located nearby.

Contact: Olympic National Park, 600 East Park Avenue, Port Angeles, WA 98362; 360/565-3130, fax 360/565-3147.

Staircase

 9

This camp is located near the Staircase Rapids of the North Fork of the Skokomish River, about one mile from where it empties into Lake Cushman. The elevation is 765 feet. A major trailhead at the camp leads to the backcountry of Olympic National Park, and other trails are nearby. See an Olympic National Park and U.S. Forest Service map for details. A beautiful two-mile loop trail running along the river is closed as of spring 2002 due to a bridge closure. Call before planning this hike. Other trails are accessible nearby. Stock facilities are also available nearby.

Location: On the North Fork of the Skokomish River in Olympic National Park; see the Olympic Peninsula and Coastal Washington, map 5, grid d6.

Campsites, facilities: There are 56 sites for tents or RVs up to 21 feet long. Picnic tables and fire grills are provided. Restrooms and drinking water are available. Some facilities are wheelchair-accessible. Leashed pets are permitted in camp.

Reservations, fees: No reservations. There is a $10 per-night fee, plus $10 national park entrance fee per vehicle. Senior discount available. Open year-round.

Directions: From Olympia on I-5, take U.S. 101 and drive north about 37 miles to the town of Hoodsport and Lake Cushman Road (County Road 119). Turn left (west) and drive 17 miles to the camp at the end of the road (set about one mile above the inlet of Lake Cushman). The last several miles of the road are unpaved.

Contact: Olympic National Park, 600 East Park Avenue, Port Angeles, WA 98362; 360/565-3130, fax 360/565-3147.

Lilliwaup Creek

  7

This camp is set along Lilliwaup Creek, a quiet and primitive setting. Fishing for trout is available here, as well as at nearby Lake Cushman, Melbourne, and Prices lakes.

Location: On Lilliwaup Creek in Bert Cole State Forest; see the Olympic Peninsula and Coastal Washington, map 5, grid b1; see the Olympic Peninsula and Coastal Washington, map 5, grid d7.

Campsites, facilities: There are 13 sites for tents or small trailers. Picnic tables, fire grills, vault toilets, and tent pads are provided. No drinking water is available. Garbage must be packed out. Leashed pets are permitted.

Reservations, fees: No reservations; no fee. Open mid-April through October

Directions: From Olympia on I-5, turn north on U.S. 101 and drive 41 miles to Lilliwaup (four miles north of Hoodsport). Continue north on U.S. 101 for seven miles to Jorsted

Creek Road (Forest Road 24). Turn left and drive 1.5 miles to a fork. Bear left at the fork (still Forest Road 24) and drive five miles to the camp.

Contact: Department of Natural Resources, South Puget Sound Region, 950 Farman Avenue North, Enumclaw, WA 98022; 360/825-1631, fax 360/825-1672.

Melbourne

  7

This primitive camp is on Melbourne Lake at about 1,000 feet in a little-known, rustic setting. Melbourne Lake is a small, lesser-known lake on the southeast flank of the Olympic Mountains in Hood Canal State Forest. It provides fishing for bass and trout. If you want quiet, and don't mind a lack of facilities, this is a good drive-to option.

Location: On Melbourne Lake in Hood Canal State Forest; see the Olympic Peninsula and Coastal Washington, map 5, grid d7.

Campsites, facilities: There are five sites for tents or small trailers. Picnic tables, fire grills, vault toilets, and tent pads are provided. No drinking water is available. Garbage must be packed out. Leashed pets are permitted.

Reservations, fees: No reservations; no fee. Open mid-April through September.

Directions: From Olympia on I-5, turn north on U.S. 101 and drive 41 miles to Lilliwaup (four miles north of Hoodsport). Continue north on U.S. 101 for seven miles to Jorsted Creek Road (Forest Road 24). Turn left and drive 1.5 miles to a fork. Bear left at the fork (still Forest Road 24) and drive four miles to a gravel road. Turn left on the gravel road and drive 1.7 miles to a T, turn left, and drive one mile to the camp at Melbourne Lake.

Contact: Department of Natural Resources, South Puget Sound Region, 950 Farman

Avenue North, Enumclaw, WA 98022; 360/825-1631, fax 360/825-1672.

76 Lake Cushman State Park

 10

This state park is set in the foothills of the Olympic Mountains on the shore of Lake Cushman. It features a blue-water mountain lake that is 10 miles long, eight miles of park shoreline, forested hillsides, and awesome views of snowcapped peaks. Beach access and good trout fishing are other highlights. The park has eight miles of hiking trails and five miles of bike trails. In fall, mushrooming is popular. Windsurfing, waterskiing, and swimming are all popular here. An 18-hole golf course is nearby.

Location: On Lake Cushman; see the Olympic Peninsula and Coastal Washington, map 5, grid e7.

Campsites, facilities: There are 50 tent sites, 30 with full hookups for trailers or RVs up to 60 feet long, and two primitive sites. Picnic tables and fire grills are provided. Restrooms, drinking water, flush toilets, showers, a picnic area, an amphitheater, horseshoe pits, volleyball, and firewood are available. A store, a restaurant, and ice are available within one mile. Boat docks and launching facilities are located at nearby Lake Cushman. Leashed pets are permitted.

Reservations, fees: Reserve at 888/CAMP-OUT (888/226-7688); website: www.parks .wa.gov/reservations ($7 reservation fee). Sites are $15 to $22 per night, $6 per extra vehicle per night. Senior discount available. Major credit cards accepted. Open April through October.

Directions: From Olympia on I-5, take the U.S. 101 exit and drive north 37 miles to Hoodsport and Highway 119 (Lake Cushman

Road). Turn west (left) on Lake Cushman Road and drive seven miles to the park on the left.

Contact: Lake Cushman State Park, 360/877-5491; State Park information, 360/902-8844.

77 Big Creek

 7

Big Creek is an alternative to Staircase camp on the North Fork Skokomish River and Lake Cushman State Park on Lake Cushman, both of which get heavier use. The sites here are large and well spaced for privacy over 30 acres, primarily a second-growth forest. Big Creek is adjacent to the campground. A four-mile loop trail extends from camp and connects to the Mt. Eleanor Trail. A bonus are two walk-in sites (quarter-mile walk), which are located along the creek.

Location: Near Lake Cushman in Olympic National Forest; see the Olympic Peninsula and Coastal Washington, map 5, grid e7.

Campsites, facilities: There are 23 sites for tents or RVs up to 30 feet long, and two walk-in sites (requiring a quarter-mile walk). Picnic tables and fire grills are provided. Drinking water, vault toilets, and sheltered picnic tables are available. A boat dock and ramp are located at nearby Lake Cushman. Leashed pets are permitted.

Reservations, fees: No reservations. Sites are $10 per night. Senior discount available. Open May through September.

Directions: From Olympia on I-5, take Exit 104 for U.S. 101/Highway 8. Drive north on U.S. 101 for 37 miles to Hoodsport and Lake Cushman Road (Highway 119). Turn left on Lake Cushman Road and drive nine miles (two miles north of Lake Cushman State Park) to the T intersection. Turn left and the campground is on the right.

Contact: Olympic National Forest, Hood Canal Ranger District, Hoodsport Office, P.O.

Box 68, Hoodsport, WA 94548; 360/877-5254, fax 360/352-2569.

Coho

 10

This eight-acre camp is set on the shore of Wynoochee Lake, which is 4.4 miles long and covers 1,140 acres. The camp is set an elevation of 900 feet. The fishing season opens June 1 and closes October 31. Power boats, water-skiing, and personal watercraft are permitted. Points of interest include the Working Forest Trail, Wynoochee Dam Viewpoint and exhibits, and the 16-mile Wynoochee Lake Shore Trail, which circles the lake. This is one of the most idyllic drive-to settings you could hope to find.

Location: On Wynoochee Lake in Olympic National Forest; see the Olympic Peninsula and Coastal Washington, map 5, grid e4.

Campsites, facilities: There are 58 sites for tents, trailers, or RVs up to 36 feet long. Picnic tables are provided. Restrooms, flush toilets, and drinking water are available. There is a dump station nearby. Some facilities are wheelchair-accessible. Boat docks and launching facilities are available at Wynoochee Lake. Leashed pets are permitted.

Reservations, fees: No reservations. Sites are $10 to $12 per night. Senior discount available. Open May through September.

Directions: From Olympia on I-5, take Exit 104 and drive north on U.S. 101 to the Aberdeen/Highway 8 exit. Turn west on Highway 8 and drive 36 miles (it becomes Highway 12 at Elma) to Montesano. Continue two miles on Highway 12 to Wynoochee Valley Road. Turn north on Wynoochee Valley Road and drive 12 miles to Forest Road 22. Continue north on Forest Road 22 (a gravel road) to Wynoochee Lake. Just south of the lake,

bear left and drive on Forest Road 2294 (which runs along the lake's northwest shore) for one mile to the camp on the west shore of Wynoochee Lake. Obtaining a U.S. Forest Service map is helpful.

Contact: Olympic National Forest, Hood Canal Ranger District, Hoodsport Office, P.O. Box 68, Hoodsport, WA 98548; 360/877-5254.

Brown Creek

 9

Brown Creek is little known among out-of-town visitors. While this camp is accessible to two-wheel-drive vehicles, the road connects to a network of primitive, backcountry forest roads. The small campground (just six acres) is within the vast Olympic National Forest, which offers many opportunities for outdoor recreation. The wheelchair-accessible Brown Creek Nature Trail begins at the hand pump and makes a one-mile loop around the camp, featuring views of an active beaver pond. Obtain a U.S. Forest Service map to expand your trip. Note that in 2002 or 2003, this camp is scheduled to be moved out of the riparian area; check for possible short-term closures.

Location: On Brown Creek in Olympic National Forest; see the Olympic Peninsula and Coastal Washington, map 5, grid e6.

Campsites, facilities: There are seven tent sites and 12 sites for trailers or RVs up to 25 feet long. Picnic tables and fire rings are provided. Drinking water and vault toilets are available. Leashed pets are permitted.

Reservations, fees: No reservations. Sites are $5 to $10 per night. Open year-round, with limited winter facilities.

Directions: From Olympia on I-5, take Exit 104 for U.S. 101/Highway 8. Drive north on U.S. 101 for 31 miles (about six miles past Shelton) to Skokomish Valley Road. Turn left and drive five miles (the road becomes Forest Road 23). Continue on Forest Road 23 for nine miles to Forest Road 2353. Bear right (cross the bridge) and drive to Forest Road 2340. Turn right and continue to the campground sign and drive three-quarters mile to the camp. Obtaining a U.S. Forest Service map is advisable.

Contact: Olympic National Forest, Hood Canal Ranger District, Hoodsport Office, P.O. Box 68, Hoodsport, WA 94548; 360/877-5254, fax 360/352-2569.

80 LeBar Horse Camp

     9

Campers with horses or pack animals, such as mules, mollies, llamas, and goats, are allowed to camp here. The camp provides access to the Lower South Fork Skokomish Trail, a 10.9-mile trip, one-way. The camp features beautiful old-growth forest, with western hemlock and Douglas fir.

Location: In Olympic National Forest; see the Olympic Peninsula and Coastal Washington, map 5, grid e6.

Campsites, facilities: There are 13 sites for tents, trailers, or RVs up to 21 feet long for the exclusive use of campers with pack animals. Picnic tables, fire grills, and hitching posts are provided. Drinking water and vault toilets are available. Garbage must be packed out. A day-use area with picnic shelter is available nearby. Some facilities are wheelchair-accessible. Leashed pets are permitted.

Reservations, fees: No reservations. Sites are $10 per night. Senior discount available. Open May through September.

Directions: From Olympia on I-5, take Exit 104 for U.S. 101/Highway 8. Drive north on U.S. 101 for 31 miles (about six miles past Shelton) to Skokomish Valley Road. Turn left and drive five miles (the road becomes Forest Road 23). Continue on Forest Road 23 for

nine miles (it becomes Forest Road 2353). When you cross the bridge, turn left, and stay on Forest Road 2353 (do not go straight to Forest Road 2340) and drive one mile to the campground on the right.

Contact: Olympic National Forest, Hood Canal Ranger District, P.O. Box 68, Hoodsport, WA 94548; 360/877-5254, fax 360/352-2569.

81 Rest-a-While RV Park

     5

This seven-acre park, located at sea level on the Hood Canal, offers waterfront sites and a private beach for clamming and oyster gathering, not to mention plenty of opportunities to fish, boat, and scuba dive. It's an alternative to Potlatch State Park and Glen Ayr RV Park.

Location: On the Hood Canal; see the Olympic Peninsula and Coastal Washington, map 5, grid e7.

Campsites, facilities: There are 80 sites with full hookups, including some drive-through, for trailers or RVs of any length, and two tent sites. Picnic tables and fire rings are provided. Restrooms, drinking water, flush toilets, showers, bottled gas, firewood, a clubhouse, a store, a seafood market, a drive-in restaurant, laundry facilities, and ice are available. A café is within walking distance. Boat docks, launching facilities, a scuba diving shop, seasonal boat and kayak rentals, and a private beach for clamming and oyster gathering are also available. Leashed pets are permitted.

Reservations, fees: Reservations accepted. Sites are $20 to $25 per night, $2 per extra vehicle per night, $4 per person per night for more than two people. Major credit cards accepted. Open year-round.

Directions: From Olympia on I-5, take Exit 104 for U.S. 101/Highway 8. Drive north on U.S. 101 for 37 miles to Hoodsport. Continue 2.5 miles north on U.S. 101 to the park located at Milepost 329.

Contact: Rest-a-While RV Park, North 27001 U.S. Highway 101, Hoodsport, WA 98548; 360/877-9474; website: www.restawhile.com.

82 Glen-Ayr RV Park & Motel

 5

This adults-only, fully developed, nine-acre park is located at sea level on the Hood Canal, where there are opportunities to fish and scuba dive. Salmon fishing is especially excellent. Swimming and boating are two other options. The park has a spa, moorage, horseshoe pits, a recreation field, and a motel.

Location: On the Hood Canal; see the Olympic Peninsula and Coastal Washington, map 5, grid e7.

Campsites, facilities: There are 40 sites with full hookups, including some drive-through, for trailers or RVs of any length, 14 motel rooms, and two suites with kitchens. Restrooms, drinking water, flush toilets, showers, picnic tables, bottled gas, a spa, a recreation hall, horseshoe pits, and a coin-operated laundry are available. A store, a café, and ice are within one mile. A boat dock is located across the street from the park. Leashed pets are permitted.

Reservations, fees: Campers must be 18 years of age or older. Reservations accepted. Sites are $26.50 per night, $4 per person per night for more than two people. Major credit cards accepted. Open year-round.

Directions: From Olympia on I-5, take Exit 104 for U.S. 101/Highway 8. Drive north on U.S. 101 for 37 miles to Hoodsport. Continue one mile north on U.S. 101 to the park on the left.

Contact: Glen-Ayr RV Park & Motel, 25381 North U.S. 101, Hoodsport, WA 98548; 800/367-9522 or 360/877-9522.

83 Minerva Beach Resort

 5

This resort is on Hood Canal, a layover spot if you're cruising up or down U.S. 101. For the highly sensitive, road noise is discernible. While there are some permanent rentals here, they are located in a separate area, apart from the campground. Recreational opportunities at this park include salmon fishing, crabbing, and digging for oysters and clams in season; check regulations. A winery is located three miles to the north. A good side trip is nearby Potlatch State Park.

Location: On the Hood Canal; see the Olympic Peninsula and Coastal Washington, map 5, grid e7.

Campsites, facilities: There are 23 sites with full hookups for trailers or RVs up to 50 feet and 20 tent sites. Picnic tables and fire grills are provided. Restrooms, drinking water, flush toilets, coin-operated showers, cable TV, a public phone, a coin-operated laundry, limited groceries, ice, RV supplies, and LP gas are available. Horseshoe pits and a gift shop are nearby. Leashed pets are permitted.

Reservations, fees: Reservations recommended. Sites are $13 to $20 per night, $2 per person per night for more than two people. Major credit cards accepted. Open year-round.

Directions: From Tumwater/Olympia, take the U.S. 101 exit and drive north to Shelton. Continue north for 10 miles past Potlatch State Park to the resort entrance on the left.

Contact: Minerva Beach Resort, 21110 Highway 101 North, Shelton, WA 98584; 360/877-5145 or 866/500-5145; website: http://home.att.net/minerva beach.

84 Potlatch State Park

 8

This state park features good shellfish harvesting in season, and to celebrate it, hosts an annual "Shellfish Shindig" every April. The park has 9,570 feet of shoreline on the Hood Canal. There are 1.5 miles of trails for hiking and biking, but the shoreline and water brings people here, with good kayaking, windsurfing, scuba diving, clamming, and fishing. The park is named for the potlatch, which is a gift-giving ceremony of the Skokomish Indians. There are four major rivers within a 30-mile radius of the park. They are the Skokomish, Hamma Hamma, Duckabush, and Dosewallips. The park receives an annual rainfall of 64 inches.

Location: On the Hood Canal; see the Olympic Peninsula and Coastal Washington, map 5, grid f7.

Campsites, facilities: There are 18 drive-through sites with full hookups for trailers or RVs up to 60 feet long, 17 developed tent sites, and two primitive tent sites. Picnic tables and fire grills are provided. Restrooms, drinking water, flush toilets, showers, a dump station, firewood, an amphitheater, a picnic area, and interpretive programs are available. A boat launch and five mooring buoys are located at the park, and boat docks are available nearby at the Hood Canal. Leashed pets are permitted.

Reservations, fees: No reservations. Sites are $6 to $22 per night, $6 per extra vehicle per night, $7 to $16 for mooring buoys. Senior discount available. Open April through October.

Directions: From Olympia on I-5, take Exit 104 for U.S. 101/Highway 8. Drive north on U.S. 101 for 22 miles to Shelton. Continue north on U.S. 101 for 12 miles to the park on the right (located along the shoreline of Annas Bay in the Hood Canal).

Contact: Potlatch State Park, 360/877-5361; State Park information, 360/902-8844.

85 Riverview Recreation Area

 7

This five-acre camp is set along the Humptulips River. It is a pretty spot, with boating and fishing access not far from camp. It's a good layover if you're cruising U.S. 101, but is popular and relatively small; reservations are advised.

Location: On the Humptulips River; see the Olympic Peninsula and Coastal Washington, map 5, grid g1.

Campsites, facilities: There are 12 sites with full hookups, including six drive-through, for trailers or RVs of any length, eight tent sites, and four cabins. Picnic tables and fire rings are provided. Restrooms, drinking water, flush toilets, and showers are available. A store, a café, and ice are within one mile. Boat-launching facilities are located nearby at the Humptulips River. Leashed pets are permitted.

Reservations, fees: No reservations accepted. Sites are $10 to $15 per night, cabins are $45 per night. Open January through September; cabins available year-round.

Directions: From Aberdeen, drive north on U.S. 101 for 22 miles to Humptulips and Kirkpatrick Road. Turn left (west) on Kirkpatrick Road and drive one quarter-mile to the park on the left.

Contact: Riverview Recreation Area, P.O. Box 97, 8 River View Drive, Humptulips, WA 98552; 360/987-2216 (phone or fax).

86 Schafer State Park

 8

This is a unique destination, with many interesting features, including buildings constructed from native stone. This heavily wooded, rural camp covers 119 acres along the East Fork of the Satsop River. The river is well known for fishing and rafting. Fishing includes for sea-run cutthroat in summer, salmon in fall, and steelhead in late winter. There are good canoeing and kayaking spots, some with Class II and III rapids, along the Middle and West Forks of the Satsop. Two miles of hiking trails are also available. At one time, this park was the Schafer Logging Company Park and was used by employees and their families.

Location: On the Satsop River; see the Olympic Peninsula and Coastal Washington, map 5, grid g5.

Campsites, facilities: There are 34 developed tent sites, six sites with partial hookups (water and electricity) for trailers or RVs up to 40 feet long, and two primitive tent sites. Picnic tables and fire grills are provided. Restrooms, drinking water, flush toilets, showers, a covered picnic shelter, interpretive activities, a dump station, and a playground with horseshoe pits are available. Some facilities are wheelchair-accessible. Leashed pets are permitted.

Reservations, fees: No reservations accepted. Sites are $6 to $22 per night, $6 per extra vehicle per night. Senior discount available. Open May through September.

Directions: From Olympia on I-5, take Exit 104 to U.S. 101. Drive west on U.S. 101 six miles to Highway 8. Turn west on Highway 8 to Elma (Highway 8 becomes Highway 12). Continue west on Highway 12 for seven miles to East Satsop Road (four miles east of Montesano). Turn north (right) and drive five miles to the park. The park is 12 miles north of Elma.

Contact: Schafer State Park, 360/482-3852; State Park information, 360/902-8844.

87 Lake Sylvia State Park

 8

This 234-acre state park on the shore of Lake Sylvia features nearly three miles of freshwater shoreline. The park is located in a former logging camp in a wooded area set midway between Olympia and the Pacific Ocean. The park has rustic charm, with displays of old logging gear, a giant ball carved out of wood from a single log, and some monstrous-sized stumps. The lake is good for fishing and ideal for canoes, prams, or small boats with oars or electric motors; no gas motors are permitted. The park has five miles of trails for hiking and a half-mile trail that is wheelchair-accessible. Additional recreation options include trout fishing and swimming. If Lake Sylvia is full, nearby camps are East Crossing and Rainbow Cove.

Location: On Lake Sylvia; see the Olympic Peninsula and Coastal Washington, map 5, grid h4.

Campsites, facilities: There are 35 sites for tents or self-contained RVs up to 30 feet long, two primitive tent sites, and one group site for up to 10 people. Picnic tables and fire grills are provided. Drinking water and vault toilets are available. Restrooms, drinking water, flush toilets, showers, a dump station, a store, fishing supplies, a boat launch, boat rentals, a picnic area, and a playground are available. A fee is charged for showers and firewood. Laundry facilities and ice are located within one mile. Some facilities are wheelchair-accessible. Leashed pets are permitted.

Reservations, fees: No reservations accepted. Sites are $6 to $16 per night, $6 per extra vehicle per night, group site requires $25 reservation fee plus $2 per person with a 20-person minimum. Senior discount available. Open early April to early October.

Directions: From Olympia on I-5, take Exit 104 to U.S. 101. Drive west on U.S. 101 six miles to Highway 8. Turn west on Highway 8 and drive 26 miles to Montesano and the last exit, Highway 7. Take Highway 7 and drive to Pioneer (the only stoplight in town). Turn left on Pioneer and drive three blocks to Third Street. Turn right and drive two miles to the park entrance (route is well signed).

Contact: Lake Sylvia State Park, Montesano, WA 98563; 360/249-3621; State Park information, 360/902-8844.

88 Travel Inn Resort

 7

This is a membership campground, which means sites for RV travelers are available only if there is extra space. It can be difficult to get a spot from May through September, but the park opens up significantly in the off-season. There are five major rivers or lakes within 15 minutes of this camp (Satsop, Chehalis, Wynoochee, Black River, and Lake Sylvia). Nearby Lake Sylvia State Park provides multiple marked hiking trails. Additional recreation options include trout fishing, swimming, and golf (three miles away).

Location: On Lake Sylvia; see the Olympic Peninsula and Coastal Washington, map 5, grid h5.

Campsites, facilities: There are 144 sites with full or partial hookups for trailers or RVs of any length and 10 tent sites. Picnic tables and fire grills are provided. Restrooms, drinking water, flush toilets, showers, a public phone, a coin-operated laundry, two community fire pits, a gazebo, a heated swimming pool, a game room, cable TV, and a social hall are available. A grocery store and restaurant are available within one mile. Some facilities are wheelchair-accessible. Leashed pets are permitted.

Reservations, fees: Reservations required from May through September at 800/871-2888. Sites are $30 per night, plus $1 each for electricity or cable TV hookups. Open year-round.

Directions: From Olympia on I-5, take Exit 104 to U.S. 101. Drive west on U.S. 101 six miles to Highway 8. Turn west on Highway 8 and drive to Elma. Take the first Elma exit and at the stop sign at Highway 12, turn right and drive about 200 yards to the end of the highway and a stop sign. Turn right and drive about 200 yards to the resort on the right.

Contact: Travel Inn Resort, 801 East Main Street, Elma, WA 98541; 800/871-2888 or 360/482-3877.

89 Falls View

 8

A viewing area to a pretty waterfall on the Big Quilcene River is only a 150-foot walk form the campground, where you see a narrow, 100-foot cascade. That is why despite the rustic setting, this spot on the edge of the Olympic National Forest has a host of facilities and is popular. The setting is a forest of mixed conifers and rhododendrons. A one-mile scenic loop trail is located high above the river and provides views of the waterfall. A picnic area is also located near the waterfall.

Location: On the Big Quilcene River in Olympic National Forest; see the Olympic Peninsula and Coastal Washington, map 6, grid b1.

Campsites, facilities: There are 30 sites for tents, trailers, or RVs up to 21 feet long. Picnic tables are provided. Restrooms, drinking water, and flush toilets are available. Some facilities are wheelchair-accessible. Leashed pets are permitted.

Reservations, fees: No reservations. Sites are $10 per night. Senior discount available. Open May to mid-September.

Directions: From Olympia on I-5, turn north on U.S. 101 and drive approximately 70 miles to the campground entrance on the left (located about four miles south of Quilcene).

Contact: Olympic National Forest, Quilcene Ranger District, P.O. Box 280, Quilcene, WA 98376; 360/765-2200, fax 360/765-2202.

90 Rainbow Group Camp

 7

Rainbow Group Camp is in a rugged, primitive setting on the edge of Olympic National Forest. This area is heavily wooded with old-growth and new-growth forest, a variety of wildflowers, and spring-blooming rhododendrons. The Rainbow Canyon Trailhead is located at the far side of the campground. This provides a short hike to the Big Quicene River and a waterfall. It is fairly steep, but not a buttkicker. There is also considerable backcountry access provided on forest roads (obtaining a U.S. Forest Service map is advisable). The nearest is Forest Road 2730, just 0.1 mile away, and leads to spectacular scenery at the Mt. Walker Observation Area. Olympic National Park is also just a short drive away.

Location: Near Quilcene in Olympic National Forest; see the Olympic Peninsula and Coastal Washington, map 6, grid c1.

Campsites, facilities: There are nine sites for tents and small RVs that are reserved for groups up to 50 people. Picnic tables and fire grills are provided. Drinking water and vault

toilets are available. A store, a café, a coin-operated laundry, and ice are within five miles. Leashed pets are permitted.

Reservations, fees: Reservations required at 360/765-2200. Group site is $50 per night.

Directions: From I-5 at Olympia, go north on U.S. 101 and drive approximately 69 miles to the campground (about six miles past Dosewallips State Park) on the left (near Walker Pass).

Contact: Olympic National Forest, Quilcene Ranger District, P.O. Box 280, Quilcene, WA 98376; 360/765-2200, fax 360/765-2202.

91 Cove RV Park

 5

This five-acre private camp is in a rural setting, yet it's fully developed with the shore of Dabob Bay nearby. Sites are grassy and graveled with a few trees. Scuba diving is popular in this area, and this park sells air for scuba tanks. Dosewallips State Park is a short drive away and a possible side trip.

Location: Near Dabob Bay; see the Olympic Peninsula and Coastal Washington, map 6, grid c1.

Campsites, facilities: There are 32 sites with full hookups (including cable TV) for trailers or RVs up to 40 feet and six tent sites. Picnic tables and fire rings (in season) are provided. Restrooms, drinking water, flush toilets, coin-operated showers, bottled gas, a dump station, a store, a coin-operated laundry, and ice are available. Boat docks and launching facilities are on the Hood Canal 2.2 miles from the park. Leashed pets are permitted.

Reservations, fees: Reservations accepted. Sites are $14 to $18.50 per night, $3 per person per night for more than two people (over 12). Major credit cards accepted. Open year-round.

Directions: From Olympia on I-5, drive north on U.S. 101

for 60 miles to Brinnon (located about one mile north of Dosewallips State Park). Continue three miles north on U.S. 101 to the park on the right (before Milepost 303).

Contact: Cove RV Park, 303075 Highway 101, Brinnon, WA 98320; 866/796-4723 or 360/796-4723, fax 360/796-3452.

92 Seal Rock

 9

Seal Rock is a 30-acre camp set along the shore near the mouth of Dabob Bay. This is one of the few national forest campgrounds anywhere located on saltwater. It brings with it the opportunity to harvest oysters and clams in season, and an outstanding jumping-off point for scuba diving. Most campsites are set along the waterfront, spaced among trees. Carry-in boats, such as kayaks and canoes, can be launched from the north landing. The Native American Nature Trail and the Marine Biology Nature Trail begin at the day-use area. These are short walks, each less than a half mile. This camp is extremely popular in the summer, often filling up quickly.

Location: On Dabob Bay in Olympic National Forest; see the Olympic Peninsula and Coastal Washington, map 6, grid c1.

Campsites, facilities: There are 40 sites for tents, trailers, or RVs up to 21 feet long. Picnic tables and fire rings are provided. Restrooms, drinking water, flush toilets, a picnic area, and a public telephone are available. Some facilities are wheelchair-accessible, including viewing areas and trails. A camp host is on-site in summer. Boat docks and launching facilities are nearby on the Hood Canal and in Dabob Bay. Leashed pets are permitted.

Reservations, fees: No reservations. Sites are $12 per night. Senior discount available. Open mid-April through September.

Directions: From Olympia on I-5, drive north on U.S. 101 for 60 miles to Brinnon (located about one mile north of Dosewallips State Park). Continue two miles north on U.S. 101 to Seal Rock and the camp on the right.

Contact: Olympic National Forest, Quilcene Ranger District, P.O. Box 280, Quilcene, WA 98376; 360/765-2200, fax 360/765-2202.

93 Dosewallips State Park

 8

This 425-acre park is set on the shore of the Hood Canal at the mouth of Dosewallips River. It features 5,500 feet of saltwater shoreline on Hood Canal and 5,400 feet of shoreline on both sides of the Dosewallips River. All campsites are grassy and located in scenic, rustic settings. Mushrooming is available in season. Check regulations for fishing and clamming, which fluctuate according to time and season. This camp is popular because it's set right off a major highway; reservations or early arrival are advised.

Location: On Dosewallips Creek; see the Olympic Peninsula and Coastal Washington, map 6, grid c1.

Campsites, facilities: There are 90 sites, including 40 with full hookups, for tents, trailers, or RVs up to 60 feet long, and two primitive sites. Picnic tables and fire rings are provided. Restrooms, drinking water, flush toilets, coin-operated showers, a sheltered picnic area, interpretive activities, and a summer Junior Ranger Program are available. A wildlife-viewing platform, horseshoe pits, saltwater boat-launching facilities, a recreation hall, a store, a café, and laundry facilities are available nearby. Some facilities are wheelchair-accessible. Leashed pets are permitted.

Reservations, fees: Reserve at 888/CAMP-OUT (888/226-7688); website: www.parks.wa.gov/reservations ($7 reservation fee). Sites are $6 to $22 per night, $6 per extra vehicle per night. Senior discount available. Major credit cards accepted. Open year-round.

Directions: From Olympia on I-5, drive north on U.S. 101 for 61 miles (one mile south of Brinnon) to the state park entrance on the right.

Contact: Dosewallips State Park, 360/796-4415; State Park information, 360/902-8844.

94 Scenic Beach State Park

    10

Scenic Beach is an exceptionally beautiful state park, with beach access and superb views of the Olympic Mountains. It features 1,500 feet of saltwater beachfront on Hood Canal. The park is also known for its wild rhododendrons in spring. Paths that are wheelchair-accessible lead to a country garden, gazebo, rustic bridge, and large trees. Many species of birds and wildlife can often be seen here. This camp is also close to Green Mountain Forest, where there is extensive hiking. A boat ramp is one-half mile east of the park, with dock and moorage available at Seabeck, one mile east of the park. A nice touch here by park staff is that they will check out volleyballs and horseshoes during the summer.

Location: On the Hood Canal; see the Olympic Peninsula and Coastal Washington, map 6, grid c2.

Campsites, facilities: There are 50 sites for tents, trailers, or self-contained RVs up to 40 feet long. Picnic tables and fire grills are provided. Restrooms, drinking water, flush toilets, coin-operated showers, and a dump station are available. A sheltered picnic area,

horseshoe pits, and volleyball fields (from May through August) are available nearby. Some facilities are wheelchair-accessible. Leashed pets are permitted.

Reservations, fees: Reserve at 888/CAMP-OUT (888/226-7688); website: www.parks.wa.gov/reservations ($7 reservation fee). Sites are $16 per night, $6 per extra vehicle per night. Senior discount available. Open April to mid-November.

Directions: From Tacoma at I-5, turn north on Highway 16 and drive 30 miles to Bremerton to the junction with Highway 3. Turn north on Highway 3 and drive about nine miles and take the first Silverdale exit (Newberry Hill Road.). Turn left and drive approximately three miles to the end of the road. Turn right on Seabeck Highway and drive six miles to Scenic Beach Road. Turn right and drive one mile to the park.

Contact: Scenic Beach State Park; 360/830-5079; State Park information, 360/902-8844.

95 Kitsap Memorial State Park

     10

Kitsap Memorial State Park is a beautiful spot for tent campers along the Hood Canal. The park covers only 58 acres but features sweeping views of Puget Sound and 1,797 feet of shoreline. The park has 1.5 miles of hiking trails and two open grassy fields for family play. Note that the nearest boat launch is four miles away, north on State Route 3 at Salisbury County Park. An 18-hole golf course and swimming, fishing, and hiking at nearby Anderson Lake Recreation Area are among the activities available. A short drive north will take you to historic Old Fort Townsend, which is an excellent day trip.

Location: On the Hood Canal; see the Olympic Peninsula and Coastal Washington, map 6, grid b3.

Campsites, facilities: There are 25 sites for tents, trailers, or self-contained RVs up to 30 feet long, 18 sites with partial hookups (water and electricity) for trailers or RVs, and three primitive tent sites. Picnic tables and fire grills are provided. Restrooms, drinking water, flush toilets, showers, a dump station, a sheltered picnic area, firewood, and a playground are available. One boat buoy is available. Leashed pets are permitted.

Reservations, fees: No reservations. Sites are $6 to $22 per night. Senior discount available. Open year-round.

Directions: From Tacoma on I-5, turn north on Highway 16 and drive 44 miles (Highway 16 turns into Highway 3). Continue north on Highway 3 and drive six miles to Park Street. Turn left and drive 200 yards to the park entrance on the right (well marked). The park is located four miles south of the Hood Canal Bridge.

Contact: Kitsap Memorial State Park, 202 N.E. Park Street, Poulsbo, WA 98370; 360/779-3205; State Park information, 360/902-8844.

96 Captain's Landing

    8

The camp overlooks Puget Sound, right next to the water. It is very rural along Admiralty Inlet. Visiting the Point-No-Point is within walking distance, with tours available on weekends. Trout fishing at Buck Lake is three miles away. Grassy, open sites make this a good choice for campers wanting an in-town location. An 18-hole golf course and a full-service marina are close by. A wildlife sanctuary is five miles away. No open fires are permitted.

Location: In Hansville; see the Olympic Peninsula and Coastal Washington, map 6, grid a4.

Campsites, facilities: There are 22 drive-through sites with full hookups for self-contained trailers or RVs of any length, and four cabins. No restrooms are available. No fires are allowed. A store and ice are available. Boat docks, launching facilities, and boat rentals are located within one mile. Leashed pets are permitted.

Reservations, fees: Reservations accepted. Sites are $25 to $30 per night. Cabins are $75 to $150 per night. Open year-round.

Directions: From Bremerton, drive north on Highway 16 for 10 miles (Highway 16 turns into Highway 3) and continue north on Highway 3 for 11 miles to Port Gamble. Bear southeast toward Kingston (still on Highway 3) to Hansville Road (at George's Corner). Turn left on Hansville Road and drive eight miles. The park is on the right side, at the bottom of the hill.

Contact: Captain's Landing, 39118 Hansville Road NE, Hansville, WA 98340; 360/638-2257, fax 360/638-2015.

97 Green Mountain Hike-In & Horse Camp

   7

This is a prime spot—primitive but with hand-pumped water provided. The campground is operated by the Department of Natural Resources and is located in Green Mountain State Forest. There are facilities for horses, and the camp is hosted by the Backcountry Horsemen of Washington.

Location: In Green Mountain State Forest; see the Olympic Peninsula and Coastal Washington, map 6, grid d2.

Campsites, facilities: There are 12 hike-in sites for tents only. Picnic tables, fire grills, and tent pads are provided. Vault toilets, hand-pumped drinking water, a group shelter, and facilities for horses, including horse corrals, are available. Garbage must be packed out.

Reservations, fees: No reservations; no fee. A gate limits vehicular access to the camp weekends from April through September, 9 A.M. to 6 P.M. A free map and brochure are available.

Directions: From Tacoma on I-5, turn north on Highway 16 and drive 30 miles to Bremerton and the junction with Highway 3. Turn north on Highway 3 and drive a short distance to the Seabeck Highway. Turn left and drive three miles to Holly Road. Turn left on Holly Road and drive four miles to Tahuya Lake Road. Turn left and drive one mile to Green Mountain Road and the Department of Natural Resources (DNR) parking lot and trailhead. Hike four miles.

Contact: Department of Natural Resources, South Puget Sound Region, 950 Farman Avenue North, Enumclaw, WA 98022; 360/825-1631, fax 360/825-1672.

98 Fay Bainbridge State Park

 10

This camp is set on the edge of Puget Sound, a beach park that offers beautiful and great recreation. The park covers just 17 acres but features 1,420 feet of saltwater shoreline on the northeast corner of the island. You can hike several miles along the beach at low tide; the water temperature is typically about 55°F in summer. The primitive walk-in sites are heavily wooded, and the developed sites have great views of the sound. On clear days, campers can enjoys views of Mt. Rainier and Mt. Baker to the east, and at night the park provides beautiful vistas of the lights of Seattle. Clamming,

diving, picnicking, beachcombing, and kite flying are popular here. In the winter months, there is excellent salmon fishing just offshore of the park.

Location: On Bainbridge Island; see the Olympic Peninsula and Coastal Washington, map 6, grid c4.

Campsites, facilities: There are 26 sites for tents or self-contained RVs up to 30 feet long and 13 primitive tent sites. Picnic tables and fire grills are provided. Restrooms, drinking water, flush toilets, coin-operated showers, a dump station, a sheltered picnic area, horseshoes, and a playground are available. A store and a café are located within one mile. Firewood can be obtained for a fee. Some facilities are wheelchair-accessible. Boat docks, launching facilities, and mooring buoys are nearby. Leashed pets are permitted.

Reservations, fees: No reservations. Sites are $6 to $16 per night, $6 per extra vehicle per night, $7 to $16 for mooring buoys. Senior discount available. Open mid-April through early October.

Directions: From Tacoma at I-5, turn north on Highway 16 and drive 30 miles to Bremerton to the junction with Highway 3. Turn north on Highway 3 and drive 18 miles to Highway 305. Turn south on Highway 305 and drive over the bridge to Bainbridge Island and continue three miles to Phelps Road Northeast. Turn left (northeast), drive two miles to Port Madison, and continue east one mile to the park entrance (well marked).

Note: From Seattle, this camp can be more easily accessed by taking the Bainbridge Island ferry and then Highway 305 north to the northeast end of the island.

Contact: Fay Bainbridge State Park, 206/842-3931; State Park information, 360/902-8844.

99 Illahee State Park

 9

This 75-acre park features the last stand of old-growth forest in Kitsap County, including one of the largest yew trees in America. The park also features 1,785 feet of saltwater frontage. The campsites are set in a pretty, forested area, and some are grassy. The shoreline is fairly rocky, set on the shore of Port Orchard Bay, although there is a small sandy area for sunbathers. Clamming is popular here. A fishing pier is available for anglers. Note that large vessels can be difficult to launch at the ramp here. *Illahee* means "earth" or "country" in the Native American tradition.

Location: Near Bremerton; see the Olympic Peninsula and Coastal Washington, map 6, grid d4.

Campsites, facilities: There are 25 sites for tents or self-contained trailers or RVs up to 30 feet long, eight primitive tent sites, and one group site for up to 40 people. Picnic tables and fire grills are provided. Restrooms, drinking water, flush toilets, showers, firewood, and a pier are available. Boat docks, launching facilities, 56 mooring buoys, and 356 feet of moorage float space are available. A sheltered picnic area, horseshoes, volleyball, field, and a playground are available nearby. Some facilities are wheelchair-accessible. A coin-operated laundry and ice are located within one mile. Leashed pets are permitted.

Reservations, fees: No reservations. Sites are $6 to $15 per night, $6 per extra vehicle per night, mooring buoys are $7 to $16 per night. Group site requires $25 reservation plus $2 per person per night. Senior discount available. Open year-round.

Directions: On Highway 3, drive to Bremerton and the East Bremerton exit. Drive east for 7.5 miles to Sylvan Way. Turn left and drive 1.5 miles (on the bridge over Port Washington Narrows) to the park entrance road.

Contact: Illahee State Park, 360/478-6460; State Park information, 360/902-8844.

100 Manchester State Park

 9

Manchester State Park is set on the edge of Point Orchard, providing excellent lookouts across Puget Sound. The park covers 111 acres, with 3,400 feet of saltwater shoreline on Rich Passage in Puget Sound. The landscape is filled with fir and maple, which are very pretty in the fall. There are 1.9 miles of hiking trails, including an interpretive trail. The camp gets relatively little use, especially in the off-season, so you're almost always guaranteed a spot. Group and day-use reservations are available. Note that the beach is closed to shellfish harvesting. In the early 1900s, this park site was used as a U.S. Coast Guard defense installation. A gun battery remains from the park's early days, along with two other buildings that are on the register of National Historical Monuments.

Location: On Puget Sound; see the Olympic Peninsula and Coastal Washington, map 6, grid d4.

Campsites, facilities: There are 34 sites, including 15 with partial hookups (water and electricity) for tents, trailers, or self-contained RVs up to 60 feet long, three primitive tent sites, and one group site. Picnic tables and fire grills are provided. Restrooms, drinking water, flush toilets, showers, a dump station, firewood, and a sheltered picnic area are available. Some facilities are wheelchair-accessible. Leashed pets are permitted.

Reservations, fees: Reserve at 888/CAMP-OUT (888/226-7688); website: www.parks.wa.gov/reservations ($7 reservation fee). Sites are $6 to $22 per night, $6 per extra vehicle per night. Senior discount available. Major credit cards accepted. Open year-round, with limited winter facilities.

Directions: From Tacoma on I-5, turn north on Highway 16 and drive through Bethel and continue to the Sedgwick Road exit and Highway 160. Turn right (east) and drive one mile to Highway 166. Turn left and drive six miles on Highway 166 to Colby. Turn left and drive along the shore through Manchester and continue for two miles to the park. The last part of the trip is well marked.

Contact: Manchester State Park, P.O. Box 36, Manchester, WA 98353; 800/233-0321 or 360/871-4065.

101 Blake Island Boat-In State Park

 10

Blake Island offers a boat-in camp on a small island in the middle of the massive Seattle metropolitan area. At night, it can seem almost surreal. The park covers 475 acres and features magnificent views of the Seattle skyline and Olympic Mountains. It has five miles of saltwater shoreline. A three-quarter-mile nature trail and 15.5 miles of hiking and biking trails are available. Good bottom fishing is available off the reef. The tidelands make up an underwater park. Blake Island was an ancestral camping ground of the Suquamish Indian tribe, and according to legend, the renowned Chief Seattle was born here. Native American–style dinners and dancing are available at Tillicum Village, a concession on the island.

Location: Near Seattle; see the Olympic Peninsula and Coastal Washington, map 6, grid d5.

Campsites, facilities: There are 54 primitive, boat-in tent sites. Picnic tables and fire grills are provided. Drinking water, pit toilets, showers, firewood, 1,500 feet of mooring with 20 mooring buoys, and two picnic shelters with a fire pit are available. There are also interpretive activities, horseshoe pits, volleyball, and a field. Garbage must be packed out. Some facilities are wheelchair-accessible. A store and restaurant are available nearby. Leashed pets are permitted.

Reservations, fees: No reservations. Sites are $5 per night, moorage buoys are $7 to $16 per night. Senior discount available. Open year-round.

Directions: This island is best reached by launching from Bremerton, Port Orchard, or Manchester. From Manchester it is a two-mile cruise east to the island (three miles west of Seattle). Then trace the shore around to the buoy floats. There are four main camping areas located between Vashon Island and Bainbridge Island, a distance of eight miles from Seattle. The park can also be reached by tour boat; call 206/443-1244 for information.

Contact: Blake Island Boat-In State Park, 360/731-0770; State Park information, 360/902-8844.

102 Aldrich Lake

   7

This campground on Aldrich Lake is managed by the Department of Natural Resources and provides primitive camping and fishing. Robbins Lake is nearby and has day-use facilities and a hand launch for small boats. To reach Robbins Lake, follow the directions below, except after turning left on Hohobas Lane and driving one-half mile, make another left and drive one mile to the lake.

Location: On Aldrich Lake in Tahuya State Forest; see the Olympic Peninsula and Coastal Washington, map 6, grid d1.

Campsites, facilities: There are four primitive campsites for tents or small trailers. Picnic tables, fire grills, and tent pads are provided. Vault toilets and drinking water are available. A hand launch for small boats is located at the lake. Garbage must be packed out. Leashed pets are permitted.

Reservations, fees: No reservations; no fee. A free map and brochure are available. Open mid-April to mid-September.

Directions: From Tacoma on I-5, drive to the junction with Highway 16. Turn north on Highway 16 and drive 30 miles to Bremerton and Highway 3. Turn west on Highway 3 and drive nine miles to Belfair and Highway 300. Turn west on Highway 300 and drive 12 miles to the town of Tahuya and Belfair-Tahuya Road. Turn right (north) on Belfair-Tahuya Road and drive four miles to Dewatto Road. Turn left on Dewatto Road and drive two miles to Hohobas Lane. Turn left on Hohobas Lane and drive one-half mile to a Y intersection. Bear right and drive 0.7 mile to the campground entrance road. Turn right and drive 200 yards to the campground.

Contact: Department of Natural Resources, South Puget Sound Region, 950 Farman Avenue North, Enumclaw, WA 98022; 360/825-1631, fax 360/825-1672.

Twin Lakes

   7

This wooded campground is in Tahuya State Forest and managed by the Department of Natural Resources. It's free and quiet. The fishing can be decent, and other highlights include privacy, shady sites, lake views, and a boat ramp. Hiking trails are nearby. Don't forget to bring water. One anomaly: Although it is called Twin Lakes, there actually is just one lake here.

Location: In Tahuya State Forest; see the Olympic Peninsula and Coastal Washington, map 6, grid e1.

Campsites, facilities: There are six primitive campsites for tents or small trailers. Picnic tables, fire grills, and tent pads are provided. Vault toilets are available, but there is no drinking water. Garbage must be packed out. A hand launch for small boats is available at the lake. Leashed pets are permitted.

Reservations, fees: No reservations; no fee. A free map and brochure are available. Open mid-April to mid-September.

Directions: From Tacoma on I-5, drive to the junction with Highway 16. Turn north on Highway 16 and drive about 30 miles to Bremerton and Highway 3. Turn south on Highway 3 and drive eight miles southwest to the town of Belfair and Highway 300. Turn west on Highway 300 west and drive four miles to Belfair-Tahuya Road. Turn right on Belfair-Tahuya Road and drive one-half mile to Elfendahl Pass Road. Turn right on Elfendahl Pass Road and drive 2.5 miles to Goat Ranch Road. Turn left and drive 1.7 miles to Twin Lakes Road. Turn right and drive one-half mile to the camp.

Contact: Department of Natural Resources, South Puget Sound Region, 950 Farman Ave. North, Enumclaw, WA 98022; 360/825-1631, fax 360/825-1672.

 Camp Spillman

   7

Camp Spillman is one of four campgrounds (along with Tahuya River Horse Camp, Howell Lake, and Twin Lakes) set in the immediate vicinity of Tahuya State Forest. This one sits along the Tahuya River, with wooded riverside sites and trails for hikers, horses, and motorbikes.

Location: On the Tahuya River in Tahuya State Forest; see the Olympic Peninsula and Coastal Washington, map 6, grid e1.

Campsites, facilities: There are six primitive campsites for tents or small trailers. Picnic tables, fire grills, and tent pads are provided. Vault toilets and drinking water are available. Garbage must be packed out. Leashed pets are permitted.

Reservations, fees: No reservations; no fee. A free map and brochure are available. Open mid-April to mid-October.

Directions: From Tacoma on I-5, drive to the junction with Highway 16. Turn north on Highway 16 and drive about 30 miles to Bremerton and Highway 3. Turn south on Highway 3 and drive eight miles southwest to the town of Belfair and Highway 300. Turn west on Highway 300 and drive four miles to Belfair-Tahuya Road. Turn right on Belfair-Tahuya Road and drive one-half mile to Elfendahl Pass Road. Turn right on Elfendahl Pass Road and drive 2.5 miles to Goat Ranch Road. Turn left and drive two-thirds mile to the camp.

Contact: Department of Natural Resources, South Puget Sound Region, 950 Farman Ave. North, Enumclaw, WA 98022; 360/825-1631, fax 360/825-1672.

105 Robin Hood Village

 5

This wooded park is set near a state park, Olympic National Forest, Mason Lake and Lake Cushman, and Hood Canal. Nearby recreation options include an 18-hole golf course.

Location: Near the Hood Canal; see the Olympic Peninsula and Coastal Washington, map 6, grid f1.

Campsites, facilities: There are 16 sites with full or partial hookups for trailers or RVs of any length, four tent sites, and four cabins. Picnic tables are provided. Restrooms, drinking water, flush toilets, showers, a restaurant, an espresso stand, a liquor store, a massage therapist, a sauna, and a coin-operated laundry are available. Bottled gas, a dump station, a store, and ice are available within one mile. Boat docks and launching facilities are located in the park. Leashed pets are permitted.

Reservations, fees: Reservations accepted. Sites are $12 to $22 per night, cabins $85 to $200 per night. Major credit cards accepted. Open year-round.

Directions: From Tacoma, drive northeast on Highway 16 for about 30 miles to Bremerton and Highway 3. Turn south on Highway 3 and drive eight miles southwest to the town of Belfair and Highway 106. Bear right (southwest) on Highway 106 and drive 13 miles to the campground along Hood Canal.

Contact: Robin Hood Village, East 6780 Highway 106, Union, WA 98592; 360/898-2163, fax 360/898-2164.

106 Twanoh State Park

 8

This state park is set on the shore of Hood Canal at one of the warmest saltwater bodies in Puget Sound and likely the warmest saltwater beach in the state. The park covers 182 acres, with 3,167 feet of saltwater shoreline. Swimming and oyster and crab harvesting are popular here. No clamming is allowed. Winter smelting is also popular; check regulations. In late fall, the chum salmon head up in the small creek and can be seen; fishing for them is prohibited. Most of the park buildings are made of brick, stone, and round logs. They were built by the Civilian Conservation Corps in the 1930s. You'll also see extensive evidence of logging from the 1890s.

Twanoh is a Native American world for "gathering place."

Other amenities include a tennis court, horse-shoe pits, and a concession stand.

Location: Near Union; see the Olympic Peninsula and Coastal Washington, map 6, grid e1.

Campsites, facilities: There are 17 tent sites and nine sites for trailers or RVs up to 35 feet long, 13 with full and nine with partial hookups. Picnic tables and fire grills are provided. Flush toilets, a store, and a playground are available. Electricity, drinking water, sewer hookups, showers, and firewood can be obtained for a fee. Some facilities are wheelchair-accessible. Leashed pets are permitted.

Reservations, fees: No reservations. Sites are $6 to $18 per night. Open April through October.

Directions: From Bremerton, take Highway 3 southwest to Belfair and Highway 106. Turn west and drive eight miles to the park. If driving from U.S. 101, turn east on Highway 106 and drive 12 miles to the park.

Contact: Twanoh State Park, 360/275-2222; State Park information, 360/902-8844.

107 Belfair State Park

  8

Belfair State Park is set along the southern edge of the Hood Canal, offering a 65-acre park with 3,720 feet of saltwater shoreline. This park is known for its saltwater tidal flats, wetlands, and wind-blown beach grasses. Beach walking and swimming are good. The camp is set primarily amid conifer forest and marshlands on the Hood Canal with nearby streams, tideland, and wetlands. A unique swimming area is created by a gravel-rimmed pool that is separated from the Hood Canal. A children's Easter egg hunt is held here each spring. Note that the

DNR Tahuya Multiple-Use Area is nearby with trails for motorcycles, mountain biking, hiking, horseback riding, and off-road vehicles. Big Mission Creek and Little Mission Creek, both located in the park, are habitat for chum salmon during spawning season in fall.

Location: On the Hood Canal; see the Olympic Peninsula and Coastal Washington, map 6, grid e2.

Campsites, facilities: There are 137 sites for tents and 47 sites with full hookups for trailers or RVs up to 75 feet long. Picnic tables and fire grills are provided. Restrooms, drinking water, flush toilets, coin-operated showers, a bathhouse, a dump station, a swimming lagoon, and a playground with horseshoe pits are available. A store and a restaurant are located within one mile. Some facilities are wheelchair-accessible. Leashed pets are permitted.

Reservations, fees: Reserve at 888/CAMP-OUT (888/226-7688); website: www.parks.wa.gov/reservations ($7 reservation fee). Sites are $15 to $22 per night, $6 per extra vehicle per night. Senior discount available. Major credit cards accepted. Open year-round.

Directions: From Tacoma on I-5, drive to the Highway 16 west exit. Take the Highway 16 northwest and drive about 27 miles toward Bremerton and Belfair (after the Port Orchard exits, note that the highway merges into three lanes). Get in the left lane for the Belfair/State Route 3 south exit. Take that exit and turn left at the traffic signal, and take State Route 3 eight miles south to Belfair to State Route 300 (at the signal just after the Safeway). Turn right and drive three miles to the park entrance.

Contact: Belfair State Park, 360/275-0668; State Park information, 360/902-8844.

108 Jarrell Cove State Park

 8

Most visitors to this park arrive by boat. Campsites are near the docks, set on a rolling, grassy area. The park covers just 43 acres but with 3,500 feet on saltwater shoreline on the northeast end of Harstine Island in South Puget Sound. The park's dense forest presses nearly to the water's edge at high tides—a beautiful setting. At low tides, tideland mud flats are unveiled. The beach is rocky and muddy, not exactly Hawaii. Hiking and biking is limited to just one mile of trail.

Location: On Harstine Island; see the Olympic Peninsula and Coastal Washington, map 6, grid f1.

Campsites, facilities: There are 21 sites for tents, trailers, or self-contained RVs up to 30 feet long, one boat-in site, and a group camp for up to 64 people. Picnic tables and fire grills are provided. Restrooms, drinking water, flush toilets, and coin-operated showers are available. Some facilities are wheelchair-accessible. Boat docks, a marine pumpout, and 14 mooring buoys are available. A picnic area and a horseshoe pit are nearby. Leashed pets are permitted.

Reservations, fees: Reserve at 888/CAMP-OUT (888/226-7688); website: www.parks.wa.gov/reservations ($7 reservation fee). Sites are $6 to $15 per night, $7 per extra vehicle per night, $10 to $16 mooring fee, group site requires $25 reservation plus $2 per person with 20-person minimum. Senior discount available. Open year-round.

Directions: From Olympia on I-5, turn north on U.S. 101 and drive 22 miles to Shelton and Highway 3. Turn north on Highway 3 and drive about eight miles to Pickering Road. Turn right and drive to the Harstine Bridge. Turn left, cross the bridge to Harstine Island, and continue to a stop sign at North Island Drive. Turn left and drive four miles to Wingert Road. Turn left and drive one quarter-mile to the park on the left.

Contact: Jarrell Cove State Park, 360/426-9226; State Park information, 360/902-8844.

109 Jarrell's Cove Marina

   6

The marina and nearby Puget Sound are the big bonus here. This small camp features 1,000 feet of shoreline and a half mile of public beach. Clamming is available in season.

Location: Near Shelton; see the Olympic Peninsula and Coastal Washington, map 6, grid f1.

Campsites, facilities: There are four sites with partial hookups (water and electricity) for trailers or RVs up to 40 feet long. Picnic tables and barbecues are provided. Restrooms, drinking water, flush toilets, showers, bottled gas, a dump station, a store, fishing licenses, bait and tackle, a laundry room, boat docks, and boat rentals are available. Leashed pets are permitted.

Reservations, fees: Reservations accepted. Sites are $25 per night. Major credit cards accepted. Open year-round.

Directions: From Olympia on I-5, turn north on U.S. 101 and drive 22 miles to Shelton and Highway 3. Turn east on Highway 3 and drive about eight miles to Pickering Road. Turn right and drive to the Harstine Island Bridge. Turn left, cross the bridge to Harstine Island, and continue to a stop sign at North Island Drive. Turn left on North Island Drive and drive 2.8 miles to Haskell Hill Road. Turn left (west) on Haskell Hill Road and drive one mile to the marina.

Contact: Jarrell's Cove Marina, 220 East Wilson Road, Shelton, WA 98584; 360/426-8823.

110 Joemma Beach State Park

 8

This beautiful camp set along the shore of the peninsula provides an alternative to nearby Penrose Point State Park. The park covers 122 acres and features 3,000 feet of saltwater frontage on the Southeast Kitsap Peninsula. This area is often excellent for boating, fishing, and crabbing. It is a forested park with the bonus of a boat-in campsite. Hiking is limited to a trail that is less than a mile long.

Location: On Puget Sound; see the Olympic Peninsula and Coastal Washington, map 6, grid g2.

Campsites, facilities: There are 19 sites for tents, trailers, or RVs up to 35 feet long and three primitive tent sites. Picnic tables, fire grills, and tent pads are provided. Vault toilets, drinking water, boat-launching facilities, and a dock are available. Leashed pets are permitted.

Reservations, fees: Reserve at 888/CAMP-OUT (888/226-7688); website: www.parks .wa.gov/reservations ($7 reservation fee). Sites are $6 to $16, $6 per extra vehicle per night. Senior discount available. Open May through September.

Directions: From Tacoma, drive north on Highway 16 for about 10 miles to Highway 302/Key Peninsula Highway. Turn west and drive about five miles to Key Peninsula Highway. Turn south and drive about 15 miles to Whiteman Road. Turn right and drive four miles to Bay Road. Turn right and drive one mile to the park entrance (stay on the asphalt road when entering the park).

Contact: Joemma Beach State Park, 253/265-3606; State Park information, 360/902-8844.

111 Penrose Point State Park

 8

This park on Carr Inlet in Puget Sound, overlooking Lake Bay, has a remote feel, but it's actually not far from Tacoma. The park covers 152 acres, with two miles of saltwater frontage on Mayo Cove and Carr Inlet. The camp has impressive stands of fir and cedars nearby, along with ferns and rhododendrons. The park has 2.5 miles of trails for biking and hiking. Bay Lake is a popular fishing lake for trout and is located one mile from the park; a boat launch is available there. The park is known for its excellent fishing, crabbing, clamming, and oysters. The nearest boat launch to Puget Sound is located three miles away in the town of Home.

Location: On Puget Sound; see the Olympic Peninsula and Coastal Washington, map 6, grid f2.

Campsites, facilities: There are 83 developed sites for tents or self-contained RVs up to 35 feet long and one primitive tent site. Picnic tables and fire grills are provided. Restrooms, drinking water, flush toilets, coin-operated showers, a dump station, horseshoe pits, a picnic area, and a beach are available. Some facilities are wheelchair-accessible. Boat docks, a marine pump-out, and mooring buoys are nearby. Leashed pets are permitted.

Reservations, fees: Reserve at 888/CAMP-OUT (888/226-7688); website: www.parks .wa.gov/reservations ($7 reservation fee). Sites are $6 to $16 per night, $7 per extra vehicle per night, boat mooring $10 to $16 per night. Senior discount available. Major credit cards accepted. Open April through August.

Directions: From Tacoma, drive north on Highway 16 for about 10 miles to Highway

302/Key Peninsula Highway. Turn west and drive about five miles to Key Peninsula Highway. Turn south and drive 9.2 miles through the towns of Key Center and Home to Cornwall Road KPS (second road after crossing the Home Bridge). Turn left and drive 1.25 miles to 158 Avenue KPS and the park entrance.

Contact: Penrose Point State Park, 253/884-2514; State Park information, 360/902-8844.

Kopachuck State Park
 8

This park is located on Henderson Bay on Puget Sound near Tacoma. A highlight at Kopachuck are the scenic views and dramatic sunsets across the Puget Sound and Olympic Mountains. The parks covers 109 acres, with 5,600 feet of saltwater shoreline. A unique element of this park is that it includes Cutts Island (also called Deadman's Island), located one-half mile from shore, and is accessible only by boat (no camping on the island). The park has sandy beaches, located about 250 yards down the hill from the camp. Two miles of hiking trails are available. Fishing access is available by boat only. A boat launch is located not far from camp.

Location: On Puget Sound; see the Olympic Peninsula and Coastal Washington, map 6, grid f3.

Campsites, facilities: There are 41 developed sites for tents or self-contained RVs up to 35 feet long, one primitive boat-in site for kayakers (no motorized boats permitted), and one group site for up to 40 people. Picnic tables and fire grills are provided. Restrooms, drinking water, flush toilets, coin-operated showers, a dump station, a covered picnic area, a Junior Ranger Program, interpretive activities, and boat buoys are available. Some facilities are wheelchair-accessible. Leashed pets are permitted.

Reservations, fees: No reservations. Sites are $14 per night, $2 per person from primitive boat-in site, $25 reservation fee for group site, plus $2 per person with 20 person minimum. Senior discount available. Open mid-May through September.

Directions: From Tacoma on I-5, turn north on Highway 16. Drive seven miles north to the second Gig Harbor exit. Take that exit and look for the sign for Kopachuck State Park. At the sign, turn west and drive five miles (the road changes name several times) to the camp (well marked).

Contact: Kopachuck State Park, 253/265-3606; State Park information, 360/902-8844.

Gig Harbor RV Resort
 7

This is a popular layover spot for folks heading up to Bremerton. Just a short jaunt off the highway, it's pleasant, clean, and friendly. An 18-hole golf course, a full-service marina, and tennis courts are located nearby. Look for the great view of Mt. Rainier from the end of the harbor.

Location: Near Tacoma; see the Olympic Peninsula and Coastal Washington, map 6, grid f4.

Campsites, facilities: There are 93 sites, most with full or partial hookups, including 28 drive-through sites and some long-term rentals, for tents, trailers, or RVs of any length, and one cabin. Restrooms, drinking water, flush toilets, showers, bottled gas, a dump station, a club room, a coin-operated laundry, ice, a playground with horseshoe pits, a sports field, and a heated swimming pool are available. Leashed pets are permitted.

Reservations, fees: Reservations recommended in the summer. Sites are $10 to $33.50 per night, cabin $36 per night. Senior discount available. Major credit cards accepted. Open year-round.

Directions: From Tacoma, drive northwest on Highway 16 for 12 miles northwest to Burnham Drive/North Rosedale exit. Take that exit and drive a short distance to the yield sign at Burnham Drive NW. Bear right on Burnham Drive NW and drive one mile to the campground on the left.

Contact: Gig Harbor RV Resort, 9515 Burnham Drive NW, Gig Harbor, WA 98332; 253/858-8138 or 800/526-8311, fax 253/858-8399.

114 Jolly Rogers RV Park

 7

This camp covers one acre near Westport Harbor, a beachside RV park with concrete sites and nearby beach access. It's a prime spot to watch ocean sunsets, and on a clear day, snow-capped Mount Rainier is visible. Westport Light and Westhaven State Parks are nearby and offer day-use facilities along the ocean.

Location: Near Westport Harbor; see the Olympic Peninsula and Coastal Washington, map 7, grid a8.

Campsites, facilities: There are 25 sites with full hookups for tents, trailers, or RVs of any length. Restrooms, drinking water, flush toilets, showers, cable TV, and boat docks are available. Bottled gas, a store, a café, and laundry are located within one mile. Leashed pets are permitted.

Reservations, fees: Reservations accepted. Sites are $16.50 to $18.50 per night. Open year-round.

Directions: From Aberdeen, drive south on State Route 105 for 22 miles southwest to Westport and Neddie Rose Drive. Turn right (north) and drive a short distance to the park on the right (Westport Docks).

Contact: Jolly Rogers RV Park, P.O. Box 342, Westport, WA 98595; 360/268-0265, fax 360/268-0265.

115 Grizzly Joe's RV Park

 9

Grizzly Joe's is a landscaped, one-acre park with ocean views on three sides. Sites are graveled and level. Snow-capped Mount Rainier is visible, and the sunsets are spectacular. Westport Light and Westhaven State Parks are nearby with multiple recreational options.

Location: On Point Chehalis; see the Olympic Peninsula and Coastal Washington, map 7, grid a8.

Campsites, facilities: There are 35 sites with full hookups and pull-through for trailers or RVs of any length. Electricity, drinking water, sewer, and cable TV are provided. A dump station, flush toilets, showers, a patio/picnic area with fire pit, a fish-cleaning station, outdoor cooking facilities, and boat docks are available. Bottled gas, a store, a café, a laundry, firewood, and ice are located within one quarter-mile. Leashed pets and permitted.

Reservations, fees: Reservations recommended. Sites are $18 per night. Open year-round.

Directions: From Aberdeen, drive south on State Route 105 for 22 miles southwest to Westport and Neddie Rose Drive. Turn right and drive four blocks to the park at the end of the road.

Contact: Grizzly Joe's RV Park, P.O. Box 1755, 743 Neddie Rose Drive, Westport, WA 98595; 360/268-5555.

116 American Sunset RV Resort

 8

If location is everything, then this RV camp is a big winner, set on a peninsula, right on the ocean. It covers 32 acres and has its own hiking and biking trails. The park is divided into two areas: one for campers, another for long-term rentals. Nearby are Westhaven and Westport Light State Parks, popular with hikers, rock hounds, scuba divers, and surf anglers. Swimming (but not off the docks), fishing, and crabbing off the docks are also options. Monthly rentals are available in summer.

Location: Near Westport Harbor; see the Olympic Peninsula and Coastal Washington, map 7, grid a8.

Campsites, facilities: There are 120 sites with full hookups, including some drive-through, for trailers or RVs up to 50 feet, 50 tent sites, and one trailer. Picnic tables and fire rings are provided. Restrooms, drinking water, flush toilets, showers, modem hookups (in office), a dump station, a coin-operated laundry, a grocery store, propane, a seasonal heated pool, horseshoe pits, a playground, a fish-cleaning station, and a 2,400-square-foot recreation hall are available. Hookups for phone and cable TV are available for extended stays only. A marina is located three blocks away. Leashed pets are permitted.

Reservations, fees: Reservations recommended during the summer; phone 800/JOY-CAMP (800/569-2267). Sites are $13 to $22.50 per night, $5 per extra vehicle per night, trailer is $45 per night. Senior discount available. Major credit cards accepted. Open year-round.

Directions: From Aberdeen, drive south on State Route 105 for 22 miles southwest to Westport and Montesano Street (the first exit in Westport). Turn right (northeast) on Montesano and drive three miles to the resort on the left.

Contact: American Sunset RV Resort, 1209 N. Montesano Street, Westport, WA 98595; 360/268-0207 or 800/569-2267; website: www.americansunsetrv.com.

117 Coho RV Park, Motel & Charter

 4

This RV park is a spot that fishermen stake out as their base camp. Fishing is good nearby for salmon and rockfish. The park covers two acres, one of several parks in the immediate area. This one has its own fishing and whale-watching charters. Nearby Westhaven and Westport Light State Parks are popular with rock hounds, scuba divers, and surf anglers. A full-service marina is within easy walking distance.

Location: Near Westport Harbor; see the Olympic Peninsula and Coastal Washington, map 7, grid a8.

Campsites, facilities: There are 76 sites, including six drive-through, with full hookups for trailers or RVs of any length. No tents are permitted. No open campfires are allowed. Restrooms, drinking water, flush toilets, coin-operated showers, a dump station, cable TV, a coin-operated laundry, a meeting hall, ice, and fishing charters are available. Boat docks and launching facilities are located nearby. Bottled gas, a store, and a café are within one mile. Leashed pets are permitted.

Reservations, fees: Reservations accepted. Sites are $19 to $21 per night, $2 per person per night for more than two people. Major credit cards accepted. Monthly rentals available. Open year-round.

Directions: From Aberdeen, drive south on State Route 105 for 22 miles southwest to Westport and Montesano Street (the first exit in Westport). Turn right (northeast) and drive 3.5 miles to Nyhus Street. Turn left (northwest) and drive 2.5 blocks to the campground on the left.

Contact: Coho RV Park, 2501 North Nyhus Street,

Westport, WA 98595; 360/268-0111 or 800/572-0177, fax 360/268-9425; website: www.westportwa.com/coho.

Totem RV Park

 8

This two-acre park is set 300 yards from the ocean, featuring an expanse of sand dunes between the park and the ocean. The park has large, grassy sites close to Westhaven State Park, which offers day-use facilities. The owner is a fishing guide and can provide detailed fishing information. Marked biking trails and a full-service marina are within five miles of the campground. This RV parks was remodeled in 2000.

Location: In Westport; see the Olympic Peninsula and Coastal Washington, map 7, grid a8.

Campsites, facilities: There are 76 sites, most drive-through with full or partial hookups, for tents, trailers, or RVs of any length. Picnic tables are provided. Restrooms, drinking water, flush toilets, coin-operated showers, a dump station, a coin-operated laundry, and ice are available. A pavilion, barbecue facilities with kitchen, and a fish-cleaning station are also available. Bottled gas and a café are located next door. A store is located within one-half mile. Boat docks, launching facilities, and fishing charters are nearby. Leashed pets are permitted.

Reservations, fees: Reservations accepted. Sites are $15.50 to $17.50 per night. Major credit cards accepted. Open year-round.

Directions: From Aberdeen, drive southwest on State Route 105 for 18 miles to the turnoff for Westport. Turn right (north) on the State Route 105 spur and drive 4.3 miles to the docks and Nyhus Street. Turn left on Nyhus Street and drive two blocks to the park on the left.

Contact: Totem RV, P.O. Box 1166, 2421 North Nyhus Street, Westport, WA 98595; 360/268-0025 or 888/TOTEM-RV (888/868-3678).

Holand Center

 6

This pleasant, 18-acre RV park is one of several in the immediate area. The sites are graveled or grassy with pine trees between and have ample space. There is no beach access from the park, but full recreational facilities are available nearby. About half of the sites are long-term rentals.

Location: In Westport; see the Olympic Peninsula and Coastal Washington, map 7, grid a8.

Campsites, facilities: There are 80 sites with full hookups for trailers or RVs up to 40 feet long. No tents are allowed. Picnic tables are provided. Restrooms, drinking water, flush toilets, coin-operated showers, a coin-operated laundry, and storage sheds are available. Bottled gas, a store, a café, and ice are located within one mile. Boat docks and launching facilities are nearby. Leashed pets are permitted.

Reservations, fees: Reservations accepted. Sites are $20 per night. Open year-round.

Directions: From Aberdeen, drive south on State Route 105 for 22 miles to Westport. Continue on State Route 105 to Wilson Street. The park is at the corner of State Route 105 and Wilson Street.

Contact: Holand Center, 201 Wilson Street, Westport, WA 98595; 360/268-9582, fax 360/532-3818.

120 Pacific Motel and RV Park

This five-acre park has grassy, shaded sites in a wooded setting. It's near Twin Harbors and Westport Light State Parks, both of which have beach access. A full-service marina is located within two miles. About 25 percent of the sites are occupied with long-term rentals.

Location: Near Twin Harbors; see the Olympic Peninsula and Coastal Washington, map 7, grid a8.

Campsites, facilities: There are 80 sites with full hookups, including some drive-through, for trailers or RVs of any length, and five tent sites. Picnic tables and fire rings are provided. Restrooms, drinking water, flush toilets, coin-operated showers, a dump station, propane gas, a fish-cleaning station, a recreation hall with a kitchen, cable TV, a public phone and fax, laundry facilities, and a heated swimming pool (seasonal) are available. A store, a café, and ice are located within one mile. Boat-launching and boat docks are nearby in a full-service marina. Leashed pets are permitted.

Reservations, fees: Reservations accepted. Major credit cards accepted. Sites are $15 to $20 per night, $2 per person per night for more than two people. Open year-round.

Directions: From Aberdeen, drive south on State Route 105 for approximately 18 miles to the State Route 105 spur road to Westport. Turn right (north) on the State Route 105 spur road (to Westport) and drive 1.7 miles to the park on the right.

Contact: Pacific Motel and RV Park, 330 South Forrest, Westport, WA 98595; 360/268-9325, fax 360/268-6227; website: www.pacific-motelandrv.com.

121 Islander RV Park & Motel

 8

This park is located on Grays Harbor, close to Westport Light and Westhaven State Parks, which offer oceanfront day-use facilities. The park covers three acres. On-site amenities include a hair salon, a gift shop, a restaurant, a motel, live music, dancing, fishing charters, and whale-watching trips. No open campfires are permitted.

Location: On Grays Harbor; see the Olympic Peninsula and Coastal Washington, map 7, grid a8.

Campsites, facilities: There are 60 sites with full hookups, including 30 drive-through, for trailers or RVs up to 40 feet long. Restrooms, drinking water, flush toilets, showers, a coffee shop, a gift shop, a restaurant, a coin-operated laundry, ice, a heated swimming pool (in season), boat docks, and fishing charters are available. Bottled gas, a dump station, and a store are located within one mile. Leashed pets are permitted.

Reservations, fees: Reservations accepted. Sites are $20 to $25 per night. Major credit cards accepted. Open year-round.

Directions: From Aberdeen, drive south on State Route 105 for 22 miles to Westport and Montesano Street. Turn right and drive two miles (becomes Dock Street) to the docks and Westhaven Drive. Turn left and drive four blocks to Neddie Rose Avenue. Turn right and drive one block to the park on the right.

Contact: Islander RV Park & Motel, 421 East Neddie Rose, Westport, WA 98595; 360/268-9166 or 800/322-1740, fax 360/268-0902.

122 Twin Harbors State Park

 8

These campsites are close together and often crammed to capacity in the summer. The park coves 172 acres, located four miles south of Westhaven. Highlights include beach access and marked hiking trails, including the Shifting Sands Nature Trail. The most popular recreation activities are surf fishing, surfing, beachcombing, and kite flying. This park was a military training ground in the 1930s. Fishing boats can be chartered nearby in Westport.

Location: On the Pacific Ocean; see the Olympic Peninsula and Coastal Washington, map 7, grid b8.

Campsites, facilities: There are 253 sites, including 49 with full hookups, for tents, trailers, or RVs up to 35 feet long, five primitive tent sites, and one group site for up to 75 people. Picnic tables and fire grills are provided. Restrooms, drinking water, flush toilets, coin-operated showers, a dump station, interpretive activities, a picnic area with kitchen shelter and electricity, and a playground with horseshoe pits are available. A store, a café, and ice are available within one mile. Some facilities are wheelchair-accessible. Leashed pets are permitted.

Reservations, fees: Reserve at 888/CAMP-OUT (888/226-7688); website: www.parks .wa.gov/reservations ($7 reservation fee). Sites are $6 to $22 per night, $6 per extra vehicle per night. Senior discount available. Group site requires $25 reservation fee and $2 per person with 20-person minimum. Major credit cards accepted. Open mid-February through October.

Directions: From Aberdeen, drive south on State Route 105 for 17 miles to the park entrance on the left (three miles south of Westport).

Contact: Twin Harbors State Park, Twin Harbors State Park, Westport, WA 98595; 360/268-9717; State Park information, 360/902-8844.

123 Ocean Gate Resort

 5

This privately run, seven-acre park has beach access, an alternative to the publicly run Grayland Beach State Park. Fishing, beach biking, and beachcombing are highlights.

Location: In Grayland; see the Olympic Peninsula and Coastal Washington, map 7, grid b8.

Campsites, facilities: There are 24 sites with full hookups, including 12 drive-through, for trailers or RVs of any length, 20 tent sites, and six cabins. Picnic tables and fire rings are provided. Restrooms, drinking water, flush toilets, showers, a covered picnic shelter with barbecue, and a playground are available. Bottled gas, a store, a café, a laundry, and ice are available within one mile. Leashed pets are permitted.

Reservations, fees: Reservations accepted. Sites are $13 to $20 per night, $5 per extra vehicle per night, cabins are $45 to $90 per night for up to eight people. Open year-round.

Directions: From Aberdeen, drive south on State Route 105 for 21 miles to a Y intersection. Take State Route 105 left toward Grayland. The park is in Grayland on the right between Mileposts 26 and 27.

Contact: Ocean Gate Resort, P.O. Box 67, 1939 State Route 105 South, Grayland, WA 98547; 360/267-1956 or 800/473-1956; website: www.oceangateresort.net.

Best Western Shores Motel and RV Park

 **4**

This small, private park is designed for families. Beach access and golf are not far, and Twin Harbors and Grayland Beach State Parks are just a few minutes away. This is an excellent layover for tourists who want to get off U.S. 101. About one-third of the RV sites are filled with permanent rentals.

Location: In Grayland; see the Olympic Peninsula and Coastal Washington, map 7, grid b8.

Campsites, facilities: There are 30 drive-through sites with full hookups for trailers or RVs of any length. Picnic tables are provided. Restrooms, drinking water, flush toilets, showers, a community fire pit, cable TV, ice, propane, a pay phone, snacks, and a playground are available. Firewood, a store, a restaurant, and a lounge are located within one mile. Leashed pets are permitted.

Reservations, fees: Reservations recommended. Sites are $12.50 per night. Major credit cards accepted. Open year-round.

Directions: From Aberdeen, drive south on State Route 105 for 19 miles to Westport. Continue south on State Route 105 to Grayland. The RV park is located in town, right along State Route 105 on the right.

Contact: Best Western Shores Motel and RV Park, 2193 State Route 105, Grayland, WA 98547; 360/267-1611.

Grayland Beach State Park

    **8**

This state park features 7,500 feet of beach frontage. All the campsites are within easy walking distance of the ocean, with the bonus of a quarter-mile self-guided interpretive trail that provides a route from the campground to the beach. The campsites are relatively spacious for a state park, but they are not especially private. This park is popular with out-of-towners, especially during summer. Recreation options include fishing, beachcombing, and kite flying. The best spot for surfing is five miles north at Westhaven State Park.

Location: On the Pacific Ocean; see the Olympic Peninsula and Coastal Washington, map 7, grid b8.

Campsites, facilities: There are 60 sites with full-hookup for trailers or RVs up to 40 feet long and three primitive tent sites. Picnic tables and fire grills are provided. Drinking water and vault toilets are available. Restrooms, drinking water, flush toilets, and coin-operated showers are available. Some facilities are wheelchair-accessible. Leashed pets are permitted.

Reservations, fees: Reserve at 888/CAMP-OUT (888/226-7688); website: www.parks.wa.gov/reservations ($7 reservation fee). Sites are $6 to $22 per night, $6 per extra vehicle per night. Senior discount available. Open year-round.

Directions: From Aberdeen, drive south on State Route 105 for 22 miles to the park entrance. The park is just south of the town of Grayland on the right (west).

Contact: Grayland Beach State Park, 360/268-9717; State Park information, 360/902-8844.

Ocean Park Resort

  **5**

This wooded, 10-acre campground is located one-half mile from Willapa Bay. It is primarily for RVs. The sites are grassy and shaded. Fishing, crabbing, and clamming are popular in season. Ocean Park has several festivals during the summer season. During these festivals, this resort fills up. To the north, Leadbetter Point State Park provides a side-trip option.

Location: On Willapa Bay; see the Olympic Peninsula and Coastal Washington, map 7, grid e8.

Campsites, facilities: There are 70 sites with full hookups, including some drive-through, for trailers or RVs of any length, seven tent sites, and several cottages (park model trailers). Picnic tables are provided. Fire pits are provided at tent sites. Restrooms, drinking water, flush toilets, coin-operated showers, bottled gas, a recreation hall, a coin-operated laundry, ice, a playground, firewood, a hot tub, and a heated swimming pool (in season) are available. A store and a café are available within one mile. Boat docks and launching facilities are located nearby on Willapa Bay. Leashed pets are permitted.

Reservations, fees: Reservations accepted. Sites are $19 to $21, $3 per person per night for more than two people; cottages are $70 to $110 per night. Major credit cards accepted. Open year-round.

Directions: From Kelso/Longview on I-5, turn west on Highway 4 and drive 63 miles to U.S. 101. Turn south on U.S. 101 and drive 13 miles to the junction with Highway 103. Turn right (north) on Highway 103 and drive 11 miles to the town of Ocean Park and 259th Street. Turn right (east) on 259th Street and drive two blocks to the resort at the end of the road.

Contact: Ocean Park Resort, P.O. Box 339, 25904 R Street, Ocean Park, WA 98640; 360/665-4585 or 800/835-4634, fax 360/665-4130; website: www.opresort.com.

Westgate Motel and Trailer Court

 9

Highlights of this pretty and clean four-acre camp include beach access, oceanfront sites, and all the amenities. There are 28 miles of beach that can be driven on. Additional facilities within five miles of the campground include an 18-hole golf course.

Location: Near Long Beach; see the Olympic Peninsula and Coastal Washington, map 7, grid e8.

Campsites, facilities: There are 39 sites with full hookups, including 15 drive-through, for trailers or RVs of any length, and six cabins. Restrooms, drinking water, flush toilets, showers, cable TV, a recreation hall, and ice are available. A store, a café, and a coin-operated laundry are available about four miles away. Boat docks and launching facilities are located nearby on Willapa Bay. Leashed pets are permitted.

Reservations, fees: Reservations accepted. Sites are $16 to $21 per night, $1 per person per night for more than two people; cabins are $55 to $65 per night. Major credit cards accepted. Open year-round.

Directions: From Kelso/Longview on I-5, turn west on Highway 4 and drive 63 miles to U.S. 101. Turn south on U.S. 101 and drive 13 miles to the junction with Highway 103. Turn north on Highway 103 and drive 7.5 miles to the campground on the left (located at the south edge of the town of Ocean Park).

Contact: Westgate Motel and Trailer Court, 20803 Pacific Highway, Ocean Park, WA 98640; 360/665-4211.

128 Ocean Aire RV Park

 4

This camp is located in town, one-half mile from the shore of Willapa Bay. Tennis courts are one quarter-mile away, and a golf course is three miles away. Leadbetter Point State Park, about eight miles north, is open for day use and provides footpaths for walking through the state-designated natural area and wildlife refuge. Two-thirds of sites are long-term rentals, making reservations essential for the remaining sites during summer.

Location: Near Willapa Bay; see the Olympic Peninsula and Coastal Washington, map 7, grid e8.

Campsites, facilities: There are 46 sites with full hookups, including eight drive-through, for trailers or RVs of any length. No tents are allowed. Restrooms, drinking water, flush toilets, showers, picnic tables, a dump station, a coin-operated laundry, and ice are available. A store and a café are available next door. Boat rentals are nearby on Willapa Bay. Leashed pets are permitted.

Reservations, fees: Reservations accepted. Sites are $16 per night, $3 per person per night for more than two people. Open year-round.

Directions: From Kelso/Longview on I-5, turn west on Highway 4 and drive 63 miles to U.S. 101. Turn south on U.S. 101 and drive 13 miles to the junction with Highway 103. Turn north on Highway 103 and drive 11 miles to the town of Ocean Park and 259th Street. Turn right on 259th Street and drive two blocks to the camp.

Contact: Ocean Aire, 25918 R Street, Ocean Park, WA 98640; 360/665-4027.

129 Ma and Pa's Pacific RV Park

  7

We wanted to give them some kind of award for the name of this place, but we haven't figured out what to give them yet. This park covers six acres and features both beach access and spacious, grassy sites near the shore. Additional facilities found within five miles of the campground include an 18-hole golf course, marked bike trails, and a riding stable.

Location: Near Long Beach; see the Olympic Peninsula and Coastal Washington, map 7, grid f8.

Campsites, facilities: There are 53 sites with full or partial hookups for trailers or RVs of any length and an area for dispersed tent camping. Restrooms, drinking water, flush toilets, coin-operated showers, picnic tables, a coin-operated laundry, a recreation room, and ice are available. Bottled gas, a store, and a café are available within one mile. Leashed pets are permitted.

Reservations, fees: Reservations recommended. Sites are $22 per night, $2 per person per night for more than two people, $5 per extra vehicle per night, $2 pet fee. Major credit cards accepted. Open year-round.

Directions: From Kelso/Longview on I-5, turn west on Highway 4 and drive 63 miles to U.S. 101. Turn south on U.S. 101 and drive 13 miles to the junction with Highway 103. Turn north on Highway 103 and drive four miles to the park on the left.

Contact: Ma and Pa's Pacific RV Park, 10515 Pacific Highway, Long Beach, WA 98631; 360/642-3253, fax 360/642-5039; website: www.maandpasrvpark.com.

130 Andersen's RV Park on the Ocean

 7

Timing is everything here. When the dates are announced for the local festivals, the sites at this park can be booked a year in advance. It is located near Long Beach, with a path through the dunes that will get you to the beach in a flash from this five-acre camp. It is set in a flat, sandy area with gravel sites. Recreation options include beach bonfires, beachcombing, surf fishing, and clamming (seasonal). Additional facilities found within five miles of the campground include marked dune trails, a nine-hole golf course, a riding stable, and tennis courts.

Location: Near Long Beach; see the Olympic Peninsula and Coastal Washington, map 7, grid f8.

Campsites, facilities: There are 57 sites with full hookups for trailers or RVs of any length and 15 tent sites. Picnic tables are provided, but not at tent sites. Tent sites have water available only. Restrooms, drinking water, flush toilets, showers, a meeting hall, cable TV, modem hookups, a dump station, a coin-operated laundry, ice, propane, bottled gas, a fax machine, a horseshoe pit, and a playground are available. A store and a café are available within two miles. Leashed pets are permitted.

Reservations, fees: Reservations accepted. Sites are $18 to $22 per night, $2 per person per night for more than two people. Major credit cards accepted. Open year-round.

Directions: From Kelso/Longview on I-5, turn west on Highway 4 and drive 63 miles to U.S. 101. Turn south on U.S. 101 and drive 13 miles to the junction with Highway 103. Turn north on Highway 103 and drive five miles to the park on the left.

Contact: Andersen's RV Park on the Ocean, 1400 138th Street, Long Beach, WA 98631; 360/642-2231 or 800/645-6795.

131 Oceanic RV Park

 3

This two-acre park is located in the heart of downtown, within walking distance to restaurants and stores. It is also within five miles of an 18-hole golf course, marked bike trails, and a full-service marina.

Location: In Long Beach; see the Olympic Peninsula and Coastal Washington, map 7, grid f8.

Campsites, facilities: There are 20 drive-through sites with full hookups for trailers or RVs of any length. No tents are allowed. Restrooms, drinking water, flush toilets, and showers are available. Bottled gas, a dump station, a store, a café, a coin-operated laundry, and ice are located within one mile. Boat docks, launching facilities, and boat rentals are nearby. Leashed pets are permitted.

Reservations, fees: Reservations accepted. Sites are $14 to $18 per night, $2 per son per night for more than two people. Major credit cards accepted. Open year-round.

Directions: From Kelso/Longview on I-5, turn west on Highway 4 and drive 63 miles to U.S. 101. Turn south on U.S. 101 and drive 13 miles to the junction with Highway 103. Turn north on Highway 103 and drive two miles to Long Beach. Continue to the campground at the south junction of Pacific Highway (Highway 103) and Fifth Avenue on the right.

Contact: Oceanic RV Park, P.O. Box 242, 504 South Pacific Avenue, Long Beach, WA 98631; 360/642-3836.

132 Sand-Lo Motel and RV Park

 3

This tiny three-acre park is within four blocks of the beach, situated along the highway. It is also within five miles of an 18-hole golf course, a full-service marina, and a riding stable.

Location: Near Long Beach; see the Olympic Peninsula and Coastal Washington, map 7, grid f8.

Campsites, facilities: There are 15 sites with full hookups for tents, trailers, or RVs of any length. Restrooms, drinking water, flush toilets, showers, cable TV, a dump station, and a coin-operated laundry are available. A restaurant is next door. Bottled gas, a store, a café, and ice are located within one mile. Leashed pets are permitted.

Reservations, fees: Reservations accepted. Sites are $15 to $20, $1 per person per night for more than two people. Major credit cards accepted. Open year-round.

Directions: From Kelso/Longview on I-5, turn west on Highway 4 and drive 63 miles to U.S. 101. Turn south on U.S. 101 and drive 13 miles to the junction with Highway 103. Turn north on Highway 103 and drive three miles to the park on the right.

Contact: Sand-Lo Motel and RV Park, 1920 North Pacific Highway, Long Beach, WA 98631; 360/642-2600.

133 Driftwood RV Park

 2

This two-acre park has grassy, shaded sites and beach access. A fenced pet area is a bonus. Additional facilities within five miles of the campground include an 18-hole golf course and a full-service marina.

Location: Near Long Beach; see the Olympic Peninsula and Coastal Washington, map 7, grid f8.

Campsites, facilities: There are 55 sites with full hookups, including some drive-through, for trailers or RVs of any length. No tents are allowed. Restrooms, drinking water, flush toilets, showers, picnic tables, a coin-operated laundry, cable TV, and a fenced pet area are available. Bottled gas, a store, and a café are available within one mile. Leashed pets are permitted.

Reservations, fees: Reservations accepted. Sites are $20 per night, $2 per person per night for more than two people. Major credit cards accepted. Open March through October.

Directions: From Kelso/Longview on I-5, turn west on Highway 4 and drive 63 miles to U.S. 101. Turn south on U.S. 101 and drive 13 miles to the junction with Highway 103. Turn north on Highway 103 and drive two miles to the park on the right, at 14th North and Pacific.

Contact: Driftwood RV Park, P.O. Box 296, 1512 North Pacific Avenue, Long Beach, WA 98631; 360/642-2711 or 888/567-1902; website: www.driftwood-rvpark.com.

134 Sand Castle RV Park

 3

This park is set across the highway from the ocean. Although not particularly scenic, it is clean and does provide nearby beach access. The park covers two acres. It is one of several in the immediate area. Additional facilities found within five miles of the campground include a nine-hole golf course, marked bike trails, a full-service marina, and two riding stables. Note that 25 percent of the sites are permanent rentals.

Location: In Long Beach; see the Olympic Peninsula and Coastal Washington, map 7, grid f8.

Campsites, facilities: There are 38 sites with full hookups, including some drive-through, for trailers or RVs of any length. Tents are permitted only with RVs. Restrooms, drinking water, flush toilets, coin-operated showers, cableTV hookups, picnic tables, a dump station, a coin-operated laundry, and a pay phone are available. Bottled gas, a store, ice, and a café are available within one mile. Boat docks, launching facilities, and rentals are within five miles. Leashed pets are permitted.

Reservations, fees: Reservations accepted. Sites are $18 to $25, $1 per person per night for more than two people. Senior discount available in off-season. Major credit cards accepted. Open year-round.

Directions: From Kelso/Longview on I-5, turn west on Highway 4 and drive 63 miles to U.S. 101. Turn south on U.S. 101 and drive 13 miles to the junction with Highway 103. Turn north on Highway 103 and drive two miles to the park on the right.

Contact: Sand Castle RV Park, 1100 North Pacific Highway, Long Beach, WA 98631; 360/642-2174.

135 Sou'Wester Lodge, Cabins Trailer Park

   7

This is a one-of-a-kind place with a lodge that dates back to 1892. It also features vintage trailers available for rent, as well as cottages. Various cultural events are held at the park during the year, including fireside evenings with theater and chamber music. The park covers three acres, provides beach access, and is one of the few sites in the immediate area that provide spots for tent camping. This park often attracts creative people such as musicians and artists, and some will arrive for vacations in organized groups. It is definitely not for Howie & Ethel from Iowa. Fishing is a recreation option. The area features the Lewis and Clark Interpretive Center, a light-house, museums, fine dining, bicycle and boat rentals, bicycle and hiking trails, and bird sanctuaries. Additional facilities found within five miles of the campground include an 18-hole golf course, a full-service marina, and a riding stable. The lodge was originally built for U.S. Senator Henry Winslow Corbett.

Location: In Seaview on the Long Beach Peninsula; see the Olympic Peninsula and Coastal Washington, map 7, grid f8.

Campsites, facilities: There are 60 sites with full hookups, some drive-through, for trailers or RVs of any length, 10 tent sites, a historic lodge, four cottages, and 12 1950s-style trailers in vintage condition. Restrooms, drinking water, flush toilets, showers, cableTV, a coin-operated laundry, a classic video library, a picnic area with pavilion, and community fire pits and grills are available. Bottled gas, a dump station, a store, a café, and ice are located within one mile. Boat-launching facilities are nearby. Leashed pets are permitted.

Reservations, fees: Reservations accepted. Sites are $20 to $29.75, $2 per person per night for more than two people. Senior discount available in off-season. Major credit cards accepted. Open year-round.

Directions: From Kelso/Longview on I-5, turn west on Highway 4 and drive 63 miles to U.S. 101. Turn south on U.S. 101 and drive 13 miles to the junction with Highway 103 (flashing light). Turn left to stay on U.S. 101 and drive one block to Seaview Beach Access Road (38th Place). Turn left and drive toward the ocean. Look for the campground on the left.

Contact: Sou'Wester Lodge, Cabins Trailer Park, P.O. Box 102, Seaview, WA 98644; 360/642-2542.

136 Fisherman's Cove RV Park

   7

This five-acre park is located by the docks, near where the Pacific Ocean and the

Columbia River meet. It has beach and fishing access nearby and caters to fishermen. Fish- and clam-cleaning facilities are available in the park. A maritime museum, hiking trails, a full-service marina, and a riding stable are located within five miles of the park. About 15 percent of the sites are taken by full-time renters.

Location: Near Fort Canby State Park; see the Olympic Peninsula and Coastal Washington, map 7, grid f8.

Campsites, facilities: There are 51 sites with full hookups, including some drive-through, for trailers or RVs of any length and some tent sites. Restrooms, drinking water, flush toilets, coin-operated showers, cable TV hookups, a dump station, and a coin-operated laundry are available. Bottled gas, a store, and a café are located within one mile. Boat docks, launching facilities, and rentals are nearby. Leashed pets are permitted.

Reservations, fees: Reservations accepted. Sites are $10 for tents and $20 for RVs per night. Open year-round.

Directions: From Kelso/Longview on I-5, turn west on Highway 4 and drive 63 miles to U.S. 101. Turn south on U.S. 101 and drive 13 miles to the junction with Highway 103. Turn north on Highway 103 and drive two miles to Highway 100. Turn right (south) and drive to Ilwaco. At the junction of Spruce Street SW and First Street, turn right (west) on Spruce Street and drive one block to Second Avenue SW. Turn left (south) on Second Avenue SW and drive four blocks south to the campground on the right.

Contact: Fisherman's Cove RV Park, P.O. Box 921, 411 Second Ave. SW, Ilwaco, WA 98624; 360/642-3689 or 877/268-3789.

137 Ilwaco KOA

  5

This 17-acre camp is about nine miles from the beach and includes a secluded area for tents. A boardwalk is nearby, as well as the Lewis and Clark Museum, lighthouses, an amusement park, and fishing from a jetty or charter boats. Additional facilities found within five miles of the campground include a maritime museum, hiking trails, and a nine-hole golf course.

Location: Near Fort Canby State Park; see the Olympic Peninsula and Coastal Washington, map 7, grid f8.

Campsites, facilities: There are 114 sites with full hookups, including drive-through, for trailers or RVs of any length, a tent area for up to 50 tents, and four cabins. Restrooms, drinking water, flush toilets, showers, cable TV, bottled gas, a dump station, a recreation hall, a store, a laundry, ice, and a playground are available. Leashed pets are permitted.

Reservations, fees: Reservations accepted; phone 800/562-3258. Sites are $23 to $30 per night, $3.75 per person per night for more than two people; cabins are $45 to $50 per night. Major credit cards accepted. Open mid-May to mid-October.

Directions: From Kelso/Longview on I-5, turn west on Highway 4 and drive 63 miles to U.S. 101. Turn south on U.S. 101 and drive 13 miles to the junction with Highway 103. The campground is located at the junction.

Contact: Ilwaco KOA, P.O. Box 549, Ilwaco, WA 98624; 360/642-3292 (phone or fax).

Fort Canby State Park

   10

This park covers 1,882 acres, set on the Long Beach Peninsula, fronted by the Pacific Ocean. There is access to 27 miles of ocean beach and two lighthouses. The park has old-growth forest, lakes, both freshwater and saltwater marshes, streams, and tidelands. The park is the choice spot in the area for tent campers. There are two places to camp: a general camping area and the Lake O'Neil area, which offers sites right on the water. Highlights at the park include hiking trails and opportunities for surf, jetty, and ocean fishing. An interpretive center highlights the Lewis and Clark expedition and maritime and military history. North Head Lighthouse is open for touring. Colbert House Museum is open during the summer.

Location: On the Pacific Ocean; see the Olympic Peninsula and Coastal Washington, map 7, grid f8.

Campsites, facilities: There are 152 sites, including 27 sites with partial hookups (water and electricity) for tents, trailers, or RVs up to 45 feet long, three cabins, and seven yurts. Picnic tables and fire grills are provided. Restrooms, drinking water, flush toilets, coin-operated showers, a dump station, a picnic area, interpretive activities, a horseshoe pit, athletic fields, a small store, and firewood are available. Some facilities are wheelchair-accessible. Leashed pets are permitted.

Reservations, fees: Reserve at 888/CAMP-OUT (888/226-7688); website: www.parks.wa.gov/reservations ($7 reservation fee). Sites are $15 to $22 per night. Cabins and yurts are $35 per night. Senior discount available. Major credit cards accepted. Open year-round.

Directions: From the junction of Highway 4 and Highway 103 (a flashing light, south of Nemah), turn west on Highway 103 (toward Ilwaco) and drive two miles to Ilwaco and Highway 100. Turn right and drive three miles to the park entrance on the right.

Contact: Fort Canby State Park, 360/642-3078; State Park information, 360/902-8844.

  **Porter Creek**

7

This primitive, rustic campground is located about 30 miles from Olympia. It is set in the Capitol Forest along the shore of Porter Creek and is managed by the Department of Natural Resources. It offers trails for hiking, horseback riding, or motorbiking. The camp serves as a launch point for a variety of trips. A trail leaves from across the road and is routed one-half mile to Porter Falls, a hike most make. Within three miles, you can also access trails that lead to a network of 87 miles of off-road vehicle trails and 84 miles of trails for nonmotorized use, where mountain biking is popular. This is a popular camp for horseback riders, with corrals and hitching posts available.

Location: On Porter Creek in Capitol Forest; see the Olympic Peninsula and Coastal Washington, map 8, grid a6.

Campsites, facilities: There are 16 primitive sites for tents or small trailers. Picnic tables, fire grills, and tent pads are provided. Vault toilets, drinking water, corrals, hitching posts and horse-loading ramps are available. All-terrain vehicles are permitted. Leashed pets are permitted.

Reservations, fees: No reservations; no fee. Open April through October.

Directions: On I-5, drive to Exit 88 (10 miles north of Chehalis) and U.S. 12. Turn west on U.S. 12 and drive 21 miles to Porter and Porter Creek Road. Turn right (northeast) on

Porter Creek Road and drive three miles (last half mile is gravel) to a junction. Bear left and drive one-half mile to the campground on the left.

Contact: Department of Natural Resources, Central Region, 1405 Rush Road, Chehalis, WA 98532-8763; 360/748-2383, fax 360/748-2387.

Middle Waddell

 7

This wooded campground is nestled along Waddell Creek in Capitol Forest. The trails in the immediate vicinity are used primarily for all-terrain vehicles (ATVs), and it can make for some noise. There is an extensive network of ATV trails in the area. Mountain bikers tend to prefer Fall Creek camp in this area.

Location: On Waddell Creek in Capitol Forest; see the Olympic Peninsula and Coastal Washington, map 8, grid a8.

Campsites, facilities: There are 24 sites for tents, trailers, or RVs of any length. Picnic tables, fire grills, and tent pads are provided. Drinking water and vault toilets are available. A full-time campground host is at this camp. Some facilities are wheelchair-accessible. Leashed pets are permitted.

Reservations, fees: No reservations; no fee. Open April through October.

Directions: From Olympia on I-5, drive south for about 10 miles to Exit 95 and Highway 121. Turn west on Highway 121 and drive four miles to Littlerock. Continue west for one mile to Waddell Creek Road. Turn right and drive three miles and look for the campground entrance road on the left.

Contact: Department of Natural Resources, Central Region, 1405 Rush Road, Chehalis, WA 98532-8763; 360/748-2383, fax 360/748-2387.

141 Fall Creek

 7

This is something of a mountain-biking headquarters with good access to an 84-mile network of trails for nonmotorized use. Although ATVs are allowed in the campground, they are not allowed on the adjacent trails. This is a wooded camp on Fall Creek in Capitol Forest. Horse facilities are available.

Location: On Fall Creek in Capitol Forest; see the Olympic Peninsula and Coastal Washington, map 8, grid a8.

Campsites, facilities: There are eight primitive campsites for tents or small trailers. Picnic tables, fire grills, and tent pads are provided. Vault toilets, drinking water, corrals, a hitching post, and a horse-loading ramp are available. A day-use staging area is also available. Some facilities are wheelchair-accessible. Leashed pets are permitted.

Reservations, fees: No reservations; no fee. Open April through October.

Directions: From Olympia on I-5, turn north on U.S. 101 and drive four miles to the Mud Bay exit. Take that to Delphi Road and drive south for six miles to Waddell Creek Road (bear right at the junction). Continue straight on Waddell Creek Road for two miles to the Triangle (turns into Sherman Valley Road). Continue straight on Sherman Valley Road for one mile (pavement ends, becomes C-Line Road) and continue four miles to Road C-6000. Turn left and drive three miles to the campground on the right.

Contact: Department of Natural Resources, Central Region, 1405 Rush Road, Chehalis, WA 98532-8763; 360/748-2383, fax 360/748-2387.

142 Margaret McKenny

 7

This camp is used primarily as a trailhead for horseback riders and mountain bikers, with trails linked to an extensive network of trails for nonmotorized use only. Most of the campsites are well away from a stream, but seven walk-in sites are available, where a 300- to 400-foot walk down a stairway takes you to pretty streamside campsites.

Location: In Capitol Forest; see the Olympic Peninsula and Coastal Washington, map 8, grid a8.

Campsites, facilities: There are 25 primitive sites for tents or small trailers; seven sites are walk-ins. Picnic tables, fire grills, and tent pads are provided. Drinking water, vault toilets, a campfire circle, and a horse-loading ramp are available. A campground host is on site. Some facilities are wheelchair-accessible. Leashed pets are permitted.

Reservations, fees: No reservations; no fee. Open April through October.

Directions: From Olympia on I-5, drive south for about 10 miles to Exit 95 and Highway 121. Turn west on Highway 121 and drive four miles to Littlerock. Continue west for one mile to Waddell Creek Road. Turn right and drive 2.5 miles and look for the campground entrance road on the left.

Contact: Department of Natural Resources, Central Region, 1405 Rush Road, Chehalis, WA 98532-8763; 360/748-2383, fax 360/748-2387.

143 Sherman Valley

 8

This is one of several secluded camps located in the Capitol Forest and managed by the Department of Natural Resources. Sherman Valley's pleasant, shady campsites are set along the shore of Porter Creek. The forest here is primarily alder and fir trees. Hiking

trails can be found nearby (see North Creek Camp). Like nearby North Creek Camp, this camp is also used by hunters in season.

Location: On Cedar Creek in Capitol Forest; see the Olympic Peninsula and Coastal Washington, map 8, grid a7.

Campsites, facilities: There are seven primitive sites for tents or small trailers and three walk-in sites. Picnic tables, fire grills, and tent pads are provided. Vault toilets and drinking water are available. Mountain bikes are permitted on the roads only; trails are reserved for hikers. Leashed pets are permitted.

Reservations, fees: No reservations; no fee. Open April through October.

Directions: From Olympia, drive south on I-5 for 16 miles to U.S. 12. Turn west on U.S. 12 and drive 12 miles to Oakville. Continue west on U.S. 12 for 2.5 miles to D-Line Road (Cedar Creek entrance). Turn right (east) and drive 6.5 miles to the camp on the right (one lane, but paved all the way).

Contact: Department of Natural Resources, Central Region, 1405 Rush Road, Chehalis, WA 98532-8763; 360/748-2383, fax 360/748-2387.

144 North Creek

 8

This little-known, wooded campground managed by the Department of Natural Resources is set along Cedar Creek (fishing available). There are trails for hikers only (no horses, no mountain bikes). A four-mile loop trail is available that is routed out to Sherman Valley (in spring 2002, a bridge was out on this trail, with a longer alternative route available; call before planning a hike). This camp is used in the fall by hunters. An option is visiting the Chehalis River, a five-mile drive to the west. A canoe launch off U.S. 12 is available north of Oakville.

Location: On Cedar Creek; see the Olympic Peninsula and Coastal Washington, map 8, grid a7.

Campsites, facilities: There are five primitive sites for tents or small trailers. Fire grills and tent pads are provided. Vault toilets and drinking water are available. Some facilities are wheelchair-accessible. Mountain bikes are permitted on the roads only; trails are reserved for hikers. Leashed pets are permitted.

Reservations, fees: No reservations; no fee. Open April through October.

Directions: From Olympia, drive south on I-5 for 16 miles to U.S. 12. Turn west on U.S. 12 and drive 12 miles to Oakville. Continue west on U.S. 12 for 2.5 miles to D-Line Road (Cedar Creek entrance). Turn right (east) and drive 4.5 miles to the camp on the right (one lane, but paved all the way).

Contact: Department of Natural Resources, Central Region, 1405 Rush Road, Chehalis, WA 98532-8763; 360/748-2383, fax 360/748-2387.

 Mima Falls Trailhead

 10

The highlight here is the five-mile loop trail for hikers and horseback riders that leads to beautiful 90-foot Mima Falls. The campground is quiet and pretty. When combined with the drinking water, free admission, and tromp out to the waterfall, this spot is a first-rate choice. One of the unique qualities of this campground is that it provides facilities for both wheelchair users and horseback riders. The trail is not wheelchair-accessible, but the facilities mean that wheelchair users with horses can access the trip to Mima Falls. The trail runs across its brink.

Location: Near Mima Falls; see the Olympic Peninsula and Coastal Washington, map 8, grid a8.

Campsites, facilities: There is a primitive, dispersed camping area for about five tents or small trailers. Picnic tables, fire grills, and tent pads are provided. Drinking water,

vault toilets, and a horse-loading ramp are available. Some facilities are wheelchair-accessible. Leashed pets are permitted.

Reservations, fees: No reservations; no fee. Open April through October.

Directions: From Olympia, drive south on I-5 for 10 miles to Highway 121. Turn west on Highway 121 and drive four miles west to Littlerock. Continue west for one mile to Mima Road. Turn left on Mima Road and drive 1.5 miles to Bordeaux Road. Turn right on Bordeaux Road and drive one-half mile to Marksman Road. Turn right and drive two-thirds of a mile to the campground access road on the left. Turn left and drive 200 yards to the campground.

Contact: Department of Natural Resources, Central Region, 1405 Rush Road, Chehalis, WA 98532-8763; 360/748-2383, fax 360/748-2387.

Bay Center/Willapa Bay KOA

 7

This KOA is set within walking distance of a beach that seems to stretch to infinity. It is located on the shore of Willapa Bay and has a trail leading to the beach. From here you can walk for miles in either direction. The beach sand is mixed, with agates, driftwood, and seaweed. Dungeness crabs, clams, and oysters all live within the nearshore vicinity. Another bonus is that herds of Roosevelt elk roam the nearby woods. Believe it or not, there are also black bear, although they are seldom seen here. The park covers 11 acres, and the campsites are graveled and shaded.

Location: On Willapa Bay; see the Olympic Peninsula and Coastal Washington, map 8, grid c1.

Campsites, facilities: There are 55 sites with full or partial hookups, including some drive-through, for trailers or RVs of any length, 22 tent sites, and two cabins. Picnic tables are provided. Restrooms, drinking water, flush toilets, showers, bottled gas, a dump station, cable TV, modem hookups, a recreation hall, a store, firewood, a coin-operated laundry, and ice are available. There is a café nearby. Boat docks and launching facilities are about three miles from camp on Willapa Bay. Leashed pets are permitted.

Reservations, fees: Reservations accepted at 800/562-7810. Sites are $18 to $26 per night, $3 per person per night for more than two people; cabins are $35 to $37 per night. Major credit cards accepted. Open mid-March through mid-October.

Directions: From Nemah on U.S. 101, drive north for five miles to Bay Center/Dike exit (located between Mileposts 42 and 43, 16 miles south of Raymond). Turn west and drive three miles to the campground.

Contact: Bay Center/Willapa Bay KOA, Bay Center Dike Road, Bay Center, WA 98527; 360/875-6344.

147 Rainbow Falls State Park

    8

This 139-acre park is set on the Chehalis River with 3,400 feet of shoreline. The camp features stands of old-growth cedar and fir and is named after a few small cascades with drops of about 10 feet. The park has 10 miles of hiking trails, including an interpretive trail, seven miles of bike trails, and seven miles of horse trails. There is a pool at the base of Rainbow Falls for swimming. Another attraction is a small fuschia garden with more than 40 varieties. There are also several log structures built by the Civilian Conservation Corps in 1935.

Location: On the Chehalis River Bay; see the Olympic Peninsula and Coastal Washington, map 8, grid c7.

Campsites, facilities: There are 47 sites for tents or self-contained RVs up to 32 feet long, three primitive tent sites, three equestrian sites with hitching points and stock water, and one group site. Picnic tables and fire rings are provided. Restrooms, drinking water, flush toilets, coin-operated showers, a dump station, a picnic area, interpretive activities, a playground with horseshoe pits, and a softball field are available. Firewood is available just outside the park. Leashed pets are permitted.

Reservations, fees: No reservations. Sites are $6 to $16 per night, $6 per extra vehicle per night. Senior discount available. Open April through September.

Directions: From Chehalis on I-5, take Exit 77 to Highway 6. Turn west and drive 16 miles to the park entrance on the right.

Contact: Rainbow Falls State Park, 4008 Highway 6, Chehalis, WA 98532; 360/291-3767; State Park information, 360/902-8844.

148 Western Lakes

    9

You want quiet and solitude? You found it. This tiny, primitive campground is a jewel set near two lakes—Snag Lake and Western Lake (the lower lake)—in a wooded area near Western Lakes, just outside of Naselle. Snag Lake is the feature, which provides fishing for rainbow trout, brook trout, and cutthroat trout. No gas motors are permitted, so it is ideal for float tubes, prams, rowboats, or canoes (with electric motors permitted). There are some good hiking trails nearby, including a route that connects the two lakes. There is a good view of Radar Ridge from the lake and campground. A wheelchair-accessible trail is available around Snag Lake, and all campsites provide wheelchair access. It's a prime camp for travelers heading to the coast who want a day or two of privacy before they hit the crowds.

Location: Near Naselle; see the Olympic Peninsula and Coastal Washington, map 8, grid e3.

Campsites, facilities: There are five tent sites, all wheelchair-accessible. Picnic tables, fire grills, tent pads, and vault toilets are provided, but there is no drinking water. Garbage must be packed out. Leashed pets are permitted.

Reservations, fees: No reservations; no fee. Open year-round.

Directions: From Kelso/Longview on I-5, turn west on Highway 4 and drive 60 miles (near Naselle) to Milepost 3 and C-Line Road. Turn north on C-Line Road (one-lane gravel road, becomes C-4000) uphill, take the left fork at Naselle Youth Camp Entrance, and drive 2.9 miles to C-2600 (gravel one-lane road). Turn left on Road C-2600 and drive 0.9 mile (after 0.4 mile it becomes C-Line Road) to C-2650. Turn right and drive 1.2 miles to the campground on the right at Western Lake. Or for Snag Lake: At Road C-2400, turn on Road C-2400 and drive 0.6 mile to campground at Snag Lake.

Contact: Department of Natural Resources, Central Region, 1405 Rush Road, Chehalis, WA 98532-8763; 360/748-2383.

149 River's End Campground and RV Park

 6

This wooded campground spreads over five acres and has riverside access. Salmon fishing is available here. Additional facilities found within five miles of the campground include marked bike trails and a full-service marina. Also nearby is Fort Columbia State Park.

Location: Near Fort Columbia State Park; see the Olympic Peninsula and Coastal Washington, map 8, grid f1.

Campsites, facilities: There are 54 sites with full hookups, including some drive-through, for trailers or RVs of any length and 24 tent sites. Picnic tables are provided at RV sites. Fire pits are provided at tent sites. Restrooms, drinking water, flush toilets, coin-operated showers, a dump station, a recreation hall, a coin-operated laundry, firewood for a fee, a fish-cleaning station, ice, and a playground are available. Bottled gas, a store, and a café are located within one mile. Boat docks, launching facilities, and rentals are nearby on the Columbia River. Leashed pets permitted.

Reservations, fees: Reservations accepted. Sites are $14 to $20 per night, $1 per person per night for more than two people. Open April to late October.

Directions: From Kelso/Longview on I-5, turn west on Highway 4 and drive 60 miles to Highway 401. Turn south on Highway 401 and drive 14 miles to the park entrance (just south of Chinook) on the left.

Contact: River's End Campground and RV Park, P.O. Box 280, 12 Bayview Street, Chinook, WA 98614; 360/777-8317.

150 Mauch's Sundown RV Park, Inc.

 5

This is an adults-only park with about 35 percent of the sites rented long-term, usually throughout the summer. The park covers four acres, has riverside access, and is in a wooded, hilly setting with grassy sites. Nearby fishing from shore is available. It's near Fort Columbia State Park.

Location: Near Fort Columbia State Park; see the Olympic Peninsula and Coastal Washington, map 8, grid f1.

Campsites, facilities: There are 50 sites with full and partial hookups for trailers or RVs of any length. No tents, children, or large pets are permitted. Restrooms, drinking water, flush toilets, coin-operated showers, picnic tables, a dump station, cable TV, a coin-operated laundry, a store, propane gas, and ice are available. A café is located within three miles. Boat docks and launching facilities are nearby on the Columbia River. Small pets are permitted.

Reservations, fees: Reservations accepted. Sites are $8 to $20 per night, $1.50 per person per night for more than two people, $1.50 per extra vehicle per night. Open year-round.

Directions: From Kelso/Longview on I-5, turn west on Highway 4 and drive 60 miles to Highway 401. Turn south on Highway 401 and drive to U.S. 101. Take U.S. 101 to the right and continue for a half mile (do not go over the bridge) to the park on the right.

Contact: Mauch's Sundown RV Park, 158 State Route 101, Chinook, WA 98614; 360/777-8713.

151 Skamokawa Vista Park

     7

This public camp covers 70 acres and features a half-mile of sandy beach and a Lewis and Clark interpretive site installed in 2002. A short hiking trail is also nearby. There is also nearby access to the Columbia River, where fishing, swimming, and boating are all options. Additional facilities found within five miles of the campground include a full-service marina and additional tennis courts. This park is in a growth mode, and there is a good chance that additional campsites and yurts will be added by 2003. In Skamokawa, a River Life Interpretive Center is open year-round.

Location: Near the Columbia River; see the Olympic Peninsula and Coastal Washington, map 8, grid f5.

Campsites, facilities: There are 21 sites with partial hookups for trailers or RVs of any length, nine sites with no hookups for tents or RVs, and four tent sites. Picnic tables and fire grills are provided. Restrooms, drinking water, flush toilets, coin-operated showers, a dump station, firewood, tennis courts, basketball courts, and a playground are available. Bottled gas, a store, a café, and ice are located within one mile. Boat docks, launching facilities, and canoe and kayak rentals are nearby. Leashed pets are permitted.

Reservations, fees: Reservations accepted. Sites are $12 to $21 per night. Open year-round.

Directions: From Kelso/Longview on I-5, turn west on Highway 4 and drive 35 miles to Skamokawa. Continue west on Highway 4 for one-half mile to the park on the left.

Contact: Skamokawa Vista Park, Port of Wahkiakum No. 2, P.O. Box 220, 13 Vista Park Road, Skamokawa, WA 98647; 360/795-8605.

SEATTLE AND THE
SAN JUAN ISLANDS

©TOM STIENSTRA

Seattle and the San Juan Islands

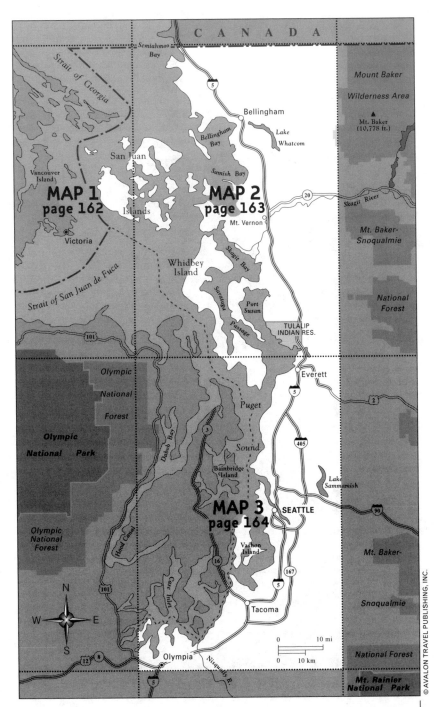

© AVALON TRAVEL PUBLISHING, INC.

Map 1

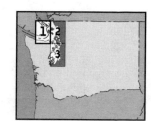

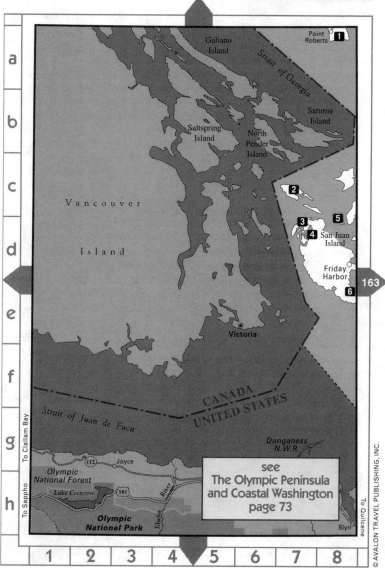

Map 2

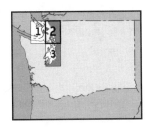

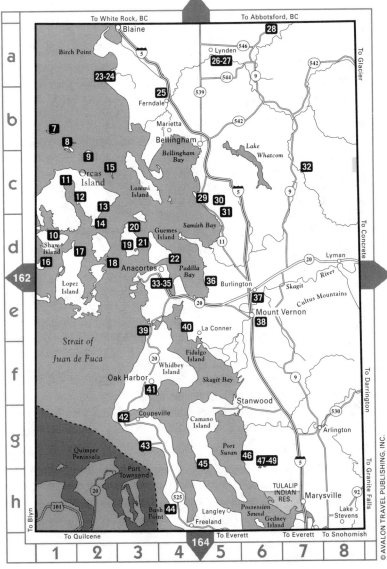

Map 3

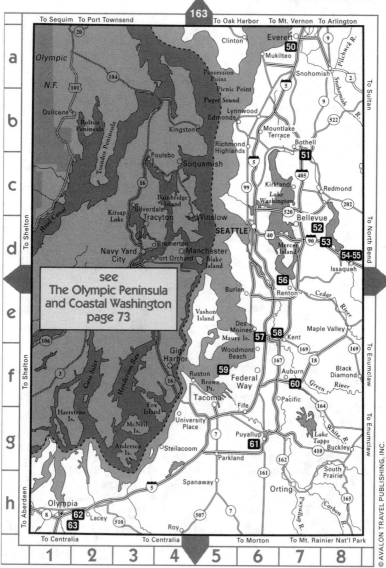

see
**The Olympic Peninsula
and Coastal Washington
page 73**

© AVALON TRAVEL PUBLISHING, INC.

Seattle and the San Juan Islands

(CONTINUED ON NEXT PAGE)

No metropolitan area in the world offers a wider array of recreation than Seattle-Tacoma and its sphere of influence. At the center are water, woods, and islands. One of our favorite views anywhere is from the top of Mt. Constitution on Orcas Island, where on a clear day you can see across an infinity of sun-swept charm. Take one look and you'll know this is why you came.

The scope of parks, campgrounds, and recreation on the islands in this region is preeminent. Even if you're traveling by car, you still have an array of excellent destinations, including many available by ferry transport. Many state parks offer gorgeous water-view campsites. Well-furnished RV parks along the I-5 corridor offer respite for vacationers in need of a layover, and hidden lakes, such as Cascade Lake on Orcas Island, will surprise you with their beauty.

But live here for even a short time and you will realize that you need some kind of boat to do it right. A power boat, sailboat, or kayak offers instant access to adventure, as well as the ability to set up boat-in campsites. With a power boat, you get instant freedom from the traffic on the I-5 corridor, as well as near-unlimited access to destinations in Puget Sound and the linked inlets, bays, and canals. Fishing can be good, too. On calm days with light breezes, roaming the peaceful waters in a sailboat amid dozens of islands provides a segue to instant tranquility. There is no better place anywhere to sea kayak, with some 25 boat-in campsites available, often with calm, sheltered waters. With near-perfect destinations like these, this area is quickly becoming the sea kayaking capital of the world.

People who live here year-round, fighting the rat maze of traffic on I-5, can easily fall into the trap of tunnel vision, never seeing beyond the line of cars ahead of them. Escape that tunnel. Scan the maps and pages in this region, and in the process, reward yourself with the best water-based adventure anywhere.

1 Whalen's RV Park

 6

This RV park is located on remote Point Roberts, where you must drive through Canada and then return south into the United States to reach it. But don't hop on the bandwagon just yet. A key here is that 80 percent of the campsites are booked for the entire summer. That makes reservations critical for anybody wishing to stay overnight. This spot is a mix of woods and water. The park has grassy sites and lots of trees. A recreation field is provided for campers. Nearby recreational options include an 18-hole golf course, a full-service marina, and tennis courts.

Location: On Point Roberts; see Seattle and the San Juan Islands, map 1, grid a8.

Campsites, facilities: There are 100 sites for tents and 50 sites with partial hookups (no sewer) for trailers or RVs of any length. Picnic tables and fire grills are provided. Restrooms, drinking water, flush toilets, coin-operated showers, a dump station, and firewood are available. A store, a café, a coin-operated laundry, and ice are located within one mile. Boat docks and launching facilities are nearby. Leashed pets are permitted.

Reservations, fees: Reservations accepted. Sites are $15 to $20 per night. Major credit cards accepted. Open from May to late October.

Directions: From Bellingham, take I-5 north through Blaine and the border customs into Canada to Highway 99 North. Continue northwest on Highway BC 99N for 18 miles to BC 17. Turn and drive six miles to the town of Tsawwassen and 56th Street. Turn west and drive to Benson Road. Turn left on Benson Road and drive one mile to Boundary Bay Road. Turn left and drive one mile to Bay View

Road. Turn left again and drive half a mile to the park on the left.

Contact: Whalen's RV Park, Roosevelt and Derby, Point Roberts, WA 98281; 360/945-2874, fax 360/945-0934.

2 Stuart Island Marine State Park Boat-In

 9

For most campers, this is really stalking the unknown. Stuart Island is a remote little spot on the edge of Canadian waters that covers 153 acres and has excellent harbors for mooring. It's the westernmost of the marine parks, making it a jumping-off point for Sucia Island, Orcas Island, and San Juan Island parks. There is good fishing at nearby Reid and Provost Harbors. On holiday weekends, it usually fills up; on summer weekends, it is typically about 70 percent filled; and on weekdays, it is about half filled. That makes it the second busiest park in the area. The park receives about 70,000 visitors per year.

Location: Northwest of San Juan Island; see Seattle and the San Juan Islands, map 1, grid c7.

Campsites, facilities: There are 22 primitive boat-in campsites, including four reserved for nonmotorized boats only. Picnic tables and fire rings are provided. Drinking water (summer season only) and composting toilets are available. There are also 22 buoys, and floats are available for overnight moorage. Garbage must be packed out. Leashed pets are permitted.

Reservations, fees: No reservations. Sites are $6 per night, moorage is $10 to $16 per night, and buoys are $7 per night. Senior discount available. Open year-round, with limited facilities in winter.

Directions: The park is on the north side of Stuart Island and is accessible only by boat. Stuart Island is located northwest of San Juan Island.

Contact: San Juan Marine Area, Star Route, Box 177, Olga, WA 98279; 360/378-2044; State Park information, 360/902-8844.

🛥 Posey Island State Park Boat-In

 9

If you want a beautiful little spot all to yourself, this can often be it. Imagine that, an island all to yourself. It's difficult to get here, however. The best way is by sea kayak, paddling in from San Juan Island out of Roche Harbor. You must arrive by nonmotorized boat; that is, only kayaks, canoes, or pelican sailboats. There are no docks or mooring buoys. This is not only one of the smallest designated campgrounds in Washington, but also one of the most idyllic and beautiful to reach by small boat. This is just a one-acre island with lots of wild flowers in spring, including chocolate lilies. No more than 16 people are permitted on the island at one time, in an attempt to keep it from being loved to death. There's not much here, and that's exactly why it is so well loved. Everything becomes simplified, and it's as if you have the entire world to yourself. And on Posey Island, you do.

Location: Near Roche Harbor; see Seattle and the San Juan Islands, map 1, grid d7.

Campsites, facilities: There are two primitive boat-in campsites. Fire rings and a composting toilet are provided. No drinking water is available. Garbage must be packed out.

Reservations, fees: No reservations. The site is $6 per night. Senior discount available. Open year-round.

Directions: This little island is located just north of Roche Harbor (on San Juan Island) and is accessible only by small boat. From Roche Harbor, you head out Wescott Bay,

turn right through Mosquito Pass, and cruise about two miles to Posey Island.

Contact: San Juan Marine Area, Star Route, Box 177, Olga, WA 98279; 360/378-2044, fax 360/856-2150.

🛥 Lakedale Resort Ferry-In

  6

This is a nice spot for visitors who want the solitude of an island camp, yet all the amenities of a privately run campground. Fishing, swimming, and boating are available at the Lakedale Lakes. A sand volleyball court, a half-court basketball area, and a grassy sports field are also on site. Roche Harbor and Wescott Bay are nearby to the north, and Friday Harbor and its restaurants are nearby to the south.

Location: On San Juan Island; see Seattle and the San Juan Islands, map 1, grid d7.

Campsites, facilities: There are 102 sites for tents and 18 sites with partial hookups (no sewer) for tents, trailers, or RVs up to 40 feet long. There are also six group sites, three tent cabins, six log cabins, and 10 luxury lodge rooms. Picnic tables and fire rings are provided. Restrooms, drinking water, flush toilets, showers, and firewood are available for a fee. A store and ice are available. Boat docks, three swimming beaches, and boat, bike, camping, and fishing gear rentals are available on site. Leashed pets are permitted.

Reservations, fees: Reservations accepted. Sites are $19 to $28 per night for tent and RV campers, $6 to $7 per extra vehicle per night, $3.25 to $5.75 per person per night for more than two people, $1 pet fee per night. Hike-in/bike-in sites are $7 per person. Major credit cards accepted. Open mid-March to mid-October for camping. Cabin rentals available year-round.

Directions: From Seattle on I-5, drive north to Burlington and Highway 20. Turn west on Highway 20 and drive 12 miles to the Highway 20 North spur, following signs to the San Juan Islands Ferry Terminal in Anacortes. Take the ferry to Friday Harbor on San Juan Island. From the ferry landing at Friday Harbor, drive two blocks on Spring Street to 2nd Street. Turn right (northwest) on 2nd Street and drive one-half mile to Tucker Avenue (it becomes Roche Harbor Road). Turn right (north) and continue 4.5 miles to the campground on the left.

Contact: Lakedale Resort, 4313 Roche Harbor Road, Friday Harbor, WA 98250; 360/378-2350 or 800/617-CAMP (800/617-2267), fax 360/378-0944; website: www.lakedale.com.

5 Jones Island Marine State Park Boat-In

 9

This small island may seem like a hidden spot, yet it is an easy boat ride out of Doe Harbor at Orcas and gets among the heaviest use of all the island campgrounds in the region, even though only nonmotorized craft are permitted. It is an ideal destination for sea kayakers. The campground is near the beach, so you don't have to carry your gear very far. The area offers good fishing and scuba diving. A note of caution: Raccoons have become pests and campers are advised to keep food well contained. Rangers here make a special request to please not feed the raccoons, deer, or other wildlife. Sunsets often provide breathtaking beauty from this island. In addition, it is set amid a national wildlife and migratory bird refuge. Another plus is that two big lawn areas are ideal for families and group camping. Note that the docks are in place from April to mid-October.

Location: Near Orcas Island; see Seattle and the San Juan Islands, map 1, grid d8.

Campsites, facilities: There are 21 primitive boat-in campsites and a group site for up to 65 people. Picnic tables and fire rings are provided. Drinking water and vault, composting, and pit toilets (pick your favorite!) are available. Boat buoys and floats are available for overnight moorage. Leashed pets are permitted.

Reservations, fees: No reservations for individual sites Reservations required for the group site. Sites are $6 per night, $10 to $16 for docking per night, $7 for a moorage buoy. Senior discount available. The group site is $25, plus $2 per person per night. Open May through September.

Directions: The campground is on tiny Jones Island, located less than one mile off the southwest tip of Orcas Island. This camp is accessible only by boat. Look for the boat buoys just offshore from the campsites.

Contact: San Juan Marine Area, Star Route, Box 177, Olga, WA 98279; 360/378-2044; State Park information, 360/902-8844.

6 Griffin Bay Boat-In

 9

This tiny, remote camp is ideal for a husband-and-wife kayak team who want the place to themselves. It receives little use, yet it's located on one of the prettiest islands in the area and is a favorite among the kayakers who know of it. Only nonmotorized boats are permitted to land. The island covers just four acres, and with one campsite and two mooring buoys, it is the smallest designated campground in Washington.

Location: On San Juan Island; see Seattle and the San Juan Islands, map 1, grid e8.

Campsites, facilities: There is one primitive boat-in campsite. A fire pit is provided. A pit toilet and three picnic sites are available. No drinking water is available.

Garbage must be packed out. Two boat buoys are available for overnight moorage.

Reservations, fees: No reservations; no fee. Open year-round.

Directions: Griffin Bay is on the southeast side of San Juan Island (south of Friday Harbor), somewhat protected by Low Point. It's accessible only by boat.

Contact: Department of Natural Resources, Northwest Region, 919 North Township Street, Sedro-Woolley, WA 98284-9395; 360/856-3500, fax 360/856-2150.

7 Patos Island State Park Boat-In

 9

If you're going to get stranded on an island, this is not a bad choice, provided you like your companion. There are good hiking trails and excellent fishing and clam-digging opportunities here. It's tiny, primitive, and used by few. Patos Lighthouse is a favorite attraction on this island. It all features great views of the Canadian islands, and sunsets are often drop-dead beautiful.

Location: Near Sucia Island; see Seattle and the San Juan Islands, map 2, grid b1.

Campsites, facilities: There are seven primitive boat-in campsites. Fire rings are provided. Vault and pit toilets are available, but there is no drinking water. Boat buoys are available for overnight moorage. Garbage must be packed out. Leashed pets are permitted.

Reservations, fees: No reservations. Sites are $6 per night, $7 per night for a mooring buoy. Senior discount available. Open year-round.

Directions: The park is on the east side of Patos Island, which is 2.5 miles northwest of Sucia Island and five miles northwest of Orcas Island. It's accessible only by boat and is the northernmost of the coastal islands.

Contact: San Juan Marine Area, Star Route, Box 177, Olga, WA 98279; 360/378-2044; State Park information, 360/902-8844.

8 Sucia Island Marine State Park Boat-In

 9

Here's a classic spot, with rocky outcrops for lookout points and good beach and fishing areas. Sucia Island covers 562 acres and provides opportunities for hiking, clamming, crabbing, canoeing, and scuba diving. Although primitive, the campground is beautiful and well worth the trip. That is why it is the busiest park in the chain of San Juan Islands. It also has the most moorage. This camp is full during summer, often even on weekdays.

Location: Near Orcas Island; see Seattle and the San Juan Islands, map 2, grid b1.

Campsites, facilities: There are 55 primitive boat-in campsites and two group sites for up to 50 people each. Picnic tables and fire rings are provided. Drinking water is available in the summer season, and vault and composting toilets and two docks are also available. Boat buoys and floats are available for overnight moorage. Garbage must be packed out. Leashed pets are permitted.

Reservations, fees: No reservations. Sites are $6 per night. Group site is $2 per person per night. Senior discount available. Open year-round.

Directions: The park is on the north side of Sucia Island, which is located 2.5 miles north of Orcas Island. It's accessible only by boat.

Contact: San Juan Marine Area, Star Route, Box 177, Olga, WA 98279; 360/378-2044; State Park information, 360/902-8844.

9 Matia Island State Park Boat-In

 9

Campsites here are located just a short walk from the docking facilities (available from April to mid-October), a big plus since many of the other island campgrounds don't have docks. Otherwise the camp is primitive, so it gets lighter use than the other campgrounds set on islands in the area. A one-mile loop trail from the campground is routed through an old-growth cedar forest. Other highlights are good fishing and beachcombing. Scuba diving is also popular.

Location: Near Orcas Island; see Seattle and the San Juan Islands, map 2, grid c2.

Campsites, facilities: There are six primitive boat-in campsites. Fire rings and composting toilets are provided. No drinking water is available. There is a boat dock, and buoys and floats are available for overnight moorage. Note that docks are in place from April to mid-October. Garbage must be packed out. Leashed pets are peritted.

Reservations, fees: No reservations. Sites are $6 per night, dock moorage is $10 to $16 per night, mooring buoys are $7 per night. Senior discount available. Open year-round, with extremely limited winter facilities.

Directions: The campground is located on the northeast side of Matia Island, which is 2.5 miles northeast of Orcas Island (located between Clark Island to the southeast, Sucia Island to the northwest, and Orcas Island to the south). It's accessible only by boat.

Contact: San Juan Marine Area, Star Route, Box 177, Olga, WA 98279; 360/378-2044; State Park information, 360/902-8844.

10 Blind Island State Park Boat-In

 9

This island has few trees and is known for its rocky shoreline. It's dangerous and ill advised to try beaching cruiser-style boats. Only nonmotorized boats are permitted, but skilled kayakers will not have difficulty landing unless the water is rough. Blind Island State Park is a designated natural area and is committed to conserving a natural environment in a minimally developed state. This is not a place for large groups to throw big barbecues, but rather a quiet place in its natural state.

Location: Near Shaw Island; see Seattle and the San Juan Islands, map 2, grid d1.

Campsites, facilities: There are four primitive boat-in campsites. Fire rings are provided. Composting and pit toilets are available, but there is no drinking water. Boat buoys are available for overnight moorage. Leashed pets are permitted.

Reservations, fees: No reservations. Sites are $6 per night, $7 for mooring buoy. Open year-round.

Directions: The campground is located just west of the Shaw Island ferry landing on little Blind Island in Blind Bay. The nearest boat ramps are at Obstruction Pass on Orcas Island or Odlin County Park on Lopez Island.

Contact: San Juan Marine Area, Star Route, Box 177, Olga, WA 98279; 360/378-2044; State Park information, 360/902-8844.

11 West Beach Resort Ferry-In

  9

Right on the beach, this resort offers salmon fishing, boating, swimming, and an apple orchard. It's an excellent alternative to Moran State Park, which is often full, and offers the same recreation opportunities. The beaches at Orcas Island are prime spots for whale-watching and beautiful views, especially at sunrise and sunset.

Location: On Orcas Island; see Seattle and the San Juan Islands, map 2, grid c1.

Campsites, facilities: There are 62 sites with partial hookups (no sewer) for tents, trailers, or RVs of any length. There are also 18 cabins. Restrooms, coin-operated showers (from

April through October only), a public phone, a store, a playground, a coin-operated laundry, ice, bottled gas, and firewood are available. A hot tub is available for a fee. Also on site are a boat ramp, a dock, a marina, and rentals. Leashed pets are permitted.

Reservations, fees: Reservations recommended. Sites are $25 to $35 per night, $5 per extra vehicle per night, $5 per pet. Major credit cards accepted. Open year-round.

Directions: From Seattle on I-5, drive north to Burlington and Highway 20. Turn west on Highway 20 and drive 12 miles to the Highway 20 North spur, following signs to the San Juan Islands Ferry Terminal in Anacortes. Take the ferry to Orcas Island. From the ferry landing, turn left and drive 11 miles on Horseshoe Highway/Orcas Road to the entrance of Eastsound. A green sign directs you left toward Moran State Park. Turn left (continuing on Orcas Road) and drive one-half mile to Enchanted Forest Road. Turn left and drive to the end of Enchanted Forest Road and the resort.

Contact: West Beach Resort, 190 Waterfront Way, Eastsound, WA 98245; 360/376-2240, fax 360/376-4746; website: www.westbeach.com.

12 Moran State Park Ferry-In

 10

This state park is drop-dead beautiful. It covers 5,252 acres with surprise lakes, hiking trails, and the best mountaintop views anywhere in the chain of islands. There are actually four separate campgrounds plus a primitive area. You can drive to the summit of Mt. Constitution, which tops out at 2,409 feet, then climb up the steps to a stone observation tower (built in 1936 by the Civilian Conservation Corps) for sensational 360-degree views of Vancouver, Mt. Baker, the San Juan

Islands, the Cascade Mountains, and several cities on the distant shores of mainland America and Canada. No RVs are allowed on the winding road to the top. There are five freshwater lakes with fishing for rainbow trout, cutthroat trout, and kokanee salmon, 33 miles of hiking trails, 11 miles of biking trails, and six miles of horse trails. The landscape features old-growth forest, primarily lodgepole pine, and several small waterfalls. Nearby recreation options include a nine-hole golf course.

Location: On Orcas Island; see Seattle and the San Juan Islands, map 2, grid c2.

Campsites, facilities: There are 136 developed sites, including some drive-through sites, for tents or RVs up to 45 feet long, 15 primitive hike-in/bike-in tent sites, and one cabin for up to 10 people. No hookups are available. Picnic tables and fire grills are provided. Restrooms, drinking water, flush toilets, coin-operated showers, a dump station, a picnic area with log kitchen shelter, and firewood are available. Boat docks, limited fishing supplies, launching facilities, and boat rentals are located at the concession stand in the park. Some facilities are wheelchair-accessible. Leashed pets are permitted.

Reservations, fees: Reserve at 888/CAMP-OUT (888/226-7688); website: www.parks.wa.gov/reservations ($7 reservation fee). Sites are $7 to $22 per night, $6 per extra vehicle per night. Reserve cabin at 800/360-4200, $114 per night. Senior discount available. Major credit cards accepted. Open year-round.

Directions: From Seattle on I-5, drive north to Burlington and Highway 20. Turn west on Highway 20 and drive 12 miles to the Highway 20 North spur, following signs to the San Juan Islands Ferry Terminal in Anacortes. Take the ferry to Orcas Island. From the ferry landing, turn left on Horseshoe Highway/Oras Road and drive 13 miles to

Moran State Park (well marked). Stop at the campground registration booth for directions to your site.

Contact: Moran State Park Ferry-In, 3572 Olga Road, Olga, WA 98245; 360/376-2326; State Park information, 360/902-8844.

13 Doe Island State Park Boat-In

 9

Doe Island has a rocky shoreline, which makes an ideal fish habitat, and the scuba diving and fishing are exceptional. Doe Island State Park is a tiny, primitive park that receives little use. Docking is available from April to mid-October.

Location: Near Orcas Island; see Seattle and the San Juan Islands, map 2, grid c2.

Campsites, facilities: There are five primitive boat-in campsites. Fire rings and vault toilets are provided. No drinking water is available. Docking and mooring buoys are available April to mid-October. Garbage must be packed out. Leashed pets are permitted.

Reservations, fees: No reservations. Sites are $6 per night, docking is $10 to $16 per night, mooring buoys are $7 per night. Senior discount available. Open year-round.

Directions: This small, secluded island is just off the southeastern shore of Orcas Island off Doe Bay. It's accessible only by boat.

Contact: San Juan Marine Area, Star Route, Box 177, Olga, WA 98279; 360/378-2044; State Park information, 360/902-8844.

14 Obstruction Pass Hike-In

 8

It takes a ferryboat ride, a tricky drive, and a half-mile walk to reach this campground, but that helps set it apart from others—you'll find a unique, primitive spot set in a forested area near the shore of Orcas Island with good hiking. The irony is that it is so unique that it is often heavily used. Moran State Park is a more developed alternative on this island, with many recreation options.

Location: On Orcas Island; see Seattle and the San Juan Islands, map 2, grid d2.

Campsites, facilities: There are nine primitive, hike-in campsites. Picnic tables and fire grills are provided. Vault toilets are available. No drinking water is available. Garbage must be packed out. Two mooring buoys are available. Leashed pets are permitted.

Reservations, fees: No reservations; no fee. Open year-round.

Directions: From Seattle on I-5, drive north to Burlington and Highway 20. Turn west on Highway 20 and drive 12 miles to the Highway 20 North spur, following signs to the San Juan Islands Ferry Terminal in Anacortes. Take the ferry to Orcas Island. Then drive on the Horseshoe Highway past Moran State Park and continue to the town of Olga and Doe Bay Road. Drive east on Doe Bay Road for one-half mile to Obstruction Pass Road. Turn right and drive 0.7 mile to Trailhead Road. Bear right and drive straight for less than a mile to the parking area. Hike one-half mile to the campground.

Contact: Department of Natural Resources, Northwest Region, 919 North Township Street, Sedro-Woolley, WA 98284-9395; 360/856-3500 or 360/856-2150.

15 Clark Island State Park Boat-In

 9

Clark Island State Park offers beautiful beaches with opportunities for scuba diving. Beachcombing and sunbathing are two other popular options. It is a short boat trip from nearby Orcas Island. You can pretend you're on a deserted Caribbean island.

Well, almost. From the campground there are excellent views of the other nearby islands. As of 2002, storm damage had temporarily closed six of the eight campsites; call for current status.

Location: Northeast of Orcas Island; see Seattle and the San Juan Islands, map 2, grid c2.

Campsites, facilities: There are eight primitive boat-in campsites. Vault toilets are available, but there is no drinking water. Fire rings are provided. Boat buoys for overnight moorage are available. Garbage must be packed out. Leashed pets are permitted.

Reservations, fees: No reservations. Sites are $6 per night, $7 per night for moorning buoy. Open year-round.

Directions: The campground, accessible only by boat, is on tiny Clark Island, located northeast of Orcas Island. Look for the moorage floats set just offshore the campsites.

Contact: San Juan Marine Area, Star Route, Box 177, Olga, WA 98279; 360/378-2044; State Park information, 360/902-8844.

16 Turn Island State Park Boat-In

 10

This spot is gorgeous, but while this is one of about 30 campgrounds in the area that can be reached only by boat, note that no docks are available at this one, just mooring buoys. This island is very small, yet just a long hop from San Juan Island off its southern tip. Quiet, primitive, and beautiful, this spot offers good trails for tromping around and year-round angling for rockfish. There are pretty beaches for shell collectors. The island is set within the San Juan Islands National Wildlife Refuge.

Location: Near Friday Harbor; see Seattle and the San Juan Islands, map 2, grid d1.

Campsites, facilities: There are 12 primitive boat-in campsites. Picnic tables and fire rings are provided. Composting toilets are available. There is no drinking water. Boat buoys are available for overnight moorage. Garbage must be packed out. Leashed pets are permitted.

Reservations, fees: No reservations. Sites are $6 per night, $7 per night for mooring buoy. Senior discount available. Open year-round.

Directions: Turn Island is located off the northeast tip of San Juan Island (in the San Juan Channel). It's accessible only by boat.

Contact: San Juan Marine Area, Star Route, Box 177, Olga, WA 98279; 360/378-2044; State Park information, 360/902-8844.

17 Spencer Spit State Park Ferry-In

 9

Spencer Spit State Park offers one of the few island campgrounds accessible to cars via ferry. There are also walk-in sites for privacy, which require anywhere from a 50-foot to a 200-yard walk to the tent sites. A sand spit, a long sliver of sand, extends far into the water and provides both a lagoon and good access to prime clamming areas. The park covers 183 acres. Picnicking, beachcombing, and sunbathing are some pleasant activities for campers looking for relaxation.

Location: On Lopez Island; see Seattle and the San Juan Islands, map 2, grid d2.

Campsites, facilities: There are 25 sites for tents or self-contained RVs up to 20 feet long, nine walk-in sites, and one group site. No hookups are provided. Picnic tables and fire grills are provided. Restrooms, drinking water, flush toilets, a picnic area, and a dump station are available, and 16 mooring buoys are available on the Cascadia Marine Trail. Boat docks and launch are within two miles.

Some facilities are wheelchair-accessible. Leashed pets are permitted.

Reservations, fees: Reserve at 888/CAMP-OUT (888/226-7688); website: www.parks.wa.gov/reservations ($7 reservation fee). Sites are $16 per night, $6 per extra vehicle per night, $7 for mooring buoys per night. Senior discount available. Call for prices for group site. Open March through October.

Directions: From Seattle on I-5, drive north to Burlington and Highway 20. Turn west on Highway 20 and drive 12 miles to the Highway 20 North spur, following signs to the San Juan Islands Ferry Terminal in Anacortes. Take the ferry to Lopez Island. The park is within four miles of the ferry terminal.

Contact: Spencer Spit State Park Ferry-In, 521A Bakerview Road, Lopez, WA 98261; 360/468-2251; State Park information, 360/902-8844.

18 James Island State Park Boat-In

 9

Small, hidden James Island provides good opportunities for hiking, fishing, and scuba diving. It's quiet and primitive, with lots of trees and a pretty beach for walking or sunbathing. Docks are in place from April to mid-October.

Location: Near Decatur Island; see Seattle and the San Juan Islands, map 2, grid d2.

Campsites, facilities: There are 12 primitive boat-in campsites, and two designated sites for nonmotorized boats. Fire rings are provided. Composting and pit toilets are available. Boat floats and buoys are available for moorage off the east side of the island. A moorage dock on the west side of the island is open from April through mid-October. Leashed pets are permitted.

Reservations, fees: No reservations. Sites are $6 per night, docking is $10 to $16 per night, moorning buoys $7 per night. Senior discount available. Open year-round.

Directions: This island is east of Decatur Island on Rosario Strait and is only accessible by boat. The campground is on the east side of the island.

Contact: San Juan Marine Area, Star Route, Box 177, Olga, WA 98279; 360/378-2044; State Park information, 360/902-8844.

19 Strawberry Island Boat-In

 9

This campground is set on a small island and is used less often than the other islands nearby because of the hazards of landing here (see the directions below). Regardless, kayakers in the region have discovered it. If you can manage to land, you'll be rewarded with a pretty, forested camp and privacy.

Location: Near Cypress Island; see Seattle and the San Juan Islands, map 2, grid d3.

Campsites, facilities: There are three primitive boat-in campsites. Picnic tables and fire grills are provided. Vault toilets are available. No drinking water is available. Garbage must be packed out.

Reservations, fees: No reservations; no fee. Open year-round.

Directions: This island is off the west coast of Cypress Island and is accessible only by small boat. From Anacortes, cruise by boat west through Guemes Channel, continue around the southern end of Cypress Island (Reef Point), and cruise north one mile to Strawberry Bay. Strawberry Island is located in Strawberry Bay. Cypress Island is just east of Strawberry Island. Note: The Department of Natural Resources cautions that strong currents and submerged rocks can make landing difficult.

Contact: Department of Natural Resources, Northwest Region, 919 North Township Street, Sedro-Woolley, WA 98284-9395; 360/856-3500, fax 360/856-2150.

20 Pelican Beach Boat-In

    9

This forested island campground offers a group shelter, beach access, and hiking trails. The 1.2-mile trail to Eagle Cliff is a must. Like Cypress Head, this scenic camp is set on the oceanfront in a well-treed area. Pelican Beach has become even more popular than Cypress Head, not only with lots of kayakers, but even commerical operations that work as outfitters and organize small groups of kayakers to venture here.

Location: On Cypress Island; see Seattle and the San Juan Islands, map 2, grid b1.

Campsites, facilities: There are four primitive boat-in campsites. Picnic tables and fire grills are provided. Composting toilets and a group picnic shelter are available. No drinking water is available. Garbage must be packed out. Six mooring buoys are available nearby.

Reservations, fees: No reservations; no fee. Open year-round.

Directions: This camp is set on the east shore of Cypress Island and is accessible only by boat. Cypress Island can be accessed by boat from Anacortes. Cruise west through Guemes Channel to Bellingham Channel (located between Cypress Island and Guemes Island). Turn north in Bellingham Channel and cruise to the campground on the southeast side of Cypress Island just north of Cypress Head.

Contact: Department of Natural Resources, Northwest Region, 919 North Township Street, Sedro-Woolley, WA 98284-9395; 360/856-3500, fax 360/856-2150.

21 Cypress Head Boat-In

    9

Cypress Head is an alternative to Pelican Beach. Primitive but pretty, this camp is situated in a forested setting, primarily Douglas fir and madrone, and is set right on Puget Sound. This camp is popular and often gets heavy use from kayakers. A trail provides access to Cypress Island Natural Resource Conservation area.

Location: On Cypress Island; see Seattle and the San Juan Islands, map 2, grid d3.

Campsites, facilities: There are five primitive, boat-in campsites. Picnic tables and fire grills are provided. Vault toilets are available. No drinking water is available. Garbage must be packed out. Five mooring buoys are available nearby.

Reservations, fees: No reservations; no fee. Open year-round.

Directions: This camp is set on the east shore of Cypress Island and is accessible only by boat. Cypress Island can be accessed by boat from Anacortes. Cruise west through Guemes Channel to Bellingham Channel (located between Cypress Island and Guemes Island). Turn north in Bellingham Channel and cruise to the campground on the southeast side of Cypress Island in Deepwater Bay (just south of Pelican Beach Campground).

Contact: Department of Natural Resources, Northwest Region, 919 North Township Street, Sedro-Woolley, WA 98284-9395; 360/856-3500, fax 360/856-2150.

22 Saddlebag Island State Park Boat-In

      9

Saddlebag Island State Park is a good cruise from Anacortes. The island is quiet and primitive, with a nice beach nearby for beachcombing and fine crabbing in the bay. Wildflowers are in bloom from April through June. This island receives moderate use.

Location: Near Guemes Island; see Seattle and the San Juan Islands, map 2, grid d4.

Campsites, facilities: There are five primitive boat-in campsites. Fire rings are provided. Vault and pit toilets are available, but there is no drinking water. Garbage must be packed out. Mooring buoys are available, but no docks. Leashed pets are permitted.

Reservations, fees: No reservations. Sites are $6 per night, mooring buoys $7 per night. Senior discount available. Open year-round.

Directions: From Seattle on I-5, drive north to Burlington and Highway 20. Turn west on Highway 20 and drive 12 miles to the Highway 20 North spur, following signs to the San Juan Islands Ferry Terminal in Anacortes. Launch your boat and cruise northeast around the southeast tip of Guemes Island. As you approach, Hat Island will be to your right, Huckleberry Island to your left, and Saddlebag Island to your center in Padilla Bay. Continue to Saddlebag Island. The camp is accessible only by boat.

Contact: San Juan Marine Area, Star Route, Box 177, Olga, WA 98279; 360/378-2044; State Park information, 360/902-8844.

23 Birch Bay State Park

     8

Birch Bay State Park covers 194 acres and features nearly two miles of beach and great views of the Canadian Gulf Islands and the Cascade Mountains. For water lovers it has the best of both worlds with 8,255 feet of saltwater shoreline and 14,923 feet of freshwater shoreline on Terrell Creek. More than 100 different species of birds, many of which are migrating on the Pacific flyway, can be seen here. The Terrell Creek Marsh Interpretive Trail extends one-half mile through both forest of black birch trees and one of the few remaining saltwater/freshwater estuaries in northern Puget Sound. Bald eagles and great blue heron feed along the banks of Terrell Creek. Several 18-hole golf courses are located nearby. The campground is divided into two loops; hookups for RVs are in the North Loop.

Location: On Birch Bay; see Seattle and the San Juan Islands, map 2, grid a2.

Campsites, facilities: There are 146 sites for tents or self-contained RVs and 20 sites with full or partial hookups for trailers or RVs up to 60 feet. Picnic tables and fire grills are provided. Flush toilets, coin-operated showers, and a dump station are available. A boat ramp, launch facilities (for boats under 16 feet only), a picnic area with sheltered kitchen with electricity, an amphitheater, basketball, interpretive activities, and a camp host are available. Some facilities are wheelchair-accessible. A store, a restaurant, a coin-operated laundry, and ice are located within one mile. Leashed pets are permitted.

Reservations, fees: Reserve at 888/CAMP-OUT (888/226-7688); website: www.parks.wa.gov/reservations ($7 reservation fee). Sites are $7 to $22 per night, $6 per extra vehicle per night. Major credit cards accepted. Open year-round.

Directions: From Bellingham, drive north on I-5 to Exit 266. At Exit 266 take Grandview west and continue seven miles to Jackson Road. Turn right on Jackson Road, and drive one mile to Helweg Road. Turn left and drive one quarter-mile to the reservation office.

Contact: Birch Bay State Park, 5105 Helweg Road, Blaine, WA 98230; 360/371-2800, fax 360/371-0455; State Park information, 360/902-8844.

24 Beachside RV Park

 8

This pretty park comes with the opportunity to view a pair of nesting eagles. The park is surrounded by evergreens and bay views, Hiking, fishing, mountain biking, and nearby golf are also options.

Location: On Birch Bay; see Seattle and the San Juan Islands, map 2, grid a2.

Campsites, facilities: There are 74 sites with full hookups, including some drive-through sites, for trailers or RVs, and 12 sites for tents. Picnic tables are provided. Restrooms, drinking water, flush toilets, showers, a group fire pit, and a coin-operated laundry are available. A grocery store mini-mart and restaurant are located within one-half mile. Leashed pets are permitted.

Reservations, fees: Reservations recommended; phone 360/371-5962. Sites are $13 to $20 per night. Major credit cards accepted. Senior discount available. Open year-round.

Directions: From Bellingham, drive north on I-5 to Exit 270. Turn west on Birch Bay-Lynden Road and drive five miles to Birch Bay Drive. Turn left and drive one mile to the park on the left.

Contact: Beachside RV Park, 7630 Birch Bay Drive, Birch Bay, WA 98230; 360/371-5962.

25 The Cedars RV Resort

 5

This campground provides more direct access from I-5 than Windmill Inn and KOA Lynden, and note that you can usually get yourself a site here. It's a nice, clean park covering 22 acres with spacious sites and trees. Horseshoe pits, a game room, and a recreation field provide possible activities for campers. Several golf courses are nearby.

Location: In Ferndale; see Seattle and the San Juan Islands, map 2, grid b4.

Campsites, facilities: There are 127 sites with full or partial hookups, including drive-through sites, for tents, trailers, or RVs of any length, and a dispersed tent camping area on grass. Picnic tables and fire pits are provided. Restrooms, drinking water, flush toilets, showers, modem hookups (at 50 sites), two RV dump stations, a coin-operated laundry, a playground with horseshoes, badminton, volleyball, a recreation room, an arcade, a pool, a small store, and ice are available. Leashed pets are permitted.

Reservations, fees: Reservations accepted. Sites are $18.50 to $27.50 per night. Major credit cards accepted. Open year-round.

Directions: From Bellingham on I-5, drive north to Ferndale and Exit 263. Take Exit 263 and turn north on Portal Way. Drive less than one mile north to the campground on the left.

Contact: The Cedars RV Resort, 6335 Portal Way, Ferndale, WA 98248; 360/384-2622, fax 360/380-6365.

26 Windmill Inn

 7

This nice little spot is set near the Nooksack River and Wiser Lake and is within 15 minutes of the Puget Sound. Because it's the last stop before the U.S.–Canadian border, the camp is used primarily as a layover for people heading north. The setting is quiet and pretty, with lots of trees and flowers. Area attractions include Mt. Baker, the quaint little shops of Lynden, and the nearby Birch Bay area, which offers many recreation options.

Location: Near the Nooksack River; see Seattle and the San Juan Islands, map 2, grid a5.

Campsites, facilities: There are eight sites for tents, trailers, or RVs of any length, and 15 motel rooms. Picnic tables are provided. Restrooms, drinking water, flush toilets, coin-operated showers, cable TV, phone hookups, and a park are available. A store, bottled gas, a café, a coin-operated laundry, and ice are available within one mile. Boat-launching facilities are located within 1.5 miles. Leashed pets are permitted.

Reservations, fees: Reservations accepted. Sites are $18 per night, $1 per person per night for more than two people. Major credit cards accepted. Open year-round.

Directions: In Bellingham on I-5, take Exit 256 for Highway 539 (called Meridian Street in Bellingham). Turn north on Highway 539 and drive 10 miles to Lynden. The campground is on the right side of the road as you enter Lynden.

Contact: Windmill Inn, 8022 Guide Meridian Road, Lynden, WA 98264; 360/354-3424, fax 360/354-8138.

27 KOA Lynden

  9

Lynden is a quaint Dutch town. The park features green lawns, flowers, and trees surrounding the mini-golf and ponds, the latter where you can fish for trout. This stars as a unique holdover spot for vacationers heading north to Canada via Highway 539 and Highway 546. Nearby recreational options include an 18-hole golf course.

Location: In Lynden; see Seattle and the San Juan Islands, map 2, grid a5.

Campsites, facilities: There are 80 tent sites and 100 sites with full or partial hookups, including 25 drive-through, for trailers or RVs of any length, and 12 cabins. Picnic tables are provided. Restrooms, drinking water, flush toilets, showers, bottled gas, a dump station, showers, firewood, a recreation hall, a store, a café (summer season only), an espresso bar, an ice cream parlor, laundry facilities, ice, a playground, miniature golf,

and a swimming pool are available. Tackle and boat rentals are available. Leashed pets are permitted.

Reservations, fees: Reservations accepted at 800/562-4779. Sites are $25 to $30 per night for two campers, $3.60 for each additional person. Cabins are $45 per night. Major credit cards accepted. Call the park for group rates. Open year-round.

Directions: From I-5 at Bellingham, take Exit 256 to Highway 539. Turn north on Highway 539 and drive 12 miles to Highway 546. Turn east on Highway 546 (Badger Road) and drive three miles to Line Road. Turn right (south) on Line Road and drive 0.5 mile to the campground on the right.

Contact: KOA Lynden, 8717 Line Road, Lynden, WA 98264; 360/354-4772, fax 360/354-7050; website: www.koa.com.

28 Sumas RV Park

   5

Located near the U.S.–Canada border, this campground is a holdover spot to spend American dollars before heading into British Columbia and making the conversion. The camp is set in the grassy flatlands; it has graveled sites and a few trees. Nearby recreation options include an 18-hole golf course and tennis courts.

Location: In Sumas; see Seattle and the San Juan Islands, map 2, grid a6.

Campsites, facilities: There are 24 tent sites and 50 sites with full or partial hookups, including 12 drive-through sites, for trailers or RVs of any length. Picnic tables and fire rings are provided. Restrooms, drinking water, flush toilets, showers, a dump station, firewood, and a ballpark are available. A store, a café, a coin-operated laundry, and ice are located within one mile.

Leashed pets are permitted.

Reservations, fees: Reservations accepted. Sites are $9 to $20 per night. Open year-round.

Directions: From I-5 at Bellingham, take Exit 256 to Highway 539. Turn north on Highway 539 and drive 12 miles to Highway 546. Turn right (east) on Highway 546 (Badger Road) and drive 14 miles (the road becomes Highway 9) to Sumas and look for Cherry Street. Turn right (south) at Cherry Street (the road becomes Easterbrook Road) and drive two blocks to the park on the left.

Contact: Sumas RV Park, 9600 Easterbrook Road, Sumas, WA 98295; 360/988-8875.

29 Larrabee State Park

  9

This 2,683-acre state park is on Samish Bay in Puget Sound and is highlighted by 8,100 feet of saltwater shoreline. The park has two freshwater lakes, coves, and tidelands. Sunsets are often beautiful. The park has 13.7 miles of hiking trails and 11.7 miles of mountain-biking trails. The landscape is primarily forested with conifers, often with dense woodlands and vegetation. It has marshlands, wetlands, streams, lakes, and Chuckanut Mountain. Fishing is available on Fragrance Lake and Lost Lake on Chuckanut Mountain, which are hike-in lakes. The area is known for Chuckanut sandstone. This was the first state park established in Washington, dating from 1915. The park lies on a beautiful stretch of coastline and offers prime spots for wildlife viewing. A relatively short drive south will take you to Anacortes, where you can catch a ferry to islands in the San Juan chain.

Location: On Samish Bay; see Seattle and the San Juan Islands, map 2, grid c5.

Campsites, facilities: There are 51 developed sites, including 26 with full hookups, for tents, trailers, or RVs up to 60 feet long, and eight primitive tent sites. Picnic tables and fire grills are provided. Restrooms, drinking water, flush toilets, coin-operated showers, a dump station, a picnic area with electricity and covered shelter, and firewood are available. Boat-launching facilities are available nearby. Leashed pets are permitted.

Reservations, fees: Reserve at 888/CAMP-OUT (888/226-7688); website: www.parks.wa.gov/reservations ($7 reservation fee). Sites are $6 to $22 per night, $6 per extra vehicle per night. Senior discount available. Major credit cards accepted. Open year-round.

Directions: From Bellingham on I-5, take Exit 250 and turn on Fairhaven Parkway. Drive less than a mile to State Route 11/Chuckanut Drive (second stoplight). Turn left (stay left at the next stoplight) and drive six miles to the park entrance on the right.

Contact: Larrabee State Park, 245 Chuckanut, Bellingham, WA 98225; 360/676-2093; State Park information, 360/902-8844.

30 Lizard Lake Hike-In

   6

Lizard Lake is located just 0.2 mile north by trail from Lily Lake, but this hike-in camp is even smaller and more isolated. It's set in a pretty, forested area. See the description of Lily Lake for more information.

Location: Near Bellingham; see Seattle and the San Juan Islands, map 2, grid c5.

Campsites, facilities: There are three primitive hike-in tent sites. Tent pads and fire grills are provided, and vault toilets are available. There is no drinking water. Garbage must be packed out. Leashed pets are permitted.

Reservations, fees: No reservations; no fee. Open year-round.

Directions: From Bellingham on I-5, drive south to Exit 240 to Samish Lake Road and drive one-half mile north to Barrel Springs Road. Turn left and drive one mile to Road SW-C-1000. Turn right and drive 1.5 miles to the Blanchard Hill Trailhead. Hike 3.2 miles, bear left, and continue three-quarters of a mile (just past Lily Lake) to the campground. A map is advisable.

Contact: Department of Natural Resources, Northwest Region, 919 North Township Street, Sedro-Woolley, WA 98284-9395; 360/856-3500, fax 360/856-2150.

31 Lily Lake Hike-In

     6

This tiny, remote hike-in campground is one of those that few people ever go to or even know about. Set on little Lily Lake, it's completely secluded and primitive; you'll have to pack in everything you need and pack out everything that's left. This is a prime area for hiking, and the nearby trails are used by hikers and horse packers alike. Fishing is an option at Lily Lake. Nearby Lizard Lake Camp provides an even smaller camp.

Location: Near Bellingham; see Seattle and the San Juan Islands, map 2, grid d5.

Campsites, facilities: There are six primitive hike-in tent sites. Tent pads and fire rings are provided. Drinking water and vault toilets are available. Garbage must be packed out. Leashed pets are allowed.

Reservations, fees: No reservations; no fee. Open year-round.

Directions: From Bellingham on I-5, drive south to Exit 240. On Samish Lake Road drive one-half mile north to Barrel Springs Road. Turn left and drive one mile to Road SW-C-1000. Turn right and drive 1.5 miles to the Blanchard Hill Trailhead. Hike 3.2 miles, bear left, and continue one-half mile to the campground. Obtaining a map is advisable.

Contact: Department of Natural Resources, Northwest Region, 919 North Township Street, Sedro-Woolley, WA 98284-9395; 360/856-3500, fax 360/856-2150.

32 Hutchinson Creek

   9

This campground is set in the forest along Hutchinson Creek near the South Fork of the Nooksack River. Managed by the Department of Natural Resources, it's rustic, beautiful, and primitive. While this camp has become known to wise locals, vacationers from out-of-town don't have much of a clue.

Location: Near the South Fork of the Nooksack River; see Seattle and the San Juan Islands, map 2, grid c7.

Campsites, facilities: There are 11 sites for tents or small trailers. Fire grills and and tent pads are provided. Vault toilets are available. There is no drinking water. Garbage must be packed out. A store is located within three miles. Leashed pets are permitted.

Reservations, fees: No reservations; no fee. Open year-round.

Directions: From Seattle, drive north on I-5 to Burlington and Highway 20. Turn east on Highway 20 and drive seven miles to Highway 9. Turn north and drive 16 miles to Acme and Mosquito Lake Road (just north of the Nooksack River Bridge). Turn east on Mosquito Lake Road, drive 2.5 miles, and look for a gravel road on the right. Turn right on the gravel road and continue for one-half mile to the campground.

Contact: Department of Natural Resources, Northwest Region, 919 North Township Street, Sedro-Woolley, WA 98284-9395; 360/856-3500, fax 360/856-2150.

Pioneer Trails RV Resort & Campground

    9

This site offers resort camping in the beautiful San Juan Islands. Tall trees, breathtaking views, cascading waterfalls, and country hospitality can all be found here. Side trips include nearby Deception Pass State Park (eight minutes away) and ferries to Victoria, British Columbia, as well as Friday Harbor, Orcas Island, and other nearby islands (it is imperative to arrive early at the ferry terminal). Horseshoes, an 18-hole golf course, relaxing spas, and lake fishing are among the nearby recreation activities.

Location: On Fidalgo Island, in the San Juan Islands; see Seattle and the San Juan Islands, map 2, grid e4.

Campsites, facilities: There are 80 sites with full or partial hookups, including some drive-through sites, for tents, trailers, or RVs, plus 24 covered wagons and five cabins. Picnic tables and fire rings are provided. Restrooms, drinking water, flush toilets, showers, a dump station, cable TV, a public phone, and a coin-operated laundry are available. A recreation hall, a playground, and a sports field are available nearby. If RV camping, leashed pets are permitted.

Reservations, fees: Reservations recommended. A three-night minimum on holidays is required. Sites are $18 to $25 per night, $5 per extra vehicle per night; covered wagons and cabins are $34 to $38. One pet is free. Major credit cards accepted. Open year-round.

Directions: From Seattle on I-5, drive north to Burlington and take Exit 230 for Highway 20 West. Drive west on Highway 20 for 12 miles. At the traffic signal, turn left (still Highway 20, toward Oak Harbor/Deception Pass)) and drive one-half mile to Miller Road. Turn right (west) on Miller Road, drive one quarter-mile, and look for the park on the right side of the road.

Contact: Pioneer Trails RV Resort & Campground, 7337 Miller Road, Anacortes, WA 98221; 360/293-5355 or 888/777-5355; website: www.pioneertrails.com.

 Fidalgo Bay Resort

     4

This park is five minutes from Anacortes and right on Fidalgo Bay for boating, fishing, and swimming, and there's a golf course two miles away. There are a few permanent rentals at this park.

Location: On Fidalgo Bay; see Seattle and the San Juan Islands, map 2, grid e4.

Campsites, facilities: There are 187 sites with full hookups, including many drive-through sites and a few sites with phone hookups, for trailers or RVs, and eight tent sites. Picnic tables are provided. Restrooms, drinking water, flush toilets, showers, modem access in the clubhouse, a large fire pit, a small boat launch, a grocery store, a dog run, and a coin-operated laundry are available. Leashed pets are permitted, but they must be kept quiet.

Reservations, fees: Reservations recommended at 800/727-5478. Sites are $25 to $40 per night, $2 per person per night for more than two people. Major credit cards accepted. Open year-round.

Directions: From Seattle on I-5, drive north to Burlington and Highway 20. Turn west on Highway 20 and drive about 14 miles to Fidalgo Bay Road. Turn right on Fidalgo Bay Road and drive one mile to the resort on the right.

Contact: Fidalgo Bay Resort, 4701 Fidalgo Bay Road, Anacortes, WA 98211; 800/727-5478 or 360/293-5353, fax 360/299-3010; website: www.fidalgobay.com.

35 Washington Park

 6

This city park is set in the woods and features many hiking trails. There is a loop route around the perimeter of the park; a 2.3-mile paved trail for vehicles, hikers, and bicyclists. The Washington State Ferry terminals are located one-half mile away, providing access to the San Juan Islands. This is a popular camp, and it's a good idea to arrive early to claim your spot.

Location: In Washington Park; see Seattle and the San Juan Islands, map 2, grid e4.

Campsites, facilities: There are 70 sites, including 45 with partial hookups and some drive-through sites, for tents, trailers, and RVs up to 40 feet, and one group tent site for up to 30 people. Restrooms, drinking water, flush toilets, coin-operated showers, a public phone, a playground, a recreation field, a dump station, and a coin-operated laundry are available. A day-use area is provided. A boat launch is also available. Leashed pets are permitted.

Reservations, fees: Reservations accepted for residents of Anacortes only. Sites are $12 to $15 per night; the group site is $50 per night. Open year-round.

Directions: From Seattle on I-5, drive north to Burlington and Highway 20. Turn west on Highway 20 and drive to Anacortes and Commercial Avenue. Turn right on Highway 20 and drive 24 blocks to 12th Street. Turn left and drive about four miles (west of the ferry landing; the road changes names several times) to Sunset Avenue. Drive straight across road to Sunset Avenue to the park entrance and campground.

Contact: Washington Park, City of Anacortes, P.O. Box 547, Anacortes, WA 98221; 360/293-1927.

36 Bay View State Park

 10

This campground set on Padilla Bay has a large, grassy area for kids, making it a good choice for families. It is a 25-acre park with 1,285 feet of saltwater shoreline, bordering 11,000 acres of Padilla Bay and the National Estuarine Sanctuary. From the park, there are views of the San Juan Islands fronting Padilla Bay. On a clear day, you can see the Olympic Mountains to the west and Mt. Rainier to the south. Kayakers should note that Padilla Bay becomes a large mud flat during low tides. Windsurfing is becoming popular, but tracking tides and wind is required. Crabbing and clamming are best at other locations along Padilla Bay or Bellingham Bay. The Breazeale Padilla Bay Interpretive Center is located one-half mile north of the park. A nice day trip is to take the ferry at Anacortes to Lopez Island (there are several campgrounds there as well).

Location: On Padilla Bay; see Seattle and the San Juan Islands, map 2, grid e5.

Campsites, facilities: There are 76 sites, some with full or partial hookups, for tents, trailers, or self-contained RVs, nine sites with full hookups for RVs up to 60 feet long, three primitive sites, and one group tent site for up to 64 people. Picnic tables and fire rings are provided. Restrooms, drinking water, flush toilets, coin-operated showers, a dump station, and a picnic area with beach shelter are available. A playground with horseshoes, volleyball, interpretive activities, windsurfing, water-skiing, swimming, clamming, crabbing, oyster gathering, and boating are available. A store and a coin-operated laundry are eight miles away in Burlington. Leashed pets are permitted. Note that some campsites are closed in winter months.

Reservations, fees: Reserve at 888/226-7688 (CAMP-OUT); website: www.parks.wa.gov/reservations ($7 reservation fee). Sites are $6 to $22 per night, $6 per extra vehicle per night. Senior discount available. Reservations required for the group camp; $25 reservation fee, plus $2 per person per night. Major credit cards accepted. Open year-round.

Directions: From Seattle on I-5, drive north to Burlington and Exit 230 for Highway 20. Turn west on Highway 20 and drive seven miles west (toward Anacortes) to Bay View-Edison Road. Turn right (north) on Bay View-Edison Road and drive four miles to the park on the right.

Contact: Bay View State Park, 1093 Bay View-Edison Road, Brighton, WA 98273; 360/757-0227; State Park information, 360/902-8844.

⯃⯅ Burlington/Anacortes KOA

      5

This is a fine KOA campground, complete with all the amenities. The sites are spacious and comfortable. Possible side trips include tours of the Boeing plant, Victoria, Vancouver Island, and the San Juan Islands.

Location: In Burlington; see Seattle and the San Juan Islands, map 2, grid e6.

Campsites, facilities: There are 120 sites, most with full or partial hookups, some are drive-through, for tents, trailers, or RVs, and nine cabins. Restrooms, drinking water, flush toilets, showers, a dump station, cable TV, a public phone, a coin-operated laundry, limited groceries, ice, LP gas, and a barbecue are available. There are also an indoor heated pool, a spa with sauna, a recreation hall, a game room, a playground, mini-golf, horseshoes, and a sports field. Leashed pets are permitted.

Reservations, fees: Reservations recommended in the summer, 800/562-9154. Sites are $19.50 to $27 per night, $2.50 to $4 per person per night for more than two people. Cabins are $38 per night. Major credit cards accepted. Open year-round.

Directions: From Seattle on I-5, drive north to Exit 232/Cook Road in Burlington. Take that exit to Cook Road. Turn right on Cook Road and drive 100 feet to Old Highway 99. Turn left and drive 3.5 miles to the campground on the right.

Contact: Burlington/Anacortes KOA, 6397 North Green Road, Burlington, WA 98233; 360/724-5511; website: www.koa.com.

⯃⯆ Riverbend RV Park

    5

Riverbend RV Park is a pleasant layover spot for I-5 travelers. While not particularly scenic, it's clean and spacious. Access to the Skagit River here is a high point, with fishing for salmon, trout, and Dolly Varden in season; check regulations. Nearby recreational options include a casino and an 18-hole golf course.

Location: On the Skagit River; see Seattle and the San Juan Islands, map 2, grid e6.

Campsites, facilities: There are 90 drive-through sites with full hookups for trailers or RVs of any length, and 25 tent sites. Picnic tables are provided at RV sites and fire pits are provided at tent sites. Restrooms, drinking water, flush toilets, coin-operated showers, a dump station, a coin-operated laundry, and a playground with horseshoe pits are available. A store, a café, ice, and a swimming pool are located within one quarter-mile. Leashed pets are permitted.

Reservations, fees: Reservations accepted. Sites are $8 to $20 per night. Major credit cards accepted. Open year-round.

Directions: From Seattle on I-5, drive north to Mt. Vernon and the College Way exit. Take the College Way exit and drive one block west to Freeway Drive. Turn right (north) and drive one quarter-mile to the park.

Contact: Riverbend RV Park, 305 West Stewart Road, Mt. Vernon, WA 98273; 360/428-4044.

39 Deception Pass State Park

  10

This state park is located at beautiful Deception Pass on the west side of Whidbey Island. The park featured 4,134 acres with almost 15 miles of saltwater shoreline and six miles of freshwater shoreline on three lakes. The landscape ranges from old-growth forest to sand dunes. This diverse habitat has attracted 174 species of birds. An observation deck is available that overlooks the Cranberry Lake wetlands. The park also features spectacular views of shoreline, mountains, and islands, often with dramatic sunsets. At one spot, rugged cliffs drop to the turbulent waters of Deception Pass. Recreation options include fishing and swimming at Pass Lake, a freshwater lake within the park. Fly-fishing for trout is a unique bonus for anglers. Note that each lake has different regulations for boating. Scuba diving is also popular. The park provides 38 miles of hiking trails, 1.2 miles of wheelchair-accessible trails, and six miles of biking trails. There are several historic Civilian Conservation Corps buildings near the campground.

Location: On Whidbey Island; see Seattle and the San Juan Islands, map 2, grid e3.

Campsites, facilities: There are 246 developed sites, including some drive-through, for tents, trailers, or self-contained RVs up to 50 feet long, and five primitive tent sites. Picnic tables and fire rings are provided. Restrooms, drinking water, flush toilets, coin-operated showers, and a dump station are available. A concession stand, an amphitheater, interpretive acitivites, a picnic area with electricity and kitchen shelter, a boat launch, boat rentals, and mooring buoys are available nearby. The facilities are wheelchair-accessible. Leashed pets are permitted.

Reservations, fees: Reserve at 888/CAMP-OUT (888/226-7688); website: www.parks.wa.gov/reservations ($7 reservation fee). Sites are $6 to $22 per night, $6 per extra vehicle per night, $7 to $16 for mooring buoys per night. Senior discount available. Major credit cards accepted. Open year-round, with limited winter services.

Directions: From Seattle on I-5, drive north to Burlington and Exit 230/Highway 20. Take that exit and drive west on Highway 20 for 12 miles to Highway 20 South. Turn south on Highway 20 South and drive six miles (across the bridge at Deception Pass) and continue to the park (three miles south of the bridge) on the right.

Contact: Deception Pass State Park, 360/675-2417; State Park information, 360/902-8844.

40 Hope Island State Park Boat-In

   8

Here's a place where you still have a chance of having an island all to yourself. This camp is lightly used. This site on the north side of Hope Island is a primitive alternative to the nearby and more developed drive-to sites. It is located between Squaxin Island and Steamboat Island. The only catch is you must have a boat to reach it. It features a 106-acre county park set in Puget Sound and a landscape covered with old-growth forests and saltwater marshes. The park has a 1.5-mile beach, the top spot. Solitude is your reward.

A little-known option is that a single campsite for kayakers was added in 2001 on the northeast tip of Skagit Island, largely a secret, and with no mooring buoy, likely to remain that way.

Location: In Skagit Bay; see Seattle and the San Juan Islands, map 2, grid e4.

Campsites, facilities: There are five primitive, boat-in campsites. Picnic tables and fire rings are provided. Pit toilets and three mooring buoys are available. No drinking water is available. Garbage must be packed out. Leashed pets are permitted.

Reservations, fees: No reservations. Sites are $5 per night, $7 to $16 for mooring buoys. Senior discount available. Open year-round.

Directions: Hope Island is in Skagit Bay, directly between the Swinomish Indian Reservation on Fidalgo Island to the east and Whidbey Island to the west. After launching from the harbor at Cornet on Whidbey Island, cruise east out of Cornet Bay and turn south (Skagit Island will be on your left). Continue one mile to Hope Island. The boating access is on the north side of the island. It's accessible only by private boat.

Contact: Hope Island State Park, 360/675-2417; State Park information, 360/902-8844.

41 Oak Harbor City Beach Park

 4

This park is popular and fills quickly on summer weekends. It is geared for RVers, with graveled sites, but is also suitable for tent campers. Fishing, swimming, boating, and sunbathing are all options at Oak Harbor City Beach Park. A full-service marina is next door. Within a few miles are an 18-hole golf course and tennis courts. Fort Ebey and Fort Casey State Parks are both reached within a short drive and are excellent side trips.

Location: In Oak Harbor; see Seattle and the San Juan Islands, map 2, grid f3.

Campsites, facilities: There are 56 sites with full hookups for trailers or RVs of any length. Restrooms, drinking water, flush toilets, showers, a dump station, coin-operated showers, and a playground are available. Bottled gas, a store, a café, a coin-operated laundry, and ice are available within one mile. Boat-launching facilities are available at Oak Harbor. Leashed pets are permitted.

Reservations, fees: No reservations. Sites are $8 to $15 per night. Open year-round.

Directions: From Seattle on I-5, drive north to Burlington and Highway 20. Turn west on Highway 20 and drive 28 miles to the intersection of Highway 20 and Pioneer Way in the town of Oak Harbor on Whidbey Island. Continue straight through the intersection onto Beeksma Drive and drive about one block to the park on the left.

Contact: Oak Harbor City Beach Park, 865 S.E. Berrington Drive, Oak Harbor, WA 98277; 360/679-5551.

42 Fort Ebey State Park

 9

This park is situated on the west side of Whidbey Island at Point Partridge. It covers 645 acres and has access to a rocky beach that is good for exploring. There are also 28 miles of trails for hiking and biking. Fort Ebey is the site of a historic World War II bunker, where concrete platforms mark the locations of the historic gun batteries. Other options here include fishing and wildlife viewing. There is limited fishing available for smallmouth bass at Lake Pondilla. It is a short walk to the lake, about 100 yards, and it is a good place to see bald eagles. The saltwater shore access provides a good spot for surfing and paragliding.

Location: On Whidbey Island; see Seattle and the San Juan Islands, map 2, grid g3.

Campsites, facilities: There are 50 developed campsites, including four sites with electricity, for tents, trailers, or self-contained RVs up to 70 feet long, and three primitive tent sites. Picnic tables and fire grills are provided. Restrooms, drinking water, flush toilets, coin-operated showers, a picnic area, and a dump station are available. Some facilities are wheelchair-accessible. Leashed pets are permitted.

Reservations, fees: Reserve at 888/CAMP-OUT (888/226-7688); website: www.parks.wa.gov/reservations ($7 reservation fee). Sites are $6 to $22 per night, $6 per extra vehicle per night. Major credit cards accepted. Senior discount available. Open year-round.

Directions: From Seattle on I-5, drive north to Burlington and Exit 230/Highway 20. Turn west on Highway 20 and drive 23 miles (Whidbey Island) to Libbey Road (eight miles past Oak Harbor). Turn right and drive 1.5 miles to Hill Valley Drive. Turn left and enter the park.

Contact: Fort Ebey State Park, 395 North Fort Ebey Road, Coupeville, WA 98239; 360/678-4636; State Park information, 360/902-8844.

43 Fort Casey State Park

  10

Fort Casey State Park features a lighthouse and sweeping views of Admiralty Inlet and the Strait of Juan de Fuca. The park has 10,180 feet of saltwater shoreline on Puget Sound at Admiralty Inlet, and includes Keystone Spit, a two-mile stretch of land separating Admiralty Inlet and Crocket Lake. The park covers 467 acres, with just 1.8 miles of hiking trails, but is a historic site, with a coast artillery post featuring two historic guns on display. The park is part of Eby's Landing National Historic Reserve. It is also a designated area for remote-control glider flying, with a parade field popular for kite flying. The lighthouse and interpretive center are open seasonally. Fishing is often good in this area, in season. Another highlight is an underwater park for divers. You can also take a ferry from here to Port Townsend on the Olympic Peninsula.

Location: On Whidbey Island; see Seattle and the San Juan Islands, map 2, grid g3.

Campsites, facilities: There are 35 developed campsites for tents, trailers, or self-contained RVs up to 40 feet long and three primitive tent sites. Picnic tables and fire grills are provided. Restrooms, drinking water, flush toilets, coin-operated showers, firewood, an interpretive center, a picnic area, and an amphitheater are available. Some facilities are wheelchair-accessible. Boat-launching facilities are located in the park. Leashed pets are permitted.

Reservations, fees: No reservations. Sites are $6 to $16 per night, $6 per extra vehicle per night. Senior discount available. Open year-round.

Directions: From Seattle on I-5, drive north to Burlington and Exit 230/Highway 20. Turn west on Highway 20 and drive 35 miles to Coupeville. Continue south on Highway 20 (adjacent to Whidbey Island Naval Air Station) and then turn right (still Highway 20, passing Crockett Lake and the Camp Casey barracks) to the park entrance.

Contact: Fort Casey State Park, 1280 Fort Casey, Coupeville, WA 98239; 360/678-4519; State Park information, 360/902-8844.

44 South Whidbey State Park

 10

This park is located on the southwest end of Whidbey Island, covering 347 acres, and provides opportunities for hiking, scuba diving, picnicking, and beachcombing along a sandy beach. There are spectacular views of Puget Sound and the Olympic Mountains. The park features old-growth forest, tidelands for clamming and crabbing, and campsites set in the seclusion of a lush forest undergrowth. Shellfish harvesting is often plentiful; check regulations. The park has 4,500 feet of saltwater shoreline on Admiralty Inlet and 3.5 miles of hiking trails.

Location: On Whidbey Island; see Seattle and the San Juan Islands, map 2, grid h4.

Campsites, facilities: There are 54 developed campsites for tents or self-contained RVs up to 45 feet long and six primitive tent sites. Picnic tables and fire grills are provided. Restrooms, drinking water, flush toilets, coin-operated showers, a dump station, a picnic area with log kitchen shelter, an amphitheater, interpretive activities, a Junior Ranger program, and firewood are available. Some facilities are wheelchair-accessible. Leashed pets are permitted.

Reservations, fees: Reserve at 888/CAMP-OUT (888/226-7688); website: www.parks.wa.gov/reservations ($7 reservation fee). Sites are $6 to $15 per night, $6 per extra vehicle per night. Senior discount available. Major credit cards accepted. Open late February through October.

Directions: From Seattle on I-5, drive north to Burlington and the Highway 20 exit. Take Highway 20 west and drive 28 miles (past Coupeville on Whidbey Island) to the Highway 525 cutoff. Turn south on Highway 525 and drive to Bush Point Road. Turn right (west) and drive to Smugglers Cove Road (the park access road, well marked). The park can also be reached easily with a ferry ride from Mulkilteo (located southeast of Everett) to Clinton (this also makes a great bike trip to the state park).

Contact: South Whidbey State Park, 360/331-4559; State Park information, 360/902-8844.

45 Camano Island State Park

   10

This park features panoramic views of Puget Sound, the Olympic Mountains, and Mt. Rainier. This camp is set at a southwest point at Camano Island, near Lowell Point and Elger Bay along the Saratoga Passage. The campsites are quiet and private in this wooded park. The parks covers 134 acres and features 6,700 feet of rocky shoreline and beach, three miles of hiking trails, and just one mile of bike trails. Good inshore angling for rockfish is available year-round, and salmon fishing is also good in season. Clamming is excellent during low tides in June. An underwater park is provided for divers. There is also a self-guided nature trail.

Location: On Camano Island; see Seattle and the San Juan Islands, map 2, grid g5.

Campsites, facilities: There are 87 developed campsites for tents or self-contained RVs up to 45 feet, one primitive tent site, and one group camp for up to 200 people. Picnic tables and fire grills are provided. Restrooms, drinking water, flush toilets, coin-operated showers, firewood, a dump station, a playground, a sheltered picnic area with kitchen shelter, summer interpretive programs, an amphitheater, and a large field for ballgames in the day-use area are available. Boat-launching facilities are located in the park.

Leashed pets are permitted. An 18-hole golf course is nearby.

Reservations, fees: No reservations accepted for family camping. Reservations required for the group camp at 360/387-3031. Sites are $6 to $15 per night, $6 per extra vehicle per night. Senior discount available. The group reservation fee is $25, plus $2 per person per night. Open year-round.

Directions: From Seattle on I-5, drive north (17 miles north of Everett) to Exit 212. Take Exit 212 to Highway 532. Drive west on Highway 532 to Stanwood and continue three miles (to Camano Island) to a fork. Bear left at the fork and continue south on East Camano Drive (the road becomes Elger Bay Road) to Mountain View Road. Turn right and drive two miles (climbs a steep hill) and continue to Lowell Point Road. Turn left and continue to the park entrance of the road. (The park is 14 miles southwest of Stanwood).

Contact: Camano Island State Park, 360/387-3031; State Park information, 360/902-8844.

46 Kayak Point County Park

    5

This camp usually fills on summer weekends. It covers 430 acres on Port Susan. It provides good windsurfing and whale-watching. This large, wooded county park is set on the shore of Puget Sound, with an 18-hole golf course nearby. A 100-yard pier is available, good for crabbing and fishing.

Location: On Puget Sound; see Seattle and the San Juan Islands, map 2, grid g6.

Campsites, facilities: There are 34 sites with partial hookups (water and electricity), including some drive-through sites, for tents, trailers, or RVs up to 32 feet long, and 10 yurts with heat and electricity for up to five people. Picnic tables and fire rings are provided. Restrooms, drinking water, flush toilets, showers, firewood, a picnic area whith covered shelter, and a 300-foot fishing pier are available. Boat docks and launching facilities are located in the park. Some facilities are wheelchair-accessible. Leashed pets are permitted.

Reservations, fees: No reservations for campsites. Reservations available for yurts. Sites are $12 to $17 per night. Yurts are $35 per night. Major credit cards accepted. Open year-round.

Directions: From Seattle on I-5, drive north past Everett to Exit 199 (Tulalip) at Marysville. Take Exit 199, bear left on Tulalip Road, and drive west for 13 miles (road name changes to Marine Drive) through the Tulalip Indian Reservation to the park entrance road on the left (marked for Kayak Point). Turn left and drive a half mile to the park.

Contact: Kayak Point County Park, Snohomish County, 15422 Marine Drive, Stanwood, WA 98292; 425/388-6600 or 360/652-7992.

47 Wenberg State Park

    8

This state park is set along the east shore of Lake Goodwin, where the trout fishing can be great. Power boats are allowed, and a seasonal concession stand provides food and fishing supplies. Lifeguards are on duty in the summer. The park covers 46 acres with 1,140 feet of shoreline frontage on the lake. Hiking is limited to a one-half-mile trail. This is a popular weekend spot for Seattle area residents.

Location: On Lake Goodwin; see Seattle and the San Juan Islands, map 2, grid g6.

Campsites, facilities: There are 46 developed tent sites and 30 sites with partial hookups (water and electricity), including some drive-through, for trailers or RVs up to 50 feet long. Picnic tables and fire grills are provided. Restrooms, drinking water, flush toilets, coin-operated showers, a dump station, a sheltered picnic area, a store, and a playground are available. Boat-launching facilities are located on Lake Goodwin. Leashed pets are permitted.

Reservations, fees: Reserve at 888/CAMP-OUT (888/226-7688); website: www.parks.wa.gov/reservations ($7 reservation fee). Sites are $16 to $22 per night, $6 per extra vehicle per night. Senior discount available. Major credit cards accepted. Open year-round.

Directions: From Seattle on I-5, drive north to Exit 206 (10 miles north of Everett). Take Exit 206/Smokey Point, turn west, and drive 2.4 miles to Highway 531. Bear right on Highway 531 and drive 2.7 miles to East. Lake Goodwin Road. Turn left and drive 1.6 miles to the park entrance on the right.

Contact: Wenberg State Park, 360/652-7417; State Park information, 360/902-8844.

Cedar Grove Shores RV Park

    5

This wooded resort is set on the shore of Lake Goodwin near Wenberg State Park. This camp is a busy place in summer. Trout fishing, water-skiing, and swimming are the highlights. Tent campers should try Lake Goodwin Resort. An 18-hole golf course is nearby.

Location: On Lake Goodwin; see Seattle and the San Juan Islands, map 2, grid g6.

Campsites, facilities: There are 48 sites with full hookups, including some drive-through, for trailers or RVs. No tents are permitted. Restrooms, drinking water, flush toilets, coin-operated showers, a coin-operated laundry, a dump station, bottled gas, ice, a clubhouse, a recreation room, horseshoe pits, and firewood

are available. A store and a café are located within one mile. Boat docks and launching facilities are available within 1,000 feet on Lake Goodwin. Some facilities are wheelchair-accessible. Leashed pets are permitted.

Reservations, fees: Reservations accepted. Sites are $20 to $27 per night, $4 per person (under 18 free) per night for more than two people. Major credit cards accepted. Open year-round.

Directions: From Seattle on I-5, drive north to Exit 206 (10 miles north of Everett). Take Exit 206/Smokey Point and drive west for 2.2 miles to Lakewood Road. Turn right and drive 3.2 miles to Westlake Goodwin Road. Turn left (the park is marked) and drive three-quarters mile to the park on the left.

Contact: Cedar Grove Shores RV Park, 16529 West Lake Goodwin Road, Stanwood, WA 98292; 360/652-7083 or 866/342-4981.

49 Lake Goodwin Resort

    5

This private campground is set on Lake Goodwin, which is known for good trout fishing. Motorboats are permitted on the lake, and an 18-hole golf course is located nearby. Other activities include swimming in the lake, horseshoe pits, shuffleboard, and a recreation field.

Location: On Lake Goodwin; see Seattle and the San Juan Islands, map 2, grid g6.

Campsites, facilities: There are 85 sites with full or partial hookups, including eight drive-through sites, for trailers or RVs of any length, 11 tent sites, and four cabins. Picnic tables and fire grills are provided. Restrooms, drinking water, flush toilets, coin-operated showers, bottled gas, a dump station, recreation equipment, a store, a coin-operated laundry, ice, a playground, and firewood are available. Boat moorage, a fishing pier, and boat rentals are located nearby on Lake Goodwin. Small leashed pets are permitted in RV sites only.

Reservations, fees: Reservations accepted; phone 800/242-8169. Sites are $18 to $30 per night; cabins are $60 to $85 per night. Major credit cards accepted. Open year-round.

Directions: From Seattle on I-5, drive north to Exit 206 (10 miles north of Everett). Take Exit 206/Smokey Point, turn west, and drive two miles to Highway 531. Bear right on Highway 531 and drive to a stop sign at Lakewood Road. Turn right at Lakewood Road and drive 3.5 miles to the park on the left.

Contact: Lake Goodwin Resort, 4726 Lakewood Road, Stanwood, WA 98292; 360/652-8169, fax 360/652-4025.

50 Lakeside RV Park

 6

This camp can be a crapshoot for vacationers in summer, with 100 of the 150 RV spaces dedicated to permanent rentals; the remaining 50 spaces get filled nightly with vacationers all summer. The park is landscaped with annuals, roses, other perennials, and shrubs, which provide privacy and gardens for each site. There's an artificially constructed pond stocked with trout year-round, providing fishing for a fee.

Location: In the town of Everett; see Seattle and the San Juan Islands, map 3, grid a7.

Campsites, facilities: There are 150 sites (50 nonpermanent), including some drive-through, with full hookups for trailers and RVs, and nine tent sites. Restrooms, drinking water, flush toilets, showers, a coin-operated laundry, propane gas, a playground, a modem hookup, and pay phones are available. Some facilities are wheelchair-accessible. Leashed pets are permitted.

Reservations, fees: Reservations recommended at 800/468-7275. Sites are $31.31 to $34.79 per night. Senior discount available. Major credit cards accepted. Open year-round.

Directions: From Seattle on I-5, drive north to Everett and Exit 186. Take Exit 186 and turn west on 128th Street, and drive about two miles to Old Highway 99. Turn left (south) on Old Highway 99 and drive one quarter-mile to the park on the left.

Contact: Lakeside RV Park, 12321 Highway 99 South, Everett, WA 98204; 425/347-2970 or 800/468-7275, fax 206/347-9052.

51 Lake Pleasant RV Park

 6

This park is set on Lake Pleasant, a large, developed camp geared primarily toward RVers. The setting is pretty, with lakeside sites and plenty of trees. Just off the highway, it's a popular camp, so expect lots of company, especially in summer. This is a good spot for a little trout fishing. Note that half of the 196 sites are permanent rentals. All sites are paved.

Location: On Lake Pleasant; see Seattle and the San Juan Islands, map 3, grid c7.

Campsites, facilities: There are 196 sites with full hookups, including half available for overnight use and some drive-through sites, for trailers or RVs up to 42 feet. Picnic tables are provided. Restrooms, drinking water, flush toilets, showers, cable TV, modem access, a dump station, a public phone, a coin-operated laundry, a playground, and LP gas are available. Some facilities are wheelchair-accessible. Leashed pets are permitted.

Reservations, fees: Reservations recommended. Sites are $28 per night. Major credit cards accepted. Open year-round.

Directions: From the junction of I-5 and I-405 (just south of Seattle), take I-405 and drive to Exit 26. Take that exit to the Bothell/Everett Highway over the freeway and drive south for about one mile; look for the park on the left side. It's marked by a large sign.

Contact: Lake Pleasant RV Park, 24025 Bothell/Everett Highway SE, Bothell, WA 98021; 425/487-1785 or 800/742-0386.

52 Trailer Inns RV Park
 5

This park features all the amenities for RV travelers. It's close to Lake Sammamish State Park as well. Nearby recreation options include an 18-hole golf course, hiking trails, marked bike trails, and tennis courts.

Location: Near Lake Sammamish State Park Pleasant; see Seattle and the San Juan Islands, map 3, grid d7.

Campsites, facilities: There are 103 sites, including half that are permanently rented and some drive-through sites, with full or partial hookups for trailers or RVs of any length. Picnic tables are provided. Restrooms, drinking water, flush toilets, showers, bottled gas, a recreation hall, an indoor swimming pool, a laundry room, ice, and a playground are available. A spa and sauna, a store, and a café are available within one mile. Leashed pets are permitted.

Reservations, fees: Reservations accepted. Sites are $18 to $33 per night. Major credit cards accepted. Open year-round.

Directions: At the junction of I-405 and I-90 south of Seattle, turn east on I-90 and drive 1.5 miles to Exit 11A. Take Exit 11A (a two-avenue exit) and stay to the right lane for 150th Avenue SE. After the lanes split, stay to the left lane and drive to the intersection of 150th Avenue SE and 37th. Continue straight through the light and look for the park entrance at the fifth driveway on the right (about one mile from I-90).

Contact: Trailer Inns RV Park and Recreation Center, 15531 Southeast 37th Street, Bellevue, WA 98006; 425/747-9181, 509/248-1142 or 800/659-4684.

53 Vasa Park Resort

 5

I was giving a seminar in Bellevue one evening when a distraught-looking couple walked in and pleaded, "Where can we camp tonight?" I answered, "Just look in the book," and this camp is where they ended up. It was the easiest sale ever made. This is the most rustic of the parks in the immediate Seattle area. The resort is on the western shore of Lake Sammamish, and the state park is at the south end of the lake. An 18-hole golf course, hiking trails, and marked bike trails are close by. The park is within easy driving distance of Seattle.

Location: On Lake Sammamish Pleasant; see Seattle and the San Juan Islands, map 3, grid d8.

Campsites, facilities: There are 16 sites with partial hookups (water and electricity) for tents, trailers, and RVs, and six sites with full hookups for trailers or RVs of any length. Picnic tables are provided. Restrooms, drinking water, flush toilets, coin-operated showers, a dump station, a playground, and a boat-launching facility are available. Bottled gas, firewood, a store, and a café are located within one mile. Leashed pets are permitted within the campsites only.

Reservations, fees: Reservations accepted. Sites are $20 to $25 per night, $3.25 per person per night for more than two people. Open mid-May to mid-October.

Directions: In Bellevue, drive east on I-90 to Exit 13. Take Exit 13 to West Lake Sammamish

Parkway SE and drive north for one mile; the resort is on the right.

Contact: Vasa Park Resort, 3560 West Lake Sammamish Parkway SE, Bellevue, WA 98008; 425/746-3260.

54 Issaquah Village RV Park

    7

Although Issaquah Village RV Park doesn't allow tents, it's set in a beautiful environment ringed by the Cascade Mountains, making it a scenic alternative in the area. Lake Sammamish State Park is just a few miles north. Most of the sites are asphalt, and 20 percent are long-term rentals.

Location: In Issaquah; see Seattle and the San Juan Islands, map 3, grid d8.

Campsites, facilities: There are 112 sites, including three drive-through sites, with full hookups, for trailers or RVs of any length. No tents are allowed. Restrooms, drinking water, flush toilets, showers, cable TV, a dump station, a public phone, a coin-operated laundry, and LP gas are available. Picnic areas and a playground are also available. Some facilities are wheelchair-accessible. Leashed pets are permitted.

Reservations, fees: Reservations recommended. Sites are $28 to $33 per night. Major credit cards accepted. Open year-round.

Directions: From Seattle on I-405 (preferred) or I-5, drive to the junction of I-90. Take I-90 east and drive 17 miles to Issaquah and Exit 17. Take Exit 17 for Front Street and turn left; drive under the freeway and look for the first right. Take the first right for a very short distance and keep bearing right on the frontage road that parallels the freeway. Drive one quarter-mile to the park on the left.

Contact: Issaquah Village RV Park, 650 First Avenue NE, Issaquah, WA 98027; 425/392-9233 or 800/258-9233.

55 Blue Sky RV Park

    5

Blue Sky RV Park is situated in an urban setting just outside of Seattle. It's a good off-the-beaten-path alternative to the more crowded metro area, yet still only a short drive from the main attractions in the city. Nearby Lake Sammamish State Park provides more rustic recreation opportunities, including hiking and fishing. All sites are paved and level.

Location: Near Lake Sammamish State Park; see Seattle and the San Juan Islands, map 3, grid d8.

Campsites, facilities: There are 51 sites with full hookups, including some long-term rentals, for trailers or RVs. Restrooms, drinking water, flush toilets, showers, cable TV, a coin-operated laundry, and a covered picnic pavilion with barbecue are available. Leashed pets are permitted.

Reservations, fees: No reservations. Sites are $28 per night, $5 per person per night for more than two people. Open year-round.

Directions: From Seattle on I-5, drive to the junction with Highway 90. Turn east on Highway 90 and drive 22 miles to Exit 22 (Preston/Falls City exit). Take that exit to SE 82nd Street. Turn right on SE 82nd Street and drive a very short distance to 302nd Avenue SE. Turn left and drive one-half mile to the campground entrance at the end of the road.

Contact: Blue Sky RV Park, 9002 302nd Avenue SE, Issaquah, WA 98027; 425/222-7910.

56 Aqua Barn Ranch

     4

This is a large park with spacious sites—a good layover spot for campers who want to avoid the metro-area crowds. You'll find all the amenities, including a pool and hot tub.

Numerous recreation options are available in the Seattle area, just 20 minutes north. New owners took over the operation in 2001, and changes are likely.

Location: South of Seattle; see Seattle and the San Juan Islands, map 3, grid e7.

Campsites, facilities: There are 200 sites, including 90 with full hookups and many permanent renters, the rest with partial hookups for trailers or RVs. No tents are allowed. Restrooms, drinking water, flush toilets, showers, a dump station, a public phone, a coin-operated laundry, ice, a restaurant, some picnic tables, and LP gas are available. Recreational facilities include horseshoe pits, a game room, an indoor heated swimming pool, and a playground. Some facilities are wheelchair-accessible. Leashed pets are permitted.

Reservations, fees: No reservations. Sites are $20 to $30 per night, $1.50 per person per night for more than two people. Major credit cards accepted. Open year-round, with limited winter facilities.

Directions: From the junction of I-5 and I-405 south of Seattle, turn east on I-405 and drive to the Enumclaw/Maple Valley exit (Exit 4). Take that exit and turn right (there are no other options) and drive about three miles to the campground on the right.

Contact: Aqua Barn Ranch, 15227 S.E. Renton-Maple Valley Highway, Renton, WA 98058; 425/255-4618.

57 Saltwater State Park

    7

This state park is located halfway between Tacoma and Seattle. The cities jointly and literally buried a hatchet in the park as a symbol of an end to their mutual competition. Campers still don't have it so peaceful, though. The camp is set on the flight path of Seattle-Tacoma International Airport, so it is often noisy from the jets. The park features tide pools and marine life, including salmon spawning in McSorley Creek in the fall. Scuba diving is good here with a nearby underwater reef. There are three trails for hiking and biking and four buildings from the 1930s built by the Civilian Conservation Corps. There are beautiful views of Maury and Vashon Islands and of the Olympic Mountains. Beaches offer clamming and picnic facilities, and scuba diving is a popular pastime.

Location: Near Seattle; see Seattle and the San Juan Islands, map 3, grid e6.

Campsites, facilities: There are 52 sites for tents or self-contained RVs up to 50 feet long. Picnic tables and fire grills are provided. Restrooms, drinking water, flush toilets, showers, a dump station, a playground, a picnic area, horseshoe pits, volleyball, interpretive activities, and firewood are available. A store, a restaurant, and ice are located within one mile. Some facilities are wheelchair-accessible. Boat buoys are nearby on Puget Sound. Leashed pets are permitted.

Reservations, fees: No reservations. Sites are $15 per night, $6 per extra vehicle per night. Senior discount available. Open April through mid-September.

Directions: From the junction of I-5 and Highway 516 (located between Seattle and Tacoma three miles south of SeaTac International Airport), take Highway 516 and drive west for two miles to Highway 509. Turn left and drive one mile to the park access road on the right. Turn right (well marked) and drive one-half mile to the park on the shore of Puget Sound.

Contact: Saltwater State Park, 206/764-4128; State Park information, 360/902-8844.

58 Seattle/Tacoma KOA

 5

This is a popular urban campground, not far from the highway yet in a pleasant setting. The sites are spacious, all drive-through to accommodate large RVs. A public golf course is located nearby. During the summer, a tour of Seattle can be taken from the campground. The tour highlights include the Space Needle, Pikes Place Market, Safeco Field, and Puget Sound.

Location: In Kent; see Seattle and the San Juan Islands, map 3, grid e6.

Campsites, facilities: There are 134 drive-through sites, most with full hookups and the rest with partial hookups, for trailers or RVs, and 18 tent sites. Restrooms, drinking water, flush toilets, showers, a dump station, a public phone, a coin-operated laundry, limited groceries, bottled gas, ice, RV supplies, free movies, and a pancake breakfast are available. A large playground, a game room, a heated swimming pool, and a recreation hall are also available. Some facilities are wheelchair-accessible. Leashed pets are permitted.

Reservations, fees: Reservations recommended. Sites are $28 to $45 per night, $2.95 per person per night for more than two people. Major credit cards accepted. Open year-round.

Directions: On I-5 in Seattle, take Exit 152 for 188th Street/Orillia. Drive east on Orillia and drive 2.5 miles (the road becomes 212th Street) to the campground on the right.

Contact: Seattle/Tacoma KOA, 5801 South 212th Street, Kent, WA 98032; 253/872-8652 or 800/562-1892, fax 206/872-9221.

59 Dash Point State Park

 8

This urban state park set on Puget Sound features unobstructed water views. The park covers 398 acres with 3,301 feet of saltwater shoreline, with 11 miles of trails for hiking and biking. Fishing, windsurfing, swimming, boating, and mountain biking are all popular. Tacoma offers a variety of activities and attractions, including the Tacoma Art Museum (with a children's gallery); the Washington State Historical Society Museum; the Seymour Botanical Conservatory at Wrights Park; Point Defiance Park, Zoo, and Aquarium; the Western Washington Forest Industries Museum; and the Fort Lewis Military Museum.

Location: Near Tacoma; see Seattle and the San Juan Islands, map 3, grid f5.

Campsites, facilities: There are 110 tent sites and 28 sites for trailers or RVs up to 35 feet long. Picnic tables and fire grills are provided. Restrooms, drinking water, flush toilets, showers, a dump station, a playground, an amphitheater, interpretive activities, two sheltered picnic areas, and firewood are available. Leashed pets are permitted.

Reservations, fees: Reserve at 888/CAMP-OUT (888/226-7688); website: www.parks.wa.gov/reservations ($7 reservation fee). Sites are $6 to $16 per night, $6 per extra vehicle per night. Senior discount available. Open year-round.

Directions: On I-5, drive to Exit 143/320th Street. Take that exit and turn west on 320th Street and drive four miles to 47th Street (a T intersection). Turn right on 47th Street and drive to Highway 509 (another T intersection). Turn left on Highway 509/Dash Pint Road and drive two miles to the park. Note: The camping area is on the west side of the road; the day-use area is on the east side of the road.

Contact: Dash Point State Park, 253/593-2206; State Park information, 360/902-8844.

60 Game Farm Wilderness Park

    6

The Game Farm Wilderness Park is just minutes from downtown Auburn. Located along the scenic Stuck River, it was demarked with group outings in mind. Mt. Rainier, the Seattle waterfront, and the Cascade Mountains are all only a short drive away.

Location: On the Stuck River in Auburn; see Seattle and the San Juan Islands, map 3, grid f7.

Campsites, facilities: There are six group campsites with partial hookups (water and electricity) for tents, trailers, and RVs, with four sleeping units per site and a maximum of 16 people per site. Picnic tables and fire grills are provided. Restrooms, drinking water, flush toilets, a picnic shelter, and a dump station are available. Some facilities are wheelchair-accessible. Leashed pets are permitted.

Reservations, fees: Reservations required to be made in-person at the Parks and Recreation Department. Group sites are $25 per night for city residents and $35 for nonresidents, with a two-week maximum. Open April through October.

Directions: On I-5 (north of Tacoma), drive to Exit 142 and Highway 18. Turn east on Highway 18 and drive to the Auburn/Enumclaw exit. Take that exit and drive to the light at Auburn Way. Turn left on Auburn Way South and drive one mile to Howard Road. Exit to the right on Howard Road and drive 0.2 mile to the stop sign at R Street. Turn right on R Street and drive 1.5 miles to Stuck River Drive SE (just over the river). Turn left and drive one quarter-mile upriver to the park on the left at 2401 Stuck River Drive.

Contact: City of Auburn Parks and Recreation Department, 25 West Main Street, Auburn, WA 98001; 253/931-3043.

61 Majestic Mobile Manor RV Park

 7

This clean, pretty park along the Puyallup River with views of Mt. Rainier caters to RVers. Nearby recreation options within 10 miles include an 18-hole golf course, a full-service marina, and tennis courts. For information on the attractions in Tacoma, see the description of Dash Point State Park.

Location: On the Puyallup River; see Seattle and the San Juan Islands, map 3, grid g6.

Campsites, facilities: There are 118 sites with full hookups, including half reserved for long-term rentals, for trailers or RVs of any length, and 12 tent sites available May to October only. Restrooms, drinking water, flush toilets, showers, bottled gas, a dump station, a recreation hall, a store, a coin-operated laundry, ice, and a swimming pool are available. Leashed pets and motorbikes are permitted.

Reservations, fees: Reservations accepted. Sites are $16 to $24 per night, $2 per person per night for more than two people. Open year-round.

Directions: From near Tacoma on I-5, take Exit 135 to Highway 167. Drive east on Highway 167 (River Road) for four miles to the park on the right.

Contact: Majestic Mobile Manor RV Park; 7022 River Road, Puyallup, WA 98371; 253/845-3144 or 800/348-3144, fax 253/841-2248; website: www.majesticrvpark.com.

62 Olympia Campground

    7

This campground in a natural, wooded setting has all the comforts. Nearby recreation options include an 18-hole golf course, hiking trails, marked bike trails, and tennis courts.

Location: Near Olympia; see Seattle and the San Juan Islands, map 3, grid h1.

Campsites, facilities: There are 95 sites with full or partial hookups, including 40 drive-through, for tents, trailers, or RVs of any length, and two cabins. Picnic tables are provided. Fire rings are provided at some sites. Restrooms, drinking water, flush toilets, showers, bottled gas, a dump station, a recreation hall, a store, a coin-operated laundry, ice, a playground, a heated swimming pool in the summer, and firewood are available. A gas station is nearby. A café is located within two miles. Leashed pets are permitted with permission.

Reservations, fees: Reservations accepted. Sites are $18 to $26 per night for two people, $4 per person per night for more than two people. Cabins are $39 per night for two people. Major credit cards accepted. Open year-round.

Directions: From Olympia on I-5, take Exit 101 to Airdustrial Way. Bear east for one quarter-mile to Center Street. Turn right on Center Street and drive one mile to 83rd Avenue. Turn right on 83rd Avenue and drive one-eighth mile to the park on the left.

Contact: Olympia Campground, 1441 83rd Avenue SW, Olympia, WA 98512; 360/352-2551.

63 Nisqually Plaza RV Park

 5

This campground is located on McAlister Creek, where salmon fishing and boating are popular. Nearby recreation opportunities include an 18-hole golf course and the Nisqually National Wildlife Refuge, which offers seven miles of foot trails for viewing a great variety of flora and fauna.

Location: Near McAlister Creek; see Seattle and the San Juan Islands, map 3, grid h1.

Campsites, facilities: There are 51 sites with full hookups, including six drive-through, for trailers or RVs of any length. Picnic tables are provided. Restrooms, drinking water, flush toilets, coin-operated showers, a telephone, cable TV, a store, a café, a coin-operated laundry, ice, a playground, and a seasonal swimming pool are available. Some facilities are wheelchair-accessible. Boat-launching facilities are nearby. Leashed pets are permitted.

Reservations, fees: Reservations accepted. Sites are $22 per night, $2 per person per night for more than two people. Open year-round.

Directions: In Olympia on I-5, take Exit 114 and drive a short distance to Martin Way. Turn right and drive a short distance to the first road (located between two gas stations), a private access road for the park. Turn right and drive to the park.

Contact: Nisqually Plaza RV Park, 10220 Martin Way East, Olympia, WA 98516; 360/491-3831.

©TOM STIENSTRA

The Northern Cascades

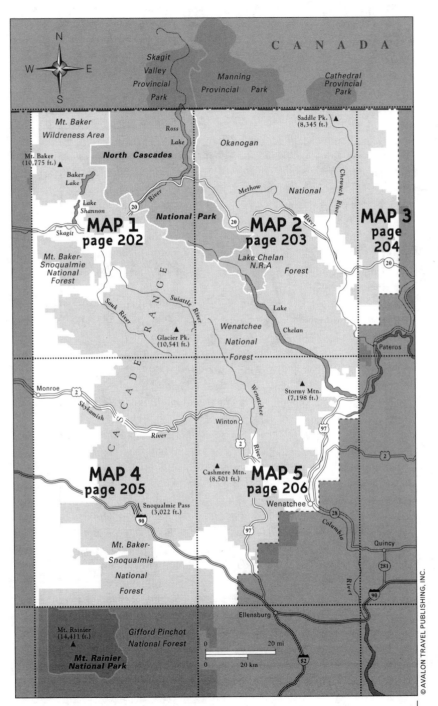

Map 1

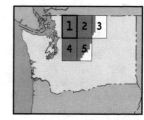

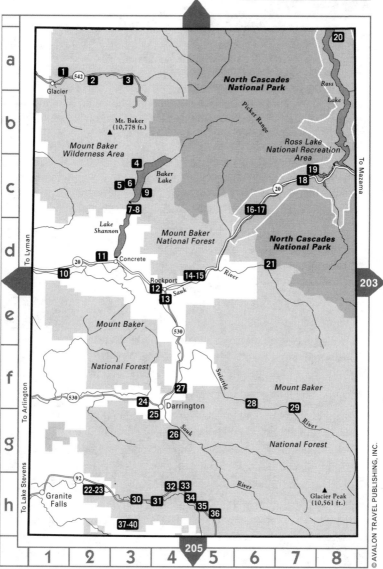

© AVALON TRAVEL PUBLISHING, INC.

Map 2

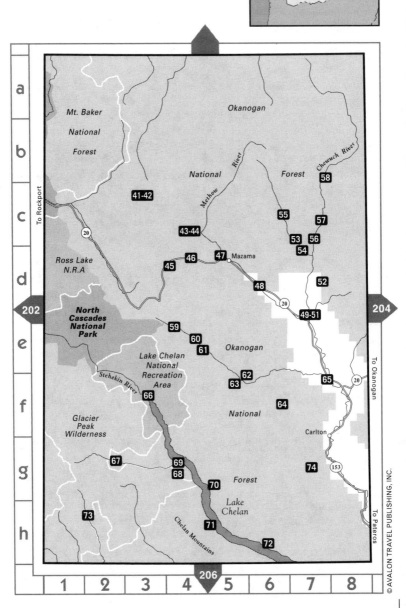

To Rockport

a

b

c

d

202

e

f

g

h

Mt. Baker
National
Forest

Okanogan

National

Forest

Methow River

Chewuch River

58

41-42

55

57

53   56
43-44   54
46 47 Mazama
45   48

20

52

49-51

Ross Lake
N.R.A.

North
Cascades
National
Park

59
60
61

Okanogan

Lake Chelan
National
Recreation
Area

62
63

65

20

To Okanogan

Stehekin River

66

64

Carlton

Glacier
Peak
Wilderness

National

67

69
68   Forest

70

74   153

Lake
Chelan

73

Chelan Mountains

71

72

To Pateros

1   2   3   4   5   6   7   8

204

206

© AVALON TRAVEL PUBLISHING, INC.

Map 3

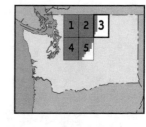

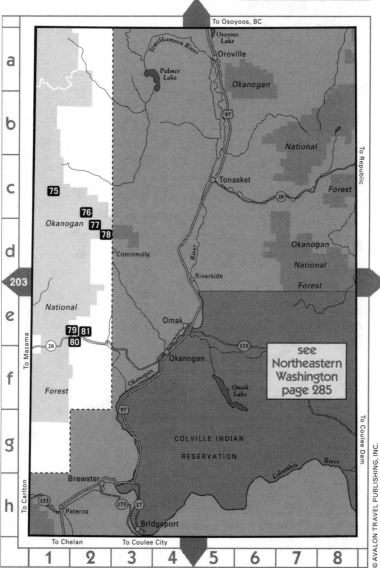

To Osoyoos, BC

Similkameen River

Osoyoos Lake

Oroville

Palmer Lake

Okanogan

97

National

Tonasket

20

Forest

Okanogan

National

Forest

75

Okanogan

76

77

78

Conconully

Riverside

National

Omak

79 **81**

80

20

155

Okanogan

see
Northeastern
Washington
page 285

Forest

Omak
Lake

97

COLVILLE INDIAN

RESERVATION

Columbia River

Brewster

153

173 17

Pateros

Bridgeport

To Mazama

To Carlton

To Chelan

To Coulee City

To Republic

To Coulee Dam

203

© AVALON TRAVEL PUBLISHING, INC.

1 2 3 4 5 6 7 8

Map 4

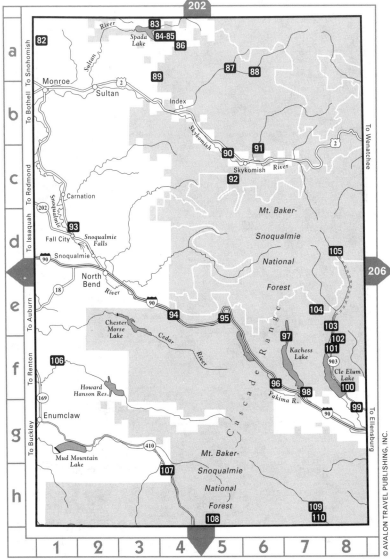

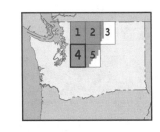

© AVALON TRAVEL PUBLISHING, INC.

Map 5

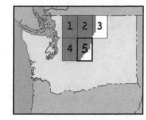

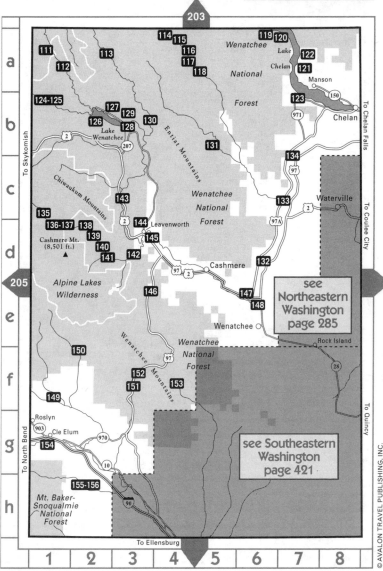

a

b

205

c

d

e

f

g

h

111

112

113

114 115

116

117

118

119 120

122

121

Wenatchee

National

Forest

Lake
Chelan

Manson

150

123

971

Chelan

To Chelan Falls

124-125

127 129

126 128 130

Lake
Wenatchee

2

207

131

Entiat Mountains

To Skykomish

Chiwaukum Mountains

143

Wenatchee
National
Forest

134

97

133

97A

Waterville

2

To Coulee City

135

136-137 138

139

140

141

142

Cashmere Mt.
(8,501 ft.)
▲

144 Leavenworth

145

Alpine Lakes
Wilderness

146

97 2

Cashmere

132

147

148

see
Northeastern
Washington
page 285

Wenatchee ○

Rock Island

28

To Quincy

150

Wenatchee Mountains

Wenatchee
National
Forest

97

152

151

153

149

Roslyn

903 Cle Elum

970

154

To North Bend

10

see Southeastern
Washington
page 421

155-156

90

Mt. Baker-
Snoqualmie
National
Forest

To Ellensburg

1 2 3 4 5 6 7 8

© AVALON TRAVEL PUBLISHING, INC.

The Northern Cascades

(CONTINUED ON NEXT PAGE)

Mt. Baker rises like a diamond in a field of coal. It is the centerpiece in a forested landscape with hundreds of lakes, rivers, and hidden campgrounds. The only limit here is weather. The northern Cascades are deluged with the nation's highest snowfall in winter; Mt. Baker often receives a foot a day for weeks. While that shortens the recreation season to just a few months in summer, it has another effect as well. With so many recreation destinations available for such a short time—literally hundreds over the course of three or four months—many remain largely undiscovered.

The vast number of forests, lakes, and streams can make choosing your destination the most difficult decision of all. With so many stellar spots available, newcomers will be well served starting at the state parks, which offer beautiful settings that are easy to reach. Many camps set along roads provide choice layover spots for vacationing travelers.

After awhile, though, searching for the lesser-known camps in the national forests becomes more appealing. Many beautiful spots are set alongside lakes and streams, often with trailheads for hikes into nearby wilderness. These areas are among the wildest in America, featuring abundant wildlife, good fishing, and great hiking.

It's true that anybody can get an overview of the area by cruising the highways and camping at the roadside spots we list. But you can take this one the extra mile. Your dream spot may be waiting out there.

1 Douglas Fir

 10

This camp features river views from some campsites, set along the Nooksack River. It is a beautiful camp, set amid old-growth Douglas fir, silver fir, and western hemlock. Trout fishing is available on the river, and there are hiking trails in the area, with a nearby trailhead at Silver Fir Camp.

Location: On the Nooksack River in Mt. Baker-Snoqualmie National Forest; see the Northern Cascades, map 1, grid a1.

Campsites, facilities: There are 30 sites for tents, trailers, or RVs up to 31 feet long. Picnic tables and fire grills are provided. Drinking water and vault toilets are available. A store, a café, a coin-operated laundry, and ice are located within five miles. Leashed pets are permitted.

Reservations, fees: Reservations recommended. Reserve at 877/444-6777 ($8.65 reservation fee) or website: www.reserveusa.com. Sites are $12 per night. Open May through September, with self-service access the remainder of the year.

Directions: From Bellingham on I-5, take the Highway 542 exit and drive 31 miles to Glacier. Continue two miles northeast on Highway 542 to the campground on the left.

Contact: Mt. Baker-Snoqualmie National Forest, Mt. Baker Ranger District, Sedro-Woolley, WA 98284; 360/856-5700, fax 360/856-1934.

2 Excelsior Group Camp

 6

This campground is set near the Nooksack River less than one mile from Nooksack Falls and 1.5 miles from the site of the Excelsior Mine. The Excelsior Pass Trailhead is about five minutes away. There are numerous hiking trails available within a 30-minute drive in the Mt. Baker Wilderness.

Location: Near the Nooksack River in Mt. Baker-Snoqualmie National Forest; see the Northern Cascades, map 1, grid a2.

Campsites, facilities: There is one group site for up to 100 people. Picnic tables, vault toilets, and fire grills are provided, but there is no drinking water. Leashed pets are permitted.

Reservations, fees: Reservations required. Reserve at 877/444-6777 ($8.65 reservation fee) or website: www.reserveusa.com. The group site fee is $60 to $150 per night. Open May through September.

Directions: From Bellingham on I-5, take the Highway 542 exit and drive 37.5 miles (6.5 miles east of Glacier) to the camp on the right.

Contact: Mt. Baker-Snoqualmie National Forest, Mt. Baker Ranger District, Sedro-Woolley, WA 98284; 360/856-5700, fax 360/856-1934.

3 Silver Fir

 9

This campground is set on the North Fork of the Nooksack River. It is within 30 minutes of the Heather Meadows area, which provides some of the best hiking trails in the entire region. In addition, Artist Ridge is just a one-mile round-trip for views of Mt. Baker and Mt. Shuksan. The first part of the trail to the first viewpoint is wheelchair-accessible. Fishing is available nearby, and in the winter the area becomes a cross-country ski area. You're strongly advised to obtain a U.S. Forest Service map in order to take maximum advantage of the recreational opportunities in the area.

Location: On the North Fork of the Nooksack River in Mt. Baker-Snoqualmie National Forest; see the Northern Cascades, map 1, grid a3.

Campsites, facilities: There are 20 sites for tents, trailers, or RVs up to 21 feet long. Picnic tables and barbecue grills are provided.

Drinking water, vault toilets, and a group picnic shelter are available. Leashed pets are permitted.

Reservations, fees: Reservations accepted; phone 877/444-6777 or access the website: www.reserveusa.com ($8.65 reservation fee). Sites are $12 per night. Senior discount available. Open May through September.

Directions: From I-5 at Bellingham, turn east on Highway 542 and drive 31 miles to Glacier. Continue east on Highway 542 for 12.5 miles to the campground on the right.

Contact: Mt. Baker-Snoqualmie National Forest, Mt. Baker Ranger District, 810 State Route 20, Sedro-Woolley, WA 98284; 360/856-5700, fax 360/856-1934.

4 Park Creek

    6

This pretty camp is set at 800 feet on Park Creek amid a heavily wooded area comprising old-growth Douglas fir and western hemlock. Park Creek is a feeder stream to nearby Baker Lake. It's primitive and small but gets its fair share of use.

Location: Near Baker Lake in Mt. Baker-Snoqualmie National; see the Northern Cascades, map 1, grid c3.

Campsites, facilities: There are 12 sites for tents or small RVs. Picnic tables are provided. Vault toilets are available, but there is no drinking water. Boat docks, launching facilities, and rentals are nearby on Baker Lake. Leashed pets are permitted.

Reservations, fees: Reservations required; phone 877/444-6777 or access the website: www.reserveusa.com ($8.65 reservation fee). Sites are $8 per night. Senior discount available. Open mid-May to early September.

Directions: From I-5 at Burlington, turn east on State Route 20 and drive approximately 24 miles to Milepost 82 and Baker Lake Highway (Forest Road 11). Turn north on Baker

Lake Highway and drive about 19.5 miles to Forest Road 1144. Turn left (northwest) and drive about 200 yards to the campground on the left. Obtaining a U.S. Forest Service map is helpful.

Contact: Mt. Baker-Snoqualmie National Forest, Mt. Baker Ranger District, 810 State Route 20, Sedro-Woolley, WA 98284; 360/856-5700, fax 360/856-1934.

5 Boulder Creek

 8

This camp provides an alternative to Horseshoe Cove. It is set on Boulder Creek about one mile from the shore of Baker Lake. Fishing is fair here for rainbow trout, but typically far better at Baker Lake. A boat launch is located at Panorama Point, about 15 minutes away. Wild berries can be found in the area in season. The campground offers prime views of Mt. Baker.

Location: Near Baker Lake in Mt. Baker-Snoqualmie National Forest; see the Northern Cascades, map 1, grid c3.

Campsites, facilities: There are eight tent sites and two group sites. Picnic tables and fire grills are provided. Pit toilets are available, but there is no drinking water. Boat docks and launching facilities are nearby on Baker Lake. Leashed pets are permitted.

Reservations, fees: Reservations required for group sites and are available for some family sites; phone 877/444-6777 or access the website: www.reserveusa.com ($8.65 reservation fee). Family sites are $8 per night; group sites are $55 per night. Senior discount available. Open mid-May to early September.

Directions: From I-5 at Burlington, turn east on State Route 20 and drive approximately 24 miles to Milepost 82 and Baker Lake Highway (Forest Road 11). Turn north on

Baker Lake Highway and drive 17.4 miles to the campground on the right.

Contact: Mt. Baker-Snoqualmie National Forest, Mt. Baker Ranger District, 810 State Route 20, Sedro-Woolley, WA 98284; 360/856-5700, fax 360/856-1934.

6 Panorama Point

    10

The camp is true to its name, with incredible scenic views of Mt. Baker, Mt. Shuk, Baker Lake, and Anderson Mountain. Panorama Point is a well-maintained campground on the northwest shore of Baker Lake. The reservoir is one of the better fishing lakes in the area, often with good prospects for rainbow trout. Power boating and water-skiing are permitted. Hiking trails are nearby.

Location: On Baker Lake in Mt. Baker-Snoqualmie National Forest; see the Northern Cascades, map 1, grid c3.

Campsites, facilities: There are 16 sites for tents, trailers, or RVs up to 21 feet long. Picnic tables are provided. Well water and vault toilets are available. A store and ice are located within one mile. A boat ramp is adjacent to the camp. Boat docks and rentals are nearby. Leashed pets are permitted.

Reservations, fees: Reservations accepted for some sites; phone 877/444-6777 or access the website: www.reserveusa.com ($8.65 reservation fee). Sites are $12 per night. Senior discount available. Open May to mid-September.

Directions: From I-5 at Burlington, turn east on State Route 20 and drive approximately 24 miles to Milepost 82 and Baker Lake Highway (Forest Road 11). Turn north on Baker Lake Highway and drive 18.7 miles to the campground entrance on the right on the shore of Baker.

Contact: Mt. Baker-Snoqualmie National Forest, Mt. Baker Ranger District, 810 State Route 20 Sedro-Woolley, WA 98284; 360/856-5700, fax 360/856-1934.

7 Horseshoe Cove

   9

This camp is set along 5,000-acre Baker Lake. Anglers will often find good fishing for rainbow trout and kokanee salmon. Other highlights are swimming access from the campground and a boat ramp. Some hiking trails can be found nearby. The Baker Lake Basin has many trails, and the Mt. Baker National Recreation area is located within 30 minutes.

Location: On Baker Lake in Mt. Baker-Snoqualmie National ; see the Northern Cascades, map 1, grid c3.

Campsites, facilities: There are eight sites for tents only and 34 sites for tents, trailers, or RVs up to 25 feet long. Picnic tables and fire grills are provided. Drinking water and flush toilets are available. A boat ramp and swimming beach are adjacent to camp. Leashed pets are permitted.

Reservations, fees: Reservations accepted for some sites, phone 877/444-6777 or access the website: www.reserveusa.com ($8.65 reservation fee). Sites are $12 per night. Senior discount available. Open May through September; one loop remains open through the off-season on a no-service, no-fee basis.

Directions: From I-5 at Burlington, turn east on State Route 20 and drive approximately 24 miles to Milepost 82 and the Baker Lake Highway (Forest Road 11). Turn north on Baker Lake Highway and drive about 14.8 miles to Forest Road 1118. Turn east on Forest Road 1118 and drive two miles to the campground. A U.S. Forest Service map is recommended.

Contact: Mt. Baker-Snoqualmie National Forest, Mt. Baker Ranger District, 810 State Route 20, Sedro-Woolley, WA 98284; 360/856-5700, fax 360/856-1934.

8 Bay View North Group & South Group

  9

These are both group camps set along Baker Lake. They are located in forest, mostly wooded. It is not dense forest, and there is an open feel to the area here. Many sites are close to the water. Baker Lake covers 5,000 acres with fishing for rainbow trout and kokanee salmon.

Location: On Baker Lake in Mt. Baker-Snoqualmie National Forest; see the Northern Cascades, map 1, grid c3.

Campsites, facilities: There are two group sites at separate camps for 25 people with tents, trailers, or RVs at each site. Picnic tables and fire grills are provided. Vault toilets are available. No drinking water is available. A boat ramp is located nearby near Horseshoe Cove Camp. Leashed pets are permitted.

Reservations, fees: Reserve at 877/444-6777 ($8.65 reservation fee) or website: www.reserveusa.com. Sites are $75 per night. Major credit cards accepted. Open mid-May through mid-September, weather permitting.

Directions: From I-5 at Burlington, turn east on State Route 20 and drive approximately 24 miles to Milepost 82 and the Baker Lake Highway (Forest Road 11). Turn north on Baker Lake Highway and drive about 14.8 miles to Forest Road 1118. Turn east on Forest Road 1118 and drive two miles to the campground (adjacent to Horseshoe Cove). A U.S. Forest Service map is recommended.

Contact: Mt. Baker-Snoqualmie National Forest, Mt. Baker Ranger District, 810 State Route 20, Sedro-Woolley, WA 98284; 360/856-5700, fax 360/856-1934.

9 Maple Grove Hike-In, Boat-In

 9

Looking for a quiet spot on the edge of a popular lake? Here it is. This rustic campground is on the shore of Baker Lake and is hike-in or boat-in only. Many camps on this lake fill on summer weekends and boating activity is high, including fishing, power boating, and water-skiing. Privacy and great mountain views are your reward for the extra effort, and it's all free.

Location: On Baker Lake in Mt. Baker-Snoqualmie National ; see the Northern Cascades, map 1, grid c3.

Campsites, facilities: There are five primitive tent sites that are accessible only by boat or on foot. Picnic tables and fire grills are provided. Vault toilets are available. No drinking water is available. Boat-launching facilities are located nearby on Baker Lake. Leashed pets are permitted.

Reservations, fees: No reservations; no fee. Open year-round.

Directions: From I-5 at Burlington, turn east on State Route 20 and drive approximately 24 miles to Milepost 82 and Baker Lake Highway (Forest Road 11). Turn north on Baker Lake Highway and drive 13.3 miles to Forest Road 1106. Turn east (right) on Forest Road 1106 and drive across Baker Dam to Forest Road 1107. Turn left and drive one-half mile to the parking area and the trailhead on the left. To reach the camp by boat, launch at one of the campgrounds on the west side of the lake (Horseshoe Cove is the closest) or take Trail 610/Baker Lake Trail (located on the east side of the

lake, one-half mile north of the dam) and walk in four miles to the camp. Obtaining a U.S. Forest Service map is recommended.
Contact: Mt. Baker-Snoqualmie National Forest, Mt. Baker Ranger District, 810 State Route 20, Sedro-Woolley, WA 98284; 360/856-5700, fax 360/856-1934.

10 Rasar State Park

     8

This park borders North Cascade National Park and is also near 10,778-foot Mt. Baker and the Baker River watershed. Fishing and hiking are the attractions here. The elevation is 4,000 feet.
Location: On the Skagit River; see the Northern Cascades, map 1, grid d1.
Campsites, facilities: There are 39 sites, including 22 with full hookups for tents, trailers, and RVs, primitive hike-in/bike-in sites, and 10 walk-in sites at which there are three four-person Adirondack shelters available. Picnic tables and fire grills are provided. Restrooms, drinking water, flush toilets, coin-operated showers, and a kitchen shelter are available. Firewood gathering is prohibited. Leashed pets are permitted.
Reservations, fees: No reservations. Sites are $6 to $22 per night, $65 per extra vehicle per night. Open year-round, weather permitting.
Directions: From Seattle, drive north on I-5 to Burlington and the Highway 20 exit. Turn east on Highway 20/North Cascade Highway and drive 20 miles to Lusk Road. Turn right on Lusk Road and drive three-quarters mile to Cape Horn Road. Turn left on Cape Horn Road and drive two miles to the park entrance.
Contact: Rasar State Park, 38730 Cape Horn Road, Concrete, WA 98237; phone 360/826-3942; State Park information, 360/902-8844.

11 Creekside Campground

   6

This pretty, wooded campground is centrally located to nearby recreational opportunities at Baker Lake and the Skagit River. Trout fishing is good here. Tackle is available nearby. Horseshoe pits and a recreation hall are also available.
Location: Near the Skagit River; see the Northern Cascades, map 1, grid d2.
Campsites, facilities: There are 29 sites for tents, trailers, or RVs up to 40 feet long. Picnic tables are provided. Restrooms, drinking water, flush toilets, showers, a dump station, a store, a laundry room, and a playground are available. A café is located within one mile. Leashed pets and motorbikes are permitted.
Reservations, fees: Reservations recommended. Sites are $10 to $22 per night. Open year-round.
Directions: From Seattle, drive north on I-5 to Exit 232 (Cook Road). Take the exit up and over the highway to the flashing light and Cook Road. Turn left on Cook Road (Highway 20) and drive four miles to the light at Highway 20. Turn left at Highway 20 and drive 17 miles to Baker Lake Road (near Grasmere/Concrete). Turn left on Baker Lake Road and drive a quarter mile to the camp.
Contact: Creekside Campground, 39602 Baker Lake Road, Concrete, WA 98237; 360/826-3566.

12 Rockport State Park

   8

This state park covers 670 acres and is set at the foot of Sauk Mountain (5,400 feet). This area was never logged, creating a natural forest with a canopy so dense that minimal sunlight penetrates to the ground.

It features more than 600 acres of old-growth Douglas firs in the park. There are five miles of hiking trails amid this forest. In addition, there is a steep but climbable trail that extends three miles (one-way) to the top of Sauk Mountain. The summit offers good views of the Skagat Valley and the North Cascades. A bonus at this camp are four Adirondack shelters, which have three sides and a roof. The Skagit River, which is a good steelhead stream, runs nearby. Rafting and kayaking are allowed on the Skagit, with the put-in not at the park, but on nearby State Route 20.

Location: Near the Skagit River; see the Northern Cascades, map 1, grid e3.

Campsites, facilities: There are 50 sites with full hookups for trailers or RVs up to 45 feet long, three primitive tent sites, eight developed, walk-in tent sites, four Adirondack shelters, and one group tent site. Picnic tables and fire grills are provided. Restrooms, flush toilets, showers, and a dump station are available. Firewood is available for a fee. Some facilities are wheelchair-accessible. A store, gas, and ice are located within one mile. Leashed pets are permitted.

Reservations, fees: Reservations required for the group site only, phone 360/853-8461. Sites are $15 to $21 per night, $6 per extra vehicle per night. Adirondack shelters are $21 per night. The group site is $25, plus $2 per person per night. Open April to late October.

Directions: From I-5 at Burlington, turn east on State Route 20 and drive 37 miles to Milepost 96. Look for the park entrance (one mile west of Rockport) on the right.

Contact: Rockport State Park, 5051 State Route 20, Concrete, WA 98237; 360/853-8461; State Park information, 360/902-8844.

13 Howard Miller Steelhead Park

  5

This is a Skagit County Park that provides grassy sites and access to the Skagit River. The river is designated a Wild and Scenic River. The steelhead fishing is often good in season. Campsites at this spot are sunny and spacious. A bald eagle sanctuary is located at the east end of the park. November through January is the best time to see bald eagles here. This camp is most popular in July, August, and September, when the weather is best, but also attracts visitors in early winter who arrive primarily for bald eagle watching.

Location: On the Skagit River; see the Northern Cascades, map 1, grid e3.

Campsites, facilities: There are 49 sites, including 18 with electrical and water hookups and 30 with electrical hookups, for tents, trailers, or RVs of any length, and 10 sites for tents. Some sites can accommodate group camps. Picnic tables and fire pits are provided. Restrooms, drinking water, flush toilets, showers, a dump station, a clubhouse, a picnic shelter, Adirondacks (three-sided, roofed shelters), and a playground with horseshoe pits are available. A store and ice are located within one mile. Boat-launching facilities are located on the Skagit River. Some facilities and sites are wheelchair-accessible. Leashed pets are permitted.

Reservations, fees: Reservations recommended ($2 reservation fee). Sites are $12 to $16 per night, $3 per extra vehicle per night. Major credit cards accepted. Call for group rates. Open year-round.

Directions: On I-5, drive to Exit 230/State Route 20 at Burlington. Turn east on

State Route 20, and drive 44 miles to Rockport and Rockport-Darrington Road (Highway 530). Turn south and drive three blocks to the camp on the right.

Contact: Howard Miller Steelhead Park, P.O. Box 127, Rockport, WA 98283; 360/853-8808, fax 360/853-7315.

14 Wilderness Village and RV Park

 6

This RV park is located near the Skagit River. It is cool and wooded, with nice, grassy sites and nearby access to the river and fishing. Horseshoe pits and a sports field offer recreation alternatives. Rockport State Park and hiking trails are nearby. Bald eagles can often be viewed on the Skagit River in December and January. A one-mile trail, round-trip, can be accessed here along the river.

Location: Near the Skagit River; see the Northern Cascades, map 1, grid d4.

Campsites, facilities: There are 32 drive-through sites with full hookups for trailers or RVs of any length and 20 tent sites. Picnic tables and fire rings are provided. Restrooms, flush toilets, coin-operated showers, cable TV, a recreation hall, and a coin-operated laundry are available. A café and ice are located within two miles. Leashed pets are permitted.

Reservations, fees: Reservations accepted. Sites are $11 to $17 per night. Open year-round.

Directions: From Burlington, drive east on State Route 20 for 44 miles to Rockport. Continue east on State Route 20 for five miles to the park. The park is between Mileposts 102 and 103 on the right.

Contact: Wilderness Village and RV Park, 57588 State Route 20, Rockport, WA 98283; 360/873-2571.

15 Skagit River Resort

 9

This beautiful camp is nestled in the trees along the Skagit River. The resort covers 125 acres, including 1.5 miles of river frontage. A feature is a restaurant called "The Eatery," which has received awards for its pecan pie and is also known for its home-style meals. Fishing, river walks, and nearby hiking trails among the glaciers and waterfalls can be accessed close to the campground. There are also three hydroelectric plants nearby that offer tours. Recreational facilities include horseshoes and a sports field for volleyball, croquet, and badminton. This resort is popular from July through September, when reservations are often required to get a spot.

Location: On the Skagit River; see the Northern Cascades, map 1, grid d5.

Campsites, facilities: There are 48 sites with full hookups, including some pull-through sites, for tents, trailers, and RVs, plus 34 cabins and mobile homes. Restrooms, drinking water, flush toilets, coin-operated showers, a dump station, a public phone, a coin-operated laundry, horseshoe pits, a sports field for volleyball, croquet, and badminton, and a restaurant are available. Leashed pets are permitted.

Reservations, fees: Reservations recommended. Sites are $10 to $20 per night. Cabins are $54 to $119. Major credit cards accepted. There is an added charge for pets in the cabins. Open year-round.

Directions: From Burlington, drive east on State Route 20 for 44 miles to Rockport. Continue east on State Route 20 for six miles to the campground on the left (between Mileposts 103 and 104).

Contact: Skagit River Resort, 58468 Clark Cabin Road, Rockport, WA 98283; 800/273-2606, 360/873-2250, fax 360/873-4077; website: www.northcascades.com.

16 Goodell Creek & Goodell Creek Group

 7

Goodell Creek Campground is an alternative to the nearby and larger Newhalem Creek Campground. This one is set at 500 feet elevation, where Goodell Creek pours into the Skagit River in the Ross Lake National Recreation Area. It's a popular put-in site for raft trips downriver. That makes the group sites popular here. No firewood gathering is permitted.

Location: On Goodell Creek and the Skagit River in Ross Lake National Recreation Area; see the Northern Cascades, map 1, grid c6.

Campsites, facilities: There are 21 campsites for tents or RVs up to 22 feet long and two group sites (Upper and Lower Goodell). Picnic tables and fire rings are provided. Vault toilets and a picnic shelter are available. Drinking water is available in the family sites, but not in the group sites. Leashed pets are permitted.

Reservations, fees: No reservations for family sites. Reservations required for group sites only; phone 360/873-4590, extension 17. Family sites are $10 per night, group sites $25 per night. Senior discount available. Open year-round, but there are no services (and no fees) in the winter.

Directions: On I-5, drive to Exit 230/State Route 20 at Burlington. Turn east on State Route 20, and drive 46 miles to Marblemount. Continue on State Route 20 for 13 miles east to the campground entrance.

Contact: North Cascades National Park Headquarters, 810 State Route 20, Sedro-Woolley, WA 98284; 360/856-5700, fax 360/856-1934.

17 Newhalem Creek & Newhalem Creek Group

 7

This spot is set along the Skagit River west of Newhalem at 500 feet elevation. Good hiking possibilities abound in the immediate area, and naturalist programs are available. Be sure to visit the North Cascades Visitor Center at the top of the hill from the campground. No firewood gathering is permitted here. If this camp is full, try Goodell Creek Campground, located just one mile west on State Route 20.

Location: Near the Skagit River in Ross Lake National Recreation Area; see the Northern Cascades, map 1, grid c6.

Campsites, facilities: There are 129 sites for tents or RVs up to 32 feet long and two group sites for up to 24 people each. Picnic tables and fire grills are provided. Flush toilets, drinking water, and a dump station are available. The group camp has a covered pavilion. Some facilities are wheelchair-accessible. Leashed pets are permitted.

Reservations, fees: No reservations for family sites. Reservations required for group camps at 360/873-4590, extension 17. Family sites are $12 per night, group sites are $32 per night. Senior discount available. Open mid-May to mid-October.

Directions: On I-5, drive to Exit 230/State Route 20 at Burlington. Turn east on State Route 20, and drive 46 miles to Marblemount. Continue 14 miles east on State Route 20 to the camp.

Contact: North Cascades National Park Headquarters, 810 State Route 20, Sedro-Woolley, WA 98284; 360/856-5700, fax 360/856-1934.

18 Gorge Lake

 9

This small camp is set near the north shore of Gorge Lake, with lake views from many sites, and close to Colonial Creek and Goodell Creek. There is some tree cover. The elevation is 900 feet. This is a very narrow lake with trout fishing; check regulations. The camp is not well known and gets low use. One problem here is that the lake level can fluctuate (but not as much as Ross Lake), leaving the camps high and dry. No firewood gathering is permitted. There are two other lakes nearby on the Skagit River—Diablo Lake and Ross Lake.

Location: On Gorge Lake on Skagit River in Ross Lake National Recreation Area; see the Northern Cascades, map 1, grid c7.

Campsites, facilities: There are six sites for tents, trailers, or RVs up to 22 feet long. Picnic tables and fire grills are provided. Vault toilets are available. No drinking water is available. Garbage must be packed out. A boat ramp is nearby. Leashed pets are permitted.

Reservations, fees: No reservations; no fee. Open late May through October.

Directions: From I-5 near Burlington, take exit 230 for State Route 20. Turn east on State Route 20 and drive 46 miles to Marblemount. Continue east on State Route 20 for another 20 miles to the junction with Diablo Road. Bear left and drive 0.6 miles to the campground on the right.

Contact: North Cascades National Park Headquarters, 810 State Route 20, Sedro-Woolley, WA 98284; 360/856-5700, fax 360/856-1934.

🔟 Colonial Creek

    7

Colonial Creek Campground (elevation 1,200 feet) sits along the shore of Diablo Lake in the Ross Lake National Recreation Area. The five-mile-long lake offers many hiking and fishing possibilities. A naturalist program and guided walks are available during the summer months. No firewood gathering is permitted at this campsite.

Location: On Diablo Lake in Ross Lake National Recreation Area; see the Northern Cascades, map 1, grid c7.

Campsites, facilities: There are 164 campsites for tents or trailers, including a few walk-in tent sites; 18 lakefront sites remain open through the winter, but no services are available. Picnic tables and fire grills are provided. Flush toilets, drinking water, a dump station, three boat docks, and a boat ramp are available. Some facilities are wheelchair-accessible. Leashed pets are permitted.

Reservations, fees: No reservations accepted. Sites are $12 per night. Senior discount available. Open mid-April to mid-October; 18 lakefront sites are open through the winter (no services provided).

Directions: From I-5 at Burlington, take Exit 230 and drive east to State Route 20. Turn east on State Route 20, drive 46 miles to Marblemount, and continue east on State Route 20 for 24 miles to the campground entrance.

Contact: North Cascades National Park Headquarters, 810 State Route 20, Sedro-Woolley, WA 98284; 360/856-5700, fax 360/856-1934.

2️⃣0️⃣ Hozomeen

   9

Hozomeen campground is just inside the U.S.–Canada border at the northeast end of Ross Lake, at 1,600 feet elevation. It takes quite an effort to get here, which tends to weed out all but the most stalwart campers. This is good news for those few, for they will find a quiet, uncrowded camp in a beautiful setting. No firewood gathering is permitted here.

Location: On Ross Lake in Ross Lake National Recreation Area; see the Northern Cascades, map 1, grid a8.

Campsites, facilities: There are 122 sites for tents or RVs up to 22 feet long. Picnic tables and fire grills are provided. Vault toilets are available. No drinking water is available. Garbage must be packed out. A boat launch on Ross Lake is available nearby. Leashed pets are permitted.

Reservations, fees: No reservations; no fee. Open late May through October.

Directions: This campground is accessible only through Canada. From the town of Hope, British Columbia, turn south on Silver-Skagit Road; it is a narrow dirt/gravel road, which is often rough. Drive south for 39 miles to the campground at the north end of Ross Lake.

Contact: North Cascades National Park Headquarters, 810 State Route 20, Sedro-Woolley, WA 98284; 360/856-5700, fax 360/856-1934.

21 Marble Creek

 7

This primitive campground is set on Marble Creek amid a setting of old-growth Douglas fir and western hemlock. Fishing for rainbow trout is possible here. A trailhead to Hidden Lake just inside the boundary of North Cascades National Park can be found about five miles from camp at the end of Forest Road 1540. See a U.S. Forest Service map for details.

Location: On Marble Creek in Mt. Baker-Snoqualmie National Forest; ; see the Northern Cascades, map 1, grid d6.

Campsites, facilities: There are 24 sites for tents, trailers, or RVs up to 22 feet long. Picnic tables and fire grills are provided. Vault toilets are available, but there is no drinking water. Leashed pets are permitted.

Reservations, fees: Reserve at 877/444-6777 ($8.65 reservation fee) or website: www.re-serveusa.com. Sites are $8 per night. Senior discount available. Open mid-May to mid-September.

Directions: From I-5, drive to Exit 230/State Route 20 at Burlington. Turn east on State Route 20, and drive 46 miles to Marblemount and Forest Road 15 (Cascade River Road). Cross the bridge, turn east on Cascade River Road, and drive eight miles to Forest Road 1530. Turn south on Forest Road 1530 and drive one mile to the campground. Obtaining a U.S. Forest Service map is advised.

Contact: Mt. Baker-Snoqualmie National Forest, Mt. Baker Ranger District, 810 State Route 20, Sedro-Woolley, WA 98284; 360/856-5700, fax 360/856-1934.

22 Turlo

 8

Turlo is set at 900 feet along the South Fork of the Stillaguamish River, the westernmost camp located on this stretch of Highway 92. A U.S. Forest Service Public Information Center is nearby. Riverside campsites are available, and the fishing can be good here. A few hiking trails can be found in the area; see a U.S. Forest Service map or consult the nearby information center for trail locations.

Location: On the South Fork of the Stillaguamish River in Mt. Baker-Snoqualmie National Forest; see the Northern Cascades, map 1, grid h2.

Campsites, facilities: There are 19 sites for tents or RVs up to 31 feet long. Picnic tables are provided. Vault toilets, drinking water, and firewood are available. Some facilities are wheelchair-accessible. A store, a café, and ice are located one mile away. Leashed pets are permitted.

Reservations, fees: Reserve at 877/444-6777 ($8.65 reservation fee) or website: www.reserveusa.com. Sites are $12 to $16 per night, $5 per extra vehicle per night. Open mid-May to late September.

Directions: From Seattle, drive north on I-5 to Everett

and U.S. 2. Turn east on U.S. 2 and drive five miles to Highway 9. Turn north and drive four miles to Highway 92. Turn east on Highway 92 and drive approximately 15 miles to the town of Granite Falls. Continue another 11 miles east on Highway 92 to the campground entrance on the right.

Contact: Mt. Baker-Snoqualmie National Forest, Darrington Ranger District, 1405 Emmens Street, Darrington, WA 98241; 360/436-1155.

23 Verlot

 9

This pretty campground is set along the South Fork of the Stillaguamish River. Some campsites provide river views. The camp is a short distance from the Lake Twenty-Two Research Natural Area and the Maid of the Woods Trail. A U.S. Forest Service map details backroads and hiking trails. Fishing is another recreation option.

Location: On the South Fork of the Stillaguamish River in Mt. Baker-Snoqualmie National Forest; see the Northern Cascades, map 1, grid h2.

Campsites, facilities: There are 26 sites for tents, trailers, or RVs up to 31 feet long. Picnic tables and fire rings are provided. Restrooms, drinking water, and flush toilets are available. A store, a café, and ice are located within one mile. Leashed pets are permitted.

Reservations, fees: Reservations accepted. Reserve at 877/444-6777 ($8.65 reservation fee) or website: www.reserveusa.com). Sites are $12 to $16 per night, $5 per extra vehicle per night. Open mid-May to late September.

Directions: From Seattle, drive north on I-5 to Everett and U.S. 2. Turn east on U.S. 2 and drive five miles to Highway 9. Turn north and drive four miles to Highway 92. Turn east on Highway 92 and drive approximately 15 miles to the town of Granite Falls, and continue

another 11.6 miles east on Highway 92 to the campground entrance on the right.

Contact: Mt. Baker-Snoqualmie National Forest, Darrington Ranger District, 1405 Emmens Street, Darrington, WA 98241; 360/436-1155.

24 Squire Creek County Park

 7

This pretty RV park is set amid old-growth forest, primarily Douglas fir and cedar, along Squire Creek. It is a family-oriented park and often fills on summer weekends. The park covers 12.2 acres, and a feature are several nearby trailheads. A trail from the park provides a 4.5-mile loop that heads toward White Horse Mountain. Other trailheads are located within five miles in nearby Snoqualmie-Mt. Baker National Forest, about three miles from the boundaries of the Boulder River Wilderness. No alcohol is permitted in this park.

Location: On Squire Creek; see the Northern Cascades, map 1, grid f3.

Campsites, facilities: There are 34 drive-through sites for tents, trailers, or RVs up to 25 feet long and two sites for trailers up to 70 feet long. No hookups are provided. Picnic tables and fire rings are provided. Restrooms, drinking water, flush toilets, a dump station, and firewood are available. Some facilities are wheelchair-accessible. A store is located three miles east in Darrington. Leashed pets are permitted.

Reservations, fees: No reservations accepted. Sites are $10 to $15 per night. Senior discount available. Open year-round.

Directions: From Seattle, drive north on I-5 to Exit 208 and the junction with Highway 530. Turn east on Highway 530 and drive 26 miles to the park on the left. The park is at Milepost 45.2.

Contact: Squire Creek County Park, Snohomish County; 425/388-6600 or 360/436-1283.

25 Cascade Kamloops Trout Farm and RV Park

   5

Campers will find a little bit of both worlds at this campground—a rustic quietness with all facilities available. A bonus is a trout pond, which is stocked year-round. No boats are allowed. Nearby recreation options include marked hiking trails, snowmobiling, cross-country skiing, river rafting, and tennis.

Location: In Darrington; see the Northern Cascades, map 1, grid g4.

Campsites, facilities: There are 32 sites with full hookups for trailers or RVs of any length and four tent sites. Picnic tables and fire rings are provided. Restrooms, drinking water, flush toilets, showers, a dump station, firewood, a coin-operated laundry, a trout pond, and a recreation hall are available. Bottled gas, a store, a café, and ice are located within one mile. Leashed pets are permitted.

Reservations, fees: Reservations accepted. Sites are $14 to $18 per night, $2 per person per night for more than two people over 12. Open year-round.

Directions: From Seattle, drive north on I-5 to Exit 208 and the junction with Highway 530. Turn east on Highway 530 and drive 32 miles to Darrington and Madison Street. Turn right on Madison Street and drive about four blocks to Darrington Street. Turn right and drive two blocks to the park on the right.

Contact: Cascade Kamloops Trout Farm and RV Park, 1240 Darrington Street, Darrington, WA 98241; 360/436-1003; website: www.glacierview.net/kamloops.

26 Clear Creek

    8

This nice, secluded spot is set in old-growth fir on the water but doesn't get heavy use. It's set at the confluence of Clear Creek and the Sauk River, a designated Wild and Scenic River. Fishing is available for rainbow trout, Dolly Varden trout, whitefish, and steelhead in season. A trail from camp leads about one mile up to Frog Pond.

Location: On Clear Creek and the Sauk River in Mt. Baker-Snoqualmie National Forest; see the Northern Cascades, map 1, grid g4.

Campsites, facilities: There are 13 sites for tents, trailers, or RVs up to 21 feet long. Picnic tables and fire grills are provided. Vault toilets and firewood are available. There is no drinking water. Some facilities are wheelchair-accessible. A store, a café, a coin-operated laundry, and ice are located within four miles. Leashed pets are permitted.

Reservations, fees: Reserve at 877/444-6777 ($8.65 reservation fee) or website: www.reserveusa.com. Sites are $8 per night. Senior discount available. Open late May to mid-October.

Directions: From Seattle, drive north on I-5 to Exit 208 and the junction with Highway 530. Turn east on Highway 530 and drive 32 miles to Darrington and Forest Road 20 (Mountain Loop Highway). Turn south on Forest Road 20 and drive 3.3 miles to the campground entrance on the left.

Contact: Mt. Baker-Snoqualmie National Forest, Darrington Ranger District, 1405 Emmens Street, Darrington, WA 98241; 360/436-1155, fax 360/436-1309.

27 William C. Dearinger

 7

This secluded campground is on the Sauk River and is managed by the Department of Natural Resources. It may be difficult to reach, but that's why you'll probably be the only one here. It's pretty, with lots of trees and sites overlooking the river.

Location: On the Sauk River; see the Northern Cascades, map 1, grid f4.

Campsites, facilities: There are 12 sites for tents or small trailers. Picnic tables, fire grills, and tent pads are provided. Vault toilets and firewood are available, but there is no drinking water. Garbage must be packed out. Leashed pets are permitted.

Reservations, fees: No reservations; no fee. Open year-round.

Directions: From Seattle, drive north on I-5 to Exit 208 and the junction with Highway 530. Turn east on Highway 530 and drive 32 miles to Darrington. Continue on Highway 530 one-third mile to Mountain Loop Road. Turn east on Mountain Loop Road and drive one-half mile; then continue straight for five miles to East Sauk Prairie Road. Turn left and drive two-thirds mile to Road SWD 5000. Bear right on Road SWD 5000 and drive 2.7 miles. Bear left for one mile to Road SWD 5400. Turn left on SWD 5400 and drive one quarter-mile to the campground.

Contact: Department of Natural Resources, Northwest Region, 919 North Township Street, Sedro-Woolley, WA 98284-9395; 360/856-3500.

28 Buck Creek

 9

Quiet and remote, this primitive campground is set along Buck Creek near its confluence with the Suiattle River in the Glacier Peak Wilderness. An interpretive trail runs along Buck Creek and provides access for fishing on the stream for rainbow trout, Dolly Varden, whitefish, and steelhead in season. There's a large (18 feet by 18 feet) Adirondack shelter by the creek and stands of old-growth timber. A zigzagging trail routed into the Glacier Peak Wilderness is accessible about one mile west of camp. See a U.S. Forest Service map for specifics.

Location: Near the Suiattle River in Mt. Baker-Snoqualmie National Forest; see the Northern Cascades, map 1, grid f6.

Campsites, facilities: There are 26 sites for tents, trailers, or RVs up to 30 feet long. Picnic tables and fire grills are provided. Vault toilets and firewood are available. No drinking water is available. Leashed pets are permitted.

Reservations, fees: Reserve at 877/444-6777 ($8.65 reservation fee) or website: www.reserveusa.com. Sites are $8 per night. Senior discount available. Open June to early October.

Directions: From Seattle, drive north on I-5 to Exit 208 and the junction with Highway 530. Turn east on Highway 530 and drive 32 miles to Darrington. Continue 7.5 miles on Highway 530 to Forest Road 26 (Suiattle River Road). Turn right (southeast) on Forest Road 26 and drive 14 miles to the campground on the left. Obtaining a U.S. Forest Service map is essential.

Contact: Mt. Baker-Snoqualmie National Forest, Darrington Ranger District, 1405 Emmens Street, Darrington, WA 98241; 360/436-1155, fax 360/436-1309.

29 Sulphur Creek

 8

This camp is set near the Suiattle River near the border of the Glacier Peak Wilderness. The Suiattle gets a lot of silt from glacier melt, and most anglers prefer to fish the nearby creeks instead. The nearby Suiattle River Trail provides streamside access. This camp is also a good base camp for a wilderness expedition, with a trailhead located about one quarter-mile south of the campground that provides access to a route leading deep into the backcountry. The trail hooks up with the Pacific Crest Trail.

Location: On the Suiattle River in Mt. Baker-Snoqualmie National Forest; ; see the Northern Cascades, map 1, grid f7.

Campsites, facilities: There are 20 sites for tents, trailers, or RVs up to 15 feet long. Picnic tables and fire grills are provided. Downed wood can be gathered and used for firewood. Vault toilets are available. There is no drinking water. Leashed pets are permitted.

Reservations, fees: Reserve at 877/444-6777 ($8.65 reservation fee) or website: www.reserveusa.com. Sites are $8 per night. Senior discount available. Open June through September.

Directions: From Seattle, drive north on I-5 to Exit 208 and the junction with Highway 530. Turn east on Highway 530 and drive 32 miles to Darrington. Continue 7.5 miles to Forest Road 26 (Suiattle River Road), turn right, and drive 22 miles southeast on Forest Road 26 to the campground on the right.

Contact: Mt. Baker-Snoqualmie National Forest, Darrington Ranger District, 1405 Emmens Street, Darrington, WA 98241; 360/436-1155, fax 360/436-1309.

30 Gold Basin

 9

This is the largest campground in Mt. Baker-Snoqualmie National Forest, and since it's loaded with facilities, it's a favorite with RVers. The campground is set at 1,100 feet along the South Fork of the Stillaguamish

River, with riverside sites, easy access, and a wheelchair-accessible interpretive trail. This area once provided good fishing, but a slide upstream puts clay silt into the water, and it has hurt the fishing. Rafting and hiking are options.

Location: On the South Fork of the Stillaguamish River in Mt. Baker-Snoqualmie National Forest; see the Northern Cascades, map 1, grid h3.

Campsites, facilities: There are 10 tent sites and 83 sites for tents, trailers, or RVs up to 60 feet long, and two group sites for up to 50 people. Picnic tables and fire rings are provided. Drinking water, restrooms, vault toilets, showers, and firewood are available. A store, a café, and ice are located within 2.5 miles. Some facilities are wheelchair-accessible. Leashed pets are permitted.

Reservations, fees: Some sites can be reserved; phone 877/444-6777 or access the website: www.reserveusa.com ($8.65 reservation fee). Sites are $14 per night; the group site is $100 per night. Open mid-May to early October.

Directions: From Seattle, drive north on I-5 to Everett and Highway 92. Turn east on Highway 92 and drive about 15 miles to the town of Granite Falls and Mountain Loop Highway (Forest Road 7). Continue east on Mountain Loop Highway for 13.5 miles to the campground entrance on the left.

Contact: Mt. Baker-Snoqualmie National Forest, Darrington Ranger District, 1405 Emmens Street, Darrington, WA 98241; 360/436-1155, fax 360/436-1309.

31 Esswine Group Camp

 6

This small, quiet camp is a great place for a restful group getaway. The lack of drinking water is the only drawback. Fishing access

is available nearby. The Boulder River Wilderness is located to the north; see a U.S. Forest Service map for trailhead locations.

Location: In Mt. Baker-Snoqualmie National Forest; see the Northern Cascades, map 1, grid h4.

Campsites, facilities: This is a specially designated group campground for tents or small RVs for up to 25 people. Picnic tables are provided. Vault toilets and firewood are available, but there is no drinking water. A store, a café, and ice are located within four miles. Leashed pets are permitted.

Reservations, fees: Reservations required; phone 877/444-6777 or access the website: www.reserveusa.com. The fee is $60 per night. Open mid-May through September.

Directions: From Seattle, drive north on I-5 to Everett and Highway 92. Turn east on Highway 92 and drive about 15 miles to the town of Granite Falls and Mountain Loop Highway (Forest Road 7). Continue northeast on Mountain Loop Highway for 16 miles to the campground entrance on the left.

Contact: Mt. Baker-Snoqualmie National Forest, Darrington Ranger District, 1405 Emmens Street, Darrington, WA 98241; 360/436-1155, fax 360/436-1309.

32 Boardman Creek

 7

Roomy sites and river access highlight this pretty riverside camp. The fishing can be excellent near here for rainbow trout, Dolly Varden, whitefish, and steelhead in season. Forest roads in the area will take you to several backcountry lakes, including Boardman Lake, Lake Evan, and Ashland Lakes. Get a U.S. Forest Service map, set up your camp, and go for it.

Location: On the South Fork of the Stillaguamish River in Mt. Baker-Snoqualmie

National Forest; see the Northern Cascades, map 1, grid h4.

Campsites, facilities: There are eight sites for tents, trailers, or RVs of any length. Picnic tables and fire grills are provided. Vault toilets and firewood are available. No drinking water is available. Leashed pets are permitted.

Reservations, fees: No reservations; sites are $8 per night. Senior discount available. Open late May to early September.

Directions: From Seattle, drive north on I-5 to Everett and Highway 92. Turn east on Highway 92 and drive about 15 miles to the town of Granite Falls and Mountain Loop Highway (Forest Road 7). Continue northeast on Mountain Loop Highway for 16.5 miles to the campground entrance on the left.

Contact: Mt. Baker-Snoqualmie National Forest, Darrington Ranger District, 1405 Emmens Street, Darrington, WA 98241; 360/436-1155, fax 360/436-1309.

33 Bedal

 9

This campground is set at the confluence of the North and South Forks of the Sauk River. It offers shaded sites, river views, and good fishing. It's a bit primitive. North Fork Falls is about one mile up the North Fork of the Sauk from camp and worth the trip.

Location: On the Sauk River in Mt. Baker-Snoqualmie National Forest; see the Northern Cascades, map 1, grid h4.

Campsites, facilities: There are 18 sites for tents, trailers, or RVs up to 21 feet long. Picnic tables and fire grills are provided. Vault toilets and a picnic shelter are available. No drinking water is available. Some facilities are wheelchair-accessible. A U.S. Forest Service district office is located 17 miles from the campground, in Darrington.

Reservations, fees: Reserve at 877/444-6777 ($8.65 reservation fee) or website:

www.reserveusa.com. Sites are $8 per night. Senior discount available. Open May to early September.

Directions: From Seattle, drive north on I-5 to Exit 208 and the junction with Highway 530. Turn east on Highway 530 and drive 32 miles to Darrington and Forest Road 20 (Mountain Loop Highway). Turn right (south) on Forest Road 20 and drive 17 miles to the campground on the right. Obtaining a U.S. Forest Service map is advised.

Contact: Mt. Baker-Snoqualmie National Forest, Darrington Ranger District, 1405 Emmens Street, Darrington, WA 98241; 360/436-1155, fax 360/436-1309.

34 Red Bridge

 9

Red Bridge is another classic spot, one of several in the vicinity, and a good base camp for a backpacking expedition. The campground is set at 1,300 feet on the South Fork of the Stillaguamish River near Mallardy Creek. It has pretty, riverside sites with old-growth fir. A trailhead two miles east of camp leads to Granite Pass in the Boulder River Wilderness.

Location: On the South Fork of Stillaguamish River in Mt. Baker-Snoqualmie National Forest; see the Northern Cascades, map 1, grid h4.

Campsites, facilities: There are 14 sites for tents, trailers, or RVs up to 31 feet long. Picnic tables are provided. Vault toilets are available, but there is no drinking water. Some facilities are wheelchair-accessible. Leashed pets are permitted.

Reservations, fees: Reserve at 877/444-6777 ($8.65 reservation fee) or website: www.reserveusa.com. Sites are $10 per night. Open late May to mid-September.

Directions: From Seattle, drive north on I-5 to Everett and Highway 92. Turn east on Highway 92 and drive about 15 miles to the town of Granite Falls and Mountain Loop Highway (Forest Road 7). Continue northeast on Mountain Loop Highway for 18 miles to the campground entrance on the right.

Contact: Mt. Baker-Snoqualmie National Forest, Darrington Ranger District, 1405 Emmens Street, Darrington, WA 98241; 360/436-1155, fax 360/436-1309.

35 Tulalip Millsite Group Camp

 7

This campground is set along the South Fork of the Stillaguamish River, nearby to several other camps: Turlo, Verlot, Gold Basin, Esswine, Boardman Creek, Coal Creek Bar, and Red Bridge. A trailhead about one mile east of camp leads north into the Boulder River Wilderness. Numerous creeks and streams crisscross this area, providing good fishing prospects.

Location: On the South Fork of the Stillaguamish River in Mt. Baker-Snoqualmie National Forest; see the Northern Cascades, map 1, grid h5.

Campsites, facilities: This is a designated group camp for up to 60 people. Picnic tables and fire grills are provided. Vault toilets are available, but there is no drinking water. Leashed pets are permitted.

Reservations, fees: Reserve at 877/444-6777 ($8.65 reservation fee) or website: www.reserveusa.com. Sites are $75 per night. Open mid-May to late September.

Directions: From Seattle, drive north on I-5 to Everett and Highway 92. Turn east on Highway 92 and drive about 15 miles to the town of Granite Falls and Mountain Loop Highway (Forest Road 7). Continue east on Mountain Loop

Highway for 18.5 miles to the campground entrance on the right.

Contact: Mt. Baker-Snoqualmie National Forest, Darrington Ranger District, 1405 Emmens Street, Darrington, WA 98241; 360/436-1155, fax 360/436-1309.

36 Coal Creek Group Camp

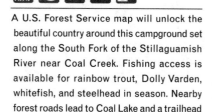 8

A U.S. Forest Service map will unlock the beautiful country around this campground set along the South Fork of the Stillaguamish River near Coal Creek. Fishing access is available for rainbow trout, Dolly Varden, whitefish, and steelhead in season. Nearby forest roads lead to Coal Lake and a trailhead that takes you to other backcountry lakes.

Location: On the South Fork of the Stillaguamish River in Mt. Baker-Snoqualmie National Forest; see the Northern Cascades, map 1, grid h5.

Campsites, facilities: There is one group site for tents or small RVs for up to 25 people. Picnic tables and fire grills are provided. Vault toilets and firewood are available. There is no drinking water. Leashed pets are permitted.

Reservations, fees: Reserve at 877/444-6777 ($8.65 reservation fee) or website: www.reserveusa.com. Sites are $60 per night for the entire camp. Open mid-May to late September.

Directions: From Seattle, drive north on I-5 to Everett and Highway 92. Turn east on Highway 92 and drive about 15 miles to the town of Granite Falls and Mountain Loop Highway (Forest Road 7). Continue northeast on Mountain Loop Highway for 23.5 miles to the campground entrance on the left.

Contact: Mt. Baker-Snoqualmie National Forest, Darrington Ranger District, 1405 Emmens Street, Darrington, WA 98241; 360/436-1155, fax 360/436-1309.

37 Beaver Plant Lake Hike-In

8

This campground is on Beaver Plant Lake, one of four campgrounds detailed in the area (the others are Upper Ashland Lake, Lower Ashland Lake, and Twin Falls Lake camps). Excellent hiking trails are a highlight of the region. One hiking trail networks with the four lakes. From this trail, you can also access the Bald Mountain Trail, which then connects to the Cutthroat Trail. It's a nine-mile hike from Beaver Plant Lake to Cutthroat Lake.

Location: On Beaver Plant Lake; see the Northern Cascades, map 1, grid h3.

Campsites, facilities: There are six tent sites. Fire grills are provided. A vault toilet and firewood are available. There is no drinking water. Garbage must be packed out. Leashed pets are permitted.

Reservations, fees: No reservations; no fee. Open mid-June through October.

Directions: From Seattle, drive north on I-5 to Everett and Highway 92. Turn east on Highway 92 and drive about 15 miles to the town of Granite Falls and Mountain Loop Highway (Forest Road 7). Continue east on Mountain Loop Highway for 15 miles to Forest Road 4020. Turn right (south) on Forest Road 4020 and drive 2.5 miles to Forest Road 4021. Turn right on Forest Road 4021 and drive two miles to the Ashland Lakes Trailhead. From the trailhead, hike 2.1 miles to the campground.

Contact: Department of Natural Resources, Northwest Region, 919 North Township Street, Sedro-Woolley, WA 98284-9395; 360/856-3500, fax 360/856-2150.

38 Upper Ashland Lake Hike-In

9

Reaching this primitive and beautiful camp requires a short hike that's well worth the effort. The site is little known, so you can expect quiet and privacy. Several good hiking trails can be found near camp. A map available from the Department of Natural Resources is helpful.

Location: Near Upper Ashland Lake; see the Northern Cascades, map 1, grid h3.

Campsites, facilities: There are six tent sites. Fire grills are provided. A vault toilet and firewood are available, but there is no drinking water. Garbage must be packed out. Leashed pets are permitted.

Reservations, fees: No reservations; no fee. Open mid-June through October.

Directions: From Seattle, drive north on I-5 to Everett and Highway 92. Turn east on Highway 92 and drive about 15 miles to the town of Granite Falls and Mountain Loop Highway. Turn north on Mountain Loop Highway and drive 15 miles to Forest Road 4020. Turn right (south) on Forest Road 4020 and drive 2.5 miles to Forest Road 4021. Turn right on Forest Road 4021 and drive 2.6 miles to the Ashland Lakes Trailhead. From the trailhead, hike two miles to the campground.

Contact: Department of Natural Resources, Northwest Region, 919 North Township Street, Sedro-Woolley, WA 98284-9395; 360/856-3500, fax 360/856-2150.

39 Lower Ashland Lake Hike-In

 8

This campground is on Lower Ashland Lake, set adjacent to Upper Ashland Lake; see the description of Upper Ashland Lake for details.

Location: On Lower Ashland Lake; see the Northern Cascades, map 1, grid h3.

Campsites, facilities: There are five tent sites. Fire rings are provided. A vault toilet and firewood are available, but there is no drinking water. Garbage must be packed out. Leashed pets are permitted.

Reservations, fees: No reservations; no fee. Open mid-June through October.

Directions: From Seattle, drive north on I-5 to Everett and Highway 92. Turn east on Highway 92 and drive about 15 miles to the town of Granite Falls and Mountain Loop Highway. Turn north on Mountain Loop Highway and drive 15 miles to Forest Road 4020. Turn right (south) on Forest Road 4020 and drive 2.5 miles to Forest Road 4021. Turn right on Forest Road 4021 and drive two miles to the Ashland Lakes Trailhead. From the trailhead, hike three miles to the campground.

Contact: Department of Natural Resources, Northwest Region, 919 North Township Street, Sedro-Woolley, WA 98284-9395; 360/856-3500, fax 360/856-2150.

40 Twin Falls Lake Hike-In

 10

This is a beautiful site, with lake views from some campsites, along with two nearby waterfalls. The first waterfall is a gorgeous 100-foot cascade into the lake. You are advised to avoid the second waterfall (at the outlet), where wet, slippery rocks have caused falls and fatalities. People willing to grunt a little will find good hiking, backpacking, and trout fishing at this site. It's a beautiful and secluded area, yet it's not a long drive from Seattle.

Location: On Twin Falls Lake; see the Northern Cascades, map 1, grid h3.

Campsites, facilities: There are five tent sites. Fire grills are provided and a vault toilet and firewood is available. No drinking water is available. Garbage must be packed out. Leashed pets are permitted.

Reservations, fees: No reservations; no fee. Open mid-June through October.

Directions: From Seattle, drive north on I-5 to Everett and Highway 92. Turn east on Highway 92 and drive about 15 miles to the town of Granite Falls and Mountain Loop

Highway (Forest Road 20). Continue on Mountain Loop Highway for 15 miles to Forest Road 4020. Turn south on Forest Road 4020 and drive 2.5 miles to Forest Road 4021. Turn right on Forest Road 4021 and drive two miles to the Ashland Lakes Trailhead. Hike in 4.5 miles from the trailhead.

Contact: Department of Natural Resources, Northwest Region, 919 North Township Street, Sedro-Woolley, WA 98284-9395; 360/856-3500.

41 Harts Pass Walk-In

  10

At 6,198 feet, Harts Pass is one of the highest drive-through mountain passes in Washington. It features great panoramic views of Mt. Gardner, Silver Star, Tower, Golden Horn, Mt. Azurite, Ballard, Crater Mountain, Mt. Baker (on a clear day), Jack Mountain, the Pickets Range, Pasayten Peak, and Mt. Robinson. This pretty little campground is near the Pasayten Wilderness, which offers 500 miles of trails leading to alpine meadows and glacier-fed lakes and streams, and along ridges to spectacular mountain heights. The Pacific Crest Trail passes near the camp and offers a great view of the northern Cascade Range. No trailers permitted on access road.

Location: Near the Pasayten Wilderness in Okanogan and Wenatchee National Forests; see the Northern Cascades, map 2, grid c3.

Campsites, facilities: There are five walk-in tent sites requiring a 50-foot walk. No RVs or trailers. Picnic tables and fire grills are provided. Vault toilets are available, but there is no drinking water. Garbage must be packed out. Leashed pets are permitted.

Reservations, fees: No reservations accepted. Sites are $5 per night. Senior discount available. Open mid-July to late September.

Directions: From Burlington, drive east on State Route 20 and for 120 miles to Mazama Road. Turn left on Mazama Road and drive one quarter-mile to County Road 9140. Turn left and drive northwest for seven miles to Lost River, where the pavement ends and the road soon becomes Forest Road 5400. Continue on Forest Road 5400 for 12.5 miles northwest to the campground (across from a guard station). Note: Forest Road 5400 is a narrow, curving road with steep slide cliffs that is closed to trailers. Drive slowly and yield to trucks.

Contact: Okanogan and Wenatchee National Forests, Methow Valley Visitor Center, 24 West Chewuch Road, Winthrop, WA 98862; 509/996-4000, fax 509/997-9770.

42 Meadows

  9

This campground is about one mile from Harts Pass and offers the same opportunities. It is set adjacent to the Pacific Crest Trail. In summer, the camp is beautiful, set in an area of spruce and subalpine fir, with lots of wildflowers in the spring. No trailers are permitted on the access road.

Location: Near the Pacific Crest Trail in Okanogan and Wenatchee National Forests; see the Northern Cascades, map 2, grid c3.

Campsites, facilities: There are 14 tent sites. Picnic tables and fire grills are provided. Vault toilets are available, but there is no drinking water or garbage service; pack out refuse. Leashed pets are permitted.

Reservations, fees: No reservations accepted. Sites are $5 per night. Senior discount available. Open mid-July to late September.

Directions: From Burlington, drive east on State Route 20 and for 120 miles to Mazama Road. Turn left on Mazama Road and drive one quarter-mile to County Road 9140. Turn left and drive northwest for seven miles to Lost River, where the pavement ends and the road soon becomes Forest Road 5400. Continue on Forest Road 5400 for 12.5 miles to Forest Road 5400-500. Turn south (left) and drive one mile to the campground. Note: Forest Road 5400 is a narrow, curving road with steep slide cliffs that is closed to trailers. Drive slowly and yield to trucks.

Contact: Okanogan and Wenatchee National Forests, Methow Valley Visitor Center, 24 West Chewuch Road, Winthrop, WA 98862; 509/996-4000, fax 509/997-9770.

43 Ballard

   6

Ballard is set at an elevation of 2,521 feet, about one-half mile from River Bend. Numerous hiking trails can be found in the area, including access to the West Fork Methow and Los River Monument Creek trails. It is possible to hike west and eventually hook up with the Pacific Crest Trail. See the description of Early Winters Campground for area information. Stock are not permitted in the campground, but a hitching rail and stock truck dock are available at the Robinson Creek Trailhead near the campground, where there are several primitive sites.

Location: Near the Methow River in Okanogan and Wenatchee National Forests; see the Northern Cascades, map 2, grid c4.

Campsites, facilities: There are six sites for tents, trailers, or RVs up to 20 feet long. Picnic tables and fire grills are provided. Vault toilets are available, but there is no drinking water. Garbage must be packed out. Leashed pets are permitted. No livestock is permitted in camp.

Reservations, fees: No reservations. Sites are $3 per night, $3 per extra vehicle per night. Senior discount available. Open June through October, weather permitting.

Directions: From Burlington, drive east on State Route 20 for 120 miles to Mazama Road. Turn left on Mazama Road and drive one quarter-mile to County Road 9140. Turn left and drive northwest for seven miles to Lost River, where the pavement ends and the road soon becomes Forest Road 5400. Continue northwest on Forest Road 5400 for two miles to the campground on the left.

Contact: Okanogan and Wenatchee National Forests, Methow Valley Visitor Center, 24 West Chewuch Road, Winthrop, WA 98862; 509/996-4000, fax 509/997-9770.

44 River Bend

    6

This campground is located along the Methow River at 2,600 feet, about two miles from the boundary of the Pasayten Wilderness. Several trails near the camp provide access to the wilderness, and another trail follows the Methow River west for about eight miles before hooking up with the Pacific Crest Trail near Azurite Peak; a U.S. Forest Service map will show you the options. See trip notes for Ballard Camp for more information about the area.

Location: On the Methow River in Okanogan and Wenatchee National Forests; see the Northern Cascades, map 2, grid c4.

Campsites, facilities: There are five sites for tents, trailers, or RVs up to 16 feet long. Picnic tables and fire grills are provided. Vault toilets are available. No drinking water is available. Garbage must be packed out. Leashed pets are permitted.

Reservations, fees: No reservations. Sites are $3 per night, $3 per extra vehicle per night. Senior discount available. Open June to late September.

Directions: From Burlington, drive east on State Route 20 for 120 miles to

Mazama Road. Turn left on Mazama Road and drive one quarter-mile to County Road 9140. Turn left and drive northwest for seven miles to Lost River, where the pavement ends and the road soon becomes Forest Road 5400. Continue northwest on Forest Road 5400 for two miles to Forest Road 5400-600. Bear left (west) on Forest Road 5400-600 and drive one-half mile to the campground on the left.

Contact: Okanogan and Wenatchee National Forests, Methow Valley Visitor Center, 24 West Chewuch Road, Winthrop, WA 98862; 509/996-4000, fax 509/997-9770.

45 Lone Fir

  9

Lone Fir is set at 3,640 feet along the banks of Early Winters Creek. The area has had some timber operations in the past, but there no nearby clear-cuts. To the west is Washington Pass Overlook, which offers a spectacular view. Anglers can fish in the creek, and many hiking and biking trails criss-cross the area, including the trailhead for Cutthroat Lake. A U.S. Forest Service map will provide details. A loop trail through the campground woods is wheelchair-accessible for four-tenths of a mile. See the description of Early Winters Camp for more information.

Location: On Early Winters Creek in Okanogan and Wenatchee National Forests; see the Northern Cascades, map 2, grid d4.

Campsites, facilities: There are 27 sites for tents, trailers, or RVs up to 20 feet long. Picnic tables and fire grills are provided. Vault toilets are available. No drinking water is available. Garbage must be packed out. Leashed pets are permitted.

Reservations, fees: No reservations. Sites are $6 per night, $6 per extra vehicle per

night. Senior discount available. Open June to late September.

Directions: From Burlington, drive east on State Route 20 for 107 miles to the campground (11 miles west of Mazama) on the right.

Contact: Okanogan and Wenatchee National Forests, Methow Valley Visitor Center, 24 West Chewuch Road, Winthrop, WA 98862; 509/996-4000, fax 509/997-9770.

46 Klipchuck

 7

This camp is located at an elevation of 3,000 feet along Early Winters Creek. The camp area is set amid majestic trees, primarily Douglas fir and subalpine firs. Klipchuck provides hiking aplenty, but note that rattlesnakes are occasionally seen in this area. A short loop trail from the camp leads about five miles up and over Delancy Ridge to Driveway Butte and down to the creek. Another trail starts nearby on Forest Road 200 (Sandy Butte-Cedar Creek Road) and goes two miles up Cedar Creek to lovely Cedar Creek Falls. Still another option is a two-mile trail along Early Winters Creek from the campground. This region is best visited in the spring and fall, with summer hot and dry. See the description of Early Winters for more information.

Location: On Early Winters Creek in Okanogan and Wenatchee National Forests; see the Northern Cascades, map 2, grid d4.

Campsites, facilities: There are 46 sites for tents, trailers, or RVs up to 34 feet long. Sites can be combined to accommodate groups. Picnic tables and fire grills are provided. Drinking water and vault toilets are available. Some facilities are wheelchair-accessible. Leashed pets are permitted.

Reservations, fees: No reservations. Sites are $8 per night, $8 per extra vehicle per night. Senior discount available. Open June to late September.

Directions: From Burlington, drive east on State Route 20 for 115 miles to Forest Road 300. (If you reach the Methow River Valley, you have gone four miles past the turnoff.) Turn left (marked) and drive northwest one mile to the camp at the end of the road.

Contact: Okanogan and Wenatchee National Forests, Methow Valley Visitor Center, 24 West Chewuch Road, Winthrop, WA 98862; 509/996-4000, fax 509/997-9770.

47 Early Winters

 6

This campground has an unusual configuration, being located on each side of the highway. Featured are great views of Goat Wall. The confluence of Early Winters Creek and the Methow River mark the site of this campground. The elevation is 2,160 feet. Campsites are flat, with the landscape on open land in a sparse lodgepole pine forest, providing an arid feel to the area. Several hiking trails can be found within five miles, including one that leads south to Cedar Creek Falls. Other possible side trips are to Goat Wall to the north and the town of Winthrop to the south, which boasts a historical museum, a state fish hatchery, and Pearrygin Lake State Park.

Location: On Early Winters Creek in Okanogan and Wenatchee National Forests; see the Northern Cascades, map 2, grid d5.

Campsites, facilities: There are 13 sites for tents, trailers, or RVs up to 24 feet long. Picnic tables and fire grills are provided. Drinking water and vault toilets are available. There is a small store and snack bar in Mazama, about two miles away. Leashed pets are permitted.

Reservations, fees: No reservations. Sites are $6 per night, $6 per extra vehicle per night. Senior discount available. Open June through October, weather permitting.

Directions: From Burlington, drive east on State Route 20 for 116 miles to the campground (if you reach County Road 1163 near Mazama, you have gone two miles too far).

Contact: Okanogan and Wenatchee National Forests, Methow Valley Visitor Center, 24 West Chewuch Road, Winthrop, WA 98862; 509/996-4000, fax 509/997-9770.

48 Rocking Horse Ranch

 7

The camp is good for campers with horses. This ranch is set in the lovely Methow River Valley, which is flanked on both sides by national forest. There are numerous trails nearby and a horse stable at the ranch. Owen Wister, who wrote the novel, *The Virginian,* lived in the nearby town of Winthrop at the turn of the 20th century. Portions of the novel were based on his experiences in this area. Horse rentals and guided trips are available if you want to try to relive the stuff of legends.

Location: In the Methow River Valley; see the Northern Cascades, map 2, grid d6.

Campsites, facilities: There are 25 tent sites and 10 drive-through sites with full or partial hookups for trailers or RVs of any length. Picnic tables are provided. Restrooms, flush toilets, showers, a dump station, a horse stable, corrals, horseshoe pits, volleyball, and firewood are available. Some facilities are wheelchair-accessible. Leashed pets are permitted.

Reservations, fees: Reservations accepted. Sites are $12 to $15 per night. Open April to late October.

Directions: From Winthrop, drive west on State Route 20 for nine miles to the campground on the right.

Contact: Rocking Horse Ranch, Star Route, 18381 State Route 20, Winthrop, WA 98862; 509/996-2768; website: www.rockinghorse winthrop.com.

49 Pine-Near RV Park

 7

This camp is an adequate layover spot for State Route 20 cruisers and a good alternative camp to the more crowded sites at Pearrygin Lake. The Methow River is nearby; see the description of KOA Methow River for information on the various activities available in the Winthrop area.

Location: On the Methow River; see the Northern Cascades, map 2, grid e7.

Campsites, facilities: There are 40 tent sites and 28 sites with full hookups, including 14 drive-through, for trailers or RVs of any length. Three mobile homes are for rent on a per-night basis. Picnic tables are provided. Restrooms, flush toilets, coin-operated showers, a dump station, and a coin-operated laundry are available. A store, bottled gas, and a café are located within one mile. Leashed pets are permitted.

Reservations, fees: Reservations accepted. Sites are $10 to $18 per night. Major credit cards accepted. Open year-round.

Directions: From Winthrop, drive east on State Route 20 one block north of Riverside Drive to Castle Avenue. Turn right (east) and drive three blocks to the park on the left.

Contact: Pine-Near RV Park, Route 1, P.O. Box 400-32, Winthrop, WA 98862; 509/996-2391.

50 KOA Methow River-Winthrop

 7

Here's another campground set along the Methow River, which offers opportunities for fishing, boating, swimming, and rafting. The park has a free shuttle into Winthrop, an interesting town with many restored, early-1900s buildings lining the main street, including the Shafer Museum, which displays lots of period items. If you would like to observe wildlife, take a short, two-mile drive southeast out of Winthrop on County Road 9129 on the east side of the Methow River. Turn east on County Road 1631 into Davis Lake, and follow the signs to the Methow River Habitat Management Area Headquarters. Depending on the time of year, you may see mule deer, porcupine, bobcat, mountain lion, snowshoe hare, black bear, red squirrel, and many species of birds. If you're looking for something tamer, other nearby recreation options include an 18-hole golf course and tennis courts.

Location: On the Methow River; see the Northern Cascades, map 2, grid e7.

Campsites, facilities: There are 70 sites with full or partial hookups, including some drive-through sites, for trailers or RVs of any length, and 35 tent sites. There are also 17 one- or two-room cabins. Picnic tables and fire grills are provided. Restrooms, drinking water, flush toilets, showers, firewood, a dump station, a recreation hall, modem hookups, bike and video rentals, a store, a laundry room, ice, a playground, and a swimming pool are available. Bottled gas and a café are located within one mile. There is a courtesy shuttle to and from Winthrop. Leashed pets are permitted.

Reservations, fees: Reservations accepted, phone 800/562-2158. Sites are $20 to $26 per night, $4 per person per night for more than two people, $2 per child 5–17 per night; cabins are $37 to $51 per night. Major credit cards accepted. Open mid-April to November.

Directions: From Winthrop, drive east on State Route 20 for one mile to the camp on the left. The camp is between Mileposts 194 and 195.

Contact: KOA Methow River-Winthrop, 1114 State Route 20, Winthrop, WA 98862; 509/996-2258.

51 Big Twin Lake Campground

 5

As you might figure from the name, this campground is set along the shore of Twin Lakes. There are views of the lake from all campsites, with a sweeping lawn and shade trees. No gas motors are permitted on the lake. Flyfishing is good for rainbow trout, with special regulations in effect: one-fish limit, single barbless hook, artificials only. This is an ideal lake for a float tube, rowboat with a casting platform, or a pram. See the description of KOA Methow River for information on the various activities available in the Winthrop area.

Location: On Twin Lakes; see the Northern Cascades, map 2, grid e7.

Campsites, facilities: There are 50 sites with full or partial hookups, including 18 drive-through sites for trailers or RVs of any length, and 35 tent sites. Picnic tables and fire grills are provided. Restrooms, drinking water, flush toilets, coin-operated showers, a dump station, firewood, ice, and a playground are available. Boat docks, launching facilities, and rentals can be obtained on Big Twin Lake. Leashed pets are permitted.

Reservations, fees: Reservations accepted. Sites are $13 to $19 per night, $3 per extra vehicle per night. Senior discount available. Open April to late October.

Directions: From Winthrop, drive east on State Route 20 for three miles to Twin Lakes Road. Turn right (west) on Twin Lakes Road and drive two miles to the campground on the right.

Contact: Big Twin Lake Campground, Route 2, Box 705, Winthrop, WA 98862; 509/996-2650; website: www.methownet.com/bigtwin.

52 Pearrygin Lake State Park

 8

Pearrygin Lake is created from underground springs and Pearrygin Creek, the lifeblood for this setting and the adjacent 578-acre state park. It is located in the beautiful Methow Valley, ringed by the North Cascade Mountains. The park is known for its expansive green lawns that lead to 8,200 feet of waterfront and sandy beaches. Old willows and ash provide shade. The camp is often frequented by red-winged and yellow-headed blackbirds, as well as marmots. The area is ideal for wildflower and wildlife viewing in the spring. The campground has access to a sandy beach and facilities for swimming, boating, fishing, and hiking. The sites are set close together and don't offer much privacy, but they are spacious, and a variety of recreation options make it worth the crunch.

Location: On Pearrygin Lake; see the Northern Cascades, map 2, grid d7.

Campsites, facilities: There are 53 tent sites and 30 sites with full hookups for tents or RVs up to 60 feet in length. Picnic tables and fire grills are provided. Restrooms, drinking water, flush toilets, coin-operated showers, a dump station, and firewood for a fee are available. A store, a deli, and ice are located within one mile. Some facilities are wheelchair-accessible. Boat-launching and dock facilities are available. Leashed pets are permitted.

Reservations, fees: Reserve at 888/CAMP-OUT (888/226-7688); website: www.parks.wa.gov/reservations ($7 reservation fee);

reservations accepted from April 15. Sites are $6 to $22 per night, $6 per extra vehicle per night. Senior discount available. Major credit cards accepted. Open April through October.

Directions: From Winthrop and State Route 20, drive north through town (road changes to East Chewuch Road). Continue 1.5 miles north from town to Bear Creek Road. Turn right and drive 15 miles to the end of the pavement and look for the cattle guard and the park entrance on the right. Turn right, drive over the cattleguard, and continue to the campground.

Contact: Pearrygin Lake State Park, 509/996-2370; State Park information, 360/902-8844.

53 Flat

  6

This campground is set along Eightmile Creek two miles from where it empties into the Chewuch River. The elevation is 2,858 feet. Buck Lake is about three miles away. This is the closest of six camps to County Road 1213. Other options are Honeymoon, Nice, and Falls Creek.

Location: On Eightmile Creek in Okanogan and Wenatchee National Forests; see the Northern Cascades, map 2, grid c7.

Campsites, facilities: There are 12 sites for tents, trailers, or RVs up to 18 feet long. Picnic tables and fire grills are provided, but there is no drinking water. Vault toilets are available. Garbage must be packed out. Leashed pets are permitted.

Reservations, fees: No reservations. Sites are $3 per night, $3 per extra vehicle per night. Senior discount available. Open June to late September.

Directions: From Burlington, drive east on State Route 20 for 134 miles to Winthrop and County Road 1213 (West Chewuch Road). Turn north on West Chewuch Road and drive 6.5 miles (the road becomes Forest Road 51.)

Continue on Forest Road 51 and drive three miles to Forest Road 5130 (Eightmile Creek Road). Turn left (northwest) and drive two miles to the campground on the left.

Contact: Okanogan and Wenatchee National Forests, Methow Valley Visitor Center, 24 West Chewuch Road, Winthrop, WA 98862; 509/996-4000, fax 509/997-9770.

54 Nice

   6

Nice is along Eightmile Creek about four miles from Buck Lake. A beaver pond in the area is often fun for youngsters to explore. A trail leading into the Pasayten Wilderness can be found at the end of Forest Road 5130. Pearrygin Lake State Park is just a few miles to the south, near Winthrop. Note: There is no turnaround area for trailers or RVs.

Location: On Eightmile Creek in Okanogan and Wenatchee National Forests; see the Northern Cascades, map 2, grid d7.

Campsites, facilities: There are three tent sites. Picnic tables and fire grills are provided. Vault toilets are available, but there is no drinking water. Garbage must be packed out. Leashed pets are permitted.

Reservations, fees: No reservations. Sites are $3 per night, $3 per extra vehicle per night. Senior discount available. Open June to late September.

Directions: From Burlington, drive east on State Route 20 for 134 miles to Winthrop and County Road 1213 (West Chewuch Road). Turn north on West Chewuch Road and drive 6.5 miles (the road becomes Forest Road 51.) Continue on Forest Road 51 and drive three miles to Forest Road 5130 (Eightmile Creek Road). Turn left (northwest) and drive four miles to the campground on the left.

Contact: Okanogan and Wenatchee National Forests, Methow Valley Visitor Center, 24 West Chewuch Road, Winthrop, WA 98862; 509/996-4000, fax 509/997-9770.

Honeymoon

 8

This small camp is set at 3,280 feet along Eightmile Creek. If you continue north seven miles to the end of Forest Road 5130, you'll reach a trailhead that provides access to the Pasayten Wilderness. See a U.S. Forest Service map for details. Why is it named Honeymoon? Well, it seems that a forest ranger and his bride chose this quiet and secluded spot along the creek to spend their wedding night.

Location: On Eightmile Creek in Okanogan and Wenatchee National Forests; see the Northern Cascades, map 2, grid c6.

Campsites, facilities: There are six sites for tents, trailers, or small RVs up to 18 feet long. Picnic tables and fire grills are provided. Vault toilets are available, but there is no drinking water. Garbage must be packed out. Leashed pets are permitted.

Reservations, fees: No reservations accepted. Sites are $3 per vehicle. Senior discount available. Open June to late September.

Directions: From Burlington, drive east on State Route 20 and for 134 miles to Winthrop and County Road 1213/West Chewuch Road. Turn north on County Road 1213/West Chewuch Road and drive 6.5 miles (where it merges with Forest Road 5130). Continue north on Forest Road 5130 for 10 miles to the campground on the right.

Contact: Okanogan and Wenatchee National Forests, Methow Valley Visitor Center, 24 West Chewuch Road, Winthrop, WA 98862; 509/996-4000, fax 509/997-9770.

Falls Creek

 7

Falls Creek is a quiet and pretty campground located at the confluence of its namesake, Falls Creek, and the Chewuch River, about a 20-minute drive out of Winthrop. The elevation is 2,100 feet. Highlights include fishing access and a quarter-mile trail (wheelchair-accessible) to a waterfall located across the road from the campground.

Location: On the Chewuch River in Okanogan and Wenatchee National Forests; see the Northern Cascades, map 2, grid c7.

Campsites, facilities: There are seven sites for tents, trailers, or RVs up to 18 feet long. Picnic tables and fire grills are provided. Vault toilets are available. No drinking water is available. Some facilities are wheelchair-accessible. Leashed pets are permitted.

Reservations, fees: No reservations. Sites are $3 per night, $3 per extra vehicle per night. Senior discount available. Open June to late September.

Directions: From Burlington, drive east on State Route 20 for 134 miles to Winthrop and County Road 1213 (West Chewuch Road). Turn north on West Chewuch Road and drive 6.5 miles (becomes Forest Road 51.) Continue on Forest Road 51 and drive 5.2 miles to the campground on the right. Obtaining a U.S. Forest Service map is advised.

Contact: Okanogan and Wenatchee National Forests, Methow Valley Visitor Center, 24 West Chewuch Road, Winthrop, WA 98862; 509/996-4000, fax 509/997-9770.

Chewuch

 6

Chewuch Camp is set along the Chewuch River at an elevation of 2,278 feet, surrounded by ponderosa pines. It is a small camp where catch-and-release fishing is a highlight. There are also hiking and biking trails in the area. By traveling north, you can access trailheads that lead into the Pasayten Wilderness. See a U.S. Forest Service map for specific locations. This camp provides an option to the more developed nearby Falls Creek Campground.

Location: On the Chewuch River in Okanogan and Wenatchee National Forests; see the Northern Cascades, map 2, grid c7.

Campsites, facilities: There are four sites for tents, small trailers, and small self-contained RVs up to 16 feet long. Picnic tables and fire grills are provided. Vault toilets are available. No drinking water is available. Garbage must be packed out. Leashed pets are permitted.

Reservations, fees: No reservations. Sites are $3 per vehicle. Senior discount available. Open June to late September.

Directions: From Burlington, drive east on State Route 20 for 134 miles to Winthrop and County Road 1213/West Chewuch Road. Turn north on County Road 1213/West Chewuch Road and drive 6.5 miles (where it merges with Forest Road 51). Continue north on Forest Road 51 for seven miles to the campground on the right.

Contact: Okanogan and Wenatchee National Forests, Methow Valley Visitor Center, 24 West Chewuch Road, Winthrop, WA 98862; 509/996-4000, fax 509/997-9770.

all have corrals, hitching rails, truck docks, and water for the stock at the trailheads, but no live stock are permitted in the campground itself. Trails leading into the Pasayten Wilderness leave from both locations. Contact the U.S. Forest Service for details.

Location: On the Chewuch River in Okanogan and Wenatchee National Forests; see the Northern Cascades, map 2, grid b7.

Campsites, facilities: There are three tent sites and two sites for tents, small trailers, or RVs up to 16 feet long. Fire grills are provided. Vault toilets are available, but there is no drinking water. Garbage must be packed out. Leashed pets are permitted, but no livestock are permitted in camp.

Reservations, fees: No reservations. Sites are $3 per night. Senior discount available. Open June to late September.

Directions: From Burlington, drive east on State Route 20 for 134 miles to Winthrop and County Road 1213/West Chewuch Road. Turn north on County Road 1213/West Chewuch Road and drive 6.5 miles (where it merges with Forest Road 51). Continue north on Forest Road 51 for 11 miles to the campground on the right.

Contact: Okanogan and Wenatchee National Forests, Methow Valley Visitor Center, 24 West Chewuch Road, Winthrop, WA 98862; 509/996-4000, fax 509/997-9770.

58 Camp 4

    6

Camp 4 is the smallest and most primitive of the three camps along the Chewuch River (the others are Chewuch and Falls Creek). It is set at an elevation of 2,400 feet. Trailers are not recommended. There are three trailheads five miles north of camp: two at Lake Creek and another at Andrews Creek. They

59 Roads End

     8

This quiet trailhead camp is located at the end of Twisp River Road. Roads End is set at 3,600 feet along the Twisp River at a major trailhead that provides fishing access and a chance to hike for mountain views and explore the Lake Chelan-Sawtooth Wilderness. The trail intersects with the Copper Creek Trail and the Pacific Crest Trail about nine miles from the camp. A U.S. Forest Service map is essential. Note that this camp is closed in the off-season to protect bull trout, an endangered species.

Location: On the Twisp River in Okanogan and Wenatchee National Forests; see the Northern Cascades, map 2, grid e4.

Campsites, facilities: There are four sites for tents, small trailers, or RVs up to 16 feet long. Picnic tables and fire grills are provided. Vault toilets are available. No drinking water is available. Garbage must be packed out. Leashed pets are permitted.

Reservations, fees: No reservations. Sites are $6 per night, $6 per extra vehicle per night. Senior discount available. Open late May to early September.

Directions: On I-5, drive to Exit 230/State Route 20 at Burlington. Turn east on State Route 20, and drive 145 miles to Twisp and County Road 9114 (Twisp River Road). Turn west on County Road 9114 (Twisp River Road) and drive 11 miles (becomes Forest Road 44). Continue west for 13.5 miles to the campground. Obtaining a U.S. Forest Service map is advisable.

Contact: Okanogan and Wenatchee National Forests, Methow Valley Visitor Center, 24 West Chewuch Road, Winthrop, WA 98862; 509/996-4000, fax 509/997-9770.

60 South Creek

 6

Although small, quiet, and little known, South Creek Campground packs a wallop with good recreation options. It's set at the confluence of the Twisp River and South Creek at a major trailhead that accesses the Lake Chelan-Sawtooth Wilderness. The South Creek Trailhead provides a hike to Louis Lake. The elevation at the camp is 3,100 feet. See a U.S. Forest Service map for details.

Location: On the Twisp River in Okanogan and Wenatchee National Forests; see the Northern Cascades, map 2, grid e4.

Campsites, facilities: There are four sites for tents or small trailers, plus a few sites with parking for RVs up to 30 feet in length. No drinking water is available. Picnic tables and fire grills are provided. A vault toilet is available. No garbage service; pack out refuse. Leashed pets are permitted.

Reservations, fees: No reservations. Sites are $3 per night, $3 per extra vehicle per night. Senior discount available. Open late May to early September.

Directions: From Burlington, drive east on State Route 20 for 145 miles to Twisp and County Road 9114 (Twisp River Road). Turn west on County Road 9114 (Twisp River Road) and drive 22 miles (becomes Forest Road 44). Continue west (becomes Forest Road 4440) to the campground on the left.

Contact: Okanogan and Wenatchee National Forests, Methow Valley Visitor Center, 24 West Chewuch Road, Winthrop, WA 98862; 509/996-4000, fax 509/997-9770.

61 Poplar Flat

 7

This campground is set at 2,900 feet along the Twisp River. This area provides many wildlife-viewing opportunities, including for deer, black bear, and many species of birds. Several trails in the area follow streams, including the Twisp River Trail, and some provide access to the Lake Chelan-Sawtooth Wilderness. Twisp River Horse Camp, across the river from the campground, has facilities for horses.

Location: On the Twisp River in Okanogan and Wenatchee National Forests; see the Northern Cascades, map 2, grid e4.

Campsites, facilities: There are 16 sites for tents, trailers, or RVs up to 22 feet long and one double site for up to 12 people. Picnic tables and fire grills are provided. Drinking water and vault toilets are available. A day-use picnic area with a shelter is nearby. Some facilities are wheelchair-accessible. Leashed pets are permitted.

Reservations, fees: No reservations. Sites are $3 per night, $3 per extra vehicle per night. Senior discount available. Open May to September.

Directions: From Burlington, drive east on State Route 20 for 145 miles to Twisp and County Road 9114 (Twisp River Road). Turn west on County Road 9114 (Twisp River Road) and drive 11 miles (becomes Forest Road 44). Continue west for 9.5 miles to the campground on the left.

Contact: Okanogan and Wenatchee National Forests, Methow Valley Visitor Center, 24 West Chewuch Road, Winthrop, WA 98862; 509/996-4000, fax 509/997-9770.

62 War Creek

 6

This trailhead camp is set at 2,400 feet with several routes into the Lake Chelan-Sawtooth Wilderness. The War Creek Trail, Eagle Creek Trail, and Oval Creek Trail all provide wilderness access and trout fishing. Backpackers can extend this trip into the Lake Chelan National Recreation Area, finishing the trip at the shore of Lake Chelan and the National Park Service outpost. It's a 15-mile trek. Rattlesnakes are occasionally spotted in this region in the summer.

Location: On the Twisp River in Okanogan and Wenatchee National Forests; see the Northern Cascades, map 2, grid f5.

Campsites, facilities: There are 10 sites for tents, trailers, or RVs up to 22 feet long. Drinking water, fire grills, and picnic tables

are provided. Vault toilets and firewood are available. Leashed pets are permitted.

Reservations, fees: No reservations. Sites are $6 per night, $6 per extra vehicle per night. Senior discount available. Open May to September.

Directions: On I-5, drive to Exit 230/State Route 20 at Burlington. Turn east on State Route 20, and drive 145 miles to Twisp and County Road 9114 (Twisp River Road). Turn west on County Road 9114 (Twisp River Road) and drive 11 miles (becomes Forest Road 44). Continue west on Forest Road 44 for 3.5 miles to the campground on the left.

Contact: Okanogan and Wenatchee National Forests, Methow Valley Visitor Center, 24 West Chewuch Road, Winthrop, WA 98862; 509/996-4000, fax 509/997-9770.

63 Twisp River Horse Camp

 7

This camp is only for horses and their owners. It is set on the Twisp River at an elevation of 3,000 feet. The camp features access to trails about three miles away. This features the North Fork Twisp River Trail, which leads to Copper Pass, and the South Fork Twisp River Trail, which leads to Lake Chelan National Recreation Area and Twisp Pass. The South Creek Trail is also available and is routed out from camp also to Lake Chelan National Recreation Area.

Location: On Twisp River in Okanogan and Wenatchee National Forests; see the Northern Cascades, map 2, grid f5.

Campsites, facilities: There are 12 sites for tents, trailers, or RVs up to 30 feet long. Picnic tables and fire grills are provided. Vault toilets are available. No drinking water is available. Garbage must be packed out. For horses, a loading ramp, hitching rails, and feed stations are available. Leashed pets are permitted.

Reservations, fees: Northwest Forest Pass ($30 annual fee) or $5 daily fee per parked vehicle is required. Senior discount available. Open May to September.

Directions: On I-5, drive to Exit 230/State Route 20 at Burlington. Turn east on State Route 20, and drive 145 miles to Twisp and County Road 9114 (Twisp River Road). Turn west on County Road 9114 (Twisp River Road) and drive 11 miles (becomes Forest Road 44). Continue west on Forest Road 44 for 3.5 miles to War Creek Campground on the left. Continue 250 yards to Forest Road 4430. Turn left (drive over the bridge) and drive approximately nine miles to the campground on the right.

Contact: Okanogan and Wenatchee National Forests, Methow Valley Visitor Center, 24 West Chewuch Road, Winthrop, WA 98862; 509/996-4000, fax 509/997-9770.

64 Blackpine Lake

 7

This campground features great views of some local peaks. About one-third of the campsites have views; the rest are set in a forest of Douglas fir and Ponderosa pine. This popular spot often fills up on summer weekends and occasionally even during the week. Fishing is available for stocked rainbow trout. Note that boating is permitted, but no gas motors are permitted; electric motors are allowed. An interpretive trail is less than a quarter-mile long and is routed around the north end of the lake.

Location: On the Blackpine Lake in Okanogan and Wenatchee National Forests; see the Northern Cascades, map 2, grid f6.

Campsites, facilities: There are 23 sites for tents, trailers, or RVs. Picnic tables and fire grills are provided. Drinking water and vault toilets are available. A boat launch and two floating docks are available nearby. Some facilities are wheelchair-accessible. Leashed pets are permitted.

Reservations, fees: No reservations. Sites are $8 per night, $8 per extra vehicle per night. Senior discount available. Open May to September.

Directions: From Burlington, drive east on State Route 20 for 145 miles to Twisp and County Road 9114 (Twisp River Road). Turn west on County Road 9114 (Twisp River Road) and drive 10 miles to County Road 1090. Turn left and drive over a bridge (becomes Forest Road 43) and continue eight miles to the campground on the right.

Contact: Okanogan and Wenatchee National Forests, Methow Valley Visitor Center, 24 West Chewuch Road, Winthrop, WA 98862; 509/996-4000, fax 509/997-9770.

65 River Bend RV Park

 6

The shore of the Methow River skirts this campground. Trout fishing, river rafting, and swimming are popular here, and there is a nice separate area for tent campers set right along the river. The description of KOA Methow River details the recreation possibilities available within 10 miles.

Location: Near the Methow River; see the Northern Cascades, map 2, grid f7.

Campsites, facilities: There are 69 sites with full hookups, including 30 drive-through sites and 31 riverfront sites, for RVs and trailers of any length, and 35 tent sites. Picnic tables and fire pits are provided. Restrooms, flush toilets, coin-operated showers, a dump station, firewood, a store, a coin-operated laundry, ice, a playground with horseshoe pits, bottled gas, modem access, and RV storage are available. Leashed pets are permitted.

Reservations, fees: Reservations accepted. Sites are $15 to $20 per night, $2 per person per night for more than two people, $1 for children over 5; a few permanent rentals are available. Major credit cards accepted. Open year-round.

Directions: From Twisp, drive west on State Route 20 for two miles to the campground on the right.

Contact: River Bend RV, 19961 State Route 20, Twisp, WA 98856; 509/997-3500 or 800/686-4498; website: www.riverbendrv.com.

Weaver Point Boat-In

 7

This boat-in campground on Lake Chelan gets high use on summer weekends. It is the largest campground in the Stehekin area. The only direct access to Stehekin is by boat or a four-mile hike to Stehekin Landing from the campground. It's a fairly easy tromp, with no steep grades.

Location: On Lake Chelan in Lake Chelan National Recreation Area; see the Northern Cascades, map 2, grid f3.

Campsites, facilities: There are 22 sites accessible only by boat, ferry, or float plane. Picnic tables and fire grills are provided. Drinking water and vault toilets are available. Garbage must be packed out. Food storage lockers are available and must be used. Two floating docks are available for boats.

Reservations, fees: No reservations, no fee; $5 per day docking fee. Open year-round, with limited facilities in winter.

Directions: From Wenatchee, drive on U.S. 97 about 40 miles to Chelan and the ferry. Take the ferry and proceed to Weaver Point. Note that this is not a scheduled stop; you must request this stop in advance. The campground

is also directly accessible by float plane. (Call Chelan Airways at 509/682-5555 for more information.)

Contact: North Cascades National Park Headquarters, 810 State Route 20, Sedro-Woolley, WA 98284; 360/856-5700, fax 360/856-1934. Lake Chelan Boat Company, 509/682-2224; website: www.ladyofthelake.com.

Holden Ballpark Ferry-In, Hike-In

 7

Getting here is half the fun, with ferryboat rides provided by the Lake Chelan Boat Company that emphasize fun and education along with transportation. Several trails to lakes in the Glacier Peak Wilderness are accessible from a trail next to the campground, which is set along Railroad Creek. Because this area is situated on the eastern slope of the Cascade Range, it's more arid; however, there is no shortage of glacier-fed streams and lakes in the area. See a U.S. Forest Service map for details. Less than one mile from the campground is the Holden Mine site, which was Washington's largest copper and zinc mine until it closed in 1957. Many of the buildings from the mining town have been preserved, and Holden Village offers housing and meals for travelers as space allows.

Location: Near the Glacier Peak Wilderness in Wenatchee National Forest; see the Northern Cascades, map 2, grid g2.

Campsites, facilities: There are two primitive tent sites that are accessible only by boat or ferry, followed by a 12-mile hike or bus trip via Holden Village up the Railroad Creek Valley. Picnic tables and fire rings are provided. One Wallowa (nonenclosed platform) pit toilet is available, but there is no drinking water. Garbage must be packed out. Be prepared to protect food from bears;

bearproof food hangs or canisters are required. Leashed pets are permitted.

Reservations, fees: No reservations; no fee. For ferry fees, which vary according to boat and age of passenger, phone 509/682-2224; typically the fee is in the $25 range. Open May through September.

Directions: From Wenatchee, drive north on U.S. 97 about 40 miles to Chelan and the ferry. Take the ferry and proceed 41 miles northwest to Lucerne. In Lucerne, take the bus 12 miles west to Holden Village. The campground is at the end of the road.

Contact: Okanogan and Wenatchee National Forests, Chelan Ranger District, 428 West Woodin Avenue, Chelan, WA 98816; 509/682-2576, fax 509/682-9004. Lake Chelan Boat Company, 509/682-2224; website: www.lady ofthelake.com.

68 Domke Lake Ferry-In, Hike-In

 9

Little known and little used, this spot is a perfect jumping-off point for a wilderness backpacking trip. Domke Lake is about one mile long and one-half mile wide and offers good fishing by boat. Trails continue past the lake into the Glacier Peak Wilderness. See a U.S. Forest Service map for details. It is set at 2,210 feet and is one of three national forest campgrounds near Domke Lake.

Location: Near the Glacier Peak Wilderness in Wenatchee National Forest; see the Northern Cascades, map 2, grid g4.

Campsites, facilities: There are eight tent sites accessible only by boat, ferry, or float plane. Picnic tables and fire rings are provided. Pit toilets are available, but there is no drinking water. Garbage must be packed out. Boat rentals are available nearby at Domke Lake Resort. Be prepared to protect food from bears; bearproof food

hangs or canisters are required. Leashed pets are permitted.

Reservations, fees: No reservations; no camping fee. A $5 per-day docking charge is required at Lucerne or Refrigerator Harbor campgrounds. For ferry fees, which vary according to boat and age of passenger, phone 509/682-2224; typically the fee is in the $25 range. Open May to late October.

Directions: From Wenatchee, drive north on U.S. 97 for 40 miles to Chelan and the ferry. Take the ferry and proceed 41 miles to Lucerne. From Lucerne, hike, bike, or motorbike on Trail 1280 for 2.5 miles to Domke Lake and the campground. The campground is also directly accessible by float plane. (Call Chelan Airways at 509/682-5555 for more information.)

Contact: Okanogan and Wenatchee National Forests, Chelan Ranger District, 428 West Woodin Avenue, Chelan, WA 98816; 509/682-2576, fax 509/682-9004. Lake Chelan Boat Company, 509/682-2224; website: www.lady ofthelake.com.

69 Lucerne

 10

This camp was named after Lucerne, Switzerland, with mountains reaching to 8,000 feet flanking each side of Lake Chelan. This campground is set along the shore of 55-mile-long Lake Chelan, the third deepest lake in North America, at 1,500 feet. This is one of 13 national forest campgrounds on Lake Chelan but the only national forest camp in the vicinity that offers drinking water. Fishing, hiking, and boating are among your options here. Refrigerator Harbor and Domke Falls campgrounds are nearby. See the description of Holden for information on the Holden Mine and Village, which is also nearby.

Location: On Lake Chelan in Wenatchee National Forest; see the Northern Cascades, map 2, grid g4.

Campsites, facilities: There are two tent sites accessible only by boat, ferry, or float plane. Picnic tables and fire rings are provided. Drinking water, pit toilets, and boat docks and basin are available. Garbage must be packed out. Leashed pets are permitted.

Reservations, fees: No reservations; no camping fee; $5 per day docking charge. For ferry fees, which vary according to boat and age of passenger, phone 509/682-2224; typically the fee is in the $25 range. Open April through October.

Directions: From Wenatchee, drive north on U.S. 97 for 40 miles to Chelan and the ferry. Take the ferry and proceed to Lucerne, 41 miles northwest of the town of Chelan on the west shore of Lake Chelan. (This spectacular voyage costs about $22 round-trip. For more information, call 509/682-2224.)

Contact: Wenatchee National Forest, Chelan Ranger District, 428 West Woodin Avenue, Chelan, WA 98816; 509/682-2576, fax 509/682-9004. Lake Chelan Boat Company, 509/682-2224; website: www.ladyofthelake.com.

 70 Prince Creek

10

This camp is set along the east shore of Lake Chelan at the mouth of Prince Creek, 18 miles south of Stehekin on Trail 1247. It's a busy camp on summer weekends. A trail from camp follows Prince Creek into the Lake Chelan-Sawtooth Wilderness and then connects to a network of other trails, all of which lead to various lakes and streams. A U.S. Forest Service map shows details. Be prepared to protect food from bears; bearproof food hangs or canisters are required. The elevation is 1,100 feet.

Location: On Lake Chelan in Wenatchee National Forest; see the Northern Cascades, map 2, grid g5.

Campsites, facilities: There are six tent sites accessible only by boat, ferry, or float plane. Picnic tables and fire rings are provided. Pit toilets are available, but there is no drinking water. Garbage must be packed out. A floating dock can accommodate about three boats.

Reservations, fees: No reservations, no fee; $5 per day docking fee. Open May to mid-November.

Directions: From Wenatchee, drive on U.S. 97 about 40 miles to Chelan and the ferry. Take the ferry and proceed to Prince Creek, 35 miles from Chelan. Note that the ferry will not stop here if water level does not allow for safe landing. The campground is also directly accessible by float plane. (Call Chelan Airways at 509/682-5555 for more information.)

Contact: Wenatchee National Forest, Chelan Ranger District, 428 West Woodin Avenue, Chelan, WA 98816; 509/682-2576, fax 509/682-9004. Lake Chelan Boat Company, 509/682-2224; website: www.ladyofthelake.com.

71 Graham Harbor Creek

 10

This campground is set along Lake Chelan at the mouth of Graham Harbor Creek. It is set on the west side of Lake Chelan, with one of the best boat moorings for winds out of the north. It's one of the more remote and primitive campgrounds on giant Lake Chelan. Fishing and boating are the main recreation attractions here. The elevation is 1,100 feet. Be prepared to protect food from bears; bearproof food hangs or canisters are required.

Location: On Lake Chelan in Wenatchee National Forest; see the Northern Cascades, map 2, grid h5.

Campsites, facilities: There are five tent sites accessible only by boat, ferry, or float plane. Picnic tables and fire rings are provided. Pit toilets are available, but there is no drinking water. Garbage must be packed out. A floating dock can accommodate about 10 boats.

Reservations, fees: No reservations, no camping fee; $5 docking fee per boat per day. Open year-round.

Directions: From Wenatchee, drive on U.S. 97 about 40 miles to Chelan and the ferry. Take the ferry and proceed to Graham Harbor Creek (the ferry does not schedule stopping at this campground, but will usually stop here if you request it in advance). The campground is also directly accessible by float plane. (Call Chelan Airways at 509/682-5555 for more information.)

Contact: Okanogan and Wenatchee National Forests, Chelan Ranger District, 428 West Woodin Avenue, Chelan, WA 98816; 509/682-2576, fax 509/682-9004. Lake Chelan Boat Company, 509/682-2224; website: www.lady ofthelake.com.

72 Deer Point Boat-In

 9

Here's another little-known spot set along the shore of Lake Chelan. If you want to camp on the remote east shore, this is one of eight camps. This campground provides good protection from down-lake winds, but is exposed to up-lake winds. Fishermen at Lake Chelan often use this spot as their boat-in camp headquarters. Be prepared to protect food from bears; bearproof food hangs or canisters are required.

Location: On Lake Chelan in Wenatchee National Forest; see the Northern Cascades, map 2, grid h6.

Campsites, facilities: There are five tent sites accessible only by boat, ferry, or float plane. Picnic tables and fire rings are provided. Pit toilets are available, but there is no drinking water. A floating dock can accommodate about eight boats.

Reservations, fees: No reservations, no camping fee; $5 per day docking fee. Open May through October.

Directions: From Wenatchee, drive north on U.S. 97 about 40 miles to Chelan and the ferry. Take the ferry and proceed to Deer Point (the ferry does not schedule stopping at this campground, but will usually stop here if you request it in advance).

Contact: Okanogan and Wenatchee National Forests, Chelan Ranger District, 428 West Woodin Avenue, Chelan, WA 98816; 509/682-2576, fax 509/682-9004. Lake Chelan Boat Company, 509/682-2224; website: www.lady ofthelake.com.

73 Phelps Creek

 7

This campground is set at an elevation of 2,800 feet at the confluence of Phelps Creek and the Chiwawa River. There's a key trailhead for backpackers and horseback riders nearby that provides access to the Glacier Peak Wilderness and Spider Meadows. The Phelps Creek Trail is routed out to Spider Meadows, a five-mile hike one-way, and the Buck Creek Trail extends into the Glacier Peak Wilderness. The Chiwawa River is closed to fishing to protect endangered species. It's advisable to obtain a U.S. Forest Service map.

Location: On the Chiwawa River in Wenatchee National Forest; see the Northern Cascades, map 2, grid h2.

Campsites, facilities: There are seven sites for tents or trailers less than 30 feet long.

Picnic tables and fire grills are provided. Pit toilets are available, but there is no drinking water. Garbage must be packed out. Horse facilities including loading ramps and high lines are nearby. Leashed pets are permitted.

Reservations, fees: Northwest Forest Pass ($30 annual fee) or $5 daily fee per parked vehicle is required. Senior discount available. Open mid-June to mid-October.

Directions: From Seattle, drive north on I-5 to Everett and U.S. 2. Turn east on U.S. 2 and drive 87 miles to State Route 207. Turn north on State Route 207 and drive four miles to Chiwawa Loop Road. Turn right (east) on Chiwawa Loop Road and drive 1.4 miles to Chiwawa Valley Road (Forest Road 6200). Bear left (north) and continue for 23.6 miles to the campground.

Contact: Okanogan and Wenatchee National Forests, Lake Wenatchee and Leavenworth Ranger District, Lake Wenatchee Office, 22976 State Route 207, Leavenworth, WA 98826; 509/763-3103, fax 509/763-3211.

74 Foggy Dew

 6

This private, remote campground is set at the confluence of Foggy Dew Creek and the North Fork of Old Creek. The elevation is 2,400 feet. Several trails for hiking and horseback riding nearby provide access to various backcountry lakes and streams. To get to the trailheads, follow the forest roads near camp. Bicycles are allowed on Trails 417, 429, and 431. There is also access to a motorcycle-use area. See a U.S. Forest Service map for options.

Location: On Foggy Dew Creek in Okanogan and Wenatchee National Forests; see the Northern Cascades, map 2, grid g7.

Campsites, facilities: There are 13 sites for tents, trailers, or RVs. Picnic tables and fire grills are provided. Vault toilets are available.

No drinking water is available. Garbage must be packed out. Leashed pets are permitted.

Reservations, fees: No reservations. Sites are $5 per night, $5 per extra vehicle per night. Senior discount available. Open late May to early September.

Directions: From Burlington, drive east on State Route 20 for 145 miles to Twisp. Continue east on State Route 20 for three miles to Highway 153. Turn south on Highway 153 and drive 12 miles to County Road 1029 (Gold Creek Road). Turn right (south) and drive one mile to Forest Road 4340. Turn right (west) and drive four miles to the campground on the left.

Contact: Okanogan and Wenatchee National Forests, Methow Valley Visitor Center, 24 West Chewuch Road, Winthrop, WA 98862; 509/996-4000, fax 509/997-9770.

75 Tiffany Springs

 7

This camp is less than a one-mile hike from Tiffany Lake, set at an elevation of 6,800 feet. Tiffany Mountain rises 8,200 feet in the distance. The lake provides fishing for rainbow trout and brook trout. There are also some good hiking trails in the area. The Tiffany Mountain area provides a network of 26 miles of hiking trails, accessed from either here at Tiffany Springs or at Tiffany Lake. No other campgrounds are in the vicinity, and it's advisable to obtain a U.S. Forest Service map of the area.

Location: Near Tiffany Lake in Okanogan National Forest; see the Northern Cascades, map 3, grid c1.

Campsites, facilities: There are six tent sites for trailers or RVs up to 15 feet long. Picnic tables are provided. Vault toilets are available, but there is no drinking water. Garbage must be packed out. Leashed pets are permitted.

Reservations, fees: Northwest Forest Pass ($30 annual fee) or $5 daily fee per parked vehicle is required. Open July to late September.

Directions: From East Wenatchee, drive north on U.S. 97 for 88 miles to Okanogan and County Road 9229. Turn north and drive 17.5 miles northwest to Conconully and County Road 2017. Turn left on County Road 2017 and drive 1.5 miles to Forest Road 37. Turn right (northwest) and drive 21 miles to Forest Road 39. Turn right (northeast) on Forest Road 39 and proceed 7.5 miles to the campground on the left.

Contact: Okanogan and Wenatchee National Forests, Tonasket Ranger District, 1 West Winesap Avenue, Tonasket, WA 98855; 509/486-2186, fax 509/486-5161.

76 Salmon Meadows

   6

This camp is located at 4,500 feet along Salmon Creek. The highlight here is a spectacular wildflower display in the spring in an adjacent meadow. The camp features a forest setting, mainly Douglas fir, spruce, and some western larch. Trails from the campground are routed out to Angel Pass, two miles one-way, for views of the Tiffany area.

Location: On Salmon Creek in Okanogan National Forest; see the Northern Cascades, map 3, grid c2.

Campsites, facilities: There are seven sites for tents, small trailers, or RVs. Picnic tables and fire grills are provided. Vault toilets are available, but there is no drinking water. Garbage must be packed out. Some facilities are wheelchair-accessible. Leashed pets are permitted.

Reservations, fees: No reservations. Sites are $5 per night, $5 per extra vehicle per night. Senior discount available. Open mid-May to mid-September.

Directions: From East Wenatchee, drive north on U.S. 97 for 88 miles to Okanogan and County Road 9229. Turn left (north) on County Road 9229 and drive 17.5 miles to Conconully and County Road 2361. Continue northwest on County Road 2361 and drive four miles (becomes Forest Road 38) to Kerr Campground. Continue past Kerr for four miles to the campground on the right.

Contact: Okanogan and Wenatchee National Forests, Tonasket Ranger District, 1 West Winesap Avenue, Tonasket, WA 98855; 509/486-2186, fax 509/486-5161.

77 Kerr

    6

This camp is located at 3,100 feet along Salmon Creek, about four miles north of Conconully Reservoir, and is one of many campgrounds near the lake. Fishing prospects are marginal for trout here. There are numerous recreation options available at Conconully Reservoir, including far better fishing.

Location: On Salmon Creek in Okanogan National Forest; see the Northern Cascades, map 3, grid d2.

Campsites, facilities: There are 13 sites for tents, trailers, or RVs up to 21 feet long. Picnic tables and fire grills are provided. Vault toilets are available, but there is no drinking water. Garbage must be packed out. Some facilities are wheelchair-accessible. Leashed pets are permitted.

Reservations, fees: No reservations. Sites are $5 per night, $5 per extra vehicle per night. Senior discount available. Open mid-May to mid-September.

Directions: From East Wenatchee, drive north on U.S. 97 for 88 miles to Okanogan and County Road 9229. Turn left (north) on County Road 9229 and drive 17.5 miles to

Conconully and County Road 2361. Continue northwest on County Road 2361 and drive four miles (becomes Forest Road 38) to the campground on the left.

Contact: Okanogan and Wenatchee National Forests, Tonasket Ranger District, 1 West Winesap Avenue, Tonasket, WA 98855; 509/486-2186, fax 509/486-5161.

Oriole

 6

This camp is located at 2,900 feet along Salmon Creek, with a creek view from some of the campsites. This forest setting features Western larch and lodgepole pine, with the campsites well spaced. This is a primitive camp, similar to Kerr and Salmon Meadows, also set on Salmon Creek.

Location: On Salmon Creek in Okanogan National Forest; see the Northern Cascades, map 3, grid d2.

Campsites, facilities: There are 10 sites for tents or small RVs. Picnic tables and fire grills are provided. Vault toilets are available, but there is no drinking water. Garbage must be packed out. Some facilities are wheelchair-accessible. Leashed pets are permitted.

Reservations, fees: No reservations. Sites are $5 per night, $5 per extra vehicle per night. Senior discount available. Open mid-May to mid-September.

Directions: From East Wenatchee, drive north on U.S. 97 for 88 miles to Okanogan and County Road 9229. Turn left (north) on County Road 9229 and drive 17.5 miles to Conconully and County Road 2361. Continue northwest on County Road 2361 and drive 2.5 miles to Forest Road 025. Turn left and drive 0.5 mile (crossing the creek) to the campground on the left.

Contact: Okanogan and Wenatchee National Forests, Tonasket Ranger District, 1 West

Winesap Avenue, Tonasket, WA 98855; 509/486-2186, fax 509/486-5161.

Loup Loup

 6

This camp provides a good setup for large groups of up to 100 people. It is located next to the Loup Loup Ski Area at 4,200 feet. The camp features a setting of Western larch trees, with good access to biking and hiking trails and the ski area.

Location: Near Loup Loup Ski Area in Okanogan National Forest; see the Northern Cascades, map 3, grid e1.

Campsites, facilities: There are 25 sites for tents, trailers, or RVs up to 21 feet long. Picnic tables and fire rings are provided. Drinking water, vault toilets, and a dump station are available. Leashed pets are permitted.

Reservations, fees: No reservations. Sites are $6 per night, $6 per extra vehicle per night. Open May through September, weather permitting.

Directions: From East Wenatchee, drive north on U.S. 97 for 88 miles to Okanogan and Highway 20. Turn west and drive 21 miles to Forest Road 42. Turn right (north) on Forest Road 42 and drive one mile to the campground on the left.

Contact: Okanogan and Wenatchee National Forests, Methow Valley Visitor Center, 24 West Chewuch Road, Winthrop, WA 98862; 509/997-4000, fax 509/997-9770.

80 JR

 7

This camp is located at 3,900 feet along Frazier Creek near the Loup Loup summit and ski area. Some of the recreation possibilities in the surrounding area include fishing, hunting, cross-country skiing, snowmobiling, hiking, and bicycling. This is a small layover for travelers looking for a spot on Highway 20.

Location: On Frazier Creek in Okanogan National Forest; see the Northern Cascades, map 3, grid e2.

Campsites, facilities: There are six sites for tents, trailers, or RVs up to 25 feet long. Picnic tables and fire rings are provided. Drinking water, vault toilets, and a dump station are available. Leashed pets are permitted.

Reservations, fees: No reservations. Sites are $5 per night. Senior discount available. Open late May to early September.

Directions: From East Wenatchee, drive north on U.S. 97 for 88 miles to Okanogan and Highway 20. Turn west and drive 22 miles to the campground on the right.

Contact: Okanogan and Wenatchee National Forests, Methow Valley Visitor Center, 24 West Chewuch Road, Winthrop, WA 98862; 509/997-4000, fax 509/997-9770.

81 Sportsman's Camp

 6

This is a popular camp with hunters in season, who may bring horses, which are allowed in the camp, although there are no stock facilities. This camp is shady and grassy with a small stream. Some roads in the area can be used by hikers and bikers. Highway 20 east of I-5 is a designated scenic route.

Location: On Sweat Creek, in Lower Loomis State Forest; see the Northern Cascades, map 3, grid e2.

Campsites, facilities: There are six pull-through sites for tents, trailers, or RVs up to 30 feet and a small, dispersed area for tents. Picnic tables and fire pits are provided. Vault toilets are available, but there is no drinking water. Garbage must be packed out.

A gazebo shelter with a fire pit is also available. Leashed pets are permitted.

Reservations, fees: No reservations; no fee. Open year-round, weather permitting.

Directions: From East Wenatchee, drive north on U.S. 97 for 88 miles to Okanogan and Highway 20. Turn west and drive 15 miles to Sweat Creek Road. Turn left on Sweat Creek Road and drive one mile to the campground on the right.

Contact: Department of Natural Resources, Northeast Region, P.O. Box 190, Colville, WA 99114-0190; 509/684-7474, fax 509/684-7484.

82 Flowing Lake County Park

 6

This campground has a little something for everyone, including swimming, power boating, water-skiing, and good fishing on Flowing Lake. The campsites are in a wood setting (that is, no lake view), and it is a one-quarter-mile walk to a beach. A one-mile nature trail is nearby. Note that private homes are on the lake and all visitors are asked to respect the privacy of the owners.

Location: Near Snohomish; see the Northern Cascades, map 4, grid a1.

Campsites, facilities: There are 40 drive-through sites, most with partial hookups (water and electricity) for tents, trailers, or RVs up to 30 feet long. Picnic tables and fire grills are provided. Restrooms, drinking water, flush toilets, coin-operated showers, a dump station, and firewood are available. A picnic area with covered shelter, a fishing dock, a playground, boat docks, and launching facilities are available nearby. Some facilities are wheelchair-accessible. Leashed pets are permitted.

Reservations, fees: No reservations. Sites are $10

to $15 per night. Open year-round with limited winter facilities.

Directions: From Seattle, drive north on I-5 to Everett and U.S. 2. Turn east on U.S. 2, drive to Milepost 10, and look for 100 Street SE (Westwick Road). Turn left and drive five miles (becomes 171st Street SE) to 48th Street Southeast. Turn right and drive about one-half mile into the park at the end of the road.

Contact: Flowing Lake County Park, Snohomish County; 360/568-2274 or 425/388-6600.

83 Cutthroat Lakes Hike-In

  9

Reaching this spot is worth the effort. You'll find beautiful lakeside camps, trout fishing, hiking, and few other campers. The "lakes" are actually small ponds, but they're very pretty. Backpacking stoves are recommended for cooking. No firewood is available.

Location: On Bald Mountain; see the Northern Cascades, map 4, grid a4.

Campsites, facilities: There are five tent sites at this primitive, hike-in campground. Vault toilets are available, but there is no drinking water. Garbage must be packed out. Leashed pets are permitted.

Reservations, fees: No reservations; no fee. Open mid-June through October.

Directions: From Seattle, drive north on I-5 to Everett and Highway 92. Turn east on Highway 92 and drive about 15 miles to the town of Granite Falls and Mountain Loop Highway (Forest Road 7). Continue northeast on Mountain Loop for 18 miles to Forest Road 4030 (at the bridge). Turn south and drive for three miles to Forest Road 4032 (follow the Mallardy Ridge signs). Bear right and take Forest Road 4032 for one mile to the end where the trailhead begins. Hike 4.5 miles to Cutthroat Lakes.

Contact: Department of Natural Resources, Northwest Region, 919 North Township Street, Sedro-Woolley, WA 98284-9395; 360/856-3500, fax 360/852-2150.

84 Little Greider Lake Hike-In

    10

This is prime country for hiking, backpacking, and trout fishing. The primitive, wooded campground is on Little Greider Lake. It is very pretty, similar to Big Greider, and gets more use than Big Greider. But hey, the truth is that in this area, Boulder Lake is the most desirable spot of all.

Location: On Little Greider Lake; see the Northern Cascades, map 4, grid a4.

Campsites, facilities: There are nine tent sites at this primitive, hike-in campground. Fire grills and tent pads are provided. Vault toilets and firewood are available. There is no drinking water. Garbage must be packed out. Leashed pets are permitted.

Reservations, fees: No reservations; no fee. Open mid-June through October.

Directions: From Seattle, drive north on I-5 to Everett and U.S. 2. Turn east on U.S. 2 and drive 24 miles to Sultan. Continue one-half mile east to Sultan Basin Road. Turn north on Sultan Basin Road and drive 13.6 miles to a fork. Take the middle road (Road SLS 4000) and drive 8.5 miles to the Greider Lake Trailhead. From the trailhead, hike 2.5 miles to the campground.

Contact: Department of Natural Resources, Northwest Region, 919 North Township Street, Sedro-Woolley, WA 98284-9395; 360/856-3500, fax 360/856-2150.

85 Big Greider Lake Hike-In

    10

This primitive campground on Big Greider Lake is a hideaway in a gorgeous setting. Although campers are few, a lot of day hikers do make the three-mile tromp to the lake. The landscape features subalpine-type terrain. Fishing is an option. This camp provides an alternative to Little Greider Lake Campground, adjacent to Little Greider Lake.

Location: On Big Greider Lake; see the Northern Cascades, map 4, grid a4.

Campsites, facilities: There are five tent sites at this primitive, hike-in campground. Fire grills and tent pads are provided. Vault toilets and firewood are available, but there is no drinking water. Garbage must be packed out. Leashed pets are permitted.

Reservations, fees: No reservations; no fee. Open mid-June through October.

Directions: From Seattle, drive north on I-5 to Everett and U.S. 2. Turn east on U.S. 2 and drive 24 miles to Sultan. Continue one-half mile east to Sultan Basin Road. Turn north on Sultan Basin Road and drive 13.6 miles to a fork. Take the middle road (Road SLS 4000) and drive 8.5 miles to the Greider Lake Trailhead. From the trailhead, hike three miles to the campground.

Contact: Department of Natural Resources, Northwest Region, 919 North Township Street, Sedro-Woolley, WA 98284-9395; 360/856-3500, fax 360/856-2150.

86 Boulder Lake Hike-In

 10

Boulder Lake features cobalt-blue water, which is brilliant azure on sunny days. It is the most desirable of the three hike-in camps in the immediate area: Little Greider Lake and Big Greider Lake are the other two. Yet this camp gets less use than the other two because it is a bit of a longer hike-in, just under four miles. It serves as a good base camp for enjoying the beauty, hiking, and fishing.

Location: On Boulder Lake; see the Northern Cascades, map 4, grid a4.

Campsites, facilities: There are nine sites for tents at this primitive, hike-in campground. Fire grills and tent pads are provided. Vault toilets and firewood are available. There is no drinking water. Garbage must be packed out. Leashed pets are permitted.

Reservations, fees: No reservations; no fee. Open mid-June through October.

Directions: From Seattle, drive north on I-5 to Everett and U.S. 2. Turn east on U.S. 2 and drive 24 miles to Sultan. Continue one-half mile east to Sultan Basin Road. Turn north on Sultan Basin Road and drive 13.6 miles to a fork. Take the middle road (Road SLS 4000) and drive 8.5 miles to the Greider Lake Trailhead. Bear right on Road SLS 7000 and drive one mile to the Boulder Lake Trailhead. From the Boulder Lake Trailhead, hike 3.8 miles to the campground.

Contact: Department of Natural Resources, Northwest Region, 919 North Township Street, Sedro-Woolley, WA 98284-9395; 360/856-3500, fax 360/856-2150.

87 Troublesome Creek

 9

This campground is set along the North Fork of the Skykomish River among old-growth pine and fir. Highlights include a half-mile nature trail adjacent to the camp and rafting and good fishing in the river. A must-do trip here is the hike out to Blanca Lake. The trailhead is a short drive, then hike 3.5 miles to the lake, which is drop-dead beautiful with blue-green water fed by glacier-melt.

Location: On the North Fork of the Skykomish River in Mt. Baker-Snoqualmie National

Forest; see the Northern Cascades, map 4, grid a5.

Campsites, facilities: There are 24 sites for tents, trailers, or RVs up to 21 feet long and six walk-in tent sites requiring about a 100-foot walk. Picnic tables and fire rings are provided. Drinking water and vault toilets are available. Some facilities are wheelchair-accessible. Leashed pets are permitted.

Reservations, fees: Some sites, including three that are wheelchair-accessible, may be reserved; phone 877/444-6777 or access the website: www.reserveusa.com ($8.65 reservation fee). Sites are $12 per night, $6 per extra vehicle per night. Senior discount available. Open Memorial Day through Labor Day.

Directions: From Seattle, drive north on I-5 to Everett and U.S. 2. Turn east on U.S. 2 and drive 36 miles to the town of Index and Forest Road 63 (Index-Galena Road). Turn left (northeast) on Forest Road 63 and drive 12 miles to the campground on the right.

Contact: Mt. Baker-Snoqualmie National Forest, Skykomish Ranger District, P.O. Box 305, Skykomish, WA 98288; 360/677-2414, fax 425/744-3265.

88 San Juan

 7

This camp is highlighted by old-growth Douglas fir and cedar and the adjacent North Fork of the Skykomish River. Campsites vary in size. It is similar to nearby Troublesome Creek Campground; see that camp for more trip notes. Note that no fishing is permitted at the river.

Location: On the North Fork of the Skykomish River in Mt. Baker-Snoqualmie National Forest; see the Northern Cascades, map 4, grid a6.

Campsites, facilities: There are nine sites for tents, trailers, or RVs. Picnic tables and fire grills are provided. Vault toilets are available. No drinking water is available. Leashed pets are permitted.

Reservations, fees: No reservations. Sites are $8 per night, $4 per extra vehicle per night. Senior discount available. Open May through October, weather permitting.

Directions: From Seattle, drive north on I-5 to Everett and U.S. 2. Turn east on U.S. 2 and drive 36 miles to the town of Index and Forest Road 63 (Index-Galena Road). Turn left (northeast) on Forest Road 63, drive 12 miles to Troublesome Creek Campground (on the right), and continue two miles to the campground on the right.

Contact: Mt. Baker-Snoqualmie National Forest, Skykomish Ranger District, P.O. Box 305, Skykomish, WA 98288; 360/677-2414, fax 425/744-3265.

89 Wallace Falls State Park Walk-In

 8

The Wallace Falls State Park Management Area is a 4,735-acre camping park with shoreline on the Wallace River, Wallace Lake, Jay Lake, Show Lake, and the Skykomish River. Features are a 265-foot waterfall, old-growth conifer forests, and fast-moving rivers and streams. Mountain lions have been spotted near Wallace Falls. Peregrine falcons inhabit the rock cliffs of the Index Town Wall, 12 miles east of Wallace Falls. Rock climbing is permitted here. The campground is located in a heavily treed area at the trailhead to the falls. The trail leads along the Wallace River and is a lovely hike. The park has 12 miles of hiking trails, including a one-quarter-mile interpretive trail, five miles of biking trails, and is extremely busy on summer days. Fishing, rafting, kayaking, canoeing, and swimming are popular at Big Eddy, a satellite park located five miles east. Fishing for trout and steelhead, in season, is a sidelight.

Location: Near Gold Bar; see the Northern Cascades, map 4, grid b3.

Campsites, facilities: There are six walk-in tent sites. Picnic tables and fire grills are provided. Flush toilets and drinking water are available. A picnic area with kitchen shelters is available nearby. Some facilities are wheelchair-accessible. Leashed pets are permitted.

Reservations, fees: No reservations accepted. Sites are $11 per night, $6 per extra vehicle per night. Open February through October.

Directions: From Seattle, drive north on I-5 to Everett and U.S. 2. Turn east on U.S. 2, drive 28 miles to the town of Gold Bar, and look for the sign for Wallace Falls State Park. Turn northeast at the sign and drive two miles to the park.

Contact: Wallace Falls State Park, 360/793-0420; State Park information, 360/902-8844.

90 Money Creek Campground

 5

You have a little surprise waiting for you here. Trains go by regularly day and night, and the first time it happens while you're in deep sleep, you might just launch a hole right through the top of your tent. The Burlington Northern rail runs along the western boundary of the campground. By now you've got the picture—that this can be a noisy camp. Money Creek Campground is on the Skykomish River, with hiking trails a few miles away. The best of these is the Dorothy Lake Trail. Renovation of this camp is set for 2002; it will remain open.

Location: On the Skykomish River in Mt. Baker-Snoqualmie National Forest; see the Northern Cascades, map 4, grid c5.

Campsites, facilities: There are 24 sites for tents, trailers, or RVs up to 21 feet long.

Picnic tables are provided. Vault toilets and drinking water are available. A store, a café, and ice are located within 3.5 miles. Some facilities are wheelchair-accessible. Leashed pets are permitted.

Reservations, fees: Some sites can be reserved; phone 877/444-6777 or access the website: www.reserveusa.com ($8.65 reservation fee). Sites are $12 per night, $6 per extra vehicle per night. Senior discount available. Open Memorial Day Weekend through Labor Day Weekend.

Directions: From Seattle, drive north on I-5 to Everett and U.S. 2. Turn east on U.S. 2 and drive 46 miles to Old Cascade Highway, 11 miles east of Index. Turn south on Old Cascade Highway and drive across the bridge to the campground.

Contact: Mt. Baker-Snoqualmie National Forest, Skykomish Ranger District, P.O. Box 305, Skykomish, WA 98288; 360/677-2414, fax 425/744-3265.

91 Beckler River

7

Located on the Beckler River at an elevation of 900 feet, this camp has scenic riverside sites in second-growth timber, primarily Douglas fir, cedar, and bigleaf maple. Fishing at the campground is poor; it's better well up the river. The Skykomish Ranger Station is just a couple of miles away; maps are available for sale.

Location: On the Beckler River in Mt. Baker-Snoqualmie National Forest; see the Northern Cascades, map 4, grid c6.

Campsites, facilities: There are 27 sites for tents, trailers, or RVs up to 21 feet long. Picnic tables and fire grills are provided. Vault toilets and drinking water are available. A store, a café, and ice are located within two miles. Some sites and facilities are wheelchair-accessible. Leashed pets are permitted.

Reservations, fees: Some sites can be reserved; phone 877/444-6777 or access the website: www.reserveusa.com ($8.65 reservation fee). Sites are $12 per night, $6 per extra vehicle per night. Senior discount available. Open Memorial Day through Labor Day.

Directions: From Seattle, drive north on I-5 to Everett and U.S. 2. Turn east on U.S. 2 and drive 49 miles to Skykomish. Continue east on U.S. 2 for one-half mile to Forest Road 65. Turn north (left) on Forest Road 65 and drive 1.6 miles to the camp on the left.

Contact: Mt. Baker-Snoqualmie National Forest, Skykomish Ranger District, P.O. Box 305, Skykomish, WA 98288; 360/677-2414, fax 425/744-3265.

92 Miller River Group

 8

This campground is located along the Miller River, a short distance from the boundary of the Alpine Lakes Wilderness. If you continue another seven miles on Forest Road 6410, you'll get to a trailhead leading to Dorothy Lake, a 1.5-mile hike. This pretty lake is two miles long. The trail continues past the lake to many other backcountry lakes. The group limit in wilderness is 12 people. A U.S. Forest Service map is essential.

Location: Near the Alpine Lakes Wilderness in Mt. Baker-Snoqualmie National Forest; see the Northern Cascades, map 4, grid c5.

Campsites, facilities: This is a group camp with 18 sites for up to 100 people with tents, trailers, or RVs. Picnic tables and fire grills are provided. Vault toilets, drinking water, a group barbecue, and a 24-foot group table are available. Some facilities are wheelchair-accessible. A store, a café, and ice are within five miles. Leashed pets are permitted.

Reservations, fees: Reservations required, phone 877/444-6777 or access the website: www.reserveusa.com ($8.65 reservation fee). Sites are $75 for the first 50 people, $125 for 51 to 75, and $150 for 76 to 100 campers. Open mid-May to late September.

Directions: From Seattle, drive north on I-5 to Everett and U.S. 2. Turn east on U.S. 2 and drive 46 miles to Old Cascade Highway, 11 miles east of Index. Turn south on Old Cascade Highway (across the bridge) and drive one mile to Forest Road 6410. Turn right (south) and drive two miles to the campground on the left.

Contact: Mt. Baker-Snoqualmie National Forest, Skykomish Ranger District, P.O. Box 305, Skykomish, WA 98288; 360/677-2414, fax 425/744-3265.

93 Snoqualmie River Campground & RV Park

 7

If you're in the Seattle area and stuck for a place for the night, this pretty 10-acre park set along the Snoqualmie River may be a welcome option. Activities include fishing, swimming, road biking, and rafting. Nearby recreation options include several nine-hole golf courses. A worthwhile side trip is beautiful Snoqualmie Falls, 3.5 miles away in the famed Twin Peaks country.

Location: On the Snoqualmie River; see the Northern Cascades, map 4, grid d1.

Campsites, facilities: There are 50 sites, including 12 long-term rentals, for trailers or RVs of any length, and about 50 tent sites. Picnic tables are provided. Restrooms, drinking water, flush toilets, showers, firewood, and a playground are available. Bottled gas, a store, a café, and ice are located within two miles. Boat-launching facilities are located within one-half mile. Leashed pets are permitted.

Reservations, fees: Reservations accepted. Sites are $21 to $25 per night, $3.50 per person per night for more than two people. Some pets may be charged fees. Open April through October.

Directions: From the junction of I-5 and I-90 south of Seattle, turn east on I-90. Drive east for 26 miles to Exit 22 (Preston-Fall City). Take that exit and turn north on Preston-Fall City Road and drive 4.5 miles to SE 44th Place. Turn east and drive one mile to the campground at the end of the road.

Contact: Snoqualmie River Campground & RV Park; 425/222-5545.

94 Tinkham

 9

About half the campsites face the Snoqualmie River, making this a pretty spot. Fishing can be good; check regulations. The camp is set at an elevation of 1,600 feet. The creek provides hiking options. This camp is often used as a overflow for Denny Creek Camp. Wilderness trails for the Alpines Lakes Wilderness are located 5 to 10 miles away from the camp.

Location: On the Snoqualmie River in Mt. Baker-Snoqualmie National Forest; see the Northern Cascades, map 4, grid e4.

Campsites, facilities: There are 48 sites for tents, trailers, or RVs up to 35 feet long. Picnic tables and fire pits are provided. Drinking water and vault toilets are available. Firewood is available for purchase. Some facilities are wheelchair-accessible. Leashed pets are permitted.

Reservations, fees: Some sites can be reserved; phone 877/444-6777 or access the website: www.reserveusa.com ($8.65 reservation fee). Sites are $12 per night, $6 per

extra vehicle per night. Open mid-May to mid-September.

Directions: In Seattle on I-5, turn east on I-90. Drive east on I-90 to Exit 42. Take that exit and turn right on Tinkham Road (Forest Road 55), and drive southeast 1.5 miles to the campground on the left. Obtaining a U.S. Forest Service map is advisable.

Contact: Mt. Baker-Snoqualmie National Forest, Snoqualmie Ranger District, North Bend office, 42404 SE North Bend Way, North Bend, WA 98045; 425/888-1421, fax 425/888-1910.

95 Denny Creek

 9

This camp is set at 1,900 feet along Denny Creek, which is pretty with nearby recreation access. The campground is secluded in an area of Douglas fir, hemlock, and cedar, with hiking trails available in addition to swimming and rafting opportunities. The Denny Creek Trail starts from the campground and provides a 4.5-mile round-trip hike that features Keckwulee Falls and Denny Creek Waterslide. You can climb to Hemlock Pass to Melakwa Lake. There is access for backpackers into the Alpine Lakes Wilderness.

Location: On Denny Creek; see the Northern Cascades, map 4, grid e5.

Campsites, facilities: There are 33 sites, some with electricity, for tents or trailers up to 35 feet long and one group site for up to 35 people. Picnic tables and fire grills are provided. Drinking water, vault toilets, and a dump station are available. Firewood is available for purchase. Some facilities are wheelchair-accessible. Leashed pets are permitted.

Reservations, fees: Reserve at 877/444-6777 ($8.65 reservation fee) or website:

www.ReserveUsa.com. Sites are $12 to $16 per night, $6 per extra vehicle per night. The group site is $75 per night. Senior discount available. Open late May to early October, weather permitting.

Directions: In Seattle on I-5, turn east on I-90. Drive east on I-90 to Exit 47. Take that exit, cross the freeway, and at the T intersection turn right and drive one quarter-mile to Denny Creek Road (Forest Road 58). Turn left on Denny Creek Road and drive two miles to the campground on the left.

Contact: Mt. Baker-Snoqualmie National Forest, Snoqualmie Ranger District, North Bend office, 42404 SE North Bend Way, North Bend, WA 98045; 425/888-1421, fax 425/888-1910.

96 Crystal Springs

   5

This campground is just off I-90, and if you think that means lots of highway noise, well, you are correct. This camp is worth knowing as an overflow campground from the more desirable Kachess Campground. It is set at 2,400 feet, featuring the Yakima River and some old-growth trees. It's a short drive to Kachess and Keechelus Lakes. Both lakes have boat ramps. The Pacific West Ski Area is at the north end of Keechelus Lake.

Location: On Yakima River in Wenatchee National Forest; see the Northern Cascades, map 4, grid f6.

Campsites, facilities: There are 22 sites, including some drive-through sites, and two double sites for tents, trailers, or RVs up to 21 feet long. Picnic tables and fire grills are provided. Drinking water, vault toilets, and firewood are available. Leashed pets are permitted.

Reservations, fees: No reservations. Sites are $12 to $24 per night, $10 per extra vehicle

per night. Senior discount available. Open mid-May to mid-September.

Directions: In Seattle on I-5, turn east on I-90. Drive east on I-90 for 60 miles to Exit 62. Take that exit and turn right (south) on Forest Road 54, and drive one-half mile to the campground on the right.

Contact: Okanogan and Wenatchee National Forests, Cle Elum Ranger District, West Second Street, Cle Elum, WA 98922; 509/674-4411, fax 509/674-1530.

97 Kachess & Kachess Group

     8

This is the only campground on the shore of Kachess Lake, but note that the water level can drop significantly in summer during low-rain years. It is the most popular campground in the local area, often filling in July and August, especially on weekends. Recreation opportunities include water-skiing, fishing, hiking, and bicycling. A trail from camp heads north into the Alpine Lakes Wilderness; see a U.S. Forest Service map for details. The elevation is 2,300 feet.

Location: On Kachess Lake in Wenatchee National Forest; see the Northern Cascades, map 4, grid e7.

Campsites, facilities: There are 120 sites, including 30 double sites, for tents, trailers, or RVs up to 32 feet long. A group site is also available. Picnic tables and fire grills are provided. Drinking water and vault toilets are available. Restrooms and dump stations are located at Kachess Lake. Some facilities are wheelchair-accessible. Leashed pets are permitted but aren't allowed in swimming areas.

Reservations, fees: Some sites can be reserved; Reserve at 877/444-6777 ($8.65 reservation fee) or website: www .ReserveUsa.com. Sites are $13 to $26 per night, $10 per extra vehicle per night. The group fee is $80 per night. Senior discount available. Open late May to mid-September.

Directions: In Seattle on I-5, turn east on I-90. Drive east on I-90 for 59 miles to Exit 62. Take that exit to Forest Road 49 and turn northeast; drive 5.5 miles to the campground on the right at the end of the paved road.

Contact: Okanogan and Wenatchee National Forests, Cle Elum Ranger District, West Second Street, Cle Elum, WA 98922; 509/674-4411, fax 509/674-1530.

98 Lake Easton State Park

 8

This campground offers many recreational opportunities. For starters, it's set along the shore of Lake Easton on the Yakima River in the Cascade foothills. The landscape features old-growth forest, dense vegetation, and freshwater marshes, with the park covering 516 acres of the best of it. Two miles of trails for hiking and biking are available. The park provides opportunities for both summer and winter recreation, including swimming, fishing, boating, cross-country skiing, and snowmobiling. Note that high-speed boating is not recommended because Lake Easton is a shallow reservoir with stumps often hidden just below the water surface. Nearby recreation options include an 18-hole golf course and hiking trails. Kachess Lake and Keechelus Lake are just a short drive away.

Location: On Lake Easton; see the Northern Cascades, map 4, grid f7.

Campsites, facilities: There are 92 developed tent sites and 45 sites with hookups for trailers or RVs up to 60 feet long, and two primitive tent sites. Picnic tables and fire grills are provided. Restrooms, drinking water, flush toilets, showers, a dump station, an amphitheater, a playground with basketball and horseshoe pits, and firewood are available. A café and ice are located within one mile. Some facilities are wheelchair-accessible. Boat-launching facilities and floats are located on Lake Easton. Leashed pets are permitted.

Reservations, fees: Reserve at 888/CAMP-OUT (888/226-7688); website: www.parks.wa.gov/reservations ($7 reservation fee). Sites are $6 to $22 per night, $6 per extra vehicle per night. Senior discount available. Major credit cards accepted. Open May through mid-October, with limited winter facilities.

Directions: From Seattle, drive east on I-90 for 68 miles to Exit 70, and the park entrance on the right (it is located one mile west of the town of Easton).

Contact: Lake Easton State Park, P.O. Box 26, Easton, WA 98925; 360/902-8844 or 509/656-2586.

99 Cayuse Horse Camp

 6

This camp is for horse campers only. It's located along the Cle Elum River at major trailheads for horses and hikers and marked trails for bikers. The elevation is 2,400 feet. See Salmon La Sac Campground for further information.

Location: On the Cle Elum River in Wenatchee National Forest; see the Northern Cascades, map 4, grid g8.

Campsites, facilities: There are 13 sites, including three double sites, for tents, trailers, or RVs with some sites 25 feet and some up to 40 feet long. Picnic tables and fire pits are provided. Drinking water and vault toilets are available. Stock facilities include corrals, troughs, and hitching posts. Bring your own stock feed. Leashed pets are permitted.

Reservations, fees: Some sites are available by reservation. Reserve at 877/444-6777 ($8.65 reservation fee) or website: www.reserveusa.com. Sites are $12 per night, $10 per night for each additional vehicle. Senior discount available. Open from mid-May to mid-September, depending on weather.

Directions: In Seattle on I-5, turn east on I-90. Drive east on I-90 for 78 miles to Exit 80 (two miles before Cle Elum). Take that exit and turn north on Bullfrog Road; drive four miles to Highway 903. Continue north on Highway 903 for 18 miles to the campground on the right.

Contact: Okanogan and Wenatchee National Forests, Cle Elum Ranger District, West Second Street, Cle Elum, WA 98922; 509/674-4411, fax 509/674-1530.

100 Wish Poosh

 7

This is a popular camp on the shore of Cle Elum Lake. It fills up on summer weekends and holidays. It is great during midweek, when many sites are usually available. While the lake is near the camp, note that the lake level can be drawn down significantly in low-rainfall years. Water-skiing, sailing, fishing, and swimming are among recreation possibilities. The camp is set an elevation of 2,400 feet.

Location: On Cle Elum Lake in Wenatchee National Forest; see the Northern Cascades, map 4, grid f8.

Campsites, facilities: There are 34 sites, including five double sites, for tents, trailers, or RVs up to 21 feet long. Picnic tables and fire grills are provided. Restrooms, drinking water, flush toilets, showers, and firewood are available. Boat-launching facilities are located on Cle Elum Lake. Restaurant and ice are available nearby. Leashed pets are permitted.

Reservations, fees: No reservations. Sites are $12 to $24 per night, $10 per extra vehicle per night. Senior discount available. Open mid-May to mid-September.

Directions: In Seattle on I-5, turn east on I-90. Drive east on I-90 for 78 miles to Exit 80 (two miles before Cle Elum). Take that exit, turn north on Bullfrog Road, and drive four miles to Highway 903. Continue north on Highway 903 for nine miles to the campground on the left.

Contact: Okanogan and Wenatchee National Forests, Cle Elum Ranger District, West Second Street, Cle Elum, WA 98922; 509/674-4411, fax 509/674-1530.

101 Cle Elum River & Cle Elum Group

 6

The gravel roads in the campground make this setting a bit more rustic than nearby Salmon La Sac. It services as a valuable overflow campground for Salmon La Sac and is similar in setting and opportunities. The group site fills most summer weekends. A trailhead is nearby for access into the Alpine Lakes Wilderness.

Location: On the Cle Elum River in Wenatchee National Forest; see the Northern Cascades, map 4, grid f8.

Campsites, facilities: There are 23 sites, including some pull-through, for tents, trailers, or RVs up to 21 feet long, and a group site for up to 100 people. Picnic tables and fire grills are provided. Drinking water and vault toilets are available. Leashed pets are permitted.

Reservations, fees: No reservations for family sites. Reservation required for group site: 877/444-6777 ($8.65 reservation fee) or website: www.ReserveUsa.com. Sites are $10 per night, $8 per extra vehicle per night.

Group site is $100 per night. Senior discount available. Open late May to mid-September.
Directions: In Seattle on I-5, turn east on I-90. Drive east on I-90 for 78 miles to Exit 80 (two miles before Cle Elum). Take that exit, turn north on Bullfrog Road, and drive four miles to Highway 903. Continue north on Highway 903 for 17 miles to the campground on the left.
Contact: Okanogan and Wenatchee National Forests, Cle Elum Ranger District, West Second Street, Cle Elum, WA 98922; 509/674-4411, fax 509/674-1530.

 Red Mountain
6

This alternative to nearby Wish Poosh has two big differences: there is no drinking water, and it's not on Cle Elum Lake. The camp is along the Cle Elum River one mile from the lake, just above where the river feeds into it. The elevation is 2,200 feet.
Location: On the Cle Elum River in Wenatchee National Forest; see the Northern Cascades, map 4, grid f8.
Campsites, facilities: There are 10 sites for tents and small RVs. Picnic tables and fire grills are provided. Pit toilets and firewood are available, but there is no drinking water. Leashed pets are permitted.
Reservations, fees: No reservations. Sites are $7 per vehicle per night, with a two-vehicle maximum. Senior discount available. Open mid-May to late November.
Directions: In Seattle on I-5, turn east on I-90. Drive east on I-90 for 78 miles to Exit 80 (two miles before Cle Elum). Take that exit and turn north on Bullfrog Road; drive four miles to Highway 903. Continue north on Highway 903 for 19 miles to the campground on the left.
Contact: Okanogan and Wenatchee National Forests, Cle Elum Ranger District, West

Second Street, Cle Elum, WA 98922; 509/674-4411, fax 509/674-1530.

Salmon La Sac
 6

This is a base camp for backpackers and day hikers, and is also popular with kayakers. It's located along the Cle Elum River at 2,400 feet, about one quarter-mile from a major trailhead, the Salmon La Sac Trailhead. Hikers can follow creeks heading off in several directions, including into the Alpine Lakes Wilderness. A campground host is available for information.
Location: On the Cle Elum River in Wenatchee National Forest; see the Northern Cascades, map 4, grid e8.
Campsites, facilities: There are 99 sites, including 12 double sites, for tents, trailers, or RVs up to 21 feet long. Picnic tables and fire grills are provided. Drinking water and vault toilets are available. Leashed pets are permitted.
Reservations, fees: Some sites can be reserved: 877/444-6777 ($8.65 reservation fee) or website: www.ReserveUsa.com. Sites are $13 to $26 per night, $10 per extra vehicle per night. Senior discount available. Open late May to mid-September.
Directions: In Seattle on I-5, turn east on I-90. Drive east on I-90 for 78 miles to Exit 80 (two miles before Cle Elum). Take that exit, turn north on Bullfrog Road, and drive four miles to Highway 903. Continue north on Highway 903 for 21 miles to the campground on the left.
Contact: Okanogan and Wenatchee National Forests, Cle Elum Ranger District, West Second Street, Cle Elum, WA 98922; 509/674-4411, fax 509/674-1530.

104 Owhi Walk-In

 9

This spot has everything you need for a drive-to wilderness experience. Well, everything but drinking water. It's located on the shore of Cooper Lake, near the boundary of the Alpine Lakes Wilderness. The campsites require a walk of 100 to 300 feet. Some sites have lake views, whereas others have lots of vegetation and provide privacy. Another highlight are old-growth Douglas fir and western hemlock. A nearby trailhead provides access to several lakes in the wilderness and extends to the Pacific Crest Trail; see a U.S. Forest Service map for details. Fishing, swimming, and canoeing are all popular at Cooper Lake. No motors, including electric motors, are permitted at the lake, making it ideal for canoes, float tubes, and prams. The campground is minimally developed. The elevation is 2,800 feet.

Location: On Cooper Lake in Wenatchee National Forest; see the Northern Cascades, map 4, grid e7.

Campsites, facilities: There are 21 walk-in tent sites. Picnic tables and fire grills are provided. Vault toilets are available, but there is no drinking water. Primitive boat-launching facilities are nearby. Leashed pets are permitted.

Reservations, fees: No reservations. Sites are $7 per vehicle per night, with a two-vehicle maximum. Senior discount available. Open mid-June to late September.

Directions: In Seattle on I-5, turn east on I-90. Drive east on I-90 for 78 miles to Exit 80 (two miles before Cle Elum). Turn north on Bullfrog Road and drive four miles to Highway 903. Turn left (north) on Highway 903 and drive 19 miles to Forest Road 46. Turn left (west) on Forest Road 46 and drive five miles to Forest Road 4616 (pavement ends).

Turn right and drive less than one-half mile to the campground. Campsites are located 100 to 300 feet from the parking lot.

Contact: Okanogan and Wenatchee National Forests, Cle Elum Ranger District, West Second Street, Cle Elum, WA 98922; 509/674-4411, fax 509/674-1530.

105 Fish Lake Walk-In

 10

This campground is way out there and just a short jaunt to the Alpine Lakes Wilderness. The camp is nestled along the shore of tiny Tucquala Lake, a jewel near the headwaters of the Cle Elum River. Fishing is available for trout. The campsites require a 100- to 300-foot walk. The elevation is 3,400 feet. There are numerous opportunities to access trails into the backcountry.

Location: On Tucquala Lake in Wenatchee National Forest; see the Northern Cascades, map 4, grid d8.

Campsites, facilities: There are five tent sites. Picnic tables and fire grills are provided. Vault toilets are available, but there is no drinking water. Garbage must be packed out. Leashed pets are permitted.

Reservations, fees: No reservations; no fee. Open July through September.

Directions: In Seattle on I-5, turn east on I-90 and drive 78 miles to Exit 80 (two miles before Cle Elum). Take Exit 80 and turn north on Bullfrog Road; drive four miles to Highway 903. Continue north on Highway 903 for 19 miles to Forest Road 4330. Bear right and drive 11 miles to the campground entrance on the right. Park and walk 100 to 300 feet to the sites. The access road is rough; no trailers are permitted.

Contact: Wenatchee National Forest, Cle Elum Ranger District, West Second Street, Cle Elum, WA 98922; 509/674-4411, fax 509/674-1530.

106 Kanaskat-Palmer State Park

 8

This wooded campground offers private campsites along the Green River. This park covers 320 acres with two miles of river frontage. It is set on a small, low plateau in a forest setting. In summer, the river is ideal for expert-level rafting and kayaking. This park is used as a put-in spot for the rafting run down the Green River Gorge. This area has much mining history and coal mining continues, as well as cinnabar mining (the base ore for mercury). Nearby Flaming Geyser gets its name from a coal seam. In winter, the river attracts a run of steelhead. The park has three miles of hiking trails.

Location: On the Green River; see the Northern Cascades, map 4, grid f1.

Campsites, facilities: There are 31 tent sites and 19 drive-through sites with partial hookups (electricity) for trailers or RVs up to 50 feet long. Picnic tables are provided. Restrooms, drinking water, flush toilets, showers, a sheltered picnic area, horseshoe pits, and a dump station are available. Some facilities are wheelchair-accessible. Boat rentals can be found nearby on the Green River. Leashed pets are permitted.

Reservations, fees: Reserve at 888/CAMP-OUT (888/226-7688); website: www.parks .wa.gov/reservations ($7 reservation fee). Sites are $15 to $22 per night, $6 per extra vehicle per night. Senior discount available. Major credit cards accepted. Open year-round, with limited facilities in the winter.

Directions: From Puyallup at the junction of Highway 167 and Highway 410, turn southeast on Highway 410 and drive 25 miles to Enumclaw and Farman Road. Turn northeast on Farman Road and drive nine miles to the park on the left.

Contact: Kanaskat-Palmer State Park, 360/886-0148; State Park information, 360/902-8844.

107 Dalles

 10

This campground is along the confluence of Minnehaha Creek and the White River. *Dalles* means "rapids." A nature trail is nearby, and the White River entrance to Mt. Rainier National Park is about 14 miles south on Highway 410. The camp sits amid a grove of old-growth trees; a particular point of interest is a huge old Douglas fir that is 9.5 feet in diameter and more than 235 feet tall. This is one of the prettiest camps in the area. It gets moderate use in summer.

Location: In Mt. Baker-Snoqualmie National Forest; see the Northern Cascades, map 4, grid h7.

Campsites, facilities: There are 44 sites for tents, trailers, or RVs up to 21 feet long. Picnic tables and fire grills are provided. Vault toilets, drinking water, and firewood are available. There is a large shaded picnic area for day use. Leashed pets are permitted.

Reservations, fees: Reservations accepted for some sites; phone 877/444-6777 or access the website: www.reserveusa.com ($8.65 reservation fee). Sites are $12 per night, $6 per extra vehicle per night. Senior discount available. Open mid-May to late September.

Directions: From Enumclaw, drive east on Highway 410 for 25.5 miles to the campground (three miles inside the forest boundary) on the right.

Contact: Mt. Baker-Snoqualmie National Forest, White River Ranger District, 450 Roosevelt Avenue East, Enumclaw, WA 98022; 360/825-6585, fax 360/825-0660.

108 Corral Pass

 10

This is the most remote of the campgrounds in the area. Set at 5,600 feet, it's primitive, quiet, and an ideal base camp for a hiking trip. Groups of horse-packers heading into the adjacent Norse Peak Wilderness frequent the camp. The best trip is the two-mile backpack up to Hidden Lake and then along a river canyon for four miles to Echo Lake. Several trails nearby lead to backcountry fishing lakes and streams. See a U.S. Forest Service map for details. In late summer and fall, visitors can find wild berries in the area.

Location: In Mt. Baker-Snoqualmie National Forest; see the Northern Cascades, map 4, grid h5.

Campsites, facilities: There are 20 tent sites. Picnic tables and fire grills are provided. Vault toilets and a horse-loading ramp are available, but there is no drinking water. Garbage must be packed out. Downed firewood can be gathered. Leashed pets are permitted.

Reservations, fees: No reservations; Northwest Forest Pass ($30 annual fee) or $5 daily fee per parked vehicle is required. Open July to late September.

Directions: From Enumclaw, drive east on Highway 410 for 30 miles to Forest Road 7174 (near Silver Springs Camp). Turn east (left) and drive six miles to the camp on the right. It's a curvy dirt road that is not suitable for trailers or RVs.

Contact: Mt. Baker-Snoqualmie National Forest, White River Ranger District, 450 Roosevelt Avenue East, Enumclaw, WA 98022; 360/825-6585, fax 360/825-0660.

109 Crow Creek

 5

This campground on the Little Naches River is popular with off-road bikers and four-

wheel-drive cowboys, similar to the following camp, Kaner Flat, except that there is no drinking water. It is set at 2,900 feet. A trail heading out from the camp leads into the backcountry and then forks in several directions. One route leads to the American River, another follows West Quartz Creek, and another goes along Fife's Ridge into the Norse Peak Wilderness (where no motorized vehicles are permitted). See a U.S. Forest Service map for details. There is good seasonal hunting and fishing in this area.

Location: On the Little Naches River in Wenatchee National Forest; see the Northern Cascades, map 4, grid h7.

Campsites, facilities: There are 15 sites for tents, trailers, or RVs up to 30 feet long. Picnic tables and fire grills are provided. Vault toilets are available, but there is no drinking water. Downed firewood may be gathered. Leashed pets are permitted.

Reservations, fees: No reservations accepted. Sites are $7 per night, $5 per extra vehicle per night. Senior discount available. Open mid-April to late November.

Directions: From Yakima, drive northwest on U.S. 12 for 18 miles to Highway 410. Bear northwest on Highway 410 and drive 24.5 miles to Forest Road 1900. Turn northwest and drive 2.5 miles to Forest Road 1902. Turn west and drive one-half mile to the campground on the right.

Contact: Okanogan and Wenatchee National Forests, Naches Ranger District, 10061 U.S. Highway 12, Naches, WA 98937; 509/653-2205, fax 509/653-2638.

110 Kaner Flat

 7

This campground is set near the Little Naches River, at an elevation of 2,678 feet. It is located at the site of a wagon-train camp on the Old Naches Trail, a route used in the

1800s by wagon trains, Native Americans, and the U.S. Cavalry on their way to West side markets. The Naches Trail is now used by motorcyclists and narrow-clearance four-wheel-drive enthusiasts. This camp is popular among them, similar to Crow Creek campground. This camp is larger, so it handles more multiple user groups.

Location: Near the Little Naches River in Wenatchee National Forest; see the Northern Cascades, map 4, grid h7.

Campsites, facilities: There are 41 sites for tents, trailers, or RVs up to 30 feet long, including two wheelchair-accessible sites. Picnic tables and fire grills are provided. Drinking water and vault toilets are available. Some facilities are wheelchair-accessible. Leashed pets are permitted.

Reservations, fees: No reservations accepted. Sites are $9 per night, $5 for each additional vehicle. Senior discount available. Open mid-May to late November.

Directions: From Yakima, drive northwest on U.S. 12 for 18 miles to Highway 410. Bear northwest on Highway 410 and drive 25 miles to Forest Road 1900. Turn northwest and drive 2.5 miles to the campground on the right.

Contact: Okanogan and Wenatchee National Forests, Naches Ranger District, 10061 U.S. Highway 12, Naches, WA 98937; 509/653-2205, fax 509/653-2638.

111 White River Falls

 9

Although very primitive, this quiet and beautiful campground is a perfect spot for those seeking solitude in the wilderness. It's next to White River Falls on the White River and close to a major trailhead that connects to a network of hiking trails into the Glacier Peak Wilderness. There is no viewing platform or fence at White River Falls, and viewing can be dangerous. People have slipped here and fallen to their deaths. There is no trailer turnaround at the camp. The elevation is 2,100 feet.

Location: On the White River in Wenatchee National Forest; see the Northern Cascades, map 5, grid a1.

Campsites, facilities: There are five tent sites. Picnic tables and fire grills are provided. Pit toilets are available, but there is no drinking water. Garbage must be packed out. Leashed pets are permitted.

Reservations, fees: No reservations; no fee. Open June to mid-October.

Directions: From Leavenworth, drive west on U.S. 2 for 14 miles to Coles Corner and State Route 207. Turn north and drive 10 miles to Forest Road 6400 (White River Road). Turn right and drive 9.9 miles to the campground on the left.

Contact: Okanogan and Wenatchee National Forests, Lake Wenatchee and Leavenworth Ranger District, Lake Wenatchee Office, 22976 State Route 207, Leavenworth, WA 98826; 509/763-3103, fax 509/763-3211.

112 Napeequa Crossing

 8

A trail across the road from this camp on the White River heads east for about 3.5 miles to Twin Lakes in the Glacier Peak Wilderness. It's definitely worth the hike, with scenic views and wildlife observation as your reward. But note that Twin Lakes is closed to fishing. Sightings of osprey, bald eagles, and golden eagles can brighten the trip. This is also an excellent spot for fall colors.

Location: On the White and Napequa Rivers in Wenatchee National Forest; see the Northern Cascades, map 5, grid a1.

Campsites, facilities: There are five sites for tents, trailers, or RVs up to 30 feet long. Picnic tables and fire grills are provided.

Pit toilets are available, but there is no drinking water. Garbage must be packed out. Leashed pets are permitted.

Reservations, fees: No reservations; no fee. Open year-round, weather and snow level permitting.

Directions: From Leavenworth, drive west on U.S. 2 for 14 miles to Coles Corner and State Route 207. Turn north and drive 10 miles to Forest Road 6400 (White River Road). Turn right and drive 5.9 miles to the campground on the left.

Contact: Okanogan and Wenatchee National Forests, Lake Wenatchee and Leavenworth Ranger District, Lake Wenatchee Office, 22976 State Route 207, Leavenworth, WA 98826; 509/763-3103, fax 509/763-3211.

Chiwawa Horse Camp

  8

This camp is not designated solely for horse campers, as many horse camps are. It is rather for all users, but features many facilities for horseback riding. It is seldom full, but is popular among equestrians. Two short trails that are specifically designed for physically challenged visitors lead around the campground, covering about a mile. A trailhead at the camp also provides access to a network of backcountry trails. The elevation is 2,000 feet.

Location: In Wenatchee National Forest; see the Northern Cascades, map 5, grid a2.

Campsites, facilities: There are 21 sites, including seven drive-through sites, for tents, trailers, or RVs up to 30 feet long. Picnic tables and fire grills are provided. Drinking water and vault toilets are available. Garbage must be packed out. Horse facilities include mounting ramps, high lines, water troughs, and a loading ramp. Some fa-

cilities are wheelchair-accessible. Leashed pets are permitted.

Reservations, fees: Northwest Forest Pass ($30 annual fee) or $5 daily fee per parked vehicle is required. Open year-round, weather and snow level permitting.

Directions: From Seattle, drive north on I-5 to Everett and U.S. 2. Turn east on U.S. 2 and drive 87 miles to State Route 207, one mile west of Winton. Turn north on State Route 207 and drive 4.5 miles to Chiwawa Loop Road. Turn right and drive two miles to Chiwawa Valley Road/Forest Road 6200. Turn left and drive 15 miles to the campground on the right.

Contact: Okanogan and Wenatchee National Forests, Lake Wenatchee and Leavenworth Ranger District, Lake Wenatchee Office, 22976 State Route 207, Leavenworth, WA 98826; 509/763-3103, fax 509/763-3211.

Cottonwood

  8

Cottonwood Camp is set along the Entiat River, adjacent to a major trailhead leading into the Glacier Peak Wilderness. Note that dirt bikes are allowed on four miles of trail, the Entiat River Trail, to Myrtle Lake, but no motorcycles or mountain bikes are allowed inside the boundary of the Glacier Peak Wilderness; violators will be prosecuted by backcountry rangers. In other words, cool your jets. Let backpackers have some peace and quiet. A U.S. Forest Service map details the backcountry. A bonus near the camp is good berry picking in season. Trout fishing is another alternative. The camp is set at an elevation of 3,100 feet.

Location: On the Entiat River in Wenatchee National Forest; see the Northern Cascades, map 5, grid a4.

Campsites, facilities: There are 25 sites for tents or small RVs. Picnic tables and fire grills are provided. Drinking water and vault toilets are available. Some facilities are wheelchair-accessible. A campground host is available in summer. Leashed pets are permitted.

Reservations, fees: No reservations accepted. Sites are $8 per vehicle per night. Senior discount available. Open June to mid-October.

Directions: From Seattle, drive north on I-5 to Everett and U.S. 2. Turn east on U.S. 2 and drive 120 miles to U.S. 97-A. Turn north on U.S. 97-A and drive 18.5 miles to Entiat River Road. Turn left (northwest) and drive 38 miles to the campground on the left.

Contact: Okanogan and Wenatchee National Forests, Entiat Ranger District, P.O. Box 476, Entiat, WA 98822; 509/784-1511.

115 North Fork

 8

This is one of seven campgrounds nestled along the Entiat River. North Fork is located near the confluence of the Entiat and the North Fork of the Entiat River. Highlights of this pretty, shaded camp include river fishing access and Entiat Falls, which are located about one-half mile downstream. Note: No fishing is permitted in the vicinity of Entiat Falls to protect the bull trout; check regulations. The elevation is 2,500 feet.

Location: On the Entiat River in Wenatchee National Forest; see the Northern Cascades, map 5, grid a4.

Campsites, facilities: There are eight tent sites and one site for a small RV. Picnic tables and fire grills are provided. Drinking water and pit toilets are available. Leashed pets are permitted.

Reservations, fees: No reservations. Sites are $7 per vehicle per night. Senior discount available. Open June to mid-October.

Directions: From Seattle, drive north on I-5 to Everett and U.S. 2. Turn east on U.S. 2 and drive 120 miles to U.S. 97-A. Turn north on U.S. 97-A and drive 18.5 miles to Entiat River Road. Turn northwest and drive 33 miles to the campground on the left.

Contact: Okanogan and Wenatchee National Forests, Entiat Ranger District, P.O. Box 476, Entiat, WA 98822; 509/784-1511.

116 Silver Falls

 10

This campground is set in an enchanted spot at the confluence of Silver Creek and the Entiat River. A trail from camp leads one-half mile to the base of beautiful Silver Falls. This trail continues in a loop trail for another mile past the falls, parallel to the river. Fishing is available above Entiat Falls, located two to three miles upriver from Silver Falls. The elevation at the camp is 2,400 feet.

Location: On the Entiat River in Wenatchee National Forest; see the Northern Cascades, map 5, grid a4.

Campsites, facilities: There are 30 sites for tents, trailers, or RVs up to 21 feet long, plus one group site for 30 to 50 people. Picnic tables and fire grills are provided. Drinking water and vault toilets are available. A camp host is available in summer. Some facilities are wheelchair-accessible. Leashed pets are permitted.

Reservations, fees: Reservations required for groups only. Family sites are $9 per vehicle per night; the group site is $60 a night. Senior discount available. Open mid-May to mid-October.

Directions: From Seattle, drive north on I-5 to Everett and U.S. 2. Turn east on U.S. 2 and drive 120 miles to U.S. 97-A. Turn north on U.S. 97-A and drive 18.5 miles to Entiat River Road. Turn left (northwest) and drive 30 miles to the campground on the left.

Contact: Okanogan and Wenatchee National Forests, Entiat Ranger District, P.O. Box 476, Entiat, WA 98822; 509/784-1511.

117 Lake Creek/Entiat

    7

This camp is located at the confluence of Lake Creek and the Entiat River, at a trail crossroads. It ties into the Mad Lake Trail System, where all-purpose trails are available for hiking and mountain biking. Another trail ties into a loop system that features the Devils Backbone to Ramona Park. There is also linkage available to a network of trails in the Lake Creek Basin in the Chelan Mountains, and several others head south and west into the Entiat Mountains. Consult a U.S. Forest Service map for more details on backcountry routes. No fishing is available in the vicinity of Entiat Falls. Note that there is another Lake Creek Camp in the Lake Wenatchee and Leavenworth Ranger District.

Location: On the Entiat River in Wenatchee National Forest; see the Northern Cascades, map 5, grid a4.

Campsites, facilities: There are 18 tent sites. Picnic tables and fire grills are provided. Drinking water and composting toilets are available. Some facilities are wheelchair-accessible. Leashed pets are permitted.

Reservations, fees: No reservations. Sites are $8 per night per vehicle. Senior discount available. Open May to mid-October.

Directions: From Seattle, drive north on I-5 to Everett and U.S. 2. Turn east on U.S. 2 and drive 120 miles to U.S. 97-A. Turn north on U.S. 97-A and drive 18.5 miles to Entiat River

Road. Turn northwest and drive 28 miles to the campground on the left.

Contact: Okanogan and Wenatchee National Forests, Entiat Ranger District, P.O. Box 476, Entiat, WA 98822; 509/784-1511.

118 Fox Creek

   7

This camp is located along the Entiat River near Fox Creek. Fishing is prohibited in the vicinity of Entiat Falls; check regulations. This camp features several campsites that are closer to the river than nearby Lake Creek Campground and is the more popular of the two. The elevation is 2,100 feet. Contact the U.S. Forest Service for details.

Location: On the Entiat River in Wenatchee National Forest; see the Northern Cascades, map 5, grid a5.

Campsites, facilities: There are 16 tent sites. Picnic tables and fire grills are provided. Drinking water and composting toilets are available. Leashed pets are permitted.

Reservations, fees: No reservations. Sites are $8 per night per vehicle. Senior discount available. Open May to mid-October.

Directions: From Seattle, drive north on I-5 to Everett and U.S. 2. Turn east on U.S. 2 and drive 120 miles to U.S. 97-A. Turn north on U.S. 97-A and drive 18.5 miles to Entiat River Road. Turn northwest and drive 27 miles to the campground on the left.

Contact: Okanogan and Wenatchee National Forests, Entiat Ranger District, P.O. Box 476, Entiat, WA 98822; 509/784-1511.

119 Snowberry Bowl

   7

Snowberry Bowl is set less than four miles from Twenty-Five Mile Creek State Park and Lake Chelan. The elevation is 2,000 feet, nestled amid a forest of Douglas fir and Ponderosa

pine, which provide privacy screening. The camp is most often used as an overflow camp when the state park fills up. It opened in 2001 and is not well known. Drinking water is available starting summer 2002.

Location: Near Lake Chelan in Wenatchee National Forest; see the Northern Cascades, map 5, grid a6.

Campsites, facilities: There are seven sites for tents, trailers, or RVs up to 40 feet long and two double sites for up to 15 people each. Picnic tables, fire grills, and tent pads on sand are provided. Drinking water and vault toilets are available. Some facilities are wheelchair-accessible. Leashed pets are permitted.

Reservations, fees: No reservations. Sites are $9 per night, $18 for double sites. Senior discount available. Open year-round, with limited winter facilities.

Directions: From Chelan, drive south on Highway 97A for three miles to South Lakeshore Road. Turn right and 13.5 miles (passing the state park) to Shady Pass Road. Turn left and drive 2.5 miles to a Y intersection with Slide Ridge Road. Bear left and drive 0.5 mile to the campground on the right.

Contact: Okanogan and Wenatchee National Forests, Chelan Ranger District, 428 West Woodin Avenue, Chelan, WA 98816; 509/682-2576, fax 509/682-9004.

120 Twenty-Five Mile Creek State Park

 8

This campground is located on Twenty-Five Mile Creek near where it empties into Lake Chelan. This park is a 235-acre marine camping park on the forested south shore of Lake Chelan. The park separates the mountain from the lake and is surrounded by spectacular scenery, featuring a rocky terrain with forested areas. The park is known for its

boat access. Exploration of the uplake wilderness portions of Lake Chelan is possible by using this park as your launching point. Fishing access for trout and salmon is close by. Fishing supplies, a dock, a modern marina, and boat moorage are available. There is also a small wading area for kids. Forest Road 5900, which heads west from the park, accesses several trailheads leading into the U.S. Forest Service lands of the Chelan Mountains. Obtain a U.S. Forest Service map of Wenatchee National Forest for details. Note that a ferry can take visitors to a roadless community at the head of the lake.

Location: Near Lake Chelan; see the Northern Cascades, map 5, grid a6.

Campsites, facilities: There are 53 sites for tents and 21 sites with full or partial hookups for trailers or RVs up to 30 feet long. Picnic tables and fire grills are provided. Drinking water and vault toilets are available. A dump station, firewood for sale, a boat dock, a fishing pier, a marina, a boat ramp, boat moorage, a picnic area, gasoline, and a grocery store are available nearby.

Reservations, fees: Reserve at 888/CAMP-OUT (888/226-7688); website: www.parks .wa.gov/reservations ($7 reservation fee). Sites are $15 to $22 per night. Senior discount available. Major credit cards accepted. Open April to October.

Directions: From Chelan, drive south on Highway 97A for three miles to South Lakeshore Road. Turn right and drive 15 miles to the park on the right.

Contact: Twenty-Five Mile Creek State Park, Route 1, P.O. Box 142A, Chelan, WA 98816; 509/687-3710; State Park information, 360/902-8844. Lake Chelan Boat Company, 509/682-2224; website: www.ladyofthelake.com.

121 Kamei Campground & RV Park

 6

This resort is on Lake Wapato, about two miles from Lake Chelan. Note that this is a seasonal lake that closes midsummer. If you have an extra day, take the ferryboat ride on Lake Chelan.

Location: On Lake Wapato; see the Northern Cascades, map 5, grid a7.

Campsites, facilities: There are 50 sites, some with partial hookups, for tents, trailers, or RVs of any length. Picnic tables are provided. Restrooms, drinking water, flush toilets, showers, and ice are available. Boat docks, launching facilities, and rentals are nearby. Leashed pets are permitted.

Reservations, fees: Reservations accepted beginning in January. Call for reservation and site fees. Open late April through July.

Directions: From Chelan, drive west on Highway 150 for seven miles to Wapato Lake Road. Turn north on Wapato Lake Road and drive three miles to the resort on Wapato Lake Road.

Contact: Kamei Resort, Wapato Lake Road Route 1, Manson, WA 98831; 509/687-3690.

122 Mitchell Creek Boat-In

 8

This is one of 13 national forest campgrounds set on Lake Chelan. It can be reached only by boat, although with advance notice it can be possible to arrange a ferry ride to this campsite; it is not a scheduled stop.

Location: On Lake Chelan in Wenatchee National Forest; see the Northern Cascades, map 5, grid a7.

Campsites, facilities: There are six tent sites accessible only by boat, ferry, or float plane. Picnic tables and fire rings are provided. Pit toilets and a group shelter are

available, but there is no drinking water. Garbage must be packed out. An on-site floating dock has a 17-boat capacity.

Reservations, fees: No reservations, no camping fee; $5 per-day docking fee. Open May to late October.

Directions: From Wenatchee, drive north on U.S. 97-A for 40 miles to the town of Chelan. Take the ferry to Mitchell Creek, 15 miles from Chelan. Note that the ferry will not stop here if the water level does not allow for safe landing. The campground is also directly accessible by float plane. (Call Chelan Airways at 509/682-5555 for more information.)

Contact: Okanogan and Wenatchee National Forests, Chelan Ranger District, 428 West Woodin Avenue, Chelan, WA 98816; 509/682-2576, fax 509/682-9004. Lake Chelan Boat Company, 509/682-2224; website: www.lady-ofthelake.com.

123 Lake Chelan State Park

 10

This is the recreation headquarters for Lake Chelan. The park provides boat docks and concession stands on the shore of the 55-mile lake. The parks covers 127 acres, featuring 6,000 feet of shoreline on the forested south shore. Summers tend to be hot and dry, but expansive lawns provide a fresh feel, especially in the early evenings, looking out on the lake. A daily ferry service provides access to the roadless community at the head of the lake. The word *chelan* is Native American and translates to both "lake" and "blue water." See the descriptions of Holden Ballpark, Domke Lake, Lucerne, Deer Point, Graham Harbor, and Prince Creek for some of the recreation options available. Water sports include fishing, swimming, scuba diving, and water-skiing.

Location: On Lake Chelan; see the Northern Cascades, map 5, grid b7.

Campsites, facilities: There are 109 developed tent sites, 35 sites with full or partial hookups for trailers or RVs up to 30 feet, and two primitive tent sites. Picnic tables and fire grills are provided. Restrooms, drinking water, flush toilets, showers, firewood, a picnic area with kitchen shelter, a dump station, a store, a restaurant, ice, a playground, a beach area, a boat dock, and launching facilities and moorage are available. Some facilities are wheelchair-accessible.

Reservations, fees: Reserve at 888/CAMP-OUT (888/226-7688); website: www.parks.wa.gov/reservations ($7 reservation fee). Sites are $6 to $22 per night, $6 per extra vehicle per night. Major credit cards accepted. Senior discount available. Open mid-March through October.

Directions: From Wenatchee, drive north on U.S. 97-A for 27 miles to State Route 971 (Navarre Coulee Road). Turn left (north) and drive seven miles to the end of the highway at South Lakeshore Road. Turn right, then immediately look for the park entrance to the left.

Contact: Lake Chelan State Park, 509/687-3710; State Park information, 360/902-8844.

124 Soda Springs

  7

This campground is set along Little Wenatchee River Road and is a small, quiet, closer-to-civilization alternative to Tumwater Camp. But note that it is without drinking water and with no trailer turnaround. It's off the beaten path in a pleasant wooded area, at an elevation of 2,000 feet. A small, cold soda spring is located next to the campground. There are some excellent hiking trails nearby.

Location: On the Little Wenatchee River in Wenatchee National Forest; see the Northern Cascades, map 5, grid b1.

Campsites, facilities: There are five tent sites. Picnic tables and fire grills are provided. Pit toilets are available, but there is no drinking water. Garbage must be packed out. Leashed pets are permitted.

Reservations, fees: No reservations; no fee. Open May to late October, weather permitting.

Directions: From Seattle, drive north on I-5 to Everett and U.S. 2. Turn east on U.S. 2 and drive 87 miles to State Route 207. Turn north on State Route 207 and drive 11 miles to Forest Road 6500. Turn left (west) on Forest Road 6500 for seven miles to the campground on the left.

Contact: Okanogan and Wenatchee National Forests, Lake Wenatchee Ranger District, 22976 State Route 207, Leavenworth, WA 98826; 509/763-3103, fax 509/763-3211.

125 Lake Creek/Wenatchee

 6

Fishing for rainbow trout can be good at this camp, which is set in a remote and primitive spot along the Little Wenatchee River. Berry picking is a bonus in late summer. The elevation is 2,300 feet. Note that there is another Lake Creek Camp in the Entiat Ranger District.

Location: On the Little Wenatchee River in Wenatchee National Forest; see the Northern Cascades, map 5, grid b1.

Campsites, facilities: There are eight sites for tents, trailers, or RVs of any length. Picnic tables and fire grills are provided, but there is no drinking water. Pit toilets are available. Garbage must be packed out. Leashed pets are permitted.

Reservations, fees: No reservations; no fee. Open May to late October, weather permitting.

Directions: From Seattle, drive north on I-5 to Everett and U.S. 2. Turn east on U.S. 2 and drive 87 miles to State Route 207. Turn north on State Route 207 and drive 11 miles to Forest Road 6500. Turn left (west) on Forest Road 6500 and drive 9.5 miles to the campground on the left.

Contact: Okanogan and Wenatchee National Forests, Lake Wenatchee and Leavenworth Ranger District, Lake Wenatchee Office, 22976 State Route 207, Leavenworth, WA 98826; 509/763-3103, fax 509/763-3211.

126 Glacier View

  9

This is a popular campground on the southwestern shore of Lake Wenatchee, near the head of the lake. It's a happening spot for boating, swimming, fishing, and windsurfing, and it fills up on summer weekends. Fishing is average. There are also some good hiking trails in the area and a golf course within a 10-minute drive. The camp is set at an elevation of 1,900 feet. Insider's note: The walk-in sites are set on the lake's shore, requiring a walk of about 100 feet.

Location: On Lake Wenatchee in Wenatchee National Forest; see the Northern Cascades, map 5, grid b2.

Campsites, facilities: There are 23 sites for tents and small RVs. Trailers are not recommended. Picnic tables and fire grills are provided. Drinking water and pit toilets are available. A primitive boat launch for small boats is available. Leashed pets are permitted.

Reservations, fees: No reservations. Sites are $11 per night. Senior discount available. Open June through September, weather permitting.

Directions: From Leavenworth, drive north on State Route 207 and drive 3.5 miles to Cedar Brae Road. Turn left (west) and drive 5.5 miles (becomes Forest Road 6607), and continue to the campground at the end of the road.

Contact: Okanogan and Wenatchee National Forests, Lake Wenatchee and Leavenworth Ranger District, Lake Wenatchee Office, 22976 State Route 207, Leavenworth, WA 98826; 509/763-3103, fax 509/763-3211.

127 Lake Wenatchee State Park

  8

Lake Wenatchee is the centerpiece for a 489-acre park with two miles of waterfront. Lake Wenatchee is fed by glaciers and the Wenatchee River, and the park is bisected by the river. That helps make the park a natural wildlife area, and visitors should be aware of bears; all food must be stored in bearproof facilities. Lake Wenatchee is set in a transition zone between the wet, western Washington woodlands and the sparse pine and fir of the eastern Cascades. Thanks to a nice location and drive-in sites that are spaced just right, you can expect plenty of company at this campground. The secluded campsites are set at the southeast end of Lake Wenatchee, which offers plenty of recreation opportunities, with a boat ramp nearby. There are eight miles of hiking trails, seven miles of bike trails, five miles of horse trails in and around the park, plus a 1.1-mile interpretive snowshoe trail in winter. Note that no horse facilities are available right in the park. In winter, there are 11 miles of multiuse trails and 23 miles of cross-country skiing trails.

Location: On Lake Wenatchee; see the Northern Cascades, map 5, grid b3.

Campsites, facilities: There are 197 sites for tents or self-contained RVs and two primitive tent sites. Picnic tables and fire grills are provided. Restrooms, drinking water, flush toilets, showers, a dump station, a store, ice, firewood, a restaurant, a playground, and horse rentals are available. Some facilities are wheelchair-accessible. Boat docks, launching facilities, rentals, and golf are nearby. Leashed pets are permitted.

Reservations, fees: Reserve at 888/CAMP-OUT (888/226-7688); website: www.parks.wa.gov/reservations ($7 reservation fee). Sites are $6 to $15 per night, $6 per extra vehicle per night. Senior discount available. Open year-round, with limited winter facilities.

Directions: From Leavenworth, drive west on U.S. 2 for 15 miles to State Route 207 at Coles Corner. Turn right (north) and drive three miles to the park entrance.

Contact: Lake Wenatchee State Park, State Route 207, Leavenworth, WA 98826; 509/763-3101; State Park information, 360/902-8844.

128 Nason Creek

 7

This campground is on Nason Creek near Lake Wenatchee, bordering Lake Wenatchee State Park. Recreation activities include swimming, fishing, and water-skiing. Boat rentals, horseback riding, and golfing are available nearby.

Location: Near Lake Wenatchee in Wenatchee National Forest; see the Northern Cascades, map 5, grid b3.

Campsites, facilities: There are 73 sites, including some drive-through, for tents, trailers, or RVs of any length. Picnic tables and fire grills are provided. Restrooms, drinking water, flush toilets, showers, and electricity are available. Some facilities are wheelchair-accessible. Boat-launching facilities are nearby.

Reservations, fees: No reservations. Sites are $11 per night. Senior discount available. Open May to mid-October.

Directions: From Seattle, drive north on I-5 to Everett and U.S. 2. Turn east on U.S. 2 and drive 87 miles to State Route 207, one mile west of Winton. Turn north on State Route 207 and drive 3.5 miles to Cedar Brae Road. Turn west and drive 100 yards to the campground.

Contact: Okanogan and Wenatchee National Forests, Lake Wenatchee and Leavenworth Ranger District, Lake Wenatchee Office, 22976 State Route 207, Leavenworth, WA 98826; 509/763-3103, fax 509/763-3211.

129 Midway Village and Grocery

 5

This private campground is located one mile from Lake Wenatchee State Park and Fish Lake, which is noted for good fishing year-round. There is good hiking and mountain biking out of the camp. Nearby recreation options include boating, fishing, water-skiing, swimming, windsurfing, hiking, and bike riding. The average annual snowfall is 12 feet. There is a snowmobile trail across the road from Midway Village. Snowmobile races are held in winter months within one quarter-mile of the campground. Winter options include cross-country skiing, dogsledding (25 miles east of Stevens Pass Ski Area), snowshoeing, and ice fishing.

Location: On the Wenatchee River; see the Northern Cascades, map 5, grid b3.

Campsites, facilities: There are 18 sites with full hookups for trailers or RVs up to 40 feet long. Picnic tables and barbecues are provided. Restrooms, flush toilets, showers, a store, firewood, a café, a coin-operated laundry, ice, bottled gas, and a playground with horseshoe pits and volleyball are available. Boat docks, launching facilities, and rentals are nearby. Leashed pets are permitted.

Reservations, fees: Reservations accepted. Sites are $9 to $15 per night. Major credit cards accepted. Open year-round.

Directions: From Seattle, drive north on I-5 to Everett and U.S. 2. Turn east on U.S. 2 and drive 88 miles over Steven's Pass to Coles Corner at State Route 207. Turn left (north) on State Route 207 and drive four miles, crossing the bridge over the Wenatchee River to a Y intersection. Turn right at the Y and drive one quarter-mile to the park on the right.

Contact: Midway Village and Grocery, 14193 Chiwawa Loop Road, Leavenworth, WA 98826; 509/763-3344.

130 Goose Creek

 7

This camp is used primarily by motorcycle riders, with trails for dirt bikes available directly from the camp. A main trail is linked to the Entiat off-road vehicle trail system, so this camp gets high use during the summer. The camp is set near a small creek.

Location: On Goose Creek in Wenatchee National Forest; see the Northern Cascades, map 5, grid b3.

Campsites, facilities: There are 29 sites for tents, trailers, or RVs of any length. Picnic tables and fire rings are provided. Drinking water and pit toilets are available. Leashed pets are permitted.

Reservations, fees: No reservations. Sites are $7 per vehicle per night. Senior discount available. Open May to mid-October.

Directions: From Seattle, drive north on I-5 to Everett and U.S. 2. Turn east on U.S. 2 and drive 87 miles to State Route 207, one mile

west of Winton. Turn north on State Route 207 and drive 4.5 miles to Chiwawa Loop Road. Turn right and drive two miles to Chiwawa Valley Road/Forest Road 6200. Turn left and drive three miles to Forest Road 6100. Turn right and drive 0.25 mile to the camp on the right.

Contact: Okanogan and Wenatchee National Forests, Lake Wenatchee and Leavenworth Ranger District, Lake Wenatchee Office, 22976 State Route 207, Leavenworth, WA 98826; 509/763-3103, fax 509/763-3211.

131 Pine Flat

 5

This camp has ready access to the Mad River off-road vehicle (ORV) area and is popular with bikers and ORV enthusiasts. There are more than 100 miles of trails, which are ideal for quads and dirt bikes. It ties into many loop trails. The elevation is 1,600 feet.

Location: Near Entiat River, in Wenatchee National Forest; see the Northern Cascades, map 5, grid b5.

Campsites, facilities: There are seven tent sites and one group site, which can accommodate up to 50 campers. Picnic tables and fire grills are provided. Drinking water and vault toilets are available.

Reservations, fees: Reservations required only for group site; phone 509/784-1511. Sites are $5 per night per vehicle; the group site is $60 per night. Senior discount available. Open late May through October, weather permitting.

Directions: From Wenatchee, drive north on U.S. 97-A for 18.5 miles to Entiat River Road. Turn (left) northwest on County Road 371/Entiat River Road and drive nine miles to Forest Road 5700. Continue northwest on Forest Road 5700 for one mile to the campground on the left.

Contact: Wenatchee National Forest, Entiat Ranger District, P.O. Box 476, Entiat, WA 98822; 509/784-1511, fax 509/784-1150.

132 Lincoln Rock State Park

  5

Lincoln Rock State Park is an 80-acre park set along the shore of Lake Entiat. The lake was created by the Rocky Reach Dam on the Columbia River. The park is named for a basalt outcropping that is said to resemble the profile of Abraham Lincoln. The park features lawns and shade trees amid an arid landscape. There are two miles of hiking and bike trails, paved and flat. Water sports include swimming, boating, and water-skiing. Beavers are occasionally visible in the Columbia River.

Location: On Lake Entiat; see the Northern Cascades, map 5, grid d6.

Campsites, facilities: There are 67 sites with partial or full hookups for trailers or RVs up to 65 feet long and 27 sites for tents or self-contained RVs. Picnic tables and fire grills are provided. Restrooms, drinking water, flush toilets, coin-operated showers, a dump station, a playground, athletic fields, horseshoe pits, a swimming beach, an amphitheater, three picnic shelters with electricity, and firewood are available. Some facilities are wheelchair-accessible. Boat docks, moorage, and launching facilities are located on Lake Entiat. Leashed pets are permitted.

Reservations, fees: Reserve at 888/CAMP-OUT (888/226-7688); website: www.parks.wa.gov/reservations ($7 reservation fee). Sites are $15 to $22 per night, $6 per extra vehicle per night. Senior discount available. Major credit cards accepted. Open March through mid-October.

Directions: From East Wenatchee, drive northeast on U.S. 2 for seven miles to the park on the left.

Contact: Lincoln Rock State Park, 509/884-8702; State Park information, 360/902-8844.

133 Entiat City Park

 8

If you're hurting for a spot for the night, you can usually find a campsite here. Lake Entiat is actually a dammed portion of the Columbia River. Access to nearby launching facilities makes this a good camping spot for boaters.

Location: On the Columbia River; see the Northern Cascades, map 5, grid c7.

Campsites, facilities: There are 25 tent sites and 31 sites with partial hookups (water and electricity) for trailers or RVs of any length. Picnic tables are provided. Restrooms, drinking water, flush toilets, coin-operated showers, a dump station, a playground, bottled gas, a store, a café, a laundry room, and ice are available. Boat docks and launching facilities are nearby. No open fires, dogs, or alcohol are permitted.

Reservations, fees: Reservation available at 800/736-8428. Sites are $20 per night, $2 per extra vehicle per night. Open mid-April to mid-September.

Directions: From Wenatchee, drive north on U.S. 97-A for 16 miles to Entiat; the park entrance on the right (Shearson Street is adjacent on the left). Turn right and drive to the park along the shore of Lake Entiat.

Contact: Entiat City Park, P.O. Box 228, Entiat, WA 98822; 800/736-8428, 509/784-1500.

134 Daroga State Park

 5

This 90-acre state park is set along 1.5 miles of shoreline along the Columbia River. It is set on the elevated edge of the desert "scablands." This camp fills up quickly on summer weekends. The Desert Canyon Golf Course is two miles away. Fishing, along with walking and biking trails, are available out of the camp.

Location: On Columbia River; see the Northern Cascades, map 5, grid c7.

Campsites, facilities: There are 28 sites with partial hookups (water and electricity), including eight drive-through sites, for tents, trailers, and RVs up to 45 feet long, 17 walk-in or boat-in sites (requiring a one-quarter-mile trip), and two group sites for 20 to 100 people. Picnic tables and fire pits are provided. Restrooms, drinking water, flush toilets (near RV sites) and vault toilets (near walk-in sites), showers, a dump station, a swimming beach, boat-launching facilities and docks, a playground with baseball field, basketball courts, softball and soccer fields, and a picnic area with kitchen shelter are available. Leashed pets are permitted.

Reservations, fees: No reservations for family sites. Reservations for group sites only; reserve at 888/CAMP-OUT (888/226-7688); website: www.parks.wa.gov/reservations ($7 reservation fee). Sites are $6 to $22, $6 per extra vehicle per night; group site is $25 plus $2 per person per night, $14 per RV per night. Senior discount available. Open mid-March to mid-October, weather permitting.

Directions: From East Wenatchee, drive north on Highway 97 (east side of Columbia River) for 18 miles to the camp. For boat-in camps, launch boats from the ramp at the park and drive one quarter-mile.

Contact: Daroga State Park, 509/664-6380; State Park information, 360/902-8844.

Blackpine Creek Horse Camp

  8

Blackpine Creek Horse Camp is for horse campers only, a base camp for horse pack trips. It is set on Black Pine Creek near Icicle Creek, at a major trailhead leading into the Alpine Lakes Wilderness. It's one of seven rustic camps on the creek, with the distinction of being the only one with facilities for horses. The elevation is 3,000 feet.

Location: Near the Alpine Lakes Wilderness in Wenatchee National Forest; see the Northern Cascades, map 5, grid c1.

Campsites, facilities: There are 10 drive-through sites for tents, trailers, or RVs up to 21 feet long. Picnic tables and fire grills are provided. Drinking water and vault toilets are available. Horse facilities, including a loading ramp, are also available. Leashed pets are permitted.

Reservations, fees: No reservations. Sites are $9 per vehicle per night. Senior discount available. Open mid-May to late October.

Directions: From Seattle, drive north on I-5 to Everett and U.S. 2. Turn east on U.S. 2 and drive 103 miles to Leavenworth and County Road 76 (Icicle River Road). Turn south and drive 19.2 miles to the campground on the left.

Contact: Okanogan and Wenatchee National Forests, Leavenworth Ranger District, 600 Sherbourne, Leavenworth, WA 98826; 509/548-6977, fax 509/548-5817.

Rock Island

    8

Rock Island is one of several campgrounds in the immediate area along Icicle Creek, about one mile from the trailhead that takes hikers into the Alpine Lakes Wilderness. This is a pretty spot, with good fishing access. The elevation is 2,900 feet.

Location: Near the Alpine Lakes Wilderness in Wenatchee National Forest; see the Northern Cascades, map 5, grid d1.

Campsites, facilities: There are 22 sites for tents, trailers, or RVs up to 21 feet long. Picnic tables and fire grills are provided. Drinking water and vault toilets are available.

Some facilities are wheelchair-accessible. Leashed pets are permitted.

Reservations, fees: No reservations accepted. Sites are $9 per vehicle per night. Senior discount available. Open May to late October.

Directions: From Seattle, drive north on I-5 to Everett and U.S. 2. Turn east on U.S. 2 and drive 103 miles to Leavenworth and County Road 76 (Icicle River Road). Turn south and drive 17.7 miles to the campground.

Contact: Okanogan and Wenatchee National Forests, Leavenworth Ranger District, 600 Sherbourne, Leavenworth, WA 98826; 509/548-6977, fax 509/548-5817.

137 Chatter Creek

 8

Icicle and Chatter Creeks are the backdrop for this creekside campground. The elevation is 2,800 feet. Trails lead out in several directions from the camp into the Alpine Lakes Wilderness.

Location: Near the Alpine Lakes Wilderness in Wenatchee National Forest; see the Northern Cascades, map 5, grid d1.

Campsites, facilities: There are 12 sites for tents, trailers, or RVs up to 21 feet long, and one group site for up to 45 people. Picnic tables and fire grills are provided. Drinking water and vault toilets are available. Leashed pets are permitted.

Reservations, fees: Reservations required only for group sites, phone 800/274-6104 (reservation fee). Rates are $89 per night for single sites and $60 per night for group sites. Senior discount available. Open May to late October.

Directions: From Seattle, drive north on I-5 to Everett and U.S. 2. Turn east on U.S. 2 and drive 103 miles to Leavenworth and County Road 76 (Icicle River Road). Turn south and drive 16.1 miles to the campground on the right.

Contact: Okanogan and Wenatchee National Forests, Leavenworth Ranger District, 600 Sherbourne, Leavenworth, WA 98826; 509/548-6977, fax 509/548-5817.

138 Ida Creek

 8

This campground is one of several small, quiet camps along Icicle and Ida Creeks, with recreation options similar to Chatter Creek and Rock Island campgrounds.

Location: On Icicle Creek in Wenatchee National Forest; see the Northern Cascades, map 5, grid d2.

Campsites, facilities: There are five tent sites and five sites for tents, trailers, or RVs up to 21 feet long. Picnic tables and fire grills are provided. Drinking water and vault toilets are available. Some facilities are wheelchair-accessible. Leashed pets are permitted.

Reservations, fees: No reservations. Sites are $8 per night. Senior discount available. Open May to late October.

Directions: From Seattle, drive north on I-5 to Everett and U.S. 2. Turn east on U.S. 2 and drive 103 miles to Leavenworth and County Road 76 (Icicle River Road). Turn south and drive 14.2 miles to the campground on the left.

Contact: Okanogan and Wenatchee National Forests, Leavenworth Ranger District, 600 Sherbourne, Leavenworth, WA 98826; 509/548-6977, fax 509/548-5817.

139 Johnny Creek

 8

This campground is split into two parts on both sides of the road, along Icicle and Johnny Creeks. It is fairly popular. Upper Johnny has a forest setting, whereas Lower Johnny is set alongside the creek, with adjacent forest. The elevation is 2,300 feet. See Bridge Creek Camp for area information.

Location: On Icicle Creek in Wenatchee National Forest; see the Northern Cascades, map 5, grid d2.

Campsites, facilities: There are 65 sites for tents, trailers, or RVs up to 30 feet long. Picnic tables and fire grills are provided. Drinking water and vault toilets are available. Some facilities are wheelchair-accessible. Leashed pets are permitted.

Reservations, fees: No reservations. Sites are $9 per night. Senior discount available. Open May to late October.

Directions: From Seattle, drive north on I-5 to Everett and U.S. 2. Turn east on U.S. 2 and drive 103 miles to Leavenworth and County Road 76 (Icicle River Road). Turn south and drive 12.4 miles to the campground (with camps on each side of the road).

Contact: Okanogan and Wenatchee National Forests, Leavenworth Ranger District, 600 Sherbourne, Leavenworth, WA 98826; 509/548-6977, fax 509/548-5817.

140 Bridge Creek

 8

This is a small, quiet spot along Icicle and Bridge Creeks. The elevation is 1,800 feet. About two miles south of the camp at Eightmile Creek is a trail that accesses the Alpine Lakes Wilderness. See a U.S. Forest Service map for details. Horseback-riding opportunities are within four miles and golf is within five miles.

Location: On Icicle Creek in Wenatchee National Forest; see the Northern Cascades, map 5, grid d2.

Campsites, facilities: There are six tent sites and one group site for up to 100 people. Picnic tables and fire grills are provided. Drinking water and vault toilets are available. The group site does not have drinking water available. Leashed pets are permitted.

Reservations, fees: Reservations required only for groups; phone 800/274-6104. Single sites are $9 per vehicle per night, and group sites are $60 per night. Senior discount available. Open mid-April to late October.

Directions: From Seattle, drive north on I-5 to Everett and U.S. 2. Turn east on U.S. 2 and drive 103 miles to Leavenworth and County Road 76 (Icicle River Road). Turn south and drive 9.4 miles to the campground on the left.

Contact: Okanogan and Wenatchee National Forests, Leavenworth Ranger District, 600 Sherbourne, Leavenworth, WA 98826; 509/548-6977, fax 509/548-5817.

141 Eightmile

 8

This camp is set in the vicinity of trout fishing and hiking. Trailheads are located within two miles of the campground along Icicle and Eightmile Creeks. This provides access to fishing, as well as a backpacking route into the Alpine Lakes Wilderness. The elevation is 1,800 feet. Horseback-riding opportunities are within four miles and golf is within five miles.

Location: Near the Alpine Lakes Wilderness in Wenatchee National Forest; see the Northern Cascades, map 5, grid d2.

Campsites, facilities: There are 45 sites for tents, trailers, or RVs up to 21 feet long and one group site for up to 70 people. Picnic tables and fire grills are provided. Drinking water and vault toilets are available. Some facilities are wheelchair-accessible. Leashed pets are permitted.

Reservations, fees: Reservations required only for group sites; phone 800/274-6104 (reservation fee). Rates are $10 per night per vehicle for single sites, and $60 per night for group sites. Senior discount available. Open mid-April to late October.

Directions: From Seattle, drive north on I-5 to Everett and U.S. 2. Turn east on U.S. 2 and drive 103 miles to Leavenworth and County Road 76 (Icicle River Road). Turn south and drive eight miles to the campground on the left.

Contact: Okanogan and Wenatchee National Forests, Leavenworth Ranger District, 600 Sherbourne, Leavenworth, WA 98826; 509/548-6977, fax 509/548-5817.

142 Icicle River RV Resort

 9

Icicle River RV Resort is one of three campgrounds in the immediate area. The others are Pine Village Resort and Chalet Trailer Park. Note that no tent camping is permitted here, but six cabins are available for rent. This pretty, wooded spot is set along the Icicle River, where fishing and swimming are available. The park is clean and scenic and even has its own putting green. An 18-hole golf course and hiking trails are nearby.

Location: On Icicle River; see the Northern Cascades, map 5, grid d3.

Campsites, facilities: There are 100 sites with full or partial hookups for trailers or RVs of any length and six rustic cabins. Picnic tables and fire pits (at some sites) are provided. Restrooms, drinking water, flush toilets, showers, modem access, a hot tub, and bottled gas are available. Firewood is available for a fee. A putting green, horseshoe pits, and two pavilions are available nearby. Leashed pets are permitted.

Reservations, fees: Reservations accepted. Sites are $25 to $27 per night, $4 per extra vehicle per night, $4 per person per night for more than two people. Major credit cards accepted. Open April through mid-December, weather permitting.

Directions: From Seattle, drive north on I-5 to Everett and U.S. 2. Turn east on U.S. 2 and drive 103 miles to Leavenworth and County Road 76 (Icicle River Road). Turn south and drive three miles to the park on the left.

Contact: Icicle River RV Resort, 7305 Icicle Road, Leavenworth, WA 98826; 509/548-5420; website: www.icicleriverrv.com.

143 Tumwater

 7

This large, popular camp provides a little bit of both worlds. It's a good layover for campers cruising U.S. 2. But there are also two forest roads nearby, each less than a mile long, which end at trailheads that provide access to the Alpine Lakes Wilderness. If you don't like to hike, no problem. The camp is on the Wenatchee River in Tumwater Canyon. This section of river is closed to fishing. The elevation is 2,050 feet.

Location: Near the Alpine Lakes Wilderness in Wenatchee National Forest; see the Northern Cascades, map 5, grid c3.

Campsites, facilities: There are 84 sites for tents, trailers, or RVs up to 30 feet long, and one group site for up to 75 people. Drinking water, fire grills, and picnic tables are provided. Flush toilets are available. Some facilities are wheelchair-accessible. Leashed pets are permitted.

Reservations, fees: Reservations required only for the group site, phone 800/274-6104 (reservation fee). Rates are $12 per night for vehicle for single sites, and $80 for group sites. Senior discount available. Open May to mid-October.

Directions: From Seattle, drive north on I-5 to Everett and U.S. 2. Turn east on U.S. 2 and drive 93 miles to the campground (10 miles west of Leavenworth).

Contact: Okanogan and Wenatchee National Forests,

Lake Wenatchee and Leavenworth Ranger District, Lake Wenatchee Office, 22976 State Route 207, Leavenworth, WA 98826; 509/763-3103, fax 509/763-3211.

Pine Village KOA/ Leavenworth

  8

This lovely resort is near the "Bavarian village" of Leavenworth, to which the park provides a free shuttle in the summer. The spectacularly scenic area is surrounded by the Cascade Mountains and set among Ponderosa pines. The camp has access to the Wenatchee River, not to mention many luxurious extras, including a hot tub and a heated pool. The park allows campfires and has firewood available. Nearby recreation options include an 18-hole golf course and hiking trails. Make a point to spend a day in Leavenworth if possible; it offers authentic German food and architecture, along with music and art shows in the summer.

Location: Near the Wenatchee River; see the Northern Cascades, map 5, grid d3.

Campsites, facilities: There are 60 sites, including 22 drive-through, for trailers or RVs up to 40 feet, 40 tent sites, and 20 cabins and two cottages. Picnic tables and fire grills are provided. Restrooms, drinking water, flush toilets, showers, a dump station, firewood, a recreation hall, cable TV, a store, a laundry room, ice, a playground with horseshoe pits and volleyball, a spa, a heated swimming pool, and a beach area are available. Some facilities are wheelchair-accessible. Bottled gas and a café are located within one mile. Leashed pets are permitted.

Reservations, fees: Reservations accepted at 800/562-5709. Sites are $21 to $36 per night, $5 per extra vehicle per night, $4.50 per person per night for more than two people. Cabins and cottages are $45 to $59. Major credit cards accepted. Open April to November.

Directions: From Seattle, drive north on I-5 to Everett and U.S. 2. Turn east on U.S. 2 and drive 103 miles to Leavenworth. Continue east on U.S. 2 for one quarter-mile to River Bend Drive. Turn north and drive one-half mile to the campground on the right.

Contact: Pine Village KOA/Leavenworth, 11401 River Bend Drive, Leavenworth, WA 98826; 509/548-7709 (phone or fax); website: www.koa.com.

Chalet RV Park

  5

This park along the Wenatchee River near Leavenworth is within walking distance of quaint "Bavarian village" shops and restaurants. A pleasant grassy area is provided for tents. Nearby recreation options include an 18-hole golf course and fishing hiking, biking, and swimming opportunities.

Location: On the Wenatchee River; see the Northern Cascades, map 5, grid d3.

Campsites, facilities: There are 29 sites with full or partial hookups, including some drive-through, for tents, trailers, or RVs of any length, a grassy area for tents, and 10 mobile home rentals. Picnic tables are provided. Restrooms, drinking water, flush toilets, showers, a dump station, and propane are available. Bottled gas, a store, a café, a coin-operated laundry, and ice can be found within one mile. Leashed pets are permitted.

Reservations, fees: No reservations. Sites are $22 to $24 per night, $4 per extra vehicle per night, $4 per person per night for more than two people. Open early May through early October.

Directions: From Seattle, drive north on I-5 to Everett and U.S. 2. Turn east on U.S. 2 and drive 103 miles to Leavenworth and Duncan Road. Turn south and drive 150 feet to the campground on the right.

Contact: Chalet RV Park, P.O. Box 288, Leavenworth, WA 98826; 509/548-4578.

146 Blu Shastin RV Park

6

This park is set in a mountainous area near Penshastin Creek. Gold panning in the river is a popular activity here, and during the gold rush, the Penshastin was the best-producing river in the state. The camp has sites on the river bank and plenty of shade trees. A heated pool, a recreation field, and horseshoe pits provide possible activities in the park. Hiking trails and marked bike trails are nearby.

Location: Near Penshastin Creek; see the Northern Cascades, map 5, grid e3.

Campsites, facilities: There are 86 sites with full hookups, including four drive-through sites, for tents, trailers, or RVs of any length. Picnic tables and fire rings are provided. Restrooms, drinking water, flush toilets, showers, a dump station, a recreation hall, firewood, a coin-operated laundry, ice, a playground, horseshoes, badminton, volleyball, and a heated swimming pool are available. Bottled gas, a store, and a café are located within seven miles. Leashed pets are permitted.

Reservations, fees: Reservations recommended. Sites are $20 to $25 per night. Major credit cards accepted. Open year-round, weather permitting.

Directions: From Leavenworth, drive south on U.S. 2 for four miles to U.S. 97. Turn south on U.S. 97 and drive seven miles to the park on the right.

Contact: Blu Shastin RV Park, 3300 Highway 97, Penshastin, WA 98847; 509/548-4184 or 888/548-4184.

147 Wenatchee River County Park

5

This camp is set along the Wenatchee River, situated between the highway and the river. It is not the greatest setting, with some highway noise, but it is convenient for RV campers. You can usually get a tree-covered site in the campground, despite it being a small park. The adjacent river is fast-moving and provides white-water rafting, with a put-in spot at the park. Fishing is typically poor.

Location: On Wenatchee River; see the Northern Cascades, map 5, grid e6.

Campsites, facilities: There are 80 sites, including 40 with full hookups, 40 with partial hookups for tents, and some drive-through sites for trailers and RVs, and 17 tent sites. Picnic tables and fire grills are provided. Restrooms, drinking water, flush toilets, and showers are available. A store and a restaurant are within one mile. Leashed pets are permitted.

Reservations, fees: Reservations available at 509/667-7503. Sites are $15 to $22. $5 per extra vehicle per night. Major credit cards accepted. Open April through September.

Directions: From Wenatchee and U.S. 2, drive west on U.S. 2 for 4.7 miles to the campground on the left.

Contact: Chelan County Commissioner, 350 Orondo Avenue, Wenatchee, WA 98801; 509/667-7503 or 509/667-6215.

148 Wenatchee Confluence State Park

    10

This 197-acre state park is set at the confluence of the Wenatchee and Columbia Rivers. The park features expansive lawns shaded by deciduous trees and fronted by the two rivers. The park has something of a dual personality. The north portion of the park is urban and recreational, while the southern section is a designated natural wetland area. There are 10.5 miles of paved trail for hiking, biking, and in-line skating. A pedestrian bridges crosses the Wenatchee River. An interpretive hiking trail is available in the Horan Natural Area. Other recreation possibilities include fishing, swimming, boating, and water-skiing. Sports enthusiasts are provided with playing fields and tennis and basketball courts. Daroga State Park and Lake Chelan to the north offer side trip possibilities.

Location: On the Columbia River; see the Northern Cascades, map 5, grid e6.

Campsites, facilities: There are 51 sites with full hookups for trailers or RVs up to 65 feet long, eight developed tent sites, and a group site for tents for up to 300 people. Picnic tables and fire grills are provided. Restrooms, drinking water, flush toilets, coin-operated showers, a boat launch, a dump station, a swimming beach, a playground, and athletic fields are available. Some facilities are wheelchair-accessible. Leashed pets are permitted.

Reservations, fees: Reserve at 888/CAMP-OUT (888/226-7688); website: www.parks.wa.gov/reservations ($7 reservation fee). Sites are $15 to $22 per night, $6 per extra vehicle per night. Major credit cards accepted from mid-May to mid-September. Senior discount available. Open year-round.

Directions: From Wenatchee and U.S. 2, take the Easy Street exit and drive south to Penny Road. Turn left and drive a short distance to Chester Kimm Street. Turn right and drive to a T intersection and Old Station Road. Turn left on Old Station Road and drive past the railroad tracks to the park on the right. The park is 1.3 miles from U.S. 2.

Contact: Wenatchee Confluence State Park, 333 Olds Station Road, Wenatchee, WA 98801; 509/664-6373; State Park information, 360/902-8844.

149 Indian Horse Camp

    6

This campground along the Middle Fork of the Teanaway River is in a primitive setting, with sunny, open sites along the water. Fishing for brook trout is best here in May and June. Quiet and solitude are highlights of this little-used camp. It's an easy drive from here to trailheads accessing the Mt. Stuart Range. Be sure to bring your own drinking water.

Location: On the Middle Fork of the Teanaway River; see the Northern Cascades, map 5, grid f1.

Campsites, facilities: There are 10 campsites for tents or small trailers. Picnic tables, fire grills, and tent pads are provided. Pit toilets are available, but there is no drinking water. Garbage must be packed out. Some saddle-stock facilities are available, including hitching posts and corrals. Some facilities are wheelchair-accessible. Leashed pets are permitted.

Reservations, fees: No reservations; no fee. Open year-round, weather permitting (heavy snows are generally expected from December through March).

Directions: From Seattle, drive east on I-90 for 80 miles to Cle Elum and Exit 85 and Highway 970. Turn east on Highway 970 and drive

6.9 miles to Teanaway Road. Turn left on Teanaway Road and drive 7.3 miles to West Fork Teenaway Road. Turn left and drive 0.6 mile to Middle Fork Teanaway Road. Turn right and drive 3.9 miles to the campground on the left.
Contact: Department of Natural Resources, Southeast Region, 713 Bowers Road, Ellensburg, WA 98926-9301; 509/925-8510, fax 509/925-8522.

150 Beverly

     8

This primitive campground is set on the North Fork of the Teanaway River, a scenic area of the river. It is primarily a hiker's camp, with several trails leading up nearby creeks and into the Alpine Lakes Wilderness. Self-issued permits are required for wilderness hiking. Fishing is poor for cutthroat trout. The elevation is 3,100 feet.
Location: On the North Fork of the Teanaway River in Wenatchee National Forest; see the Northern Cascades, map 5, grid f2.
Campsites, facilities: There are 13 sites for tents, trailers, or RVs up to 21 feet long. Picnic tables and fire grills are provided. Vault toilets are available, but there is no drinking water. Garbage must be packed out. Leashed pets are permitted.
Reservations, fees: No reservations. Sites are $5 per night per vehicle. Open June to mid-November.
Directions: In Seattle on I-5, turn east on I-90. Drive east on I-90 for 80 miles to Cle Elum and Exit 86. Take Exit 86 to Highway 970. Turn east on Highway 970 and drive eight miles to Teanaway Road (County Road 970). Turn left (north) on Teanaway Road and drive 13 miles to the end of the paved road. Bear right (north) on Forest Road 9737 and drive four miles to campground on the left.
Contact: Okanogan and Wenatchee National Forests, Cle Elum Ranger District, West Second Street, Cle Elum, WA 98922; 509/674-4411, fax 509/674-1530.

151 Mineral Springs

   6

This campground at the confluence of Medicine and Swauk Creeks is one of five campgrounds along U.S. 97. Note that this camp is set along a highway, so there is some highway noise. Fishing, berry picking, and hunting are good in season in this area. It is at an elevation of 7,700 feet. Most use the camp as a one-night layover spot.
Location: On Swauk Creek in Wenatchee National Forest; see the Northern Cascades, map 5, grid f3.
Campsites, facilities: There are 12 sites for tents, trailers, or RVs up to 21 feet long. Picnic tables and fire rings are provided. Drinking water and vault toilets are available. Leashed pets are permitted. A restaurant is nearby.
Reservations, fees: No reservations accepted. Sites are $10 per night, $8 per extra vehicle per night. Senior discount available. Open mid-May to late September.
Directions: From Seattle, drive east on I-90 for 80 miles to Cle Elum and Exit 85 and Highway 970. Turn northeast on Highway 970 drive 12 miles to U.S. 97. Continue northeast (the road becomes U.S. 97) and drive about seven miles to the campground on the left.
Contact: Okanogan and Wenatchee National Forests, Cle Elum Ranger District, 830 West Second Street, Cle Elum, WA 98922; 509/674-4411, fax 509/674-4794.

152 Swauk

     6

Some decent hiking trails can be found at this campground along Swauk Creek. A short loop trail, about a one-mile round-trip, is the most popular. Fishing is marginal, and there is some highway noise from U.S. 97. The elevation is 3,200 feet. Three miles east of the camp on Forest Road 9716 is the Swauk Forest Discovery Trail. This interpretive trail is three miles long and explains some of the effects of logging and U.S. Forest Service management of the forest habitat.

Location: On Swauk Creek in Wenatchee National Forest; see the Northern Cascades, map 5, grid f3.

Campsites, facilities: There are 22 sites, including two double sites, for tents, trailers, or RVs. Fire grills and picnic tables are provided. Pit toilets and firewood are available, but there is no drinking water. Leashed pets are permitted.

Reservations, fees: No reservations. Sites are $10 to $20 per night, $8 per extra vehicle per night. Senior discount available. Open mid-April to late September.

Directions: In Seattle on I-5, turn east on I-90. Drive east on I-90 for 80 miles to Cle Elum and Exit 86. Take Exit 86 to County Road 970. Turn east on County Road 970 and drive 12 miles to U.S. 97. Turn north on U.S. 97 and drive 10 miles to the campground on the right (near Swauk Pass).

Contact: Okanogan and Wenatchee National Forests, Cle Elum Ranger District, West Second Street, Cle Elum, WA 98922; 509/674-4411, fax 509/674-1530.

153 Ken Wilcox Horse Camp

 8

First note that the last couple miles of road are pretty rough, suitable only for high-clearance vehicles or pickups. It is set at an elevation of 5,500 feet, at launch point for an extensive trail system. This scenic camp near Haney Meadows has been adopted by a local equestrian association that helps maintain the horse trails. Mountain bikers

also use this camp; note that when bikes and horses meet on a trail, bikes must give way, even if it involves dismounting the bike and carrying it off the trail.

Location: Near Swauk Creek at Haney Meadows in Wenatchee National Forest; see the Northern Cascades, map 5, grid f4.

Campsites, facilities: There are 25 sites for tents, trailers, or RVs up to 25 feet. Fire pits and vault toilets are provided. No drinking water is available. Garbage must be packed out. Stock facilities include hitching equipment, including rails and rings for suspending a high line.

Reservations, fees: Northwest Forest Pass ($30 annual fee) or $5 daily fee per parked vehicle is required. Open early July to mid-October (the access road is not plowed).

Directions: In Seattle on I-5, turn east on I-90. Drive east on I-90 for 80 miles to Cle Elum and Exit 86. Take Exit 86 to County Road 970. Turn east on County Road 970 and drive 12 miles to U.S. 97. Turn north on U.S. 97 and drive 15 miles to the summit of Swauk Pass and Forest Road 9716. Turn right on Forest Road 9716 (gravel) and drive about four miles to Forest Road 9712. Turn left on Forest Road 9712 and drive about five miles to the camp on the left.

Contact: Okanogan and Wenatchee National Forests, Cle Elum Ranger District, West Second Street, Cle Elum, WA 98922; 509/674-4411, fax 509/674-1530.

154 Trailer Corral

 7

This wooded campground along the Yakima River offers a choice of grassy or graveled sites. Nearby recreation options include an 18-hole golf course, marked hiking trails, and tennis courts.

Location: On the Yakima River; see the Northern Cascades, map 5, grid g1.

Campsites, facilities: There are 23 sites with full hookups for trailers or RVs of any length, three tent sites, and six cabins. Picnic tables are provided. Restrooms, flush toilets, showers, a dump station, firewood, and a coin-operated laundry are available. A store is located within one mile. Boat-launching facilities are nearby. Leashed pets are permitted.

Reservations, fees: Reservations accepted. Sites are $14 to $18 per night. Cabins are $35 to $42. Major credit cards accepted. Open year-round.

Directions: From Seattle, drive east on I-90 for 80 miles to Cle Elum and Exit 85 and Highway 970. Turn east on Highway 970 and drive 1.5 mile to the park on the left.

Contact: Trailer Corral, 2781 Highway 970, Cle Elum, WA 98922; 509/674-2433.

155 Taneum

 7

This is a rustic spot along Taneum Creek with an elevation of 2,400 feet. It is set several miles away from the camps popular with the off-road vehicle crowd. This is more of a quiet getaway, not a base camp. Ponderosa pines add to the setting. Trout fishing is popular here in the summer. The camp receives moderate use.

Location: On Taneum Creek in Wenatchee National Forest; see the Northern Cascades, map 5, grid h2.

Campsites, facilities: There are 13 sites for trailers or RVs up to 21 feet long and one double site. Picnic tables and fire rings are provided. Drinking water and firewood are available. Some facilities are wheelchair-accessible. Leashed pets are permitted.

Reservations, fees: No reservations accepted. Rates are $8 to $20 per night for single sites, and $8 for each additional vehicle. Senior discount available. Open May to late September.

Directions: From Ellensburg, drive northeast on U.S. 90 for about 12 miles to Thorp Prairie Road. Turn south on Thorp Prairie Road and drive four miles (crossing back over the freeway) to Taneum Road. Turn right and drive west for three miles (it becomes Forest Road 33). Continue west for three miles to the campground on the left.

Contact: Okanogan and Wenatchee National Forests, Cle Elum Ranger District, 830 West Second Street, Cle Elum, CA 98922; 509/674-4411, fax 509/674-4794.

156 Icewater Creek

 7

Icewater Creek Camp is similar to Taneum Camp, except that the trees are smaller and the sites are a bit more open. It is most popular with off-road motorcyclists because there are two ORV trails leading from the camp, both of which network to an extensive system of off-road riding trails. The best route extends along South Fork Taneium River area. Fishing is fair, primarily for six- to eight-inch cutthroat trout.

Location: On Taneum Creek in Wenatchee National Forest; see the Northern Cascades, map 5, grid h2.

Campsites, facilities: There are 14 sites for trailers or RVs up to 26 feet long. Picnic tables and fire rings are provided. Drinking water and firewood are available. Some facilities are wheelchair-accessible. Leashed pets are permitted.

Reservations, fees: No reservations accepted. Rates are $8 for single sites, and $6 for each additional vehicle. Senior discount available. Open May to late September.

Directions: From Ellensburg, drive northeast on U.S. 90 for about 12 miles to Thorp

Prairie Road. Turn south on Thorp Prairie Road and drive four miles (crossing back over the freeway) to Taneum Road. Turn right and drive west for three miles (it becomes Forest Road 33). Continue west for 4.5 miles to the campground on the left.

Contact: Okanogan and Wenatchee National Forests, Cle Elum Ranger District, 830 West Second Street, Cle Elum, CA 98922; 509/674-4411, fax 509/674-4794.

NORTHEASTERN
WASHINGTON

Northeastern Washington

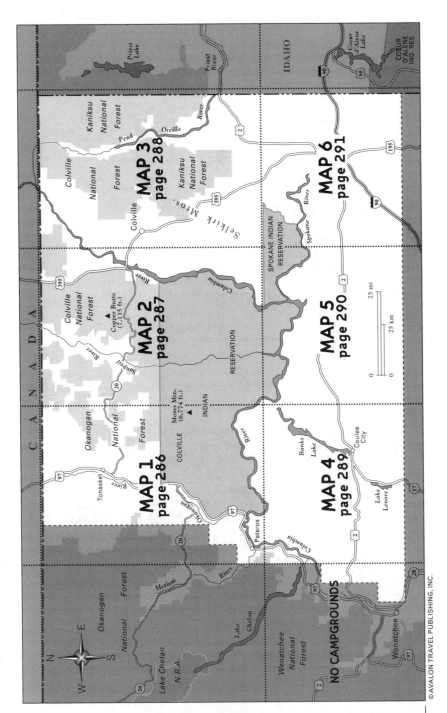

© AVALON TRAVEL PUBLISHING, INC.

Map 1

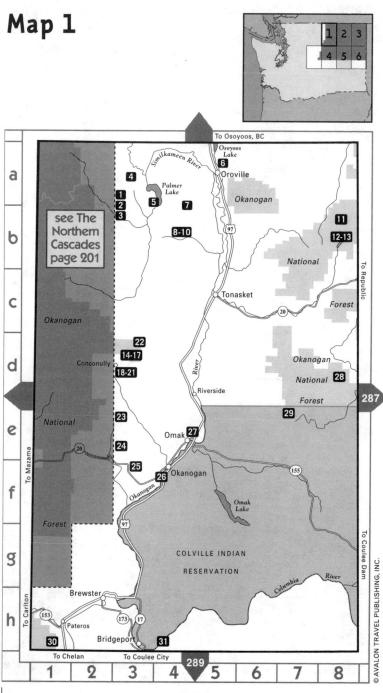

see The Northern Cascades page 201

To Osoyoos, BC

Similkameen River

Osoyoos Lake

6
Oroville

4

Palmer Lake

1
2
3

5

7

Okanogan

8-10

97

National

11

12-13

Tonasket

20

Forest

To Republic

Okanogan

22

14-17

Conconully

18-21

Okanogan

National

28

River

Riverside

Forest

287

29

23

Omak **27**

24

To Mazama

20

25

26 Okanogan

155

Okanogan

Omak Lake

97

COLVILLE INDIAN

RESERVATION

Columbia River

To Coulee Dam

Brewster

To Cariton

153

173 17

Pateros

30

Bridgeport

31

To Chelan

To Coulee City **289**

1 2 3 4 5 6 7 8

© AVALON TRAVEL PUBLISHING, INC.

Map 2

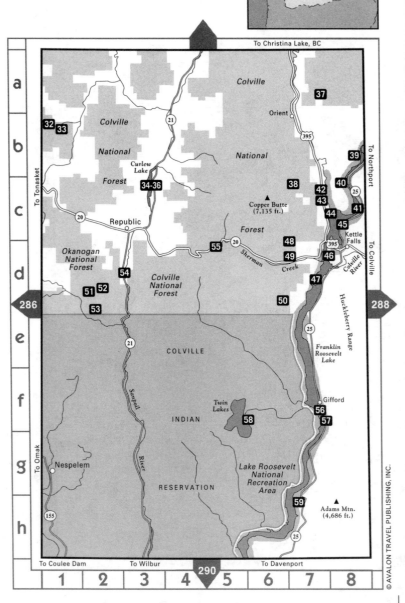

© AVALON TRAVEL PUBLISHING, INC.

Map 3

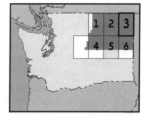

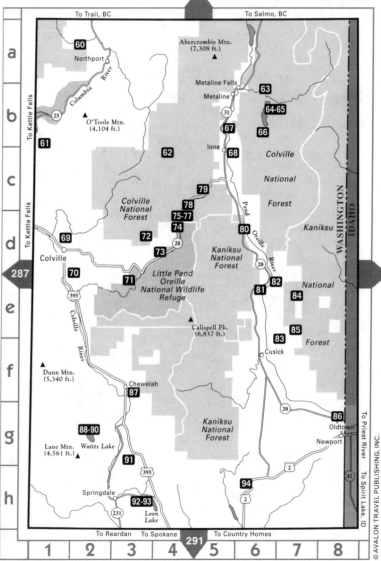

To Trail, BC   To Salmo, BC

a

60

Northport

Abercrombie Mtn.
(7,308 ft.) ▲

b

25

O'Toole Mtn.
(4,104 ft.) ▲

61

Metaline Falls

Metaline

31

63

64-65

67

66

62

Ione

68

Colville

Columbia River

To Kettle Falls

c

79

78

75-77

74

72

Colville
National
Forest

National

Forest

80

Kaniksu

d

69

73

20

287

Colville

70

71

395

Little Pend
Oreille
National Wildlife
Refuge

Kaniksu
National
Forest

Pend Oreille River

20

81

82

84

National

WASHINGTON
IDAHO

e

Colville River

Calispell Pk.
(6,837 ft.) ▲

83

85

Forest

Cusick

f

Dunn Mtn.
(5,340 ft.) ▲

Chewelah

87

20

86

Oldtown

To Priest River

g

88-90

Lane Mtn.
(4,561 ft.) ▲ *Waitts Lake*

Kaniksu
National
Forest

Newport

2

Oldtown

41

To Spirit Lake, ID

h

91

395

Springdale

231

92-93

*Loon
Lake*

94

2

To Reardan   To Spokane   **291**   To Country Homes

© AVALON TRAVEL PUBLISHING, INC.

1   2   3   4   5   6   7   8

Map 4

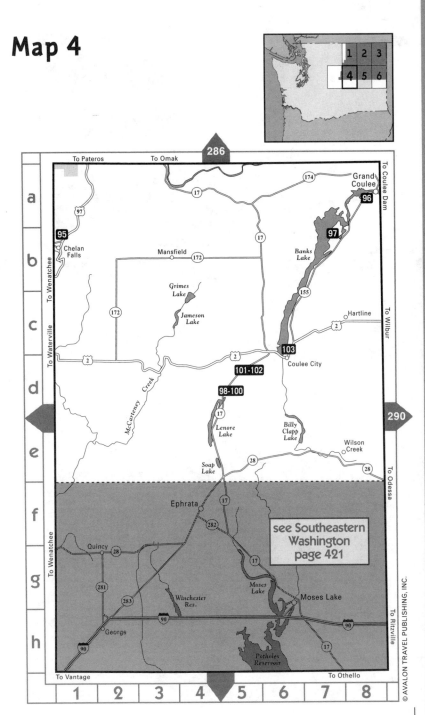

To Pateros To Omak **286**

To Coulee Dam

a

174 Grand Coulee

17 **96**

97

95

Chelan Falls

Mansfield 172

b

To Wenatchee

Banks Lake

17

Grimes Lake

155

c

172

Jameson Lake

Hartline

2

To Waterville

2 **103**

To Wilbur

101-102

Coulee City

98-100

d

To Wenatchee

McCartney Creek

17

Lenore Lake

Billy Clapp Lake

290

Wilson Creek

e

Soap Lake

28

28

To Odessa

Ephrata 17

f

282

see Southeastern Washington page 421

Quincy 28

17

g

To Wenatchee

281

Moses Lake

Moses Lake

28.3

Winchester Res.

h

90

George

90

To Ritzville

90

Potholes Reservoir

17

To Vantage

To Othello

1 2 3 4 5 6 7 8

© AVALON TRAVEL PUBLISHING, INC.

Map 5

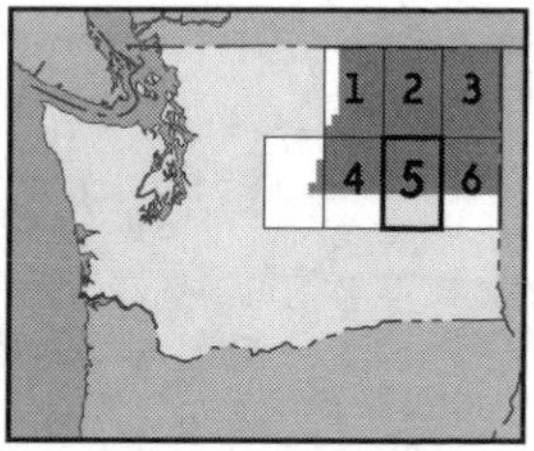

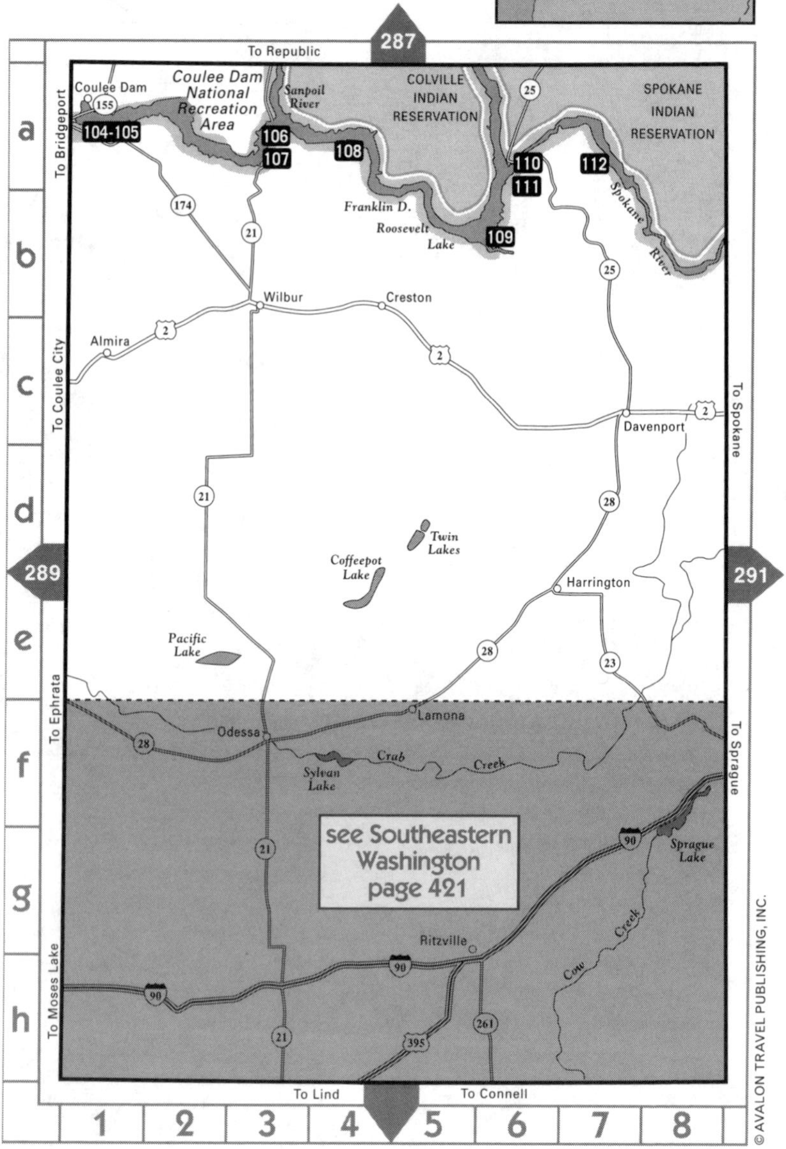

see Southeastern Washington page 421

To Republic

287

Coulee Dam

155

104-105

Coulee Dam National Recreation Area

Sanpoil River

106
107

108

COLVILLE INDIAN RESERVATION

25

SPOKANE INDIAN RESERVATION

110
111

112

Franklin D. Roosevelt Lake

109

Spokane River

174

21

To Bridgeport

To Coulee City

Wilbur

Creston

Almira

2

25

2

To Spokane

Davenport

2

21

28

Twin Lakes

Coffeepot Lake

289

291

Harrington

Pacific Lake

28

23

To Ephrata

Lamona

Odessa

Crab Creek

To Sprague

28

Sylvan Lake

21

90

Sprague Lake

To Moses Lake

21

Ritzville

90

Crab Creek

261

90

395

To Lind

To Connell

© AVALON TRAVEL PUBLISHING, INC.

Map 6

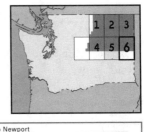

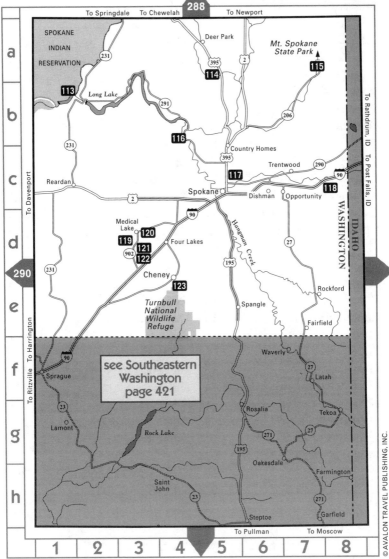

see Southeastern Washington page 421

Northeastern Washington

A lot of people call this area "God's country." You know why? Because nobody else could have thought of it. The vast number of lakes, streams, and national forests provides an unlimited land of adventure. You could spend a lifetime here—your days hiking, fishing, and exploring, your nights camping out and staring up at the stars.

And that's exactly what some people do, like our friend Rich Landers, the outdoors writer for the *Spokane Spokesman-Review*. People know they have it good here, living on the threshold of a fantastic land of adventure, but with a population base in Spokane that creates a financial center for career opportunities.

The landscape features a variety of settings. The national forests (Colville, Kaniksu, Wenatchee), set in the northern tier of the state, are ideal for people looking for a mountain hideaway. You'll find remote ridges and valleys with conifers, and many small streams and lakes. In the valleys, the region is carved by the Pacific Northwest's largest river system, featuring the Columbia River and Franklin D. Roosevelt Lake and the Spokane River. These are best for campers interested in water views, boating, and full facilities.

While many well-known destinations are stellar, our favorites are the lesser-known sites. There are dozens of such camps in this area, often along the shore of a small lake, that provide good fishing and hiking. You could search across the land and not find a better region for outdoor adventure. This is a wilderness to enjoy.

◼ Cold Springs

 8

It's quite a drive to get here, but you'll be happy you made the effort to reach this pretty forested camp. Campsites are located near a small stream amid a forest of lodgepole pine, Western larch, and several species of fir, including Douglas fir. Trails for horseback riding, hiking, and snowmobiling run through the area. Because the camp is little known and remote, it's advisable to obtain a map of the area from the Department of Natural Resources.

Location: Near Cold Creek; see Northeastern Washington, map 1, grid a3.

Campsites, facilities: There are nine campsites for tents or small trailers. Picnic tables, fire grills, and tent pads are provided. Vault toilets and drinking water are available. Leashed pets are permitted.

Reservations, fees: No reservations; no fee. Open year-round.

Directions: From Wenatchee, drive north on U.S. 97 for 120 miles to Tonasket and Forest Street. Turn left and drive 0.2 mile (crossing the Okanogan River) to Highway 7. Turn right (north) on Highway 7 (Loomis-Oroville Highway) and drive five miles. At the fork, continue on Loomis-Oroville Highway for about 12 miles to Toats Coulee Road, 2.1 miles north of Loomis. Turn left and drive 5.5 miles to the Toats Coulee Lower Site camp. Continue 0.1 mile to the upper site at the junction of roads. Take Road OM-T-1000 for 2.1 miles to Cold Creek Road. Turn right (gravel road) and drive 0.4 mile. Bear right and continue 1.8 miles. Bear left and drive 2.7 miles to the camp, past the picnic area.

Contact: Department of Natural Resources, Northeast Region, P.O. Box 190, Colville, WA 99114-0190; 360/902-1234 or 509/684-7474, fax 509/684-7484.

◼ North Fork Nine Mile

 6

Dear and black bears frequent this campground situated in the forest along the North Fork of Toats Coulee Creek and Nine Mile Creek. This camp is popular in the fall with hunters. Trout fishing is fair at Toats Coulee Creek; check regulations. It's advisable to obtain a map that details the area from the Department of Natural Resources.

Location: On the North Fork of Toats Coulee Creek; see Northeastern Washington, map 1, grid b3.

Campsites, facilities: There are 11 campsites for tents or small trailers. Picnic tables, fire grills, and tent pads are provided. Vault toilets and drinking water are available. Leashed pets are permitted.

Reservations, fees: No reservations; no fee. Open year-round.

Directions: From Wenatchee, drive north on U.S. 97 for 120 miles to Tonasket and Forest Street. Turn left and drive 0.2 mile (crossing the Okanogan River) to Highway 7. Turn right (north) on Highway 7 (Loomis-Oroville Highway) and drive five miles. At the fork, continue on Loomis-Oroville Highway for about 12 miles to Toats Coulee Road, 2.1 miles north of Loomis. Turn left and drive 5.5 miles to the Toats Coulee Lower Site camp. Continue 0.1 mile to the upper site at the junction of roads. Take Road OM-T-1000 for 2.5 miles to the campground on the right.

Contact: Department of Natural Resources, Northeast Region, P.O. Box 190, Colville, WA 99114-0190; 360/902-1234 or 509/684-7474, fax 509/684-7484.

3 Toats Coulee

 6

These are actually two primitive campsites set a short distance apart. The camp is in a wooded spot along Toats Coulee Creek. Trout fishing is available; check regulations. The best hiking is located 10 miles northwest in the Pasayten Wilderness (to reach this trailhead, continue driving up the campground road). These camps are popular in the fall for hunters. In the winter, a road for snowmobile use follows the South Fork of Toats Coulee Creek, swinging south and then heading east along Cecil Creek. Contact the Department of Natural Resources for details.

Location: On Toats Coulee Creek; see Northeastern Washington, map 1, grid b3.

Campsites, facilities: There are nine sites for tents or small trailers. Picnic tables, fire grills, and tent pads are provided. Vault toilets are available. There is no drinking water. Garbage must be packed out. Leashed pets are permitted.

Reservations, fees: No reservations; no fee. Open year-round.

Directions: From Wenatchee, drive north on U.S. 97 for 120 miles to Tonasket and Forest Street. Turn left and drive 0.2 mile (crossing the Okanogan River) to Highway 7. Turn right (north) on Highway 7 (Loomis-Oroville Highway) and drive five miles. At the fork, continue on Loomis-Oroville Highway for about 12 miles to Toats Coulee Road, 2.1 miles north of Loomis. Turn left and drive 5.5 miles to the lower campsite on the left. Continue 0.1 mile to the upper campsite, located at the junction of Road OM-T-2000 and Road OM-T-1000).

Contact: Department of Natural Resources, Northeast Region, P.O. Box 190, Colville, WA 99114-0190; 360/902-1234 or 509/684-7474, fax 509/684-7484.

4 Chopaka Lake

 8

This campground provides a classic setting for the expert angler. It's nestled along the western shore of Chopaka Lake, which is extremely popular with trout anglers. No boat motors are permitted on the lake. That makes it a winner for flyfishers (barbless hooks required) using float tubes.

Location: On Chopaka Lake; see Northeastern Washington, map 1, grid a3.

Campsites, facilities: There are 15 campsites for tents or small trailers. Picnic tables, fire grills, and tent pads are provided. Vault toilets, drinking water, a fishing platform, and primitive boat-launching and dock facilities are available. Some facilities are wheelchair-accessible. Leashed pets are permitted.

Reservations, fees: No reservations; no fee. Open year-round.

Directions: From Wenatchee, drive north on U.S. 97 for 120 miles to Tonasket and Forest Street. Turn left and drive 0.2 mile (crossing the Okanogan River) to Highway 7. Turn right (north) on Highway 7 (Loomis-Oroville Highway) and drive five miles. At the fork, continue on Loomis-Oroville Highway for about 12 miles to Toats Coulee Road, 2.1 miles north of Loomis. Turn left and drive 1.5 miles. Turn right onto a steep, one-lane road and drive 3.4 miles. Bear left, drive 1.7 miles, turn right, and drive two miles to the campground.

Contact: Department of Natural Resources, Northeast Region, P.O. Box 190, Colville, WA 99114-0190; 360/902-1234 or 509/684-7474, fax 509/684-7484.

5 Palmer Lake

 9

This shorefront camp is the only one at Palmer Lake. The campsites are set close to the lake's shore, which is very scenic. It fills

up during the summer, even on weekdays, often with visitors from Canada. Fishing is often good for kokanee salmon and rainbow trout. Power boating and water-skiing are permitted. The winter range of the deer is in the Sinlahekin Valley to the south of Palmer Lake. There are numerous migration routes in the region. Wildlife that can be spotted includes the endangered bighorn sheep, cougar, bald and golden eagles, black bear, and grouse.

Location: On Palmer Lake; see Northeastern Washington, map 1, grid b3.

Campsites, facilities: There are six campsites for tents or small trailers. Picnic tables, fire grills, and tent pads are provided. Vault toilets and a fishing pier are available, but there is no drinking water. Garbage must be packed out. A primitive boat launch is located at the opposite end of the lake; four-wheel-drive is required. Leashed pets are permitted.

Reservations, fees: No reservations; no fee. Open year-round, weather permitting.

Directions: From Wenatchee, drive north on U.S. 97 for 120 miles to Tonasket and Forest Street. Turn left and drive 0.2 mile, crossing the Okanogan River, to Highway 7. Turn right (north) on Highway 7 (Loomis-Oroville Highway) and drive 18.5 miles, 8.5 miles past Loomis. Stay to the right and drive to the camp at the north end of the lake.

Contact: Department of Natural Resources, Northeast Region, P.O. Box 190, Colville, WA 99114-0190; 360/902-1234 or 509/684-7474, fax 509/684-7484.

6 Osoyoos Lake State Park

      9

The park is set along the shore of Osoyoos Lake, a 14-mile-long lake created from the Okanogan River, located south of the Canadian Rockies. The park covers 47 acres and provides a base of operations for a fishing vacation. The lake provides rainbow trout, kokanee salmon, smallmouth bass, crappie, and perch. Water sports are also popular in the summer, and in winter, it is an ideal location for ice skating, ice fishing, and snow play. Expansive lawns lead down to the sandy shore of the lake. The park also features a war veteran's memorial. Osoyoos Lake is a winter nesting area for geese. A nine-hole golf course is located nearby. A history note: Many years ago, the area was the site of the annual *okanogan* (rendezvous) of the Washington and British Columbia Indians. They would gather and share supplies of fish and game for the year. Fishing gear and concessions are available at the park.

Location: On Osoyoos Lake; see Northeastern Washington, map 1, grid a5.

Campsites, facilities: There are 80 sites, including one site with full hookups, for tents or self-contained RVs up to 45 feet long, and six primitive tent sites. Picnic tables and fire grills are provided. Restrooms, flush toilets, showers, a dump station, a store, a café, firewood, and a playground with horseshoes and volleyball are available. A coin-operated laundry facility and ice are located within one mile. Boat-launching and dock facilities are nearby. Leashed pets are permitted.

Reservations, fees: Reserve at 888/CAMP-OUT (888/226-7688); website: www.parks.wa.gov/reservations ($7 reservation fee). Sites are $6 to $22 per night, $6 per extra vehicle per night. Major credit cards accepted. Open year-round, with limited facilities in winter.

Directions: From Oroville, on U.S. 97 just south of the Canadian border, drive north on U.S. 97 for one mile to the park entrance on the right.

Contact: Osoyoos Lake State Park, 509/476-3321; State Park information, 360/902-8844.

⑦ Sun Cove Resort

 9

This beautiful resort is surrounded by trees and hills and set along the shore of Wannacut Lake, a spring-fed lake that doesn't get much traffic. The lake is approximately three miles long and 2.5 miles wide. An eight-mph speed limit is enforced for boats. Fishing, swimming, boating, and hiking are all summertime options. The park provides full facilities, including a heated pool, a playground, and a recreation hall. For the horsy set, a guided trail and overnight rides are available one mile from the resort.

Location: On Wannacut Lake; see Northeastern Washington, map 1, grid b4.

Campsites, facilities: There are 22 tent sites and 26 drive-through sites with hookups for trailers or RVs of any length and two sites up to 38 feet long, two cottages, and 10 motel units with kitchens. Picnic tables are provided. Restrooms, flush toilets, showers (fee), a dump station, a recreation hall, a store, a café, a laundry room, ice, a playground, and a swimming pool are available. Some facilities are wheelchair-accessible. Boat docks, launching facilities, and rentals are also available. Leashed pets are permitted.

Reservations, fees: Reservations accepted. Sites are $20 per night. Major credit cards accepted. Open late April through October.

Directions: From Oroville (on U.S. 97 just south of the Canadian border), drive west on Ellemehan Mountain Road for about six miles to Wannacut Lake Road. Turn left (south) and drive five miles to the resort at the end of the road.

Contact: Sun Cove Resort, 93 East Wannacut Lane, Oroville, WA 98844; 509/476-2223.

⑧ Spectacle Lake Resort

   7

This pleasant resort on the shore of long, narrow Spectacle Lake has grassy, shaded sites. Sites are usually available here, although reservations are accepted. Recreation options include boating, fishing, swimming, water-skiing, and hunting (in season).

Location: On Spectacle Lake; see Northeastern Washington, map 1, grid b4.

Campsites, facilities: There are 40 sites with full hookups for tents, trailers, or RVs of any length, and 12 motel rooms with kitchenettes. Picnic tables are provided. Restrooms, flush toilets, showers, bottled gas, a dump station, a store, a coin-operated laundry, ice, a playground, a recreation hall, an exercise room, and a heated swimming pool are available. Boat docks, launching facilities, and rentals are also available nearby. Leashed pets are permitted.

Reservations, fees: Reservations accepted. Sites are $16 per night, $1 per person per night for more than two people. Major credit cards accepted. Open mid-April to late October.

Directions: In Tonasket on U.S. 97, turn west (left if arriving from south), cross the bridge, and continue to Highway 7. Turn right on Highway 7 and drive about 12 miles to Holmes Road. Turn left (south) on Holmes Road and drive one-half mile to McCammon Road. Turn right (west) and drive one block to the park at the end of the road.

Contact: Spectacle Lake Resort, 10 McCammon Road, Tonasket, WA 98855; 509/223-3433; website: www.spectaclelakeresort.com.

9 Rainbow Resort

      7

This resort on Spectacle Lake is an alternative to Spectacle Lake Resort. Major renovations were completed in late 2000. The camp features pretty lake views and full facilities. Nearby activities include swimming, fishing, hunting, tennis, and horseback riding, including overnight trail rides.

Location: On Spectacle Lake; see Northeastern Washington, map 1, grid b4.

Campsites, facilities: There are 54 sites with full hookups for trailers or RVs of any length, including 34 drive-through sites, and 14 tent sites with electricity and water. Picnic tables and fire pits are provided. Restrooms, flush toilets, showers, ice, a recreation room, horseshoes, volleyball, boat docks, boat rentals, and launching facilities are available. Leashed pets are permitted.

Reservations, fees: Reservations accepted. Sites are $20 per night. Major credit cards accepted. Senior discount available. Open April through October.

Directions: From Ellisford, turn west on Loomis Highway and drive 9.5 miles to the resort on the left.

Contact: Rainbow Resort, 761 Loomis Highway, Tonasket, WA 98855; 509/223-3700 or 800/347-4375.

10 Spectacle Falls Resort

     8

Spectacle Falls Resort is set on the shore of Spectacle Lake. It is open only as long as fishing is available, which means an early closing in July. Be sure to phone ahead of time to verify that the resort is open. Nearby recreation options include hiking, swimming, fishing, tennis, and horseback riding, including guided trails and overnight rides. Rainbow Resort provides an option.

Location: On Spectacle Lake; see Northeastern Washington, map 1, grid b4.

Campsites, facilities: There are 20 drive-through sites with full hookups for trailers or RVs of any length, 10 tent sites, and four mobile homes available for rent. Picnic tables are provided. Restrooms, flush toilets, showers, a dump station, ice, boat docks, launching facilities, and boat rentals are available. Leashed pets are permitted.

Reservations, fees: Reservations accepted. Sites are $16 per night, $2 per person per night for more than two people, $2 per extra vehicle per night. Open mid-April to late July.

Directions: From Tonasket on U.S. 97, turn northwest on Loomis Highway and drive 15 miles to the resort on the left.

Contact: Spectacle Falls Resort, 879 Loomis Highway, Tonasket, WA 98855; 509/223-4141.

11 Lost Lake

     7

This camp is set on the shore of Lost Lake at 3,800 feet. It keeps visitors happy as a launch point for fishing, swimming, hiking, hunting, and horseback riding. Only electric motors are permitted on the lake (that is, no gas motors). The lake is similar to Beth and Beaver Lakes (see Beth Lake and Beaver Lake camp listings), but is more round. The Big Tree Botanical Area is about one mile away. Note that the group site is often booked one year in advance.

Location: On Lost Lake in Okanogan National Forest; see Northeastern Washington, map 1, grid b8.

Campsites, facilities: There are 18 single and double sites for tents, trailers, or RVs up to 31 feet long. There is also one group unit available by reservation only. Picnic tables and fire rings are provided. Drinking water and vault toilets are available. Boat docks and launching facilities are nearby. Leashed pets are permitted.

Reservations, fees: Reservations required for the group site; phone 509/486-2186. Single and multiple sites are $8 per vehicle per night; group rates are $40 for up to 25 people, $60 for 26 to 50 people, and $80 for 51 to 100 people. Senior discount available. Open mid-May to mid-September.

Directions: From East Wenatchee, drive north on U.S. 97 for 20 miles to Tonasket and Highway 20. Turn east on Highway 20 and drive 20 miles to Bonaparte Lake Road (County Road 4953). Turn left (north) and drive six miles to Forest Road 32. Turn right (north) and drive three miles to Forest Road 33. Bear left (northwest) and drive three miles to a four-way intersection. Turn left on Forest Road 33-050 and drive 0.3 miles to the campground on the right.

Contact: Okanogan and Wenatchee National Forests, Tonasket Ranger District, 1 West Winesap Avenue, Tonasket, WA 98855; 509/486-2186, fax 509/486-5161.

12 Bonaparte Lake

 7

This campground is located on the southern shore of Bonaparte Lake at an elevation of 3,600 feet. The lake is stocked with rainbow trout, brook trout, and mackinaw trout. See the description of Bonaparte Lake Resort for lake recreation information. Several trails nearby provide access to Mt. Bonaparte Lookout. Consult a U.S. Forest Service map for details.

Location: On Bonaparte Lake in Okanogan National Forest; see Northeastern Washington, map 1, grid b8.

Campsites, facilities: There are 15 single and 10 multiple sites for tents, trailers, or RVs up to 31 feet long, plus three bike-in/hike-in sites (require a walk of less than 100 feet), and one group site that can accommodate up to 30 people. Picnic tables and fire grills are provided. Drinking water and vault toilets are available. A dump station, a store, a café, and ice are available within one mile. Boat docks and launching facilities are also available. Some facilities are wheelchair-accessible, including a wheelchair-accessible fishing dock. Leashed pets are permitted.

Reservations, fees: No reservations accepted. Sites are $8 per night. Senior discount available. Open mid-May to mid-September.

Directions: From East Wenatchee, drive north on U.S. 97 for 20 miles to Tonasket and Highway 20. Turn east on Highway 20 and drive 20 miles to Bonaparte Lake Road (County Road 4953). Turn left (north) and drive six miles to Bonaparte Lake and Forest Road 32 and the campground on the left.

Contact: Okanogan and Wenatchee National Forests, Tonasket Ranger District, 1 West Winesap Avenue, Tonasket, WA 98855; 509/486-2186, fax 509/486-5161.

13 Bonaparte Lake Resort

 6

Fishing is popular at this resort, which is set on the southeast shore of Bonaparte Lake. A 10-mph speed limit keeps the lake quiet, ideal for fishing. Other recreational activities include hiking and hunting in the nearby U.S. Forest Service lands and snowmobiling and cross-country skiing in the winter.

Location: On Bonaparte Lake; see Northeastern Washington, map 1, grid b8.

Campsites, facilities: There are 35 sites, including most with full hookups and some drive-through sites, for trailers or RVs of any length, 10 tent sites, and 10 cabins. Picnic tables are provided. Restrooms, flush toilets, showers, bottled gas, a dump station, firewood, a recreation hall, a store, a restaurant, a laundry room, ice, a playground, boat docks, launching facilities, and boat rentals are available. Leashed pets (licensed drivers only) are permitted.

Reservations, fees: Reservations accepted. Sites are $8 to $14 per night; cabins are $35 to $55 per night. Open April through October.

Directions: From East Wenatchee, drive north on U.S. 97 for 20 miles to Tonasket and Highway 20. Turn east on Highway 20 and drive 20 miles to Bonaparte Lake Road (County Road 4953). Turn left (north) and drive six miles to Bonaparte Lake and the resort on the left.

Contact: Bonaparte Lake Resort, 615 Bonaparte Road, Tonasket, WA 98855; 509/486-2828; website: www.bonapart@nuinet.com.

14 Jack's RV Park and Motel

 5

This park is in the town of Conconully, not far from Conconully Reservoir. Horseshoe pits can be found in the park, and nearby recreation options include hiking trails, fishing, hunting (in season), and water sports (summer and winter) at the lake.

Location: Near Conconully Reservoir; see Northeastern Washington, map 1, grid d3.

Campsites, facilities: There are 57 sites with full hookups, including 20 drive-through sites, for trailers or RVs of any length. Picnic tables are provided. Restrooms, flush toilets,

showers, propane gas, and a coin-operated laundry are available. A store, a café, and ice are located within two blocks. Boat docks, launching facilities, and rentals are nearby. Leashed pets are permitted.

Reservations, fees: Reservations accepted. Sites are $18 per night, $2 per person per night for more than two people, $3 per extra vehicle per night. Major credit cards accepted. Open mid-April through October, weather permitting.

Directions: From U.S. 97 in Okanogan, turn north (left if arriving from the south) on Pine Street/Conconully Highway and drive 17.5 miles northwest to Conconully and Broadway Street. Turn right (east) and drive one block to A Avenue. Turn left (north) on A Avenue and drive less than one block to the park on the right.

Contact: Jack's RV Park and Motel, P.O. Box 98, Conconully, WA 98819; 509/826-0132 or 800/893-5668.

15 Lazy Daze RV Park

 5

This park is in downtown Conconully, a short distance from the lake. The park is geared specifically toward RVs, with shaded grassy sites. Nearby recreational opportunities include hiking, fishing, swimming, boating—and in winter, snowmobiling.

Location: Near Conconully Reservoir; see Northeastern Washington, map 1, grid d3.

Campsites, facilities: There are 43 drive-through sites with full hookups for trailers or RVs of any length. Picnic tables are provided. Restrooms, flush toilets, coin-operated showers, firewood, a coin-operated laundry, and ice are available. Bottled gas, a dump station, a store, a café, and ice are located within two blocks. Boat docks, launching facilities, and rentals are nearby. Leashed pets are permitted.

Reservations, fees: Reservations accepted. Sites are $18 per night. Senior discount available. Open April through October, weather permitting.

Directions: From U.S. 97 in Okanogan, turn north (left if arriving from the south) on Pine Street/Conconully Highway and drive 17.5 miles northwest to Conconully and Silver Street. Turn right (east) and drive one block to A Avenue. Turn right (south) on A Avenue and drive about half a block to the park on the right.

Contact: Lazy Daze RV Park, P.O. Box 67, 209 A Avenue, Conconully, WA 98819; 509/826-0326.

16 Kozy Kabins and RV Park

 7

This quiet and private park is in Conconully, with a small creek running through it and plenty of greenery. A full-service marina is located close by. If you continue northeast of town on County Road 4015, the road will get a bit narrow for awhile, but will widen again when you enter the Sinlahekin Habitat Management Area, which is managed by the Department of Fish and Game. There are some primitive campsites in this valley, especially along the shores of the lakes in the area.

Location: Near Conconully Reservoir; see Northeastern Washington, map 1, grid d3.

Campsites, facilities: There are 15 sites with full hookups for trailers or RVs up to 40 feet, six tent sites, and eight cabins. Picnic tables and fire pits are provided. Restrooms, flush toilets, coin-operated showers, and firewood are available. Bottled gas, a dump station, a store, a café, a coin-operated laundry, and ice are located within one block. Boat docks,

launching facilities, and boat rentals are nearby. Leashed pets are permitted.

Reservations, fees: Reservations accepted. Sites are $8 to $16 per night; cabins are $35 per night. Major credit cards accepted. Open year-round.

Directions: From U.S. 97 in Okanogan, turn north (left if arriving from the south) on Pine Street/Conconully Highway and drive 17.5 miles northwest to Conconully and Broadway Street. Turn right (east) and drive one block to A Avenue. The park is at the junction of A Avenue and Broadway.

Contact: Kozy Kabins and RV Park, P.O. Box 82, 111 East Broadway, Conconully, WA 98819; 509/826-6780 or 888/502-2246.

17 Maple Flats RV Park and Resort

 9

This campground near Conconully Reservoir is in a beautiful setting, situated in a valley between two lakes. Nearby recreation options include hiking and biking on the many nature trails in the area, an 18-hole golf course (15 miles away), and trout fishing in the well-stocked Upper and Lower Conconully Reservoirs.

Location: Near Conconully Reservoir; see Northeastern Washington, map 1, grid d3.

Campsites, facilities: There are 25 drive-through sites with full hookups for trailers or RVs of any length, a dispersed camping area with room for six tents, and one apartment with kitchen for rent. Picnic tables and fire pits are provided. Restrooms, flush toilets, showers, a coin-operated laundry, and a covered gazebo with electricity are available. Groceries, dining, dancing, propane, and boat, snowmobile, and jet ski rentals are located within two blocks. Boat docks and launching facilities are also nearby. Leashed pets are permitted.

Reservations, fees: Reservations accepted. Sites are $10 to $18 per night. Open April through October.

Directions: From U.S. 97 in Okanogan, turn north (left if arriving from the south) on Pine Street/Conconully Highway and drive 17.5 miles northwest to Conconully and Silver Street. Turn right (east) and drive one block to A Avenue. Turn left (north) on A Avenue and drive to the park on the right.

Contact: Maple Flats RV Park and Resort, P.O. Box 126, 310 A Avenue, Conconully, WA 98819; 509/826-4231 or 800/683-1180.

18 Conconully State Park

  9

This park is considered a fisherman's paradise, with trout, bass, and kokanee salmon. The park is set along Conconully Reservoir, covering 81 acres with 5,400 feet of shoreline. A boat launch, beach access, swimming, and fishing provide all sorts of water sports possibilities. A half-mile nature trail is available. This park dates to 1910. A side-trip option is to Sinlahekin Habitat Management Area, which is accessible via County Road 4015. This route heads northeast along the shore of Conconully Reservoir on the other side of U.S. 97. The road is narrow at first, but then becomes wider as it enters the Habitat Management Area.

Location: On Conconully Reservoir; see Northeastern Washington, map 1, grid d3.

Campsites, facilities: There are 71 sites for tents or self-contained RVs up to 60 feet long and six primitive tent sites. Picnic tables and fire grills are provided. Restrooms, flush toilets, showers, a dump station, firewood, and a playground are available. A store, a café, a coin-operated laundry, and ice are located within one mile. Boat-launching and dock facilities are nearby. A picnic area with covered shelter and electricity, horseshoe pits, a baseball field, and interpretive activities are available nearby. Leashed pets are permitted.

Reservations, fees: No reservations accepted. Sites are $6 to $16 per night, $6 per extra vehicle per night. Senior discount available. Open April through September.

Directions: On U.S. 97 at Omak, take the North Omak exit. At the base of the hill, turn right and drive two miles until you reach Conconully Road. Turn right and drive 19 miles north to the park entrance.

Contact: Conconully State Park, P.O. Box 95, Conconully, WA 98819; 509/826-7408; State Park information, 360/902-8844.

19 Conconully Reservoir Resort

  6

This resort is one of several set along the shore of Conconully Reservoir. Tents are permitted, but this is a prime vacation destination for RVers. Trout fishing, swimming, and boating are all options here.

Location: On Upper Conconully Reservoir; see Northeastern Washington, map 1, grid d3.

Campsites, facilities: There are 11 sites with full hookups for trailers or RVs of any length, four cabins, and one apartment. Picnic tables are provided. Restrooms, flush toilets, coin-operated showers, and ice are available. Bottled gas, a dump station, a store with tackle, a café, and a coin-operated laundry are located within one mile. Boat docks, launching facilities, and a variety of boat rentals are available. Leashed pets are permitted.

Reservations, fees: Reservations accepted. Sites are $21 per night, $2 per person per night for more than two people, $55 for cabins. Major credit cards accepted. Open late April to late October.

Directions: From U.S. 97 in Okanogan, turn north (left if arriving from the south) on Pine Street/Conconully Highway and drive 17.5 miles northwest to Conconully and Lake Street. Turn right on Lake Street and drive one mile to the park on the right.

Contact: Conconully Reservoir Resort, P.O. Box 131, 102 Sinlahekin Road, Conconully, WA 98819; 509/826-0813 or 800/850-0813, fax 509/826-1292; website: www.conconully lakeresort.com.

20 Liar's Cove Resort

    6

Roomy sites for RVs can be found at this camp on the shore of Conconully Reservoir. Tents are allowed, too. Fishing, swimming, boating, and hiking opportunities are located nearby.

Location: On Conconully Reservoir; see Northeastern Washington, map 1, grid d3.

Campsites, facilities: There are 30 sites with full hookups, including 20 drive-through sites for tents, trailers, or RVs up to 50 feet long, two cabins, one mobile home, and three motel rooms. Picnic tables and fire pits are provided. Restrooms, flush toilets, coin-operated showers, cable TV, and ice are available. Bottled gas, a dump station, a store, and a café are located within one mile. Boat docks, launching facilities, and boat rentals are available. Some facilities are wheelchair-accessible. Leashed pets are permitted.

Reservations, fees: Reservations accepted. Sites are $20 to $29 per night, $2 per

person per night for more than two people. Open April to through October.

Directions: From U.S. 97 in Okanogan, turn north (left if arriving from the south) on Pine Street/Conconully Highway and drive 16.5 miles northwest to Conconully and look for the park on the left. It's located one quarter-mile south of Conconully.

Contact: Liar's Cove Resort, P.O. Box 72, Conconully, WA 98819; 509/826-1288 or 800/830-1288; website: www.omakchronicle .com/liarscove.

21 Shady Pines Resort

     6

This camp is set on the western shore of Conconully Reservoir. It is near Conconully State Park and provides a possible option if the state park campground is full—a common occurrence in summer. But note that on summer weekends, this camp often fills as well. See the descriptions of Kozy Kabins and RV Park and Conconully State Park for area information.

Location: On Conconully Reservoir; see Northeastern Washington, map 1, grid d3.

Campsites, facilities: There are 23 sites for trailers or RVs of any length, including 21 sites with full hookups and 14 drive-through sites. Picnic tables and fire rings are provided. Restrooms, flush toilets, coin-operated showers, ice, and firewood are available. Bottled gas, a dump station, a store, a café, and a coin-operated laundry are located within one mile. Boat-launching facilities and boat rentals are available. Leashed pets are permitted.

Reservations, fees: Reservations accepted. Sites are $19 to $21 per night. Major credit cards accepted. Open mid-April to late October.

Directions: From U.S. 97 in Okanogan, turn north (left if arriving from the south) on Pine Street/Conconully Highway and drive 16.5 miles northwest to Conconully and Broadway Street. Turn left (west) and drive one mile. The park is on the west shore of the lake.

Contact: Shady Pines Resort, P.O. Box 44, 125 West Fork Road, Conconully, WA 98819; 509/826-2287 or 800/552-2287; website: www.shadypinesresort.com.

22 Sugarloaf

 6

Sugarloaf Lake is a small lake, about 20 acres, and this small camp is set near its shore. It provides fishing for rainbow trout, but the lake level often drops during summer, so this camp gets little use in late summer and early fall. Conconully State Park and Information Center are nearby.

Location: On Sugarloaf Lake in Okanogan National Forest; see Northeastern Washington, map 1, grid d3.

Campsites, facilities: There are five tent sites and one site for a tent, trailer, or RV up to 21 feet long. Picnic tables are provided, but there is no drinking water. No garbage service is provided, so trash must be packed out. Vault toilets and firewood are available. Boat-launching facilities are available nearby. No boats with gas motors are permitted. Leashed pets are permitted.

Reservations, fees: No reservations. Sites are $5 per night, $5 per extra vehicle per night. Senior discount available. Open mid-May to mid-September.

Directions: From East Wenatchee, drive north on U.S. 97 for 88 miles to Okanogan and County Road 9229. Turn north and drive about 17.5 miles northwest to Conconully and County Road 4015. Turn right (northwest) on

County Road 4015 and drive 4.5 miles to the campground on the left.

Contact: Okanogan and Wenatchee National Forests, Tonasket Ranger District, 1 West Winesap Avenue, Tonasket, WA 98855; 509/486-2186, fax 509/486-5161.

23 Rock Lakes

 8

This camp is set in a forested area along the shore of Rock Lake. Fishing for rainbow trout and brook trout is a plus at Rock Lake. A downer is that access for launching even car-top boats is difficult, requiring a quarter-mile hike. That makes it a better bet for float tubes. Note that the best fishing is early in the season and that the lake level often drops because of irrigation use. Some roads in the area are used by hikers and bikers. A good bet is to combine a trip here with nearby Leader Lake. Highway 20 east of I-5 is a designated scenic route.

Location: On Rock Lake; see Northeastern Washington, map 1, grid e3.

Campsites, facilities: There are eight sites for tents or small trailers. Picnic tables and fire pits are provided. Vault toilets are available, but there is no drinking water. Leashed pets are permitted.

Reservations, fees: No reservations; no fee. Open year-round.

Directions: From East Wenatchee, drive north on U.S. 97 for 88 miles to Okanogan and Highway 20. Turn west and drive 10 miles to Loup Loup Canyon Road. Turn left on Loup Loup Canyon Road and drive 4.8 miles to Rock Lakes Road. Turn left on Rock Lakes Road and drive 5.8 miles to the campground entrance. Turn left and drive one quarter-mile to the campground.

Contact: Department of Natural Resources, Northeast Region, P.O. Box 190,

Colville, WA 99114-0190; 509/684-7474, fax 509/684-7484.

24 Rock Creek

 6

This wooded campground is situated at the confluence of Rock and Loup Loup Creeks. A group picnic shelter with a barbecue is available. The camp is used primarily in the fall as a base camp for hunters and occasionally during the summer, primarily on weekends. It's advisable to obtain a map detailing the area from the Department of Natural Resources.

Location: On Rock Creek and Loup Loup Creek; see Northeastern Washington, map 1, grid e3.

Campsites, facilities: There are six sites for tents, small trailers, or RVs up to 30 feet. Picnic tables and fire pits are provided. Vault toilets, a picnic area, and drinking water are available. Leashed pets are permitted.

Reservations, fees: No reservations; no fee. Open year-round.

Directions: From East Wenatchee, drive north on U.S. 97 for 88 miles to Okanogan and Highway 20. Turn west and drive 10 miles to Loup Loup Canyon Road. Turn left on Loup Loup Canyon Road and drive 3.9 miles to the camp on the left.

Contact: Department of Natural Resources, Northeast Region, P.O. Box 190, Colville, WA 99114-0190; 509/684-7474, fax 509/684-7484.

25 Leader Lake

 7

This primitive but pretty camp is set along the shore of Leader Lake. It is just far enough off the beaten path to get missed by many travelers. The camp has forest cover. The boat ramp is a bonus, and trout fishing can be good in season. Note that the water level often drops in summer because of irrigation use.

Location: On Leader Lake; see Northeastern Washington, map 1, grid f3.

Campsites, facilities: There are 16 sites for tents or small trailers. Picnic tables and fire pits are provided. Vault toilets, a boat ramp, and a fishing pier are available, but there is no drinking water. Boat-launching facilities are nearby. Leashed pets are permitted.

Reservations, fees: No reservations; no fee. Open year-round.

Directions: From East Wenatchee, drive north on U.S. 97 for 88 miles to Okanogan and Highway 20. Turn west and drive eight miles to Leader Lake Road. Turn left and drive 0.4 mile to the campground.

Contact: Department of Natural Resources, Northeast Region, P.O. Box 190, Colville, WA 99114-0190; 509/684-7474, fax 509/684-7484.

26 American Legion Park

 6

This city park is located along the shore of the Okanogan River in an urban setting. The sites are graveled and sunny. Anglers may want to try their hand at the excellent bass fishing here. There is a historical museum at the park.

Location: On the Okanogan River; see Northeastern Washington, map 1, grid f4.

Campsites, facilities: There are 35 sites for tents, trailers, or RVs of any length. No hookups. Picnic tables are provided. Restrooms, drinking water, flush toilets, and coin-operated showers are available. A store, a café, a coin-operated laundry, and ice are located within one mile. Leashed pets are permitted.

Reservations, fees: No reservations accepted. Sites are $3 to $5 per vehicle per night. Open May to October, weather permitting.

Directions: From East Wenatchee, drive north on U.S. 97 for 88 miles to Okanogan and Highway 215. Turn left (north) on Highway 215 and drive about three miles to the campground on the right.

Contact: Okanogan City Hall, P.O. Box 752, Okanogan, WA 98840; 509/422-3600.

27 Eastside Park and Carl Precht Memorial RV Park

  6

This city park is in the town of Omak, along the shore of the Okanogan River. It covers about 10 acres, with the campsites positioned on concrete pads surrounded by grass. Trout fishing is often good here, and there is a boat ramp near the campground. Nearby recreation options include an 18-hole golf course, a pool, and a sports field.

Location: On the Okanogan River; see Northeastern Washington, map 1, grid e4.

Campsites, facilities: There are 76 drive-through sites with full hookups for trailers or RVs of any length, and 25 tent sites. Picnic tables are provided. Restrooms, flush toilets, coin-operated showers, a dump station, a swimming pool, a playground with horseshoe pits, a skateboarding park, and a fitness trail are available. A store, a café, a coin-operated laundry, and ice are located within one mile. Boat-launching facilities are nearby. Some facilities are wheelchair-accessible. Leashed pets are permitted.

Reservations, fees: No reservations. Sites are $10 to $12 per night. Open April through September, weather permitting.

Directions: From U.S. 97 in Omak, turn east (right, if coming from the south) on Highway 155 and drive 0.3 mile to the campground on the left.

Contact: City of Omak, P.O. Box 72, Omak, WA 98841; 509/826-1170.

28 Lyman Lake

 5

Little known and little used, this campground along the shore of Lyman Lake is an idyllic setting for those wanting solitude and quiet. The lake is quite small, just five acres at most, but fishing for stocked rainbow trout is an option.

Location: On Lyman Lake in Okanogan National Forest; see Northeastern Washington, map 1, grid d8.

Campsites, facilities: There are four sites for tents, trailers, or RVs up to 31 feet long. Picnic tables and fire grills are provided. Vault toilets are available, but there is no drinking water. Garbage must be packed out. Leashed pets are permitted.

Reservations, fees: No reservations; no fee. Open mid-May to mid-September.

Directions: From East Wenatchee, drive north on U.S. 97 for 119 miles to Tonasket and Highway 20. Turn east on Highway 20 and drive 12.5 miles to County Road 9455. Turn right (southeast) on County Road 9455 and drive 13 miles to County Road 3785. Turn right (south) on County Road 3785 and drive 2.5 miles to the campground entrance on the right.

Contact: Okanogan and Wenatchee National Forests, 1 West Winesap Avenue, Tonasket, WA 98855; 509/486-2186, fax 509/486-5161.

29 Crawfish Lake

 8

This pretty, remote, and primitive camp is set at 4,500 feet elevation along the shore of Crawfish Lake. Crawdads were once abundant here, but they have been depleted by overfishing. Swimming and fishing for trout are more popular.

Location: On Crawfish Lake in Okanogan National Forest; see Northeastern Washington, map 1, grid e7.

Campsites, facilities: There are 19 sites for tents, trailers, or RVs up to 31 feet long. Picnic tables and fire grills are provided. Vault toilets are available, but there is no drinking water. No garbage service is provided, so trash must be packed out. Boat-launching facilities are located on the lake. Leashed pets are permitted.

Reservations, fees: No reservations; no fee. Open mid-May to mid-September.

Directions: From East Wenatchee, drive north on U.S. 97 for 102 miles to Riverside and County Road 9320. Turn right (east) on County Road 9320 and drive 20 miles (becomes Forest Road 30) to Forest Road 30-100. Turn right and drive one-half mile to the campground on the right.

Contact: Okanogan and Wenatchee National Forests, Tonasket Ranger District, 1 West Winesap Avenue, Tonasket, WA 98855; 509/486-2186, fax 509/486-5161.

30 Alta Lake State Park

 8

This state park is nestled among the pines along the shore of Alta Lake. The park covers 181 acres, and the lake is two miles long and one-half mile wide. It brightens a region where the mountains and pines meet the desert. A feature is good trout fishing in summer, along with a boat launch and a half-mile-long swimming beach. Windsurfing is often excellent on windy afternoons. Because of many hidden rocks just under the lake surface, it can be dangerous for water-skiing. An 18-hole golf course and a riding stable are close by, and a nice one-mile hiking trail leads up to a scenic lookout. Lake Chelan is about 30 minutes away.

Location: On Alta Lake; see Northeastern Washington, map 1, grid h1.

Campsites, facilities: There are 157 developed tent sites and 32 sites with partial hookups (water and electricity) for trailers or RVs up to 40 feet long. Picnic tables and fire grills are provided. Restrooms, flush toilets, showers, electricity, firewood, and a dump station are available. A picnic area with a shelter is available nearby. A store, a café, and ice can be found within one mile. Some facilities are wheelchair-accessible. Boat-launching facilities are nearby. Leashed pets are permitted.

Reservations, fees: No reservations. Sites are $6 to $21 per night, $6 per extra vehicle per night. Senior discount available. Open April through October.

Directions: From East Wenatchee, drive north on U.S. 97 for 64 miles to Highway 153 (just south of Pateros). Turn left (northwest) on Highway 153 and drive two miles to Alta Lake Road. Turn left (southwest) and drive two miles to the park at the end of the road.

Contact: Alta Lake State Park, 509/923-2473; State Park information, 360/902-8844.

31 Bridgeport State Park

 8

Bridgeport State Park is located along the shore of Rufus Woods Lake, a reservoir on the Columbia River above Chief Joseph Dam. It's a big place, covering 748 acres, including 7,500 feet of shoreline and 18 acres of lawn, with some shade amid the desert landscape. Highlights include beach access and a boat launch. A unique feature are the "haystacks," which are unusual volcanic formations that resemble their name, the park's most striking characteristic. Fishing is best by boat because shore fishing requires a Colville Tribe Fishing License (for sale at the Bridgeport Hardware Store), in addition to a state fishing license. The lake has plenty of rainbow trout and walleye. A half-mile walking trail is available out of camp. Windsurfing in the afternoon wind and water-skiing are popular at the lake. Nearby recreation options include an 18-hole golf course.

Location: On Rufus Woods Lake; see Northeastern Washington, map 1, grid h4.

Campsites, facilities: There are 14 sites for tents or self-contained RVs and 20 sites with water and electrical hookups for trailers or RVs up to 45 feet long. Picnic tables and fire grills are provided. Restrooms, flush toilets, coin-operated showers, firewood, a picnic area, and a dump station are available. A store, a café, and ice are located within two miles. Boat docks and launching facilities are nearby on both the upper and lower portions of the reservoir. Interpretive programs are available in summer. Leashed pets are permitted.

Reservations, fees: No reservations. Sites are $15 to $22 per night. Senior discount available. Open April through October.

Directions: From East Wenatchee, drive north on U.S. 97 for 71 miles to Highway 17. Turn south on Highway 17 and drive eight miles southeast to the park entrance on the left.

Contact: Bridgeport State Park, P.O. Box 846, Bridgeport, WA 98813; 509/686-7231; State Park information, 360/902-8844.

Lake, and several hiking trails, one of which leads up to the Mt. Bonaparte Lookout.

Location: On Beth Lake in Okanogan National Forest; see Northeastern Washington, map 2, grid b1.

Campsites, facilities: There are 15 sites for tents, trailers, or RVs up to 31 feet long, plus one multiple site. Picnic tables and fire rings are provided. Drinking water and vault toilets are available. Boat-launching facilities are available nearby. Some facilities are wheelchair-accessible. Leashed pets are permitted.

Reservations, fees: No reservations accepted. Sites are $6 per vehicle per night. Senior discount available. Open mid-May to mid-September.

Directions: From East Wenatchee, drive north on U.S. 97 for 20 miles to Tonasket and Highway 20. Turn east on Highway 20 and drive 20 miles to Bonaparte Lake Road (County Road 4953). Turn left (north) and drive six miles to Bonaparte Lake and Forest Road 32. Bear right (north) and drive six miles to County Road 9480. Turn left (northwest) and drive one mile to the campground on the left.

Contact: Okanogan and Wenatchee National Forests, Tonasket Ranger District, 1 West Winesap Avenue, Tonasket, WA 98855; 509/486-2186, fax 509/486-5161.

32 Beth Lake

 7

This campground is set between Beth Lake and Beaver Lake, both small, narrow lakes stocked with rainbow trout and brook trout. The elevation is 2,800 feet. A 1.9-mile-long hiking trail (one-way) connects the two lakes. Other side trips in the area include Lost Lake, Bonaparte

33 Beaver Lake

  7

Home for this camp is along the southeastern shore of long, narrow Beaver Lake, situated at 2,700 feet elevation, one of several lakes in this area. Beth Lake, the previous listing, is nearby and accessible with an hour-long hike. The lake is stocked with trout. Fishing, swimming, hunting, and hiking are all possibilities here. See the descriptions for Beth Lake, Lost Lake, and Bonaparte Lake for information on the other lakes in the area.

Location: On Beaver Lake in Okanogan National Forest; see Northeastern Washington, map 2, grid b1.

Campsites, facilities: There are nine single and two multiple sites for tents, trailers, or RVs up to 21 feet long. Picnic tables are provided. Vault toilets are available. No drinking water is available. Boat-launching facilities are located within 100 yards of the campground. No boats with gas engines are permitted. Leashed pets are permitted.

Reservations, fees: No reservations. Sites are $6 per vehicle per night. Senior discount available. Open mid-May to mid-September.

Directions: From East Wenatchee, drive north on U.S. 97 for 20 miles to Tonasket and Highway 20. Turn east on Highway 20 and drive 20 miles to Bonaparte Lake Road (County Road 4953). Turn left (north) and drive six miles to Bonaparte Lake and Forest Road 32. Bear right (north) and drive six miles to the campground on the left.

Contact: Okanogan and Wenatchee National Forests, Tonasket Ranger District, 1 West Winesap Avenue, Tonasket, WA 98855; 509/486-2186, fax 509/486-5161.

❸❹ Curlew Lake State Park

  8

Boredom is banned at this park, which is set on the eastern shore of Curlew Lake. This park covers 123 acres, and the lake is 5.5 miles long. Fishing is often good for trout and largemouth bass at the lake, and there are additional fishable lakes and streams in the immediate region. There is also beach access, swimming, water-skiing, and hiking, with two miles of hiking and biking trails in the park. The park is also used as a base for bicycle tour groups, with mountain biking available on a fairly steep trail that provides a view of the valley. The park borders an air field. An active osprey nest can be viewed from the park. Nearby recreation options include an 18-hole golf course. The park is located in the heart of a historic gold-mining district.

Location: On Curlew Lake; see Northeastern Washington, map 2, grid c3.

Campsites, facilities: There are 25 sites with full or partial hookups for trailers or RVs up to 40 feet long, 57 developed tent sites, and five primitive tent sites. Picnic tables are provided. Restrooms, flush toilets, showers, a dump station, electricity, drinking water, sewer hookups, firewood, and boat-launching and dock facilities are available. Boat fuel is available at the marina. An amphitheater with interpretive activities is available nearby. Leashed pets are permitted.

Reservations, fees: No reservations accepted. Sites are $6 to $21 per night, $6 per extra vehicle per night. Senior discount available. Open April to through October.

Directions: From Spokane on I-90, turn north on U.S. 395 and drive 87 miles to Colville and Highway 20. Turn west on Highway 20 and continue 34 miles to Highway 21 (two miles east of Republic). Turn north and drive 7.5 miles to the park entrance on the left.

Contact: Curlew Lake State Park, 509/775-3592; State Park information, 360/902-8844.

❸❺ Tiffanys Resort

    7

Tiffanys Resort is in a pretty, wooded setting along the western shore of Curlew Lake. This 6.5-mile-long lake is good for fishing and water-skiing. Fishing can be good for rainbow trout and largemouth bass. Most of the sites are fairly spacious. This is a smaller, more private alternative to Blacks Beach Resort.

Location: On Curlew Lake; see Northeastern Washington, map 2, grid c3.

Campsites, facilities: There are 15 sites with full hookups for trailers or RVs of any length and four tent sites. Picnic tables and fire pits are provided. Restrooms, flush toilets, showers, firewood, a store, a coin-operated laundry, ice, a playground, and a swimming beach are available. Boat docks, launching facilities, and rentals are available. Leashed pets are permitted.

Reservations, fees: Reservations accepted. Sites are $18 to $19 per night. Major credit cards accepted. Open April to late October.

Directions: From Colville, drive west on Highway 20 for 36 miles into the town of Republic and Klondike Road. Turn right on Klondike Road and drive 10.2 miles (Klondike Road will turn into West Curlew Lake Road) to Tiffany Road. Turn right and drive 0.5 miles to the resort at the end of the road.

Contact: Tiffanys Resort, 58 Tiffany Road, Republic, WA 99166; 509/775-3152; website: www.tiffanysresort.com.

Blacks Beach Resort

 7

Here's another resort along Curlew Lake. This one is much larger, with beautiful waterfront sites and full facilities. Water-skiing, swimming, and fishing are all options.

Location: On Curlew Lake; see Northeastern Washington, map 2, grid c3.

Campsites, facilities: There are 120 sites with full hookups, including 60 drive-through sites, for trailers or RVs of any length, nine tent sites, and 13 lodging units. Picnic tables and fire pits are provided. Restrooms, flush

toilets, coin-operated showers, a dump station, a store, a coin-operated laundry, ice, and a playground are available. Boat docks, launching facilities, and rentals are located at the resort. Leashed pets are permitted.

Reservations, fees: Reservations accepted. Sites are $15 to $19 per night. Major credit cards accepted. April through October; three cabins are available in winter.

Directions: From Colville, drive west on Highway 20 for continue 34 miles to Highway 21 (two miles east of Republic). Turn north and drive eight miles to West Curlew Lake Road. Turn right (north) on West Curlew Lake Road and continue for one mile to the resort on the lake.

Contact: Blacks Beach Resort, 80 Black Beach Road, Republic, WA 99166; 509/775-3989; website: www.blackbeachresort.com.

⃞ Pierre Lake

 8

Pierre Lake, just 105 acres, is a quiet jewel near the Canadian border. It's only a short drive from U.S. 395, yet the campground gets relatively little use. The camp is set on the west shore of the lake. It is popular and usually fills on summer weekends. The lake has fishing for rainbow trout, cutthroat trout, brook trout, crappie, bass, and catfish. While there is no speed limit, the lake is too small for big, fast boats.

Location: On Pierre Lake in Colville National Forest; see Northeastern Washington, map 2, grid a7.

Campsites, facilities: There are 15 sites for tents, trailers, or RVs up to 24 feet long. Picnic tables and fire grills are provided. Vault toilets are available. No drinking water is available. Garbage must be packed out.

Boat docks and launching facilities are available on site. Some facilities are wheelchair-accessible. A convenience store and ice are located within seven miles. Leashed pets are permitted.

Reservations, fees: No reservations. Sites are $6 per night. Senior discount available. Open mid-April to mid-October.

Directions: From Spokane, drive north on U.S. 395 for 74 miles to Colville. Continue north on U.S. 395 for about 25 miles to Barstow and Pierre Lake Round (County Road 4013). Turn right (north) on Pierre Lake Road and drive nine miles to the campground on the west side of Pierre Lake.

Contact: Colville National Forest, Three Rivers Ranger District, 255 West 11th Street, Kettle Falls, WA 99141; 509/738-6111, fax 509/738-7701.

38 Davis Lake

 8

This tiny campground is set at 4,600 feet elevation at Little Davis Lake. It is a scenic spot, and the fishing for cutthroat trout is often good. Only small boats are permitted on the small, shallow lake, which covers just 17 acres. No gas motors are permitted, but it can be ideal for float tubes, canoes, and prams with electric motors or oars. A one-mile trail loops the lake.

Location: On Davis Lake, in Colville National Forest; see Northeastern Washington, map 2, grid c7.

Campsites, facilities: There are four sites for tents or small trailers. Picnic tables and fire grills are provided. Vault toilets are available. No drinking water is available. Garbage must be packed out. Some facilities are wheelchair-accessible. Leashed pets are permitted.

Reservations, fees: No reservations; no fee. Open April through November, weather permitting.

Directions: From Spokane, drive north on U.S. 395 for 84 miles to Kettle Falls. Continue north on U.S. 395 for nine miles to Deadman Creek Road. Turn west on Deadman Creek Road and drive about three miles to County Road 465 (Jack Knife cutoff). Turn right and drive 2.5 miles. Bear right and drive about one-half mile to County Road 480. Turn left and drive about three miles to County Road 080. Turn right and drive about three miles to Davis Lake. Note: The access road is very rough; high-clearance vehicles are recommended.

Contact: Colville National Forest, Three Rivers Ranger District, Kettle Falls, 255 West 11th Street, WA 99141; 509/738-6111, fax 509/738-7701.

39 North Gorge

 7

This is the first and northernmost of many campgrounds we discovered along the shore of 130-mile-long Franklin Roosevelt Lake, which was formed by damming the Columbia River at Coulee. This camp is set on the west shore, near the Coulee Dam National Recreation Area to the nearby south. Recreation options include water-skiing and swimming, plus fishing for walleye, trout, bass, and sunfish. During the winter, the lake level is drawn down, and a unique trip is to walk along the lake's barren edge. See the description of Spring Canyon for more recreation information.

Location: On Franklin Roosevelt Lake in Lake Roosevelt National Recreation Area; see Northeastern Washington, map 2, grid b8.

Campsites, facilities: There are 10 sites for tents, trailers, or RVs up to 26 feet. Picnic tables and fire grills are provided. Drinking water, vault toilets, boat docks, and launching facilities are available. Some facilities are wheelchair-accessible. Note that if the lake level drops below an elevation of 1,272 feet, there is no drinking water. Leashed pets are permitted.

Reservations, fees: No reservations. Sites are $5 to $10 per night; there is a $6 launch fee. Senior discount available. Open year-round.

Directions: From Spokane on I-90, drive north on U.S. 395 for 84 miles to the town of Kettle Falls and Highway 25. Turn north (right) on Highway 25 and drive 20 miles to the campground entrance.

Contact: Lake Roosevelt National Recreation Area, 1008 Crest Drive, Coulee Dam, WA 99116-1259; 509/633-9441, fax 509/633-9332.

40 Snag Cove

 8

Snag Cove has a setting similar to North Gorge campground (see previous listing). It is set amid Ponderosa pines along Franklin Roosevelt Lake. It is a small camp with just nine sites, but the nearby boat launch makes this camp a find. This camp is set on the west shore, near the Coulee Dam National Recreation Area to the nearby north.

Location: On Franklin Roosevelt Lake in Lake Roosevelt National Recreation Area; see Northeastern Washington, map 2, grid c8.

Campsites, facilities: There are nine sites for tents, trailers, or RVs up to 26 feet long. Picnic tables and fire grills are provided. Vault toilets are available. When the lake level drops, there is no drinking water. Some facilities are wheelchair-accessible. Boat-launching facilities and docks are nearby. Leashed pets are permitted.

Reservations, fees: No reservations. Sites are $5 to $10 per night, $6 boat launch fee.

Senior discount available. Open year-round, weather permitting.

Directions: From Spokane, turn north on U.S. 395 and drive 84 miles to the town of Kettle Falls. Continue north on U.S. 395 (crossing the Columbia River) for seven miles to the Hedlund Bridge turnoff. Turn right and cross Hedlund Bridge and drive 7.5 miles to the campground on the right.

Contact: Lake Roosevelt National Recreation Area, 1008 Crest Drive, Coulee Dam, WA 99116-1259; 509/633-9441, fax 509/633-9332.

41 Evans

 9

This campground is another in a series set along the shore of Franklin Roosevelt Lake. This camp is set along the eastern shoreline just south of the town of Evans. Fishing, swimming, and water-skiing are among the activities here. See the description of Spring Canyon for more information.

Location: On Franklin Roosevelt Lake in Lake Roosevelt National Recreation Area; see Northeastern Washington, map 2, grid c8.

Campsites, facilities: There are 46 sites for tents, trailers, or RVs up to 26 feet long and one group site for up to 25 people. Picnic tables and fire grills are provided. Drinking water and flush toilets are available. A boat dock, launch facilities, a dump station, and a picnic area are available nearby. Some facilities are wheelchair-accessible. Leashed pets are permitted.

Reservations, fees: No reservations for family sites; reservations for group site required at 509/633-3860. Sites are $5 to $10 per night; there is a $6 launch fee. Open year-round, with limited facilities in the winter.

Directions: From Spokane on I-90, drive north on U.S. 395 for 84 miles to the town of Kettle Falls and Highway 25. Turn north (right) on Highway 25 and drive eight miles to the campground entrance on the left.

Contact: Lake Roosevelt National Recreation Area, 1008 Crest Drive, Coulee Dam, WA 99116-1259; 509/633-9441, fax 509/633-9332.

42 Whispering Pines RV Resort & Campground

  7

This campground is set along the long, narrow Kettle River Arm of Franklin Roosevelt Lake. It is a country resort and is usually quiet and peaceful. A highlight is easy access to the lake. There is no steep walk like at so many other campgrounds at this lake. A one-mile loop nature trail is available along the lake shore, where wild turkeys and deer are often spotted. It's close to marked bike trails, a full-service marina, and tennis courts. Riding stables are available 20 miles away, and a golf course is within 15 miles. A good side trip is to Colville National Forest East Portal Interpretive Area, 10 miles away. (Drive south to the junction of Highway 20 and continue southwest for about six miles.) Highlights include a nature trail and the Bangs Mountain auto tour, a five-mile drive that takes you through old-growth forest to Bangs Mountain Vista overlooking the Roosevelt Lake-Kettle Falls area.

Location: On Franklin Roosevelt Lake; see Northeastern Washington, map 2, grid c7.

Campsites, facilities: There are 42 sites with full hookups, including 40 drive-through sites, for tents, trailers or RVs of any length, 15 tent sites, two cabins, three rental trailers, and two motel rooms with kitchens. An overflow camping area is also available. Picnic tables and fire grills are provided. Restrooms, drinking water, flush toilets, coin-operated showers, a dump station, a coin-operated laundry, a playground with horseshoe pits and volleyball, modem hookups, a store, and firewood are available. Lake swimming and fishing are on site. Leashed pets are permitted. A restaurant is available within five miles.

Reservations, fees: Reservations accepted. Sites are $11 to $21 per night, $1 to $5 per person per night for more than two people. Weekly and monthly rates are available. Call for cabin and lodging rates. Open year-round.

Directions: From Spokane, turn north on U.S. 395 and drive 84 miles to the town of Kettle Falls. Continue north on U.S. 395 for 6.5 miles (towards Canada) to the campground entrance road on the right. Turn east at the sign for the campground and drive 300 yards to the camp on the right.

Contact: Whispering Pines RV Resort and Campground, Roosevelt Road, Kettle Falls, WA 99141; 509/738-2593 (phone or fax) or 800/597-4423.

43 Kettle River

 7

This campground is set along the long, narrow Kettle River Arm of Franklin Roosevelt Lake, with campsites amid Ponderosa pines. If the lake level drops below an elevation of 1,272 feet, there is no drinking water. The nearest boat launch is at Napoleon Bridge.

Location: On Franklin Roosevelt Lake in Lake Roosevelt National Recreation Area; see Northeastern Washington, map 2, grid c7.

Campsites, facilities: There are 13 sites for tents, trailers, or RVs up to 16 feet long. Picnic tables and fire grills are provided. Vault toilets are available. When the lake level drops, there is no drinking water. Some facilities are wheelchair-accessible. Boat docks are nearby. Leashed pets are permitted.

Reservations, fees: No reservations. Sites are $5 to $10 per night. Senior discount available. Open year-round, weather permitting.

Directions: From Spokane, turn north on U.S. 395 and drive 84 miles to the town of Kettle Falls. Continue north on U.S. 395 (crossing the Columbia River) for seven miles to the campground on the right.

Contact: Lake Roosevelt National Recreation Area, 1008 Crest Drive, Coulee Dam, WA 99116-1259; 509/633-9441, fax 509/633-9332.

44 Kamloops Island

 10

This is one of the more primitive campgrounds located along Franklin Roosevelt Lake. It's located at Kamloops Island, an optimum area for water-skiing and fishing, and there are unbelievably beautiful views of water and mountains. It is located near the mouth of the Kettle River arm of the lake. While the scenic beauty merits a 10, note that the nearest boat launch is way across the lake at Kettle Falls and that if the lake level drops below an elevation of 1,272 feet, there is no drinking water.

Location: On Franklin Roosevelt Lake in Lake Roosevelt National Recreation Area; see Northeastern Washington, map 2, grid c8.

Campsites, facilities: There are 17 tent sites. Picnic tables and fire grills are provided. Vault toilets are available. When the lake level drops, there is no drinking water. Some facilities are wheelchair-accessible. Boat docks are nearby. Leashed pets are permitted.

Reservations, fees: No reservations. Sites are $5 to $10 per night. Senior discount available. Open year-round, weather permitting.

Directions: From Spokane, turn north on U.S. 395 and drive 84 miles to the town of Kettle Falls. Continue north on U.S. 395 (crossing the Columbia River) for seven miles to the Hedlund Bridge turnoff. Turn right and cross Hedlund Bridge and drive to the campground on the left.

Contact: Lake Roosevelt National Recreation Area, 1008 Crest Drive, Coulee Dam, WA 99116-1259; 509/633-9441, fax 509/633-9332.

45 Marcus Island

 8

This campground located south of Evans camp on the eastern shore of Franklin Roosevelt Lake is quite similar to that camp. Water-skiing, fishing, and swimming are the primary recreation options. See the description of Spring Canyon for information about the park and side-trip options in the area.

Location: On Franklin Roosevelt Lake in Lake Roosevelt National Recreation Area; see Northeastern Washington, map 2, grid c8.

Campsites, facilities: There are 20 sites for tents, trailers, or RVs up to 20 feet long. Picnic tables and fire grills are provided. Drinking water, vault toilets, and a picnic area are available. A boat launch and dock are available nearby. Some facilities are wheelchair-accessible. Note that if the lake level drops below an elevation of 1,272 feet, there is no drinking water. A store is located within one mile. Leashed pets are permitted.

Reservations, fees: No reservations. Sites are $5 to $10 per night, boat-launching is $6 per boat, good for seven days. Senior discount available. Open year-round, weather permitting.

Directions: From Spokane on I-90, drive north on U.S. 395 for 84 miles to the town of Kettle Falls and Highway 25. Turn north (right) on Highway 25 and drive four miles to the campground entrance on the left.

Contact: Lake Roosevelt National Recreation Area, 1008 Crest Drive, Coulee Dam, WA 99116-1259; 509/633-9441, fax 509/633-9332.

Kettle Falls

  8

This campground only occasionally fills. It's located along the eastern shore of Roosevelt Lake, about two miles south of the highway bridge near West Kettle Falls. In the summer, the rangers offer campfire programs in the evenings. Water-skiing, swimming, and fishing are all options. Local side trips include St. Paul's Mission in Kettle Falls, which was built in 1846 and is one of the oldest churches in Washington.

Location: On Franklin Roosevelt Lake in Lake Roosevelt National Recreation Area; see Northeastern Washington, map 2, grid d7.

Campsites, facilities: There are 77 sites for tents, trailers, or RVs up to 26 feet long and two group sites, one for up to 50 people and one for up to 75 people. Picnic tables and fire grills are provided. Restrooms, drinking water, flush toilets, showers, a dump station, firewood, a small marina with store, and a playground are available. A store is located within one mile. Some facilities are wheelchair-accessible. Boat docks, fuel, and launching facilities are available. Leashed pets are permitted.

Reservations, fees: No reservations for family sites; reservations required for group sites at 509/633-3860. Sites are $5 to $10 per night; there is a $6 boat-launch fee. Senior discount available. Major credit cards accepted. Open year-round, with limited facilities in winter.

Directions: From Spokane, drive north on U.S. 395 for 84 miles to the town of Kettle Falls. Continue on U.S. 395 for three miles to Kettle Park Road on the left. Turn left and drive two miles to the campground on the right.

Contact: Lake Roosevelt National Recreation Area, 1008 Crest Drive, Coulee Dam, WA 99116-1259; 509/633-9441, fax 509/633-9332.

Haag Cove

 8

This campground is tucked away in a cove along the western shore of Franklin Roosevelt Lake (Columbia River), about two miles south of Highway 20. A good side trip is to the Sherman Creek Habitat Management Area, located just north of camp. It's rugged and steep, but a good place to see and photograph wildlife, including bald eagles, golden eagles, and 200 other species of birds, along with the occasional black bear, cougar, and moose. Note that no boat launch is available at this camp, but that boat ramps are available at Kettle Falls or French Rock. Also note that no drinking water is available if the lake level drops below an elevation of 1,275 feet.

Location: On Franklin Roosevelt Lake in Lake Roosevelt National Recreation Area; see Northeastern Washington, map 2, grid d7.

Campsites, facilities: There are 18 sites for tents, trailers, or RVs up to 26 feet long. Picnic tables and fire grills are provided. Drinking water and vault toilets are available. Boat docks are available nearby. Leashed pets are permitted.

Reservations, fees: No reservations. Sites are $5 to $10 per night. Senior discount available. Open year-round, weather permitting.

Directions: From Spokane, drive north on U.S. 395 for 84 miles to the town of Kettle Falls and Highway 20. Continue on Highway

20 and drive 7.5 miles to Kettle Falls Road. Turn left (south) and drive two miles to the campground on the right.

Contact: Lake Roosevelt National Recreation Area, 1008 Crest Drive, Coulee Dam, WA 99116-1259; 509/633-9441, fax 509/633-9332.

48 Trout Lake

  8

Trout Lake is a little lake, just eight acres, that is set at an elevation of 3,100 feet. It provides fishing for rainbow trout, with prospects similar to that of Davis Lake. No gas motors are permitted, but electric motors are allowed on small boats. The nearby, five-mile-long Hoodoo Canyon Trail, accessible for hiking or biking, offers spectacular views.

Location: On Trout Lake in Colville National Forest; see Northeastern Washington, map 2, grid d7.

Campsites, facilities: There are four tent sites. Picnic tables and fire pits are provided. Vault toilets are available. No drinking water is available. Garbage must be packed out. Some facilities are wheelchair-accessible. Leashed pets are permitted.

Reservations, fees: No reservations; no fee. Open April through November, weather permitting.

Directions: From Spokane, turn north on U.S. 395 and drive 87 miles to Colville and Highway 20. Turn west on Highway 20 and drive 15 miles (crossing the Columbia River) to Trout Lake Road (Forest Road 020). Turn right on Trout Lake Road and drive five miles to the campground at the end of the road.

Contact: Colville National Forest, Three Rivers Ranger District, 255 West 11th Street, Kettle Falls, WA 99141; 509/738-6111, fax 509/738-7701.

49 Canyon Creek

 7

The campground is located 0.4 mile from the highway, just far enough to keep it from road noise. It's a popular spot for campers looking for a layover spot, with the bonus of trout fishing in the nearby creek. It is within hiking distance of the East Portal Historical Site. The camp is set in a pretty area not far from the Columbia River, which offers a myriad of recreation options. A side trip is the Bangs Mountain Auto Tour, featuring a scenic route with mountain vistas.

Location: Near the East Portal Historical Site in Colville National Forest; see Northeastern Washington, map 2, grid d7.

Campsites, facilities: There are 12 sites for tents, trailers, or RVs up to 30 feet long. Picnic tables and fire grills are provided. Vault toilets are available. No drinking water is available. Garbage must be packed out. Some facilities are wheelchair-accessible. Leashed pets are permitted.

Reservations, fees: No reservations. Sites are $6 per night. Open late May to early September.

Directions: From Spokane, drive north on U.S. 395 for 87 miles to Highway 20. Turn west on Highway 20 and drive 18 miles (crossing the Columbia River) to Forest Road 136. Turn left and drive south for one-third mile to the campground on the left.

Contact: Colville National Forest, Three Rivers, Ranger District, 255 West 11th Street, Kettle Falls, WA 99141; 509/738-6111, fax 509/738-7701.

50 Lake Ellen & Lake Ellen West

  7

Lake Ellen is an 82-acre lake that is a favorite for power boating (with no speed limit) and fishing for rainbow trout, which are a good size and plentiful early in the season. There are two small camps available here. The boat launch is located at the west end of the lake. This lake is located about three miles west of the Columbia River and the Lake Roosevelt National Recreation Area. See a U.S. Forest Service map for details.

Location: On Lake Ellen in Colville National Forest; see Northeastern Washington, map 2, grid d6.

Campsites, facilities: There are 11 sites at Lake Ellen and five sites at Lake Ellen West for tents, trailers, or RVs up to 22 feet long. Picnic tables are provided, but there is no drinking water. Vault toilets and boat docks are available. Garbage must be packed out. Some facilities are wheelchair-accessible. Leashed pets are permitted.

Reservations, fees: No reservations. Sites are $6 per night. Senior discount available. Open mid-April to mid-October.

Directions: From Spokane, drive north on U.S. 395 for 87 miles to Colville and Highway 20. Turn west on Highway 20 and drive 14 miles (crossing the Columbia River) to County Road 3. Turn left and drive south for 4.5 miles to County Road 412. Turn right on County Road 412 and drive five miles to the Lake Ellen Campground or continue another 0.7 miles to Lake Ellen West Campground.

Contact: Colville National Forest, Three Rivers Ranger District, 255 West 11th Street, Kettle Falls, WA 99141; 509/738-6111, fax 509/738-7701.

51 Swan Lake

      8

Scenic views greet visitors on the drive to and at this campground on the shore of Swan Lake, which is at an elevation of 3,700 feet. A beautiful hiking trail circles the lake, the Swan Lake Trail. Fishing for rainbow trout is an option. Swimming, boating (gas motors prohibited), mountain biking, and hiking are some of the possibilities here. It's a good out-of-the-way spot for RV cruisers seeking a rustic setting. It commonly fills on summer weekends.

Location: On Swan Lake in Colville National Forest; see Northeastern Washington, map 2, grid d2.

Campsites, facilities: There are 25 sites for tents, trailers, or RVs up to 31 feet long. Picnic tables and fire grills are provided. Drinking water and vault toilets are available. A picnic shelter with barbecue, firewood, a boat dock, and launching facilities are available nearby. Gas motors are prohibited on the lake. Leashed pets are permitted.

Reservations, fees: No reservations accepted. Sites are $12 per night, $2 per extra vehicle per night. Senior discount available. Open May through September.

Directions: From Spokane on I-90, turn north on U.S. 395 and drive 87 miles to Highway 20. Turn west on Highway 20 and drive 36 miles to the town of Republic and Highway 21. Turn south on Highway 21 and drive seven miles to Forest Road 53 (Scatter Creek Road). Turn right (southwest) on Forest Road 53 and drive eight miles to the campground at the end of the road.

Contact: Colville National Forest, Republic Ranger District, Republic, WA 99166; 509/775-3305, fax 509/775-7401.

52 Ferry Lake

  7

53 Long Lake

   9

This is one of three fishing lakes within a four-square-mile area. The others are Swan Lake and Long Lake. Gas motors are prohibited on the lake. For more information, see the descriptions of the other two campgrounds.

Location: On Ferry Lake in Colville National Forest; see Northeastern Washington, map 2, grid d2.

Campsites, facilities: There are nine sites for tents, trailers, or RVs up to 20 feet long. Fire grills and picnic tables are provided. Vault toilets and firewood are available. No drinking water is available. Garbage must be packed out. Launching facilities are nearby. Leashed pets are permitted.

Reservations, fees: No reservations. Sites are $8 per night, $2 per extra vehicle per night. Senior discount available. Open May through September, weather permitting.

Directions: From Spokane on I-90, turn north on U.S. 395 and drive 87 miles to Highway 20. Turn west on Highway 20 and drive 36 miles to the town of Republic and Highway 21. Turn south on Highway 21 and drive seven miles to Forest Road 53 (Scatter Creek Road). Turn right (southwest) on Forest Road 53 and drive about seven miles to Forest Road 5330. Turn right (north) on Forest Road 5330 and drive one mile to Forest Road 100. Turn right (north) and drive one mile to the campground on the left.

Contact: Colville National Forest, Republic Ranger District, 180 North Jefferson, Republic, WA 99166; 509/775-3305, fax 509/775-7401.

Long Lake is the third and smallest of the three lakes in this area (the others are Swan Lake and Ferry Lake). Expert fly fishermen can get a quality experience here angling for cutthroat trout. No gas motors are allowed on the lake, and fishing is restricted (fly-fishing only), but is ideal with a float tube or a pram. The lake is set adjacent to little Fish Lake, and a half-mile trail runs between the two lakes. The drive on Highway 21 south of Republic is particularly beautiful, with views of the Sanpoil River.

Location: On Long Lake in Colville National Forest; see Northeastern Washington, map 2, grid e2.

Campsites, facilities: There are 12 sites for tents, trailers, or RVs up to 21 feet long. Picnic tables and fire grills are provided. Drinking water and vault toilets are available. Garbage must be packed out. Primitive launching facilities are nearby. Leashed pets are permitted.

Reservations, fees: No reservations. Sites are $10 per night, $2 per extra vehicle per night. Open May through September.

Directions: From Spokane on I-90, turn north on U.S. 395 and drive 87 miles to Highway 20. Turn west on Highway 20 and drive 36 miles to the town of Republic and Highway 21. Turn south on Highway 21 and drive seven miles to Forest Road 53 (Scatter Creek Road). Turn right (southwest) on Forest Road 53 and drive seven miles to Forest Road 400. Turn south and drive 1.5 miles to the camp on the right.

Contact: Colville National Forest, Republic Ranger District, 180 North Jefferson, Republic, WA 99166; 509/775-3305, fax 509/775-7401.

54 Ten Mile

     7

This spot is secluded and primitive. Located about nine miles from Swan Lake, Ferry Lake, and Long Lake, this campground along the Sanpoil River is a good choice for a multi-day trip, visiting each of the lakes. The Sanpoil River provides fishing for rainbow trout, and a hiking trail leads west from camp for about 2.5 miles.

Location: On the Sanpoil River in Colville National Forest; see Northeastern Washington, map 2, grid d3.

Campsites, facilities: There are nine sites for tents, trailers, or RVs up to 21 feet long. Picnic tables and fire rings are provided. Vault toilets are available. No drinking water is available. Garbage must be packed out. Leashed pets are permitted.

Reservations, fees: No reservations. Sites are $8 per night, $2 per extra vehicle per night. Senior discount available. Open mid-May to mid-October.

Directions: From Spokane on I-90, turn north on U.S. 395 and drive 87 miles to Highway 20. Turn west on Highway 20 and drive 40 miles to Republic and Highway 21. Turn south on Highway 21 and drive 10 miles to the campground entrance on the left.

Contact: Colville National Forest, Republic Ranger District, 180 North Jefferson, Republic, WA 99166; 509/775-3305, fax 509/775-7401.

55 Sherman Pass Overlook

    6

Sherman Pass Scenic Byway (Highway 20) is routed through here, so the camp does have some road noise. This roadside campground is located near Sherman Pass (5,575 feet), one of the few high-elevation mountain passes that is maintained open year-round in Washington. Several nearby trails provide access to various peaks and vistas in the area. One of the best is the Kettle Crest National Recreation Trail, with the trailhead located one mile from the camp. This trail extends for 45 miles, generally running north to south, and provides spectacular views of the Cascades on clear days. No other campgrounds are in the immediate vicinity.

Location: At Sherman Pass in Colville National Forest; see Northeastern Washington, map 2, grid d5.

Campsites, facilities: There are nine sites for tents, trailers, or RVs up to 24 feet long. Picnic tables and fire grills are provided. Vault toilets are available. No drinking water is available. Garbage must be packed out. Some facilities are wheelchair-accessible. Leashed pets are permitted.

Reservations, fees: No reservations. Sites are $6 per night. Senior discount available. Open mid-May to late September.

Directions: From Spokane on I-90, turn north on U.S. 395 and drive 87 miles to Highway 20. Turn west on Highway 20 and drive 19.5 miles to the campground on the right.

Contact: Colville National Forest, Three Rivers Ranger District, 255 West 11th Street, Kettle Falls, WA 99141; 509/738-6111, fax 509/738-7701.

56 Cloverleaf

    8

This camp is small and primitive. It is located on the east shore of Roosevelt Lake, just south of the town of Gifford. Nearby Gifford Camp to the south provides an option. In this particular area of Roosevelt Lake, water-skiing and other high-speed boating is not advised because of submerged hazards, but fishing is fine. The tree cover in the area is primarily Ponderosa pine. See the descriptions of Springs Canyon and North Gorge for recreation details. Note that no drinking water is available if the lake level drops below 1,282 feet elevation.

Location: On Franklin Roosevelt Lake in Lake Roosevelt National Recreation Area; see Northeastern Washington, map 2, grid f7.

Campsites, facilities: There are eight tent sites. Picnic tables and fire grills are provided. Drinking water and vault toilets are available. Boat-launching facilities and a picnic area are nearby. Some facilities are wheelchair-accessible. Leashed pets are permitted.

Reservations, fees: No reservations. Sites are $5 to $10 per night; there is a $6 launch fee. Open year-round, with limited winter facilities.

Directions: From Spokane on I-90, drive west for four miles to U.S. 2. Turn west on U.S. 2 and drive 34 miles to Highway 25. Turn north (right) on Highway 25 and drive 61 miles to Davenport and the campground (located about two miles south of Gifford).

Contact: Lake Roosevelt National Recreation Area, 1008 Crest Drive, Coulee Dam, WA 99116-1259; 509/633-9441, fax 509/633-9332.

57 Gifford

 7

Fishing and water-skiing are two of the draws at this camp on the eastern shore of Franklin Roosevelt Lake (Columbia River). The nearby boat ramp is a big plus.

Location: On Franklin Roosevelt Lake in Lake Roosevelt National Recreation Area; see Northeastern Washington, map 2, grid f8.

Campsites, facilities: There are 47 sites for tents, trailers, or RVs up to 20 feet long and one group site for up to 50 people. Picnic tables and fire grills are provided. Drinking water and vault toilets are available. Boat docks and launching facilities, a dump

station, and a picnic area are nearby. Some facilities are wheelchair-accessible. Leashed pets are permitted.

Reservations, fees: No reservations for family sites. Reservations for group site required at 509/633-3860. Sites are $5 to $10 per night; $6 boat launch fee. Senior discount available. Open year-round, with limited winter facilities.

Directions: From Spokane on I-90, drive west for four miles to U.S. 2. Turn west on U.S. 2 and drive 34 miles to Davenport and Highway 25. Turn north (right) on Highway 25 and drive 60 miles to the campground (located about three miles south of Gifford) on the left.

Contact: Lake Roosevelt National Recreation Area, 1008 Crest Drive, Coulee Dam, WA 99116-1259; 509/633-9441, fax 509/633-9332.

58 Rainbow Beach Resort

 8

This quality resort is set along the shore of Twin Lakes Reservoir in the Colville Indian Reservation. This camp is busy in summer and fills up virtually every day in July and August. Nearby recreation options include hiking trails, marked bike trails, a full-service marina, and tennis courts.

Location: On Twin Lakes Reservoir; see Northeastern Washington, map 2, grid f5.

Campsites, facilities: There are 14 sites with full hookups, including five drive-through sites for trailers and RVs of any length, seven tent sites, and 26 cabins. Picnic tables are provided. Restrooms, drinking water, flush toilets, coin-operated showers, bottled gas, a dump station, firewood, a recreation hall, a store, a laundry room, ice, boat rentals, docks and launching facilities, and a playground with volleyball and horseshoe pits are available. Leashed pets are permitted.

Reservations, fees: Reservations recommended. Sites are $7 to $17 per night. Cabins are $35 to $70 per night. Pets are $4 per night. There is a small pet fee. Major credit cards accepted. Campsites are available April through October; cabins are available year-round.

Directions: From Spokane, drive north on U.S. 395 for 84 miles to the town of Kettle Falls and Highway 20. Turn east on Highway 20 and drive five miles to the turnoff for Inchelium Highway. Turn left (south) and drive about 20 miles to Inchelium and Bridge Creek-Twin Lakes County Road. Turn right (west) and drive two miles to Stranger Creek Road. Turn left and drive one quarter-mile to the resort on the right.

Contact: Rainbow Beach Resort, 18 North Twin Lakes Road, Inchelium, WA 99138; 509/722-5901, fax 509/722-7080.

59 Hunters Park

   8

This campground on a shoreline point along Roosevelt Lake (Columbia River) is a good spot for swimming, fishing, or water-skiing. It is located on the east shore of the lake adjacent to the mouth of Hunters Creek and near the town of Hunters. Note: No drinking water is available if the lake level drops below an elevation of 1,245 feet.

Location: On Franklin Roosevelt Lake in Lake Roosevelt National Recreation Area; see Northeastern Washington, map 2, grid h7.

Campsites, facilities: There are 42 sites for tents, trailers, or RVs up to 26 feet long and three group sites for up to 25 people each. Picnic tables and fire grills are provided.

Drinking water and vault toilets are available. Restrooms, drinking water, flush toilets, a dump station, and a picnic area are available. Some facilities are wheelchair-accessible. A store and ice are available within one mile. Boat docks and launching facilities are nearby. Leashed pets are permitted.

Reservations, fees: No reservations for family sites. Reservations required for group sites at 509/633-3860. Sites are $5 to $10 per night; $6 launch fee. Senior discount available. Open year-round, with limited winter facilities.

Directions: From Spokane on I-90, drive west for four miles to U.S. 2. Turn west on U.S. 2 and drive 34 miles to Davenport and Highway 25. Turn north on Highway 25 and drive 47 miles to Hunters and the campground access road on the left side (west side) of the road (well marked). Turn left at the access road and drive two miles to the campground at the end of the road.

Contact: Lake Roosevelt National Recreation Area, 1008 Crest Drive, Coulee Dam, WA 99116-1259; 509/633-9441, fax 509/633-9332.

60 Sheep Creek

    8

This campground is in a forested area along Sheep Creek, about four miles from the Columbia River and close to the Canadian border. It's a primitive camp, yet it has drinking water and is crowded with locals on the Fourth of July weekend. Sheep Creek provides trout fishing. Huckleberry picking is good in August.

Location: On Sheep Creek; see Northeastern Washington, map 3, grid a2.

Campsites, facilities: There are 11 sites for tents or small trailers. Picnic tables, fire grills, and tent pads are provided. Vault toilets, drinking water, a wheelchair-accessible fishing platform, and a group picnic shelter with barbecues are available. Restaurants and stores are located within five miles. Some facilities are wheelchair-accessible. Leashed pets are permitted.

Reservations, fees: No reservations; no fee. Open mid-April through November, weather permitting.

Directions: From Spokane, drive north on U.S. 395 for 84 miles to Kettle Falls and Highway 25. Turn north on Highway 25 and drive 33 miles to Northport. Continue north on Highway 25 for three-quarters mile to Sheep Creek Road (across the Columbia River Bridge). Turn left on Sheep Creek Road and drive 4.3 miles (on a gravel road) to the campground entrance on the right.

Contact: Department of Natural Resources, Northeast Region, P.O. Box 190, Colville, WA 99114-0190; 509/684-7474, fax 509/684-7484.

61 Williams Lake

 9

This camp is set along the shore of Williams Lake, with some of the campsites providing great views. With so many vacationers heading to nearby Franklin Roosevelt Lake, this secluded spot in a pretty, forested setting provides an alternative that is overlooked by nearly all out-of-towners. The landscape features lots of Douglas firs. This is a swimming lake, and with no motorized boats permitted, it can be ideal for canoes, kayaks, and rafts. There is a boat launch one-half mile from the camp. Only ice fishing is permitted here; check regulations.

Location: On Williams Lake; see Northeastern Washington, map 3, grid b1.

Campsites, facilities: There are eight sites for tents or small trailers. Picnic tables, fire grills, and tent pads are provided. Vault toilets, drinking water, and a boat launch are

available. Some facilities are wheelchair-accessible. Leashed pets are permitted.

Reservations, fees: No reservations; no fee. Open mid-April through November.

Directions: From Spokane, drive north for 74 miles to Colville. Continue north on U.S. 395 for two miles to Williams Lake Road. Turn north on Williams Lake Road and drive 13.7 miles to the campground entrance road on the left.

Contact: Department of Natural Resources, Northeast Region, P.O. Box 190, Colville, WA 99114-0190; 509/684-7474, fax 509/684-7484.

62 Big Meadow Lake

 8

Big Meadow Lake is set at 3,400 feet with 71 surface acres. The camp, located in a scenic area, is quiet, remote, and relatively unknown, and the lake provides trout fishing. The U.S. Forest Service has provided a wildlife-viewing platform, where osprey, ducks, geese, and occasionally even moose, elk, and cougar may be spotted. An environmental education lab is located near the campground.

Location: On Big Meadow Lake in Colville National Forest; see Northeastern Washington, map 3, grid c4.

Campsites, facilities: There are 16 sites for tents, trailers, or RVs up to 32 feet long. Fire grills, picnic tables, and vault toilets are provided, but there is no drinking water. A boat launch, restrooms, and a wheelchair-accessible nature trail and fishing pier are available. Leashed pets are permitted.

Reservations, fees: No reservations; no fee. Open May through November, weather permitting.

Directions: From Spokane, drive north on U.S. 395 for 74 miles to Colville and Highway

20. Turn east on Highway 20 and drive one mile to Colville-Aladdin Northpoint Road (County Road 9435). Turn north and drive 20 miles to Meadow Creek Road. Turn right (east) and drive six miles to the campground on the right. Note: The surface of the access road changes dramatically depending on the season.

Contact: Colville National Forest, Three Rivers Ranger District, Colville Office, 755 South Main Street, Colville, WA 99114; 509/684-7010, fax 509/684-7280.

63 Mill Pond

 6

Mill Pond Campground, located along the shore of a small reservoir just north of Sullivan Lake, is a good base camp for backpackers. Note that boat size is limited to crafts that can be carried and hand launched; about a 50-foot walk from the parking area to the lake is necessary. A 1.5-mile hiking trail (no bikes) circles Mill Pond and ties into an interpretive trail that is historical and wheelchair-accessible (located at the opposite end of the lake). For more ambitious hikes, the Hall Mountain Trail and Elk Creek Trail are nearby and provide beautiful valley and mountain views. Nearby Sullivan Lake is well known for giant but elusive brown trout and produced the state record. There are also rainbow trout in the lake. All amenities are a short drive away in Metaline Falls. See the descriptions of East and West Sullivan Lakes for other information about the area.

Location: Near Sullivan Lake in Colville National Forest; see Northeastern Washington, map 3, grid b6.

Campsites, facilities: There are 10 sites for tents, trailers, or RVs up to 25 feet long. Picnic tables and fire grills are provided. Hand-pumped water and vault toilets are available.

A dump station is located within one mile. Boats can be hand launched after a 50-foot walk; no gas motors are permitted. Leashed pets are permitted.

Reservations, fees: No reservations. Sites are $10 per night, $5 per night extra vehicle fee. Open late May to early September.

Directions: From Spokane, drive north on U.S. 395 for six miles to U.S. 2. Turn northeast on U.S. 2 and drive 30 miles to the Metaline turnoff and Highway 211 West. Turn northwest on Highway 211 West and drive 15 miles to Usk and Highway 20. Turn northwest (left) and drive 34 miles to Tiger and Highway 31. Turn left (north) on Highway 31 and drive 15 miles to the town of Metaline Falls and continue 2.5 miles Sullivan Lake Road (County Road 9345). Turn right (east) on Sullivan Lake Road and drive 7.5 miles to the campground on the east end of Mill Pond.

Contact: Colville National Forest, Sullivan Lake Ranger District, 12641 Sullivan Lake Road, Metaline Falls, WA 99153-9701; 509/446-7500, fax 509/446-7580.

64 Sullivan Lake East

 7

This is the largest campground on Sullivan Lake and by far the most popular. It fills up in summer. The camp is located on the lake's north shore. Some come here to try to catch the giant brown trout or the good numbers of smaller rainbow trout. The boating and hiking are also good. The beautiful Salmo-Priest Wilderness is located just three miles to the east. It gets light use, which means quiet, private trails. This is a prime place to view wildlife, carrying binoculars while hiking for a chance to spot the rare Woodland caribou and Rocky Mountain bighorn sheep. A nearby grass airstrip provides an opportunity for fly-in camping, but pilots should note that there are chuck holes present and holes from lots of ground squirrels, and only planes suited for primitive landing conditions should be flown in; check FAA guide to airports.

Location: On Sullivan Lake in Colville National Forest; see Northeastern Washington, map 3, grid b6.

Campsites, facilities: There are 38 sites, including some drive-through sites, for tents, trailers, or RVs up to 45 feet long. Picnic tables and fire grills are provided. Drinking water and vault toilets are available. A boat dock, launching facilities, a picnic area, a swimming platform, a camp host, and a dump station are nearby. Some facilities are wheelchair-accessible. Leashed pets are permitted.

Reservations, fees: Reserve at 877/444-6777 ($8.65 reservation fee) or website: www.reserveusa.com. Sites are $10 per night, $5 per night extra vehicle fee, and the group site is $60 per night. Senior discount available. Open late May through August.

Directions: From Spokane, drive north on U.S. 395 for six miles to U.S. 2. Turn northeast on U.S. 2 and drive 30 miles to the Metaline turnoff and Highway 211 West. Turn northwest on Highway 211 West and drive 15 miles to Usk and Highway 20. Turn northwest (left) and drive 34 miles to Tiger and Highway 31. Turn left (north) on Highway 31 and drive 15 miles to the town of Metaline Falls (Highway 31 also known as Lehigh Avenue in town) and continue 2.5 miles to Sullivan Lake Road (County Road 9345). Turn right (east) on Sullivan Lake Road and drive eight miles to Sullivan Creek Road. Turn left (east) and drive one quarter-mile to the campground on the right.

Contact: Colville National Forest, Sullivan Lake Ranger District, 12641 Sullivan Lake Road, Metaline Falls, WA 99153-9701; 509/446-7500, fax 509/446-7580.

65 Sullivan Lake West

 7

This small campground is set along the northwestern shore of Sullivan Lake and is a popular destination for boating, fishing, swimming, sailing, water-skiing, and hiking. See the previous listing for Sullivan Lake East for recreation and local details.

Location: On Sullivan Lake in Colville National Forest; see Northeastern Washington, map 3, grid b6.

Campsites, facilities: There are seven sites for tents, trailers, or RVs up to 30 feet long. Picnic tables and fire grills are provided. Drinking water and vault toilets, a picnic shelter, a boat launch, a developed swimming beach, a floating swim platform, and a camp host are available. Some facilities are wheelchair-accessible. Leashed pets are permitted.

Reservations, fees: Reserve at 877/444-6777 ($8.65 reservation fee) or website: www.reserveusa.com. Sites are $10 per night, $5 per extra vehicle per night. Senior discount available. Open late May through August.

Directions: From Spokane, drive north on U.S. 395 for six miles to U.S. 2. Turn northeast on U.S. 2 and drive 30 miles to the Metaline turnoff and Highway 211 West. Turn northwest on Highway 211 West and drive 15 miles to Usk and Highway 20. Turn northwest (left) and drive 34 miles to Tiger and Highway 31. Turn left (north) on Highway 31 and drive 15 miles to the town of Metaline Falls (Highway 31 is also known as Lehigh Avenue in town) and continue 2.5 miles to Sullivan Lake Road (County Road 9345). Turn right (east) on Sullivan Lake Road and drive 8.1 miles to the campground on the left (set at the foot of Sullivan Lake, just across the road from the Sullivan Lake Ranger Station).

Contact: Colville National Forest, Sullivan Lake Ranger District, 12641 Sullivan Lake Road, Metaline Falls, WA 99153-9701; 509/446-7500, fax 509/446-7580.

66 Noisy Creek & Noisy Creek Group

     7

This campground is situated on the southeast end of Sullivan Lake, adjacent to where Noisy Creek pours into Sullivan Lake. Note that the lake level can be drawn down for irrigation, leaving this camp well above the lake. The Noisy Creek Trail near camp heads east along Noisy Creek and then north up to Hall Mountain (elevation 6,323 feet), a distance of 5.3 miles; this is bighorn sheep country. The Lakeshore Trailhead is at the nearby day-use area. Water-skiing is allowed on the 3.5-mile-long lake, and the boat ramp near the camp provides a good launch point.

Location: On Sullivan Lake in Colville National Forest; see Northeastern Washington, map 3, grid b6.

Campsites, facilities: There are 19 sites for trailers or RVs up to 45 feet long and one group camp for up to 30 people. If the group camp is not reserved, it is available as an overflow area. Picnic tables and fire grills are provided. Drinking water and vault toilets are available. Boat-launching facilities and a picnic area are nearby. Leashed pets are permitted.

Reservations, fees: Reserve at 877/444-6777 ($8.65 reservation fee) or website: www .reserveusa.com. Sites are $10 per night, $5 extra vehicle fee. Senior discount available. Group site is $60 per night. Open late May to early September.

Directions: From Spokane, drive north on U.S. 395 for six miles to U.S. 2. Turn northeast on U.S. 2 and drive 30 miles to the Metaline turnoff and Highway 211 West. Turn

northwest on Highway 211 West and drive 15 miles to Usk and Highway 20. Turn northwest (left) and drive 34 miles to Tiger and Highway 31. Turn north on Highway 31 and drive 15 miles to the town of Metaline Falls (Highway 31 is known at Lehigh Avenue in town) and continue 2.5 miles to Sullivan Lake Road (County Road 9345). Turn east (right) on Sullivan Lake Road and drive eight miles to the campground on the right (on the south end of Sullivan Lake).

Contact: Colville National Forest, Sullivan Lake Ranger District, 12641 Sullivan Lake Road, Metaline Falls, WA 99153; 509/446-7500, fax 509/446-7580.

67 Edgewater

 6

Edgewater Camp is set on the shore of the Pend Oreille River about two miles upstream from the Box Canyon Dam. The camp is not far out of Ione, yet it has a primitive feel to it. Fishing is popular here, with largemouth bass, rainbow trout, and brown trout available, with somewhat of a problem with suckers and squawfish.

Location: On the Pend Oreille River in Colville National Forest; see Northeastern Washington, map 3, grid b5.

Campsites, facilities: There are 21 sites for tents, trailers, or RVs up to 40 feet long. Picnic tables and fire grills are provided. Drinking water and vault toilets are available. A boat launch and six picnic sites for day use are available nearby. Leashed pets are permitted.

Reservations, fees: No reservations. Sites are $10 per night, $5 per extra vehicle per night. Senior discount available. Open late May to early September.

Directions: From Spokane, drive north on U.S. 395 for six miles to U.S. 2. Turn northeast on U.S. 2 and drive 30 miles to the Metaline turnoff and Highway 211 West. Turn northwest on Highway 211 West and drive 15 miles to Usk and Highway 20. Turn northwest (left) and drive 34 miles to Tiger and Highway 31. Turn north on Highway 31 and drive 15 miles to the town of Metaline Falls (Highway 31 is known as Lehigh Avenue in town) and continue 2.5 miles to Sullivan Lake Road (County Road 9345). Turn east (right) on Sullivan Lake Road and drive one quarter-mile to County Road 3669. Turn north (left) on County Road 3669 and drive two miles to the campground entrance road on the left. Turn left and drive one quarter-mile to the campground.

Contact: Colville National Forest, Sullivan Lake Ranger District, 12641 Sullivan Lake Road, Metaline Falls, WA 99153-9701; 509/446-7500, fax 509/446-7580.

68 Ione RV Park and Motel

      8

This is a good layover for campers with RVs or trailers who want to stay in town. The park is on the shore of the Pend Oreille River, which offers fishing, swimming, several bike trails, and boating. In the winter, bighorn sheep may be spotted north of town.

Location: On the Pend Oreille River; see Northeastern Washington, map 3, grid c5.

Campsites, facilities: There are 19 sites with full hookups for trailers or RVs of any length, seven tent sites, and 11 motel rooms. Picnic tables are provided. Restrooms, drinking water, flush toilets, showers, a dump station, and a coin-operated laundry are available. A store, a café, and ice are located within one mile. Boat docks, launching facilities, and a playground are nearby. Leashed pets are permitted.

Reservations, fees: Reservations accepted. Sites are $5 to $18 per night. Major credit cards accepted. Open year-round.

Directions: From Spokane, drive north on U.S. 2 for 48 miles to the junction with Highway 211 at the Washington/Idaho border. Turn west on Highway 211 and drive 48 miles northwest to Tiger and Highway 31. Turn north on Highway 31 and drive four miles to Ione. Cross a spillway (it looks like a bridge) on Highway 31 and to the campground on the right.

Contact: Ione RV Park and Motel, P.O. Box 730, Ione, WA 99139; 509/442-3213.

69 Douglas Falls

    8

This campground in a wooded area along Mill Creek includes Douglas Falls and is just outside of town. It is a 0.2-mile walk from the campground to a beautiful overlook of a waterfall. In addition, a cabled free-span bridge is available, another unique highlight. And best of all, this camp is free!

Location: On Mill Creek; see Northeastern Washington, map 3, grid d1.

Campsites, facilities: There are 18 sites for tents or small trailers. Picnic tables, fire grills, and tent pads are provided. Vault toilets and drinking water are available. A barrier-free vault toilet, trails, and group picnic shelter with barbecue are also available. A baseball field is nearby. Leashed pets are permitted.

Reservations, fees: No reservations; no fee. Open Memorial Day weekend through November.

Directions: From Spokane, drive north on U.S. 395 for 74 miles to Colville and Highway 20. Turn east on Highway 20 and drive 1.1 miles to Aladdin Road. Turn left (north) and drive two miles to Douglas Falls Road. Turn left and drive three miles to the campground on the left.

Contact: Department of Natural Resources, Northeast Region, P.O. Box 190, Colville, WA 99114-0190; 509/684-7474, fax 509/684-7484.

70 Rocky Lake

 6

The campground is set on Rocky Lake, a shallow, weedy pond lined with a lot of rocks. This camp is good for overnight camping, but not for a long-term stay; instead go to Douglas Falls. Fishing for rainbow trout is an option. If you backtrack a bit on Rocky Lake Road, you'll see the entrance signs for the nearby Little Pend Oreille Wildlife Refuge, a premium area for hiking, fishing, hunting, and wildlife photography. It is 10 miles away.

Location: On Rocky Lake; see Northeastern Washington, map 3, grid e2.

Campsites, facilities: There are seven sites for tents or small trailers. Picnic tables, fire grills, and tent pads are provided. Vault toilets, drinking water, and a boat launch are available. Leashed pets are permitted.

Reservations, fees: No reservations; no fee. Open to overnight camping from mid-April through May and from Labor Day weekend through November. The interim period, June to early September, is open to day-use only.

Directions: From Spokane, drive north on U.S. 395 for 74 miles to Colville and Highway 20. Turn east on Highway 20 and drive six miles to Artman-Gibson Road. Turn right on Artman-Gibson Road and drive 3.2 miles to a one-lane gravel road. Turn right on the gravel road (unnamed) and drive about one-half mile. Bear left and continue another two miles to the campground.

Contact: Department of Natural Resources, Northeast Region, P.O. Box 190, Colville, WA 99114-0190; 509/684-7474, fax 509/684-7484.

71 Starvation Lake

 8

Starvation Lake is only 15 feet deep and has a weed problem, so it's okay for fishing for trout but not for swimming. It is possible to drown here from getting your feet tangled in the weeds. Osprey and bald eagles frequent the area. It's advisable to obtain a detailed map of the area. The camp is used extensively by locals during the early fishing season (end of April to early June), but is uncrowded thereafter when the fishing is then catch-and-release; check regulations. Boats must not exceed 16 feet.

Location: On Starvation Lake; see Northeastern Washington, map 3, grid e3.

Campsites, facilities: There are eight sites for tents, small trailers, or RVs; six are pull-through sites. Picnic tables and fire grills are provided. Vault toilets, drinking water, and a barrier-free fishing dock are available. Some facilities are wheelchair-accessible. Leashed pets are permitted.

Reservations, fees: No reservations; no fee. Open mid-April through November, weather permitting.

Directions: From Spokane, drive north on U.S. 395 for 74 miles to Colville and Highway 20. Turn east on Highway 20 and drive 10.5 miles to a gravel road (sign says Starvation Lake). Turn right on a gravel road and drive one-third mile to an intersection. Turn left and drive one-half mile to the campground on the right.

Contact: Department of Natural Resources, Northeast Region, P.O. Box 190, Colville, WA 99114-0190; 509/684-7474, fax 509/684-7484.

72 Little Twin Lakes

 6

Sites at this pretty, wooded campground on the shore of Little Twin Lakes have lake views and are free. Fishing is best here for cutthroat trout. It's rare to find such a nice spot on the water for free. See the description of North Gorge for more information.

Location: On Little Twin Lakes in Colville National Forest; see Northeastern Washington, map 3, grid d3.

Campsites, facilities: There are 20 sites for tents, trailers, or RVs up to 16 feet long. Fire grills and picnic tables are provided. There is no drinking water. Pit toilets and firewood are available. Boat docks and launching facilities are located nearby. Leashed pets are permitted.

Reservations, fees: No reservations; no fee. Open May to mid-November, weather permitting.

Directions: From Spokane, drive north on U.S. 395 for 74 miles to Colville and Highway 20. Turn east on Highway 20 and drive 12.5 miles to County Road 4915. Turn northeast and drive 1.5 miles to Forest Road 4939. Turn right (north) and drive 4.5 miles to the campground on the right.

Contact: Colville National Forest, Three Rivers Ranger District, Colville Office, 755 South Main Street, Colville, WA 99114; 509/684-7010, fax 509/684-7280.

73 Flodelle Creek

 8

This campground is set where hiking, hunting, and fishing are quite good. It's advisable to obtain a detailed map of the area. Off-road vehicle trails are available at this camp (see listing for Sherry Creek campground), and they are often in use, so don't count on a particularly quiet camping experience. This spot can provide good fishing, best for brook trout. Wildlife includes black bears, moose, mosquitoes, and black gnats, the latter occasionally so prevalent that they are considered wildlife. Be prepared.

Location: On Flodelle Creek; see Northeastern Washington, map 3, grid d4.

Campsites, facilities: There are eight sites for tents or small trailers. Picnic tables, fire grills, and tent pads are provided. Vault toilets and drinking water are available. Leashed pets are permitted.

Reservations, fees: No reservations; no fee. Open May through November, weather permitting.

Directions: From Spokane, drive north on U.S. 395 for 74 miles to Colville and Highway 20. Turn east on Highway 20 and drive 19.4 miles to an unnamed two-lane gravel road on the right. Turn right on that road and drive one quarter-mile to the campground entrance road on the left.

Contact: Department of Natural Resources, Northeast Region, P.O. Box 190, Colville, WA 99114-0190; 509/684-7474, fax 509/684-7484.

74 Sherry Creek

 6

This is an old fire camp set near the off-road vehicle (ORV) trail network of the Pend Orielle Lake system. It is set on Sherry Creek, about three miles from Sherry Lake. It is basically a fishing camp, with lots of brook trout and a few rainbow trout. It's advisable to obtain a detailed map of the area. Biking and hiking on the ORV trails is an option. It covers a network of 75 miles of ORV trails and can be accessed from this campground. This country has good numbers of black bear and even some moose, and because it is set next to a wetland, there can be tons of mosquitoes in summer.

Location: Near Sherry Lake; see Northeastern Washington, map 3, grid d4.

Campsites, facilities: There are three sites for tents and small trailers. Picnic tables and fire pits are provided. Vault toilets are available, but there is no drinking water or garbage service. Leashed pets are permitted.

Reservations, fees: No reservations; no fee. Open May through November, weather permitting.

Directions: From Spokane, drive north on U.S. 395 for 74 miles to Colville and Highway

20. Turn east on Highway 20 and drive 23.8 miles to a gravel road. Turn right and drive about one-half mile to the campground.

Contact: Department of Natural Resources, Northeast Region, P.O. Box 190, Colville, WA 99114-0190; 509/684-7474, fax 509/684-7484.

75 Lake Gillette

 8

This pretty and popular camp is situated right on the shore of Lake Gillette. Like neighboring East Gillette Campground, it fills up fast in the summer with off-road motorcyclists. The camp is popular with off-road vehicle (ORV) users. An ORV system can't be accessed directly from the campground, but is close. Fishing at Lake Gillette is best for cutthroat trout.

Location: On Lake Gillette in Colville National Forest; see Northeastern Washington, map 3, grid d4.

Campsites, facilities: There are 14 sites for tents, trailers, or RVs up to 31 feet long. Drinking water, fire grills, and picnic tables are provided. Vault toilets, a dump station, and an amphitheater are available. A store and ice are located within one mile. Some facilities are wheelchair-accessible. Boat docks, launching facilities, and rentals are nearby. Leashed pets are permitted.

Reservations, fees: No reservations. Sites are $8 to $14 per night. Senior discount available. Open mid-May to late September.

Directions: From Spokane, drive north on U.S. 395 for 74 miles to Colville and Highway 20. Turn east on Highway 20 and drive 20 miles to County Road 4987 (Lake Gillette Road). Turn right (east) on Lake Gillette Road and drive one-half mile to the campground on the right.

Contact: Colville National Forest, Three Rivers Ranger District, Colville Office, 755 South Main Street, Colville, WA 99114; 509/684-7010, fax 509/684-7280.

76 Gillette

 7

This beautiful and extremely popular campground is near Lake Gillette, just south of Beaver Lodge Resort and Lake Thomas, one in a chain of seven lakes. There are a few hiking trails in the area. See the description of Beaver Lodge Resort for other recreation information. Be sure to make reservations early.

Location: Near Lake Gillette in Colville National Forest; see Northeastern Washington, map 3, grid d4.

Campsites, facilities: There are 30 sites for tents, trailers, or RVs up to 31 feet long. Picnic tables and fire grills are provided. Drinking water, vault toilets, and a dump station are available. A store and ice are located within one mile. Some facilities are wheelchair-accessible. Boat docks, launching facilities, and rentals are nearby. Leashed pets are permitted.

Reservations, fees: No reservations. Sites are $8 per night. Senior discount available. Open mid-May to late September.

Directions: From Spokane, drive north on U.S. 395 for 74 miles to Colville and Highway 20. Turn east on Highway 20 and drive 20 miles to County Road 4987 (Lake Gillette Road). Turn right (east) on Lake Gillette Road and drive one-half mile to the campground on the left.

Contact: Colville National Forest, Three Rivers Ranger District, Colville Office, 755 South Main Street, Colville, WA 99114; 509/684-7010, fax 509/684-7280.

77 Beaver Lodge Resort

 9

This developed camp is along the shore of Lake Gillette, one in a chain of four lakes. A highlight in this area is the numerous opportunities for off-road vehicles (ORVs), with a network of ORV trails. In addition, hiking trails and marked bike trails are close to the camp. In winter, downhill and cross-country skiing is available.

Location: On Lake Thomas; see Northeastern Washington, map 3, grid d4.

Campsites, facilities: There are 18 sites for tents, trailers or RVs up to 40 feet, a separate tent camping area, and seven cabins. Picnic tables and fire grills are provided. Restrooms, drinking water, flush toilets, showers, gasoline, bottled gas, firewood, a recreation hall, a store, a café, ice, boat rentals, and a playground are available. A dump station is located within one mile. Boat docks and launching facilities are nearby. Leashed pets are permitted.

Reservations, fees: Reservations accepted. Sites are $10 to $16 per night; cabins are $45 to $65 per night. Major credit cards accepted. Open year-round.

Directions: From Spokane, drive north on U.S. 395 for 74 miles to Colville and Highway 20. Turn east on Highway 20 and drive 25 miles to the lodge on the right.

Contact: Beaver Lodge Resort, 2430 Highway 20 East, Colville, WA 99114; 509/684-5657.

78 Lake Thomas

 6

This camp on the shore of Lake Thomas is a less crowded alternative to the campgrounds at Lake Gillette. The lake provides fishing for cutthroat trout. Nearby options are Lake Gillette and Beaver Lodge Resort; see these listings for recreation information.

Location: On Lake Thomas in Colville National Forest; see Northeastern Washington, map 3, grid c4.

Campsites, facilities: There are 15 sites for tents and small RVs. Picnic tables, fire grills, and tent pads are provided. Drinking water, vault toilets, and firewood are available. A dump station is located within one mile. Boat docks, launching facilities, and rentals are nearby. Leashed pets are permitted.

Reservations, fees: No reservations. Sites are $8 per night. Senior discount available. Open mid-May to late September.

Directions: From Spokane, drive north on U.S. 395 for 74 miles to Colville and Highway 20. Turn east on Highway 20 and drive 20 miles to County Road 4987 (Lake Gillette Road). Turn right (east) on Lake Gillette Road and drive one mile to the campground on the left.

Contact: Colville National Forest, Three Rivers Ranger District, Colville Office, 755 South Main Street, Colville, WA 99114; 509/684-7010, fax 509/684-7280.

79 Lake Leo

 6

Lake Leo is the northernmost and quietest camp on the chain of lakes in the immediate vicinity. This lake provides fishing for cutthroat trout. Frater and Nile Lakes, both fairly small, are one mile north. In winter, there is a Nordic ski trail that starts adjacent to the camp. Fishing and boating are two recreation options here.

Location: On Lake Leo in Colville National Forest; see Northeastern Washington, map 3, grid c5.

Campsites, facilities: There are eight sites for tents,

trailers, or RVs up to 15 feet long. Picnic tables and fire grills are provided. Vault toilets are available. No drinking water is available. A boat ramp and launching facilities are nearby. Leashed pets are permitted.

Reservations, fees: No reservations. Sites are $8 per night. Senior discount available. Open mid-May to mid-September.

Directions: From Spokane on I-90, drive north on U.S. 395 for 74 miles to Colville and Highway 20. Turn east on Highway 20 and drive 23 miles to the campground entrance on the right.

Contact: Colville National Forest, Three Rivers Ranger District, Colville Office, 755 South Main Street, Colville, WA 99114; 509/684-7010, fax 509/684-7280.

80 Blueslide Resort

 7

This resort is situated along the western shore of the Pend Oreille River. It offers a headquarters for fishermen and vacationers. Four to five bass tournaments are held each spring during May and June, and the river is stocked with both rainbow trout and bass. The resort offers full facilities for anglers, including tackle, boat rentals, and a marina with the only boat gas for 53 miles. The park is lovely, with grassy, shaded sites, and is located along the waterfowl migratory path. Lots of groups camp here in the summer. Recreation options include bicycling nearby. The only other campground in the vicinity is the Outpost Resort (see next listing).

Location: On the Pend Oreille River; see Northeastern Washington, map 3, grid d6.

Campsites, facilities: There are 44 sites with full or partial hookups, including four drive-through sites, for tents, trailers or RVs of any length, seven tent sites, four motel units,

and five cabins. Picnic tables and fire pits are provided. Restrooms, drinking water, flush toilets, showers, a dump station, a meeting hall, several sports fields, a store, propane, a laundry room, ice, firewood, a playground with basketball, tetherball, volleyball, and horseshoe pits, a heated swimming pool, boat docks, launching facilities, and boat fuel are available. Leashed pets are permitted.

Reservations, fees: Reservations recommended. Sites are $14 to $18 per night, $2 per person per night for more than two people. Cabins are $47 to $65 per night. Major credit cards accepted. Open year-round, but only cabins are available in the winter.

Directions: From Spokane, drive north on U.S. 395 for six miles to U.S. 2. Turn north on U.S. 2 and drive 26 miles northeast to Highway 211. Turn left and drive 18 miles to Highway 20. Turn left and drive 22 miles to the park (located on the right at milepost 400).

Contact: Blueslide Resort, 400041 State Route 20, Cusick, WA 99119; 509/445-1327; website: www.blueslideresort.com.

81 Outpost Resort

  8

This comfortable campground in a pretty setting along the west shore of the Pend Oreille River has fairly spacious sites and views of snow-capped mountains. If you're cruising Highway 20, Blueslide Resort is located about five miles north, the nearest alternative if this camp is full.

Location: On the Pend Oreille River; see Northeastern Washington, map 3, grid e6.

Campsites, facilities: There are 12 tent sites and 12 drive-through sites with full hookups for trailers or RVs of any length. There are also four cabins. Picnic tables are provided. Flush toilets, a dump station, a store, a café, ice, electricity, drinking water, sewer hookups, showers, a swimming area, boat rentals, boat docks, and launching facilities are available. Leashed pets are permitted.

Reservations, fees: Reservations accepted. Sites are $10 to $15 per night; cabins are $40 to $65 per night. Major credit cards accepted. Open year-round, with limited winter facilities.

Directions: From Spokane, drive north on U.S. 395 for six miles to U.S. 2. Turn north on U.S. 2 and drive 34 miles to Highway 211. Turn left and drive 18 miles to Highway 20. Turn left and drive 17 miles to the park (located between mileposts 405 and 406) on the right.

Contact: Outpost Resort, 405351 Highway 20, Cusick, WA 99119; 509/445-1317 or 888/888-9064.

82 Panhandle

  9

In the tall trees and with views of the river, here's a scenic spot to set up camp along the eastern shore of the Pend Oreille River. This is a good base for a fishing or water-skiing trip. Fishing for largemouth and small-mouth bass is the most popular, with an annual bass tournament held every summer in the area. The campground is located in an area of mature trees directly across the river from the Outpost Resort. A network of hiking trails can be accessed by taking Forest Roads to the east. See a U.S. Forest Service map for details.

Location: On the Pend Oreille River in Colville National Forest; see Northeastern Washington, map 3, grid e6.

Campsites, facilities: There are 13 sites for tents, trailers, or RVs up to 32 feet long. Picnic tables and fire grills are provided. Drinking water and vault toilets are available. A small boat launch is nearby. Some facilities are wheelchair-accessible. Leashed pets are permitted.

Reservations, fees: Reserve at 877/444-6777 ($8.65 reservation fee) or website: www.reserveusa.com. Sites are $10 per night, $5 per extra vehicle per night. Senior discount available. Open late May to late September.

Directions: From Spokane, drive north on U.S. 395 for six miles to U.S. 2. Turn north on U.S. 2 and drive 30 miles to the Metaline turnoff and Highway 211 West. Take Highway 211 West and drive for 15 miles to the junction of Highway 20. Cross Highway 20, driving through the town of Usk. Continue across the Pend Oreille River to Le Clerk Road. Turn left and drive 15 miles north on Le Clerk Road to the campground on the left.

Contact: Colville National Forest, Newport Ranger District, 315 North Warren Avenue, Newport, WA 99156; 509/447-7300, fax 509/447-7301.

83 Skookum Creek

    5

This campground is set in a wooded area along Skookum Creek, about 1.5 miles from where it empties into the Pend Oreille River. It's a good canoeing spot, has drinking water, and gets little attention. And you can't beat the price of admission—free.

Location: Near the Pend Oreille River; see Northeastern Washington, map 3, grid e6.

Campsites, facilities: There are 10 sites for tents or small trailers. Picnic tables, fire grills, and tent pads are provided. Drinking water and vault toilets are available. A group picnic shelter with a barbecue is available nearby. Leashed pets are permitted.

Reservations, fees: No reservations; no fee. Open mid-April through October, weather permitting.

Directions: From Spokane, drive north on U.S. 395 for six miles to U.S. 2. Turn north on U.S. 2 and drive 48 miles to Newport and Highway 20. Turn west on Highway 20 and drive 16 miles northwest to the town of Usk. Continue east across the bridge for 0.9 mile to Le Clerc Road. Turn right on Le Clerc Road and drive 2.2 miles to a one-lane gravel road. Turn left and drive a short distance to another gravel road. Turn left and drive one quarter-mile to the campground.

Contact: Department of Natural Resources, Northeast Region, P.O. Box 190, Colville, WA 99114-0190; 509/684-7474, fax 509/684-7484.

84 Browns Lake

   8

This campground is set along the shore of Browns Lake, with lakeside sites bordering old-growth hemlock and cedar. No motorized boats are permitted on the lake, and only fly-fishing is allowed, so it can be ideal for float tubes, canoes, and prams. A 1.25-mile-long hiking trail leaves the campground and ties into a wheelchair-accessible interpretive trail with beautiful views along the way. At the end of the trail is a fishing viewing platform in the creek (Browns Creek) that feeds into the lake. South Skookum Lake is about five miles away.

Location: On Browns Lake in Colville National Forest; see Northeastern Washington, map 3, grid e7.

Campsites, facilities: There are 18 sites for tents, trailers, or RVs up to 21 feet long. Picnic tables and fire grills are provided. Vault toilets are available. No drinking water is available. A primitive boat launch is available for small boats such as canoes, rowboats, and inflatables. Some facilities are wheelchair-accessible. Leashed pets are permitted.

Reservations, fees: No reservations. Sites are $8 per night, $4 per extra vehicle per night. Senior discount available. Open late May to late September.

Directions: From Spokane, drive north on U.S. 395 for six miles to U.S. 2. Turn north on U.S. 2 and drive 30 miles to the Metaline turnoff and Highway 211 West. Turn northwest on Highway 211 West and drive for 15 miles to Usk and Highway 20. Drive north on Highway 20 a short distance to County Road 3389. Turn right (east) on County Road 3389 and drive (over the Pend Oreille River) for four miles to a fork with Forest Road 5030. Bear north and drive four miles to the campground at the end of the road.

Contact: Colville National Forest, Newport Ranger District, 315 North Warren Avenue, Newport, WA 99156; 509/447-7300, fax 509/447-7301.

85 South Skookum Lake

   7

This camp is sited at the western shore of South Skookum Lake, at the foot of Kings Mountain (elevation 4,383 feet). This is a good fishing lake and is popular with families. It is stocked with cutthroat trout. A 1.3-mile-long hiking trail circles the water, and a spur trail leads to South Baldy Lookout.

Location: On South Skookum Lake in Colville National Forest; see Northeastern Washington, map 3, grid e7.

Campsites, facilities: There are 25 sites for tents, trailers, or RVs up to 30 feet long. Picnic tables and fire rings are provided. Drinking water and vault toilets are available. A boat ramp for small boats, two docks, and a wheelchair-accessible fishing dock are available nearby. Leashed pets are permitted.

Reservations, fees: No reservations. Sites are $10 per night, $5 per extra vehicle per night. Senior discount available. Open late May to late September.

Directions: From Spokane, drive north on U.S. 395 for six miles to U.S. 2. Turn north on U.S. 2 and drive 30 miles to the Metaline turnoff and Highway 211 West. Turn northwest on Highway 211 West and drive for 15 miles to Usk and Highway 20. Drive north on Highway 20 a short distance to Kings Lake Road (County Road 3389). Turn right (east) on Kings Lake Road (County Road 3389) and drive for eight miles (over the Pend Oreille River) to the campground entrance road on the right. Turn right and drive one quarter-mile to the campground.

Contact: Colville National Forest, Newport Ranger District, 315 North Warren Avenue, Newport, WA 99156; 509/447-7300, fax 509/447-7301.

86 Pioneer Park

 8

Pioneer Park Campground is set along the shore of Box Canyon Reservoir on the Pend Oreille River near Newport. The launch and adjoining parking area are suitable for larger boats. Water-skiing and water sports are popular here. There is a wheelchair-accessible interpretive trail with a boardwalk and beautiful views of the river. Signs along the way explain the history of the Kalispel tribe.

Location: On the Pend Oreille River in Colville National Forest; see Northeastern Washington, map 3, grid g8.

Campsites, facilities: There are 17 sites for tents, trailers, or RVs up to 32 feet long.

Picnic tables and fire rings are provided. Drinking water, vault toilets, and a picnic area are available. Some facilities are wheelchair-accessible. Boat docks, launching facilities, and rentals are nearby. Leashed pets are permitted.

Reservations, fees: Reserve at 877/444-6777 ($8.65 reservation fee) or website: www .reserveusa.com. Sites are $10 per night, $5 per extra vehicle per night. Senior discount available. Open May to late September, weather permitting.

Directions: From Spokane, drive north on U.S. 395 for six miles to U.S. 2. Turn north on U.S. 2 and drive 41 miles to Newport. Continue across the Pend Oreille River to Le Clerc Road (County Road 9305). Turn left on Le Clerc Road and drive two miles to the campground on the left.

Contact: Colville National Forest, Newport Ranger District, 315 North Warren Avenue, Newport, WA 99156; 509/447-7300, fax 509/447-7301.

87 The 49er Motel and RV Park

 6

This is the heart of mining country. The park is in a mountainous setting next to a motel, with grassy sites. Nearby recreation options include a 27-hole golf course, hiking trails, and marked bike trails. This is a good deal for RV cruisers—a rustic setting right in town. In winter, note that the 49 Degrees Ski & Snowboard Parks is located 12 miles to the east.

Location: Near Chewelah; see Northeastern Washington, map 3, grid f3.

Campsites, facilities: There are 27 sites with full hookups, including most drive-through sites, for tents, trailers, or RVs up to 30 feet long, and 13 motel rooms. Picnic tables

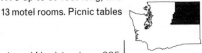

are provided. Restrooms, drinking water, flush toilets, showers, a dump station, cable TV, a spa, a recreation hall, picnic tables, and an indoor heated swimming pool are available. Bottled gas, a store, a café, ice, and a coin-operated laundry are located within one mile. Leashed pets are permitted.

Reservations, fees: Reservations accepted. Sites are $12 to $16.50 per night, with weekly and monthly rates available. Major credit cards accepted. Open year-round.

Directions: From Spokane, drive north on U.S. 395 and go 44 miles to Chewelah; the park is on the right (on U.S. 395 at the south edge of town, well marked).

Contact: The 49er Motel and RV Park, South 311 Park Street, Chewelah, WA 99109; 509/935-8613 or 888/412-1994, fax 509/935-8705.

88 Winona Beach Resort and RV Park

 9

This beautiful and comfortable resort on the shore of Waitts Lake has spacious sites and friendly folks. The park fills up in July and August, and note that cabins here are available during this time by the week, not the night. In the spring, fishing for brown trout and rainbow trout can be quite good. The trout head to deeper water in the summer, and bluegill and perch are easier to catch. Water-skiing and windsurfing are also popular.

Location: On Waitts Lake; see Northeastern Washington, map 3, grid g2.

Campsites, facilities: There are 54 sites with full hookups, including 20 lakeside sites and two drive-through sites, for tents, trailers, or RVs up to 40 feet, seven tent sites, and seven cabins. Picnic tables and fire rings are provided. Restrooms, drinking water, flush toilets, coin-operated showers, a dump station,

firewood, a snack bar, a general store, a playground with volleyball, horseshoe pits, basketball, a swimming beach, an antique store, and ice are available. Boat docks, launching facilities, and rentals are on site. Leashed pets are permitted.

Reservations, fees: Reservations accepted. Sites are $14 to $20 per night, $2 per extra vehicle per night. Cabins are $49 to $75 per night. Pets $2.50 per night. Major credit cards accepted. Open April through September.

Directions: From Spokane, drive north on U.S. 395 for 42 miles to the Valley-Waitts Lake exit. Turn west (left) at that exit and drive one mile to Highway 231. Turn right (north) on Highway 231 and drive 1.5 miles to the town of Valley and Valley-Waitts Lake Road. Turn left and drive three miles to Winona Beach Road. Turn left and drive one quarter-mile to the resort at the end of the road.

Contact: Winona Beach Resort and RV Park, 33022 Winona Beach Road, Valley, WA 99181; 509/937-2231, fax 509/937-2215; website: www.gocampingamerica.com/winona.

89 Silver Beach Resort

  6

Silver Beach Resort offers grassy sites on the shore of Waitts Lake, where fishing and water-skiing are popular. See the previous description of Winona Beach Resort and RV Park for information about the lake.

Location: On Waitts Lake; see Northeastern Washington, map 3, grid g2.

Campsites, facilities: There are 53 sites with full hookups, including four drive-through sites, for trailers or RVs up to 40 feet, and seven cabins. Picnic tables and fire pits are provided. Restrooms, drinking water, flush toilets, coin-operated showers, bottled gas, a dump station, a store, a restaurant, a coin-operated laundry, ice, a playground, boat docks, launching facilities, and boat rentals are available. Leashed pets are permitted.

Reservations, fees: Reservations accepted. Sites are $19 per night, $2 per person per night for more than two people, $2.50 pet fee per night. Cabins $68 to $79. Senior discount available. Major credit cards accepted. Open late April through September.

Directions: From Spokane, drive north on U.S. 395 for 42 miles to the Valley-Waitts Lake exit. Turn west (left) at that exit and drive six miles to Waitts Lake and the resort on the left-hand side near the shore of the lake.

Contact: Silver Beach Resort, 3323 Waitts Lake Road, Valley, WA 99181; 509/937-2811, fax 509/937-2816.

90 Waitts Lake Resort

 7

The shore of Waitts Lake is the home of this clean, comfortable resort, where lake views are available and ice fishing is popular in the winter. See the previous description of Winona Beach Resort and RV Park for information about the lake. The campsites have lake views.

Location: On Waitts Lake; see Northeastern Washington, map 3, grid g2.

Campsites, facilities: There are 13 sites with full hookups for tents, trailers, or RVs up to 40 feet. Picnic tables and fire rings are provided. Restrooms, drinking water, flush toilets, showers, a store, a year-round restaurant, firewood, boat docks, boat rentals, launching facilities, and ice are available. Leashed pets are allowed.

Reservations, fees: Reservations recommended. Sites are $18.50 per night, $5 pet fee per night. Major credit cards accepted. Open early April to late October.

Directions: From Spokane, drive north on U.S. 395 for 42 miles to the Valley-Waitts Lake exit. Turn west (left) at that exit and drive one mile to Highway 231. Turn right (north) on Highway 231 and drive 1.5 miles to the town of Valley and Valley-Waitts Lake Road. Turn left and drive three miles to the resort on the left.

Contact: Waitts Lake Resort, 3365 Waitts Lake Road, Valley, WA 99181; 509/937-2400.

91 Jump Off Joe Lake Resort

 7

Located on the edge of Jump Off Joe Lake, this wooded campground offers lake views and easy boating access. Recreational activities include boating, fishing, and swimming. Spokane and Grand Coulee Dam are both within a short drive and provide excellent side-trip options. Within 10 miles to the north is an 18-hole golf course and casino.

Location: On Jump Off Joe Lake; see Northeastern Washington, map 3, grid g3.

Campsites, facilities: There are 20 sites for tents and 20 sites with full hookups, including one drive-through site, for tents, trailers, or RVs, and five cabins. Picnic tables and fire rings are provided. Restrooms, drinking water, flush toilets, showers, a pay phone, horseshoe pits, a recreation field, a store, a swimming beach, and a barbecue are available. The camp also rents boats and has a boat ramp and dock. Some facilities are wheelchair-accessible. Leashed pets are permitted.

Reservations, fees: Reservations recommended. Sites are $15.50–17.50 per night. A pet fee of $2.50 per night is charged. Cabins are $49 to $75. Major credit cards accepted. Open April through October.

Directions: From Spokane, drive north on U.S. 395 for

about 40 miles (three miles south of the town of Valley) to the Jump Off Joe Road exit (mile marker 198). Take that exit, turn west and drive 1.2 miles to the campground on the right.

Contact: Jump Off Joe Lake Resort, 3290 East Jump Off Joe Road, Valley, WA 99181; 509/937-2133.

92 Shore Acres

 8

Located along the shore of Loon Lake at 2,400 feet elevation, this family-oriented campground has a long expanse of beach and is an alternative to Granite Point Park across the lake. See the description of Granite Point Park for details about the fishing opportunities.

Location: On Loon Lake; see Northeastern Washington, map 3, grid h3.

Campsites, facilities: There are 30 sites with full hookups for tents, trailers, or RVs up to 40 feet long and 10 cabins. Picnic tables are provided. Restrooms, drinking water, flush toilets, showers, a dump station, cable TV, a general store, firewood, propane, ice, a playground, a swimming area, boat docks, boat rentals, and launching facilities are available. Leashed pets are permitted.

Reservations, fees: Reservations recommended. Sites are $25 per night, pets $2.50 per night. Cabins are $480 to $615 per week in July and August, $80 to $100 per night the rest of the year. Major credit cards accepted. Open mid-April through September.

Directions: From Spokane, drive north on U.S. 395 for 30 miles to Highway 292. Turn west on Highway 292 and drive two miles to Shore Acres Road. Turn left and drive another two miles to the park.

Contact: Shore Acres, 41987 Shore Acres Road, Loon Lake, WA 99148; 800/900-2474 or 509/233-2474.

93 Granite Point Park

 8

This camp is located on the shore of Loon Lake, a clear, clean, spring-fed lake that covers 1,200 acres and features a sandy beach and swimming area. The campground features grass sites, no concrete. In the spring, the Mackinaw trout range from 4 to 30 pounds and can be taken by deepwater trolling (downriggers suggested). Easier to catch are the kokanee salmon and rainbow trout in the 12- to 14-inch class. A sprinkling of perch, sunfish, and bass come out of their hiding places when the weather heats up. Water-skiing and windsurfing are popular in summer months.

Location: On Loon Lake; see Northeastern Washington, map 3, grid h3.

Campsites, facilities: There are 80 sites with full hookups for trailers or RVs up to 40 feet, and 25 cottages with kitchens. Picnic tables and barbecues are provided. Restrooms, drinking water, flush toilets, showers, a recreation hall, a store, a café, a coin-operated laundry, ice, a playground with basketball, volleyball, and horseshoe pits, three swimming areas with a three-quarter-mile beach, two swimming docks, boat docks, boat rentals, and launching facilities are available. Bottled gas is located within one mile. Pets are *not* permitted.

Reservations, fees: Reservations accepted. Sites are $22 per night, $4 per person per night for more than two people. Cottages are $400 to $800 per week in July and August, and $60 to $120 per night the rest of the year. Open mid-April to mid-September.

Directions: From Spokane, drive north on U.S. 395 for 26 miles (eight miles past the town of Deer Park) to the campground on the left.

Contact: Granite Point Park, 41000 Granite Point Road, Loon Lake, WA 99148; 509/233-2100; website: www.granitepointpark.com.

94 Pend Oreille County Park

 6

This 440-acre park is wooded with hiking trails throughout. There is some road noise from U.S. 2, but it's not intolerable. This is the only campground around, and it's not a bad choice if you're looking for a layover spot. It's a good alternative to the often-crowded Mt. Spokane State Park. Nearby activities include fishing and hunting.

Location: Near Newport; map A5; see Northeastern Washington, map 3, grid h6.

Campsites, facilities: There are 34 sites for tents and two sites for trailers or RVs up to 30 feet long. No hookups are available. Picnic tables and barbecues are provided. Restrooms, drinking water, flush toilets, and showers are available. Leashed pets are permitted.

Reservations, fees: Reservations at 509/447-4821. Sites are $8 to $12 per night. Open Memorial Day Weekend to Labor Day Weekend.

Directions: From Spokane, drive north on U.S. 395 for six miles to U.S. 2. Turn north on U.S. 2 and drive 31 miles to the county park entrance on the left (west side). Or from Newport: Drive east on U.S 2 for 13 miles (past County Road 211) to the park entrance on the right.

Contact: Pend Oreille County Department of Parks and Recreation, P.O. Box 5067, Newport, WA 99156; 509/447-4821.

95 Lakeshore RV Park and Marina

 7

This municipal park and marina on Lake Chelan is a popular family camp, with fishing, swimming, boating, and hiking among the available activities. The camp fills up in the summer, including on weekdays in July and August. This RV park covers 22 acres, featuring a large marina and a 15-acre day-use area. An 18-hole championship golf course and putting green, lighted tennis courts, and a visitor scenter are nearby. A trip worth taking is the ferry ride to one of several landings on the lake; the ferry terminal is one-half mile from the park.

Location: On Lake Chelan; see Northeastern Washington, map 4, grid b1.

Campsites, facilities: There are 167 sites with full hookups for tents, trailers, or RVs of any length. Picnic tables are provided. Restrooms, flush toilets, coin-operated showers, a dump station, and a covered picnic area with a shelter are available. A store, a café, a coin-operated laundry, ice, a playground, and bottled gas are available within one mile. Boat docks and launching facilities are on site.

Reservations, fees: Reservations accepted for each year beginning January 2. Sites are $11 to $32 per night, $5 per extra vehicle per night. Major credit cards accepted. Open year-round.

Directions: From East Wenatchee, drive north on Highway 97-A for 40 miles to Chelan (after crossing the Dan Gordon Bridge, the road name changes to Saunders Street). Continue for 0.1 mile to Johnson Street. Turn left and drive 0.2 mile (becomes Highway 150/Manson Highway) to the campground on the left.

Contact: City of Chelan, P.O. Box 1669, Chelan, WA 98816; 509/682-8024, fax 509/682-8248.

96 Coulee Playland Resort

 7

This park on North Banks Lake, south of the Grand Coulee Dam, is pretty and well treed, with spacious sites for both tents and RVs.

The Grand Coulee Laser Light Show is just two miles away and is well worth a visit. Boating, fishing for many species, and water-skiing are all popular. In addition, hiking trails, marked bike trails, a full-service marina, and tennis courts are closeby.

Location: Near the Grand Coulee Dam; see Northeastern Washington, map 4, grid a8.

Campsites, facilities: There are 65 sites for tents, trailers, or RVs of any length, and one yurt, which sleeps five. Picnic tables and fire grills are provided. Restrooms, flush toilets, coin-operated showers, a dump station, a store, a coin-operated laundry, firewood, ice, a playground, boat docks, launching facilities, boat rentals, gas, and a bait-and-tackle shop are available. Bottled gas and a café are located within one mile. Pets are permitted.

Reservations, fees: Reservations accepted. Sites are $18 to $21 per night, $10 per extra vehicle per night. Major credit cards accepted. Open year-round, with limited winter facilities.

Directions: From the junction of Highway 17 and U.S. 2 (north of Ephrata), drive east on U.S. 2 for five miles to Highway 155. Turn left (north) and drive 26 miles to Grand Coulee and Electric City. The campground is just off the highway on the left.

Contact: Coulee Playland Resort, P.O. Box 457, 401 Coulee Boulevard, Electric City, WA 99123; 509/633-2671; website: www.couleeplayland.com.

97 Steamboat Rock State Park

 10

Steamboat Rock State Park is an oasis in desert surroundings. The park covers 3,522 acres and features nine miles of shoreline along Banks Lake, a reservoir created by the Grand Coulee Dam. Dominating the landscape is the columnar basaltic rock, with a surface area of 600 acres, that rises 800 feet above the lake. Two campground areas and a large day-use area are set on green lawns sheltered by tall poplars. The park has 13 miles of hiking and biking trails, and 10 miles of horse trails. There is also a swimming beach, and fishing and water-skiing are popular. So is rock climbing. A hiking trail is available that leads to Northrup Lake. Horse trails are available in nearby Northrup Canyon. Note that the one downer is mosquitoes, which are very prevalent in early summer. During the winter, the park is used by snowmobilers, cross-country skiers, and ice anglers.

Location: On Banks Lake; see Northeastern Washington, map 4, grid b7.

Campsites, facilities: There are 100 sites with full hookups for trailers or RVs up to 50 feet long, 26 sites for tents or self-contained RVs, and 92 primitive campsites. Picnic tables and fire grills are provided. Restrooms, flush toilets, a dump station, a café, and a playground with volleyball are available. Some facilities are wheelchair-accessible. Boat-launching facilities, docks, and a marine dump station are nearby. Leashed pets are permitted.

Reservations, fees: Reserve at 888/CAMP-OUT (888/226-7688); website: www.parks.wa.gov/reservations ($7 reservation fee). Sites are $15 to $22 per night, $6 per extra vehicle per night. Senior discount available. Major credit cards accepted. Open year-round, with limited winter facilities.

Directions: From East Wenatchee, drive north U.S. 2 for 70 miles to Highway 155 (five miles east of Coulee City). Turn north and drive 18 miles to the park on the left.

Contact: Steamboat Rock State Park, P.O. Box 352, Electric City, WA 99123; 509/633-1304; State Park information, 360/902-8844.

Blue Lake Resort

 6

Blue Lake Resort is in a desertlike area along the shore of Blue Lake between Sun Lakes State Park and Lake Lenore Caves State Park. Both parks are excellent side trips. Activities at Blue Lake include trout fishing, swimming, and boating. Tackle and boat rentals are available at the resort.

Location: On Blue Lake; see Northeastern Washington, map 4, grid d5.

Campsites, facilities: There are 56 sites with full or partial hookups, including six drive-through sites, for trailers or RVs of any length, 30 tent sites, and 10 cabins that sleep up to four people. Picnic tables and fire pits are provided. Restrooms, flush toilets, showers, a dump station, firewood, a store, ice, a roped swimming area, volleyball, a playground, boat docks, launching facilities, and boat rentals are available. Leashed pets are permitted.

Reservations, fees: Reservations accepted. Call for current rates. Major credit cards accepted. Open April through September.

Directions: From the junction of I-90 and Highway 17 (just south of Moses Lake), drive north on Highway 17 for 36 miles to the park on the right.

Contact: Blue Lake Resort, 31199 Highway 17 North, Coulee City, WA 99115; 509/632-5364.

Sun Village Resort

 6

Like Blue Lake Resort, this campground is situated along the shore of Blue Lake. The setting is hot desert, perfect for swimming and fishing. Late July and early August are the busiest times of the year here. See the following description of Sun Lakes State Park for information on the nearby state parks and other recreation options.

Location: On Blue Lake; see Northeastern Washington, map 4, grid d5.

Campsites, facilities: There are 95 sites, including 40 drive-through and most with full hookups, for trailers or RVs of any length, and four tent sites. Picnic tables are provided. Restrooms, flush toilets, coin-operated showers, group fire pits, bottled gas, a dump station, a coin-operated laundry, a store, a café, bait and tackle, ice, a playground, boat docks, launching facilities, and boat rentals are available. Firewood can be obtained for a fee. Leashed pets are permitted.

Reservations, fees: Reservations accepted. Sites are $18.50 per night, $4 per extra vehicle per night, $3 pet fee per night, cabins $49 to $110 per night. Major credit cards accepted. Open late April to late September.

Directions: From the junction of I-90 and Highway 17 (just south of Moses Lake), drive north on Highway 17 for 36 miles to Blue Lake and Park Lake Road. Turn right (east) on Park Lake Road (the south entrance) and drive one-half mile to the resort on the right.

Contact: Sun Village Resort, 33575 Park Lake Road NE, Coulee City, WA 99115; 509/632-5664 or 888/632-5664.

Coulee Lodge Resort

 8

This camp is set at Blue Lake, which often provides outstanding fishing for stocked trout in early spring, a mix of rainbow trout and brown trout. It is one of five camps in the general area and one of three in the immediate vicinity. Blue Lake offers plenty of summertime recreation options. A swimming beach is a highlight. See the following description of Sun Lakes State Park for details.

Location: On Blue Lake; see Northeastern Washington, map 4, grid d5.

Campsites, facilities: There are 22 sites with full hookups, including seven drive-through sites, for trailers or RVs up to 35 feet long, and 14 tent sites. Picnic tables and fire pits are provided. Restrooms, flush toilets, coin-operated showers, bottled gas, a dump station, a store, firewood, a coin-operated laundry, boat docks, boat and personal watercraft rentals, launching facilities, and ice are available. A café is located within five miles. Some facilities are wheelchair-accessible. Leashed pets are permitted.

Reservations, fees: Reservations accepted. Sites are $14 to $17 per night, $3 per extra vehicle per night, $2 pet fee per night. Major credit cards accepted. Open mid-April to October.

Directions: From the junction of I-90 and Highway 17 (just south of Moses Lake), drive north on Highway 17 for 39 miles to the north end of Blue Lake.

Contact: Coulee Lodge Resort, 33017 Park Lake Road NE, Coulee City, WA; 509/632-5565, fax 509/632-8607; website: www.couleelodge resort.com.

101 Sun Lakes State Park

 10

Sun Lakes State Park is situated on the shore of Park Lake, which is used primarily by anglers, boaters, and water-skiers. This is a 4,027-acre park with 12 miles of shoreline near the foot of Dry Falls. Dry Falls, a former waterfall, is now a stark 400-foot-high climb, 3.5 miles wide. During the Ice Age floods, this waterfall was 10 times the size of Niagara Falls. An interpretive center at Dry Falls is open May to September. Now, back to the present: There are nine lakes in the park. The Lake Lenore Caves can be reached by a trail at the north end of Lake Lenore. Nearby recreation possibilities include a nine-hole golf course and miniature golf.

Location: On Park Lake; see Northeastern Washington, map 4, grid d5.

Campsites, facilities: There are 162 sites for tents or self-contained RVs, 18 sites with full hookups for trailers or RVs up to 50 feet long, and one group campsite for up to 40 people. Picnic tables and fire pits are provided. Restrooms, flush toilets, coin-operated showers, a dump station, a café, a coin-operated laundry, ice, electricity, drinking water, sewer hookups, and firewood for sale are available. A store is located within one mile. Some facilities are wheelchair-accessible. Boat docks, launching facilities, and rentals are nearby. Leashed pets are permitted.

Reservations, fees: Reserve at 888/CAMP-OUT (888/226-7688); website: www.parks.wa .gov/reservations ($7 reservation fee). Sites are $15 to $22 per night. Senior discount available. Major credit cards accepted. Open year-round.

Directions: From Ephrata, drive northeast on Highway 28 to Soap Lake and Highway 17. Turn north on Highway 17 and drive 17 miles to the park on the right.

Contact: Sun Lakes State Park, 509/632-5583; State Park information, 360/902-8844.

102 Sun Lakes Park Resort

      6

This camp is run by the concessionaire that operates within Sun Lakes State Park. It offers full facilities and is a slightly more developed alternative to the state campground. See the description of Sun Lakes State Park.

Location: Sun Lakes State Park; see Northeastern Washington, map 4, grid d5.

Campsites, facilities: There are 110 sites with full hookups, including 64 drive-through for tents, trailers, or RVs of any length. Picnic tables and fire grills are provided. Restrooms, flush toilets coin-operated showers, bottled gas, a dump station, a store, firewood, a snack bar, a coin-operated laundry, ice, a playground, boat rentals, and a swimming pool are available. Boat docks and launching facilities are nearby. Some facilities are wheelchair-accessible. Leashed pets are permitted.

Reservations, fees: Reservations accepted. Sites are $21 to $23 per night, $6 per extra vehicle per night. Open mid-April to mid-October, weather permitting.

Directions: From Ephrata, drive northeast on Highway 28 to Soap Lake and Highway 17. Turn north on Highway 17 and drive 17 miles to the Sun Lakes Park on the right. Enter the park and drive to the resort (well marked).

Contact: Sun Lakes Park Resort, 34228 Park Lake Road NE, Coulee City, WA 99115; 509/632-5291.

103 Coulee City Park

 6

Coulee City Park is a well-maintained park located in shade trees on the southern shore of 30-mile-long Banks Lake. You can see the highway from the park, and there is some highway noise. Campsites are usually available. The busiest time of the year is Memorial Day weekend because of the local rodeo. Boating, fishing, and water-skiing are popular. An 18-hole golf course is closeby.

Location: On Banks Lake; see Northeastern Washington, map 4, grid c6.

Campsites, facilities: There are 100 tent sites and 55 sites for trailers or RVs up to 35 feet long, including 32 drive-through sites with full hookups. Picnic tables and fire rings are provided. Restrooms, flush toilets, showers, group fire pits, a dump station, and a playground are available. Bottled gas, firewood, a store, a restaurant, a café, a coin-operated laundry, and ice are located within one mile. Some facilities are wheelchair-accessible. Boat docks and launching facilities are on site.

Reservations, fees: No reservations accepted. Sites are $12 to $17 per night, $2 per extra vehicle. Open April to late October, weather permitting.

Directions: From Coulee City, drive east on U.S. 2 for 0.5 miles to the park on the left.

Contact: Coulee City Park, P.O. Box 398, Coulee City, WA 99115; 509/632-5331.

104 Spring Canyon

 6

This large, developed campground is a popular vacation destination. Fishing for bass, walleye, trout, and sunfish are popular at the Franklin Roosevelt Lake, as is water-skiing. The campground is not far from Grand Coulee Dam. Lake Roosevelt National Recreation Area offers numerous recreation options, such as free programs conducted by rangers that include guided canoe trips, historical tours, campfire talks, and guided hikes. This lake is known as a prime location to view bald eagles, especially in winter. Side-trip options include visiting the Colville Tribal Museum in the town of Coulee Dam and touring the Grand Coulee Dam Visitor Center. The dam is one of the largest concrete structures ever built. The dam is almost one mile long and twice as high as Niagara Falls. It is open for self-guided tours.

Location: On Franklin Roosevelt Lake in Lake Roosevelt National Recreation Area; see Northeastern Washington, map 5, grid a1.

Campsites, facilities: There are 87 sites for tents, trailers, or self-contained RVs up to 26 feet long and one group site for up to 25 people. Picnic tables and fire grills are provided. Restrooms, flush toilets, a dump station, a café, a picnic area, a public telephone, and a playground are available. Some facilities are wheelchair-accessible. Boat docks, launching facilities, marine fuel, and a marine dump station are available nearby. Leashed pets are permitted.

Reservations, fees: No reservations accepted. Sites are $5 to $10 per night; $6 launch fee. Senior discount available. Reservations required for group site at 509/633-3830. Open year-round, weather permitting.

Directions: From the junction of I-90 and Highway 17 (just south of Moses Lake), drive north on Highway 17 for 45 miles to U.S. 2. Turn east on U.S. 2 and drive five miles to Highway 155. Turn left (north) and drive 26 miles to Grand Coulee and Highway 174. Turn right (east) on Highway 174 and drive three miles to the campground entrance on the left.

Contact: Lake Roosevelt National Recreation Area, 1008 Crest Drive, Coulee Dam, WA 99116-1259; 509/633-9441, fax 509/633-9332.

105 Lakeview Terrace Mobile and RV Park

     6

This pleasant resort is near Franklin Roosevelt Lake, which was created by Grand Coulee Dam. It's a slightly less crowded option to the national park camps in the vicinity.

See the description of Spring Canyon for water recreation options. A full-service marina and tennis courts are nearby.

Location: Near Franklin Roosevelt Lake; see Northeastern Washington, map 5, grid a1.

Campsites, facilities: There are 20 drive-through sites with full hookups for trailers or RVs of any length and 20 tent sites. Picnic tables and fire pits are provided. Restrooms, flush toilets, coin-operated showers, a coin-operated laundry, and a playground are available. Boat docks, launching facilities, and rentals are nearby. Leashed pets are permitted.

Reservations, fees: Reservations accepted. Sites are $12 to $15 per night. Senior discount available. Major credit cards accepted. Open year-round.

Directions: From Grand Coulee, drive east on Highway 174 for 3.5 miles east to the park entrance on the left.

Contact: Lakeview Terrace Mobile and RV Park, 44900 Route 174 North, Grand Coulee, WA 99133; 509/633-2169.

106 Keller Ferry

  7

This camp is set along the shore of Franklin Roosevelt Lake, a large reservoir created by Grand Coulee Dam, about 15 miles west of camp. This lake is known for its walleye fishing, and although more than 30 species live in this lake, 90 percent of those caught are walleye. They average one to four pounds and always travel in schools. Trout and salmon often swim below the bluffs near Keller Ferry. Water-skiing, fishing, and swimming are all options here.

Location: On Franklin Roosevelt Lake in Lake Roosevelt National Recreation Area; see Northeastern Washington, map 5, grid a3.

Campsites, facilities: There are 50 sites for tents, trailers, or RVs up to 16 feet long and two group sites for up to 50 people each. Picnic tables and fire grills are provided. Drinking water and vault toilets are available. A dump station, ice, a picnic area, a public telephone, and a playground are available nearby. Boat docks, launching facilities, fuel, and a marine dump station are also available. Some facilities are wheelchair-accessible. Leashed pets are permitted.

Reservations, fees: No reservations. Sites are $5 to $10 per night; there is a $6 launch fee. Reservations required for group sites, 509/633-3830. Senior discount available. Open year-round, weather permitting.

Directions: From Spokane on U.S. 90, turn west on U.S. 2 and drive 71 miles to Wilbur and Highway 21. Turn north and drive 14 miles to the campground on the left.

Contact: Lake Roosevelt National Recreation Area, 1008 Crest Drive, Coulee Dam, WA 99116-1259; 509/633-9441, fax 509/633-9332.

107 River Rue RV Park

7

This camp is located in high desert terrain, but it is surrounded by lots of trees. Several hiking trails leave from the campground. You can fish, swim, water-ski, or rent a houseboat at Lake Roosevelt, which is one mile away. Another nearby side trip is the Grand Coulee Dam. A nine-hole golf course is available in Wilbur.

Location: Near the Columbia River; see Northeastern Washington, map 5, grid a3.

Campsites, facilities: There are 86 sites for tents, trailers, or RVs of any length, including some with full hookups, partial hookups, and some drive-through sites. Picnic tables and fire rings are provided. Restrooms, showers,

a dump station, a pay phone, limited groceries, ice, a snack bar, RV supplies, fishing tackle, and LP gas are available. Recreational facilities include a playground, volleyball, and horseshoe pits. Some facilities are wheelchair-accessible. Leashed pets are permitted.

Reservations, fees: Reservations recommended. Sites are $14 to $22 per night, $2 per person per night for more than two people. Major credit cards accepted. Open April through October.

Directions: On U.S. 2 at Wilbur, drive west on U.S. 2 for one mile to Highway 174. Turn north on Highway 174 and drive one quarter-mile to Highway 21. Turn right (north) on Highway 21 and drive 13 miles to the park on the right.

Contact: River Rue RV Park, 44892 State Route 21 North, Wilbur, WA 99185; 509/647-2647; website: www.riverrue.com.

108 Jones Bay

6

This small and primitive campground is set on Jones Bay on Franklin Roosevelt Lake. It is well known by locals and gets high use on summer weekends. The camp is set at the bottom of a canyon in a cove, with some Ponderosa pine, and is quiet most weekdays. In 2002, the boat launch is scheduled to be lengthened. Fishing for bass, walleye, trout, and sunfish are popular at the Franklin Roosevelt Lake.

Location: On Franklin Roosevelt Lake in Lake Roosevelt National Recreation Area; see Northeastern Washington, map 5, grid a4.

Campsites, facilities: There are nine sites for tents, trailers, or self-contained RVs up to 16 feet long. Picnic tables and fire grills are provided. Vault toilets are available. No drinking water is available. A boat launch and dock is nearby. Some facilities are wheelchair-accessible. Leashed pets are permitted.

Reservations, fees: No reservations accepted. Sites are $5 to $10 per night; $6 launch fee. Senior discount available. Open year-round, weather permitting.

Directions: From Spokane on U.S. 90, turn west on U.S. 2 and drive 71 miles to Wilbur and Highway 21. Turn north on Highway 21 and drive seven miles to Jones Bay Road (dirt road, marked). Turn right and drive eight miles to the campground entrance road on the right. A high-clearance vehicle is recommended.

Contact: Lake Roosevelt National Recreation Area, 1008 Crest Drive, Coulee Dam, WA 99116-1259; 509/633-9441, fax 509/633-9332.

109 Hawk Creek

 8

This is a pleasant camping spot along the shore of Roosevelt Lake (Columbia River), adjacent to the mouth of Hawk Creek. This is often a good fishing spot for walleye, trout, and bass. Note that there is no drinking water if the lake level drops below an elevation of 1,265 feet.

Location: On Franklin Roosevelt Lake in Lake Roosevelt National Recreation Area; see Northeastern Washington, map 5, grid b6.

Campsites, facilities: There are 20 sites for tents, trailers, or RVs up to 16 feet long. Picnic tables and fire grills are provided. Drinking water and vault toilets are available. Boat docks and launching facilities are nearby. Some facilities are wheelchair-accessible. Leashed pets are permitted.

Reservations, fees: No reservations. Sites are $5 to $10 per night; there is a $6 launch fee. Senior discount available. Open year-round, with limited winter facilities.

Directions: From Spokane on I-90, drive west for four miles to U.S. 2. Turn west on U.S. 2 and drive 34 miles to Davenport and Highway 25. Turn north (right) on Highway 25 and drive 23 miles to Miles-Creston Road. Turn northwest (left) and drive 10 miles to the campground at the mouth of Hawk Creek on the left.

Contact: Lake Roosevelt National Recreation Area, 1008 Crest Drive, Coulee Dam, WA 99116-1259; 509/633-9441, fax 509/633-9332.

110 Seven Bays Resort and Marina

 6

Manicured grassy, lakeside sites among deciduous trees and friendly folks running the place are the highlights of this resort on the shore of Roosevelt Lake. This is an alternative to Fort Spokane and Hawk Creek. A full-service marina sets this spot apart from the others.

Location: On Franklin Roosevelt Lake; see Northeastern Washington, map 5, grid a6.

Campsites, facilities: There are 48 sites with full hookups, including two drive-through sites, for trailers or RVs up to 50 feet, and 24 tent sites. Picnic tables are provided. Restrooms, drinking water, flush toilets, coin-operated showers, bottled gas, a dump station, a store, a café, a coin-operated laundry, and ice are available. Boat rentals, docks, and launching facilities are located at the resort. Leashed pets are permitted.

Reservations, fees: Reservations accepted. Sites are $10 to $15 per night. Major credit cards accepted. Open year-round.

Directions: From Spokane on I-90, drive west for four miles to U.S. 2. Turn west on U.S. 2 and drive 34 miles to Highway 25. Turn north on Highway 25 and drive 23 miles to Miles-Creston Road. Turn left and drive five miles to the resort on the right.

Contact: Seven Bays Resort, Route 1, 1250 Marina Drive, Seven Bays, WA 99122; 509/725-1676.

111 Fort Spokane

8

Rangers offer evening campfire programs and guided daytime activities at this modern campground on the shore of Roosevelt Lake. Living-history demonstrations are enacted at this park. This is one of 28 campgrounds on the 130-mile-long lake. A 190-mile scenic vehicle route encircles most of the lake.

Location: On Franklin Roosevelt Lake in Lake Roosevelt National Recreation Area; see Northeastern Washington, map 5, grid a6.

Campsites, facilities: There are 67 sites for tents, trailers, or RVs up to 26 feet long and two group sites for up to 30 people each. Picnic tables and fire grills are provided. Restrooms, drinking water, flush toilets, a dump station, and a playground are available. A picnic area and a public telephone are nearby. A store and ice are located within one mile. Some facilities are wheelchair-accessible. Boat docks, launching facilities, and a marine dump station are nearby. Leashed pets are permitted.

Reservations, fees: No reservations for family sites. Reservations required for group sites at 509/633-3830. Sites are $5 to $10 per night; there is a $6 launch fee. Senior discount available. Open year-round, with limited winter facilities.

Directions: From Spokane on I-90, drive west for four miles to U.S. 2. Turn west on U.S. 2 and drive 34 miles to Davenport and Highway 25. Turn north (right) on Highway 25 and drive 22 miles to the campground entrance on the right.

Contact: Lake Roosevelt National Recreation Area, 1008 Crest Drive, Coulee Dam, WA 99116-1259; 509/633-9441, fax 509/633-9332.

112 Porcupine Bay

8

This camp is extremely popular, and the sites are filled most of the summer. It is an especially good spot for campers with boats because of its proximity to a nearby dock and launch. A swimming beach is adjacent to the campground.

Location: On Franklin Roosevelt Lake in Lake Roosevelt National Recreation Area; see Northeastern Washington, map 5, grid a7.

Campsites, facilities: There are 31 sites for tents, trailers, or RVs up to 20 feet long. Picnic tables and fire grills are provided. Drinking water and vault toilets are available. Restrooms, drinking water, flush toilets, a dump station, a picnic area, a public telephone, and a playground are available. Boat docks and launching facilities are nearby. Some facilities are wheelchair-accessible. Leashed pets are permitted.

Reservations, fees: No reservations. Sites are $5 to $10 per night; $6 boat launch fee. Senior discount available. Open year-round, weather permitting.

Directions: From Spokane on I-90, drive west for four miles to U.S. 2. Turn west on U.S. 2 and drive 34 miles to Davenport and Highway 25. Turn north (right) on Highway 25 and drive 19 miles to Porcupine Bay Road. Turn right (east) and drive 4.3 miles to the campground at the end of the road.

Contact: Lake Roosevelt National Recreation Area, 1008 Crest Drive, Coulee Dam, WA 99116-1259; 509/633-9441, fax 509/633-9332.

113 Long Lake Camp and Picnic Area

 8

This campground is located about 45 minutes from Spokane. The camp is set on a terrace above the lake (Spokane River), where fishing can be good for rainbow trout and occasional brown trout. This is also a large water recreation area, popular for power boating, water-skiing, and personal watercraft. It is crowded in summer, getting a lot of use from residents of the Spokane area.

Location: On the Spokane River; see Northeastern Washington, map 6, grid b1.

Campsites, facilities: There are 12 sites for tents or small trailers. Picnic tables, fire grills, and tent pads are provided. Drinking water and vault toilets are available. A boat launch, a dock, a swimming beach, and a day-use area are nearby. Most of the facilities are wheelchair-accessible.

Reservations, fees: No reservations; no fee. Open April through September.

Directions: From Spokane on I-90, drive west for four miles to U.S. 2. Turn west on U.S. 2 and drive 21 miles to Reardan and Highway 231. Turn north on Highway 231 and drive 14.2 miles to Long Lake Dam Road (Highway 291). Turn right and drive 4.7 miles to the campground entrance on the right.

Contact: Department of Natural Resources, Northeast Region, P.O. Box 190, Colville, WA 99114-0190; 509/684-7474, fax 509/684-7484.

114 Dragoon Creek

 5

This spot is frequented by locals but is often missed by out-of-town vacationers. It is set along Dragoon Creek, a tributary to the Little Spokane River. The campsites are set in a forest of Ponderosa pine and Douglas fir. It is fairly close to U.S. 395, but it's quiet and rustic. The Department of Natural Resources offers a map that details the region.

Location: Near the Little Spokane River; see Northeastern Washington, map 6, grid a5.

Campsites, facilities: There are 22 sites for tents or small trailers. Picnic tables, fire grills, and tent pads are provided. Vault toilets and drinking water are available. Leashed pets are permitted.

Reservations, fees: No reservations; no fee. Open April through September.

Directions: From Spokane, drive north on U.S. 395 for 10.2 miles to Dragoon Creek Road. Turn left on Dragoon Creek Road and drive 0.4 mile to the campground entrance at the end of the road.

Contact: Department of Natural Resources, Northeast Region, P.O. Box 190, Colville, WA 99114-0190; 509/684-7474, fax 509/684-7484.

115 Mt. Spokane State Park

 8

This is one of the better short trips available out of Spokane. This state park is set on the slopes of Mt. Spokane (5,883 feet). Its little brother, Mt. Kit Carson (5,180 feet), sits alongside it. The park covers 13,643 acres in the Selkirk Mountains and features a stunning view from the top of Mt. Spokane. The lookout takes in Washington, Idaho, Montana, and Canada. The park has 86 miles of hiking trails, occasionally routed into old-growth forest and amid granite outcroppings. The Mt. Spokane Ski Resort operates here in winter. The park receives an average of 300 inches of snow.

Location: On Mt. Spokane; see Northeastern Washington, map 6, grid a7.

Campsites, facilities: There are 12 sites for tents, trailers, or self-contained RVs up to 30 feet long. Picnic tables and fire grills are provided. Restrooms, drinking water, and flush toilets are available. A picnic area with kitchen shelter, interpretive activities, and a café are available nearby, and a coin-operated laundry is within one mile. Leashed pets are permitted.

Reservations, fees: No reservations. Sites are $15 per night, $6 per extra vehicle per night. Open June through September, weather permitting.

Directions: From Spokane, drive north on U.S. 395 for six miles to U.S. 2. Turn north on U.S. 2 and drive six miles to Highway 206. Turn northeast on Highway 206 and drive 15 miles north to the park.

Contact: Mt. Spokane State Park, 509/456-4169; State Park information, 360/902-8844.

116 Riverside State Park

    8

This 10,000-acre park is set along the Spokane and Little Spokane Rivers, featuring freshwater marshes and a beautiful countryside. There are many recreation options. Fishing is available for bass, crappie, and perch. There are 55 miles of hiking and biking trails, featuring the 37-mile Centennial Trail, and 25 miles of trails for horseback riding, as well as riding stables nearby. The park also has a 600-acre riding area for dirt bikes in summer and snowmobiles in winter. An 18-hole golf course is located nearby. A local point of interest is the unique Bowl and Pitcher Lava Formation in the river.

Location: Near Spokane; see Northeastern Washington, map 6, grid b4.

Campsites, facilities: There are 22 tent sites, 17 sites with partial hookups for tents, trailers, or RVs up to 45 feet long, and three primitive tent sites. Picnic tables and fire grills are provided. Restrooms, drinking

water, flush toilets, showers, a picnic area with kitchen shelter and electricity, a dump station, interpretive programs, and firewood are available. A store, a restaurant, and ice are located within three miles. Group camping can be accommodated. Boat-launching facilities and dock are located on site. Leashed pets are permitted.

Reservations, fees: Reservations accepted only for RV sites; 888/CAMP-OUT (888/226-7688); website: www.parks.wa.gov /reservations ($7 reservation fee). Senior discount available. Sites are $6 to $22 per night, $6 per extra vehicle per night. Open year-round.

Directions: In Spokane on I-90, take Exit 280/Maple Street North (cross the Maple Street Bridge), and drive north 1.1 miles to Maxwell Street (becomes Pettit Street). Turn left (west) and drive 1.9 miles, bearing left along the Spokane River to the park entrance. From the park entrance, continue for 1.5 miles on Aubrey L. White Parkway to the campground.

Contact: Riverside State Park, Box 65, Nine Mile Falls, WA 99026; 509/456-3964; State Park information, 360/902-8844.

117 Trailer Inns RV Park

    5

This large RV park is a perfect layover on the way to Idaho. It's as close to a hotel as an RV park can get. Nearby recreation options include an 18-hole golf course, a racquet club, and tennis courts. See the description of Overland Station for information on attractions in Spokane.

Location: In Spokane; see Northeastern Washington, map 6, grid c5.

Campsites, facilities: There are 97 sites with full hookups, including 30 drive-through sites, for tents, trailers, or RVs of any length.

Picnic tables are provided. Restrooms, drinking water, flush toilets, showers, bottled gas, cable TV, a TV room, a coin-operated laundry, ice, and a playground are available. A dump station, a store, and a café are within one mile. Leashed pets are permitted.

Reservations, fees: Reservations accepted. Sites are $15 to $21 per night, $3 per extra vehicle per night. Major credit cards accepted. Open year-round.

Directions: Note that your route will depend on your direction: In Spokane eastbound on I-90, take Exit 285 (Sprague Avenue/Eastern Road) to Eastern Road. Drive 0.1 mile on Eastern Road to Fourth Avenue. Turn right (west) on Fourth Avenue and drive two blocks to the campground. In Spokane westbound on I-90, take Exit 284 (Havana Street). Drive one block south on Havana Street to Fourth Avenue. Turn left (east) on Fourth Avenue and drive one mile to the park.

Contact: Trailer Inns RV Park, 6021 East Fourth Avenue, Spokane, WA 99212; 509/535-1811 or 800/659-4864.

118 KOA Spokane

5

This KOA campground is close to the shore of the Spokane River. Also nearby is the Centennial Trail, as well as an 18-hole golf course and tennis courts. See the description of Overland Station for information on attractions in Spokane.

Location: On the Spokane River; see Northeastern Washington, map 6, grid c8.

Campsites, facilities: There are 150 sites with full hookups, including 109 drive-through sites, for trailers or RVs of any length, 50 tent sites, and three cabins. Picnic tables are provided. Restrooms, drinking water, flush toilets, showers, cable TV, a

dump station, showers, a recreation hall, a playground, a store, a laundry room, ice, modem access, and a swimming pool are available. Some facilities are wheelchair-accessible. A café is located within two miles. Leashed pets are permitted.

Reservations, fees: Reservations accepted at 800/562-3309. Sites are $20 to $30 per night. Major credit cards accepted. Open March through November.

Directions: From Spokane, drive east on I-90 for 13 miles to Exit 293. Take that exit to Barker Road. Turn north on Barker Road and drive 1.5 miles to the campground on the left.

Contact: KOA Spokane, 3025 North Barker, Otis Orchards, WA 99027; 509/924-4722 or 800/562-3309; website: www.koa.com.

119 West Medical Lake Resort

7

This site is primarily a fish camp for anglers. There are actually two lakes: West Medical is the larger of the two and has better fishing, with boat rentals available; Medical Lake is just one-quarter-mile wide and a half-mile long, and boating is restricted to rowboats, canoes, kayaks, and sailboats The lakes got their names from the wondrous medical powers once attributed to these waters. This family-operated shorefront resort, one of several campgrounds on Medical Lake, is a popular spot for Spokane locals.

Location: On West Medical Lake; see Northeastern Washington, map 6, grid d3.

Campsites, facilities: There are 20 tent sites and 20 sites with full hookups for trailers or RVs. At tent sites, fire pits are provided. Picnic tables, restrooms, drinking water, flush toilets, showers, a café, bait, tackle, and ice are available. Boat and fishing docks, launching facilities, a fish-cleaning station, and boat and barge rentals are nearby. Leashed pets are permitted.

Reservations, fees: Reservations recommended. Call for pricing. Open late April through September.

Directions: In Spokane on I-90, drive west to Exit 264 and Salnave Road. Take that exit and turn north on Salnave Road; drive six miles to Fancher Road. Turn right (west) and drive 200 yards. Bear left on Fancher Road and drive 200 yards to the campground.

Contact: West Medical Lake Resort, 1432 West Fancher Road, Medical Lake, WA 99022; 509/299-3921.

120 Picnic Pines on Silver Lake

 8

This shorefront resort on Silver Lake caters primarily to RVers, although tent campers are welcome. Fishing can be excellent here. Nearby recreation options include marked bike trails, a full-service marina, and tennis courts. See the description of West Medical Lake Resort for further details.

Location: On Silver Lake; see Northeastern Washington, map 6, grid d3.

Campsites, facilities: There are 18 sites, six with full hookups and 12 with electricity, for trailers or RVs up to 35 feet in length, and 13 tent sites. Hookups are available only from mid-March to mid-October. Picnic tables and fire pits are provided. Restrooms, drinking water, flush toilets, showers, a store, a restaurant, a lounge, a bait shop, boat docks, boat rentals, launching facilities, ice, and a swimming beach are available. Bottled gas and a coin-operated laundry are located within two miles. Leashed pets are permitted.

Reservations, fees: Reservations accepted. Sites are $15 to $17 per night. Major credit cards accepted. Open year-round.

Directions: In Spokane on I-90, drive west to Exit 270 and Medical Lake Road. Take that exit and turn west on Medical Lake Road; drive three miles to Silver Lake Road. Turn left and drive one-half mile to the park on the left.

Contact: Picnic Pines on Silver Lake, South 9212 Silver Lake Road, Medical Lake, WA 99022; 509/299-6902.

121 Mallard Bay Resort

 8

This resort is on the shore of Clear Lake, which is two miles long, one-half-mile wide, and used for water-skiing, windsurfing, and sailing. Most of the campsites are lakeshore sites on a 20-acre peninsula. Marked bike trails and tennis courts are nearby.

Location: On Clear Lake; see Northeastern Washington, map 6, grid d3.

Campsites, facilities: There are 50 sites with partial hookups (water and electricity) for tents, trailers, or RVs of any length, plus two cabins. Picnic tables and fire pits are provided. Restrooms, drinking water, flush toilets, showers, bottled gas, a dump station, a store, a tackle shop, ice, swimming facilities with a diving board, a playground, a basketball court, boat docks, launching facilities, a fishing pier, fish-cleaning stations, and boat rentals are available. Leashed pets are permitted.

Reservations, fees: Reservations accepted. Sites are $16 per night, $3 per extra vehicle per night. Cabins are $39 per night. Open mid-April to mid-September.

Directions: In Spokane on I-90, drive west to Exit 264 and Salnave Road. Take that exit and turn north on Salnave Road; drive 1.5 miles to a junction signed by Mallard Bay Resort. Turn right at that sign and drive one-half mile on a dirt road to the resort at the end of the road.

Contact: Mallard Bay Resort, 14601 Salnave Road, Cheney, WA 99004; 509/299-3830.

122 Rainbow Cove RV and Fishing Resort

     7

This resort at Clear Lake features a 300-foot dock with benches that can be used for fishing. If you figured that most people here are anglers, well, that is correct. Fishing can be good for rainbow trout, brown trout, largemouth bass, crappie, bullhead, and catfish. Most of the campsites are at least partially shaded. Summer weekends are often busy.

Location: On Clear Lake; see Northeastern Washington, map 6, grid d3.

Campsites, facilities: There are 16 sites with partial hookups (water and electricity) for trailers or RVs up to 40 feet, four tent sites, and two rustic cabins. Picnic tables and fire pits are provided. Restrooms, drinking water, flush toilets, showers, a café, ice, bait and tackle, boat docks, boat rentals, and launching facilities and moorage are available. Leashed pets are permitted.

Reservations, fees: Reservations accepted. Sites are $15 to $20 per night, $3 per person per night for more than two people. Cabins are $35 per night. Open mid-April through mid-September.

Directions: In Spokane on I-90, drive west to Exit 264 and Salnave Road. Take that exit and turn right (north) on Salnave Road; drive a short distance to Clear Lake Road. Turn right (north) on Clear Lake Road and drive three miles to the resort on the left (well signed).

Contact: Rainbow Cove RV and Fishing Resort, 12514 South Clear Lake Road, Medical Lake, WA 99022; 509/299-3717.

123 Yogi Bear's Camp Resort

    6

This resort is located 10 minutes from downtown Spokane, yet provides a wooded, rural setting. It features towering Ponderosa pines. Highlights include an 18-hole golf course next door and several other courses within 20 minutes of the resort.

Location: West of Spokane; see Northeastern Washington, map 6, grid e4.

Campsites, facilities: There are 168 sites with full hookups, including 63 drive-through sites, for tents, trailers, or RVs up to 70 feet long, five cabins, and six bungalows. Restrooms, drinking water, flush toilets, showers, cable TV, modem-friendly phone service, a dump station, propane, a coin-operated laundry, an RV wash station, and three playgrounds are available. Other facilities include a camp store, an activity center with an indoor pool, a spa, an exercise room, a game room, a snack shack, a dog walk, and various sports facilities (volleyball, basketball, badminton, miniature golf, and daily organized recreational activities). Some facilities are wheelchair-accessible. Leashed pets are permitted.

Reservations, fees: Reservations accepted. Sites are $19 to $33 per night, $3 to $8 for more than two people. Cabins are $80, bungalows are $60 to $100. Major credit cards accepted. Open year-round.

Directions: In Spokane on I-90, drive to Exit 272 and Westbow Road. Take that exit and turn east on Westbow Road and drive to Thomas Mallen Road. Turn right (south) on Thomas Mallen Road and drive one-half mile to the campground on the right.

Contact: Yogi Bear's Camp Resort, 7520 South Thomas Mallen Road, Cheney, WA 99004; 509/747-9415 or 800/494-7275; website: www.jellystonewa.com.

©TOM STIENSTRA

Mount Rainier and the Columbia River Gorge

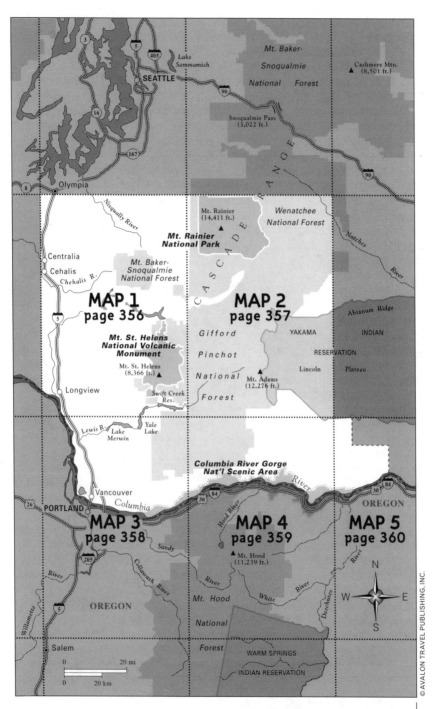

Map 1

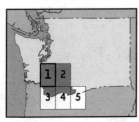

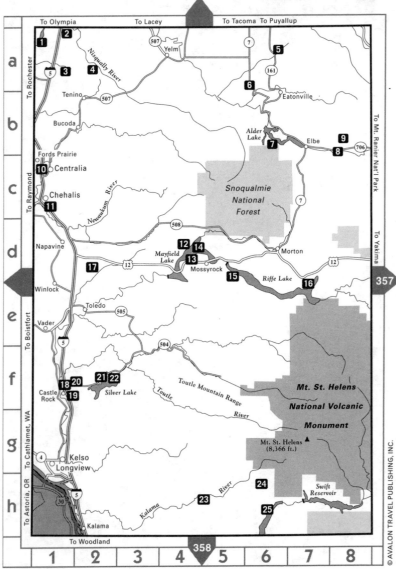

© AVALON TRAVEL PUBLISHING, INC.

Map 2

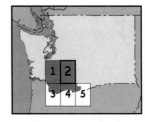

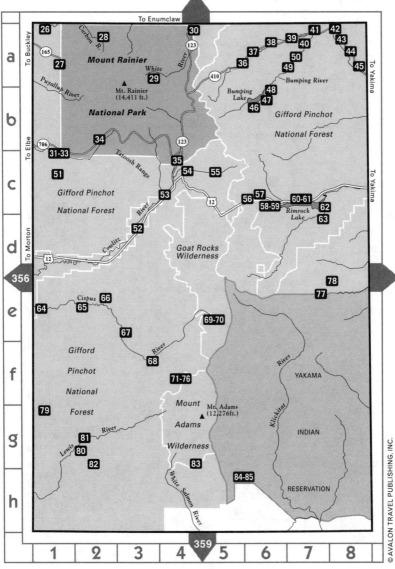

Map 3

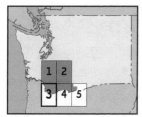

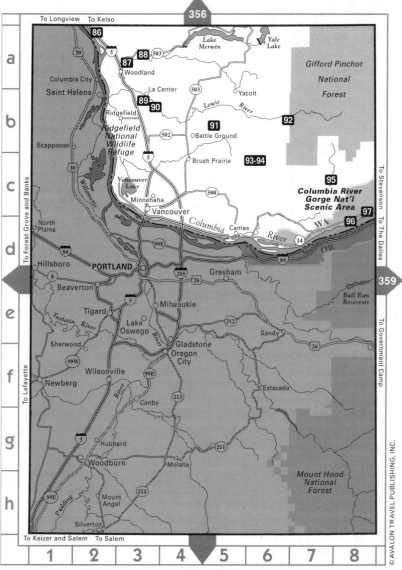

To Longview   To Kelso

a

86
30
88 503
87
Woodland
Columbia City
Saint Helens
La Center 503
89 90
Ridgefield
Lewis River
92

b

Lake
Merwin
Yale
Lake

Gifford Pinchot

National

Forest

Yacolt

Scappoose
Ridgefield
National
Wildlife
Refuge
502 Battle Ground
91
Brush Prairie
93-94

c

Vancouver
Lake
Minnehaha
Vancouver
500
95
Columbia River
Gorge Nat'l
Scenic Area
97
96

To Forest Grove and Banks

Columbia River
Camas
WA
OR
14

North
Plains

To Stevenson   To The Dalles

d

84
Hillsboro
PORTLAND
99E
205
26 Gresham
84

8
Beaverton

359

To Lafayette

e

Tigard
5
Milwaukie
212
Sandy
26
Bull Run
Reservoir

Thalatin River

Lake
Oswego

To Government Camp

Sherwood
99W
Gladstone
Oregon
City

f

Wilsonville
99E
Estacada
Newberg
213
Canby

g

5
Hubbard
211
Woodburn
Molalla
211

Mount Hood
National
Forest

h

99E
Mount
Angel
211
Silverton

Pudding River

To Keizer and Salem   To Salem

1   2   3   4   5   6   7   8

© AVALON TRAVEL PUBLISHING, INC.

Map 4

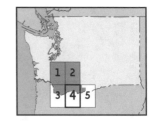

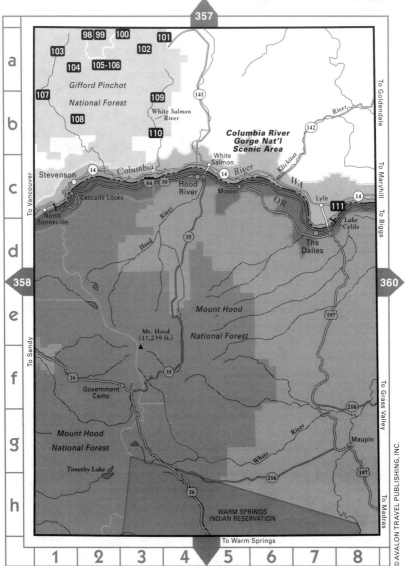

a

98 99 100 101
103 102
104 105-106

Gifford Pinchot
107
National Forest
108 109
White Salmon River
110

b

141
142

Columbia River Gorge Nat'l Scenic Area

To Goldendale

To Vancouver
Stevenson 14 Columbia White Salmon River Klickitat WA
84 30 Hood River Mosier OR

c

To Maryhill

Cascade Locks
North Bonneville

Lyle 14
111

To Biggs

Lake Celilo

d

35

Hood River

The Dalles

Mount Hood
197

e

Mt. Hood (11,239 ft.)

National Forest

To Sandy

f

26 35

Government Camp

216

To Grass Valley

g

Mount Hood National Forest

Timothy Lake

White River

Maupin
216 197

h

26

216

WARM SPRINGS INDIAN RESERVATION

To Madras

To Warm Springs

© AVALON TRAVEL PUBLISHING, INC.

1 2 3 4 5 6 7 8

Map 5

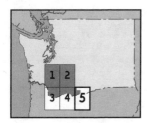

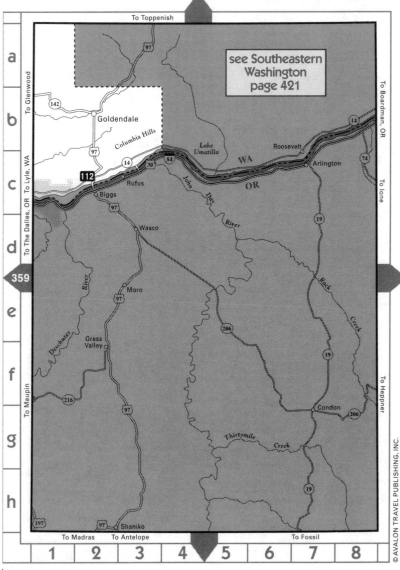

Mount Rainier and the Columbia River Gorge

(CONTINUED ON NEXT PAGE)

As you stand at the rim of the Mount St. Helens volcano, the greatest natural spectacle anywhere on the planet is at your boot tips. The top 1,300 feet of the old mountain has been blown clean off, along with the entire north flank. The half-moon crater walls drop almost 2,100 feet straight down to a lava plug dome, a mile across and still building, with a wisp of smoke emerging from its center. At its edges, the rising plumes of dust from continuous rock falls can be deceptive—you may think a small eruption is in progress. It's like looking inside the living bowels of the earth.

The plug dome gives way to the blast zone, where the mountain has completely blown out its side and pours out across 230 square miles of devastation. From here, it's largely a moonscape but for Spirit Lake on the northeast flank, where thousands of trees are still floating, log-jammed from the eruption 18 years ago. Beyond is 14,411-foot Mount Rainier to the north, 12,276-foot Mount Adams to the northeast, and 11,235-foot Mount Hood to the south, all pristine jewels in contrast to the nearby remains.

We've hiked most of the Pacific Crest Trail and climbed most of the West's highest mountains, but no view compares to this. It provides a sweeping panorama of a land that can be explored for years. The most famous spots in this region are St. Helens, Rainier, and Adam; the latter are two of the three most beautiful mountains in the Cascade Range (Mount Shasta in Northern California is the third). All of them offer outstanding touring and hiking, with excellent camps of all kinds available around their perimeters. St. Helens provides the most eye-popping views and most developed visitor centers, Rainier the most pristine wilderness, and Adams some of the best lakeside camps, with trout fishing sometimes within casting range of your tent.

That's just the beginning. The western Cascades span down river canyons and up mountain subridges, both filled with of streams and lakes. There are camps throughout. At the same time, the I-5 corridor and its network of linked highways also provide many privately developed RV parks fully furnished with everything a vacationer could desire.

1 Columbus Park

7

This spot is pretty enough along the shore of Black Lake to be selected for special events, such as weddings and reunions. The campsites are wooded and a stream (no fishing) runs through the campground. Black Lake is good for fishing. An 18-hole golf course is nearby.

Location: On Black Lake; see Mount Rainier and the Columbia River Gorge, map 1, grid a1.

Campsites, facilities: There are 23 sites with partial hookups for trailers or RVs up to 40 feet. Picnic tables are provided. Restrooms, drinking water, flush toilets, showers, a dump station, a coin-operated laundry, ice, firewood, a playground with volleyball and horseshoe pits, boat docks, and launching facilities are available. A picnic area for special events is nearby. Some facilities are wheelchair-accessible. Bottled gas, ice, and a store are located within one mile; there is a restaurant within three miles. Leashed pets are permitted.

Reservations, fees: Reservations recommended during summer. Sites are $16.20 per night. Open year-round.

Directions: From I-5 in Olympia, take the U.S. 101 exit and drive 1.7 miles northwest to Black Lake Boulevard. Turn south on Black Lake Boulevard and drive 3.5 miles to the park on the left.

Contact: Columbus Park, 5700 Black Lake Boulevard SW, Olympia, WA 98502; 360/786-9460 or 800/848-9460.

2 American Heritage Campground

6

This spacious, wooded campground situated just one-half mile off the highway is close to many activities, including an 18-hole golf course, hiking trails, marked bike trails, and tennis courts. The park features novelty cycle rentals, free wagon rides, and free nightly movies. It's exceptionally clean and pretty, making for a pleasant layover on your way up or down I-5.

Location: Near Olympia; see Mount Rainier and the Columbia River Gorge, map 1, grid a1.

Campsites, facilities: There are 72 sites with full or partial hookups for tents, trailers, or RVs of any length, 23 tent sites, and one cabin. Picnic tables and fire rings are provided. Restrooms, drinking water, flush toilets, showers, bottled gas, a dump station, a recreation hall, a group pavilion, recreation programs, a store, a coin-operated laundry, ice, a playground, a heated swimming pool, and firewood are available. Leashed pets are permitted.

Reservations, fees: Reservations accepted. Sites are $20 to $28 per night for two people, $4 per person per night for more than two people. Cabin is $40 per night. Major credit cards accepted. Open Memorial Day through Labor Day weekend.

Directions: From Olympia, drive five miles south on I-5 to Exit 99. Take that exit and drive one quarter-mile east to Kimmie Street. Turn right (south) on Kimmie Street and drive one quarter-mile to the end of the road to the campground on the left.

Contact: American Heritage Campground, 9610 Kimmie Street SW, Olympia, WA 98512; 360/943-8778.

3 Millersylvania State Park

8

This state park is set on the shore of Deep Lake and features 3,300 feet of waterfront. The park has many trails amid an abundance of old-growth cedar and fir trees, 8.6 miles of hiking trails, and 7.6 miles of bike trails.

Boating at Deep Lake is restricted to hand-launched boats, with a five-mph speed limit. A fishing dock is available at the boat-launch area. A one-mile fitness trail is another highlight. Remnants are still present on park roads of a narrow-gauge railroad and several skid trails used in the 1800s by the logging industry.

Location: On Deep Lake; see Mount Rainier and the Columbia River Gorge, map 1, grid a1.

Campsites, facilities: There are 135 developed tent sites, 52 sites for trailers or RVs up to 45 feet long, and four primitive tent sites. Picnic tables and fire grills are provided. Restrooms, drinking water, flush toilets, coin-operated showers, a dump station, a playground, boat docks and launching facilities, and firewood are available. A picnic area, summer interpretive activities, and horseshoe pits are also nearby. A store, a restaurant, and ice are located within one mile. Some facilities are wheelchair-accessible. Leashed pets are permitted.

Reservations, fees: Reserve at 888/CAMP-OUT (888/226-7688); website: www.parks.wa.gov/reservations ($7 reservation fee). Sites are $6 to $22 per night, $6 per extra vehicle per night. Senior discount available. Major credit cards accepted. Open year-round.

Directions: From Olympia, drive south on I-5 for 10 miles to Exit 95 and Highway 121. Turn east on Maytown Road (Highway 121) and drive 2.7 miles to Tilley Road. Turn left (north) and drive 1.3 miles to the park.

Contact: Millersylvania State Park, 360/753-1519; State Park information, 360/902-8844.

4 Offut Lake Resort

8

This wooded campground is on Offut Lake, just enough off the beaten track to provide a bit of seclusion. Fishing, swimming, and boating are favorite activities here. Anglers will find everything they need, including tackle and boat rentals, at the resort. Boating is restricted to a five-mph speed limit, and no gas motors are permitted on the lake. Several fishing derbies are held here every year.

Location: On Offut Lake; see Mount Rainier and the Columbia River Gorge, map 1, grid a2.

Campsites, facilities: There are 51 sites with full or partial hookups for trailers or RVs up to 40 feet in length, 25 tent sites, and 10 cabins. Picnic tables and fire rings are provided. Restrooms, drinking water, flush toilets, coin-operated showers, a picnic shelter, a dump station, firewood, a store, bait and tackle, propane gas, a laundry room, ice, and a playground with basketball and horseshoe pits are available. Boat rentals, docks are available; no gas motors permitted. Some facilities are wheelchair-accessible. Leashed pets are permitted.

Reservations, fees: Reservations accepted. Sites are $17 to $24 per night, $2 per extra vehicle per night, $1 to $2 pet fee. Cabins are $35 to $75 and tent cabins are $20 to $30. Major credit cards accepted. Open year-round.

Directions: From Olympia, drive south on I-5 for seven miles to Exit 99. Take that exit and turn east on 93rd Avenue; drive four miles to Old Highway 99. Turn south and drive four miles to Offut Lake Road. Turn left (east) and drive 1.5 miles to the resort.

Contact: Offut Lake Resort, 4005 120th Avenue SE, Tenino, WA 98589; 360/264-2438; website: www.offutlakeresort.com.

5 Rainbow Resort

 8

This wooded park along the shore of Tanwax Lake has spacious, shady sites with views of mountains, forest, and lake. Highlights include good fishing, a seasonal fishpond, and a nearby riding stable. Power boating and water-skiing can be popular on hot summer weekends.

Location: On Tanwax Lake; see Mount Rainier and the Columbia River Gorge, map 1, grid a6.

Campsites, facilities: There are about 50 sites with full hookups for tents, trailers, or RVs up to 40 feet long. Picnic tables are provided. Restrooms, drinking water, flush toilets, coin-operated showers, bottled gas, a recreation hall, a store, a coin-operated laundry, a café, ice, cable TV, boat docks, boat rentals, and launching facilities are available. Leashed pets are permitted.

Reservations, fees: Reservations accepted. Sites are $12 to $26 per night, $3 per person per night for more than two people, $3 pet fee. Senior discount available. Major credit cards accepted. Open year-round.

Directions: From Tacoma, drive south on I-5 to Exit 127 and Highway 512. Turn east on Highway 512 and drive to Highway 161. Turn south on Highway 161 and drive to Tanwax Drive. Turn left (east) on Tanwax Drive and drive 200 yards to the resort.

Contact: Rainbow Resort, 34217 Tanwax Court East, Eatonville, WA 98328; 360/879-5115.

6 Henley's Silver Lake Resort

 8

Silver Lake is a 150-acre spring-fed lake that can provide good trout fishing. This full-facility resort is set up as family vacation destination. It's one of the rare private campgrounds that caters both to tent campers and RVers. Silver Lake is beautiful and stocked with trout. Highlights include a 250-foot fishing dock and 50 rental rowboats.

Location: On Silver Lake; see Mount Rainier and the Columbia River Gorge, map 1, grid a6.

Campsites, facilities: There are 36 sites with full or partial hookups, including two drive-through, for trailers or RVs, a very large area for dispersed tent camping, and six cabins. Restrooms, drinking water, flush toilets, a public phone, snacks, boat rentals, a boat ramp, and a dock are available. Leashed pets are permitted except in the cabins.

Reservations, fees: Reservations accepted. Sites are $10 to $15 per night. Cabins are $60 per night. Open the first day of fishing season in April through October, weather permitting.

Directions: From Tacoma, drive south on I-5 for five miles to Exit 127 and Highway 512. Turn east of Highway 512 and drive two miles to Highway 7. Turn south on Highway 7 and drive 19 miles (two miles straight beyond the blinking light) to Silver Lake Road on the right (well marked). Turn right and drive one quarter-mile to the resort entrance on the left.

Contact: Henley's Silver Lake Resort, 40718 South Silver Lake Road East, Eatonville, WA 98328; 360/832-3580.

7 Alder Lake Recreation Area

 6

This recreation area at Alder Lake features three camping areas: Rocky Point, Alder Lake Park, and Boathouse. Alder Lake is a 3,065-acre lake, 7.5 miles long, often with good fishing for kokanee salmon, rainbow trout, and cutthroat trout. Rocky Point features a sunny beach and is set near the the mouth of feeder streams, often the best fishing spots on the lake. At the west end of the lake, anglers can catch catfish, perch, and crappie. The campsites are set near the water with lots of trees and shrubbery. On clear, warm summer weekends, these camps can get crowded. The camps are always booked full for summer holiday weekends in January, as soon as reservations are available. Another potential downer is that the water level fluctuates here. Power boating, water-skiing and personal watercraft are allowed at this lake. Mount Rainier Scenic Railroad leaves from Elbe regularly and makes its way through the forests to Mineral Lake. It features open deck cars, live music, and restored passenger cars.

Location: On Alder Lake; see Mount Rainier and the Columbia River Gorge, map 1, grid b6.

Campsites, facilities: There are three camping areas with approximately 125 sites with full or partial hookups for trailers or RVs of any length, 100 tent sites, and one group site with full hookups for up to 20 RVs. Alder Lake Camp is the largest and most developed; Rocky Point is a nearby overflow camp for RVs, with no tent sites available; and Boathouse Camp is smaller (24 sites), primarily for tents with some electricity hookups for self-contained trailers and RVs. Picnic tables and fire grills are provided. Drinking water and vault toilets are available. Boat docks and launching facilities are available nearby. A swimming beach, a day-use picnic area, a fishing dock, a small convenience store, and a dump station are available nearby. Some facilities are wheelchair-accessible. Leashed pets are available.

Reservations, fees: Reservations recommended. Sites are $19 to $20 per night, $6 per extra vehicle per night. Senior discount available. Group camp is $20 per night per site. Major credit cards accepted. Open

year-round, excluding December 20 through January 2.

Directions: From Chehalis, drive south on I-5 for 10 miles to U.S. 12. Turn east and drive 31 miles to Morton and Highway 7. Turn north on Highway 7 and drive 17 miles to Elbe. Bear left on Highway 7 and drive to the park entrance road on the left (on the east shore of Alder Lake). Turn left and drive 0.2 mile to the park entrance gate.

Contact: Alder Lake Park, Tacoma Power at 50324 School Road, Eatonville, WA 98328; 360/569-2778; website: www.tacomapower.com.

🖪 Sahara Creek Horse Camp

   6

While this camp is called a "horse camp," it is actually a multiple-use camp, open to others without horses. It is a pretty camp set near the foot of Mount Rainier with multiple trailheads and a camp host on site. It is popular among equestrians.

Location: Near Elbe; see Mount Rainier and the Columbia River Gorge, map 1, grid c8.

Campsites, facilities: There are 18 tent sites. Picnic tables and fire pits are provided. A covered pavilion, vault toilets, high lines, and hitching posts are available, but there is no drinking water. Garbage must be packed out. Leashed pets are permitted.

Reservations, fees: No reservations; no fee. Open year-round.

Directions: From Chehalis, drive south on I-5 for 10 miles to U.S. 12. Turn east and drive 31 miles to Morton and Highway 7. Turn north on Highway 7 and drive 17 miles to Elbe and Highway 706. Turn east (right) and drive five miles to the campground on the left.

Contact: Department of Natural Resources, South Puget Sound Region, 950 Farman Avenue North, Enumclaw, WA 98022; 360/825-1631, fax 360/825-1672.

9 Elbe Hills

 6

This is not an official, designated campground, but rather a trailhead with room for three campsites for four-wheelers. The Department of Natural Resources manages this wooded campground and provides eight miles of trails for short-wheelbase four-wheel-drive vehicles. This features a technical obstacle course. In some areas, you must have a winch to make it through the course. This area is always gated. You must obtain the key from the camp host at Sahara Creek Campground, located one mile away.

Location: Near Elbe; see Mount Rainier and the Columbia River Gorge, map 1, grid b8.

Campsites, facilities: There are three primitive sites for tents or small trailers. Picnic tables and fire grills are provided. Vault toilets and a group shelter are available. No drinking water is available. Garbage must be packed out. Leashed pets are permitted.

Reservations, fees: No reservations; no fee. Open year-round, weather permitting.

Directions: From Chehalis, drive south on I-5 for 10 miles to U.S. 12. Turn east and drive 31 miles to Morton and Highway 7. Turn north on Highway 7 and drive 17 miles to Elbe and Highway 706. Turn east (right) and drive six miles to Stoner Road (a Department of Natural Resources access road). Turn left and drive 2.5 miles to The 9 Road. Bear right on The 9 Road and drive one mile; look for a spur road on the left. Turn left and drive about 100 yards to the four-wheel-drive trailhead.

Contact: Department of Natural Resources, South Puget Sound Region, 950 Farman Avenue North, Enumclaw, WA 98022-0068; 360/825-1631, fax 360/825-1672.

10 Peppertree West Motor Inn & RV Park

 5

If you're driving I-5 and looking for a stopover, this spot is a good choice for tent campers or RVers. Surrounded by Chehalis Valley farmland, it's near an 18-hole golf course, hiking trails, and tennis courts.

Location: In Centralia; see Mount Rainier and the Columbia River Gorge, map 1, grid c1.

Campsites, facilities: There are 42 sites with full or partial hookups, including most drive-through, for trailers or RVs of any length, and 20 tent sites. Restrooms, drinking water, flush toilets, coin-operated showers, cable TV, a dump station, a recreation hall, a coin-operated laundry, and ice are available. Boat-launching facilities are nearby. A store, propane, and a café are also nearby. Leashed pets are permitted.

Reservations, fees: Reservations accepted. Sites are $10 to $20 per night. Senior discount available. Major credit cards accepted. Open year-round.

Directions: From Centralia on I-5, take Exit 81 to Melon Street. Turn west and then take the first left to the park (located in the southeast corner of Centralia).

Contact: Peppertree West Motor Inn & RV Park, 1208 Alder Street, Centralia, WA 98531; 360/736-1124, fax 360/807-9779.

11 Stan Hedwall Park

 5

This park is set along the Newaukum River, and its proximity to I-5 makes it a good layover spot for vacation travelers. Recreational opportunities include fishing, hiking, and golf (an 18-hole course and hiking trails are nearby).

Location: On the Newaukum River; see Mount Rainier and the Columbia River Gorge, map 1, grid c1.

Campsites, facilities: There are 29 sites with partial hookups (water and electricity) for trailers or RVs of any length. Picnic tables are provided. Restrooms, drinking water, flush toilets, coin-operated showers, a dump station, cable TV, and a playground are available. Bottled gas, a store, a café, and a coin-operated laundry are located within one mile. Leashed pets are permitted.

Reservations, fees: Reservations accepted two weeks or more in advance. Sites are $15 per night. Open March through November, weather permitting.

Directions: Near Chehalis on I-5, take Exit 76 to Rice Road. Turn south and drive one-eighth mile to the park.

Contact: Stan Hedwall Park, City of Chehalis, P.O. Box 871, Chehalis, WA 98532; 360/748-0271, fax 360/748-6993.

🄬 Ike Kinswa State Park

 8

This state park is set alongside the north shore of Mayfield Lake. The park features 8.5 miles of shore, forested campsites, 2.5 miles of hiking trails, and two miles of bike trails. Mayfield Lake is a treasure trove of recreational possibilities. Fishing is a year-round affair here, with trout and tiger muskie often good. Boating, water-skiing, swimming, and driftwood collecting are all popular. The park is named after a prominent Cowlitz Indian, Ike Kinswa. Two fish hatcheries are located nearby. A spectacular view of Mount St. Helens can be found at a vista point 11 miles east. This popular campground often fills on summer weekends. Be sure to reserve well in advance.

Location: At Mayfield Lake; see Mount Rainier and the Columbia River Gorge, map 1, grid d4.

Campsites, facilities: There are 60 developed tent sites, 41 sites for trailers or RVs up to 60 feet long, and two primitive tent sites. Picnic tables and fire grills are provided. Restrooms, drinking water, flush toilets, showers, a dump station, a store, a café, a playground, a picnic area, horseshoe pits, and firewood are available. Some facilities are wheelchair-accessible. Boat docks and launching facilities are nearby. Leashed pets are permitted.

Reservations, fees: Reserve at 888/CAMP-OUT (888/226-7688); website: www.parks.wa.gov/reservations ($7 reservation fee). Sites are $6 to $21 per night, $6 per extra vehicle per night. Senior discount available. Major credit cards accepted. Open year-round.

Directions: From Longview, drive north on I-5 to Exit 68 and U.S. 12. Turn east on U.S. 12 and drive 14 miles to Silver Creek Road (State Route 122). Turn north and drive 1.9 miles to a Y intersection. Bear right on State Route 111/Harmony Road and drive 1.6 miles to the park entrance.

Contact: Ike Kinswa State Park, 873 Harmony Road, Silver Lake, WA 98585; 360/983-3402; State Park information, 360/902-8844.

🄭 Mayfield Lake Park

 7

Mayfield Lake is the centerpiece of this 50-acre park. Insider's tip: Campsites 42 to 54 here are set along the lake's shoreline. The camp has a relaxing atmosphere and comfortable, wooded sites. Fishing is primarily for trout, bass, and silver salmon. Other recreational activities include water-skiing, swimming, and boating. A great side trip is touring nearby Mount St. Helens. Note that this camp was managed for years as a county park. Tacoma Power first established new management in spring 2002.

Location: On Mayfield Lake; see Mount Rainier and the Columbia River Gorge, map 1, grid d4.

Campsites, facilities: There are 54 sites for tents, trailers, or self-contained RVs. Picnic tables and fire grills are provided. Restrooms, drinking water, flush toilets, coin-operated showers, a public phone, and a barbecue are available. A dump station is located within one-half mile. Some facilities are wheelchair-accessible. Leashed pets are permitted.

Reservations, fees: Reservations recommended. Sites are $12 to $16 per night, $5 per extra vehicle per night. Open mid-April to mid-October.

Directions: From Longview, drive north on I-5 to Exit 68 and U.S. 12. Turn east on U.S. 12 and drive 11 miles. Look for the campground entrance signs on the left.

Contact: Mayfield Lake Park, 360/985-2364; website: www.tacomapower.com.

14 Harmony Lakeside RV Park

     6

This park fills up on weekends in July and August. It is set on Mayfield Lake, a ten-mile-long lake with numerous recreational activities, including fishing, boating, and water-skiing. There are lake views from some sites. Ike Kinswa State Park is a nearby option.

Location: Near Mayfield Lake; see Mount Rainier and the Columbia River Gorge, map 1, grid d4.

Campsites, facilities: There are 80 sites with full or partial hookups for tents, trailers, or RVs of any length. Picnic tables and fire grills are provided. Restrooms, drinking water, flush toilets, coin-operated showers, a dump station, ice, firewood, a pay phone, boat docks, and launching facilities are available. Group facilities, including a banquet and

meeting room, are also available. Leashed pets are permitted.

Reservations, fees: Reservations recommended. Sites are $22 to $27 per night, $2 pet fee. Monthly rates available. Major credit cards accepted. Open year-round.

Directions: From Longview, drive north on I-5 to Exit 68 and U.S. 12. Turn east on U.S. 12 and drive 21 miles to Mossyrock (Highway 122). Turn left (north) and drive 2.3 miles to the park on the left.

Contact: Harmony Lakeside RV Park, 563 State Route 122, Silver Creek, WA 98585; 360/983-3804, fax 360/983-8345; website: www.mayfieldlake.com.

15 Mossyrock Park

 8

This park is set along the southwest shore of Riffle Lake. It is an extremely popular campground for several reasons. For anglers, it provides the best of both worlds—a both launch on Riffle Lake with coho salmon, rainbow trout, and bass, and nearby Swofford Pond, a 240-acre pond stocked with rainbow trout, brown trout, bass, catfish, and bluegill. Swofford Pond is located south of Mossyrock on Swofford Road; no gas motors are permitted. This campground provides access to a half-mile loop nature trail. On the north side of the lake, the 14,000-acre Cowlitz Wildlife Area is a nesting area for bald eagles and osprey.

Location: At Riffle Lake; see Mount Rainier and the Columbia River Gorge, map 1, grid d5.

Campsites, facilities: There are 141 sites, including 77 with full hookups, for tents, trailers, and RVs, 12 walk-in sites, one group camp with 60 sites, and a primitive group camp with 10 sites. Picnic tables and fire rings are provided. Restrooms, drinking water, flush toilets, showers, a dump station, a fishing bridge, fish-cleaning stations, a boat launch, a playground, a swimming area, a horseshoe pit, a volleyball net, and intrepretive displays are available. In summer, a camp host is available. Some facilities are wheelchair-accessible. Leashed pets are permitted.

Reservations, fees: Reservations recommended at 360/983-3900. Sites are $10 to $19 per night, $6 per extra vehicle per night. Senior discount available. Call for group site prices. Major credit cards accepted in summer. Open year-round, excluding December 20 through January 20.

Directions: On I-5, drive to Exit 68 and Highway 12 East. Take Highway 12 East and drive 21 miles to Williams Street (flashing yellow light). Turn right and drive several blocks in the town of Mossyrock to a T intersection with State Street. Turn left and drive 3.5 miles (becomes Mossyrock Road East, then Ajlure Road) to the park. Ajlure Roads lead right into the park.

Contact: Taidnapam Park, Tacoma Power, 50324 School Road, Eatonville, WA 98328; 360/497-7707; website: www.tacomapower.com.

16 Taidnapam Park

  8

This park is located at the east end of Riffle Lake. It is a 50-acre park that is nestled in the cover of Douglas fir and maple, surrounded by thousands of acres of undeveloped greenbelt. Fishing is open year-round at the lake, with coho salmon, rainbow trout, and bass available. This camp was named after the Upper Cowlitz Indians, also knowns as "Taidnapam." This camp often fills in summer; the walk-in sites are an outstanding option.

Location: At Riffle Lake; see Mount Rainier and the Columbia River Gorge, map 1, grid e7.

Campsites, facilities: There are 52 sites with full or partial hookups for tents, trailers, and RVs, 16 walk-in sites, and one group camp with 22 sites and a kitchen shelter. Picnic tables and fire rings are provided. Restrooms, drinking water, flush toilets, showers, a dump station, a fishing bridge, fish-cleaning stations, a boat launch, a playground, a swimming area, a horseshoe pit, a volleyball net, and intrepretive displays are available. Some facilities are wheelchair-accessible. Leashed pets are permitted.

Reservations, fees: Reservations recommended at 360/497-7707. Sites are $10 to $19 per night, $6 per extra vehicle per night. Senior discount available. Call for group site prices. Major credit cards accepted in summer season. Open year-round, excluding December 20 through January 20.

Directions: On I-5, drive to Exit 68 and Highway 12 East. Take Highway 12 East and drive 37 miles (five miles past Morton) to Kosmos Road. Turn right and drive 200 yards to No. 100 Chapion Haul Road (a gravel road). Turn left and drive four miles to the park.

Contact: Taidnapam Park, Tacoma Power, 50324 School Road, Eatonville, WA 98328; 360/497-7707; website: www.tacomapower.com.

17 Lewis and Clark State Park

  8

The highlight of this state park is an immense old-growth forest that contains some good hiking trails and a half-mile nature trail. This is a famous grove where half of the old-growth trees along the highway were blown down in the legendary 1962 Columbus Day storm. This was a cataclysmic result for what is one of the last major stands of old-growth forest in the state. The park covers

621 acres and features primarily Douglas fir and red cedar, wetlands, and dense vegetation. There are eight miles of hiking trails and five miles of horse trails. June is Youth Fishing Month, when youngsters age 14 and younger can fish the creek. Jackhouse tours are available year-round by appointment, where visitors can see a pioneer home built in 1845 north of the Columbia River.

Location: Near Chehalis; see Mount Rainier and the Columbia River Gorge, map 1, grid d2.

Campsites, facilities: There are 25 sites for tents, trailers, or self-contained RVs and two group camps for up to 50 people each. Picnic tables and fire grills are provided. Restrooms, drinking water, flush toilets, coin-operated showers, firewood, a picnic area, an amphitheater, horseshoe pits, volleyball, and badminton are available. Leashed pets are permitted.

Reservations, fees: No reservations. Sites are $15 per night, $6 per extra vehicle per night. Senior discount available. Group sites require $25 reservation, plus $2 per person with a 20-person minimum. Open April through September.

Directions: From Chehalis, drive south on I-5 to Exit 68 and U.S. 12. Drive east on U.S. 12 for three miles to Jackson Highway. Turn right and drive three miles to the park entrance on the right.

Contact: Lewis and Clark State Park, 4583 Jackson Highway, Winlock, WA 98596; 360/864-2643; State Park information, 360/902-8844.

⓲ River Oaks RV Park & Campground

 8

This camp is set right on the Cowlitz River, with opportunities for swimming, boating, and fishing. In most years in the spring, the river is the site of a big smelt run, and they come thick. Using a dip net, you can sometimes fill a five-gallon bucket with just a couple of dips.

Location: On the Cowlitz River; see Mount Rainier and the Columbia River Gorge, map 1, grid f1.

Campsites, facilities: There are 50 tent sites and 24 sites with full hookups, including 12 long-term rentals and 12 drive-through, for trailers or RVs. Restrooms, drinking water, flush toilets, showers, picnic tables, fire rings, firewood, a dump station, a laundry room, and ice are available. Bottled gas, a store, bait and tackle, and a café are located within one mile. Boat-launching facilities, mooring buoys, and a fishing shelter are nearby. Leashed pets are permitted.

Reservations, fees: Reservations accepted. Sites are $15 to $22 per night. Senior discount available. Open year-round.

Directions: From Castle Rock on I-5, take Exit 59 for Highway 506. Turn west on Highway 506 and drive 0.3 mile to the park on the left.

Contact: River Oaks RV Park & Campground, 491 Highway 506, Toledo, WA 98591; 360/864-2895.

⓳ Paradise Cove Resort & RV Park

 7

This wooded park is about 400 yards from the Toutle River and one-half mile from the Cowlitz River. Take your pick. Seaquest State Park and Silver Lake to the east provide two excellent, activity-filled side-trip options.

Location: Near the Toutle River; see Mount Rainier and the Columbia River Gorge, map 1, grid f1.

Campsites, facilities: There are 52 sites with full hookups, including many drive-through, for trailers or RVs of any length, and a large dispersed tent camping area. Picnic tables are provided. Restrooms, drinking water, flush toilets, showers, propane, a coin-operated laundry, a store with video rentals, and ice are available. Boat-launching facilities are nearby. Leashed pets are permitted.

Reservations, fees: Reservations accepted. Sites are $14 to $20 per night. Senior discount available. Major credit cards accepted. Open year-round.

Directions: From Longview, drive 10 miles north on I-5 to Castle Rock and Exit 52. Take Exit 52 and look for the park on Frontage Road, just off the freeway (within view of the freeway).

Contact: Paradise Cove Resort & RV Park, 112 Burma Road, Castle Rock, WA 98611; 360/274-6785.

20 Mount St. Helens RV Park

 6

This RV park is located just outside Castle Rock, only three miles from the Mount St. Helens Visitor Center. It is close to the highway. Fishing and boating are available nearby on Silver Lake.

Location: Near Silver Lake; see Mount Rainier and the Columbia River Gorge, map 1, grid f2.

Campsites, facilities: There are 90 sites with full or partial hookups for tents, trailers, or RVs. Restrooms, drinking water, flush toilets, coin-operated showers, cable TV, propane, a coin-operated laundry, a dump station, a public phone, and ice are available. Horseshoes, a recreation hall, and a playground are also provided. Some facilities are wheelchair-accessible. Leashed pets are permitted.

Reservations, fees: Reservations recommended in the summer; phone 360/274-8522.

Sites are $17 to $22 per night, $1 per person per night for more than two people. Major credit cards accepted. Open year-round.

Directions: From Longview, drive 10 miles north on I-5 to Castle Rock and Exit 49 and Highway 504. Take Exit 49 and drive east on Highway 504 for two miles to Schaffran Road. Turn left (well signed) and drive to the park at the top of the hill.

Contact: Mount St. Helens RV Park, 167 Schaffran Road, Castle Rock, WA 98611; 360/274-8522.

21 Seaquest State Park

 6

This camp is filled nightly because it is set along the paved road to the awesome Johnston Ridge Observatory, the premier lookout of Mount St. Helens. This state park is located adjacent to Silver Lake, one of western Washington's premier fishing lakes for bass and trout. Yet an equal highlight is the Mount St. Helens Visitor Center, which opened in 2000 and is located across the road from the park entrance. This 425-acre park features more than one mile of lake shoreline and a forested park with eight miles of trails for hiking and biking. The irony of the place is that some out-of-towners on vacation think that this park is located on the ocean because of its name, Seaquest. The park has nothing to do with the ocean, of course. It is named after Alfred L. Seaquest, who donated the property to the state for parkland; another anomaly is that he stipulated in his will that if liquor were ever sold on the property that the land would be transferred to Willamette University as its owner. The park is popular for day use as well as camping.

Location: Near Silver Lake; see Mount Rainier and the Columbia River Gorge, map 1, grid f2.

Campsites, facilities: There are 92 sites, including 16 with full hookups, for tents, self-contained trailers, and RVs, and four primitive tent sites. Picnic tables and fire grills are provided. Restrooms, drinking water, flush toilets, showers, a picnic area, a playground, six horseshoe pits, a ball field, a dump station, and firewood are available. A store is within one mile. Some facilities are wheelchair-accessible. Leashed pets are permitted.

Reservations, fees: Reserve at 888/CAMP-OUT (888/226-7688); website: www.parks.wa .gov/reservations ($7 reservation fee). Sites are $6 to $22 per night, $6 per extra vehicle per night. Senior discount available. Major credit cards accepted. Open year-round.

Directions: From Longview, drive 10 miles north on I-5 to Castle Rock and Exit 49 and Highway 504. Take Exit 49 and drive east on Highway 504 for six miles to the park.

Contact: Seaquest State Park, 360/274-8633; State Park information, 360/902-8844.

22 Silver Lake Motel and Resort

  8

This park is set along the shore of Silver Lake, featuring a view of Mount St. Helens. This is one of Washington's better lakes for largemouth bass and trout, as well as perch, crappie, and bluegill. Power boating and water-skiing are also popular. It's an alternative to the more crowded campground at Seaquest State Park.

Location: On Silver Lake; see Mount Rainier and the Columbia River Gorge, map 1, grid f2.

Campsites, facilities: There are 22 sites with partial hookups (water and electricity) for trailers or RVs of any length, 13 tent sites, five cabins, and six motel rooms. Picnic tables and fire grills are provided. Restrooms, drinking water, flush toilets, coin-operated showers, a store, showers, ice, boat docks, boat rentals, launching facilities, and a playground are available. A dump station is within one mile, and a café is within four miles. Leashed pets are permitted.

Reservations, fees: Reservations accepted. Sites are $15 to $22 per night, $5 per extra vehicle per night. Major credit cards accepted. Open year-round.

Directions: From Longview, drive 10 miles north on I-5 to Castle Rock and Exit 49 and Highway 504. Take Exit 49 and drive east on Highway 504 for 6.5 miles to the park on the right.

Contact: Silver Lake Motel and Resort, 3201 Spirit Lake Highway, Silver Lake, WA 98645; 360/274-6141, fax 360/274-2183; website: www.silverlake-resort.com.

23 Kalama Horse Camp

   8

This is the most popular horse camp in the area, with the enthusiastic volunteer support of local equestrians. The camp fills on weekends. One reason is a network of 53 miles of trails for equestrians that is accessible from camp. The camp is very near Mount St. Helens.

Location: Near Mount St. Helens; see Mount Rainier and the Columbia River Gorge, map 1, grid h5.

Campsites, facilities: There are 27 sites for tents, trailers, or RVs and three group sites. Picnic tables and fire grills are provided. Vault toilets are available. No drinking water is provided. Garbage must be packed out. Horse facilities include 10-by-10-foot corrals, a staging and mounting assist area, stock water, a stock loading ramp, and hitching rails. A 24-by-36-foot log cabin shelter with a picnic table and a picnic area with horseshoe pits are also available. Boat-launching facilities are located on Lake Merrill. Leashed pets are permitted.

Reservations, fees: Northwest Forest Pass ($30 annual fee) or $5 daily fee per parked vehicle is required. Open April to mid-December, weather permitting.

Directions: From Woodland on I-5, take Exit 21 for Highway 503. Drive east on Highway 503 and go 23 miles to the Highway 503 spur. Continue northeast on Highway 503 spur to Forest Road 81 (at Yale Lake, one mile south of Cougar). Turn left on Forest Road 81 and drive about eight miles to the camp on the right.

Contact: Gifford Pinchot National Forest, Mount St. Helens National Volcanic Monument, 42218 NE Yale Bridge Road, Amboy, WA 98601-0369; 360/247-3900, fax 360/247-3901.

24 Lake Merrill

 7

This site is for campers seeking a quiet setting. The campground is nestled in old-growth Douglas fir on the shore of Lake Merrill, very near Mount St. Helens. It's free and provides an alternative to the more developed parks in the area, especially along the main access roads to viewing areas of the volcano. The lake provides fishing for brown trout and cutthroat trout, but is restricted to fly-fishing only, with only nonmotorized boats permitted. This makes it ideal for fly-fishers with prams or float tubes.

Location: Near Mount St. Helens; see Mount Rainier and the Columbia River Gorge, map 1, grid h6.

Campsites, facilities: There are seven tent sites. Picnic tables, fire grills, and tent pads are provided. Vault toilets and hand-pumped drinking water are available. Some facilities are wheelchair-accessible. Boat-launching facilities are located on Lake Merrill. Leashed pets are permitted.

Reservations, fees: No reservations; no fee. Open May through November, weather permitting.

Directions: From Woodland on I-5, take Exit 21 for Highway 503. Drive east on Highway 503 for 23 miles to Highway 503 Spur. Drive northeast on Highway 503 Spur to Forest Road 81. Turn left on Forest Road 81 and drive 4.5 miles. Turn left on the access road and continue to the campground.

Contact: Department of Natural Resources, Southwest Region, P.O. Box 280, Castle Rock, WA 98611-0280; 360/577-2025 or 360/274-4196.

25 Lone Fir Resort

 4

This private campground is located near Yale Lake (the smallest of four lakes in the area) and is designed primarily for RV use, with grassy sites and plenty of shade trees. Mount St. Helens is a side-trip option. The trailhead for the summit climb is nearby at Climber's Bivouac on the south flank of the volcano; a primitive campground with dispersed sites for hikers only is available here. Note: It is the only trailhead available for the summit climb.

Location: Near Yale Lake; see Mount Rainier and the Columbia River Gorge, map 1, grid h6.

Campsites, facilities: There are 17 sites with full hookups, including three drive-through, for trailers or RVs of any length, and eight tent sites. Picnic tables are provided.

Fire pits are provided at tent sites. Restrooms, drinking water, flush toilets, showers, a laundry room, coin-operated showers, ice, a snack bar, and a swimming pool in summer are available. Bottled gas, a store, and a restaurant are within one mile. Boat docks and launching facilities are nearby. Pets and motorbikes are permitted.

Reservations, fees: Reservations accepted. Sites are $14 to $18 per night, $2 per person per night for more than two people. Senior discount available if paying cash. Major credit cards accepted. Open year-round.

Directions: In Woodland on I-5, take Exit 21 for Highway 503. Drive east on Highway 503 for 29 miles to Cougar and the resort turnoff (marked, in town, with the park visible from the road) on the left.

Contact: Lone Fir Resort, 16806 Lewis River Road, Cougar, WA 98616; 360/238-5210.

Evans Creek

 7

This primitive campground is located close to Evans Creek in an off-road-vehicle area near the northwestern corner of Mount Rainier National Park. If you're looking for a quiet, secluded spot, this isn't it. The two nearby roads that lead into the park are secondary or gravel roads and provide access to several other primitive campgrounds and backcountry trails in the park. A national forest map details the backroads and hiking trails.

Location: On Evans Creek in Mount Baker-Snoqualmie National Forest; see Mount Rainier and the Columbia River Gorge, map 2, grid a1.

Campsites, facilities: There are 27 tent sites. Picnic tables and fire grills are provided. Drinking water and vault toilets are available. Downed wood can be gathered for campfires. Garbage must be packed out. Leashed pets are permitted.

Reservations, fees: Northwest Forest Pass ($30 annual fee) or $5 daily fee per parked vehicle is required. Open mid-June to late September.

Directions: From Tacoma on I-5, turn east on Highway 167 and drive nine miles to Highway 410. Continue 11 miles east on Highway 410 to the town of Buckley and Highway 165. Turn south on Highway 165 and drive 11 miles to Forest Road 7920. Turn left and drive 1.5 miles to the campground on the right.

Contact: Mount Baker-Snoqualmie National Forest, White River Ranger District, 450 Roosevelt Avenue East, Enumclaw, WA 98022; 360/825-6585, fax 360/825-0660.

Mowich Lake Walk-In

   8

This is a walk-in camp with campsites set adjacent to and above Mowich Lake, with a lakeview from some of the sites. A 200-yard walk is required to reach the campsites. Some backpackers use the camp as a launch point for trips into the Mount Rainier Wilderness. The Wonderland Trail can be accessed at this campground. Fishing is poor for trout at this lake because it is not stocked and there is no habitat for natural spawning.

Location: Near the Carbon River in Mount Rainier National Park; see Mount Rainier and the Columbia River Gorge, map 2, grid a1.

Campsites, facilities: There are 30 walk-in tent sites. Picnic tables are available at some sites. Pit toilets are available. No drinking water is provided. No campfires are permitted; use a backpacking stove. Leashed pets are permitted in camp, but not on trails.

Reservations, fees: No reservations; no fee, except a $10 park entrance fee. Open June through October, weather permitting.

Directions: From Puyallup, drive east on Highway 167 to Highway 410. Turn east on Highway 410 and drive 11 miles to the town of Buckley and Highway 165. Turn south on Highway 165 and drive to a fork with Carbon River Park Road. Bear right and stay on Highway 165 for eight miles to the campground at the end of the road. High-clearance vehicles only are recommended for this access road.

Contact: Mount Rainier National Park, Tahoma Woods, Star Route, Ashford, WA 98304; 360/569-2211, fax 360/569-2187.

28 Ipsut Creek

 8

This camp is set at the end of Carbon River Road, primarily a trailhead camp for hikers heading into the backcountry of Mount Rainier National Park, past lakes, glaciers, waterfalls, and many other wonders. For dayhikers, the Carbon Glacier Trail is accessible from the campground, a seven-mile round-trip. The trail follows the Carbon River through the forest to the snout of the glacier; watch for falling rocks. In addition, the Carbon River Rain Forest Nature Trail begins at the Carbon River entrance to the park. This 0.3-mile loop trail explores the only inland rainforest at Mount Rainier National Park. Note that fishing is prohibited on Isput Creek above the campground at the water supply intake. The elevation is 2,300 feet.

Location: Near the Carbon River in Mount Rainier National Park; see Mount Rainier and the Columbia River Gorge, map 2, grid a2.

Campsites, facilities: There are 31 sites for tents and two group camps for up to 40 people. Picnic tables and fire rings are provided. Vault toilets are available. No drinking water is available. Leashed pets are permitted in camp, but not on trails.

Reservations, fees: No reservations. Sites are $9 per night, $5 per extra vehicle per night, plus $10 park entrance fee. Group sites

are $40 per night. Senior discount available. Open year-round, weather permitting.

Directions: From Puyallup, drive east on Highway 167 to Highway 410. Turn east on Highway 410 and drive 11 miles to the town of Buckley and Highway 165. Turn south on Highway 165 and drive to a fork with Carbon River Park Road. Bear left and drive five miles to the campground on the left. Note: The access road is subject to flooding and closure after heavy rains.

Contact: Mount Rainier National Park, Tahoma Woods, Star Route, Ashford, WA 98304; 360/569-2211, fax 360/569-2187.

29 White River

 7

This campground is set on the White River at 4,400 feet. The Glacier Basin Trail, a seven-mile round-trip, starts at the campground and leads along the Emmons Moraine to a view of the Emmons Glacier, the largest glacier in the continental United States. It is sometimes possible to spot mountain goats on the surrounding mountain slopes, as well as mountain climbers. Note that another trail near camp leads a short distance (but vertically, it's a rise of 2,200 feet) to the Sunrise Visitor Center. Local rangers recommend that trailers be left at the White River Campground and the 11-mile road trip to Sunrise be made by car. From there, you can take several trails that lead to backcountry lakes and glaciers. This camp is often used by climbers planning to summit Mount Rainier. Also note that this campground is located in what is considered to be a geo-hazard zone, where there is risk of a mud flow. It's never happened, but minor incidents have occurred upslope from the camp.

Location: On the White River in Mount Rainier National Park; see Mount

Rainier and the Columbia River Gorge, map 2, grid a3.

Campsites, facilities: There are 112 sites for tents or RVs up to 20 feet long. Picnic tables and fire grills are provided. Flush toilets and drinking water are available. A small amphitheater is nearby. Some facilities are wheelchair-accessible. Leashed pets are permitted in camp, but not on trails or in the wilderness.

Reservations, fees: No reservations accepted. Sites are $10 per night. Major credit cards accepted. Open mid-June to mid-September.

Directions: From Enumclaw, drive southeast on Highway 410 to the entrance of Mount Rainier National Park and White River Road. Turn right and drive seven miles to the campground on the left.

Contact: Mount Rainier National Park, Tahoma Woods, Star Route, Ashford, WA 98304; 360/569-2211, fax 360/569-2187.

30 Silver Springs

 9

This campground along the White River on the northeastern border of Mount Rainier National Park is a good alternative to the more crowded camps in the park. It's located in a beautiful section of old-growth forest and is very scenic, primarily with Douglas fir, cedar, and hemlock. Hiking is the choice of recreational options. A U.S. Forest Service information center is located one mile away from the campground entrance on Highway 410.

Location: In Mount Baker-Snoqualmie National Forest; see Mount Rainier and the Columbia River Gorge, map 2, grid a4.

Campsites, facilities: There are 55 sites for tents, trailers, or RVs up to 21 feet long and one group site for up to 50 people. Picnic tables and fire grills are provided. Flush toilets, drinking water, and downed firewood

for gathering are available. The group site has a picnic shelter. Some facilities are wheelchair-accessible. Leashed pets are permitted.

Reservations, fees: Reservations accepted for some sites; phone 877/444-6777 or access the website: www.reserveusa.com ($8.65 reservation fee). Sites are $12 per night; $6 extra vehicle fee. Senior discount available. Group site is $75 per night. Open mid-May to late September.

Directions: From Enumclaw, drive east on Highway 410 for 31 miles (one mile south of the turnoff for Corral Pass) to the campground entrance on the right.

Contact: Mount Baker-Snoqualmie National Forest, White River Ranger District, 450 Roosevelt Avenue East, Enumclaw, WA 98022; 360/825-6585, fax 360/825-0660.

31 Gateway Inn and RV Park

 8

This park is located less than 100 feet from the southwestern entrance to Mount Rainier National Park. In turn, it can provide a launching point for your vacation. One option is to enter the park at the Nisqually (southwestern) entrance to Mount Rainier National Park, then drive on Nisqually Paradise Road for about five miles to Longmire Museum; general park information and exhibits about the plants and geology of the area are available. If you then continue into the park for 10 more miles, you'll arrive at the Jackson Visitor Center in Paradise, which has more exhibits and an observation deck. This is the only road into the park that's open year-round. Winter activities in the park include cross-country skiing, snowshoeing, and innertubing down slopes.

Location: Near Mount Rainier National Park; see Mount Rainier and the Columbia River Gorge, map 2, grid c1.

Campsites, facilities: There are 16 sites with full hookups for trailers or RVs of any length, a dispersed area for up to seven tents, and nine cabins. Picnic tables are provided. Drinking water and portable toilets are available. A restaurant, a gift shop, and a mini-mart are nearby. Leashed pets are permitted.

Reservations, fees: Reservations accepted. Sites are $12 to $22 per night. Cabins are $69 to $89 per night, $10 per person per night for more than two people. Senior discount available. Major credit cards accepted. Open April through September.

Directions: From Chehalis, drive south on I-5 for 10 miles to U.S. 12. Turn east and drive 31 miles to Morton and Highway 7. Turn north on Highway 7 and drive 17 miles to Elbe and Highway 706. Turn east on Highway 706 and drive 13 miles to the campground on the right.

Contact: Gateway Inn and RV Park, 38820 Highway 706 East, Ashford, WA 98304; 360/569-2506; website: www.gatewaytom-trainier.com.

32 Mounthaven Resort

 6

This campground is located within one-half mile of the Nisqually entrance to Mount Rainier National Park. See the previous description of Gateway Inn and RV Park for information about the national park. A creek runs through this wooded camp.

Location: Near Mount Rainier National Park; see Mount Rainier and the Columbia River Gorge, map 2, grid c1.

Campsites, facilities: There are 17 sites with full hookups for trailers or RVs of any length, one tent site, and 11 furnished cabins. Picnic tables and fire grills are provided. Restrooms, drinking water, flush toilets, one shower, a coin-operated laundry, firewood, and a playground are available. A restaurant and a store are within one mile. Leashed pets are permitted.

Reservations, fees: Reservations accepted. Sites are $15 to $20 per night. Cabins are $69 to $199 per night. Major credit cards accepted. Open year-round.

Directions: From Chehalis, drive south on I-5 for 10 miles to U.S. 12. Turn east and drive 31 miles to Morton and Highway 7. Turn north on Highway 7 and drive 17 miles to Elbe and Highway 706. Turn east on Highway 706 and drive to Ashford; continue for six miles to the campground on the right.

Contact: Mounthaven Resort, 38210 Highway 706 East, Ashford, WA 98304; 800/456-9380 or 360/569-2594; website: www.mounthaven.com.

33 Sunshine Point

 7

This is one of several campgrounds in Mount Rainier National Park located near the Nisqually entrance. The others are Ipsut Creek, Cougar Rock, White River, and Ohanapecosh. The elevation is 2,000 feet. See the previous description of Gateway Inn and RV Park for information about nearby sights and facilities.

Location: In Mount Rainier National Park; see Mount Rainier and the Columbia River Gorge, map 2, grid c1.

Campsites, facilities: There are 18 sites for tents or RVs up to 25 feet long. Picnic tables and fire rings are provided. Drinking water and pit toilets are available. Some facilities are wheelchair-accessible. Leashed pets are permitted in the camp, but not on trails or in the wilderness.

Reservations, fees: Reservations accepted. Sites are $10 per night, $5 per extra vehicle per night, plus $10 park entrance fee. Senior discount available. Major credit cards accepted. Open year-round.

Directions: From Chehalis, drive south on I-5 for 10 miles to U.S. 12. Turn east and drive 31 miles to Morton and Highway 7. Turn north on Highway 7 and drive 17 miles to Elbe and Highway 706. Turn east on Highway 706 and drive 12 miles to the park entrance. The campground is just inside the park entrance on the right.

Contact: Mount Rainier National Park, Tahoma Woods, Star Route, Ashford, WA 98304; 360/569-2211, fax 360/569-2187.

34 Cougar Rock

 9

Cougar Rock is a national park campground set at 3,180 feet at the foot of awesome Mount Rainier. To the east is Paradise, a beautiful 1.2-mile loop trail. It begins at the visitors center and provides stellar views of Mount Rainier and the Nisqually Glacier. Fishing tends to be marginal. Like all national parks, no trout are stocked, and lakes without natural fisheries provide zilch. See previous listing for Gateway Inn and RV Park for information on the nearby park sights and visitors centers.

Location: In Mount Rainier National Park; see Mount Rainier and the Columbia River Gorge, map 2, grid b2.

Campsites, facilities: There are 173 sites for tents or RVs up to 30 feet long and five group sites for up to 24 to 40 people each. Picnic tables and fire rings are provided. Restrooms, drinking water, flush toilets, a dump station, and an amphitheater are available. A camp store is located two miles away. Some facilities are wheelchair-accessible. Leashed pets are permitted.

Reservations, fees: Reserve at 800/365-CAMP (800/365-2267) or website: http://reservations.nps.gov/. Sites are $12 per night, plus $10 park entrance fee, $6 per extra vehicle per night. Senior discount available. Group sites are $40 to $64 per night.

Major credit cards accepted. Open mid-May to mid-October.

Directions: From Tacoma, drive south on I-5 for five miles to Highway 512. Turn east of Highway 512 and drive two miles to Highway 7. Turn south on Highway 7 and drive to Elbe and Highway 706. Continue east on Highway 706 and drive 12 miles to the park entrance. Continue 11 miles to the campground entrance on the left (about two miles past the Longmire developed area).

Contact: Mount Rainier National Park, Tahoma Woods, Star Route, Ashford, WA 98304; 360/569-2211, fax 360/569-2187.

35 Ohanapecosh

 8

This camp is set at an elevation of 1,914 feet, at the foot of North America's most beautiful volcano, 14,410-foot Mount Rainier. It is also set along the Ohanapecosh River and the Ohanapecosh Visitor Center, with exhibits on the history of the forest, plus visitor information. A half-mile loop trail leads from the campground, behind the visitors center, to Ohanapecosh Hot Springs. The Silver Falls Trail, a three-mile loop trail, follows the Ohanapecosh River to 75-foot Silver Falls. Warning: Do not climb on the wet rocks near the waterfall; they are wet and slippery. Note that Stevens Canyon Road heading west and Highway 123 heading north are closed by snowfall in winter.

Location: On the Ohanapecosh River in Mount Rainier National Park; see Mount Rainier and the Columbia River Gorge, map 2, grid c4.

Campsites, facilities: There are 188 sites for tents or RVs up to 30 feet long and one group site for up to 25 people. Picnic tables are provided. Flush toilets, drinking water, and a dump station are available. An amphitheater is nearby. Some facilities are wheelchair-accessible. Leashed pets are permitted in camp, but not on trails.

Reservations, fees: Reservations accepted up to five months in advance for the late June to early September season; phone 800/365-CAMP (800/365-2267) or access the website: www.reservations.nps.gov. Sites are $12 per night, plus $10 per vehicle park entrance fee. Senior discount available. Group site is $40 per night. Major credit cards accepted. Open mid-May through September.

Directions: On I-5, drive to Exit 68 (south of Chehalis) and U.S. 12. Turn east on U.S. 12 and drive 72 miles (seven miles past Packwood) to Highway 123. Turn north and drive five miles to the Ohanapecosh entrance to the park. As you enter the park, the camp is on the left, next to the visitors center.

Contact: Mount Rainier National Park, Tahoma Woods, Ashford, WA 98304; 360/569-2211, fax 360/569-2187.

36 Lodgepole

  6

This campground is set at an elevation of 3,500 feet, along the American River, just eight miles east of the boundary of Mount Rainier National Park. See the previous description of Gateway Inn and RV Park for information on Mount Rainier. Fishing access is available nearby. The campground was remodeled in 2001.

Location: On the American River in Wenatchee National Forest; ; see Mount Rainier and the Columbia River Gorge, map 2, grid a5.

Campsites, facilities: There are 33 sites for tents, trailers, or RVs up to 20 feet long. Picnic tables and fire grills are provided. Drinking water, vault toilets, garbage service, and firewood are available. Leashed pets are permitted.

Reservations, fees: No reservations accepted. Sites are $11 to $14 per night, $5 for each additional vehicle. Senior discount available. Open late May to late October.

Directions: From Yakima, drive northwest on U.S. 12 for 18 miles to Highway 410. Bear northwest on Highway 410 and drive 40.5 miles (eight miles east of the national park boundary) to the campground on the right.

Contact: Okanogan and Wenatchee National Forests, Naches Ranger District, 10061 U.S. Highway 12, Naches, WA 98937; 509/653-2205, fax 509/653-2638.

37 Pleasant Valley

  7

This campground is a good base camp for a hiking or fishing trip. A trail from the camp follows Kettle Creek up to the American Ridge and Kettle Lake in the William O. Douglas Wilderness. It joins another trail that follows the ridge and then drops down to Bumping Lake. A U.S. Forest Service map is essential. The camp is set at an elevation of 3,300 feet. You can fish here for whitefish, steelhead, trout, and salmon in season; check regulations. In the winter, the area is popular with cross-country skiers. The campground was remodeled in 2001.

Location: On the American River in Wenatchee National Forest; see Mount Rainier and the Columbia River Gorge, map 2, grid a6.

Campsites, facilities: There are 16 sites for tents, trailers, or RVs up to 32 feet long. Picnic tables and fire grills are provided. Drinking water, garbage service, vault toilets, and a picnic shelter are available. Downed firewood may be gathered. Some facilities are wheelchair-accessible. Leashed pets are permitted.

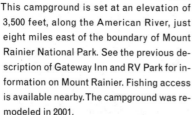

Reservations, fees: No reservations accepted. Rates are $11 to $14 per night for single sites, $22 per night for double sites, and $5 for each additional vehicle. Senior discount available. Open mid-May to mid-November.

Directions: From Yakima, drive northwest on U.S. 12 for 18 miles to Highway 410. Bear northwest on Highway 410 and drive 37 miles to the campground on the left.

Contact: Okanogan and Wenatchee National Forests, Naches Ranger District, 10061 U.S. Highway 12, Naches, WA 98937; 509/653-2205, fax 509/653-2638.

38 Hells Crossing

 7

This campground lies along the American River, at an elevation of 3,250 feet. A steep trail from the camp leads up to Goat Peak and follows the American Ridge in the William O. Douglas Wilderness. Other trails join the ridgeline trail and connect with lakes and streams. A U.S. Forest Service map details the backcountry. Fishing here is for trout, steelhead, salmon, and whitefish in season; check regulations.

Location: On the American River in Wenatchee National Forest; see Mount Rainier and the Columbia River Gorge, map 2, grid a6.

Campsites, facilities: There are 18 sites for tents, trailers, or RVs up to 20 feet long. Picnic tables and fire grills are provided. Drinking water (at the west end of camp) and vault toilets are available. Downed firewood may be gathered. Leashed pets are permitted.

Reservations, fees: No reservations accepted. Rates are $11 to $14 per night for single sites, $22 per night for double sites, and $5 for each additional vehicle. Senior discount available. Open late May to late November.

Directions: From Yakima, drive northwest on U.S. 12 for 18 miles to Highway 410. Bear northwest on Highway 410 and drive 33.5 miles northwest on Highway 410 to the campground on the right.

Contact: Okanogan and Wenatchee National Forests, Naches Ranger District, 10061 U.S. Highway 12, Naches, WA 98937; 509/653-2205, fax 509/653-2638.

39 Pine Needle Group Camp

 7

This is a reservations-only group campground on the edge of the William O. Douglas Wilderness along the American River, at an elevation of 3,000 feet. There are trails leading south into the backcountry at nearby camps; see a U.S. Forest Service map. The camp is easy to reach, rustic, and beautiful. Fishing access is for whitefish, trout, steelhead, and salmon in season. For a side trip, Bumping Lake is available to the south, where boating, fishing, and swimming are all possible options.

Location: On the American River in Wenatchee National Forest; see Mount Rainier and the Columbia River Gorge, map 2, grid a7.

Campsites, facilities: There are six group sites for tents, trailers, or RVs up to 21 feet long, with a maximum capacity of 60 campers and eight vehicles. Picnic tables and fire grills are provided. Pit toilets are available, but there is no drinking water. Note that drinking water is available 2.5 miles west at Hells Crossing Campground (see previous listing). Garbage must be packed out. Downed firewood may be gathered. Leashed pets are permitted.

Reservations, fees: Reservations required. Sites are $20 per night on weekdays and $40 per night on weekends. Discounts are available for three or more consecutive days. Open mid-May to late October.

Directions: From Yakima, drive northwest on U.S. 12 for 18 miles to Highway 410. Bear northwest on Highway 410 and drive 30.5 miles to the campground on the left.

Contact: Okanogan and Wenatchee National Forests, Naches Ranger District, 10061 U.S. Highway 12, Naches, WA 98937; 509/653-2205, fax 509/653-2638.

40 Cedar Springs
 6

The Bumping River is the locale of this camp, set an elevation of 2,800 feet. Fishing here follows the seasons for trout, steelhead, and whitefish; check regulations. If you continue driving southwest for 11 miles on Forest Road 1800/Bumping River Road, you'll get to Bumping Lake, where recreation options abound.

Location: On the Bumping River in Wenatchee National Forest; see Mount Rainier and the Columbia River Gorge, map 2, grid a7.

Campsites, facilities: There are 15 sites for tents, trailers, or RVs up to 22 feet long, including two multi-family sites. Picnic tables and fire grills are provided. Drinking water, vault toilets and firewood are available. Leashed pets are permitted.

Reservations, fees: No reservations accepted. Rates are $11 to $14 per night for single sites, $22 per night for double sites, and $5 for each additional vehicle. Senior discount available. Open late May to late November.

Directions: From Yakima, drive northwest on U.S. 12 for 18 miles to Highway 410. Bear northwest on Highway 410 and drive 28.5 miles to the campground access Road (Forest Road 1800/Bumping River Road). Turn southwest and drive one-half mile to the campground on the left.

Contact: Okanogan and Wenatchee National Forests, Naches Ranger District, 10061 U.S. Highway 12, Naches, WA 98937; 509/653-2205, fax 509/653-2638.

41 Indian Flat Group Camp
 7

This is a reservations-only group campground set along the American River. The elevation is 2,600 feet. Fishing access is available for trout, steelhead, and whitefish in season; check regulations. A trail that starts just across the road from camp leads into the backcountry, west along Fife's Ridge, and farther north to the West Quartz Creek drainage. A U.S. Forest Service map details the adventure possibilities.

Location: On the American River in Wenatchee National Forest; see Mount Rainier and the Columbia River Gorge, map 2, grid a7.

Campsites, facilities: There are group sites for tents, trailers, or RVs up to 30 feet long, with a maximum capacity of 65 campers and 22 vehicles. Picnic tables and fire grills are provided. Drinking water, vault toilets, and firewood are available. Garbage must be packed out. Leashed pets are permitted.

Reservations, fees: Reservations required. Sites are $45 per night on week days and $125 per night on weekends. Discounts are available for three or more consecutive days. Open late May to late October.

Directions: From Yakima, drive northwest on U.S. 12 for 18 miles to Highway 410. Bear northwest on Highway 410 and drive 27 miles to the campground on the left.

Contact: Okanogan and Wenatchee National Forests, Naches Ranger District, 10061 U.S. Highway 12, Naches, WA 98937; 509/653-2205, fax 509/653-2638.

42 Little Naches
 5

This campground on the Little Naches River near the American River, 24 miles from Mount Rainier, is just 0.1 mile off the road, and the easy access is a major attraction for highway cruisers. The location right next to the highway means you can hear highway noise, and at four sites, you can see highway vehicles. A buffer of trees between the highway and the campground is a plus for other sites. This camp is a destination for off-road motorcyclists and jeep campers because there is a 200-mile network of off-road trails. It is possible, for instance, to reach Cle Elum from here without driving on asphalt. Fishing access is available from camp. The elevation is 2,562 feet.

Location: On the Little Naches River in Wenatchee National Forest; see Mount Rainier and the Columbia River Gorge, map 2, grid a8.

Campsites, facilities: There are 21 sites for tents, trailers, or RVs up to 20 feet long, with several sites accessible for RVs up to 32 feet long and two multifamily sites. Picnic tables and fire grills are provided. Drinking water, vault toilets, and garbage service are available. Some facilities are wheelchair-accessible. Leashed pets are permitted.

Reservations, fees: No reservations accepted. Rates are $11 to $14 per night for single sites, and $5 for each additional vehicle. Senior discount available. Open late May to late November.

Directions: From Yakima, drive northwest on U.S. 12 for 18 miles to Highway 410. Bear northwest on Highway 410 and drive 25 miles to the campground access road (Forest Road 1900). Turn left and drive 100 yards to the campground on the left.

Contact: Okanogan and Wenatchee National Forests, Naches Ranger District, 10061 U.S. Highway 12, Naches, WA 98937; 509/653-2205, fax 509/653-2638.

43 Cottonwood

 7

Pretty, shaded sites and riverviews are the main draw at this camp along the Naches River. Sawmill Flat, Little Naches, Crow Creek, Kaner Flat, and Halfway Flat campgrounds provide nearby alternatives. The elevation here is 2,300 feet. The fishing is similar to that of the other camps.

Location: On the Naches River in Wenatchee National Forest; see Mount Rainier and the Columbia River Gorge, map 2, grid a8.

Campsites, facilities: There are 16 sites for tents, trailers, or RVs up to 22 feet long. Picnic tables and fire grills are provided. Drinking water, vault toilets, and garbage service are available. A store, a café, and ice are available nearby. Some facilities are wheelchair-accessible. Leashed pets are permitted.

Reservations, fees: No reservations accepted. Sites are $11 to $14 per night, $5 for each additional vehicle. Senior discount available. Open April through November.

Directions: From Yakima, drive northwest on U.S. 12 for 18 miles to Highway 410. Turn left (northwest) on Highway 410 and drive 17.5 miles to the campground on the left.

Contact: Okanogan and Wenatchee National Forests, Naches Ranger District, 10061 U.S. Highway 12, Naches, WA 98937; 509/653-2205, fax 509/653-2638.

44 Sawmill Flat

 6

This campground on the Naches River near Halfway Flat is used more by off-road motorcyclists than others. It offers fishing access and a hiking trail that leads west from Halfway Flat Campground for several miles into the backcountry; note that you must wade across the river to reach Halfway Flat from Sawmill Flat. Fishing is primarily for trout in summer, whitefish in winter; check regulations. Another trailhead is located at Boulder Cave to the south. See a U.S. Forest Service map for details.

Location: On the Naches River in Wenatchee National Forest; see Mount Rainier and the Columbia River Gorge, map 2, grid a8.

Campsites, facilities: There are 24 sites for tents, trailers, or RVs up to 24 feet long. Picnic tables and fire grills are provided. Drinking water, vault toilets, a dump station, and an Adirondack group shelter are available. Downed firewood may be gathered. Some facilities are wheelchair-accessible, including one campsite. A camp host is available in summer. Leashed pets are permitted.

Reservations, fees: No reservations accepted. Rates are $11 to $14 per night for single sites, $5 for each additional vehicle. Senior discount available. Open April through November.

Directions: From Yakima, drive northwest on U.S. 12 for 18 miles to Highway 410. Bear northwest on Highway 410 and drive 23.5 miles to the campground on the left.

Contact: Okanogan and Wenatchee National Forests, Naches Ranger District, 10061 U.S. Highway 12, Naches, WA 98937; 509/653-2205, fax 509/653-2638.

45 Halfway Flat

 7

Fishing, hiking, and off-road vehicle (ORV) opportunities abound at this campground along the Naches River. A motorcycle trail leads from the campground into the backcountry adjacent to the William O. Douglas Wilderness; no motorized vehicles are permitted in the wilderness itself, however. This campground is not peaceful and quiet. It is something of a chameleon; that is, sometimes primarily a family campground, but at other times dominated by ORV users. It was remodeled in 2001.

Location: On the Naches River in Wenatchee National Forest; see Mount Rainier and the Columbia River Gorge, map 2, grid a8.

Campsites, facilities: There are nine sites for tents, trailers, or RVs up to 27 feet long. Picnic tables and fire grills are provided. Drinking water, vault toilets, garbage service, and firewood are available. Leashed pets are permitted.

Reservations, fees: No reservations accepted. Sites are $7 per night. Senior discount available. Open April to late November.

Directions: From Yakima, drive northwest on U.S. 12 for 18 miles to Highway 410. Turn left (northwest) on Highway 410 and drive 17 miles to the campground on the left.

Contact: Okanogan and Wenatchee National Forests, Naches Ranger District, 10061 U.S. Highway 12, Naches, WA 98937; 509/653-2205, fax 509/653-2638.

46 Lower Bumping Lake

 7

This camp is set at 3,200 feet near Bumping Lake amid a forest of primarily lodgepole pine. This is a popular campground, with a variety of water activities at Bumping Lake, including water-skiing, fishing (salmon and trout), and swimming. A boat ramp is available near the camp. There are also several hiking trails that go into the William O. Douglas Wilderness area surrounding the lake.

Location: On Bumping Lake in Wenatchee National Forest; see Mount Rainier and the Columbia River Gorge, map 2, grid b6.

Campsites, facilities: There are 23 sites for tents, trailers, or RVs up to 50 feet long. Picnic tables and fire grills are provided. Drinking water, vault toilets, and a dump station are available. Some facilities are wheelchair-accessible. Boat-launching facilities are located nearby at Upper Bumping Lake Campground. Leashed pets are permitted.

Reservations, fees: No reservations. Sites are $11 to $14 per night, $22 for a double site, $5 for each additional vehicle. Senior discount available. Open mid-May to late November, weather permitting.

Directions: From Yakima, drive northwest on U.S. 12 for 18 miles to Highway 410. Turn left (northwest) on Highway 410 and drive 28.5 miles to Forest Road 1800. Turn left (southwest) and drive 11 miles (along the Bumping River); look for the campground entrance road on the right (now paved all the way).

Contact: Wenatchee National Forest, Naches Ranger District, 10061 Highway 12, Naches, WA 98937; 509/653-2205, fax 509/653-2638.

Upper Bumping Lake

  7

Woods and water—this spot has them both. The lake is cold and stocked with trout, and the nearby boat launch makes this a winner for campers with boats. This popular camp fills up quickly on summer weekends. A variety of water activities are allowed at Bumping Lake, including water-skiing, fishing (salmon and trout), and swimming. Six picnic sites are adjacent to the boat facilities. There are also several hiking trails that go into the William O. Douglas Wilderness area surrounding the lake. This is one of the more developed camps in the area and was remodeled in 2001.

Location: On Bumping Lake in Wenatchee National Forest; see Mount Rainier and the Columbia River Gorge, map 2, grid b6.

Campsites, facilities: There are 45 sites for tents, trailers, or RVs up to 30 feet long. Picnic tables and fire grills are provided. Drinking water, vault toilets, and firewood are available. Boat docks, launching facilities, rentals, and a dump station are nearby. Leashed pets are permitted.

Reservations, fees: No reservations accepted. Sites are $11 to $14 per night, $5 for each additional vehicle. Senior discount available. Open mid-May to late November.

Directions: From Yakima, drive northwest on U.S. 12 for 18 miles to Highway 410. Turn left (northwest) on Highway 410 and drive 28.5 miles to Forest Road 1800. Turn left (southwest) and drive 11 miles (along the Bumping River) to the end of the pavement; look for the campground entrance road on the right.

Contact: Okanogan and Wenatchee National Forests, Naches Ranger District, 10061 U.S. Highway 12, Naches, WA 98937; 509/653-2205, fax 509/653-2638.

Bumping Crossing

 5

This campground is set on the Bumping River about one mile from the boat landing at Bumping Lake. It is a more primitive option to Bumping Lake and Boat Landing. It's a good spot for a weekend trip, but remember to bring your own drinking water. Fishing and boating are often good. The elevation is 3,200 feet.

Location: On the Bumping River in Wenatchee National Forest; see Mount Rainier and the Columbia River Gorge, map 2, grid b6

Campsites, facilities: There are 12 sites for tents, trailers, or RVs up to 15 feet long. Picnic tables and fire grills are provided. Vault toilets are available, but there is no drinking water. A store, a café, and ice are located within one mile. Boat docks, launching facilities, and rentals are nearby on Bumping Lake. Leashed pets are permitted.

Reservations, fees: Northwest Forest Pass ($30 annual fee) or $5 daily fee per parked vehicle is required. Open late May to late November.

Directions: From Yakima, drive northwest on U.S. 12 for 18 miles to Highway 410. Turn left (northwest) on Highway 410 and drive 28.5 miles to Forest Road 1800. Turn left (southwest) and drive 10 miles (along the Bumping River) to the campground on the right.

Contact: Okanogan and Wenatchee National Forests, Naches Ranger District, 10061 U.S. Highway 12, Naches, WA 98937; 509/653-2205, fax 509/653-2638.

49 Cougar Flat

    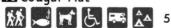 5

One of several camps in the immediate vicinity, this spot along the Bumping River is close to good fishing, and a trail from the camp follows the river and then heads up the tributaries. The elevation is 3,100 feet. See the chapter map for nearby camping options.

Location: On the Bumping River in Wenatchee National Forest; see Mount Rainier and the Columbia River Gorge, map 2, grid a7.

Campsites, facilities: There are 12 sites for tents, trailers, or RVs up to 20 feet long. Picnic tables and fire grills are provided. Drinking water and vault toilets are available. Some facilities are wheelchair-accessible. Leashed pets are permitted.

Reservations, fees: No reservations accepted. Sites are $10 to $14 per night; $5 for each additional vehicle. Senior discount available. Open late May to mid-September.

Directions: From Yakima, drive northwest on U.S. 12 for 18 miles to Highway 410. Turn left (northwest) on Highway 410 and drive 28.5 miles to Forest Road 1800. Turn left (southwest) and drive six miles (along the Bumping River) to the campground on the left.

Contact: Okanogan and Wenatchee National Forests, Naches Ranger District, 10061 U.S. Highway 12, Naches, WA 98937; 509/653-2205, fax 509/653-2638.

50 Soda Springs

      6

Highlights of this camp along Bumping Creek include natural mineral springs and a nature trail. The mineral spring is located next to a trail across the river from the campground, where the water bubbles up out of the ground. It is a coldwater spring that is popular with some campers for soaking and drinking. Many campers use this camp for access to nearby Bumping Lake. Fishing access is available. A sheltered picnic area is provided.

Location: On the Bumping River in Wenatchee National Forest; see Mount Rainier and the Columbia River Gorge, map 2, grid a7.

Campsites, facilities: There are 26 sites for tents, trailers, or RVs up to 30 feet in length. Picnic tables and fire grills are provided. Drinking water, vault toilets, a dump station, firewood, several picnic shelters with fireplaces, and garbage service are available. Some facilities are wheelchair-accessible. Leashed pets are permitted.

Reservations, fees: No reservations accepted. Sites are $11 to $14 per night, $5 for each additional vehicle. Senior discount available. Open May to late November.

Directions: From Yakima, drive northwest on U.S. 12 for 18 miles to Highway 410. Turn left (northwest) on Highway 410 and drive 28.5 miles to Forest Road 1800. Turn left (southwest) and drive five miles (along the Bumping River) to the campground on the left.

Contact: Okanogan and Wenatchee National Forests, Naches Ranger District, 10061 U.S. Highway 12, Naches, WA 98937; 509/653-2205, fax 509/653-2638.

51 Big Creek

   8

This camp is useful as an overflow spot for Mount Rainier and Puget Sound area campers. It is set along a stream next to a rural residential area, in a forest setting made up of Douglas fir, western hemlock, western red cedar, and bigleaf and vine maple. RV drivers should note that the turning radius required is fairly tight.

Location: On Big Creek in Gifford Pinchot National Forest; see Mount Rainier and the Columbia River Gorge, map 2, grid c1.

Campsites, facilities: There are 28 sites for tents, trailers, or RVs up to 25 feet long. Picnic tables and fire rings are provided. Drinking water and vault toilets are available. Leashed pets are permitted.

Reservations, fees: Reservations recommended; phone 877/444-6777 or access the website: www.reserveusa.com ($8.65 reservation fee). Sites are $11 for a single, $22 for a double site per night, $5 for each additional vehicle. Senior discount available. Open late May through mid-September.

Directions: On I-5, drive to Exit 68 (south of Chehalis) and U.S. 12. Turn east on U.S. 12 and drive 62 miles to Packwood and Forest Road 52/Skate Creek Road. Turn left (northwest) and drive 23 miles to the campground on the left.

Contact: Gifford Pinchot National Forest, Cowlitz Valley Ranger District, P.O. Box 670, Randle, WA 98377-0670; 360/497-1100, fax 360/497-1102.

52 Packwood Trailer and RV Park

   6

This is a pleasant campground, especially in the fall when the maples turn. Groups are welcome. Mount Rainier National Park is just 25 miles north, and this camp is a good alternative if the park is full. Nearby recreation options include a riding stable and tennis courts.

Location: In Packwood; see Mount Rainier and the Columbia River Gorge, map 2, grid d3.

Campsites, facilities: There are 88 sites, most with full hookups, for trailers or RVs of any length, and 15 tent sites. Picnic tables are provided. Restrooms, flush toilets, showers, a dump station, a store, cable TV, and a coin-operated laundry are available. A café and bottled gas are available within walking distance. Leashed pets are permitted.

Reservations, fees: Reservations accepted. Sites are $11 to $20 per night. Major credit cards accepted. Open year-round.

Directions: On I-5, drive to Exit 68 (south of Chehalis) and U.S. 12. Turn east on U.S. 12 and drive 65 miles to Packwood. The park is on the north side of the highway in town at 19285 U.S. Highway 12.

Contact: Packwood Trailer and RV Park, P.O. Box 309, Packwood, WA 98361; 360/494-5145.

53 La Wis Wis

 9

This camp is ideally located for day trips to Mount Rainier and Mount St. Helens. It's set at an elevation of 1,400 along the Clear Fork of the Cowlitz River, near the confluence with the Ohanapecosh River. Trout fishing is an option. The landscape features an old-growth forest, a mix of Douglas fir, western hemlock, western red cedar, and Pacific yew, with an undergrowth of bigleaf maple. A 200-yard trail provides access to the Blue Hole on the Ohanapecosh River, a deep pool designated by an observation point and interpretive signs. Another trail goes less than one quarter-mile to Purcell Falls. The entrance to Mount Rainier

National Park is about seven miles south of the camp.

Location: On the Cowlitz River in Gifford Pinchot National Forest; see Mount Rainier and the Columbia River Gorge, map 2, grid c4.

Campsites, facilities: There are 115 sites for tents, trailers, or RVs up to 24 feet long. Picnic tables and fire rings are provided. Flush and vault toilets, drinking water, and firewood are available. Some facilities are wheelchair-accessible. Leashed pets are permitted.

Reservations, fees: Reserve at 877/444-6777 ($8.65 reservation fee) or website: www.reserveusa.com. Sites are $12.50 to $14.50 and $25 per night for double sites, $5 per extra vehicle per night. Senior discount available. The maximum stay is 14 days. Open mid-May to late September.

Directions: On I-5, drive to Exit 68 (south of Chehalis) and U.S. 12. Turn east on U.S. 12 and drive 69 miles (about six miles past Packwood) to Forest Road 1272. Turn left and drive one-half mile to the campground on the left.

Contact: Gifford Pinchot National Forest, Cowlitz Valley Ranger District, P.O. Box 670, Randle, WA 98377-0670; 360/497-1100, fax 360/497-1102.

54 Summit Creek

     5

This is a primitive campground nestled in the trees along Summit Creek, at an elevation of 2,400 feet. It is another good base camp for trips into the Cascade Range backcountry. See the following description of Soda Springs.

Location: On Summit Creek in Gifford Pinchot National Forest; see Mount Rainier and the Columbia River Gorge, map 2, grid c4.

Campsites, facilities: There are six primitive tent sites. Picnic tables and fire rings are provided. A vault toilet is available, but there is no drinking water. Garbage must be packed out. Leashed pets are permitted.

Reservations, fees: No reservations; no fee. Open mid-June to early September.

Directions: On I-5, drive to Exit 68 (south of Chehalis) and U.S. 12. Turn east on U.S. 12 and drive 75 miles (two miles past the Highway 123 turnoff) to Forest Road 45. Turn left and drive three miles (becomes Forest Road 4510) to the campground.

Contact: Gifford Pinchot National Forest, Cowlitz Valley Ranger District, P.O. Box 670, Randle, WA 98377-0670; 360/497-1100, fax 360/497-1102.

55 Soda Springs

 6

Soda Springs is set at 3,200 feet along Summit Creek and the border for the William O. Douglas Wilderness. This primitive camp is ideal as a jumping-off base camp for a backpacking expedition or daily hiking trips in the Cascade Range. One trail out of camp leads three miles up to Jug Lake in the Douglas Wilderness. There are several trails and lakes to choose as destinations. Obtain a U.S. Forest Service map for details.

Location: On Summit Creek in Gifford Pinchot National Forest; see Mount Rainier and the Columbia River Gorge, map 2, grid c5.

Campsites, facilities: There are six primitive tent sites. Picnic tables and fire rings are provided. A vault toilet is available, but there is no drinking water. Garbage must be packed out. Leashed pets are permitted.

Reservations, fees: Northwest Forest Pass ($30 annual fee) or $5 daily fee per parked vehicle is required. Open early-June to late October.

Directions: On I-5, drive to Exit 68 (south of Chehalis) and U.S. 12. Turn east on U.S. 12 and drive 75 miles (two miles past the Highway 123 turnoff) to Forest Road 45. Turn left and drive one mile (becomes Forest Road 4510) to the camp on the right.

Contact: Gifford Pinchot National Forest, Cowlitz Valley Ranger District, P.O. Box 670, Randle, WA 98377-0670; 360/497-1100, fax 360/497-1102.

56 White Pass

 7

This campground on the shore of Leech Lake at an elevation of 4,500 feet is near trails leading into the Goat Rocks Wilderness to the south and the William O. Douglas Wilderness to the north. A trailhead for the Pacific Crest Trail is also nearby. Beautiful Leech Lake is popular for fly-fishing for rainbow trout. Note that this is the only type of fishing allowed here; check regulations. White Pass Ski Area is located across the highway, less than one quarter-mile away. No gas motors on boats are permitted at Leech Lake.

Location: On Leech Lake in Wenatchee National Forest; see Mount Rainier and the Columbia River Gorge, map 2, grid c6.

Campsites, facilities: There are 16 sites for tents, trailers, or RVs up to 20 feet long. Picnic tables and fire grills are provided. Vault toilets and firewood are available, but there is no drinking water. A store, a café, a coin-operated laundry, and ice are located within one mile. Boat-launching facilities are nearby. No gas motors on boats are allowed; electric motors are permitted. Leashed pets are permitted.

Reservations, fees: No reservations accepted. Sites are $7 per night, $5 per extra vehicle per night. Senior discount available. Open late May to late October.

Directions: On I-5, drive to Exit 68 (south of Chehalis) and U.S. 12. Turn east on U.S. 12 and drive 84 miles (three miles past the White Pass Ski Area) to the campground entrance road on the left side. Turn north and drive 200 yards to Leech Lake and the campground.

Contact: Okanogan and Wenatchee National Forests, Naches Ranger District, 10061 U.S. Highway 12, Naches, WA 98937; 509/653-2205, fax 509/653-2638.

57 Dog Lake

 5

This campground is on the shore of Dog Lake at 3,400 feet elevation. Fishing can be good for native rainbow trout, and the lake is good for hand-launched boats, such as canoes and prams. Nearby trails lead into the William O. Douglas Wilderness. See a U.S. Forest Service map for details.

Location: On Dog Lake in Wenatchee National Forest; see Mount Rainier and the Columbia River Gorge, map 2, grid c6.

Campsites, facilities: There are 11 sites for tents, trailers, or RVs up to 20 feet long. Picnic tables and fire grills are provided. Vault toilets are available, but there is no drinking water. Leashed pets are permitted. No horses are allowed in the campground.

Reservations, fees: No reservations accepted. Sites are $7 per night, $5 per extra vehicle per night. Senior discount available. Open late May to late November.

Directions: On I-5, drive to Exit 68 (south of Chehalis) and U.S. 12. Turn east on U.S. 12 and drive 87 miles (six miles past the White Pass Ski Area) to the campground entrance road on the left side.

Contact: Okanogan and Wenatchee National Forests, Naches Ranger District, 10061 U.S. Highway 12, Naches, WA 98937; 509/653-2205, fax 509/653-2638.

58 Clear Lake North

  7

This campground is set along the shore of Clear Lake at an elevation of 3,100 feet. A five-mph speed limit keeps the lake quiet and ideal for fishing, often good for rainbow trout. It is stocked regularly in the summer. Clear lake is the forebay for Rimrock Lake. Swimming is allowed. This camp is primitive and gets relatively little use.

Location: On Clear Lake in Wenatchee National Forest; see Mount Rainier and the Columbia River Gorge, map 2, grid c6.

Campsites, facilities: There are 33 sites for tents, trailers, or RVs up to 22 feet long. Picnic tables and fire grills are provided. Vault toilets and garbage service are available. There is no drinking water at Clear Lake North, but there is drinking water at Clear Lake South Campground. Some facilities are wheelchair-accessible. Boat docks, launching facilities, and rentals are nearby. Leashed pets are permitted.

Reservations, fees: No reservations accepted. Sites are $9 per night, $5 per extra vehicle per night. Senior discount available. Open mid-April to late November.

Directions: From Yakima, drive northwest on I-12 for 17 miles to the junction with Highway 410. Turn west on U.S. 12 and drive 31 miles to Forest Road 1200. Turn left (south) and drive one quarter-mile to Forest Road 1200-740. Continue south for one-half mile to the campground.

Contact: Okanogan and Wenatchee National Forests, Naches Ranger District, 10061 U.S. Highway 12, Naches, WA 98937; 509/653-2205, fax 509/653-2638.

59 Clear Lake South

 7

This campground (elevation 3,100 feet) is located near the east shore of Clear Lake, which is the forebay for Rimrock Lake. Fishing and swimming are options. For winter travelers, several sno-parks in the area offer snowmobiling and cross-country skiing. There are many hiking trails to the north; see a U.S. Forest Service map.

Location: In Wenatchee National Forest; see Mount Rainier and the Columbia River Gorge, map 2, grid c6.

Campsites, facilities: There are 23 sites for tents, trailers, or RVs up to 22 feet long. Picnic tables and fire grills are provided. Drinking water and vault toilets are available. Downed firewood may be gathered. Boat-launching facilities are nearby. Leashed pets are permitted.

Reservations, fees: No reservations accepted. Sites are $9 per night, $5 per extra vehicle per night. Open mid-April to late November.

Directions: From Yakima, drive northwest on I-82 for 17 miles to the junction with Highway 410. Turn west on U.S. 12 and drive 31 miles to Forest Road 1200. Turn left (south) and drive one mile to Forest Road 1200-740. Continue south and drive one quarter-mile to the campground.

Contact: Okanogan and Wenatchee National Forests, Naches Ranger District, 10061 U.S. Highway 12, Naches, WA 98937; 509/653-2205, fax 509/653-2638.

60 Silver Beach Resort

 8

This resort along the shore of Rimrock Lake is one of several camps in the immediate area. It's very scenic, with beautiful lakefront sites. Hiking trails, marked bike trails, a full-service marina, and a riding stable are close by.

Location: On Rimrock Lake; see Mount Rainier and the Columbia River Gorge, map 2, grid c7.

Campsites, facilities: There are 97 sites, most with full hookups, for tents, trailers, or RVs up to 40 feet, three cabins with kitchens, and 16 motel rooms. Picnic tables and fire pits are provided. A restroom, coin-operated showers, a café, a store, a dump station, bait and tackle, bottled gas, propane, ice, a playground, a hot tub, boat docks, launching facilities, and boat and personal watercraft rentals are available. Leashed pets are permitted.

Reservations, fees: Reservations accepted. Sites are $13 to $18 per night, $5 per extra vehicle per night; cabins are $75 per night. Major credit cards accepted. Open year-round, with limited winter facilities.

Directions: From Yakima, drive northwest on U.S. 12 for 40 miles to the resort on the left.

Contact: Silver Beach Resort, 40350 Highway 12, Rimrock, WA 98937; 509/672-2500.

61 Indian Creek

 7

Fishing, swimming, and water-skiing are among the activities at this shorefront campground on Rimrock Lake (elevation 3,000 feet). The camp is adjacent to Rimrock Lake Marina and Silver Beach Resort. This is a developed lake and an extremely popular campground, often filling on summer weekends. Fishing is often good for rainbow trout. Many excellent hiking trails to the north, about 5 to 10 miles from the campground, are routed into the William O. Douglas Wilderness, including the treasured Indian Creek Trail into the wilderness.

Location: On Rimrock Lake in Wenatchee National Forest; see Mount Rainier and the Columbia River Gorge, map 2, grid c7.

Campsites, facilities: There are 39 sites for tents, trailers, or RVs up to 32 feet long. Picnic tables and fire grills are provided. Drinking water and vault toilets are available. Downed firewood may be gathered. A café, a store, ice, boat docks, launching facilities, and rentals are nearby. Leashed pets are permitted.

Reservations, fees: No reservations accepted. Sites are $11 to $14 per night, $5 per extra vehicle per night. Open late May to mid-September.

Directions: From Yakima, drive northwest on I-82 for 17 miles to the junction with Highway 410. Turn west on U.S. 12 and drive 20 miles to Rimrock Lake and the campground entrance at the lake.

Contact: Okanogan and Wenatchee National Forests, Naches Ranger District, 10061 U.S. Highway 12, Naches, WA 98937; 509/653-2205, fax 509/653-2638.

62 Peninsula

 7

Fishing for silvers and rainbow trout, swimming, and water-skiing are all allowed at Rimrock Lake (elevation 3,000 feet), where this shorefront recreation area and camp is located. The lake is stocked regularly in summer and is popular. The nearby vicinity of a boat ramp is a big plus. This is one of several camps on the lake. A point of interest is a nearby emergency airstrip here, a grass landing runway. A nearby sno-park offers wintertime fun, including cross-country skiing and snowmobiling.

Location: On Rimrock Lake in Wenatchee National Forest; see Mount Rainier and the Columbia River Gorge, map 2, grid c7.

Campsites, facilities: There is a dispersed camping area for tents, trailers, or RVs up to 20 feet long. Vault toilets and picnic tables are available, but there is no drinking water. Boat docks and launching facilities are nearby. Leashed pets are permitted.

Reservations, fees: Northwest Forest Pass ($30 annual fee) or $5 daily fee per parked vehicle is required. Senior discount available. Open mid-April to late November.

Directions: From Yakima, drive northwest on I-82 for 17 miles to the junction with Highway 410. Turn west on U.S. 12 and drive 22 miles to Forest Road 1200. Turn south (left) and drive three miles (across the cattleguard) to Forest Road 711. Turn right (west) and drive a short distance to the campground.

Contact: Okanogan and Wenatchee National Forests, Naches Ranger District, 10061 U.S. Highway 12, Naches, WA 98937; 509/653-2205, fax 509/653-2638.

63 South Fork

 8

This campground (at 3,000 feet) is set along the South Fork of the Tieton River, less than one mile from where it empties into Rimrock Lake. Note that fishing is prohibited to protect the bull trout. By traveling a bit farther south on Tieton River Road, you can see the huge Blue Slide, an enormous prehistoric rock and earth slide that has a curious blue tinge to it.

Location: On the South Fork of the Tieton River in Wenatchee National Forest; see Mount Rainier and the Columbia River Gorge, map 2, grid d7.

Campsites, facilities: There are nine sites for tents, trailers, or RVs up to 20 feet long. Picnic tables and fire grills are provided. Vault toilets and garbage service are available, but there is no drinking water. Leashed pets are permitted.

Reservations, fees: No reservations accepted. Sites are $7 per night, $5 per extra vehicle per night. Open late May to mid-October.

Directions: From Yakima, drive northwest on I-82 for 17 miles to the junction with Highway 410. Turn west on U.S. 12 and drive 22 miles to Forest Road 1200. Turn south (left) and drive four miles to Forest Road 1203. Bear left and drive 0.75 mile to Forest Road 1203-517. Turn right and drive 200 feet to the campground.

Contact: Okanogan and Wenatchee National Forests, Naches Ranger District, 10061 U.S. Highway 12, Naches, WA 98937; 509/653-2205, fax 509/653-2638.

64 Iron Creek

 7

This popular U.S. Forest Service campground is set along the Cispus River near its confluence with Iron Creek. Trout fishing is available. The landscape features a forested setting of primarily Douglas fir, western red cedar, and old-growth forest on fairly flat terrain. The camp is also located along the access route that leads to the best viewing areas on the eastern flank for Mount St. Helens. It is a 25-mile drive to Windy Ridge Vista Point, for a breathtaking view of Spirit Lake and the blast zone of the volcano.

Location: On the Cispus River in Gifford Pinchot National Forest; see Mount Rainier and the Columbia River Gorge, map 2, grid e1.

Campsites, facilities: There are 98 sites for tents, trailers, or RVs. Picnic tables and fire rings are provided. Drinking water, vault toilets, and firewood are available. Some facilities are wheelchair-accessible. Leashed pets are permitted.

Reservations, fees: Reserve at 877/444-6777 ($8.65 reservation fee) or website: www .reserveusa.com. Rates are $12.50 to $14.50 per night, $25 per night for a double site, $5 per extra vehicle per night. Senior discount available. Open mid-May to late September.

Directions: From Olympia, drive south on I-5 to Exit 68 and U.S. 12. Turn east on U.S. 12 and drive 48 miles to Randle and Highway 131. Turn south on Highway 131 and drive one mile (becomes Forest Road 25). Continue south on Forest Road 25 and drive nine miles to a fork. Bear left at the fork, continue across the bridge, turn left, and drive two miles to the campground entrance on the left (along the south shore of the Cispus River).

Contact: Gifford Pinchot National Forest, Cowlitz Valley Ranger District, P.O. Box 670, Randle, WA 98377-0670; 360/497-1100, fax 360/497-1102.

65 Tower Rock

 5

This campground along the Cispus River is an option to nearby Iron Creek and North Fork. It has shaded and sunny sites, with lots of trees and plenty of room. The camp is set fairly close to the river, with some sites featuring river frontage. It is also fairly flat and forested with Douglas fir, western hemlock, red cedar, and bigleaf maple. Fishing for trout is popular here.

Location: On the Cispus River in Gifford Pinchot National Forest; see Mount Rainier and the Columbia River Gorge, map 2, grid e2.

Campsites, facilities: There are 22 sites for tents, trailers, or RVs up to 21 feet long. Picnic tables and fire grills are provided. Drinking water, vault toilets, and firewood are available. A small store and a trout pond are nearby. Leashed pets are permitted.

Reservations, fees: Reserve at 877/444-6777 ($8.65 reservation fee) or website: www.reserveusa.com. Sites are $11.50 to $13.50 per night, $5 per extra vehicle per night. Senior discount available. Open mid-May to late September.

Directions: From Olympia, drive south on I-5 to Exit 68 and U.S. 12. Turn east on U.S. 12 and drive 48 miles to Randle and Highway 131. Turn south on Highway 131 and drive one mile to Forest Road 23. Turn left on Forest Road 23 and drive eight miles to the campground entrance road on the right.

Contact: Gifford Pinchot National Forest, Cowlitz Valley Ranger District, P.O. Box 670, Randle, WA 98377-0670; 360/497-1100, fax 360/497-1102.

66 North Fork & North Fork Group

 6

This campground set along the North Cispus River offers single sites, double sites, and a group camp, with river flowing between the sites for individual and group use. The elevation is 1,500 feet. The campsites are set back from the river in a well-forested area. A national forest map details the backcountry access to the Valley Trail, which is routed up the Cispus River Valley for about 15 miles. This provides access for hikers, bikers, all-terrain vehicles, and horses. Note that if you explore Road 2300-083 for 15 miles west you will find Layser Cave, a Native American archeological site that is open to the public.

Location: On the Cispus River in Gifford Pinchot National Forest; see Mount Rainier and the Columbia River Gorge, map 2, grid e2.

Campsites, facilities: There are 33 sites for tents, trailers, or RVs up to 31 feet long and an adjacent group camp with three sites. Picnic tables and fire grills are provided. Drinking water, vault toilets, and firewood are available. Leashed pets are permitted.

Reservations, fees: Reserve at 877/444-6777 ($8.65 reservation fee) or website: www.reserveusa.com. Sites are $11.50 to $13.50 per night, $23 for double sites, $5 per extra vehicle per night. Senior discount available. Open mid-May to late September.

Directions: From Olympia, drive south on I-5 to Exit 68 and U.S. 12. Turn east on U.S. 12 and drive 48 miles to Randle and Highway 131. Turn south on Highway 131 and drive one mile to Forest Road 23. Bear left and drive 11 miles to the campground on the left.

Contact: Gifford Pinchot National Forest, Cowlitz Ranger District, P.O. Box 670, Randle, WA 98377; 360/497-1100, fax 360/497-1102.

67 Blue Lake Creek

 7

This camp is set at an elevation of 1,900 feet along Blue Lake Creek. It is a significant camp for all-terrain vehicle (ATV) owners, with access to a network of ATV trails here. There is nearby access to the Valley Trail, with features 25 to 30 miles of trail. This is also near the launch point for the 3.5-mile hike to Blue Lake, with the trailhead about one-half mile from camp.

Location: Near Blue Lake in Gifford Pinchot National Forest; see Mount Rainier and the Columbia River Gorge, map 2, grid e3.

Campsites, facilities: There are 11 sites for tents, trailers, or RVs up to 31 feet long. Picnic tables and fire rings are provided. Drinking water and vault toilets are available. Firewood can be gathered outside of the campground area. Leashed pets are permitted.

Reservations, fees: Reserve at 877/444-6777 ($8.65 reservation fee) or website: www.reserveusa.com. Sites are $10.50 per night, $5 per extra vehicle per night. Senior discount available. Open mid-May to late September.

Directions: From Olympia, drive south on I-5 to Exit 68 and U.S. 12. Turn east on U.S. 12 and drive 48 miles to Randle and Highway 131. Turn south on Highway 131 and drive one mile to Forest Road 23. Turn south and drive about 10 miles to the campground on the left.

Contact: Gifford Pinchot National Forest, Cowlitz Ranger District, P.O. Box 670, Randle, WA 98377; 360/497-1100, fax 360/497-1102.

68 Adams Fork

 7

This campground is set at 2,600 feet elevation along the Upper Cispus River near Adams Creek and is popular with off-road vehicle (ORV) enthusiasts. Most of the campsites are small, but a few are large enough for comfortable RV use. The area has many towering trees. There are many miles of trails designed for use by ORVs. A trail that is just one-half mile away leads north to Blue Lake, which is about a five-mile hike (one-way) from the camp. The Cispus River provides trout fishing.

Location: On the Cispus River in Gifford Pinchot National Forest; see Mount Rainier and the Columbia River Gorge, map 2, grid f3.

Campsites, facilities: There are 24 sites for tents, trailers, or RVs up to 21 feet long. Picnic tables and fire grills are provided. Drinking water and vault toilets are available.

Firewood may be gathered outside the campground area. Some facilities are wheelchair-accessible. Leashed pets are permitted.

Reservations, fees: Reservations accepted; phone 877/444-6777 or access the website: www.reserveusa.com ($8.65 reservation fee). Rates are $11 per night for single sites, $22 per night for double sites, and group sites are $15 to $27 per night, $5 per extra vehicle per night. Senior discount available. Open May to late October.

Directions: On I-5, drive to Exit 68 (south of Chehalis) and U.S. 12. Turn east on U.S. 12 and drive 48 miles to Randle and U.S. 131. Turn right (south) and drive one mile to Forest Road 23. Turn left (southeast) and drive 18 miles to Forest Road 21. Turn left (southeast) on Forest Road 21 and drive five miles to Forest Road 56. Turn right on Forest Road 56 and drive 200 yards to the campground on the left.

Contact: Gifford Pinchot National Forest, Cowlitz Valley Ranger District, P.O. Box 670, Randle, WA 98377; 360/497-1100, fax 360/497-1102.

69 Walupt Lake

 8

This popular spot is a good base camp for a multiday vacation. It is set at 3,900 feet elevation along the shore of Walupt Lake. The trout fishing is often good here; check regulations. But note that only small boats are advisable here because the launch area at the lake is shallow and it can take a four-wheel-drive vehicle to get a boat in and out. A swimming beach is nearby. In addition, several nearby trails lead into the backcountry and to other smaller alpine lakes. One trail out of the campground leads to the upper end of the lake, then launches off to the Goat Rocks Wilderness, which is an outstanding hike. The

trail is also excellent for horseback rides. See a U.S. Forest Service map for details.

Location: On Walupt Lake in Gifford Pinchot National Forest; see Mount Rainier and the Columbia River Gorge, map 2, grid e5.

Campsites, facilities: There are 44 sites for tents, trailers, or RVs up to 22 feet long. Picnic tables are provided. Drinking water and vault toilets are available. Fire rings are located next to the campground. There is primitive boat access with a 10-mph speed limit; no water-skiing is allowed. Leashed pets are permitted.

Reservations, fees: Reservations accepted; phone 877/444-6777 or access the website: www.reserveusa.com ($8.65 reservation fee). Sites are $11.50 to $23 per night, $5 for each additional vehicle. Senior discount available. Open mid-June to mid-September.

Directions: On I-5, drive to Exit 68 (south of Chehalis) and U.S. 12. Turn east on U.S. 12 and drive 62 miles to Forest Road 21 (2.5 miles southwest of Packwood). Turn right (southeast) and drive 20 miles to Forest Road 2160. Turn left (east) and drive 4.5 miles to the campground.

Contact: Gifford Pinchot National Forest, Cowlitz Valley Ranger District, P.O. Box 670, Randle, WA 98377-0670; 360/497-1100, fax 360/497-1102.

70 Walupt Horse Camp

 7

This camp is for horse campers only, set about one mile from Walupt Lake, which is good for trout fishing. Several trails lead from the lake into the backcountry of the southern Goat Rocks Wilderness, which has 50 miles of trails that can be used by horses, along with other trails outside of the wilderness boundary. If you have planned a multiday horse packing trip, you should bring in your own feed for the horses. Feed must be pellets or processed grain only. Hay is not permitted in the wilderness. The lake has a 10-mph speed limit for boats.

Location: Near the Goat Rocks Wilderness in Gifford Pinchot National Forest; see Mount Rainier and the Columbia River Gorge, map 2, grid e5.

Campsites, facilities: There are nine sites for equestrians in tents, trailers, or RVs up to 18 feet long. Picnic tables and fire grills are provided. Drinking water, vault toilets, and firewood are available. Garbage must be packed out. A horse ramp, high lines, and tethering areas are available. Leashed pets are permitted.

Reservations, fees: Northwest Forest Pass ($30 annual fee) or $5 daily fee per parked vehicle is required. Senior discount available. Open June through October, weather permitting.

Directions: On I-5, drive to Exit 68 (south of Chehalis) and U.S. 12. Turn east on U.S. 12 and drive 62 miles to Forest Road 21 (2.5 miles southwest of Packwood). Turn right (southeast) and drive 16.5 miles to Forest Road 2160. Turn left (east) and drive 3.5 miles to the campground on the right.

Contact: Gifford Pinchot National Forest, Cowlitz Valley Ranger District, Packwood, WA 98361; 360/494-0600, fax 360/494-0602.

71 Olallie Lake

  9

This campground is located at 4,200 feet on the shore of Olallie Lake, a small alpine lake that is one of several in the area fed by streams coming off the glaciers on nearby Mount Adams (elevation 12,276 feet). Trout fishing is good here in early summer. The campsites are close to the lake, with gorgeous views of Mount Adams across the

lake. Several of the campsites are small, in one larger area with room for RVs. A word to the wise: Mosquitoes can be a problem in the spring and early summer.

Location: On Olallie Lake in Gifford Pinchot National Forest; see Mount Rainier and the Columbia River Gorge, map 2, grid f4.

Campsites, facilities: There are five sites for tents, trailers, or RVs up to 21 feet long. Picnic tables and fire rings are provided. Pit toilets are available, but there is no drinking water. Firewood may be gathered outside the campground area. Boat-launching facilities are nearby, but all gasoline motors are prohibited on the lake. Leashed pets are permitted.

Reservations, fees: No reservations accepted. Sites are $9 per night, and $9 for each additional vehicle. Senior discount available. Open July to late September.

Directions: From Chehalis, drive south on I-5 for 10 miles to Exit 68 and U.S. 12. Turn east on U.S. 12 and drive 48 miles to Randle and U.S. 131. Turn south and drive one mile to Forest Road 23. Turn left (southeast) and drive 29 miles to Forest Road 2329. Turn left (northeast) and drive one mile to a junction with Forest Road 5601. Bear left and drive one-half mile to the campground on the right.

Contact: Gifford Pinchot National Forest, Cowlitz Valley Ranger District, P.O. Box 670, Randle, WA 98377-0670; 360/497-1100, fax 360/497-1102.

72 Takhlakh Lake

 9

This campground is situated along the shore of Takhlakh Lake, one of five lakes in the area, all accessible by car. It's a beautiful place, set at 4,500 feet elevation, but alas, mosquitoes abound until late July. A viewing area

(Mount Adams is visible across the lake) is available for visitors, while the more ambitious can go berry picking, fishing, and hiking. This lake is much better than nearby Horseshoe Lake, and in turn, the fishing is much better, especially for trout early in the season. The Takhlakh Meadow Loop Trail provides a 1.5-mile hike, a barrier-free trail.

Location: On Takhlakh Lake in Gifford Pinchot National Forest; see Mount Rainier and the Columbia River Gorge, map 2, grid f4.

Campsites, facilities: There are 54 sites for tents, trailers, or RVs up to 21 feet long. Drinking water and picnic tables are provided. Vault toilets are available. Firewood may be gathered outside the campground area. Boat-launching facilities are available in the day-use area, but all gasoline motors are prohibited on the lake. Some facilities are wheelchair-accessible. Leashed pets are permitted.

Reservations, fees: Reservations accepted; phone 877/444-6777 or access the website: www.reserveusa.com ($8.65 reservation fee). Sites are $11 to $13 per night, $5 for each additional vehicle. Senior discount available. Open mid-June to late September.

Directions: From Chehalis, drive south on I-5 for 10 miles to Exit 68 and U.S. 12. Turn east on U.S. 12 and drive 48 miles to Randle and U.S. 131. Turn south and drive one mile to Forest Road 23. Turn left (southeast) and drive 29 miles to Forest Road 2329. Turn left (northeast) and drive 1.5 miles to the campground entrance road on the right.

Contact: Gifford Pinchot National Forest, Cowlitz Valley Ranger District, P.O. Box 670, Randle, WA 98377-0670; 360/497-1100, fax 360/497-1102.

73 Cat Creek

 5

This small, rustic camp is set along Cat Creek at its confluence with the Cispus River about

10 miles from the summit of Mount Adams. It gets a lot of all-terrain vehicle (ATV) use. It is a forested setting. A trail starts less than one mile from camp and leads up along Blue Lake Ridge to Blue Lake. See trip notes for Adams Fork camp. Obtaining a U.S. Forest Service map is advised.

Location: On Cat Creek and the Cispus River in Gifford Pinchot National Forest; see Mount Rainier and the Columbia River Gorge, map 2, grid f4.

Campsites, facilities: There are five sites for tents, trailers, or RVs up to 15 feet long. Picnic tables and fire grills are provided. Pit toilets and firewood are available, but there is no drinking water. Garbage must be packed out. Firewood may be gathered outside the campground area. Leashed pets are permitted.

Reservations, fees: Northwest Forest Pass ($30 annual fee) or $5 daily fee per parked vehicle is required. Open mid-May to late October.

Directions: On I-5, drive to Exit 68 (south of Chehalis) and U.S. 12. Turn east on U.S. 12 and drive 48 miles to Randle and U.S. 131. Turn right (south) and drive one mile to Forest Road 23. Turn left (southeast) and drive 18 miles to Forest Road 21. Turn left (southeast) on Forest Road 21 and drive six miles to the campground.

Contact: Gifford Pinchot National Forest, Cowlitz Valley Ranger District, P.O. Box 670, Randle, WA 98377; 360/497-1100, fax 360/497-1102.

74 Horseshoe Lake

 9

This camp is set on the shore of picturesque Horseshoe Lake, a 10-acre lake. The campsites are poorly defined, more like camping areas, with some close to the lake. A trail

runs partway around the lake and is open to mountain bikes and horse riders (which occasionally come from another nearby camp). Fishing is just fair in the lake for trout, which is stocked infrequently. The water is too cold for most visitors to want to swim in. A trail from the camp goes up to nearby Green Mountain (elevation 5,000 feet), about a three-mile round-trip. This is a multiuse trail, but it can tie into the High Lakes Trail system. Another trail heads up the north flank of Mount Adams. See a U.S. Forest Service map for details. Berry picking is an option in the late summer months.

Location: On Horseshoe Lake in Gifford Pinchot National Forest; see Mount Rainier and the Columbia River Gorge, map 2, grid f4.

Campsites, facilities: There are 11 sites for tents, trailers, or RVs up to 16 feet long. Picnic tables are provided. Vault toilets are available, but there is no drinking water. Firewood may be gathered outside the campground area. Primitive launching facilities are located on the lake, but all gasoline motors are prohibited on the water. Leashed pets are permitted.

Reservations, fees: Northwest Forest Pass ($30 annual fee) or $5 daily fee per parked vehicle is required. Open mid-June to late September.

Directions: From Chehalis, drive south on I-5 for 10 miles to Exit 68 and U.S. 12. Turn east on U.S. 12 and drive 48 miles to Randle and U.S. 131. Turn south and drive one mile to Forest Road 23. Turn left (southeast) and drive 29 miles to Forest Road 2329. Turn left (northeast) and drive seven miles (bearing right at the junction with Forest Road 5601) to Forest Road 078 (bearing right at the junction with Forest Road 5601). Turn left on Forest Road 078 and drive 1.5 miles to the campground on the left.

Contact: Gifford Pinchot National Forest, Cowlitz Valley Ranger District, P.O. Box 670, Randle, WA 98377-0670; 360/497-1100, fax 360/497-1102.

75 Keene's Horse Camp

 7

This camp is for equestrians only. It is set at 4,200 feet along the South Fork of Spring Creek on the northwest flank of Mount Adams (elevation 12,276 feet). The Pacific Crest Trail passes within a couple miles of the camp. Several trails lead from here into the backcountry and to several alpine meadows. The meadows are fragile, so walk along their outer edges. See notes for Walupt Horse Camp. In summer 2002, a portion of campground was moved out of a riparian area.

Location: On the South Fork of Spring Creek in Gifford Pinchot National Forest; see Mount Rainier and the Columbia River Gorge, map 2, grid f4.

Campsites, facilities: There are 12 sites in two areas for tents, trailers, or RVs up to 21 feet long. Picnic tables and fire grills are provided. Pit toilets, water troughs, a mounting ramp, corrals, manure bins, and hitching facilities (high lines) are available, but there is no drinking water. Some facilities are wheelchair-accessible. Firewood may be gathered outside the campground area. Leashed pets are permitted.

Reservations, fees: Northwest Forest Pass ($30 annual fee) or $5 daily fee per parked vehicle is required. Open July to late September.

Directions: On I-5, drive to Exit 68 (south of Chehalis) and U.S. 12. Turn east on U.S. 12 and drive 48 miles to Randle and U.S. 131. Turn right (south) and drive one mile to Forest Road 23. Turn left (southeast) and drive 18 miles to Forest Road 21. Turn left (southeast) on Forest Road 21 and drive five miles to Forest Road 56. Turn right on Forest Road 56 and drive five miles to Forest Road 5603. Turn right and drive five miles to Forest Road 2329. Turn right and drive two miles to the camp on the right.

Contact: Gifford Pinchot National Forest, Cowlitz Valley Ranger District, P.O. Box 670, Randle, WA 98377-0670; 360/497-1100, fax 360/497-1102.

76 Killen Creek

     7

This wilderness trailhead camp is ideal as a launch point for backpackers. The campground set along Killen Creek at the foot of Mount Adams (elevation 12,276 feet) marks the start of a three-mile trail that leads up the mountain and connects with the Pacific Crest Trail. It's worth the effort. The Killen Trail goes up to secondary ridges and shoulders of Mount Adams for stunning views. Berry picking is another summertime option.

Location: Near Mount Adams in Gifford Pinchot National Forest; see Mount Rainier and the Columbia River Gorge, map 2, grid f4.

Campsites, facilities: There are eight sites for tents, trailers, or RVs up to 21 feet long. Picnic tables and fire are provided. Pit toilets are available, but there is no drinking water. Garbage must be packed out. Firewood may be gathered outside the campground area. Leashed pets are permitted.

Reservations, fees: Northwest Forest Pass ($30 annual fee) or $5 daily fee per parked vehicle is required. Open July to late September.

Directions: On I-5, drive to Exit 68 (south of Chehalis) and U.S. 12. Turn east on U.S. 12 and drive 48 miles to Randle and U.S. 131. Turn right (south) and drive one mile to Forest Road 23. Turn left (southeast) and drive 29 miles to Forest Road 2329. Turn left (northeast) and drive six miles to Forest Road 073. Turn left (west) and drive 200 yards to the campground.

Contact: Gifford Pinchot National Forest, Cowlitz Valley Ranger District, P.O. Box 670, Randle, WA 98377-0670; 360/497-1100, fax 360/497-1102.

77 Clover Flats

    8

This campground is in the subalpine zone on the slope of Darland Mountain, which peaks at 6,982 feet. Trails connect the area with the Goat Rocks Wilderness, six miles to the west. Contact the Department of Natural Resources or Wenatchee National Forest for details. See the description of Ahtanum Camp for information on winter snowmobiling.

Location: Near the Goat Rocks Wilderness; see Mount Rainier and the Columbia River Gorge, map 2, grid e7.

Campsites, facilities: There are nine campsites for tents or small trailers. Picnic tables, fire grills, and tent pads are provided. Pit toilets and drinking water are available. Garbage must be packed out. Leashed pets are permitted.

Reservations, fees: No reservations; no fee. Open year-round, weather permitting (heavy snows are generally expected from mid-November through early April).

Directions: From Yakima, drive south on I-82 for two miles to Union Gap and Ahtanum Road. Turn right (west) and drive 20 miles to Tampico and Road A-3000 (North Fork Road). Turn right (west) and drive 9.5 miles to the Ahtaman Camp. Continue to a junction with A-2000 (Middle Fork Road). Bear left and drive nine miles to the camp on the left. Note: The last few miles of Road A-2000 are very steep, with a 12 percent grade. High-clearance vehicles only are recommended.

Contact: Department of Natural Resources, Southeast Region, 713 Bowers Road, Ellensburg, WA 98926-9301; 509/925-8510, fax 509/925-8522.

78 Tree Phones

     7

This forested campground is set along the Middle Fork of Ahtanum Creek, an elevation of 4,800 feet. It is close to hiking, motorbiking, and horseback-riding trails. A shelter with a wood stove is available year-round for picnics. During summer, there are beautiful wildflower displays. See the description of Ahtanum Camp for snowmobiling information.

Location: On the Middle Fork of Ahtanum Creek; see Mount Rainier and the Columbia River Gorge, map 2, grid e8.

Campsites, facilities: There are 14 campsites for tents or small trailers. Picnic tables, fire grills, and tent pads are provided. Drinking water and vault toilets are available. A 20-by-40-foot snow shelter and saddle-stock facilities are also available. Some facilities are wheelchair-accessible. Leashed pets are permitted.

Reservations, fees: No reservations; no fee. Open year-round, weather permitting (heavy snows are expected from late November through March).

Directions: From Yakima, drive south on I-82 for two miles to Union Gap and Ahtanum Road. Turn right (west) and drive 20 miles to Tampico and Road A-3000 (North Fork Road). Turn right (west) and drive 9.5 miles to the Ahtaman Camp. Continue to a junction with A-2000 (Middle Fork Road). Bear left and drive six miles to the camp. Note: High-clearance vehicles only are recommended.

Contact: Department of Natural Resources, Southeast Region, 713 Bowers Road, Ellensburg, WA 98926-9301; 509/925-8510, fax 509/925-8522.

79 Green River Horse Camp

  8

Got a horse? This is your spot. Don't have a horse. Pick some other camp. This camp is for equestrians only. It is set on the Green River near an area of beautiful, old-growth timber, but the campsites themselves are in a reforested clear-cut, with trees about 20 to 30 feet tall. There is access to great trails into the Mount St. Helens blast area. The lookout from Windy Ridge is one of the most drop-dead awesome views in North America of Spirit Lake, the blast zone, and the open crater of Mount St. Helens. The campsite features high lines at each site, and the access is designed for easy turning and parking with horse trailers.

Location: Near Green River in Gifford Pinchot National Forest; see Mount Rainier and the Columbia River Gorge, map 2, grid g1.

Campsites, facilities: There are eight sites for up to two trailer rigs or three vehicles each. Picnic tables, fire grills, and high lines are provided. Vault toilets are available. No drinking water is provided. Stock water facilities are available starting 2002; call for confirmation. Garbage must be packed out. Drinking water is available five miles north at Norway Pass Trailhead. Leashed pets are permitted.

Reservations, fees: Northwest Forest Pass ($30 annual fee) or $5 daily fee per parked vehicle is required. Open mid-May through November, weather permitting.

Directions: From Olympia, drive south on I-5 to Exit 68 and U.S. 12. Turn east on U.S. 12 and drive 48 miles to Randle and Highway 131. Turn right (south) and drive one mile (becomes Forest Road 25). Continue south and drive 19 miles to Forest Road 99. Turn right (west, toward Windy Ridge) and drive 8.5 miles to Forest Road 26. Turn right (north) and drive five miles to Forest Road 2612 (gravel). Turn left (west) and drive about two miles to the campground entrance on the left. Note: Due to past flooding events, Forest Road 26 has deteriorated. For the last seven miles, high-clearance, four-wheel-drive vehicles are recommended.

Contact: Gifford Pinchot National Forest, Mount St. Helens National Volcanic Monument, 42218 NE Yale Bridge Road, Amboy, WA 98601; 360/247-3900, fax 360/247-3901.

80 Lower Falls

 10

This camp is set in the primary viewing area for six major waterfalls on the Lewis River. The spectacular Lewis River Trail is available for hiking or horseback riding, and there is a wheelchair-accessible loop. Several other hiking trails in the area branch off along backcountry streams. The sites are paved and set among large fir trees on a gently sloping ground, with access roads designed for easy RV parking. Note that above the falls, the calm water in the river looks safe, but it is not! Stay out. In addition, the trail goes along cliffs, providing beautiful views but potentially dangerous hiking. The elevation is 1,400 feet.

Location: On the Lewis River in Gifford Pinchot National Forest; see Mount Rainier and the Columbia River Gorge, map 2, grid g2.

Campsites, facilities: There are 42 sites for tents, trailers, or RVs up to 35 feet long and two group sites for up to 20 people each. Picnic tables and fire grills are provided. Drinking water and composting toilets are available. Leashed pets are permitted.

Reservations, fees: Reserve at 877/444-6777 ($8.65 reservation fee) or website: www .reserveusa.com. Rates are $14 per night for single sites, $20 per night for double sites, $5 per extra vehicle per night. Senior discount available. Group site is $22 to $27 per night. Open May through September.

Directions: From Woodland on I-5, take Exit 21 for Highway 503. Drive east on Highway 503 for 23 miles to Highway 503 Spur. Drive north-

east on Highway 503 Spur for seven miles (becomes Forest Road 90). Continue east on Forest Road 90 for 21 miles to the campground (along the Lewis River) on the right.

Contact: Gifford Pinchot National Forest, Mount St. Helens National Volcanic Monument, 42218 NE Yale Bridge Road, Amboy, WA 98601-0369; 360/247-3900, fax 360/247-3901.

81 Lewis River Horse Camp

 7

During summer, this camp is reserved for equestrians only. The camp is not particularly scenic, but the area around it is. There are six waterfalls nearby on the Lewis River, for example. There are many trails, all of which are open to mountain bikers and some to motorcycles. The spectacular Lewis River Trail is available for hiking, mountain biking, or horseback riding, and there is a wheelchair-accessible loop. Several other hiking trails in the area branch off along backcountry streams. See a U.S. Forest Service map for details.

Location: Near the Lewis River and Quartz Creek in Gifford Pinchot National Forest; see Mount Rainier and the Columbia River Gorge, map 2, grid g2.

Campsites, facilities: There are nine sites for tents, trailers, or RVs. Picnic tables and fire rings are provided. A composting toilet is available. No drinking water is provided. Garbage must be packed out. Horse facilities include high lines, stock water, and three corrals. Leashed pets are permitted.

Reservations, fees: Northwest Forest Pass ($30 annual fee) or $5 daily fee per parked vehicle is required. Open May through November, weather permitting.

Directions: From Woodland on I-5, take Exit 21 for Highway 503. Drive east on Highway 503 and drive 23 miles to Highway 503 Spur. Drive northeast on Highway 503 Spur for seven miles (becomes Forest Road 90). Continue east on Forest Road 90 for 27 miles to Forest Road 93. Turn left and drive one mile to the campground (along the Lewis River) on the right.

Contact: Gifford Pinchot National Forest, Mount St. Helens National Volcanic Monument, 42218 NE Yale Bridge Road, Amboy, WA 98601-0369; 360/247-3900, fax 360/247-3901.

82 Tillicum & Saddle

 8

These are two pretty camps that are primitive but well forested and within walking distance of several recreation options. A trail from the Tillicum camp leads southwest past little Meadow Lake to Squaw Butte, then over to Big Creek, approximately 4.5 miles. It's a nice hike, as well as an excellent ride for mountain bikers. This is a premium area for picking huckleberries in August and early September. The Lone Butte area to the south is about five miles away and provides a side trip. Nearby Saddle camp, located one mile to the east, receives little use. There are two lakes nearby, Big and Little Mosquito Lakes, which are fed by Mosquito Creek. So, while we're on the subject, mosquito attacks in late spring and early summer can be like squadrons of World War II bombers moving in. The Pacific Crest Trail passes right by camp.

Location: Near Meadow Lake in Gifford Pinchot National Forest; see Mount Rainier and the Columbia River Gorge, map 2, grid g2.

Campsites, facilities: There are eight sites for tents only and 37 sites for tents, trailers, or RVs up to 18 feet long. Picnic tables and fire grills are provided. Drinking water, pit toilets, and firewood are available. Garbage must be packed out. Leashed pets are permitted.

Reservations, fees: No reservations. Northwest Forest Pass ($30 annual fee) or $5 daily

fee per parked vehicle is required. Open mid-June to late September.

Directions: From Vancouver (Washington) on I-205, take Highway 14 and drive east for 66 miles to Highway 141. Turn north on Highway 141 and drive 25 miles to Trout Lake and County Road 141 (Forest Road 24). Turn left (west) and drive two miles to a fork. Bear left at the fork and drive 20 miles (becomes Forest Road 24) to the campground on the left.

Contact: Gifford Pinchot National Forest, Mount St. Helens National Volcanic Monument, 42218 NE Yale Bridge Road, Amboy, WA 98601; 360/247-3900, fax 360/247-3901.

83 Morrison Creek

 7

Here's a prime yet little-known spot. It's located along Morrison Creek at an elevation of 4,600 feet near the southern slopes of Mount Adams (12,276 feet). Nearby trails will take you to the snowfields and alpine meadows of the Mount Adams Wilderness. In particular, the Shorthorn Trail is accessible from this campground.

Location: On Morrison Creek in Gifford Pinchot National Forest; see Mount Rainier and the Columbia River Gorge, map 2, grid g4.

Campsites, facilities: There are 12 tent sites. Picnic tables and fire rings are provided in some sites. Vault toilets are available, but there is no drinking water. Garbage must be packed out. Leashed pets are permitted.

Reservations, fees: Northwest Forest Pass ($30 annual fee) or $5 daily fee per parked vehicle is required. Open July to late September.

Directions: From Hood River, Oregon, drive north on Highway 35 (over the Columbia River) to Highway 14. Turn left and drive two miles to Highway 141. Turn right (north) on Highway 141 and drive 20 miles to County Road 17 (just 200 yards east of the town of

Trout Lake). Turn right (north) and drive two miles to Forest Road 80. Turn right (north) and drive 3.5 miles to Forest Road 8040. Bear left (north) and drive six miles to the campground on the left. The access road is rough and not recommended for trailers or RVs.

Contact: Gifford Pinchot National Forest, Mount Adams Ranger District, 2455 Highway 141, Trout Lake, WA 98650; 509/395-3400, fax 509/395-3424.

84 Island Camp

 8

This campground in a forested area along Bird Creek is close to lava tubes and blowholes. It's about a three-quarter-mile walk to see this strange slit in the ground, which is about one foot wide (too small to climb into and explore). Bird Creek provides a chance to fish for brook trout in late spring. In the winter, the roads are used for snowmobiling. A snowmobile shelter with a wood stove is available year-round for picnics. See the following description of Maryhill State Park for information on the nearby Klickitat Habitat Management Area.

Location: On Bird Creek; see Mount Rainier and the Columbia River Gorge, map 2, grid h5.

Campsites, facilities: There are six campsites for tents or small trailers. Picnic tables, fire grills, and tent pads are provided. Vault toilets are available, but there is no drinking water. Garbage must be packed out. Leashed pets are permitted.

Reservations, fees: No reservations; no fee. Open year-round.

Directions: From Yakima, drive south on I-82 for 15 miles to U.S. 97. Turn south and drive 49 miles to Goldendale and Highway 142. Turn right (west) and drive 10 miles to Counts Road. Turn right (northwest) and drive 26 miles to Glenwood, and continue for one quarter-mile to Bird Creek Road. Turn right

and drive 0.9 mile to K-3000 Road (still Bird Creek Road). Turn left, drive over the cattle guard, and drive 1.2 miles to Road S-4000. Turn right and drive 1.3 miles to Road K-4000. Turn left and drive 3.4 miles to Road K-4200. Turn left and drive 1.1 miles to the campground entrance on the left. Turn left and drive one quarter-mile to the campground.

Contact: Department of Natural Resources, Southeast Region, 713 Bowers Road, Ellensburg, WA 98926-9301; 509/925-8510, fax 509/925-8522.

85 Bird Creek

 7

This campground is set in a forested area of old-growth Douglas fir and Ponderosa pine along Bird Creek. It is one of two camps in the immediate area. (The other, also a primitive site, is Island Camp.) This spot lies just east of the Mount Adams Wilderness and is within three miles of Island Camp, where there are snowmobile trails. See the following description of Maryhill State Park for information on the nearby Klickitat Habitat Management Area.

Location: Near the Mount Adams Wilderness; see Mount Rainier and the Columbia River Gorge, map 2, grid h6.

Campsites, facilities: There are 12 campsites for tents or small trailers. Picnic tables, fire grills, and tent pads are provided. Pit and vault toilets are available, but there is no drinking water. Garbage must be packed out. Some facilities are wheelchair-accessible. Leashed pets are permitted.

Reservations, fees: No reservations; no fee. Open May to mid-October, weather permitting.

Directions: From Yakima, drive south on I-82 for 15 miles to U.S. 97. Turn south and drive 49 miles to Goldendale and Highway 142. Turn right (west) and drive 10 miles to Counts Road. Turn right (northwest) and drive 26 miles to Glenwood. From the post office in Glenwood, continue one quarter-mile to Bird Creek Road. Turn right and drive 0.9 mile. Turn left (still Bird Creek Road), cross the cattle guard to Road K-3000, and drive 1.2 miles to Road S-4000 (gravel). Turn right and drive 1.3 miles to Road K-4000. Turn left and drive two miles to the campground on the left.

Contact: Department of Natural Resources, Southeast Region, 713 Bowers Road, Ellensburg, WA 98926-9301; 509/925-8510, fax 509/925-8522.

86 Camp Kalama RV and Campground

  6

This option to Louis Rasmussen RV Park has a more rustic setting, with open and wooded areas and some accommodations for tent campers. It's set along the Kalama River, where salmon and steelhead fishing is popular. A full-service marina is nearby.

Location: On the Kalama River; see Mount Rainier and the Columbia River Gorge, map 3, grid a2.

Campsites, facilities: There are 118 sites with full or partial hookups, including drive-through, for trailers or RVs of any length, and 50 tent sites. Picnic tables are provided. Restrooms, drinking water, flush toilets, coin-operated showers, fire pits, cable TV, bottled gas, a dump station, a store, a café, a beauty shop, a banquet room, firewood, a coin-operated laundry, ice, boat-launching facilities, a beach area, and a playground are available. Some facilities are wheelchair-accessible. Leashed pets are permitted.

Reservations, fees: Reservations accepted. Sites are $16 to $25.50, $1.50 per person per night for more than two adults, $1 pet

fee. Senior discount available. Major credit cards accepted. Open year-round.

Directions: From near Kalama (between Kelso and Woodland) on I-5, take Exit 32 and drive south on the frontage road for one block to the campground.

Contact: Camp Kalama RV and Campground, 5055 North Meeker Drive, Kalama, WA 98625; 360/673-2456 or 800/750-2456, fax 360/673-2324.

87 Woodland

 7

This is an optimum spot for people who are touring Washington on I-5 but want a quiet setting along the way. The campground is nestled in an area of evergreen and deciduous trees (maple and red alder), so it's private. It is about three miles off the highway. A popular side trip is a visit to the Hulda Klager Lilac Gardens in Woodland a few miles away, which is best visited in spring when the lilacs are blooming.

Location: Near Woodland; see Mount Rainier and the Columbia River Gorge, map 3, grid a3.

Campsites, facilities: There are 10 sites for tents or small trailers. Picnic tables, fire grills, and tent pads are provided. Vault toilets, drinking water, horseshoe pits, volleyball and basketball courts, and a playground are available. Some facilities are wheelchair-accessible. Leashed pets are permitted.

Reservations, fees: No reservations; no fee. Open May to September.

Directions: From Woodland on I-5, take Exit 21 and drive east for 100 yards to East CC Street. Turn right and drive across the Lewis River to just south of the bridge to County Road 1. Turn right on County Road 1 and drive one quarter-mile to 389th Street. Turn left on 389th Street and drive 2.5 miles to the campground on the left.

Contact: Department of Natural Resources, Southwest Region, P.O. Box 280, Castle Rock, WA 98611-0280; 360/577-2025 or 360/274-4196.

88 Lewis River RV Park

    7

This park is set along the Lewis River. Fishing can be good in season. It's a pleasant camp, with a choice of paved or grassy shaded sites. An 18-hole golf course is nearby.

Location: On the Lewis River; see Mount Rainier and the Columbia River Gorge, map 3, grid a3.

Campsites, facilities: There are 90 sites with full or partial hookups, including 30 long-term rentals, two drive-through, for tents, trailers, or RVs of any length. Picnic tables are provided. Restrooms, drinking water, flush toilets, showers, fire rings, firewood, a dump station, a store, a coin-operated laundry, ice, and a swimming pool are available. Boat-launching facilities are nearby on the Lewis River. Leashed pets are permitted.

Reservations, fees: No reservations. Sites are $16 to $20 per night. Major credit cards accepted. Open year-round.

Directions: In Woodland on I-5, take Exit 21 for Highway 503. Drive east on Highway 503 (Lewis River Road) for four miles to the park on the right.

Contact: Lewis River RV Park, 3125 Lewis River Road, Woodland, WA 98674; 360/225-9556.

89 Paradise Point State Park

 8

This park is named for the serenity that once blessed this area. It has lost much of that peacefulness since the freeway went in next to the park. To reduce traffic noise, stay at one of the wooded sites at the small apple orchard. The sites in the grassy areas have little noise buffer. This park covers 88 acres and features 1,680 feet of river frontage. There is a two-mile hiking trail that is good for families and children. Note that the boat ramp is dirt, primitive, nonfunctional when the water level drops, and recommended for car-top boats only. Fishing on the East Fork of the Lewis River is a bonus.

Location: On the East Fork of the Lewis River; see Mount Rainier and the Columbia River Gorge, map 3, grid b3.

Campsites, facilities: There are nine primitive tent sites and 70 sites for tents or self-contained RVs up to 40 feet long. Picnic tables and fire grills are provided. Restrooms, drinking water, flush toilets, showers, a dump station, firewood, an amphitheater, and summer interpretive programs are available. A primitive, dirt boat-launching area is located nearby on the East Fork of the Lewis River. Leashed pets are permitted.

Reservations, fees: Reserve at 888/CAMP-OUT (888/226-7688); website: www.parks.wa .gov/reservations ($7 reservation fee). Sites are $6 to $14, $6 per extra vehicle per night. Major credit cards accepted. Open mid-May through September.

Directions: From Vancouver (Washington), drive north on I-5 for 15 miles to Exit 16 (La Center/Paradise Point State Park exit). Take that exit and turn right, then almost immediately at Paradise Park Road, turn left and drive one mile to the park.

Contact: Paradise Point State Park, 360/263-2350; State Park information, 360/902-8844.

90 Big Fir Campground and RV Park

 6

This campground is in a heavily wooded, rural area not far from Paradise Point State Park. It's nestled among hills with shaded gravel sites and wild berries. See the previous description of Paradise Point State Park for details on the area.

Location: Near Paradise Point State Park; see Mount Rainier and the Columbia River Gorge, map 3, grid b3.

Campsites, facilities: There are 37 sites with full hookups, including three drive-through, for trailers or RVs of any length, and 33 tent sites. Picnic tables are provided. Restrooms, drinking water, flush toilets, coin-operated showers, volleyball, croquet, a horseshoe pit, board games, a store, and ice are available. Boat-launching facilities are located within 1.5 miles. Leashed pets are permitted.

Reservations, fees: Reservations accepted. Sites are $14 to $20 per night. Major credit cards accepted. Open year-round.

Directions: From Vancouver (Washington), drive north on I-5 to Exit 14 (Ridgefield exit). Take that exit to Highway 269. Drive east on Highway 269 (the road changes names several times) for two miles to 10th Avenue. Turn right and drive to the first intersection at 259th Street. Turn left and drive two miles to the park on the right (route is well marked).

Contact: Big Fir Campground and RV Park, 5515 NE 259th Street, Ridgefield, WA 98642; 360/887-8970 or 800/532-4397.

91 Battle Ground Lake State Park

  8

The centerpiece for this state park is Battle Ground Lake, a spring-fed lake that is stocked with trout and provides a popular fishing lake for bass and catfish as well. The lake is of volcanic origin, fed by water from underground lava tubes, and is considered a smaller version of Crater Lake in Oregon. The park covers 280 acres, primarily conifers,

in the foothills of the Cascade Mountains. There are 10 miles of trails for hiking and biking, including a trail around the lake, and five miles of trails for horses; a primitive equestrian camp is also available. The lake is good for swimming and fishing, and it has a nice beach area; no motorized boats are allowed. If you're traveling on I-5 and looking for a layover, this camp 15 minutes from the highway is ideal. In July and August, there are several local fairs and celebrations. Like many of the easy-access state parks on I-5, it fills up quickly on weekends. The average annual rainfall is 35 inches.

Location: On Battle Ground Lake; see Mount Rainier and the Columbia River Gorge, map 3, grid b5.

Campsites, facilities: There are 35 sites for tents, trailers, or self-contained RVs up to 50 feet long and 15 primitive tent sites. Picnic tables and fire grills are provided. Restrooms, drinking water, flush toilets, showers, a dump station, a store, firewood, a restaurant, a sheltered picnic area, an amphitheater, summer interpretive programs, a playground with horseshoe pits, and an athletic field are available. Some facilities are wheelchair-accessible. Boat-launching facilities and rentals are nearby. Leashed pets are permitted.

Reservations, fees: Reserve at 888/CAMP-OUT (888/226-7688); website: www.parks.wa.gov/reservations ($7 reservation fee). Sites are $6 to $15 per night. Major credit cards accepted. Senior discount available. Open year-round.

Directions from I-5 southbound: On I-5, take Exit 14 and drive (well marked) to the city of Battle Ground and continue to the east end of town to Grace Avenue. Turn left and drive three miles (a marked route) to the park.

Directions from I-5 northbound: On I-5, take Exit 9 and drive (well marked) to the city of Battle Ground and continue to the east end of town to Grace Avenue. Turn left and drive three miles (a marked route) to the park.

Contact: Battle Ground Lake State Park, 360/687-4621; State Park information, 360/902-8844.

92 Sunset

 9

This campground is located at an elevation of 1,000 feet along the East Fork of the Lewis River. Fishing, hiking, huckleberry picking, and mushroom hunting are some of the favored pursuits of visitors. Scenic Sunset Falls is located just upstream of the campground. A barrier-free viewing trail leads to an overlook.

Location: On the East Fork of the Lewis River in Gifford Pinchot National Forest; see Mount Rainier and the Columbia River Gorge, map 3, grid b6.

Campsites, facilities: There are 10 sites for tents, trailers, or RVs up to 22 feet long and six walk-in sites. Picnic tables and fire grills are provided. Drinking water (well water) and vault toilets are available. Leashed pets are permitted.

Reservations, fees: No reservations. Sites are $13 per night, $5 per extra vehicle per night. Open year-round.

Directions: From Vancouver (Washington), drive north on I-5 about seven miles to County Road 502. Turn east on Highway 502 and drive six miles to Highway 503. Turn left and drive north for five miles to Lucia Falls Road. Turn right and drive eight miles to Moulton Falls and Old County Road 12. Turn right on Old County Road 12 and drive seven miles to the Forest Boundary and the campground entrance on the right.

Contact: Gifford Pinchot National Forest, Mount St. Helens National Volcanic Monument,

42218 NE Yale Bridge Road, Amboy, WA 98601; 360/247-3900, fax 360/247-3901.

93 Cold Creek

 6

First, don't expect to find a "cold creek" here. There just is no such thing. And second, the directions are complicated. Hey, Waylon Jennings once told me that few things worth remembering come easy, right? Well, sometimes. This campground is set in a forested area, with plenty of trails nearby for hiking and horseback riding. The camp gets minimal use. A large shelter is available at the day-use area. This camp was closed in 2000 and 2001, and the Department of Natural Resources hopes to have it reopened in 2002.

Location: On Cedar Creek; see Mount Rainier and the Columbia River Gorge, map 3, grid c5.

Campsites, facilities: There are six campsites for tents or small trailers. Picnic tables, fire grills, and tent pads are provided. Vault toilets are available. No drinking water is provided. Some facilities are wheelchair-accessible. Leashed pets are permitted.

Reservations, fees: No reservations; no fee. Open May through September.

Directions: From Vancouver (Washington), drive north on I-5 to Exit 9 and NE 179th Street. Turn east and drive 5.5 miles to Highway 503. Turn right and drive 1.5 miles to NE 159th Street. Turn left on NE 159th Street and drive three miles to 182nd Avenue. Turn right and drive one mile to NE 139th (Road L-1400). Turn left and drive eight miles to Road L-1000. Turn left and drive three miles. Turn left at the campground entrance road and drive one mile to the camp.

Contact: Department of Natural Resources, Southwest Region, P.O. Box 280, Castle Rock, WA 98611-0280; 360/577-2025 or 360/274-4196.

Rock Creek Campground and Horse Camp

 6

This camp is located in a wooded area along Rock Creek. The camp is popular among equestrians, especially on weekends, because of the Tarbell Trail, a 25-mile loop trail that is accessible from the campground and goes to the top of Larch Mountain.

Location: On Rock Creek; see Mount Rainier and the Columbia River Gorge, map 3, grid c5.

Campsites, facilities: There are 19 campsites for tents or small trailers. Picnic tables, fire grills, and tent pads are provided. Vault toilets, drinking water, a horse-loading ramp, and corrals are available. Some facilities are wheelchair-accessible. There is a campground host on site. Leashed pets are permitted.

Reservations, fees: No reservations; no fee. Open year-round, weather permitting.

Directions: From Vancouver (Washington), drive on I-5 to Exit 9 and NE 179th Street. Turn east and drive 5.5 miles to Highway 503. Turn right and drive 1.5 miles to NE 159th Street. Turn left on NE 159th Street and drive three miles to 182nd Avenue. Turn right and drive one mile to NE 139th (Road L-1400). Turn left and drive eight miles to Road L-1000. Turn left and drive 3.5 miles (passing Cold Creek Campground after three miles) to Road L-1200. Turn left and drive 200 yards to the campground on your right.

Contact: Department of Natural Resources, Southwest Region, P.O. Box 280, Castle Rock, WA 98611-0280; 360/577-2025 or 360/274-4196.

Dougan Creek

 7

This campground is small and remote, located on Dougan Creek where it empties into the Washougal River. The camp is heavily forested with second-growth Douglas fir and has pretty sites with riverviews.

Location: Near the Washougal River; see Mount Rainier and the Columbia River Gorge, map 3, grid c7.

Campsites, facilities: There are seven campsites for tents or small trailers. Picnic tables, fire grills, and tent pads are provided. Vault toilets are available. No drinking water is provided. Some facilities are wheelchair-accessible. Leashed pets are permitted.

Reservations, fees: No reservations; no fee. Open mid-May to mid-September.

Directions: From Vancouver (Washington) on I-205, take Highway 14 and drive east for 20 miles to Highway 140. Turn north on Highway 140 and drive five miles to Washougal River Road. Turn right on Washougal River Road and drive about seven miles until you come to the end of the pavement and pass the picnic area on the left. The campground is just beyond the picnic area.

Contact: Department of Natural Resources, Southwest Region, P.O. Box 280, Castle Rock, WA 98611-0280; 360/577-2025 or 360/274-4196.

Beacon Rock Resort

 7

This trailer park is set along the Columbia River, a short distance from Beacon Rock State Park. See the following description of the state park for details. Nearby recreation options include a nine-hole golf course four miles away and two 18-hole golf courses, 8 and 12 miles away, respectively.

Location: On the Columbia River; see Mount Rainier and the Columbia River Gorge, map 3, grid d8.

Campsites, facilities: There are 20 sites with full hookups, including three drive-through, for trailers or RVs up to 45 feet, and a grassy area for tents. Picnic tables and fire rings are provided. Restrooms, drinking water, flush toilets, coin-operated showers, bottled gas, firewood, a store, a recreation hall, a coin-operated laundry, and ice are available. Boat-launching facilities are located within one quarter-mile on the Columbia River. Leashed pets are permitted.

Reservations, fees: Reservations accepted with a deposit. Sites are $12 to $17 per night, $2 per person per night for more than two people. Open year-round.

Directions: From Vancouver (Washington) on I-205, take Highway 14 and drive east for 27 miles to Skamania. Look for the park along Highway 14 on the right at the corner of Moorage Road.

Contact: Beacon Rock Resort, 62 Moorage Road, Skamania, WA 98648; 509/427-8473.

97 Beacon Rock State Park

 8

This state park is highlighted by Beacon Rock, the second largest monolith in the world, which overlooks the Columbia River Gorge. The park is located in the heart of the Columbia River Gorge National Scenic Area. The Beacon Rock Summit Trail, a 1.8-mile round-trip hike, provides panoramic views of the gorge. The rock is also excellent for rock climbing, with the climbing season running from mid-July to January. Beacon Rock was originally named by Lewis and Clark on their expedition to the Pacific Ocean in 1805. The park covers nearly 5,000 acres and includes 9,500 feet of shoreline along the Columbia River and more then 20 miles of nearby roads open for hiking, mountain biking, and horseback riding. An eight-mile loop trail to Hamilton Mountain (2,300 feet) is one of the best hikes, featuring even better views than from Beacon Rock. Fishing is available on the Lower Columbia river below Bonneville Dam for sturgeon, salmon, steelhead, smallmouth bass (often excellent), and walleye in season; check regulations.

Location: On the Columbia River; see Mount Rainier and the Columbia River Gorge, map 3, grid c8.

Campsites, facilities: There are 25 developed sites for tents or self-contained RVs up to 40 feet long, one hike-in/bike-in site, and one group site for up to 200 people. Picnic tables and fire grills are provided. Restrooms, drinking water, flush toilets, coin-operated showers, a picnic area with kitchen shelter and electricity, and a playground are available. Some facilities are wheelchair-accessible. Boat docks and launching facilities are on site. Leashed pets are permitted.

Reservations, fees: No reservations for family sites. Reservations required for group camp. Reserve at 888/CAMP-OUT (888/226-7688); website: www.parks.wa.gov/reservations ($25 reservation fee). Family sites are $6 to $16 per night, $5 launch fee, $10 to $16 for boat mooring. Senior discount available. Group site requires $25 reservation fee plus $2 per person with a 20-person minimum. Open April to October.

Directions: From Vancouver (Washington) on I-205, take Highway 14 and drive east for 35 miles. The park straddles the highway; follow the signs to the campground.

Contact: Beacon Rock State Park, 34841 State Route 14, Skamania, WA 98648; 509/427-8265; State Park information, 360/902-8844.

98 Cultus Creek

      7

This camp is set at an elevation of 4,000 feet along Cultus Creek, on the edge of the Indian Heaven Wilderness. This camp is close to trails that will take you into the backcountry, which has numerous small meadows and lakes among the old-growth stands of fir and pines. Horse trails are available as well. It is about a two-mile climb to access the Pacific Crest Trail. This camp is popular during the fall huckleberry season, when picking is good here, but gets light use the rest of the year. The sites are graveled and level, situated amid gentle terrain.

Location: Near the Indian Heaven Wilderness in Gifford Pinchot National Forest; see Mount Rainier and the Columbia River Gorge, map 4, grid a2.

Campsites, facilities: There are 43 sites for tents, trailers, or RVs up to 32 feet long. Picnic tables and fire grills are provided. Drinking water, vault toilets, and firewood are available. Garbage must be packed out. Some facilities are wheelchair-accessible. Leashed pets are permitted.

Reservations, fees: No reservations. Northwest Forest Pass ($30 annual fee) or $5 daily fee per parked vehicle is required. Open June through September.

Directions: From Vancouver (Washington) on I-205, take Highway 14 east and drive 66 miles to State Route 141. Turn north on State Route 141 and drive 28 miles (becomes Forest Road 24) and continue two miles to a junction. Turn right (staying on Forest Road 24) and drive 13.5 miles to the campground.

Contact: Gifford Pinchot National Forest, Mount Adams Ranger District, 2455 Highway 141, Trout Lake, WA 98650; 509/395-3400, fax 509/395-3424.

99 Smokey Creek

  7

This primitive, little-used campground is set in an area of old-growth Douglas fir along Smokey Creek. A trail leading into the Indian Heaven Wilderness passes near the camp. Berry picking can be good here in summer

and early fall. The elevation is 3,700 feet. See the description of Tillicum and Saddle, Walupt Horse Camp, and Morrison Creek for details on more recreation options in the immediate area.

Location: Near the Indian Heaven Wilderness in Gifford Pinchot National Forest; see Mount Rainier and the Columbia River Gorge, map 4, grid a2.

Campsites, facilities: There are three sites for trailers or RVs up to 22 feet long. Picnic tables and fire rings are provided. Pit toilets are available, but there is no drinking water. Garbage must be packed out. Leashed pets are permitted.

Reservations, fees: No reservations. Northwest Forest Pass ($30 annual fee) or $5 daily fee per parked vehicle is required. Open late June to late September.

Directions: From Vancouver (Washington) on I-205, take Highway 14 east and drive 66 miles to State Route 141. Turn north on State Route 141 and drive 28 miles (becomes Forest Road 24) and continue two miles to a junction. Turn right (staying on Forest Road 24) and drive seven miles to the campground.

Contact: Gifford Pinchot National Forest, Mount Adams Ranger District, 2455 Highway 141, Trout Lake, WA 98650; 509/395-3400, fax 509/395-3424.

100 Little Goose & Little Goose Horse Camp

 5

This campground is near Little Goose Creek (located between Smokey and Cultus campgrounds). Huckleberry picking is quite good in August and early September. It's close to the road and sometimes dusty. Note that the access road is paved but is rough and not recommended for RVs or trailers. Campers with horse trailers must drive slowly.

This camp has sites ranging from good to poor and is lightly used in fall. Several trails are available leading out from the campground. The elevation is 4,000 feet. See the description of Tillicum and Saddle, Walupt Horse Camp, and Morrison Creek camps for more details of the area.

Location: On Little Goose Creek in Gifford Pinchot National Forest; see Mount Rainier and the Columbia River Gorge, map 4, grid a3.

Campsites, facilities: There are 10 sites for tents, trailers, or RVs up to 18 feet long and one site for campers with stock animals. Picnic tables and fire grills are provided. Pit toilets are available. No drinking water is available. Garbage must be packed out. Leashed pets are permitted.

Reservations, fees: No reservations. Northwest Forest Pass ($30 annual fee) or $5 daily fee per parked vehicle is required. Open June to late September.

Directions: From Vancouver (Washington) on I-205, take Highway 14 east and drive 66 miles to State Route 141. Turn north on State Route 141 and drive 28 miles (becomes Forest Road 24) and continue two miles to a junction. Turn right (staying on Forest Road 24) and drive eight miles (one mile past Smokey Creek) to the campground.

Contact: Gifford Pinchot National Forest, Mount Adams Ranger District, 2455 Highway 141, Trout Lake, WA 98650; 509/395-3400, fax 509/395-3424.

Trout Lake Creek

 7

This spot is a popular base camp for folks fishing at Trout Lake (five miles away). Many will fish at the lake during the day, where fishing is good for stocked rainbow trout, then return to this camp for the night. Some bonus brook trout are occasionally caught at Trout Lake. The camp is set along a creek in a forest of Douglas fir. In season, berry picking can be good here.

Location: On Trout Lake Creek in Gifford Pinchot National Forest; see Mount Rainier and the Columbia River Gorge, map 4, grid a3.

Campsites, facilities: There are 17 sites for tents, trailers, or RVs up to 32 feet long. Picnic tables and fire rings are provided. Pits toilets are available. Garbage must be packed out. Leashed pets are permitted.

Reservations, fees: Northwest Forest Pass ($30 annual fee) or $5 daily fee per parked vehicle is required. Senior discount available. Open May through September.

Directions: From Hood River, Oregon, drive north on Highway 35 (over the Columbia River) to Highway 14. Turn left and drive two miles to Highway 141. Turn right (north) on Highway 141 and drive 25 miles north to Forest Road 88. Turn right and drive four miles to Forest Road 8810. Turn right and drive 1.5 miles to Forest Road 8810-010. Turn right and drive one quarter-mile to the campground on the right.

Contact: Gifford Pinchot National Forest, Mount Adams Ranger District, 2455 Highway 141, Trout Lake, WA 98650; 509/395-3400, fax 509/395-3424.

 Peterson Prairie & Peterson Prairie Group

 8

Here's a good base camp if you want to have a short ride to town as well as access to the nearby wilderness areas. This is a prime spot for huckleberry picking in the fall. A trail from the camp leads about one mile to nearby ice caves; a stairway into the caves provides access to see a variety of ice formations. A sno-park in the area is open for winter recreation, with snowmobiling and cross-country skiing trails. The elevation is 2,800 feet.

Location: Near the town of Trout Lake in Gifford Pinchot National Forest; see Mount Rainier and the Columbia River Gorge, map 4, grid a3.

Campsites, facilities: There are 23 sites for tents, trailers, or RVs up to 32 feet long, one group site for up to 50 people, and one historic cabin. Picnic tables and fire grills are provided. Drinking water, vault toilets, and firewood are available. A camp host is available in summer. Some facilities are wheelchair-accessible. Leashed pets are permitted.

Reservations, fees: Reservations required for the group site only; phone 877/444-6777 or access the website: www.reserveusa.com ($8.65 reservation fee). Rates are $13 to $26 per night for individual sites and double sites, $5 per extra vehicle per night; $29 per night for the group site. Senior discount available. Open May to late September.

Directions: From Hood River, Oregon, drive north on Highway 35 (over the Columbia River) to Highway 14. Turn left and drive two miles to Highway 141. Turn right (north) on Highway 141 and drive 25.5 miles to Forest Road 24 (5.5 miles beyond and southwest of the town of Trout Lake). Bear right (west) and drive 2.5 miles to the campground on the left.

Contact: Gifford Pinchot National Forest, Mount Adams Ranger District, 2455 Highway 141, Trout Lake, WA 98650; 509/395-3400, fax 509/395-3424.

103 Paradise Creek

 9

This camp is located deep in Gifford Pinchot National Forest among old-growth woods, primarily Douglas fir, cedar, and western hemlock, at the confluence of Paradise Creek and the Wind River. Its gets light use despite easy access and easy RV parking. The campsites are well shaded. Lava Butte is a short distance from the camp and is accessible by trail, a 1.2-mile round-trip hike from the campground, providing a good view of the valley. Fishing is closed here. The elevation is 1,500 feet.

Location: On Paradise Creek and the Wind River in Gifford Pinchot National Forest; see Mount Rainier and the Columbia River Gorge, map 4, grid a1.

Campsites, facilities: There are 42 sites for tents, trailers, or RVs up to 25 feet long. Picnic tables and fire grills are provided. Drinking water and vault toilets are available. Some facilities are wheelchair-accessible. Leashed pets are permitted.

Reservations, fees: Reserve at 877/444-6777 ($8.65 reservation fee) or website: www.reserveusa.com. Sites are $9 to $18 per night, $5 per extra vehicle per night. Open mid-May to mid-November.

Directions: From Vancouver (Washington), take Highway 14 east and drive 50 miles to Carson and the Wind River Highway (County Road 30). Turn north on the Wind River Highway and drive 20 miles to the camp on the right.

Contact: Gifford Pinchot National Forest, Wind River Work Center, 1262 Hemlock Road, Carson, WA 98610; 509/427-3200, fax 509/427-3215.

104 Falls Creek Horse Camp

 5

This camp is at the threshold of a great launch point for hiking, horseback riding, and mountain biking. There are 90 miles of trail for horses and hiking and 40 miles for mountain bikes. The camp is set along the Race Track Trail adjacent to the western border of Indian Heaven Wilderness. A wilderness trailhead is available right at the camp. While this is a multiple-use campground, note that the sites are small and the turnaround is tight for RVs.

Location: Near the Pacific Crest Trail in Gifford Pinchot National Forest; see Mount Rainier and the Columbia River Gorge, map 4, grid a1.

Campsites, facilities: There are six sites for tents, small trailers, or RVs up to 15 feet long. Picnic tables and fire grills are provided. Pit toilets are available, but there is no drinking water. Garbage must be packed out. Leashed pets are permitted.

Reservations, fees: Northwest Forest Pass ($30 annual fee) or $5 daily fee per parked vehicle is required. Open mid-June to November.

Directions: From Vancouver (Washington) on I-205, take Highway 14 and drive east for 50 miles to Carson and the Wind River Highway (County Road 30). Turn north on the Wind River Highway and drive six miles to Forest Road 65. Turn left (north) and drive 15 miles to the campground on the left.

Contact: Gifford Pinchot National Forest, Wind River Work Center, 1262 Hemlock Road, Carson, WA 98610; 509/427-3200, fax 509/427-3215.

105 Crest Horse Camp

 6

This small, primitive, multiple-use camp is set near the Pacific Crest Trail, adjacent to the eastern boundary of the Indian Heaven Wilderness. It is an excellent jumping-off spot for wilderness treks with horses or other stock animals. This is a forested setting, primarily second-growth Douglas fir.

Location: Bordering Big Lava Bed in Gifford Pinchot National Forest; see Mount Rainier and the Columbia River Gorge, map 4, grid a2.

Campsites, facilities: There are three sites for tents, trailers, or RVs. Picnic tables and fire pits are provided. A vault toilet and high lines (for horses) are available. No drinking water is provided. Garbage must be packed out. Leashed pets are permitted.

Reservations, fees: No reservations. Northwest Forest Pass ($30 annual fee) or $5 daily fee per parked vehicle is required. Open mid-May to mid-November, weather permitting.

Directions: From Vancouver (Washington), take Highway 14 east and drive 50 miles to Carson and the Wind River Highway (County Road 30). Turn north and drive nine miles to Forest Road 6517. Turn right (east) on Forest Road 6517 and drive 1.5 miles to Forest Road 65. Turn left (north) on Forest Road 65 and drive about 10 miles to Forest Road 60. Turn right and drive two miles to the camp on the right.

Contact: Gifford Pinchot National Forest, Wind River Work Center, 1262 Hemlock Road, Carson, WA 98610; 509/427-3200, fax 509/427-3215.

106 Goose Lake

   9

This campground is set along the shore of beautiful Goose Lake at an elevation of 3,200 feet. It can be crowded in summer. Fishing for trout is available, as well as berry picking. The northern edge of Big Lava Bed is adjacent to the camp. While the lake is quite pretty, the camp itself is set well above the lake and is not as nice as the lake itself. A five-mph speed limit is enforced on the lake.

Location: On Goose Lake in Gifford Pinchot National Forest; see Mount Rainier and the Columbia River Gorge, map 4, grid a3.

Campsites, facilities: There are 25 tent sites and one site for trailers or RVs up to 18 feet long. Picnic tables and fire rings are provided. Vault toilets and firewood for sale are available, but there is no drinking water. A camp host is on site. A boat ramp is nearby. Leashed pets are permitted.

Reservations, fees: Reserve at 877/444-6777 ($8.65 reservation fee) or website: www.reserveusa.com. Sites are $13 to $15 per night, $5 per extra vehicle per night. Senior discount available. Open mid-June to mid-September.

Directions: From Vancouver (Washington) on I-205, take Highway 14 east and drive 46 miles to County Road 30/Wind River Road. Turn left and drive six miles to Panther Creek Road and Forest Road 65. Turn right and drive 10 miles to a four-way intersection called Four Corners. Turn right on Forest Road 60 and drive 10 miles to the campground on the left.

Contact: Gifford Pinchot National Forest, Mount Adams Ranger District, 2455 Highway 141, Trout Lake, WA 98650; 509/395-3400, fax 509/395-3424.

107 Beaver

 7

This is the closest campground north from Stevenson in the Columbia Gorge. It is set along the Wind River, with pretty, shaded sites. No fishing is permitted. The campsites are paved and a large grassy day-use area is nearby. Hiking highlights are two nearby trailheads. Two miles north is the trailhead for the Trapper Creek Wilderness, with 30 miles of trails, including a loop possibility. Three miles north is the Falls Creek Trail. The elevation is 1,100 feet.

Location: On the Wind River in Gifford Pinchot National Forest; see Mount Rainier and the Columbia River Gorge, map 4, grid b1.

Campsites, facilities: There are 26 sites for tents, trailers, or RVs up to 25 feet long and one group site for up to 40 campers. Picnic tables and fire grills are provided. Drinking water and pit toilets are available. Some facilities are wheelchair-accessible. Leashed pets permitted.

Reservations, fees: Reservations accepted for family sites and required for group site. Reserve at 877/444-6777 ($8.65 reservation fee) or website: www.reserveusa.com. Sites are $11 to $22 per night, $5 per extra vehicle per night. Senior discount available. The group site is $65 per night. Open mid-April to late September.

Directions: From Vancouver (Washington), take Highway 14 east and drive 50 miles to Carson and the Wind River Highway (County Road 80). Turn left (north) and drive 12 miles to the campground entrance (three miles past Stabler) on the left.

Contact: Gifford Pinchot National Forest, Wind River Work Center, 1262 Hemlock Road, Carson, WA 98610; 509/427-3200, fax 509/427-3215.

108 Panther Creek & Panther Creek Horse Camp

 8

This campground is set along Panther Creek in second-growth forest, with an old-growth forest adjacent to the campground. The forest is primarily Douglas fir, with some western hemlock. The sites are well-defined, and despite a paved road to the campground and easy parking and access, the campground gets light use. It is 3.5 miles from the Wind River, an option for those who enjoy fishing, hiking, and horseback riding. The Pacific Crest Trail is accessible from the adjacent Panther Creek Horse Camp. The elevation is 1,000 feet.

Location: On Panther Creek in Gifford Pinchot National Forest; see Mount Rainier and the Columbia River Gorge, map 4, grid b2.

Campsites, facilities: There are 33 sites for tents, trailers, or RVs up to 25 feet long, and at the adjacent horse camp, one equestrian site, with a stock loading ramp. Picnic tables

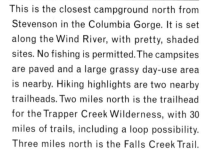

and fire rings are provided. Drinking water and pits toilets are available. Garbage must be packed out. Leashed pets are permitted.

Reservations, fees: Reserve at 877/444-6777 ($8.65 reservation fee) or website: www.reserveusa.com. Sites are $9 to $18 per night, $5 per extra vehicle per night. Senior discount available. Open mid-May to mid-September.

Directions: From Vancouver (Washington), take Highway 14 east and drive 50 miles to Carson and the Wind River Highway (County Road 30). Turn north and drive nine miles to Forest Road 6517 (just past Stabler). Turn right (east) on Forest Road 6517 and drive 1.5 miles to the campground entrance road on the right.

Contact: Gifford Pinchot National Forest, Wind River Work Center, 1262 Hemlock Road, Carson, WA 98610; 509/427-3200, fax 509/427-3215.

facilities are wheelchair-accessible. Leashed pets are permitted.

Reservations, fees: Reservations accepted; phone 877/444-6777 or access the website: www.reserveusa.com ($8.65 reservation fee). Sites are $11 per night, $5 for each additional vehicle. Senior discount available. Open mid-May to mid-September.

Directions: From Hood River, Oregon, drive north on Highway 35 for one mile over the Columbia River to Highway 14. Turn left on Highway 14 and drive about five miles to Cook and County Road 1800. Turn right (north) and drive 14 miles (becomes Cook-Underwood Road, then Willard Road, then Oklahoma Road) to the campground entrance at the end of the paved road.

Contact: Gifford Pinchot National Forest, Wind River Work Center, 1262 Hemlock Road, Carson, WA 98610; 509/427-3200, fax 509/427-3215.

109 Oklahoma

 7

This pretty campground is set along Little White Salmon River at an elevation of 1,700 feet. Fishing can be excellent in this area. It is stocked in the spring with rainbow trout. The camp gets light use. It features some open meadow, but is generally flat. It is close to the Columbia River Gorge, with paved road all the way into the campground, with easy RV parking. As to why they named the camp "Oklahoma," who knows? If you do, drop me a line.

Location: On the Little White Salmon River in Gifford Pinchot National Forest; see Mount Rainier and the Columbia River Gorge, map 4, grid b3.

Campsites, facilities: There are 23 sites for tents, trailers, or RVs up to 22 feet long. Drinking water, fire rings, and picnic tables are provided. Vault toilets are available. Some

110 Moss Creek

 7

This campground is set at 1,400 feet elevation, about one mile from the Little White Salmon River. It is a short distance from Willard and Big Cedars County Park. Good fishing prospects for trout can be found here in the spring, usually with few other people around. The camp is lightly used. The sites are generally small but are shaded and still functional for most RVs. The road is paved all the way to the campground.

Location: On the Little White Salmon River in Gifford Pinchot National Forest; see Mount Rainier and the Columbia River Gorge, map 4, grid b3.

Campsites, facilities: There are 17 sites for tents, trailers, or RVs up to 32 feet long. Picnic tables and fire grills are provided. Drinking water and vault toilets are available. Some facilities are wheelchair-accessible.

A camp host is available in the summer. Leashed pets are permitted.

Reservations, fees: Reservations accepted; phone 877/444-6777 or access the website: www.reserveusa.com ($8.65 reservation fee). Sites are $11 per night; $5 for each additional vehicle. Senior discount available. Open mid-May to mid-September.

Directions: From Hood River, Oregon, drive north on Highway 35 and for one mile over the Columbia River to Highway 14. Turn left on Highway 14 and drive about five miles to Cook and County Road 1800. Turn right (north) and drive 10 miles (becomes Cook-Underwood Road, then Willard road, then Oklahoma Road) to the campground entrance on the right.

Contact: Gifford Pinchot National Forest, Wind River Work Center, 1262 Hemlock Road, Carson, WA 98610; 509/427-3200, fax 509/427-3215.

111 Horsethief Lake State Park

     10

This is a 338-acre park with 7,500 feet of Columbia River shoreline. It also adjoins the 3,000-acre Dalles Mountain Ranch State Park. Horsethief Butte dominates the skyline, set adjacent to the lake. Horsethief Lake is approximately 90 acres, created by The Dalles Dam, and is a part of the Columbia River. Lupine and balsam root bloom in mid-April and create spectacular fields of purple and gold. Rockclimbing in the park is popular, but the river canyon is often windy, especially in late spring and early summer. Most people find the place as a spot camp while driving along the Columbia River Highway. There are hiking trails and access to both the lake and the Columbia River. Non-powered boats are allowed, and anglers can try for trout and bass. Guided tours on weekends feature pictographs and petroglyphs;

reservations required at 509/767-1159. See the following description of Maryhill State Park for information on other recreation options in the region.

Location: Near Dalles Dam; see Mount Rainier and the Columbia River Gorge, map 4, grid c8.

Campsites, facilities: There are 12 sites, most with partial hookups, for tents or self-contained RVs up to 30 feet long, and two primitive tent sites. Picnic tables and fire grills are provided. Drinking water, flush toilets, firewood, a dump station, a horseshoe pit, and a picnic area are available. A store and a café are located within two miles. Boat-launching facilities are located on both the lake and the river. Leashed pets are permitted.

Reservations, fees: No reservations accepted. Sites are $6 to $22 per night, $6 per extra vehicle per night. Senior discount available. Open April to late October.

Directions: From The Dalles in Oregon, turn north on Highway 197, cross over the Columbia River, and drive four miles to Highway 14. Turn right (east) and drive two miles to Milepost 85 and the park entrance on the right.

Contact: Horsethief Lake State Park; 360/902-8844 or 509/767-1159.

112 Maryhill State Park

   8

This 99-acre park has 4,700 feet of frontage along the Columbia River. Fishing, water-skiing, and windsurfing are among the recreation possibilities. The climate here is pleasant from March through mid-November. Two interesting places can be found near Maryhill: one is a full-scale replica of Stonehenge, located on a bluff overlooking the Columbia River, about one mile from the park. The other is the historic Mary Hill home, which is open to the public; Mary Hill's husband, Sam Hill, constructed the Stonehenge replica.

Location: On the Columbia River; see Mount Rainier and the Columbia River Gorge, map 5, grid c2.

Campsites, facilities: There are 50 sites with full hookups for trailers or RVs up to 50 feet long and 20 tent sites, including three primitive sites. Picnic tables and fire pits are provided. Restrooms, flush toilets, showers, a dump station, a store, and a picnic area with covered shelters are available. A café is within one mile. Some facilities are wheelchair-accessible. Boat docks and launching facilities are nearby. Leashed pets are permitted.

Reservations, fees: No reservations. Sites are $16 to $22 per night, $6 per extra vehicle per night. Senior discount available. Major credit cards accepted. Call 360/902-8844 for group camping information. Open year-round.

Directions: From Goldendale and U.S. 97, drive 12 miles south to the park on the left.

Contact: Maryhill State Park; 360/902-8844 or 509/773-5007.

©TOM STIENSTRA

Southeastern Washington

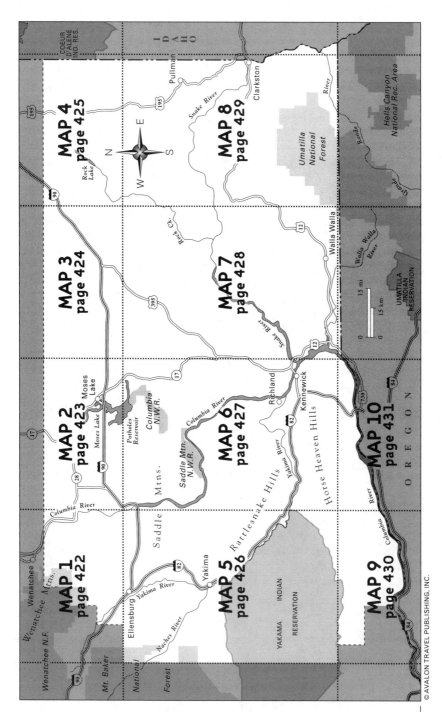

MAP 1
page 422

MAP 2
page 423

MAP 3
page 424

MAP 4
page 425

MAP 5
page 426

MAP 6
page 427

MAP 7
page 428

MAP 8
page 429

MAP 9
page 430

MAP 10
page 431

IDAHO

COEUR D'ALENE IND. RES.

Hells Canyon National Rec. Area

Umatilla National Forest

Pullman

Clarkston

Walla Walla

Snake River

Rock Lake

Rock Ck.

Moses Lake

Potholes Reservoir

Columbia N.W.R.

Saddle Mtn. N.W.R.

Saddle Mtns.

Columbia River

Richland

Kennewick

Rattlesnake Hills

Horse Heaven Hills

Yakima River

YAKAMA INDIAN RESERVATION

Yakima

Ellensburg

Yakima River

Naches River

National Forest

Wenatchee Mtns.

Wenatchee N.F.

Mt. Baker

Columbia River

UMATILLA INDIAN RESERVATION

Walla Walla River

Grande Ronde River

OREGON

Snake River

Columbia River

N E S W

0   15 mi
0   15 km

© AVALON TRAVEL PUBLISHING, INC.

Map 1

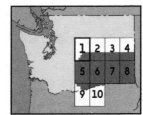

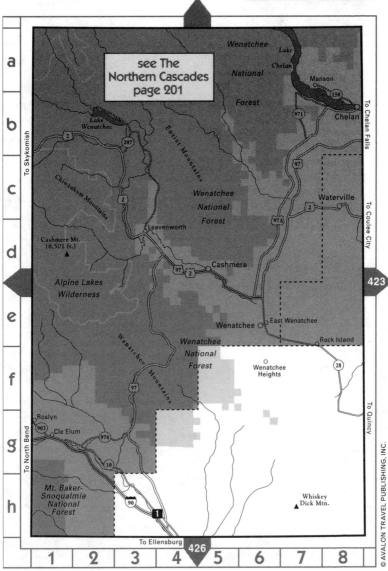

see The
Northern Cascades
page 201

Map 2

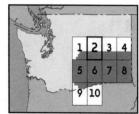

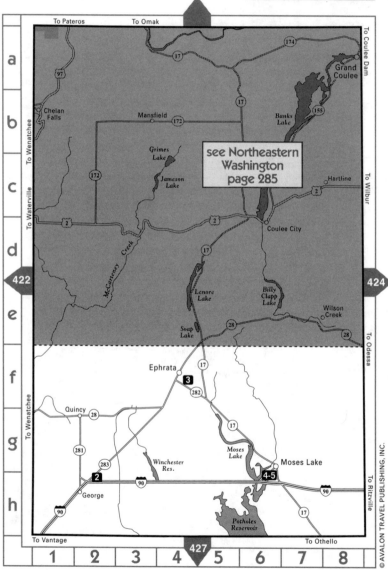

To Pateros   To Omak

To Coulee Dam

a

97

Grand
Coulee

b

To Wenatchee

Chelan
Falls

Mansfield   172

Banks
Lake

155

172

Grimes
Lake

see Northeastern
Washington
page 285

Hartline

To Wilbur

c

To Waterville

Jameson
Lake

2

2

Coulee City

d

422

424

McCartney Creek

172

17

Lenore
Lake

Billy
Clapp
Lake

Wilson
Creek

e

Soap
Lake

28

28

To Odessa

f

Ephrata   17

3

282

g

To Wenatchee

Quincy   28

17

281

Moses
Lake

Moses Lake

283

Winchester
Res.

4-5

To Ritzville

2

90

90

90

h

George

17

90

Potholes
Reservoir

To Vantage   427

To Othello

1   2   3   4   5   6   7   8

© AVALON TRAVEL PUBLISHING, INC.

Map 3

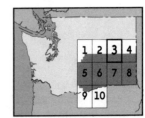

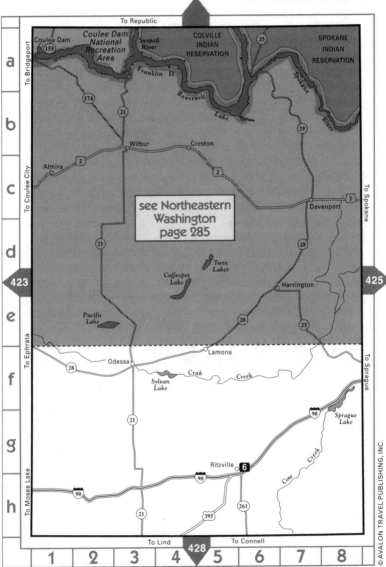

see Northeastern Washington page 285

© AVALON TRAVEL PUBLISHING, INC.

Map 4

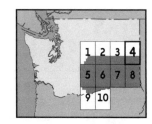

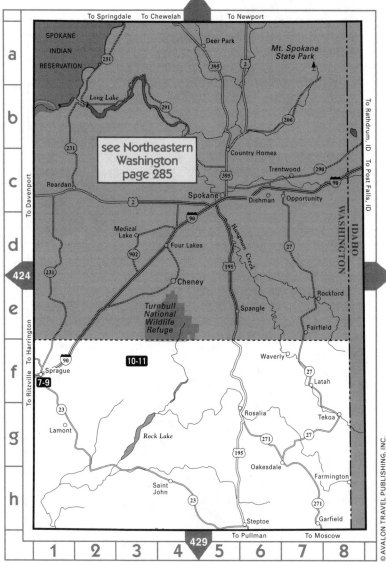

To Springdale   To Chewelah   To Newport

SPOKANE
INDIAN
RESERVATION

Deer Park

Mt. Spokane
State Park

231

395

2

Long Lake

291

206

see Northeastern Washington page 285

231

Country Homes

Trentwood

290

395

Spokane

Dishman

Opportunity

90

2

Reardan

To Davenport

Medical Lake

Four Lakes

Hangman Creek

27

902

195

231

Cheney

Turnbull National Wildlife Refuge

Spangle

Rockford

Fairfield

To Harrington

To Ritzville

90

10-11

Waverly

Sprague

27

7-9

Latah

23

Rosalia

Tekoa

Lamont

Rock Lake

271

27

195

Oakesdale

Farmington

Saint John

23

271

Steptoe

Garfield

To Pullman   To Moscow

IDAHO
WASHINGTON

To Rathdrum, ID   To Post Falls, ID

424

429

429

Map 5

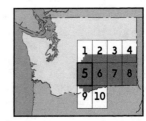

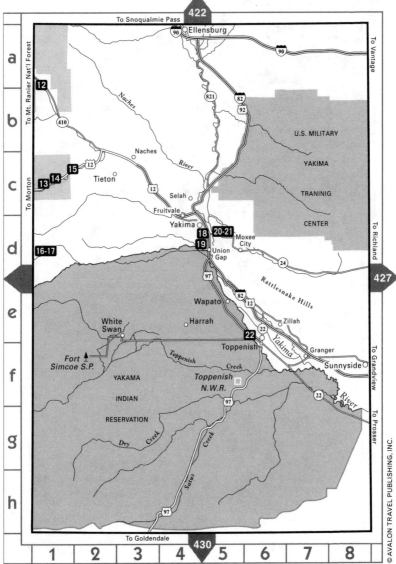

Map 6

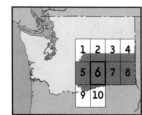

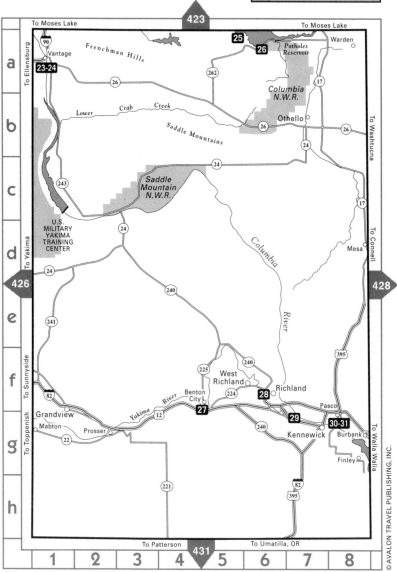

© AVALON TRAVEL PUBLISHING, INC.

Map 7

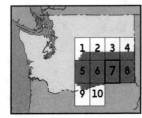

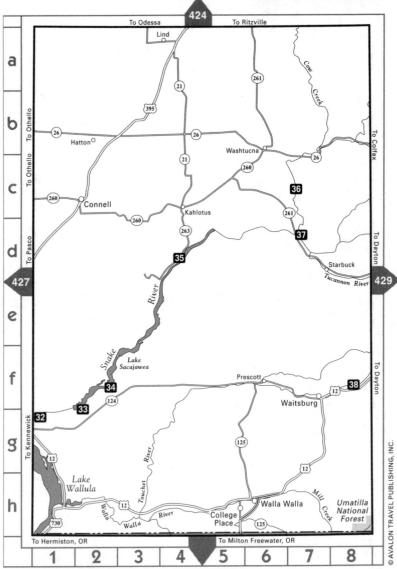

Map 8

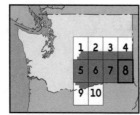

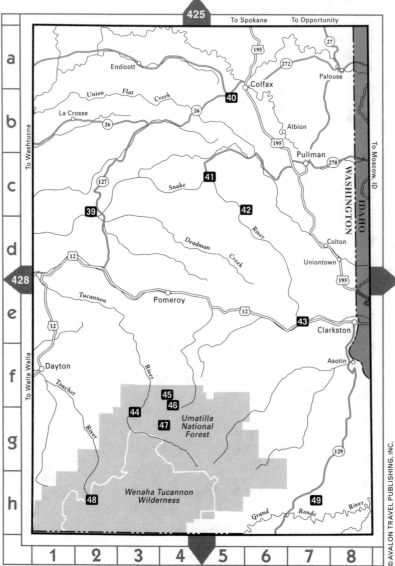

Map 9

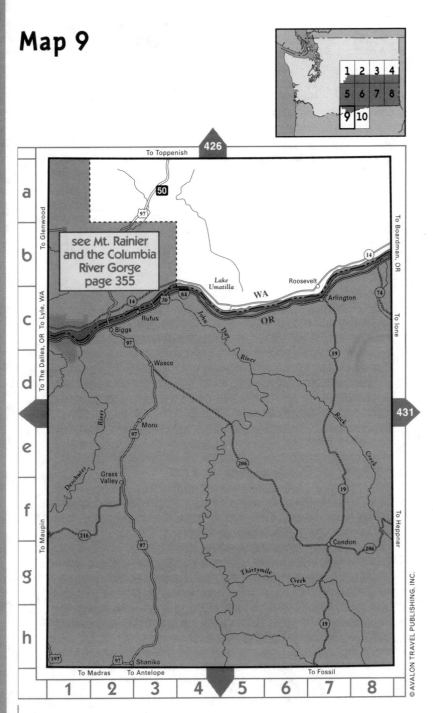

see Mt. Rainier and the Columbia River Gorge page 355

© AVALON TRAVEL PUBLISHING, INC.

Map 10

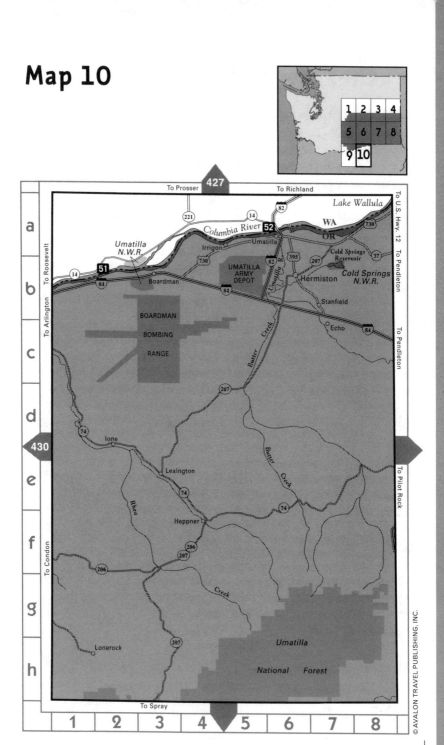

Southeastern Washington

The expansive domain of southeastern Washington is a surprise for many newcomers. Instead of the high mountains of the Cascades, there are rolling hills. Instead of forests, there are miles of wheat fields (Washington's second-largest export crop behind lumber). Instead of a multitude of streams, there are giant rivers—the Columbia and Snake. There is just one pocket of mountains and somewhat sparse forest, set in the southeast corner of the state, a remote sector of Umatilla National Forest.

The Lewis and Clark expedition was routed through this area some two-hundred years ago, and today, several major highways, including I-82 and U.S. 395, bring out-of-town visitors passing through en route to other destinations. A network of camps are set along these highways, including RV parks that have been created to serve the needs of travelers. Of the 16 parks, the 13 state parks offer the best campgrounds. The prettiest picture you will find is Palouse Falls, where a gorgeous fountain of water pours through a desert gorge.

◻ Ellensburg KOA

 8

This is one of the few campgrounds in a 25-mile radius, and it's exceptionally clean and scenic. It offers well-maintained, shaded campsites along the Yakima River. Rafting and fly-fishing on the nearby Yakima River are also popular. Other nearby recreation options include an 18-hole golf course, tennis courts, and horseback-riding rentals. The Kittitas County Historical Museum is in town at Third and Pine Streets.

Location: On the Yakima River; see Southeastern Washington, map 1, grid h4.

Campsites, facilities: There are 100 sites for trailers or RVs of any length, including 48 drive-through sites, some with full hookups and the rest with water and electricity, and 25 tent sites. Picnic tables are provided. Restrooms, flush toilets, showers, a dump station, a video arcade, a store, a coin-operated laundry, ice, a playground, video rentals, a horseshoe pit, volleyball, a seasonal wading pool, and a heated swimming pool are available. Bottled gas and a café are located within one mile. Extra parking is available for horse trailers, vans and boats. Leashed pets are permitted.

Reservations, fees: Reservations accepted. Sites are $20 to $35 per night, $3 per person per night for more than two people, $3 per extra vehicle per night. Major credit cards accepted. Open year-round.

Directions: From Seattle, drive east on I-90 for 106 miles to Exit 106 (near Ellensburg). Take that exit and continue one quarter-mile to Thorp Highway. Turn right at Thorp Highway and drive a short distance to the KOA entrance (well marked).

Contact: Ellensburg KOA, 32 Thorp Highway South, Ellensburg, WA 98926; 509/925-9319 or 800/562-7616, fax 509/925-3607; website: www.koa.com.

◻ Shady Tree RV Park

 8

This is an oasis in a desertlike area, with shade trees and grassy sites. A natural outdoor amphitheater just eight miles away seats 2,000 and is the scene of major concerts from June through September. Another option is Martha Lake, small and public, within one mile of Moses Lake State Park, about 30 miles away.

Location: Near George; see Southeastern Washington, map 2, grid h2.

Campsites, facilities: There are 30 tent sites and 41 sites with full hookups for trailers or RVs of any length; four are drive-through sites. Picnic tables are provided. A restroom with flush toilets, showers, a dump station, a horseshoe pit, and a coin-operated laundry are available. Leashed pets are permitted.

Reservations, fees: No reservations accepted. Sites are $18 to $20 per night, $2 per person per night for more than two people over age 12. Open year-round.

Directions: From Spokane, drive west on I-90 to Exit 151 (two miles east of George). Take that exit and bear right to the campground right at the corner (just off the highway at the intersection of Highways 281 and 283).

Contact: Shady Tree RV Park, 1099 Highway 283 North, Quincy, WA 98848; 509/785-2851.

◻ Oasis RV Park and Golf

 5

This can be an extremely warm, arid area during the summer months, but, fortunately, Oasis RV Park offers shaded sites. There are two fishing ponds at the resort: one has crappie, while the other is for kids, fishing for trout and bass. There is also a nine-hole golf course at the park. Mineral baths are located just a few miles north.

Location: Near Soap Lake; see Southeastern Washington, map 2, grid f4.

Campsites, facilities: There are 38 tent sites and 68 sites with full hookups for trailers or RVs of any length; 10 are drive-through sites. Picnic tables are provided. A restroom with flush toilets and coin-operated showers is available. A nine-hole golf course, a dump station, a store, propane gas, a coin-operated laundry, ice, a swimming pool, and a fishing pond for children are available. A café is located within one mile. Leashed pets are permitted.

Reservations, fees: Reservations recommended. Sites are $15 to $20 per night. Major credit cards accepted. Senior discount available. Open year-round, with limited winter facilities.

Directions: From Spokane, drive west on I-90 to the Moses Lake exit and Highway 17. Turn northeast and drive 17 miles to the Y junction with Highway 282. Take Highway 282 and drive four miles to Highway 281/283 (a stoplight). Turn left and drive 1.25 miles to the park on the right (just before reaching the town of Ephrata).

Contact: Oasis RV Park and Golf, 2541 Basin Street SW, Ephrata, WA 98823; 509/754-5102 or 877/754-5102.

4 Big Sun Resort

 5

This park is a short distance from Moses Lake State Park, which is open for day-use only. Moses Lake is the primary appeal, where you will find shady picnic spots with tables and fire grills, beach access, and moorage floats. Water-skiing is allowed on the lake.

Location: Near Moses Lake State Park; see Southeastern Washington, map 2, grid h6.

Campsites, facilities: There are 10 tent sites and 42 sites with full hookups for trailers or RVs of any length; 13 are drive-through sites.

Picnic tables and fire pits are provided. A restroom with flush toilets and pay showers is available. A coin-operated laundry, ice, cable TV, rowboat rentals and launch facilities, and a playground are available. A dump station, a store, and a restaurant are located within one mile. Boat docks, launching facilities, and rentals are nearby. Leashed pets are permitted.

Reservations, fees: Reservations accepted. Sites are $13.50 to $22 per night, $2 per person ($1 per child) per night for more than two people. Major credit cards accepted. Open March through October.

Directions: From Spokane, drive west on I-90 to Moses Lake and Exit 176. Take that exit to Broadway and drive one-half mile to Burress Avenue. Turn west on Burress Avenue and drive one block to the park.

Contact: Big Sun Resort, 2300 West Marina, Moses Lake, WA 98837; 509/765-8294.

5 Willows Trailer Village

 5

One of two campgrounds in the area, this one has grassy, shaded sites, horseshoe pits, barbecues, and a recreation field. See the description of Big Sun Resort for information on recreation spots in the vicinity. Note there are some permanent site rentals at this RV park, but they are separated by a landscape barrier.

Location: Near Moses Lake State Park; see Southeastern Washington, map 2, grid h6.

Campsites, facilities: There are 20 tent sites and 65 drive-through sites, most with full hookups, for trailers or RVs of any length. Electricity, drinking water, and picnic tables are provided. A restroom with flush toilets, coin-operated showers, bottled gas, a store, ice, a coin-operated laundry, and a playground with a horseshoe pit are available.

There is also a hair salon on site. Leashed pets are permitted.

Reservations, fees: Reservations accepted with deposits. Sites are $14.50 to $20.50 per night, $3 per person per night for more than two people. Open year-round.

Directions: From Spokane, drive west on I-90 to Moses Lake and Exit 179 and Highway 17. Turn south and drive 2.5 miles to Road M. Turn right (west) and drive one quarter-mile to the park on the left.

Contact: Willows Trailer Village, 1347 Road M Southeast, Moses Lake, WA 98837; 509/765-7531 (phone or fax).

₆ Best Inn Suites and RV

   7

If all you have is a tent, well, this is the only site to stake it within a radius of 25 miles. The nearest fishing is at Sprague Lake, 22 miles north on U.S. 395. Burroughs Historical Museum is a possible side trip in town. An 18-hole golf course and tennis courts are nearby, just across the street.

Location: In Ritzville; see Southeastern Washington, map 3, grid h6.

Campsites, facilities: There are 39 drive-through sites with full hookups for tents, trailers, or RVs of any length. Picnic tables and cable TV hookups are provided. Restrooms, flush toilets, showers, a dump station, a coin-operated laundry, modem hookups, ice, a playground, a hot tub, and a seasonal swimming pool are available. Some facilities are wheelchair-accessible. Bottled gas, a store, a gift shop, a café, and a restaurant are located within one mile. Leashed pets are permitted.

Reservations, fees: Reservations accepted. Sites are $10 to $25 per night. Senior discount available. Major credit cards accepted. Open mid-April to mid-October.

Directions: From Pasco, take U.S. 395 and drive 85 miles north to Ritzville to I-90. Take I-90 east and drive one-half mile to Exit 221. Take that exit and drive 0.25 mile to Smitty's Boulevard. Turn right and drive a short distance to the hotel/RV check-in on the left.

Contact: Best Inn and RV and Suites, 1513 Smitty's Boulevard, Ritzville, WA 99169; 509/659-1007 or 800/237-8466, fax 509/659-1025; website: www.hotels/west.com.

₇ Four Seasons Campground & Resort

 7

This campground along the shore of Sprague Lake, one of the top fishing waters in the state, has spacious sites with plenty of vegetation. The fishing for rainbow trout is best in May and June, with some bass in spring and fall. Because there is an abundance of natural feed in the lake, the fish reach larger sizes here than in neighboring lakes. Walleye up to 11 pounds are taken here. Perch, crappie, blue gill, and catfish are also abundant. In late July through August, a fair algae bloom is a turnoff for swimmers and water-skiers.

Location: On Sprague Lake; see Southeastern Washington, map 4, grid f1.

Campsites, facilities: There are 38 sites with full or partial hookups, including some drive-through sites, for trailers or RVs, 25 tent sites, and four furnished cabins for up to six people. Picnic tables and fire grills are provided. Restrooms, drinking water, flush toilets, coin-operated showers, a dump station, firewood, ice, a store with fishing tackle, a fish-cleaning station, a small basketball court, and a swimming pool are available. Boat and fishing docks, launching facilities, and rentals are nearby. Leashed pets are permitted.

Reservations, fees: Reservations accepted. Sites are $15 to $19 per night, pets $1 per night. Cabins are $65 to $75 per night. Open March through October, weather permitting.

Directions: From Spokane, drive west on I-90 for about 40 miles to Exit 245. Take Exit 245 and drive south to Fourth Street. Turn right and drive one block to B Street. Turn left and drive two blocks to First Street. Turn right and drive one-half mile to a Y intersection. Bear right to Doerschlag Road and drive one mile to Lake Road. Turn left and drive four miles to Bob Lee Road. Turn left and drive one mile to the campground at the end of the road.

Contact: Four Seasons Campground & Resort, 2384 North Bob Lee Road, Sprague, WA 99032; 509/257-2332; website: www.four seasonscampground.com.

8 Sprague Lake Resort

 5

This developed campground is on the shore of Sprague Lake, about 35 miles from Spokane. It's a pleasant, grassy setting with about 100 cottonwood and native trees on the property. See listing for Four Seasons Campground and Resort for more information about Sprague Lake.

Location: On Sprague Lake; see Southeastern Washington, map 4, grid f1.

Campsites, facilities: There are 30 drive-through sites with full or partial hookups for trailers or RVs of any length and 50 tent sites. Picnic tables and fire grills are provided. Restrooms, drinking water, flush toilets, coin-operated showers, a dump station, a small store, a coin-operated laundry, ice, firewood for sale, a playground, boat docks, launching facilities, and rentals are available. Leashed pets are permitted.

Reservations, fees: Reservations accepted. Sites are $15 to $19 per night, $1 per person per night for more than two people. Open April through October.

Directions: In Spokane, drive west on I-90 to the Sprague Business Center exit. Take that exit to Sprague Lake Road and drive two miles to the resort on the left (well signed).

Contact: Sprague Lake Resort, 1999 Sprague Lake Resort Road, Sprague, WA 99032; 509/257-2864; website: www.spraguelake resort.com

9 Fox's Last Roundup Motel & RV Park

 5

This park is located just on the outskirts of Sprague. It is set in a meadowlike area, flat with a rural feel and open, grassy sites. Fishing is excellent year-round at nearby Sprague Lake. In the fall, hunters will sometimes base RVs and trailers at this park and launch their trips from here.

Location: Near Sprague Lake; see Southeastern Washington, map 4, grid f1.

Campsites, facilities: There are 13 sites, including some drive-through, for tents, trailers, or RVs of any length, plus a grass area for tents. Restrooms, drinking water, flush toilets, showers, a coin-operated laundry, a gift shop, a store, and ice are available. Bottled gas and a café are located within one mile. Leashed pets are permitted.

Reservations, fees: Reservations accepted. Sites are $12 to $16 per night. Major credit cards accepted. Open year-round.

Directions: From Spokane, drive west on I-90 for 35 miles to Sprague and Exit 245. Take Exit 245 and drive one-half mile south on Highway 23 to Fourth Street. Turn right (west) and drive one block to B Street. Turn right (north) and drive three blocks to First Street. Turn right (east) on First Street and drive one block to the park on the right.

Contact: Fox's Last Roundup Motel & RV Park, 312 East First Street, Sprague, WA 99032; 509/257-2583, fax 509/257-2615.

⑩ Klink's Williams Lake Resort

  6

This family-oriented resort is set on the shore of Williams Lake, which is just under three miles long and is popular for swimming and water-skiing. The resort has a swimming area with a floating dock and diving board. This lake is also one of the top fishing lakes in the region for rainbow trout and cutthroat trout. The lake is bordered in some areas by rocky cliffs. Note that about 100 permanent residents live at the resort. See the description of Peaceful Pines Campground for information on nearby Turnbull National Wildlife Refuge.

Location: On Williams Lake; see Southeastern Washington, map 4, grid f3.

Campsites, facilities: There are 60 sites with full or partial hookups, including one drive-through site, for trailers or RVs of any length, 15 tent sites, and three log cabins. Picnic tables are provided. Restrooms, drinking water, flush toilets, coin-operated showers, bottled gas, a dump station, firewood, a store, a café, a restaurant, ice, a playground, boat docks, launching facilities, and boat rentals are available. Leashed pets are permitted.

Reservations, fees: Reservations accepted. Sites are $16 to $19 per night. Major credit cards accepted. Open mid-April to October.

Directions: From Spokane, drive west on I-90 for 10 miles to Exit 270 and Highway 904. Turn south on Highway 904 and drive four miles to Cheney and Cheney Plaza Road. Turn left (south) on Cheney Plaza Road and drive 11.2 miles to Williams Lake Road. Turn right (west) and drive 2.2 miles to the campground on the left.

Contact: Klink's Williams Lake Resort, 18617 West Williams Lake Road, Cheney, WA 99004; 509/235-2391.

⑪ Bunker's Resort

  8

This campground is on the shore of Williams Lake. See the description of Williams Lake Resort for information on the lake and the description of Peaceful Pines Campground for information on nearby Turnbull National Wildlife Refuge.

Location: On Williams Lake; see Southeastern Washington, map 4, grid f3.

Campsites, facilities: There are 10 drive-through sites with full or partial hookups for trailers or RVs of any length, 10 sites for tents, and four furnished cabins. Fire pits are provided at tent sites. Picnic tables, restrooms, drinking water, flush toilets, showers, bottled gas, a dump station, a restaurant, a store, ice, boat and fishing docks, launching facilities, and rentals are available. Leashed pets are permitted.

Reservations, fees: Reservations accepted. Sites are $12 to $21.50 per night; cabins are $55 to $70 per night. Major credit cards accepted. Open mid-April through September.

Directions: From Spokane, drive west on I-90 for 10 miles to Exit 270 and Highway 904. Turn south on Highway 904 and drive six miles to Cheney and Mullinex Road. Turn left (south) on Mullinex Road and drive 12 miles to the resort.

Contact: Bunker's Resort, 36402 South Bunker Landing Road, Cheney, WA 99004; 509/235-5212.

12 Squaw Rock Resort

 8

This park situated in a stand of old-growth fir and pine on the Naches River is close to a host of activities, including trout fishing, hiking trails, marked bike trails, and a riding stable. The park has a pool and hot tub. The nearby town of Naches, located southeast of the campground on State Route 410, offers all services.

Location: On the Naches River; see Southeastern Washington, map 5, grid b1.

Campsites, facilities: There are 65 sites, most with full hookups, for trailers or RVs of any length, 25 tent sites, five cabins, and four motel rooms. Picnic tables are provided. Restrooms, flush toilets, showers, bottled gas, a dump station, cable TV, a recreation hall, a store, a café, ice, a playground, a hot tub, and a swimming pool are available. Leashed pets are permitted.

Reservations, fees: Reservations accepted. Sites are $15 to $22 per night, $2 per person per night for more than two people. Major credit cards accepted. Open year-round.

Directions: From Yakima, drive northwest on U.S. 12 for 18 miles to State Route 410. Continue straight on State Route 410 and drive 15 miles to the campground on the left.

Contact: Squaw Rock Resort, 15070 State Route 410, Naches, WA 98937; 509/658-2926, fax 509/658-2927; website: http://iyp.uswestdex.com:80/squawrockresort.

13 Hause Creek

  7

Several creeks converge at this campground along the Tieton River (elevation 2,500 feet). The Tieton Dam, which creates Rimrock Lake, is just upstream. This is one of the larger,

more developed camps in the area. Willows is a primitive alternative.

Location: On the Tieton River in Wenatchee National Forest; see Southeastern Washington, map 5, grid c1.

Campsites, facilities: There are 42 sites for tents, trailers, or RVs up to 30 feet long. Picnic tables and fire grills are provided. Drinking water and flush toilets are available. Some facilities are wheelchair-accessible. Boat docks, launching facilities, and rentals are located on Rimrock Lake. Leashed pets are permitted.

Reservations, fees: Reservations accepted; phone 877/444-6777 or access the website: www.reserveusa.com ($8.65 reservation fee). Sites are $11 to $14 per night, $22 for double sites, $5 per extra vehicle per night. Senior discount available. Open late May to late November.

Directions: From Yakima, drive northwest on I-82 for 17 miles to the junction with Highway 410. Turn west on U.S. 12 and drive 22 miles to the campground on the left.

Contact: Okanogan and Wenatchee National Forests, Naches Ranger District, 10061 U.S. Highway 12, Naches, WA 98937; 509/653-2205, fax 509/653-2638.

14 Willows

 5

This primitive, beautiful, and easily accessible camp can be found on the Tieton River at 2,400 feet elevation. Rimrock Lake to the west provides many recreation options, and hiking trails leading into the William O. Douglas Wilderness are within driving distance.

Location: On the Tieton River in Wenatchee National Forest; see Southeastern Washington, map 5, grid c1.

Campsites,   facilities: There are 15 sites for tents, trailers, or RVs up to 20 feet long. Picnic tables and fire grills are provided. Drinking water, vault toilets, and garbage service are available. Leashed pets are permitted.

Reservations, fees: No reservations accepted. Sites are $11 to $14 per night, $5 per extra vehicle per night. Senior discount available. Open April to late November.

Directions: From Yakima, drive northwest on I-82 for 17 miles to the junction with Highway 410. Turn west on U.S. 12 and drive 16 miles to the campground on the left.

Contact: Okanogan and Wenatchee National Forests, Naches Ranger District, 10061 U.S. Highway 12, Naches, WA 98937; 509/653-2205, fax 509/653-2638.

15 Windy Point
    5

This campground, located along the Tieton River at an elevation of 2,000 feet, is more isolated than the camps set westward toward Rimrock Lake. Drinking water is a bonus. Fishing access is available.

Location: On the Tieton River in Wenatchee National Forest; see Southeastern Washington, map 5, grid c1.

Campsites, facilities: There are 15 sites for tents, trailers, or RVs up to 22 feet long. Picnic tables and fire grills are provided. Drinking water and vault toilets are available. Garbage service and firewood are available nearby. Leashed pets are permitted.

Reservations, fees: No reservations accepted. Sites are $11 to $14 per night, $5 per extra vehicle per night. Senior discount available. Open April to late November.

Directions: From Yakima, drive northwest on I-82 for 17 miles to the junction with Highway 410. Turn west on U.S. 12 and drive nine miles to the campground on the left.

Contact: Okanogan and Wenatchee National Forests, Naches Ranger District, 10061

U.S. Highway 12, Naches, WA 98937; 509/653-2205, fax 509/653-2638.

16 Snow Cabin
   7

Located in an area of old-growth timber, this place is popular with horse campers, who use it to access old logging roads. There are cutthroat trout in Ahtanum Creek, and fishing is permitted. The landscape is filled primarily with Douglas fir. Some who have visited this camp may remember that saddle-stock facilities were once available. They have been removed.

Location: On the North Fork of Ahtanum Creek; see Southeastern Washington, map 5, grid d1.

Campsites, facilities: There are eight sites for tents or small trailers. Picnic tables, fire grills, and tent pads are provided. Pit toilets are available, but there is no drinking water. Garbage must be packed out. Leashed pets are permitted.

Reservations, fees: No reservations; no fee. Open year-round, weather permitting.

Directions: From Yakima, drive south on I-82 for two miles to Union Gap and Ahtanum Road. Turn right (west) and drive 20 miles to Tampico and Road A-3000 (North Fork Road). Turn right (west) and drive 9.5 miles to Road A-3000 (North Fork Ahtanum Road). Turn right (west) and drive 5.6 miles (bearing left for the last mile) to the Gray Rock Trailhead. From Gray Rock, continue 1.5 miles to the campground on the left. Note: High-clearance vehicles only are recommended.

Contact: Department of Natural Resources, Southeast Region, 713 Bowers Road, Ellensburg, WA 98926-9301; 509/925-8510, fax 509/925-8522.

Ahtanum & Ahtanum Meadows

   7

These two campgrounds are simply separated by Ahtanum Creek, but both are primitive sites with the same limited facilities. For a good side trip, drive 14 miles to the Darland Mountain viewpoint at 6,900 feet. The road gets very steep near the lookout and is not suitable for RVs or trailers. In the winter, this area offers 60 miles of groomed trails for snowmobilers. A snow shelter is provided at Tree Phones Campground. Contact the Department of Natural Resources for a map.

Location: On Ahtanum Creek; see Southeastern Washington, map 5, grid d1.

Campsites, facilities: There are 11 campsites for tents or small trailers at Ahtanum Meadows and nine sites at Ahtanum. Picnic tables, fire grills, and tent pads are provided. Vault and pit toilets and drinking water are available. Some facilities are wheelchair-accessible. Leashed pets are permitted.

Reservations, fees: No reservation; no fee. Open year-round, weather permitting.

Directions: From Yakima, drive south on I-82 for two miles to Union Gap and Ahtanum Road. Turn right (west) and drive 20 miles to Tampico and Road A-3000 (North Fork Road). Turn right (west) and drive nine miles to the Ahtanum Meadows campground entrance on the left. To reach Antanum, continue one-half mile to the campground on the left. Note: High-clearance vehicles only are recommended.

Contact: Department of Natural Resources, Southeast Region, 713 Bowers Road, Ellensburg, WA 98926-9301; 509/925-8510, fax 509/925-8522.

Circle H RV Ranch

  8

This pleasant, centrally located, and clean park with a Western flavor has comfortable, spacious sites among ornamental trees and roses. Nearby recreation options include an 18-hole golf course, hiking trails, marked bike trails, and a riding stable. See the description of KOA Yakima for information on points of interest in Yakima.

Location: In Yakima; see Southeastern Washington, map 5, grid d4.

Campsites, facilities: There are 64 sites with full hookups for trailers or RVs of any length, including 16 drive-through sites, and 12 tent sites. Picnic tables are provided. Restrooms, flush toilets, showers, two recreation halls, a coin-operated laundry, a hot tub, modem hookups, two playgrounds with horseshoes, a tennis court, volleyball and basketball, a video arcade, a mini-golf course, and a swimming pool are available. Bottled gas, a store, a café, and ice are located within one mile. Mini-storage units are available for a fee. Leashed pets are permitted.

Reservations, fees: Reservations accepted. Sites are $16.64 to $20 per night, $2 per person per night for more than two people. Major credit cards accepted. Open year-round.

Directions: In Yakima on I-82, take Exit 34 and drive one block to South 18th Street. Turn right (north) and drive one quarter-mile to the campground on the right.

Contact: Circle H RV Ranch, 1107 South 18th Street, Yakima, WA 98901; 509/457-3683, fax 509/457-3683; website: http://circlehrv park.uswestdex.com.

19 Trailer Inn RV Park

 7

Like the Trailer Inn RV Park in Spokane, this spot has many of the luxuries you'd find in a hotel, including a pool, a hot tub, a sauna, on-site security, and a large-screen TV. An 18-hole golf course, hiking trails, marked bike trails, and tennis courts are close by. It's especially pretty in the fall when the sycamores turn. See the description of KOA Yakima for information on some of the points of interest in Yakima.

Location: In Yakima; see Southeastern Washington, map 5, grid d4.

Campsites, facilities: There are 152 sites with full hookups for tents, trailers, or RVs of any length; 30 are drive-through sites. Picnic tables are provided. Restrooms, flush toilets, showers, bottled gas, a dump station, a recreation hall, a coin-operated laundry, ice, an indoor heated swimming pool, a whirlpool, a TV room with a 52-inch screen, a dog walk, an enclosed barbecue (no open fires permitted), and a playground are available. A store and a café are located within one block. Leashed pets are permitted.

Reservations, fees: Reservations accepted. Sites are $17 to $24 per night, $5 per person per night for more than two people, $5 per extra vehicle per night. Major credit cards accepted. Open year-round.

Directions: In Yakima on I-82, take Exit 31 and drive south for one block on North First Street to the park on the right (west side of the road).

Contact: Trailer Inn RV Park, 1610 North First Street, Yakima, WA 98901; 509/452-9561; website: www.trailerinnrv.usquestdex.com.

20 Yakima Sportsman State Park

 8

This park is on the flood plain of the Yakima River and is an irrigated area in an otherwise desert landscape. Several deciduous trees shade the camping and picnic areas. More than 140 bird species have been identified in the park. It is a popular layover spot for visitors attending events in the Yakima area. There is a fishing pond for children (no anglers over age 15 are allowed). Hiking is permitted along two miles of unpaved roadway on the river dike. Kayaking and rafting are possible at this park on the Yakima River. No swimming is allowed. Nearby recreation options include an 18-hole golf course and hiking trails. See the description of KOA Yakima for information on other points of interest in Yakima.

Location: On the Yakima River; see Southeastern Washington, map 5, grid d5.

Campsites, facilities: There are two primitive tent sites, 28 sites for tents or self-contained RVs, and 37 drive-through sites with full hookups for trailers or RVs up to 60 feet in length. Picnic tables and fire grills are provided. Flush toilets, a dump station, and a playground are available. Showers and firewood can be obtained for an extra fee. Some facilities are wheelchair-accessible. A store and ice are within one mile. Leashed pets are permitted.

Reservations, fees: Reservations accepted. Sites are $6 to $21 per night, $6 per extra vehicle per night. Major credit cards accepted. Senior discount available. Open year-round.

Directions: In Yakima, drive on I-82 to Milepost 34 and the Highway 24 exit. Turn east on Highway 24 and drive one mile to Keys Road.

Turn left and drive one mile to the park entrance on the left.

Contact: Yakima Sportsman State Park; 360/902-8844 or 509/575-2774.

21 KOA Yakima

 6

This campground along the Yakima River offers well-maintained, shaded sites and fishing access. Some points of interest in Yakima are the Yakima Valley Museum and the Yakima Trolley Lines, which offer rides on restored trolley cars originally built in 1906. Indian Rock Paintings State Park is located five miles west of Yakima on U.S. 12. Nearby recreation options include an 18-hole golf course, hiking trails, marked bike trails, and tennis courts. A casino is located 15 miles to the east.

Location: On the Yakima River; see Southeastern Washington, map 5, grid d5.

Campsites, facilities: There are 120 sites, some with full hookups, the rest with water and electricity for trailers or RVs of any length, 40 tent sites, and seven cabins. Picnic tables are provided. Restrooms, flush toilets, showers, bottled gas, a dump station, a recreation hall, a store, a coin-operated laundry, ice, a pool, a playground with horseshoes, a basketball court, fishing ponds, firewood, bike rentals, and boat rentals including paddleboats are available. A café is located within one mile. Leashed pets permitted.

Reservations, fees: Reservations accepted. Sites are $35 to $46 per night, $3 per person per night for more than two people; cabins are $35 to $46 per night. Major credit cards accepted. Open year-round.

Directions: In Yakima, drive on I-82 to Milepost 34 and the Highway 24 exit. Turn east on Highway 24 and drive one mile to Keys Road. Turn north on Keys Road and drive 300 yards to the campground on the left.

Contact: KOA Yakima, 1500 Keys Road, Yakima, WA 98901; 509/248-5882 or 800/562-5773; website: www.koa.com.

22 Yakama Nation RV Resort

 3

The park is set within the Yakama Indian Reservation (the tribe spells its name differently from the river and town), where a casino and movie theater are near the resort. The Toppenish National Wildlife Refuge, the best side trip, is almost always a good spot to see a large variety of birds. For information, phone 509/545-8588. Nearby Toppenish, a historic Old West town with a museum, is also worth a side trip.

Location: Near the Yakima River; see Southeastern Washington, map 5, grid e6.

Campsites, facilities: There are 125 sites with full hookups for RVs of any length, one tent site, and 14 tepees for up to 10 people each. Picnic tables and fire pits are provided. Restrooms, flush toilets, showers, modem hookups, a dump station, garbage service, a playground, a recreation room, an exercise room, a jogging track, ball courts, bicycle rentals, a heated pool, and a coin-operated laundry are available. A picnic shelter with drinking water, propane, and a sink is available in the tent area. A restaurant and grocery store are located within 1.5 miles. Leashed pets are permitted.

Reservations, fees: Reservations recommended; phone 800/874-3087. Sites are $14 to $26 per night, $2 per person per night for more than two people. Teepees are $30 per night for five campers, plus $3 each additional person. Major credit cards accepted. Open year-round.

Directions: From Yakima, drive south on U.S. 97 for 16 miles to the resort on the right.

Contact: Yakama Nation RV Resort, 280 Buster Road, Toppenish, WA 98948; 509/865-2000 or 800/874-3087; website: www.yakama nation.com.

 Ginkgo-Wanapum State Park

    7

Ginkgo Petrified Forest State Park is one of the most unusual fossil forests in the world, and it is registered as a national natural landmark. It makes up one of two separate parks here that are linked, with the other being Wanapum State Recreation Area. Camping is permitted only at Wanapum, which is seven miles south of the main entrance at Ginkgo. The park is the site of an ancient petrified forest, and there is an interpretive center and trail. The petrified forest is open weekends and holidays from November through March. Ginkgo is set along Wanapum Lake in the course of the Columbia River. This is a huge recreation area, covering 7,740 acres surrounding the 27,000 acres of Wanapum Lake. Options include hiking (three miles of trails), swimming, boating, water-skiing, and fishing. There are also several historical Civilian Conservation Corps structures from the 1930s. The campground at Wanapum is set up primarily for RVs, with full hookups, restrooms, and showers. Note that the park always fills up during the Gorge concert season.

Location: On the Columbia River and Wanapum Lake; see Southeastern Washington, map 6, grid a1.

Campsites, facilities: There are 50 sites with full hookups for trailers or RVs up to 60 feet. Picnic tables, fire grills, and flush toilets are provided. Showers and firewood are available for an extra fee. Boat docks, launching facilities, and a picnic area are nearby. Leashed pets are permitted.

Reservations, fees: Reserve at 888/CAMP-OUT (888/226-7688); website: www.parks.wa .gov/reservations ($7 reservation fee). Sites are $21 per night, $6 per extra vehicle per night. Senior discount available. Open April through October.

Directions: From Spokane, drive west on I-90 to the Vantage Highway/Huntzinger Road (Exit 136). Take that exit, turn south on Vantage Highway/Huntzinger Road, and drive three miles south to the park on the right.

Contact: Ginkgo-Wanapum State Park, Vantage, WA 98950; 360/902-8844 or 509/856-2700.

 Vantage Riverstone Resort

6

This campground offers pleasant, grassy sites overlooking the Columbia River a short distance from the state park (see Ginkgo-Wanapum State Park, south of I-90). This is the only campground in the immediate area that provides space for tent camping. The next closest camp is 12 miles away at Shady Tree RV Park in George.

Location: On the Columbia River; see Southeastern Washington, map 6, grid a1.

Campsites, facilities: There are 50-plus tent sites and 50 sites with full hookups for trailers or RVs of any length. Picnic tables, a restroom with flush toilets, showers, a dump station, a recreation hall, a coin-operated laundry, ice, a playground, and a heated indoor swimming pool are available. A store and a café are located next to the resort. Boat docks and launching facilities are nearby. Leashed pets are permitted.

Reservations, fees: Reservations accepted. Sites are $19 to $23 per night. Major credit cards accepted. Open year-round.

Directions: From Spokane, drive west on I-90 to Vantage and the Vantage Highway (Exit 136). Take that exit, turn north, and drive north for three blocks to the resort on the left.

Contact: Vantage Riverstone Resort, P.O. Box 1101, Vantage, WA 98950; 509/856-2230, fax 509/856-2802; website: www.vantagewa.com.

25 Potholes State Park

    8

This park is on Potholes Reservoir, also known as O'Sullivan Reservoir (because of the O'Sullivan Dam), where fishing is the highlight. Trout, walleye, crappie, and perch are among the species taken here. Water-skiing and hiking (three miles of hiking trails) are two other options. There is a sand beach near the campground. The surrounding terrain is desertlike with freshwater marshes. A side trip to the Columbia Wildlife Refuge, located two miles east of the park, is recommended. Note that Potholes Reservoir is often confused with the Potholes Lakes themselves, which are a 30- to 45-minute drive from the park.

Location: On Potholes Reservoir; see Southeastern Washington, map 6, grid a5.

Campsites, facilities: There are 121 sites for tents, trailers, or RVs up to 50 feet long; 60 have full hookups. Picnic tables and fire grills are provided. Flush toilets, a dump station, a store, a playground, and a picnic area with a shelter are available. Showers and firewood can be obtained for a fee. Boat-launching facilities and rentals are nearby. Leashed pets are permitted.

Reservations, fees: Reserve at 888/CAMP-OUT (888/226-7688); website: www.parks.wa

.gov/reservations ($7 reservation fee). Sites are $6 to $21 per night, $6 per extra vehicle per night. Senior discount available. Open year-round.

Directions: From I-90 at Moses Lake, take Exit 179 and Highway 17. Turn south and drive nine miles to Highway 262/O'Sullivan Dam Road. Turn right (west) and drive 11 miles to the resort on the southern shore of Potholes Reservoir (well signed).

Contact: Potholes State Park, 6762 Highway 262 East, Othello, WA 99344; 360/902-8844.

26 Mar Don Resort

     7

This resort is located on Potholes Reservoir with opportunities for fishing, swimming, and boating. A marina, tackle, and boat rentals are all available. Hiking trails and marked bike trails are close by. There is also a 25-unit motel and two rental homes at the resort. A café and cocktail lounge are a nice bonus for many visitors. The Columbia National Wildlife Refuge is located to the nearby south, providing exceptional bird-watching, with pelicans and kingfishers common and bald eagles and migratory sandhill cranes often seen.

Location: Near Potholes Reservoir; see Southeastern Washington, map 6, grid a6.

Campsites, facilities: There are 275 sites for tents, trailers, or RVs of any length, including 187 with full or partial hookups and seven with drive-through sites. Electricity, drinking water, and picnic tables are provided. A restroom with flush toilets, coin-operated showers, bottled gas, a dump station, a game room, a store, a coin-operated laundry, ice, a playground, boat moorage, boat rentals, and launching facilities are available. Some facilities are wheelchair-accessible. Leashed pets are permitted.

Reservations, fees: Reservations recommended. Sites are $18 to $23 per night, $5 per extra vehicle per night, $3 per pet per night. Major credit cards accepted. Open year-round.

Directions: From Spokane, drive west on I-90 to Moses Lake and Exit 179 and Highway 17. Turn south and drive nine miles to Highway 262. Turn west and drive 10 miles to the resort on the southern shore of Potholes Reservoir.

Contact: Mar Don Resort, 8198 Highway 262 Southeast, Othello, WA 99344; 509/346-2651 or 800/416-2736; website: www.mardonresort.com

27 Beach RV Park

 8

If it's getting late, you'd best stop here because its the only option for a long stretch. This park along the shore of the Yakima River is a pleasant spot, with spacious RV sites and a large grassy area with poplar trees and shrubs providing privacy between sites. Nearby recreation options include an 18-hole golf course, a full-service marina, and tennis courts. The park was bought in 2000, and the new owner installed a deck overlooking the river.

Location: On the Yakima River; see Southeastern Washington, map 6, grid f5.

Campsites, facilities: There are 39 sites with full hookups for tents, trailers, or RVs of any length; five are drive-through sites. Electricity, drinking water, sewer hookups, and cable TV are provided. Flush toilets, showers, a coin-operated laundry, and ice are available. Bottled gas, a dump station, a store, and a café are located within one mile. Boat-launching facilities are nearby. Leashed pets are permitted.

Reservations, fees: Reservations accepted. Sites are $13 to $20 per night. Open year-round.

Directions: From Pasco, drive west on U.S. 12 past Richland and continue eight miles to Exit 96 and the Benton City/West Richland exit. Take that exit and drive one block north to Abby Avenue. Turn left (west) and drive 1.5 blocks to the park on the left.

Contact: Beach RV Park, 113 Abby Avenue, Benton City, WA 99320; 509/588-5959 (phone or fax); website: www.angelfire.com/wa2/beachrvpark.

28 Desert Gold RV Park and Motel

 6

This is a nice RV park located about one mile from the Columbia River. Nearby recreation options include an 18-hole golf course, hiking trails, a full-service marina, and tennis courts. You can also visit the Department of Energy public information center at the Hanford Science Center. The RV park has a pool and spa if you just want to relax without going anywhere.

Location: Near the Columbia River; see Southeastern Washington, map 6, grid f6.

Campsites, facilities: There are 90 sites with full hookups for trailers or RVs of any length, including 15 drive-through sites, and 29 motel rooms including 19 with kitchenettes. Picnic tables and cable TV are provided. Flush toilets, showers, bottled gas, a dump station, a store, a coin-operated laundry, ice, a game/meeting room, video rentals, and a seasonal hot tub and swimming pool are available. A café is located within one mile. Boat docks and launching facilities are nearby on the Columbia River. Leashed pets are permitted.

Reservations, fees: Reservations accepted. Sites are $20 per night, $1.50 per person per night for more than two people. Major credit cards accepted. Open year-round.

Directions: In Richland on I-182, take Exit 3 (Queensgate). Turn right and drive to Columbia Park Trail (the first left). Turn left and drive about two miles to the park.

Contact: Desert Gold RV Park and Motel, 611 Columbia Park Trail, Richland, WA 99352; 509/627-1000 or 800/788-GOLD (800/788-4653), fax 509/627-3467.

29 Columbia Park

  7

This campground is set in a grassy suburban area on the Columbia River, adjacent to 605-acre Columbia Park. Nearby activities include water-skiing on the Columbia River, an 18-hole golf course, hiking trails, marked bike trails, tennis courts, and Frisbee golf. The sun can feel like a branding iron during the summer here.

Location: On the Columbia River; see Southeastern Washington, map 6, grid g7.

Campsites, facilities: There are 58 sites, including 30 with partial hookups (water and electricity), for tents, trailers, or RVs; 14 are drive-through. Picnic tables and fire grills are provided. Drinking water, restrooms, flush toilets, showers, a dump station, ice, and a playground with horseshoes are available. Firewood can be obtained for a fee. Group picnic shelters, a snack bar, and a public telephone are available nearby. Some facilities are wheelchair-accessible. A store and a café are located within one mile. Boat docks and launching facilities are nearby. Leashed pets are permitted.

Reservations, fees: Reservations accepted at 509/585-4529. Sites are $7 to $11 per night. Major credit cards accepted. Open year-round.

Directions: In Kennewick on U.S. 395/Highway 240, drive west toward the Columbia River to the first exit, signed Columbia Park. Take that exit and continue to the campground along the highway. The campground is located adjacent to Columbia Park.

Contact: Columbia Park Campground, 6515 Columbia Park Trail, Kennewick, WA 99336; 509/585-4529 or 509/585-5293.

30 Greentree RV Park

 6

This shady park in urban Pasco is close to an 18-hole golf course, hiking trails, a full-service marina, and tennis courts. The Franklin County Historical Museum, which is located in town, and the Sacajawea State Park Museum and Interpretive Center, located three miles southeast of town, both offer extensive collections of Native American artifacts. One bonus here: Parking is available for extra vehicles. Also note that about 15 site rentals are permanent.

Location: In Pasco; see Southeastern Washington, map 6, grid g8.

Campsites, facilities: There are 40 sites with full hookups for trailers or RVs of any length. A coin-operated laundry and coin-operated showers are available. Bottled gas, a store, a café, and ice are located within one mile. Boat docks, launching facilities, and rentals are nearby. Leashed pets are permitted.

Reservations, fees: Reservations accepted. Sites are $18 per night; call for weekly and monthly rates. Open year-round.

Directions: In Pasco on I-182, take Exit 13 onto Fourth Avenue and continue a short distance to the park entrance driveway on the right. Turn right and enter the park.

Contact: Greentree RV Park, 2103 North Fifth Avenue, No. 69, Pasco, WA 99301; 509/547-6220 (phone or fax).

31 Arrowhead RV Park

    5

This is a decent layover spot in Pasco. Nearby recreation options include an 18-hole golf course, a full-service marina, and tennis courts.

Location: Near the Columbia River; see Southeastern Washington, map 6, grid g8.

Campsites, facilities: There are 35 tent sites and 80 sites with full hookups for trailers or RVs of any length; 33 are drive-through sites. Electricity (30 Amp), drinking water, sewer hookups, and picnic tables are provided. Flush toilets, showers, a pay phone, and a coin-operated laundry are available. A store and a café are located within walking distance. Small pets are permitted.

Reservations, fees: Reservations accepted. Sites are $20 to $30 per night for two people, $6 per person and $4 per child per night for more than two people. Open year-round.

Directions: In Pasco on U.S. 395 North, take the Hillsboro Street exit, turn east, and drive a short distance to Commercial Avenue. Turn right (south) and drive one quarter-mile to the park entrance on the right.

Contact: Arrowhead RV Park, 3120 Commercial Avenue, Pasco, WA 99301; 509/545-8206.

32 Hood Park

   6

This is a 99-acre park on Lake Wallula. All the campsites are paved at the main campground, with an overflow camping area and boat camping also available. This park is a more developed, nearby alternative to Columbia Park Campground and provides access for swimming and boating. There are hiking trails throughout the park, along with two stocked fishing ponds. Other recreation options include basketball and horseshoes. McNary Wildlife Refuge is right next door, and Sacajawea State Park is within four miles.

Location: On Lake Wallula; see Southeastern Washington, map 7, grid g1.

Campsites, facilities: There are 69 sites for tents, trailers, or RVs up to 60 feet long, including 25 pull-through sites, and an overflow camping area with 90 sites. Picnic tables and fire grills are provided. Drinking water, restrooms, flush toilets, showers, a dump station, a playground, horseshoe pits, a basketball court, a swimming beach, a covered picnic area, public phones, and an amphitheater are available. Summer programs are also available. A restaurant and convenience store are located within two miles. Some facilities are wheelchair-accessible. Boat docks and launching facilities are nearby. Leashed pets are permitted.

Reservations, fees: Reservations accepted; phone 877/444-6777 or access the website: www.reserveusa.com ($8.65 reservation fee). Sites are $14 to $16 per night, and $7 per night in the overflow area and for boat camping. Senior discount available. Open April through September. The gates are locked from 10 P.M. to 6 A.M.

Directions: In Pasco, drive southeast on U.S. 12 for three miles to the junction with Highway 124. Turn left (east) on Highway 124 and drive an extremely short distance to the park entrance on the right.

Contact: U.S. Army Corps of Engineers, 2763 Monument Drive, Burbank, WA 99323; 509/547-7781, fax 509/543-3201.

Charbonneau Park

 6

This shorefront camp is a centerpiece for a 244-acre park that is set along the Snake River just above Ice Harbor Dam. It is a good spot for fishing, boating, swimming, and water-skiing. An overflow camping area provides an insurance policy if the numbered sites are full. At Lake Sacajawea, the dam's visitors center (open daily from April through October) features exhibits and a view through Lucite glass of a salmon fish ladder.

Location: On the Snake River; see Southeastern Washington, map 7, grid f2.

Campsites, facilities: There are 54 sites for sites for tents, trailers, or RVs up to 60 feet long, including 18 pull-through sites with full hookups, and an overflow camping area. Picnic tables and fire grills are provided. Flush toilets, showers, tent pads, a dump station, a public telephone, a playground with volleyball net, and summer campground programs are available. Some facilities are wheelchair-accessible. A marina with boat docks, launching facilities, a marine dump station, a swimming beach, a store, ice, and group shelters with electricity are nearby. Leashed pets are permitted.

Reservations, fees: Reservations accepted; phone 877/444-6777 or access the website: www.reserveusa.com ($8.65 reservation fee). Sites are $14 to $18 per night. Overflow and boat camping is $7 per night. Senior discount available. Open April through October with full facilities and gate closure from 10 P.M. to 6 A.M.; there are limited facilities and no fee the rest of the year.

Directions: In Pasco, drive southeast on U.S. 12 for five miles to Highway 124. Turn east and drive eight miles to Sun Harbor Road. Turn north and drive two miles to the park.

Contact: U.S. Army Corps of Engineers, Route 6, Box 693, Pasco, WA 99301-9165; 509/547-7781.

Fishhook Park

 6

If you're driving along Highway 124 and you need a spot for the night, make the turn on Fishhook Park Road and check out this wooded camp along the Snake River. It is a nice spot within a 46-acre park set on Lake Sacajawea. Some lawn area is provided, along with places to swim, fish, and water-ski. It is a one-mile walk along railroad tracks to access a fishing pond. This park is popular on summer weekends.

Location: On the Snake River; see Southeastern Washington, map 7, grid f2.

Campsites, facilities: There are 20 tent-only sites and 41 sites with partial hookups (electricity and water) for tents, trailers, or RVs up to 45 feet long; eight are drive-through sites. Picnic tables and fire grills are provided. Drinking water, flush toilets, showers, a dump station, a public telephone, and a playground are available. Some facilities are wheelchair-accessible. Campground programs are available in the summer. Boat docks, launching facilities, a swimming beach, and group shelters with electricity are nearby. Leashed pets are permitted.

Reservations, fees: Reservations accepted; phone 877/444-6777 or access the website: www.reserveusa.com ($8.65 reservation fee). Sites are $10 to $18 per night, and boat camping is $7 per night. Senior discount available. Open April through September. Park gates are locked from 10 P.M. to 6 A.M.

Directions: In Pasco, drive southeast on U.S. 12 for five miles to Highway 124. Turn east and drive 18 miles to Fishhook Park Road. Turn left on Fishhook Park Road and drive four miles to the park.

Contact: U.S. Army Corps of Engineers, 2763 Monument Drive, Burbank, WA 99323; 509/547-7781, fax 509/543-3201.

35 Windust

6

Windust is the only game in town, with no other campgrounds within a 20-mile radius. The camp is located along the shore of Lake Sacajawea near the Lower Monumental Dam on the Snake River. The park covers 54 acres. Swimming, water-skiing, and fishing are popular.

Location: On Lake Sacajawea; see Southeastern Washington, map 7, grid d4.

Campsites, facilities: Open camping areas at both ends of the park provide space for 24 tents, trailers, or RVs. Picnic tables and fire grills are provided. Vault toilets and garbage bins are available year-round. Flush toilets are available from April through September. Drinking water, a playground and horseshoe pit, a swimming beach, covered sun shelters, and a public telephone are available nearby. Some facilities are wheelchair-accessible. Boat docks and launching facilities are nearby. Leashed pets are permitted.

Reservations, fees: Reservations accepted; phone 877/444-6777 or access the website: www.reserveusa.com ($8.65 reservation fee). Sites are $8 per night, and boat camping is $7 per night. Senior discount available. Open year-round, with limited facilities and no fee from October through March.

Directions: From Pasco, drive east on U.S. 12 for four miles to Pasco/Kahlotus Highway. Turn east and drive 28 miles to Burr Canyon Road. Turn right on Burr Canyon

Road and drive 5.2 miles to the park (from the north, the Burr Canyon Road becomes Highway 263).

Contact: U.S. Army Corps of Engineers, 2763 Monument Drive, Burbank, WA 99323; 509/547-7781, fax 509/543-3201.

36 Palouse Falls State Park

 10

This remote state park is well worth the trip. Spectacular 198-foot Palouse Falls is a sight not to miss. A quarter-mile wheelchair-accessible trail has been completed to a waterfall overlook. The park is set at the confluence of the Snake and Palouse Rivers, and it does not receive heavy use, even in summer. The park covers 1,282 acres and features a waterfall observation shelter, shaded picnic facilities, historical displays, and an abundance of wildlife.

Location: On the Snake and Palouse Rivers; see Southeastern Washington, map 7, grid c7.

Campsites, facilities: There are 10 primitive campsites for tents, self-contained trailers, or RVs up to 40 feet long. Picnic tables and fire grills are provided. Pit toilets, a picnic area, and a dump station are available. Some facilities are wheelchair-accessible. Leashed pets are permitted.

Reservations, fees: No reservations accepted. Sites are $8 per night, $6 per extra vehicle per night. Senior discount available. Open April to late September, weather permitting.

Directions: From Starbuck, drive northwest on Highway 261 for 16.4 miles (crossing the river) to the park entrance and Palouse Falls Road. Turn right and drive to the park.

Contact: Palouse Falls State Park, 360/902-8844; or State Park information, 509/646-3252.

37 Lyon's Ferry State Park

 8

This state park covers 1,282 acres, is located at the confluence of the Snake and Palouse Rivers, and is loaded with activities. One feature is the nearby terrain. It is part of hundreds of square miles of "peeled ground" that spans from Spokane west to the Cascades and south to the Snake River, which some geologists call "the strangest landscape this side of Mars." A three-quarter-mile trail leads to a lookout point with interpretive plaques. In addition, another short hike from camp can take you to the Marmes Rock Shelter, where the Marmes Man—the oldest human remains ever found in the Western hemisphere—was unearthed in 1968. Many other recreation options include boating, fishing, swimming, and waterskiing. Note that high winds can occur suddenly and surprise many boaters. A good side trip is a visit to beautiful 198-foot Palouse Falls, located 10 miles north.

Location: On the Snake River; see Southeastern Washington, map 7, grid d7.

Campsites, facilities: There are 49 sites, including 12 pull-through sites with full hookups, for tents, trailers, or RVs up to 45 feet along, and two primitive tent sites. Picnic tables and fire grills are provided. Restrooms, flush toilets, coin-operated showers, and a dump station are available. A bathhouse, a sheltered picnic area, a snack bar, a boat dock, and a boat launch and moorage are available nearby. Some facilities are wheelchair-accessible. Leashed pets are permitted.

Reservations, fees: No reservations accepted. Sites are $6 to $21 per night, $6 per extra vehicle per night. Moorage fee $7 to $16 per night. Senior discount available. Open April through September.

Directions: From Starbuck, drive northwest on Highway 261 for 14.2 miles (crossing the river) to the park entrance (just north of the river on the right). Turn right and drive to the park.

Contact: Lyon's Ferry State Park, 360/902-8844; or State Park information, 509/646-3252.

38 Lewis and Clark Trail State Park

 8

Fishing for rainbow trout and brown trout can be excellent here. The park is set on 37 acres with frontage along the Touchet River. The landscape is an unusual mixture of old-growth forest and riparian habitat featuring long-leafed Ponderosa pine and cottonwood amid the surrounding arid prairie grasslands. An interpretive display explains much of it, as well as the history of the area. A Saturday evening living-history program depicts the story of Lewis and Clark and the site's history here on the original Lewis and Clark Trail. Also note: If it's getting late and you need to stop, consider this camp because it's the only one within 20 miles. In winter, cross-country skiing and snow-shoeing are good here.

Location: On the Lewis and Clark Trail; see Southeastern Washington, map 7, grid f8.

Campsites, facilities: There are 25 sites for tents, self-enclosed trailers, or RVs up to 28 feet long and four primitive tent sites. Picnic tables and fire grills are provided. Restrooms, flush toilets, showers, firewood, and a dump station are available. Two fire circles, an amphitheater, a picnic area, badminton, a baseball field, and a volleyball court are available nearby. A store, a café, and ice are located within one mile. Leashed pets are permitted.

Reservations, fees: No reservations accepted. Sites are $6 to $15 per night, $6 per extra vehicle per night. Open year-round, with limited winter facilities.

Directions: From Walla Walla, drive east on U.S. 12 for 22 miles to Waitsburg. Bear right on U.S. 12 and drive east for 4.5 miles to the park entrance on the left.

Contact: Lewis and Clark Trail State Park, Route 1, P.O. Box 90, Dayton, WA 99328; 509/337-6457; or State Park information, 360/902-8844.

39 Central Ferry State Park

 8

This is the only campground within a 20-mile radius, yet it's a great spot to hunker down and enjoy the world. It is a 185-acre park set on 10,000-acre Lake Bryan, a reservoir set on the Snake River, created by Little Goose Dam. Boating is popular at the desert lake, with summer daytime temperatures in the 90s and even 100s occasionally. Despite the lake, the surrounding terrain is dry, courtesy of just eight inches of average rainfall per year, with geologic evidence of basaltic lava flows. The park is named after a ferry that once operated in this area. A beach, swimming, boating, water-skiing, swimming, and fishing for bass and catfish are all options here. Navigational locks are on the lake.

Location: On the Snake River; see Southeastern Washington, map 8, grid c2.

Campsites, facilities: There are eight primitive tent sites and 60 sites with full hookups for trailers or RVs up to 45 feet long. There is also one group camp accommodating up to 100 people. Picnic tables and fire grills are provided. Restrooms, flush toilets, coin-operated showers, a dump station, a group fire ring, a day-use picnic area with covered kitchen shelter, a swim beach and bathhouse, beachside shade structures, volleyball courts, and three horseshoe pit areas are available. A store and a restaurant are within five miles. Some facilities are wheelchair-accessible. Boat docks, launching facilities, and a fishing pier are within the park. Leashed pets are permitted.

Reservations, fees: Reserve at 888/CAMP-OUT (888/226-7688); website: www.parks.wa.gov/reservations ($7 reservation fee). Sites are $6 to $22 per night, $6 per extra vehicle per night. Senior discount available. For group camp reservations, phone 509/549-3551; group sites are $25 per night plus $2 per night per camper and $13 per night per RV. Major credit cards accepted. Open mid-March to mid-November.

Directions: From Spokane, drive south on U.S. 195 for 59 miles to Highway 26. Turn west on Highway 26 and drive 17 miles southwest to the town of Dusty and Highway 127. Turn south on Highway 127 and drive 17 miles to the park entrance on the right (set on the north shore of the Snake River).

Contact: Central Ferry State Park, 10152 State Route 127, Pomeroy, WA 99347; 509/549-3551; State Park information, 360/902-8844.

40 Palouse Empire Fairgrounds & Horse Camp

 6

The camp consists primarily of a large lawn area with shade trees, set just off the road. The highway, surprisingly, is relatively limited. All sites are on grass. The park covers 47 acres, with paved trails available around the adjacent fairgrounds. This is an agricultural area, with rolling hills, and it is considered the "Lentil Capital of the World." Horse campers are encouraged to stay here, with wash racks, corrals, arenas, and water troughs. This camp fills up for the Whitman County Fair in mid-September. They turn back the clock every Labor Day weekend with the annual "Threshing Bee," where there are demonstrations of historical farming practices dating back to the early 1900s, including the use of draft horses.

Location: west of Colfax, Whitman County; see Southeastern Washington, map 8, grid b5.

Campsites, facilities: There are 60 sites with partial hookups (water and electricity) for tents, trailers, or RVs of any length. Large groups can be accommodated. Picnic tables are provided. Restrooms, drinking water, flush toilets, showers, and a dump station are available. Some facilities are wheelchair-accessible. Restaurants, gas, and supplies are available 4.5 miles away in Colfax. Leashed pets are permitted.

Reservations, fees: No reservations accepted. Sites are $15 per night, horse stalls $10 per night. Open year-round with limited winter facilities.

Directions: From Colfax and Highway 26, drive west on Highway 26 for 4.5 miles to the fairgrounds on the right.

Contact: Palouse Empire Fairgrounds & Horse Camp, Whitman County, North 310 Main, Colfax, WA 99111; 509/397-6238; website: www.whitmancounty.org.

⁴¹ Boyer Park and Marina

 7

This 99-acre park on the north shore of Lake Bryan is two miles from the Lower Granite Dam. It features 3.5 miles of trails for hiking and biking, and the lake is popular for water-skiing and fishing for sturgeon, steelhead, and salmon. The camp features shade trees, with all campsites paved and bordered by a grassy day-use area. It is flat and open and gets hot here in summer. The camp is well above the water level, typically about 100 feet above the lakeshore. The camp commonly fills on summer weekends.

Location: on Lake Bryan on the Snake River; see Southeastern Washington, map 8, grid c5.

Campsites, facilities: There are 28 sites, including 12 with full hookups and 16 with partial hookups (no sewer) for tents, trailers, or RVs up to 40 feet long. Picnic tables and fire grills are provided. Restrooms, drinking water, flush toilets, showers, and a dump station are available. Some facilities are wheelchair-accessible. A coin-operated laundry, covered shelters, a swimming area, a snack bar, a store, ice, gas, and public phones are available. A restaurant, a marina, boat docks, a boat launch, and a marine dump station are nearby. Leashed pets are permitted.

Reservations, fees: Reservations at 509/397-3208; sites are $10 to $22 per night. Senior discount available. Major credit cards accepted. Open year-round with limited winter facilities.

Directions: From U.S. 195 at Colfax, turn southwest on Almota Road and drive 17 miles to the park and campground.

Contact: Port of Whitman County, West 105 Island Street, Colfax, WA 99111; 509/397-3208 or 509/397-3791.

⁴² Wawawai County Park

 7

This park covers just 49 acres but is set near the inlet to Lower Granite Lake, about one quarter-mile to the lake. The camp itself is set on a hillside, with all sites paved. Some sites have views of a bay, but not the entire lake. Tree cover is a plus. So is a half-mile loop trail that leads to a bird-viewing platform, and a diverse amount of wildlife and geology, making interpretive hikes with naturalists often popular. One strange note is that an underground house built in 1980 has been converted to a ranger's residence. This camp often fills on summer weekends.

Location: on Lower Granite Lake, Whitman County; see Southeastern Washington, map 8, grid c6.

Campsites, facilities: There are nine sites for tents, self-contained trailers, or RVs up to 24 feet long. No hookups are available. Picnic tables and fire grills are provided. Drinking water and vault toilets are available. A playground with a volleyball net and a group covered shelter is available nearby. Some facilities are wheelchair-accessible. Leashed pets are permitted.

Reservations, fees: No reservations; sites are $10 per night. Open year-round with limited winter facilities and no fee from mid-October to mid-April.

Directions: From Colfax, drive south on U.S. 195 for 16 miles to Wawawai-Pullman Road (located just west of Pullman). Turn right (west) and drive about 10 miles to Wawawai Road. Turn right on Wawawai Road (signed) and drive to the park on Lower Granite Lake.

Contact: Wawawai County Park, Whitman County, North 310 Main, Colfax, WA 99111; 509/397-6238; website: www.whitman county.org.

43 Chief Timothy State Park

🏃 🏊 🎣 🚤
🐕 🤸 ♿ 🚐 ⛺ 8

This unusual state park is set on a bridged island in the Snake River and is accessible to cars. The park covers 282 acres with two miles of shoreline. It is a desert landscape, with the park set on an island composed of glacial tills. There are 2.5 miles of hiking trails, and in addition, water sports are available here, including fishing, swimming, boating, water-skiing, and sailing, plus docks for boating campers, a beach area, and an interpretive center focusing on the Lewis and Clark expedition. Outfitters in Clarkston will take you sight-seeing up the Grand Canyon of the Snake River. Call the Clarkston Chamber of Commerce at 509/758-7712 for details.

Location: On the Snake River; see Southeastern Washington, map 8, grid e7.

Campsites, facilities: There are 58 sites, including 25 with full hookups and eight with partial hookups (water and electricity) for tents, trailers, or RVs up to 60 feet long and two primitive tent sites. Picnic tables and fire grills are provided. Restrooms, flush toilets, showers, a dump station, a picnic area, a small store, and a playground with volleyball courts and horseshoe pits are available. Firewood can be obtained for a fee. Some facilities are wheelchair-accessible. Boat docks and launching facilities are nearby. Leashed pets are permitted.

Reservations, fees: Reserve at 888/CAMP-OUT (888/226-7688); website: www.parks.wa.gov/reservations ($7 reservation fee). Sites are $6 to $22 per night, $6 per extra vehicle per night. Senior discount available. Major credit cards accepted. Open year-round, with limited winter facilities.

Directions: From Clarkston on the Washington/Idaho border, drive west on U.S. 12 for seven miles to the signed park entrance road on the right. Turn north and drive one mile to the park, which is set on a bridged island in the Snake River.

Contact: Chief Timothy State Park, Highway 12, Clarkston, WA 99403; 509/758-9580; or State Park information, 360/902-8844.

44 Tucannon

 8

For people willing to rough it, this backcountry camp in Umatilla National Forest is the place, with plenty of hiking, fishing, and hunting, all in a rugged setting. The camp is set along the Tucannon River, which offers a myriad of options for vacationers. This camp is popular from early spring (best time for fishing) through fall (when it makes a good hunting camp). In summer, several nearby ponds are stocked with trout, making it a good family destination. There is some tree cover. The elevation is 2,600 feet.

Location: In Umatilla National Forest; see Southeastern Washington, map 8, grid f3.

Campsites, facilities: There are 13 sites for tents, trailers, or RVs up to 21 feet long. Picnic tables and fire grills are provided. Vault toilets are available, but there is no drinking water. Garbage must be packed out. Two covered shelters are available nearby. Leashed pets are permitted.

Reservations, fees: No reservations; no fee. Open May to late November, weather permitting.

Directions: From Clarkston, drive west on U.S. 12 for 37 miles to Pomeroy. Continue west for five miles to Tatman Mountain Road (signed for Camp Wooten). Turn left (south) and drive 19 miles (becomes Forest Road 47). Once inside the national forest boundary, continue southwest on Forest Road 47 for four miles to the campground on the left.

Contact: Umatilla National Forest, Pomeroy Ranger District, 71 West Main Street, Pomeroy, WA 99347; 509/843-1891, fax 509/843-4621.

45 Alder Thicket

 7

This is probably the first time you've heard of this place. Hardly anybody knows about it, in-

cluding people who live relatively nearby in Walla Walla. It is set at an elevation of 5,100 feet, making it a prime base camp for a backcountry hiking adventure in summer or a jumping-off point for a hunting trip in the fall. This is a primitive camp, but it's great if you're looking for quiet and solitude. Note: During summer, drinking water is available six miles away at the Clearwater Guard Station.

Location: In Umatilla National Forest; see Southeastern Washington, map 8, grid f4.

Campsites, facilities: There are five sites for tents, trailers, or RVs up to 21 feet long. Picnic tables and fire grills are provided. Vault toilets are available, but there is no drinking water. Garbage must be packed out. Some facilities are wheelchair-accessible. Leashed pets are permitted.

Reservations, fees: No reservations; no fee. Open mid-May to mid-November, weather permitting.

Directions: From Clarkston, drive west on U.S. 12 for 37 miles to Pomeroy and Highway 128. Turn south and drive seven miles to a fork. At the fork, continue straight to Forest Road 40 (15 miles from Pomeroy to the national forest boundary) and continue 3.5 miles to the campground on the right.

Contact: Umatilla National Forest, Pomeroy Ranger District, 71 West Main Street, Pomeroy, WA 99347; 509/843-1891, fax 509/843-4621.

46 Big Springs

 8

This camp is set at an elevation of 5,000 feet. In the fall, Big Springs is used primarily by hunters, while come summer this nice, cool site is a possible base camp for a backpacking trip. Although quite primitive with little in the way of activity options, this is a perfect spot to get away from it all. It's advisable to obtain a U.S. Forest Service map. During summer, drinking water is available at the Clearwater Guard Station, located three miles to the southwest on Forest Road 42.

Location: In Umatilla National Forest; see Southeastern Washington, map 8, grid f4.

Campsites, facilities: There are eight tent sites. Picnic tables are provided. Vault toilets are available, but there is no drinking water. Some facilities are wheelchair-accessible. Leashed pets are permitted.

Reservations, fees: No reservations; no fee. Open mid-May to mid-November.

Directions: From Clarkston, drive west on U.S. 12 for 37 miles to Pomeroy and Highway 128. Turn south and drive 25 miles to Forest Road 42 (to the Clearwater Lookout Tower). Turn left and continue on Forest Road 42 for five miles to the campground entrance road (Forest Road 4225). Turn left and drive to the campground at the end of the road.

Contact: Umatilla National Forest, Pomeroy Ranger District, 71 West Main Street, Pomeroy, WA 99347; 509/843-1891, fax 509/843-4621.

47 Teal Spring

 8

The views of the Tucannun drainage and the Wenaha-Tucannon Wilderness are astonishing from the nearby lookout. Teal Springs Camp is set at 5,600 feet elevation and is one of several small, primitive camps in the area. There are good day-hiking options on trails in the immediate area. A U.S. Forest Service map details the backcountry roads, trails, and streams. Hunting is popular in the fall.

Location: In Umatilla National Forest; see Southeastern Washington, map 8, grid g4.

Campsites, facilities: There are five sites for tents, trailers, or RVs up to 26 feet long. Vault toilets are available, but there is no drinking water. Picnic tables and fire grills

are provided. Garbage must be packed out. Some facilities are wheelchair-accessible. Leashed pets are permitted.

Reservations, fees: No reservations; no fee. Open June to mid-November.

Directions: From Clarkston, drive west on U.S. 12 for 37 miles to Pomeroy and Highway 128. Turn south and drive 25 miles to Forest Road 42 (to the Clearwater Lookout Tower). Turn left and continue on Forest Road 42, and drive one mile to the campground entrance road. Turn right and drive 200 yards to the campground.

Contact: Umatilla National Forest, Pomeroy Ranger District, 71 West Main Street, Pomeroy, WA 99347; 509/843-1891, fax 509/843-4621.

48 Godman

 8

This tiny, little-known spot bordering a wilderness area is set at 6,050 feet elevation and features drop-dead gorgeous views at sunset, as well as a wilderness trailhead. It is primarily used as a base camp for backcountry expeditions. A trailhead provides access to the Wenaha-Tucannon Wilderness for both hikers and horseback riders. Horse facilities are available less than one quarter-mile away. There are also opportunities for mountain biking, but note that bikes are forbidden past the wilderness boundary.

Location: Near the Wenaha-Tucannon Wilderness in Umatilla National Forest; see Southeastern Washington, map 8, grid h2.

Campsites, facilities: There are eight sites for tents, trailers, or RVs up to 15 feet long, plus one cabin that can accommodate up to eight people. Picnic tables and fire grills are provided. Vault toilets are available, but there is no drinking water. Garbage must be packed out. Some facilities are wheelchair-accessible. Facilities are available nearby for up to six people with horses, including hitching rails and a spring, with an additional fee for more than six. Leashed pets are permitted.

Reservations, fees: No reservations accepted. There is no fee for the campsites, but cabins are $30 a night plus $5 per person. Open mid-June to late October; cabin is available year-round.

Directions: From Walla Walla, drive northeast on U.S. 12 for 32 miles to Dayton and North Fork Touchet River Road. Turn right on North Fork Touchet River Road and drive 14 miles southeast to the national forest boundary; continue to Kendall Skyline Road. Turn left (south) and drive 11 miles to the campground on the left.

Contact: Umatilla National Forest, Pomeroy Ranger District, 71 West Main Street, Pomeroy, WA 99347; 509/843-1891, fax 509/843-4621.

49 Fields Spring State Park
  8

This 792-acre state park is located in the Blue Mountains, set in a forested landscape atop Puffer Butte, offering a spectacular view of three states and the Grande Ronde River. A hiking trail leads up to Puffer Butte at 4,500 feet, which offers a panoramic view of the Snake River Canyon, the Wallowa Mountains, and Idaho, Oregon, and Washington. This park is noted for its variety of bird life and wildflowers. There are seven miles of mountain-biking trails, along with three miles of hiking trails. In winter, there are opportunities for cross-country skiing, snowmobiling, snowshoeing, and general snow play. Basalt is dominant across the landscape. Not many people know about this spot, yet it's a good one tucked away in the southeast corner of

the state. It also has a designated environmental learning center. Two day-use areas with boat launches, managed by the Department of Fish and Game, are within about 25 miles of the park. One is the Snake River Access, 22.5 miles south of Asotin on Snake River Road; the other is the Grande Ronde River Access, 24 miles south of Asotin on the same road.

Location: Near Puffer Butte; see Southeastern Washington, map 8, grid h7.

Campsites, facilities: There are 20 sites for tents or self-contained RVs up to 30 feet long and four primitive tent sites. Picnic tables and fire grills are provided. Restrooms, drinking water, flush toilets, a dump station, two picnic shelters with electricity, two sheltered fire circles, a playground with horseshoe pits, a softball field, and volleyball courts are available. Showers and firewood can be obtained for a fee. A store, a restaurant, and ice are located within one mile. Some facilities are wheelchair-accessible. Leashed pets are permitted.

Reservations, fees: No reservations accepted. Sites are $6 to $15 per night, $6 per extra vehicle per night. Senior discount available. Open year-round, with limited winter facilities.

Directions: From Clarkston, turn south on Highway 129 and drive 28.5 miles (just south of Rattlesnake Pass) to the park entrance on the left (east) side of the road.

Contact: Fields Spring State Park, P.O. Box 86, Anatone, WA 99401; 509/256-3332; State Park information, 360/902-8844.

50 Brooks Memorial State Park
 7

This 700-acre park is located between the barren hills of the South Yakima Valley and the lodgepole pine forests of the Simcoe Mountains. It is set at an elevation of nearly 3,000

feet. Highlights include nine miles of hiking trails, a 1.5-mile-long nature trail that runs along the Little Klickitat River, and occasional excellent fishing for trout. You can extend your trip into the mountains, where you'll find open meadows with a panoramic view of Mt. Hood. Nature talks are provided at the environmental learning center. Other activities near the park include stargazing at the Goldendale Observatory, visiting the Maryhill Museum, viewing the replica of Stonehenge on State Route 14, and driving the historic Columbia Highway in nearby Oregon. The Yakima Indian Nation is located two miles north of the park.

Location: Near the Goldendale Observatory; see Southeastern Washington, map 9, grid a3.

Campsites, facilities: There are 22 developed sites for tents or self-contained RVs, 23 sites with water and electrical hookups for trailers or RVs up to 50 feet long, and two primitive tent sites. Picnic tables and fire grills are provided. Restrooms, flush toilets, a dump station, and a playground are available. Showers can be obtained for a fee. A picnic area with covered shelters and electricity and a ballfield are nearby. A store is located within one mile. Leashed pets are permitted.

Reservations, fees: No reservations accepted. Sites are $6 to $21 per night, $6 per extra vehicle per night. Open year-round, with limited winter facilities.

Directions: From Toppenish, drive south on U.S. 97 for 40 miles to the park on the right (well marked).

Contact: Brooks Memorial State Park; 360/902-8844 or 509/773-5382.

51 Crow Butte State Park

 8

How would you like to be stranded on a romantic island? Well, this park offers that possibility. This state park is set on an island in the Columbia River and is the only campground in a 25-mile radius. The park is sometimes referred to as "The Maui of the Columbia," covering 1,312 acres with several miles of shoreline. It is set on the Lewis and Clark Trail, with the camp situated in a partially protected bay. A mile-long path leads to the top of a butte, where you can see Mt. Hood, Mt. Adams, and the Columbia River Valley, the highlight of 3.5 miles of hiking trails. Water-skiing, sailboarding, fishing, swimming, and hiking are among the possibilities here. One downer: Keep an eye out for rattlesnakes, which are occasionally spotted. The Umatilla National Wildlife Refuge is adjacent to the park and allows fishing and hunting in specified areas.

Location: On the Columbia River; see Southeastern Washington, map 10, grid b2.

Campsites, facilities: There are two primitive tent sites and 50 sites with full hookups for tents, trailers, or RVs up to 60 feet long, including 24 pull-through sites and one group camp. Fire grills and picnic tables are provided. Restrooms, flush toilets, coin-operated showers, a sheltered picnic area, a swimming beach, and a dump station are available. Some facilities are wheelchair-accessible. Boat-launching and moorage facilities are nearby. A store is open on weekends. Leashed pets are permitted.

Reservations, fees: Reserve at 888/CAMP-OUT (888/226-7688); website: www.parks.wa.gov/reservations ($7 reservation fee). Sites are $6 to $21 per night, $6 per extra vehicle per night. Group site is $35 plus $10 per person. Moorage fees are $7 to $16 per night. Senior discount available. Open year-round, with limited winter facilities.

Directions: From the junction of I-82/U.S. 395 and Highway 20 at Plymouth, just north of the Columbia River, turn west on

Highway 14. Drive to Paterson and continue west for 13 miles to the park entrance road at Milepost 155 on the right. Turn right and drive one mile (across the bridge) to the park on the island.

Contact: Crow Butte State Park, P.O. Box 217, Paterson, WA 99345; 360/902-8844 or 509/875-2644.

52 Plymouth Park

  7

Plymouth Park is a family and RV-style campground set on Lake Umatilla on the Columbia River. It is a 112-acre park, but it is not at the shore of the lake, rather about a one-quarter-mile drive to the water. The camp has tree cover, which is a nice plus, and it fills up most summer weekends. Each campsite has a tent pad.

Location: on Lake Umatilla, Benton County; see Southeastern Washington, map 10, grid a6.

Campsites, facilities: There are 32 sites, including 28 pull-through sites and 16 with partial hookups (no sewer) for tents, trailers, or RVs up to 40 feet long. Picnic tables and fire grills are provided. Restrooms, drinking water, flush toilets, showers, a dump station, and a coin-operated laundry are available. A boat dock, boat launch, swimming areas, and covered shelters are available nearby. A store and a restaurant are within two miles. Some facilities are wheelchair-accessible. Leashed pets are permitted.

Reservations, fees: Reserve at 877/444-6777 ($8.65 reservation fee) or website: www .reserveusa.com. Senior discount available. Major credit cards accepted. Open April through October.

Directions: From Richland and I-82, drive south on I-82 for about 30 miles to Highway 14. Turn west on Highway 14 and drive two miles to the Plymouth exit. Take that exit and drive to Christy Road; continue for 200 yards to the park entrance on the left.

Contact: U.S. Army Corps of Engineers, Portland District; 509/783-1270 or 541/506-7818.

RESOURCE GUIDE

Resource Guide

National Forests

The Forest Service provides many secluded camps and allows camping anywhere except where it is specifically prohibited. If you ever want to clear the cobwebs from your head and get away from it all, this is the way to go.

Many Forest Service campgrounds are remote and have no drinking water. You usually don't need to check in or make reservations, and sometimes there is no fee. At many Forest Service campgrounds that provide drinking water, the camping fee is often only a few dollars, with payment made on the honor system. Because most of these camps are in mountain areas, they are subject to winter closure due to snow or mud.

Dogs are permitted in national forests with no extra charge. Always carry documentation of current vaccinations.

Northwest Forest Pass

A Northwest Forest Pass is required for certain activities in some Washington national forests and at North Cascades National Park in Washington. The pass is required for parking at participating trailheads, rustic camping areas, boat launches, picnic areas, and visitors centers.

Daily passes cost $5 per vehicle; annual passes are $30 per vehicle. You can buy Northwest Forest Passes at national forest offices and dozens of retail outlets and online vendors. Holders of Golden Age and Golden Access (not Golden Eagle) cards can buy the Northwest Forest Pass at a 50 percent discount at national forest offices only, or at retail outlets for the retail price. Major credit cards are accepted at most retail and online outlets but not at forest service offices.

More information about the Northwest Forest Pass program, including a listing of retail and online vendors, can be obtained at the following websites: www.fs.fed.us/r6/feedemo/ or www.naturenw.org.

National Forest Reservations

Some of the more popular camps, and most of the group camps, are on a reservation system. Reservations can be made up to 240 days in advance and up to 360 days in advance for groups. To reserve a site, call 877/444-6777 or visit the website: www.reserveusa.com. The reservation fee is usually $8.65 for a camp site in a national forest, but group site reservation fees are higher. Major credit cards are accepted. Holders of Golden Age or Golden Access passports receive a 50 percent discount for campground fees, except for group sites.

National Forest Maps

National Forest maps are among the best you can get for the price. They detail all backcountry streams, lakes, hiking trails, and logging roads for access. They usually cost $8 and can be obtained in person at forest service offices. Maps can also be purchased through Nature of the Northwest, an interpretive center, by telephone at 503/872-2750 or by website: www.naturenw.org

Forest Service Information

Forest Service personnel are most helpful for obtaining camping or hiking trail information. Unless you are buying a map or Northwest Forest Pass, it is advisable to call to get the best service. For specific information on a national forest, contact the following offices:

Colville National Forest, 765 South Main Street, Colville, WA 99114; 509/684-7000, fax 509/684-7280; website: www.fs.fed.us/r6/colville

Gifford Pinchot National Forest, 10600 N.E. 51st Circle, Vancouver, WA 98682; 360/891-5000, fax 360/891-5045; website: www.fs.fed.us/gpnf

Mount Baker-Snoqualmie National Forest, 21905 64th Avenue West, Mountlake Terrace, WA 98043; 425/775-9702, 800/627-0062, fax 425/744-3255; website: www.fs.fed.us/r6/mbs

Okanogan and Wenatchee National Forests, 215 Melody Lane, Wenatchee, WA 98801; 509/662-4335, fax 509/662-4368; website: www.fs.fed.us/r6/wenatchee

Olympic National Forest, 1835 Black Lake Blvd. SW, Olympia, WA 98512-5623; 360/956-2402, fax 360/956-2330; website: www.fs.fed.us/r6/olympic

National Parks

The national parks in Washington are natural wonders, ranging from the spectacular Mount Rainier National Park to the lava-strewn Mount St. Helens National Volcanic Monument to the often fog-bound Olympic National Park. Reservations are available at some of the campgrounds at these parks and recreation areas. Various discounts are available for holders of Golden Age and Golden Access passports, including a 50 percent reduction of camping fees (group camps not included).

For information about each of the national parks in Washington, contact the parks directly at the following telephone numbers or addresses:

Lake Roosevelt National Recreation Area, 1008 Crest Drive, Coulee Dam, WA 99116-1259; 509/633-9441; fax 509/633-9332; website: www.nps.gov/laro

Mount Rainier National Park, Tahoma Woods, Star Route, Ashford, WA 98304-9751; 360/569-2211, fax 360/569-2170; website: www.nps.gov/mora

Olympic National Park, 600 East Park Avenue, Port Angeles, WA 98362-6798; 360/565-3130, fax 360/565-3147; website: www.nps.gov/olym

North Cascades National Park, Service Complex, 810 State Route 20, Sedro Woolley, WA 98284-9394; 360/856-5700, fax 360/856-1934; website: www.nps.gov/noca

Mount St. Helens National Volcanic Monument, 42218 N. E. Yale Bridge Road, Amboy, WA 98601; 360/247-3900, fax 360/247-3901; website: www.fs.fed.us/gpnf

State Parks

The Washington State Parks system provides many popular camping spots in spectacular settings. The camps include drive-in numbered sites, tent spaces, and picnic tables, with showers and bathrooms provided. Reservations are often a necessity during the summer. Although some parks are well known, there are still some little-known gems in the state parks system where campers can enjoy seclusion, even in the summer.

More than 50 of the state park campgrounds are on a reservation system, and campsites can be booked up to nine months in advance at these parks. Reservations can be made by telephone at 888/CAMPOUT (888/226-7688) or online at website: www.parks.wa.gov/reservations. The reservation number is open from 7 A.M. to 8 P.M. (Pacific Standard Time) every day of the year, except Christmas Day and New Year's Day, and with shortened hours on Christmas Eve and New Year's Eve. Major credit cards are accepted for reservations, and credit cards are accepted at some of the parks during the summer. A $7 reservation fee is charged for a campsite, and the reservation fee for group sites is higher. Discounts are available for pass holders of disabled, limited-income, off-season senior citizen and disabled veterans status.

General information regarding Washington State Parks can be obtained by telephoning 360/902-8844 or accessing the website: www.parks.wa.gov. For more information, contact: Washington State Parks and Recreation Commission, P.O. Box 42650, Olympia, WA 98504-2669.

State Department of Natural Resources

The Department of Natural Resources manages more than five million acres of public land in Washington. All of it is managed under the concept of "multiple use," designed to provide the greatest number of recreational opportunities while still protecting natural resources.

The campgrounds in these areas are among the most primitive, remote, and least known of the camps listed in the book. The campsites are usually free, and you are asked to remove all litter and trash from the area, leaving only your footprints behind. Due to budget cutbacks, some of these campgrounds have been closed in recent years; expect more closures in the future.

In addition to maps of the area it manages, the Department of Natural Resources also has U.S. Geological Survey maps and U.S. Army Corps of Engineers maps. For information, write or telephone the Department of Natural Resources at its state or regional addresses:

State of Washington, 1111 Washington Street SE, P.O. Box 47000, Olympia, WA 98504-7000, 360/902-1000 or 800/527-3305, fax 360/902-1775; website: www.wa.gov/dnr

Central Region, 1405 Rush Road, Chehalis, WA 98532-8763; 360/748-2383, fax 360/748-2387

Northeast Region, 225 S. Silke Road, P.O. Box 190, Colville, WA 99114-0190; 509/684-7474, fax 509/684-7484

Northwest Region, 919 N. Township Street, Sedro-Woolley, WA 98284-9384; 360/856-3500, fax 360/856-2150

Olympic Region, 411 Tillicum Lane, Forks, WA 98331-9271; 360/374-6131, fax 360/374-5446

South Puget Sound Region, 950 Farman Avenue N., Enumclaw, WA 98022-9282; 360/825-1631, fax 360/825-1672

Southeast Region, 713 Bowers Road, Ellensburg, WA 98926-9301; 509/925-8510, fax 509/925-8522

Southwest Region, 601 Bond Road, P.O. Box 280, Castle Rock, WA 98611-0280; 360/577-2025, fax 360/274-4196

U.S. Army Corps of Engineers

Some of the family camps and most of the group camps operated by the U.S. Army Corps of Engineers are on a reservation system. Reservations can be made up to 240 days in advance and up to 360 days in advance for groups. To reserve a site, call 877/444-6777 or visit the website: www.reserveusa.com. The reservation fee is usually $8.65 for a camp site, but group site reservation fees are higher. Major credit cards are accepted. Holders of Golden Age or Golden Access passports receive a 50 percent discount for campground fees, except for group sites.

Walla Walla District, 201 North 3rd Avenue, Walla Walla, WA 99362-1876; 509/527-7700, fax 509/527-7800; website: www.nww.usace.army.mil

Other Resources

Tacoma Power, P.O. Box 11007, Tacoma, WA 98411; 253/502-8000; website: www.tacomapower.com

U.S. Geological Survey, Branch of Information Services, P.O. Box 25286, Federal Center, Denver, CO 80225; 303/202-4700 or 888/ASK-USGS (888/275-8747); website: earthexplorer.usgs.gov/>http://earthexplorer.usgs.gov

Washington Department of Fish and Wildlife, 600 Capitol Way N., Olympia, WA 98501-1091; 360/902-2200, fax 360/902-2230; website: www.wa.gov/wdfw

Washington Department of Transportation, Washington State Highway Information, 800/695-ROAD (800/695-7623); Greater Seattle Area Information, 206/DOT-HIWY (206/368-4499); website: www.wsdot.wa.gov

Index

Canoeing and Kayaking

Horseback Riding

Blackpine Creek Horse Camp: 272
Camp Spillman: 134
Cayuse Horse Camp: 255–256
Chiwawa Horse Camp: 262
Circle H RV Ranch: 441
Crest Horse Camp: 414
Cultus Creek: 410–411
Falls Creek Horse Camp: 413–414
Green Mountain Hike-In and Horse Camp: 130–131
Green River Horse Camp: 401–402
Horseshoe Lake: 398–399
Indian Horse Camp: 278–279
Kalama Horse Camp: 374–375
Keene's Horse Camp: 399–400
Ken Wilcox Horse Camp: 280
Lake Wenatchee State Park: 268
LeBar Horse Camp: 122
Lewis River Horse Camp: 402–403
Little Goose & Little Goose Horse Camp: 411–412
Mima Falls Trailhead: 155
Moran State Park Ferry-In: 172
Porter Creek: 152
Riverside State Park: 349
Rocking Horse Ranch: 231–232
Sahara Creek Horse Camp: 367
Snow Cabin: 440
Steamboat Rock State Park: 340
Tarbell Trail: 409
Twisp River Horse Camp: 238–239
Walput Horse Camp: 396–397
Walput Lake: 396

Howard Miller Steelhead Park: 215–216
Hozomeen: 218–219
Hunters Park: 322
Hutchinson Creek: 181
hypothermia: 15, 44–45

I

Icewater Creek: 281–282
Icicle Creek: 272
Icicle River RV Resort: 275
Ida Creek: 273
Ike Kinswa State Park: 369
Illahee State Park: 132
Ilwaco KOA: 151
Indian Creek: 392
Indian Flat Group Camp: 383
Indian Heaven Wilderness: 413
Indian Horse Camp: 278–279
Indian Reservations: Quinalt: 116
Indian Rock Paintings State Park: 443
insects, protection from: 32–38
Ione RV Park and Motel: 327
Ipsut Creek: 377
Iron Creek: 393–394
Island Camp: 404
Islander RV Park & Motel: 143
Issaquah Village RV Park: 193

J

Jack's RV Park and Motel: 301
James Island State Park Boat-In: 175
Jarrell's Cove Marina: 137
Jarrell Cove State Park: 137
Joemma Beach State Park: 138
Johnny Creek: 273–274
Johnson Ridge Observatory: 373
Jolly Rogers RV Park: 140
Jones Bay: 345–346
Jones Island Marine State Park Boat-In: 169
JR: 246–247
July Creek Walk-In: 115–116
Jump Off Joe Lake Resort: 337–338

K

Kachess & Kachess Group: 254–255
Kalaloch: 105
Kalama Horse Camp: 374–375
Kamei Campground & RV Park: 266

Off-Road Vehicle Trails

Remote or Hike-In Campsites

Trailheads

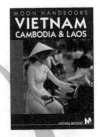

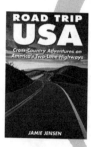

Maps